9/05

D1074610

by

Stephen Chenault and Mac Golden

with contributions by

Davis Chenault and Gary Gygax

Acknowledgments

Contributing Writers: Todd Grey, Christian Harris, Mark Sandy, and Mark Barthel
Cover: Doug Kovacs
Title and Border Design: Kieran Yanner
Interior Art: Jim Branch, Bryan Swartz, Jason Walton, Phil Avelli, Juha Harju, Kelli Nelson, Chris Seaman, and Dave Zenz
Cartography: Davis Chenault, Mac Golden, and Jim Branch
Editors: Nicole Chenault, Mac Golden

In memory of the many to try, of the many to fail, and those few who lived to tell the tale. All those characters helped forge the Winter Dark, 1985-2000.

A Note from the Authors

The Codex of Erde is a campaign setting and source book. It is more than that however, it is a tapestry. One that relates the tale of an ongoing story. It is a tale only partially told, awaiting the final threads of completion.

The setting is not particular to any gaming style but, rather, one that can easily accommodate many styles. Herein you will find, amongst many other things, a detailed history of the world of Erde. This history has a clear beginning and a clear ending. The Winter Dark Wars are over and the world has been born again in the After Winter's Dark, and it is now yours to develop and create. Some forty countries are discussed, their governments, heraldry and rulers identified, and their economic strengths outlined. However, these represent only a shell of what it takes for a Referee to run a game. The details, the texture, will come from you. To help you along, gods, guilds, magic items, spells, classes, languages and races are all outlined, adding more color to the overall tapestry that you, in the end, must weave.

What Erde does offer is a setting with an internal consistency. There are reasons, supplied to the Referee, why the Stone Dwarves are bound to their halls in Roheisen Hohle. There is a reason the trolls of Gottland-Ne rule from a throne called the "Elephant's Back." This is the history of Erde, marking it a world with depth, purpose and feeling, a world where there is a reason for being. The elements of fantasy that we have all come to know and love are here, elves, dwarves, halflings, dragon, orcs and so forth. They are woven into the cultural geography of a world rich in magic and adventure.

It should be noted that the subjects of population and scale are not seriously addressed in the book. We believe that Referee's and Players must take the initiative in any campaign setting. It is their responsibility to develop that setting into one which reflects there own gaming style and ideas. By populating a country we would set the tone of its development, one which may differ from your own. Instead we offer a simple economic rating, a mechanic for each area, which allows you to know its basic elements. You must flesh this economy out with a population. Scale is addressed in the same manner. If you need the world to be larger than it is, discard the scale supplied on the maps. Make it larger.

Concerning the map, we decided to forego placing a fold out or tear map in the book. Though it seems a good idea, our experience shows that it invariably leads to a damaged product. Instead eight black and white maps are found in the terrain section, more details are added and discussed. The large color map is sold separately.

As far as the language of the work is concerned, we freely confess that we have borrowed heavily from our European neighbors, particularly German and French. Many of the words are taken directly from history, some are a conglomeration of words. This has two purposes. The first, is that it has allowed us to set a tone for a region without creating a whole new language. For instance, the Dwarven world in Erde is based largely on German. The names are based on German and some times translate directly over. The word Erde is German. By doing this we have created a consistent feel for the Dwarves, for language is the heart of any culture. The second reason for doing this, is that it allows you to expand upon what we have given. If you want to run a game in the Punj and the Rhuneland look to Russia, for names of personages or places. Dwarves, Aachen and Augsberg look to German. Angouleme, French. Kayomar, English. The Gnomes, fierce in Erde, look to Scandanavia. Brindisium, Latin Rome. Tagea, Greek. The old Aenochians, Outremere, Egyptian. This of course does not exclude using purely fantasy names, as we have many. The Orcs, Gelderland, Luneberg Plains, etc. For the use of their languages we would like to thank the whole of Europe for having such beautiful languages and such a rich cultural history.

Troll Lord Games is dedicated to bringing you quality products, but they are products which require a different type of gamer. They are products which necessitate a gamer to be creative, to expand on what we have given and battle or role play your way through Worlds of Epic adventure.

The Codex of Erde is a tapestry that you, the Referee and Player, must finish weaving. The final threads are yours, and will by your hand make the world whole.

~Stephen Chenault, Mac Golden, Davis Chenault, Todd Grey

Table of Contents

The History of the World

This being an account of the Days before Days & the creation of the world – The Dwarven Songs & the Goblin-Dwarf Wars – The Coming of Man – The Imperial Wars and how these ended in tragedy – That Age of Winter's Dark – Those Winter Dark Wars & the rise of the Young Kingdoms in the Realms of Aenoch and Ethrum, those that are called the Lands of Ursal.

These Histories are gathered from a great many sources. From the Mammoth Scrolls, to the Books of Jaren, Master of the Order of the Scintillant Dawn, to the Lothian Chronicles and more besides.

The All Father & the Beginning of Time

Excerpts from the "Histories," the second volume of the Books of Jaren which number thirteen, "The Days before Days." Compiled and written by Jaren, Master of the Order of the Scintillant Dawn, in the years 798-800oy.

The Days before Days

In the beginning, the Void existed without shape or form, and the All Father moved across the face of the Void, pondering the great emptiness. He saw the great Dragon Inzae, and realized there was life apart from himself. The All Father wondered at this and sought to master meaning in existence. To this end, he set about creating all manner of things.

He fashioned creatures from his thoughts. For behold the All Father knew the Language of Creation, and he understood that life begets life. These creatures, slivers of the All Father, failed to embody what he imagined so he lay them aside. In this way, a great many beings came into existence, powerful manifestations of the All Father's memories or imaginings. Most of these creations were benign, but some few possessed great intelligence, and they knew the differences between good and evil.

The All Father then saw that the dragon Inzae hung in the emptiness, spinning upon herself, creating a maelstrom of chaos about her. She split the fabric of the universe in her thrashings, opening rifts, portals and doors to other planes. Unbeknownst to Inzae, the All Father settled upon her chaos and shaped it in his mind's eye. And lo, the All Father made the world from the Maelstrom. He named it in his voice and it became the crucible of his mind. He pounded substance from the Maelstrom and made fire, earth, air and water. He fashioned these elements into the world, binding them together. So the flat plane of Erde came into being in the Void, and from its edges spilled the substance of his creation and it mingled with the Maelstrom.

The substance of creation fell upon Inzae and she marveled at it, for she knew nothing of the All Father's presence in the Maelstrom. Surrounding herself with the heat of fire, the rush of wind, the cold hard earth, and the liquid blanket of water, she began to form and mold. From these elements, and others whose nature passes all knowing, Inzae configured her own world, one which lay upon the underside of Erde, bound to it and a part of the whole. With it she caused the mountains to grow, the seas to pool, the skies to dash, and the warmth of the day to radiate.

Thus, there came to be two worlds in the Void, one astride the other, bound together. This is the tale of Erde, however, and the stories of Inzae have little to do with the making of the All Father's world, hung flat and empty upon the back of the Maelstrom.

The All Father, full of creation, came to the world. The land was dark and though he knew of it, he could not see its beauty. He stood thus for a great while, until the earth rumbled and exploded. In the great column of fire which rose above the land he saw the beauty of his creation: the rivers, the mountains, the skies. But the fire burned out and the All Father was dismayed, for in sooth, the flames awoke a great lust in him to see his creation in the light.

He fashioned a maiden from his soul and gave her light within. She gloried in it and rose on high, above the lands of the All Father. She glowed there, casting a pale light upon the world. In later years the people of the world called her the Maiden of Night. But the All Father was not altogether pleased so he set to fashioning another maiden, and lit her afire so that she burned from the outside. She too rose into the heavens. There she burned brighter than her sister, washing the All Father's creation in light. He marveled at its beauty. And the Maiden of Light diminished the light of her sister, and the Maiden of Night was unhappy. These beings were called the Twin Sisters by the dwarves and early kingdoms of men, and they were worshiped as gods.

The All Father marveled at his creation for time without reckoning. His face and arms turned red and he knew warmth. But at last he came to miss the cool of the darkness. He pondered his own desires, seeking a solution to his hunger for the dark and the light. He saw then the rivalry between the Twin Sisters and he laughed aloud. He gave them steeds and chariots and gave them the heavens to race in, promising them that she who won would be given command of the heavens. So the twin sisters raced over the world, laughing and goading, but never catching one another. And the All Father marveled for the world changed with the racing of the Maidens. As the Maidens spun about Erde, it waxed warm then became cold, it snowed then rained, and things lived then died. Thus, the seasons came to be.

It is said, by those few Sentients who remember the All Father in his days of glory, that the first time he felt rain upon his face that he knew such joy that he danced and shook the world. The falling rain washed his burnt arms and face and pleased him so that he stomped and stomped. And tis said that his footprints can still be seen, even after the reshaping of the world, in the bottoms of the Amber Sea.

During this long age of peace the Dragon Inzae discovered the All Father and learned of his creation upon the back of the Maelstrom. She saw life upon the firmament and wondered at it, for such things were a mystery to her. She rose up through the Maelstrom and came to the All Father, resting at his feet upon the top of the world, upon the very slopes of Mount Thangondrim. She beseeched him to grant her the knowledge of creation. The All Father had not forgotten that his world rested upon the Maelstrom created by the Dragon and spoke to her of the Language saying, "All things come from the Language of Creation, even you and I, and to master it is to master all things. You used the Language to create the Maelstrom though you knew it not. For my part I know the language in its entirety and I will teach it to you gladly."

So he set about teaching her the Language. Inzae struggled with the language for long ages, trying to unravel it, but the Language is the root of all things and few can master the magic of it, only two in the history of time. Inzae's mind was of a different bent and she could not master it wholly altogether. So the All Father set down the language in a monumental tomb, the pages of which were black and the cover as well. These glyph and runes were for Inzae to ponder over and to use whenever she would. This tomb, which the Dwarves call the Obsidian Book, is the only place but for one that this root of all creation was set to print. The other, the tunnels of the Rings of Brass, had the script set upon them but none now remember where they lay, and the Mammoth Scrolls are but shades of these things. Inzae thanked the All Father and returned to her own world to fashion things wondrous and great.

The All Father reveled in his own creation. He saw some of his earlier creations come from the Void and settle in the world. These creatures were benign for the most part, incomplete things made from the All Father's youth. They were strange to him for he had forgotten them and he paid them no heed and let them roam as they would, they were few in number and bothered him little. But there were three which stood out from the others, powerful beings, filled with the lusts of the All Father and they were called, in the tongues of men, Corthain, Thorax and Mordius.

These beings commanded power in many different ways. Corthain held memories of the All Father's goodness; he was lawful in his actions, meticulous, and careful, and he fashioned a realm of wonder beneath the skies of the Twin Sisters. Mordius, his sister, was filled with the All Father's thoughts of beauty and wholeness. She wandered the world in a state of awe, and spent many seasons pondering the world about her. But Thorax was altogether different. Filled with the lust of dark places, he stalked the underworld, brooding in his pits in a constant unreasoning rage.

And so, it came to pass that they made constant war upon one another. The unreasoned hatred of Thorax perplexed Mordius and enraged Corthain. They made battle upon the world until they drew the All Father's attention. He watched them, and soon discovered that where the Twin Sisters were pieces of him, these gods were but figments of his memory, and therefore possessed desires entirely their own. He learned too that these creatures were far more powerful than he imagined they could ever be, and it made him wonder about the safety of his creation.

In those days the world was flat and unbound. The All Father turned his attention to its edges and called forth a great mist to bind the world on all sides. This mist has many names but is called in the tongues of the Dwarves, the Karontung, which means, the "Ever Flowing Beard." Men call it the Wall of the World. Beyond lay the Void and creatures could not easily pass from one plane to the other. Those who tried were lost in the seething clouds and lived out their days in abject loneliness, for the Void was not empty as its name implied. Within it were many beings, and too there were many scattered thoughts of the All Father, thoughts which took shape in the great unknown. And the Wall of the World kept the creatures of the Void from passing into the All Father's creation, and for years without count, the world remained safe from harm.

The All Father lingered in the world for many ages, and laughed and reveled at the racing of the Twin Sisters. He marveled at the seasons and marveled even more when he saw the world take shapes of its own accord. Grasses grew, and strange plants as well, rising from the soils of the world. There were other things, creatures which lived as memories of his original thoughts and they who stole into the world before the Wall of the World was made whole.

At last the All Father returned to his labors. He divided the lands into seven continents, gathered water from the skies and clouds, and filled the empty basins between them with wide and deep oceans. For many ages thereafter he wandered the lands, shaping the world as he went. In this manner the great mountains, ridges and hills came to be. Some places he passed over, leaving them flat and open. He carved rivers into the firmament so that what water remained on the land could flow freely.

But then the All Father grew lonely in his world. The Twin Sisters paid him little heed in their race, and the gods and other figments hid themselves for fear of being banished to the Void. So he sat upon the highest peak in the world, what the Dwarves and men call, Mount Thangondrim, the "throne of the sky," and pondered this new dilemma. His beard and hair grew to great lengths until he knew at last that he was older than he had been, and that his moods were less hasty. This knowledge gave him insight into the shaping of Life.

He brought the Trees into the world, and gave them life and knowledge of all the makings of his creation. In this manner they knew his mind and loved the All Father like none before nor any ever after for they knew the Language of Creation.

The first Trees lived as Sentient creatures and moved across the land. They never hurried, but rather, moved slowly, methodically, reveling in the world of the All Father's making. Some settled in places and stayed there ever after, and in the space of many years, great forests of these Sentients grew across the world. 'Tis said that the All Father loved the Sentients more than all of his creations. He walked amongst them, talking of the world in the early days of its making, and he knew joy in their company.

The Sentients lived long, being mirrors of the All Father, but in time of years they settled, the bark of flesh decayed, and they withered back into the earth from which they came. The seedlings they dropped proved less than the elders, some could not move, some could not speak, and others were simple trees, rooted to the ground.

The All Father looked upon the world of his creation and saw the beauty of it all, the rivers and oceans, the deep forests of trees, the rising mountains and ridges, and their valleys and dales. He saw the wonder of colors that the Maiden of Light left as she spun around the world. He loved the cool of the dark when the Maiden of Night rode across the heavens. And he could see into the Void where the memories of his thoughts shone like points of distant light.

So the world stood at creation and the All Father was pleased.

 f the Beginning of Days & the Dwarves of Old

But it had ever been the All Father's joy to fashion things, great and small. So he turned once more to the labors of creation. Into the great forests and plains, rivers and seas, mountains and hills and swamps, the All Father placed other living things, beasts, fish and birds. These were simple tasks, made with only slivers of his self. Few of them knew his mind, or even their own. These animals wandered the world, propagating, and evolving, heedless of their creators desires or intentions. The Sentients seemed to enjoy the company, for few of these animals caused them harm, and those few who did, never did so intentionally.

For his part the All Father watched in amazement when, after many years, certain of these creatures changed, seemingly of their own accord, becoming creatures altogether different from his original intent. But he did not worry. Rather, he watched and enjoyed their continued evolution.

In time the All Father grew incurious with his world and wondered

what next he could create. He thought upon the Dragon Inzae and the beauty of her form. She came unbidden to him for she too sought more knowledge of creation. So in exchange for a gift of a tree, Inzae lay a great clutch of eggs. And the All Father was pleased.

He took the eggs, laid warm earth upon them, and sat over them singing the Language of Creation across their leathery shells. When at last they hatched, he was amazed. Their serpentine forms slid forth and into the world. They bore many colors, but the first was

more striking than all the others. And it was Frafnog and he was ever the greatest.

In this way the Dragons came to be. They carried the intelligence of Inzae and the wisdom of the All Father, and so, many possessed an understanding of the Language of Creation that no others could command. In those days, they were powerful beyond imagining and plentiful in number. They soared upon the heights, commanding the wind, or they plunged to the deepest of the seas, breathing water. They fought terrific duels in the clouds and across the lands. And had there been any but the gods to see them, they would have stood in awe at the ferocity of their battles with fire, ash, acid and lightning, and they would have seen great storms of wind, rain and ice, as well as other things beyond knowing.

At times the Dragons made war, singly or in pairs, upon the gods, driving Thorax, Mordius and Corthain before them. Thorax fought one such duel with the blue Dragon, Ineltex, to great loss. He sought to drag the beast to the underworld and wrestled with her. But she tore from his grasp and ripped his left eye from its socket. She took the eye to the heights of the world and swallowed it. There it burned within her, solidified, until she vomited it forth. The jewel has ever been sought by man, dwarf, and beast, and is said to be filled with wondrous power.

Frafnog, First Born, ruled his kin in these early days and like the Sentients, he knew the mind of the All Father and spoke the Language of Creation. Even now, nestled in the heart of the Kolkrab Mountains, he alone, of all Erde, remembers the Days before Days.

The world knew peace and grew in abundance for days without number. But the All Father grew listless once more and sought to add to his perfection.

He looked upon the Sentients and studied them. They had spread throughout the world. He saw how they settled in the earth and devoured time as food. He brought his attention to the beasts of the field. They remained simple, if beautiful. He then looked to the Dragons. He wondered at them, their grace in flight, their rage in battle, and how they moved across the world searching for the joy of life. He looked upon all these things in awe. And at last he returned to his labors, shaping the greatest and most fell of his creations. For after the Dwarves the world would never be the same.

The All Father labored long and hard upon his forges, pounding upon the substance of creation. At first he could not shape his vision and he became angry. As his anger rose so did the speed with which he worked. He shook the stuff in his hands, bellowed it, and finally broke his great hammer, Iergild, the shards of which fell to the earth as great metal slabs and were used ever after in the shaping of magical weaponry. He howled then in rage and he shaped the substance with his own hands, bending it to his insurmountable will. At last, tired and spent, the All Father brought the Dwarves into being. They were odd to him, not filled with the beauty of the world, but rather its strength and his anger. He looked upon them for a great while, until at last he scattered them across the plains and mountains to see what they would do.

The Dwarves were different from all his other creations, for they did not know his mind and they sought to shape the world for themselves. It is written in the Mammoth Scrolls that some Dwarves stood as giants amongst their kin and that these, forged before the Iergild hammer broke, possessed much of the knowledge of the All Father. They set themselves apart from the others for they believed in their own greatness.

The Dwarves traveled everywhere, into the forests, across the seas, and atop mountains and hills. They did not propagate quickly like the trees, but slowly like the Dragons. And, they built things. They could not master the Language of Creation, but they used pieces of it in their labors. And indeed they were the last, apart from powerful sorcerers, who ever used the language.

Unlike any of his other creations, the Dwarves surprised the All Father in their desire to fashion things from the world. This bemused him for a great while and he watched them build homes from wood and stone. He watched as they entered the cavernous worlds beneath the mountains to make halls and as they fashioned boats to cross the open waters, an idea that never occurred to the All Father. He saw them as different from all his other makings. He saw in them desires not his own, wonders that he had not placed within them. He watched them grow. And because they did not know his mind, they feared him at first and fled from him.

The Dwarves became plentiful, and in those days occupied the whole of the world but for the skies. They called to the Twin Sisters, and eventually to the gods. The gods began to interact with them, finding in them an independence that did not mark the purity of the All Father's other makings. Corthain found their strength wondrous and sought to shape their future, and Mordius enjoyed their shaping, which seemed to alter rather than destroy things. Thorax saw in them an ally, creatures to use to make war upon his siblings, who he had grown to hate.

Into this came Inzae. She stole through the Maelstrom and came to the world of the All Father, hungry for knowledge. She came upon the tribes of Greater Dwarves, and she wove a spell of charming about them, bidding them come to Inzae.

"I shall give over to you the whole of my world to do fashion in your own image," she beguiled. Many acquiesced and followed, though some, as is told, stayed behind. Lonely creatures, the Greater Dwarves that followed fled into the wilderness, where in time, they became a people wholly apart from their kin.

The Greater Dwarves were the forebearers of the Giants, but those who went to Inzae fell from the memories of the world and no word of them came again to Erde until the Dwarven Smiths of Norgorad-Kam uncovered the tunnels between the worlds and fashioned the Rings of Brass.

Despite this, the All Father came to the Dwarves, seeking to guide them and help them master the forge. They learned from him and became greater smiths than ever he imagined. Most notable of these are the lines of Angrod, from which descended Dolgan King of Grundliche Hohle and Helgostohl the Iron shapers. They took his teachings to heart and explored the world of the forge. They were ever the masters of creation for these gifts from the All Father, but they took what he taught and used it in their own manner. They

shaped objects from the elements. Where the All Father had used only the substance of the Void, the Dwarves used all things, they used brass and iron, jewels and gold, and made wondrous things. This, however, the All Father could not fathom, and he left them to their own devices, watching in bemusement as they rethought and remade his creations.

For these reasons, so it is said, the All Father tired of the Dwarves and turned his back on the world. He retreated to the heavens in solitude, watching the mad races of the Twin Sisters as their heaven bound chariots thundered across the skies. And it was for this absence that he grew ignorant of the world and did not see the tragedy that it would come.

So in time the Dwarves waxed powerful beneath the sun, and they named their world Erde. They named Kings to rule over their people and holy men, All Fathers, to guide them. They had in them a great lust for the making of beautiful things, and it is said that it was a reflection of the lust of the All Father, for ever in his shaping of the world did he seek beauty.

Songs of the Dwarves

Being a History of the First Years of the Dwarves. Excerpts from the Mammoth Scrolls, those Dwarven parchments which recount the history of the Dwarves as the Dwarves reckon it. As translated & interpreted by Ephun Aul, Historian and Chronicler.

Of their Kings, Histories, and the Origins of Man

In the days of the first Kingdoms there was peace. The Dwarves called themselves "the Folk," and with an ever increasing population, the Folk spread throughout the lands building towns and villages. They discovered that they enjoyed the underground most of all. There, they were protected from the elements, rain and snow affecting them little or not at all. Too, they found protection from the fancies of the Dragons, some of which hunted the Dwarves. So the Dwarves tunneled beneath the hills and mountains, making halls of stone. They crafted all manner of things great and small, yet they were young in their craft and spent many years perfecting it. Few artifacts remain from these early days, and those that do are prized, not for their perfect shape, but rather because they are relics from a time when the Dwarves were young.

As is told, the Dwarves labored with the All Father, learning what craft he would teach of the Language of Creation, casting it into form and shape. They founded Kingdoms under mountains. The greatest of these, Gorthurag, First Home, they carved from the stone of Mount Austrien, that is in the vulgate, "God's Forge." Here, their greatest Kings ruled, springing from the line of Argrind, called Darkeye. The pains of his labors upon the forge brought the Dwarves into a new age, an age which heralded the perfection of their craft. From his hand sprang the Axe of the All Father, shaped from Iergild metal. It was then and still remains, the most holy of items in all the Dwarven hordes. Argrind ruled Gorthurag for many years, and the Dwarves waxed great and powerful.

When he "returned to stone," as the Dwarven folk style death, his people, filled with the wonder of his memory, began migrating further from the spires of Mount Austrien. These days are termed the Great Migrations in the Mammoth Scrolls. The Kingdom of Grausumhart, Grimjaw in the Vulgate, was founded beneath the Crusp Mountains. In the space of a few centuries this great Kingdom rivaled Gorthurag in all but its history. Her line, under the Uthkin Kings, challenged that of Argrind for rule over the Folk.

Some Dwarves turned their craftsmen to the construction of boats, and these mastered the art of sailing the waters of the world, river, lake and sea. Upon their great ships they plied the oceans, exploring the whole of the world and settling in distant lands. Yet only the eldest of the Dwarves remember, for after the Great Goblin-Dwarf Wars, when so many of the Folk drowned, the passage over water became anathema for the Dwarves. To this day, they hesitate to even cross broad streams. But in those days, they possessed no fear and battled the seas with vigor. The outposts they founded became Dwarven kingdoms in later days, of which Grundliche Hohle and Alanti were but two. The latter of which, in time, became the most wondrous of all Dwarven Kingdoms before its loss beneath the oceans of Erde.

The Mammoth Scrolls relate that the Dwarves could fashion ships that could master not only the water, but the sky as well. They recount tales of great boats, with mast and sail, plying the air of the heavens in quests for the unknown. Some proof supports these legends, for in the plains beyond the Rhodope Mountains, elders speak of such a craft which pirated the caravans of Aufstrag during the Age of the Winter Dark.

As is told, some Dwarves settled far from the mountain homes of their kin, even before the coming of Argrind. These folk lived wholly above ground, preferring the light of day and open spaces to the deeps of the world. In time, before the first Kingdoms arose, they grew in stature and numbers. Thirteen tribes of these men spread across the lands, living mostly in the north, where the cold ruled. But they slowly moved into the southern lands as well. And for the most part they lived with the Dwarves in harmony.

A note on the etymology of the word men. Some argue that the tales recounted in the Mammoth Scrolls that use the word "men" are actually bastardizing the Dwarven word, "Muen," which means, simply, "tall." Many historians assert this as proof that the men of the world sprang from Dwarven roots. In the Dwarf tongue there are no words which relate to males being men, as there are in the Vulgate. Rather, they designate sex in the ending of a word. A male Dwarven smith is a Schumeiden, whereas a female smith would be a Schumeidun.

These men faced a different world than their Dwarven kin. Living above ground they fought the elements, as well as animals and Dragons. They became superstitious and began to call upon the powers of nature, and in doing so, they captured the attention of Mordius. She walked amongst them, guiding them and giving them aid where she could. She learned to love men as she loved no other. These became dedicated to her worship, and ever after did man become enthralled with the words of gods.

The Dwarves were bound to a different fate. Thorax, who had settled in the deeps, followed the evolution of the Dwarves and in time of years, when he felt they would hear him, he approached. Argrind Darkeye, young and full of power, faced the scar-faced god and heard his words. Thorax wove a spell around his language, using his tongue to bemuse and fool Argrind King. But the King laughed him off and forbid Thorax the right to remain in his halls. In rage, Thorax fell upon the King and the two fought a great battle. Dwarves aplenty hurled themselves upon Thorax, and the halls ran with blood for days after.

Though lo, Argrind King, cased in iron, used the Axe of the Dwarven Lords to drive his foe from the room. Thorax, encased in armor of his own design, fell beneath the strength of the Iergild, seeing in it the fire of the All Father. He fled the halls in fear and rage, cursing the Dwarves, the world, and the All Father.

Victory leads to tragedy, and Argrind King's victory Thorax proved true. Thorax fled the halls into the deep north, where his sister Mordius dwelt in peace amongst the men of those parts. He watched her, stalking her from afar. All the while raging against her place in the pantheons of men. She thrived in her role, becoming ever greater, and he desired the same adoration and power of enlightenment, but knew that he would never have it.

Thorax became so envious of his sister's enlightened beauty, it drove him rapturously mad. He plotted to slay her. Coming upon her in a grove of birch trees, he devilishly murdered her, laying her low with his great sword. Her blood splashed the trees and grass, turning the gnoll a dark red. She died beneath his blade, stunned at his outrage against her, but forgiving him all the same. Her last breath, blowing across his brow, was an offering of peace, bearing the tidings of joy. This outraged Thorax in shame. From that day hence, he became evil incarnate, the enemy of all that was good.

The men of the north, overpowered with grief by her death, knew not what to do. Some staggered hopelessly through the wilderness, caught within the grips of a terrible fear. But others were not unmade so easily, and they found hope in the blood stained ground of the grove where Mordius fell. When spring came a small host of brightly colored silver trees, mostly birch and oak, came to life, growing in the ground where her blood had been spilt. They grew larger than any other tree of Erde, excepting only those earliest Sentients, for these trees bore pieces of Mordius within. To men they were held as holy things and worshiped. And it is from this line of trees that the Great Trees of the world have sprung, and to hear the March Lords of the Eldwood speak, the Great Tree of the Druids, is one of their last.

These men hated Thorax and swore vengeance upon him. But those who were lost in the wilderness turned to him or to Corthain, or even to other powers who had slipped into to the world. They found gods in these creatures and called upon them. So it was in this fashion that evil came to the world, borne by Thorax's jealously of, his hatred for the Dwarves, and his lust for power over men.

In honor of his fallen sister, Corthain swore an oath to forever maintain a balance of power amongst the gods; he became the Justice Maker, slayer of gods and shatterer of worlds. His great contest with Thorax began in these years.

The stain of Thorax and the death of Mordius retreated in time. The Sentients from the Days before Days still wandered wild, and the Dragons made great nests across the world. For three hundred centuries Erde thrived beneath the light of the sun, and the men and Dwarves lived in harmony.

Of the Coming of the Goblins

During the long age of peace, the Dwarves perfected their arts, becoming masters of construction and the forge. They built ever deeper halls and their cities sprawled along the flanks of the great mountains. Their halls of stone stretched out beneath the world like the roots of a great tree. In Alanti, the Dwarves built their homes upon the sea. The streets and buildings, carved from beautiful marble, stretching between island realms, were a wonder to behold. It is told that the Alanti Dwarves became more learned than their fellows in the Language of Creation. And in time of years all the massed knowledge of the Folk was gathered there and placed in monumental libraries.

And then Goblins came into the world and the ages of peace ended forever. The memory of those days linger only in legend and dream.

From where the Goblin's originated, none could say. Many whispered of Dwarves turned evil, corrupted by the dark of deep places and greed. There is truth in this tale. As is told, the Dwarves were plentiful and tunneled beneath the world. They became scattered far and wide, so much so, that many lost contact with their fellows, living out their days in solitude far from their Kingdom's Halls. They became removed from the discoveries of other Dwarves, lingering in the past as their cousins moved into the future. Thorax found them thus, and made easy prey of them.

He taught them new things and convinced them that their brethren had kept these secrets in them from spite. He twisted their thoughts and buried their memories with twisted tongue, and made them hate their kin. Slowly he gathered them over time, until there was a small host of several tens of thousands.

Thorax taught them a vile brand of sorcery. And when they mastered it he revealed his true nature. He sung the song of how he was not of the Void, but rather a memory of the All Father come to life, equating himself to unlimited power. He told of how he stole away into the world of Erde and hid himself in dark places. He was not like them, for they were made of the Language of Creation, pounded from the substance of the Void. In rapt attention they listened, all the while wondering on the memory of the All Father which stood before them. In doing so they changed. Their own spite corrupted them, and their bodies shriveled, and their hair fell out. They lost the form which the All Father had cast for them, and adopted one which resembled nothing the world had seen before, a malevolent version of the Dwarves. They became Goblins.

In this they assumed, as Thorax had planned, a greater identity. They absorbed images of Thorax's memory. They learned of the All Fathers as well, and it came to pass that this knowledge was power. With it these Goblins found the secret of immortality. These earliest Goblins, the Eldritch Goblins, being powerful reflections of Thorax's memory, could die only by fell magic or strange curse.

These Eldritch Goblins were fiercely independent and fought amongst themselves continually. Thorax coaxed them into choosing a King and Queen for he knew that without leadership they would war on one another as much as the Dwarves. They chose Ichlun as their King and Oglotay as their Queen, and they were a horrid pair to see. They dug great holes deep into the earth. Using magic more than skill, they carved out a Kingdom, a realm they called Lugtrunda. And here, in the depths of the world the Goblin King mated with his Goblin Queen and she spawned, laying eggs upon the ground. The part of the Goblin host was horrified, for this was utterly unnatural, a bestial thing. But Oglotay nested with her eggs, mothering them, all the while laying more. So came into the world the Goblin Kin, those drones, warriors and slaves, who do the bidding of the Eldritch Goblins.

Legends speak of other Goblin Queens, but none bear the mark of truth. There is only the one, and in later days she returned to the Goblins, it is said, even to the halls of Ichlin-Yor, or in our tongue Ngorondoro.

The first encounters of Goblin and Dwarf are not known to the chroniclers, but mention is made of the Kav-Orun, the cave dwellers, in the year 5123df. And again, forty years later the Mammoth Scrolls record a letter which mentions these same folk with the following:

Master Rudlung has reported that when the corridor collapsed, it opened into a cavern just to the left of our own, running parallel to it. He found there one of the Kav-Orun in possession of an uncut (undetermined) stone. The Kav-Orun proceeded to shout obscenities at Master Rodlung and claim the stone for his own. He retreated down the corridor. Master Rudlung thought little of it, ordered the cavern filled, and continued construction.

The Scrolls report numerous other similar incidents in the following years. But mostly the Goblins lived in their holes far from the workings of the Dwarves, designing mischief, squabbling with one another, and preparing their vengeance.

Of the Goblin-Dwarf Wars

The Goblins lived thus for many long years, nurturing hate. A hate that was not their own, but rather Thorax's. When they thought their power great enough, they issued forth from their caverns and halls in great numbers. They were bound in armor and bore weapons of iron and brass. And they made war upon the Dwarves. So began the great Goblin-Dwarf wars which brought the world so much that is evil, and yet, so much that is good.

It proved a hard time for the Dwarves. For the line of Argrind Darkeye had fallen away with the death of Argrind IX, and the great Kingdoms Grausumhart and Gorthurag made war upon one another. During these wars the Dwarves bent their crafts to making weapons and armors. They put armies into the field, enlisted the aid of men, and fought each other. They had little heart for it at first, refusing to slay their kin openly. But some inevitably fell. Thus, as the years passed and more died, they hardened, becoming accustomed to the chaos of war. The Kinship Wars began in 5207df and lasted for 200 years, ending in 5457df with the sundering of the realms. Isenharg I, cousin to Argrind, ruled in Gorthurag while the Ithkin Kings remained in Grausumhart.

The Mammoth Scrolls reckon this the end of the First Age of Dwarves and Men.

The First Goblin-Dwarf War, 5590-5593

The Goblins, under King Ichlun, issued forth from their caves, sweeping across the valleys and plains in a wave of terror and war. As is written they bore armor, shields and weapons of iron. They favored jagged knives and short swords, spiked balls and whips, so that their war was made all the more gruesome. The Dwarves, caught unaware, threw up weak defenses, but these did not hold the ferocity of the Goblin attack. The Folk fell, cut down by the host of Thorax's hate. These were largely innocent people, farmers and their kin, those who lived above ground and had no recourse to defense. They fled before the Goblins.

The terror of the attack did not last, however, for the Dwarves were fresh from their wars with each other and well armed for war. The

King of Grausamhart led the initial counter attacks against the Goblins and they were filled with such rage for the slaughter of the innocents that the Goblins could not stop him. Other Kingdoms joined him, Gothurag and Grundliche Hohle most of all. The latter Kingdom found a nest of the Goblins upon their doorstep, and there the fighting was greatest for the fathers of Dolgan King plundered the upper layers of the Ichlin-Yor, driving the Goblins to the depths of the world.

So ended the first Goblin-Dwarf war and the Dwarves heralded it as a great victory. But in truth it was not so, for the Goblins had not shown their strength, but had rather tested the Dwarves. Oglotay continued to lay eggs and Ichlun rallied his armies. In the space of a few years they came forth again, this time in even greater numbers.

The Second Goblin-Dwarf War, 5616-5640

The Mammoth Scrolls speak of an uncountable host, of fields overflowing with the Goblin Kin, led by Sorcerers and their fierce King. In this the second war the Dwarves were unmade. They fought above and below the earth. They fought on open fields with large hosts, on pony back and from the heights of mountains. They fought in castles and walled towns, vainly holding back the tide. But as is reported, the Dwarves were not as skilled in the acts of war in those days as they became in later ages. They were young and still filled with joy, mirth, and the love of beauty given to them by the All Father. And for this, they could not stand against the Goblin rage.

So fierce were the battles of this Great War that tens of thousands fell. Whole towns and villages vanished, castles burned, and the Dwarven people fled beneath the earth. The Nine Lamentations, those Dwarven death dirges, originated in these days, reminding all the Folk of the loss suffered upon the fields of battle.

Only Alanti held out against the Goblins, for those twisted creatures feared water and would not cross it. So the Sea Kings sailed their armies where they would, attacking the Goblins in the flanks and rear. They harried them ever after in the long years of Goblin Rule.

And so did the Goblins rule the world of Erde but for the Mountain Kingdoms of the Dwarves and the Sea Kingdoms of Alanti.

For 400 years the Goblin King Ichlun ruled Erde. Little is known of these days, for the Goblins did not keep histories and men were only just beginning to track the passage of the Twin Sisters through the heavens. It is known that the Goblins turned all their might to building great Keeps upon the heights above the Dwarven realms. They paid little heed to the men of the north, and fled from the raiders of Alanti. Ondluche, the Eldritch Goblin, rose in might, using his sorcery to serve King Ichlun.

The Sea Kings waxed powerful in war during the rule of the Goblin King. They mastered the construction of war ships, light arms and armor. With these weapons they harried the Goblins, driving them

from the coastal regions. They constructed towers and walled estuaries upon the continents, and grew ever bolder with attacks into the interior. They plundered the Goblin's holds, caravans and towns, slaughtering all without mercy, and retreated to the sea. Upon the few occasions the Goblins attacked, they could do little beyond throwing down the towers by the Sea.

In time, the Dwarves learned to forge weapons of iron and steel and mastered the shaping of rock and mountain. They bent themselves to the arts of war, forgetting the love of beautiful things. They spent many years in their Mountains, where the Goblins were unable to strike them. Many skirmishes were fought as Dwarves came forth and assailed the Goblins, but they were ever driven back, being divided and outnumbered. Nonetheless, they grew powerful in war, for they were ever the first-makers.

It was not until the greatest of the Dwarven smiths of Norgorad-Kam discovered the magic of the planes that the war turned. The Mammoth Scrolls speak of a forge master, nameless, who learned to create magical gates in rings of brass. These gates, forged from the Language of Creation, opened portals through the Wall of the World and into the Void and the Dwarves found they could travel great distances across Erde. Several Dwarves, wrapped in shadows, crossed the great mountains, bringing these rings to the realms of the other Dwarves.

What in fact the smiths had discovered were vast staircases constructed by the Greater Dwarves of Inzae, those same Dwarves who the Dragon God had enticed from Erde when the world was young. Trapped in Inzae, these refugees sought ever after to return to their own lands. They built great tunnels of stairs snaking through the firmament of the Maelstrom. These Dwarves possessed access to the Obsidian Book, that tomb wherein the All Father wrote down the Language of Creation for the dragon Inzae. In bits and pieces the Dwarves copied the text in runes upon the steps of their tunnels.

This was the second and final time the Language found a home in the written word.

But the tunnels failed to breach the Wall of Worlds and the Greater Dwarves left off their attempts to return to Erde as slaves or worse. The smiths of Norgorad-Kam breached the Wall of Worlds with the spells of brass and found the tunnels. They used them to move through the Maelstrom to Inzae and then back to Erde, thus traveling from one Kingdom to the next.

Using the Rings, the Dwarves were able to gather the greater part of their folk in the Halls of Gothurag under King Isenharg IV, and in the year 5812df, the Dwarves at last felt strong enough to challenge the hated Goblins.

The Third Goblin-Dwarf War, 5812-6010

So the Third Goblin-Dwarf War began, that which the Mammoth Scrolls call the Great War. Bitterly fought, this longest of the early wars destroyed the flower of both peoples and changed the Dwarves from a kindly people of craftsmen to a warrior's race. The Dwarves came forth from the deep halls of Gothurag in legions of iron and the Goblins were caught wholly unprepared. The first of the great citadels fell to the Iron Host. Though, as it is written, the Goblins soon regrouped and counterattacked.

Countless dwarves fought powerful goblins heedless of the destruction of war. They fought long horrid battles beneath the earth in dark tunnels far from the light of day. Who may say what acts of heroism and treachery went unrecorded, what desperate characters lived and died in those deep places. Who may say indeed, for not even the Dwarf histories, as told in the Mammoth Scrolls, record these dark years. They speak only of terrible times in which many a dwarf lost his beard, of plagues and famine, of horror and destruction, and death.

In the end the Iron Legions met the Goblin Horde upon the Fields of Ravens, their numbers uncountable. Here, Isenharg slew King Ichlun. With the Axe of the All Father he struck him down. It is said that when the immortal Ichlun fell that at first he called for mercy, begging Isenharg to spare him, but Isenharg's heart was like iron and he hacked off his head. A howling rose in the valley of Ravens and thundered over the heads of the Goblin Horde, and they knew fear such that they fled the field of battle, scattering to the corners of the wide world.

Thus ended the Second Age of Dwarves.

The Coming of the Sorcerers and the Fall of the Dwarves

With the fall of Ichlun, a Golden Age dawned upon the Dwarves. This is held to be the Third Age by the Mammoth Scrolls. Too, it is the age of the Sea Kings, as they came into their full glory. The Dwarves never returned to the surface of Erde to build halls of stone beneath the Twin Sisters, but they delved deeper into the earth, building wondrous tunnels and halls beneath the world. The age is called the Peace of Tunnels, for their were no disturbances of Goblins and no war.

During this Golden Age the Dwarves reached the pinnacle of their craftsmanship. In the making of all things, whether weapons of war, armor, jewels, or the construction of underground halls, or anything else they never surpassed these days. The skills of the forge learned during the late wars were bent to all things and all things made better thereby. They traded with men, striking up old friendships. The men, for their part, traded wood, beasts, pelts and the like, woven tapestries, and rugs. For this was an art the Dwarves never mastered, always relying on the men of the north and their fine spinning.

It is retold how King Imontep of the Ethrum tribe gave to Isenharg VI a lengthy tapestry depicting the great triumphs of the Dwarven Kings of Gorthurag. The tapestry, much valued by the Dwarves, hung over the throne of the King for many thousands of years. It possessed magical properties, for the men were ever the children of Mordius and bore her strange imprint upon everything they created.

In the latter years of the Peace of Tunnels, the Sea Kings of Alanti grew great in the councils of both Dwarves and men. Their colonies spread across the world and they traded goods with all the peoples. Already famed for their marbled towers and houses, they grew even greater. The wealth of the world was theirs, pearls from the oceans, platinum and gold from the Dwarves, silver and fine tapestries from the tribes of men. They built ever greater ships and cities upon the

sea, reveling in the glory of their strength. They mapped the heavens, and the course of the Twin Sisters. They charted the deep waters of the oceans and came to know the currents, their movements and variations. They were the greatest of the Dwarves and lived in peace with the world under the Alantine Kings.

Yet all things must end. As it is written, the Goblins had not been unmade in those closing years of the Second Age. They spent many years hiding in holes and caves, ever fearful of the wrath of the Iron Legions. The Dwarves forgot and paid those who yet lived little heed. And because of their neglect Ondluche made good work of his sorcery, crafting ever greater spells to exact a vengeance that was altogether his own. And the Queen, Oglotay, continued to lay eggs and the Goblins number of Goblin kin surpassed that of ages past.

In the 8603rd year as the Dwarves reckon time, Ondluche took the crown of Ichlun for his own and his people called him King.

Word of this came to the Dwarves and too late they realized the threat to the Folk. They began marshaling the Iron Legions once more, calling to the Kings of Gorthurag, Grausumhart, Grundliche Hohle, Norgorod-Kam, and the others, as well as the Sea Kings to send their armies to meet the Goblin King.

In the Fourth Goblin-Dwarf War the Goblins fought insanely to unmake all that the Dwarves had created. The armored hosts came forth in waves, they rode Dragons enslaved to their wills, the sorcerers carpeted the ground in front of the horde with vile magic, and whole armies battled while mounted on wolves. Together these forces assailed the Dwarves, who were encased in iron. The battles fought in this third war were beyond brutal, the hatred the two peoples bore each other reached a maddened lust. Dwarven warriors, male and female, fought with axe and mace, cleaving the Goblins who in turn fought with whips and chains.

For 110 years this war raged across Erde. In deep places, on high peaks, in the open, and at last upon the sea. Everywhere there was destruction and death. The dragon riders came at last to Alanti and visited war on that fair Kingdom. Alanti, with her great fleets and island cities, the most wondrous and beautiful of all dwarf realms, was thrown down and swallowed by the sea. Many of the Great Homes of the early Kings were lost as well. The war consumed the world that existed in the Days before Days, its glory lost forever.

In reprisals the Dwarves sacked the Goblin Holes and rooted out their fell Queen. Immense in size, the massive creature could not move herself, but lay upon her side, birthing eggs of Goblins all the while. They could not slay her, for the root of her lay deep in the world. But they bound her, using magic of the forge, and encased her in a temple of stone. Iron guardians they set to guard her, and they buried the temple beneath the earth. So she remained for many years, until after Winter's Dark.

None claimed victory, for the toll of war proved too great. Those who fought remembered only sorrow. The war culminated when Ondluche used his fell might to warp the world. In working a great spell to unmake the Dwarves, he splintered the mind of the slumbering All Father, opening gates into the All Father's imaginings. Thus, the multi-verse came into existence, springing out and across the Void and juxtaposing with Erde in a billion hidden places.

The All Father groaned, lay beneath the world, and died.

With this the Dwarves were thrown into consternation, and the Goblins pressed the attack. Ondluche used the power garnished from the All Father to assail Gorthurag. He brought the Kingdom down, slaying her King, Isorn III, and his seven sons. He spent many years filling the valley with mud and muck. These lands were later called the Seven Swamps as it is said that the children of Isorns haunt the valley still, calling out for their father, whose body the horrid swamp had devoured.

In the year 8733df, the King of Norgorad-Kam, Dognur VII, captured the Goblin sorcerer in his halls of Lugtundra. He cast aside his plate and axe and gathered Ondluche up in his hands. He strangled the Goblin, grinding his neck and bones to gristle in his

iron clad fist. Knowing well the Goblin curse of immortality, Dognur took the corpse, crushed it into dust and locked it in a chest of wrought iron. The chest he threw into the sea where it lay for many ages of the world.

This fourth war forever changed the world of Erde. From the fell magic of Ondluche the splintered imaginings of the All Father came to life. Faerie came into the world, with its beautiful Queen and Goddess, Wenafar, and all the magic that it promised. The immortal elves, sprung from the purest of the All Father's thoughts, came to life in the deeps of the great forests, gnomes and halflings too. All these were thoughts of the All Father, and as such, were unlike the Dwarves and Goblins, who alone of the people of the world, were pounded out of the substance of the Maelstrom and bore the mark of the Language of Creation.

There were other things as well. Dark things, orcs and demons and many more beside. And worst of all was the Unklar, the All Father's nightmare. And the world was never the same.

But these creatures were young, few in number, and knew not the world at large. Many years passed before they began to grow and explore. Only the Elves came to the world with a knowledge greater than themselves, for Wenafar, their Queen, was the incarnation of the All Father's dreams of the original trees. She loved the Elves and gave them knowledge.

For another thousand years the Dwarves reigned in Erde. Little is known about these days, for the Mammoth Scrolls do not speak of them. Indeed the last entries of those Dwarven histories refer only to the rebuilding of Grundliche Hohle and Norgorad-Kam, and the rising dominance of Grausumhart after the fourth war.

The Age of Dwarves ended soon thereafter. In 9804df the Stone Wars between Dwarf and Goblin began. This war, fought wholly underground, shattered both peoples and left their halls in smoking ruin. It was murderous war between small groups and armies with no mercy sought, nor any given. Legends speak of atrocities by both sides, of rooms of blood and bodies. In 10302, the Goblins, led by Agmaur the Immortal, plundered Grausumhart. Old King Rotterkin X made to slay Agmaur, but was felled instead, for that Goblin had a greater role to play in the years to come. The Stone Wars, fought intermittently for 500 years, left the twin folk so broken that they never again ruled in Erde. So ended the Stone Wars.

In truth, some of the Dwarven Kings which arose during the Winter Dark Wars of recent memory were powerful Lords. Dagmar III of Norgorod-Kam led a Dwarven host at the Battle of Eastfair. And there was Dolgon King, of Grundliche Hohle, who it is said was the greatest Dwarven Smith the world has ever seen. But these Lords were but shadows of the glory of yesteryear.

The songs which reference the Ages of Dwarves are sorrowful tales. Hints of the glories of a past where Erde lived in peace, and where no war or death existed. But lo, there was a time when the Dwarven Kingdoms sprawled across the world of Erde in glory and majesty. A time filled with hope and promise. But these are forgotten memories only, forgotten memories of a once great people, for the Dwarves are a spent race forever more.

Of the Age of Man

Excerpts from "The Histories," the third volume of the Books of Jaren which number 13, "First Years." Compiled and written by Jaren, Master of the Order of the Scintillant Dawn in the years 798-800oy.

First Years

For 10,000 years the Dwarves dominated Erde. With their fall, the age of Man began.

From their shallow roots the thirteen tribes of men grew. The fathers and mothers begat sons and daughters, and they multiplied and spread across the land. More adaptable than Dwarves, they settled in the forests, deserts, and plains. And in the space of many years, their Kingdoms grew upon the face of Erde. The Mammoth Scrolls reference these thirteen tribes many times, some greater, some less so. Of these the Aenoch, Ethrum, Madriu, Nieta, Engalei, and Inklu are named. These men lived long lives, mimicking the Dwarves, who 'tis said, were their ancestors. Not until the judgement of Corthain did this change.

In the early years, Man left the tunnels of their forefathers and settled in villages and towns. Slowly they divided and spread across the land. Unlike the Dwarves, who sat at the feet of the All Father, man wandered in ignorance. He kept no comprehension of the world around him and looked upon things as strange and terrifying. So in the space of years they came to worship those fragments of the All Father's memories, Corthain, Thorax, Mordius and more besides who are un-named in the annals. Of them all, Mordius took them under wing and the cult of her nature grew far and wide. It spread to all the races of man, for there were as many then as there are now. They learned from Mordius, whom they called the Mother Goddess, the workings of the world and they lived in peace for a great while.

But when Thorax learned of this worship of his sister, he stole into the glade where she slept and slew her, so that her blood ran upon the ground. The druids who paid her homage became distraught. A madness seized most men, such that they fled back into the wilderness, abandoning their villages and towns. As word of her death spread from tribe to tribe, born out by the dreams of holy men, the power she held over man began to wane. They turned to the worship of other gods, Corthain, Thorax, and the others who were first named in these days Poseidon, Toth, and Tefnut. Though in truth, Thorax paid little heed to these people, being ensnared in his own hatred for Argrind's line and the whole of the Dwarven world.

Mordius lived in many places, at many times. She had been a memory of the All Father and as such was not bound by his creation. Thus when she fell to Thorax, it was not in a singular place, but in many places, all at once. So the annals regard that all the men of the thirteen tribes who worshiped her experienced her fall. So also did they benefit by it. As is written, the trees in the groves of Morduis sprang to life, borne again with the blood of the Mother Goddess.

These trees took many shapes in the mythology of men. To the northmen the tree Yrgdsil was born and became the heart of the world. In the south, the Vines of Life, sprouted anew, giving hope to those without hope. And in the lands of the tribes of Aenoch and Ethrum, where the Grove is said to have consisted of seven oaks and seven birch, these trees became holy things. They sprouted leaves so deep in their green that they were mirrors of Mordius' eyes and the bark of the birch grew silver and became priceless as holy things. From these trees sprang the lines of the Great Trees which ever after held sway with those folk. Indeed, the chroniclers record, that it was in grim mockery of one of these descendants that the horned god fashioned the castle of Aufstrag, making its shape that of a horribly twisted oak.

In later years the various tribes of men were drawn into the Goblin-Dwarf wars. The histories of men make no reference to these days, but the Mammoth Scrolls speak of them from time to time. They reference only three of the tribes, the Engalie, Aenoch and Ethrum. This first tribe, tall and strong, dark of skin, lived in the vicinity of First Home, Gorthurag. They were the most civilized and fought alongside the Dwarves in all three wars. They built cities upon the slopes of the great mountains and learned from the Dwarves even as the Folk learned from them. But they leave the annals of history many thousands of years ago, for in the last great battles they stood true to their friends and fought alongside the Dwarves in the Stone Wars. The greater part of them perished in those days, for their homes were swallowed by the Seven Swamps. Their descendants live there still, like the Dwarves, shadows of their former selves.

The Aenoch and Ethrum are mentioned for they settled in the vicinity of three of the great Dwarven Kingdoms, Grundliche Hohle, Norgorad-Kam and Roheisen Hohle. They had much concourse with the Dwarves, and like the Engalie they learned from them. But unlike the Engalie, these folk turned to the gods for securement. They sought power over the world as the Dwarves never had. The Aenoch were far worse than the Ethrum, and were ever a self centered people. When the Goblin-Dwarf wars began they played one side against the other. Their chieftains learned the Dwarven arts of metallurgy and too, they mastered the sorceries of the Goblins. And they used these powers to evil ends.

During the Fourth Goblin Dwarf war these people joined the enemy or the Dwarves, whichever their fancy dictated, but when the world was sundered by the workings of Ondluche the Sorcerer and the All Father slain, they fell back from the armies in dismay. For in these days strange creatures came to Erde, creatures not of the natural order, not of the Language of Creation. Beastly things, with the heads of lions and bodies of dragons, flying horses, all manner of combinations that more resembled a mad sorcerers nightmares than the All Father's creations. Some resembled gods, being unlike the Dwarves or Goblins, and men took up their worship as well. Wenefar the Faerie Queen was one, but so too was Narrheit, a Lord of Chaos.

Later, even after the Stone Wars ended and the old races were spent, Thorax looked upon the fields of battle in gladness. He saw that his lust for vengeance had come to fruition for the Dwarves were almost wholly unmade and their Kingdoms in ruin. He rose to the heights of Mount Thangondrim, where the All Father had sat in days past. He stood amidst the broken remains of the All Father's forge and he laughed upon the ruin of the world.

His laughter drew the rage of Corthain, he who had ever sought to avoid the workings of Erde. Corthain remembered the death of Mordius and he saw the world in ruins, and he rose in a wrath that shook the heavens. With him came flights of Dragons, Frafnog at their head, other gods besides, some Dwarves and other creatures who had come into the world when Ondluche slew the All Father. They fell upon Thorax and his minions upon the mountain slopes.

There, Thorax stood, girded in segmented armor of plate with his great sword in hand. He wrapped himself in a blood red cloak of magical design which hid his form as a shadow at the edge of light. The battle shook the mountains and the minions of Thorax fled or died, but none save Frafnog could see the grim god, wrapped as he was, in the Cloak of Red.

That Dragon, first born, stood before Thorax like a mountain. He cornered the god upon the porch and gave him such battle that never again did Thorax dare to stand before the Drake. In the end Frafnog threw Thorax from the mountain, his very breath scorching The Cloak of Red, and melting away the god's armor.

In terror Thorax fled from his foes. He vanished into the deep places of the world to brood and ponder what next he must do. The Goblins were spent, and he could not use them and he was without ally. Then his roving mind came to the tribes of men, those creatures who he had always hated and despised. He learned then of the people of Aenoch, how they called to him with Goblin sorcery. He took the disguise of a large bull and traveled to the lands of Aenoch and spent a great while amongst those people. He saw their power, their greed for life, and began to twist it. He gathered those people together and taught them knowledge beyond their wildest imaginings. They lusted for it, and waxed in strength. They began to learn of the memories of the All Father, and sought to adopt immortality.

As word spread, men flocked to the worship of Thorax. Only the druids avoided his calls and many of the people of Ethrum. It is written, that those who stayed behind, were not wholly affected by the Judgment of Corthain, and in after years, these folk were the very same who founded the Kingdom of Kayomar.

The folk of the tribe of Aenoch rose to overwhelm the world of Erde. Led by their sorcerers, with the Bull at their head, they gathered their armies and conquered the other tribes. They styled themselves gods over Men, Dwarf and Goblin. Their Kings called themselves God Emperors, and they ruled as such. All bowed to them, but for the Great Sorcerers whoever after have plagued the rulers of man. They cut down the trees of Mordius, burnt the temples of Corthain and drove out many of the lesser powers. And ever were these people the tools of Thorax, for he saw that with the fall of the Dwarves and the power of men, he could rule in Erde where his brother could not.

His folk came to the Halls of Frafnog's lair and there hounded that most ancient of Dragons. First of the All Father's living creatures, Frafnog could not remember the number of years that were his. He slept mostly in those days, caring little for the world at large. But when the armed men came to his lair and pestered him he slew them with a swipe of his huge claw. He roused himself, in towers of flame, and in fire he fell upon the cities of man and in his anger he cared not whether they were good men or servants of Thorax. The god himself fled in fear of the fell Dragon as nothing could stand against his anger. Wenafar, the goddess of the Fay, at last interceded on behalf of man and came to the Dragon where he lay in the ruins of one of their great towns. She bid him leave off his war and let history unfold. Long they struggled, in mind if not body, until at last she convinced the Drake to return to his lair deep in the earth. But his rage had burrowed a fear in the hearts of men for the Dragons, and ever after only the greatest of those folk could stand against their might, though they knew not why.

Corthain watched in dismay as his brother set to corrupting another race upon Erde, and he saw the memory of the All Father corrupted as well. He judged this wrong and made war upon the Bull of Thorax. Corthain had never before interacted in the happenings of Erde. Thus, his power was not spent, but was much as it had been when he stole into the world in the Days before Days. And he set to fashioning a great spear. Its haft he took from a fallen oak fed by the blood of Mordius, its point he crafted from his own mind and coated it in the silvery bark of a birch of Mordius. With this spear he came to the worlds of the tribes of men, even to the tent where the Great Sorcerer reigned. The one eyed Bull was there and the gods knew each other.

The battle of Thorax and Corthain jarred the world to its foundation. The Bull gored Corthain time and again, but in turn, Corthain lanced the beast in the chest, side and neck. They trampled the sorcerers to death, crushing the tents of the army and scattering it far and wide. The battle raged for weeks and months and the blood flowed in rivers. The Men fled in terror, hiding in caves and dark places to await the battle's outcome. In the last, Corthain slew Thorax, breaking the spear in the Būll's heart. When at last Thorax died,

Corthain commanded the body to rot and it seeped into a morass of tar and ichor, never to be seen on the plane of Erde again.

Corthain turned then to the hosts of men and cast judgment upon them. "In your greed, you sought the gifts of immortality. You sought to become what you are not and for this I strike you and place upon you the curse of mortality. Forever more yours days on Erde will be short and your lives spent in hurried vanity. Forever more."

The judgment of Corthain left man in the shells of mortal being, and but for a few, they lived ever shorter lives. The god broke the Wall of Worlds and left Erde to its own devising. He dwells still, or so it is said, in the heavens of the world, a star in the midnight sky.

So ended the first years of man.

The Rule of Man & the Days of Aenoch

These texts are taken from the Lothian Chronicles, recounting the early rule of Aenoch and Ethrum, The Age of Heroes, The Catalyst War and the Waning of the World. Compiled by the Cleric Mourilee Lothian Pendagrantz, 800oy.

After the Judgment of Corthain men lived in fear for many years. As is written their lives were greatly shortened so that they lived for decades only and not centuries. Only a few men of the tribe of Ethrum, who had stood by the worship of Corthain and had not succumbed to the sorceries of Thorax, were spared Judgment. These men lived for many years and counted themselves the true men as cast in the mold of the All Father's Eyes. In later years they founded the Kingdom of Kayomar where their line survives, though greatly reduced in numbers.

In time, however, Man recovered from the Judgment and began rebuilding. They possessed the range of knowledge given to them by Thorax, the Dwarves and the Goblins. They used it to build ever greater cities. The worship of the gods resumed, though for the most part they avoided the name of Thorax and his worship. Tis true that small cults of his followers survived, as they do to this day, but his power was forever broken by the rage of Corthain and existed only in the glass eye forged by the great blue Dragon, Ineltex, in the Days before Days. Man rebuilt the Kingdoms of old, and the greatest of these, as they had before, were in the lands of Aenoch and Ethrum.

These peoples thrived where two continents touched at the straights of Ursal, once more in the shadow of the Dwarven Kingdoms. Here, the tribes of Aenoch and Ethrum permanently settled, the former in the east and the latter in the west. They turned the soil, built villages along the rivers and castles to overlook them. They built ships, plowing the waters in trade. Ships need ports and soon, great walled towns stood upon the coasts as they did before the fall of Alanti many years ago. In time, large cities grew in the interior and the people of Aenoch and Ethrum spread across the land. They began to reckon time, and they learned the travels of the stars through the

heavens. They relearned most everything set aside since the Judgment of Thorax.

In the 92nd year as men record time (11480df), the chieftains of the two peoples came together in an attempt to bind the two tribes in union. In those days a great stone bridge stretched across the straights of Ursal. It spanned 90 miles, being built upon great pylons in the water. Legends tell of a width that exceeded half a mile. The men called it simply The Ursal Bridge, but its true name resided with the Dwarves, who called it Andstein. There is no direct translation for this word in the Vulgate tongue. "And" means to bind through an oath. "Stein" means stone. Literally, the stone bind. It probably held significance as a stone creation which bound the early Dwarf Kingdoms together as would an oath.

When the chieftains came together upon the span to discuss the union of the Aenoch and Ethrum, they soon came to blows. They could not agree on the rules of law and they parted from one another in disagreement. Each returned to their lands and proclaimed their greatest leaders their Kings. So the twin Kingdoms of Aenoch and Ethrum were founded, and they mirrored each other in differences not unlike the Twin Sisters.

The lands of Aenoch grew in strength and number, greater than those of Ethrum. Their people were far more industrious, adopting the new world and the new races far more readily than their neighbors to the west. Foremost amongst their dealings were the Gnomes. A small industrious race filled with the merchants craft, they soon aided in Aenoch's economy, so much so that that realm waxed in wealth. The nine Gnome clans grew in stature and benefitted by their dealings as well, and in time of years, their clans split again and again until they now number 47, each ruled by a Thrushbeard, (chieftain).

The Kings of Aenoch waxed in wealth and power. As they outstripped their neighbors to the west, and soon began to seek out new lands. They conquered the peoples in the distant east and across the south seas. In the 207th year of their recorded history, King Olivier IV of the House Golden, proclaimed himself Emperor. He became Olivier I and he ruled his Empire from the stone halls of Al-Liosh. The Empire became fabulously wealthy, her nobles as rich as the Kings of Ethrum, the Emperor's wealth beyond description. They derided their neighbors as weak and foolish, and invited them to become a province of the Empire. This insult did not go unanswered in the west and those people spurned the easterners as tools of evil.

In the southern lands of Ethrum, near the Eldwood, the noble family of Tarvish, who rose to prominence in the fur trade, called for the King in the far off capital of Ruthan to make ready for war. When the King proved reluctant, Tarvish rose in rebellion and overthrew the dynasty. The Tarvish eventually proclaimed themselves Kings of Ethrum, though many called them Emperors and looked to them in the same manner that they did the Aenochians in the east. The Tarvish Emperors ruled in a benign fashion, but nonetheless, made their Kingdom ready for war.

Olivier's son, Olivier II, marshaled all the forces of the Empire of Aenoch, gathering them near the western span of the Ursal Bridge.

The Tarvish gathered the Ethrumanians but to no avail. In the war that followed, the wealth and power of sorcery of the Empire destroyed the westerners. In a series of set-piece battles, Olivier II overwhelmed the west and destroyed their armies. In the later days of the war, the Tarvish Emperors constructed a great wall from the northern tips of the Bergrucken to the sea. But this too failed to keep the Aenochians at bay and in the end this Great Wall of Ethrum was breached and the Tarvish overthrown. These battles men called the Isles of Mark, for upon each of the eleven fields where the armies met a great marking stone was placed by unknown hands. The unnaturally carved stones, were blank, jutting out of the ground like black monoliths.

Olivier II crowned himself God Emperor of Erde, styling his reign after his ancient predecessors. His smiths and sorcerers forged for him a crown, the Cunae Mundus Usquam, called in the Vulgate, the Cradle of the World. A reign of brutal tyranny followed his conquest. The Ethrumanians lived out their days in servitude to the Emperors in Aenoch. On occasion they rose in rebellion, and even for a time some lived under the rule of the descendants of the Tarvish in the south, near the forests of the Eldwood. But these rebellions were forcefully put down, and those in arms put to death, and the Tarvish's days were numbered.

For five centuries the lords of Aenoch ruled a sprawling empire. Vast lands across the Amber Sea fell to them and they built colonies in other lands as well. Eventually, it stretched from the eastern seas, across the straights, and into the distant west where stood the Rhodope mountains.

In truth, they did not rule completely, their Empire, but a shadow of the true God Emperors of years past, never included many of the other peoples of Erde. No Dwarven lands came under their thumb, nor did the elven tribes who lived in the forest's deeps. And the orcs made constant war from their fortresses in the swamps, hills, and mountains. Other lands viewed them not as lords, but as distant rulers of far-away lands. Not until the end of their line did the

Emperors of Aenoch bring the world of Erde together, and then it was their master, the horned god, who did so.

During the rule of the Aenochian Emperors a host of new gods came into the lands. Powerful imaginings from the splintered mind of the All Father still roamed the world. In many cases, men adopted them as their gods and fell to worshiping them. Some stole away to the forest deeps and worshiped the trees from the Days before Days, returning to the druidic worship of Mordius. It is said that a singular sapling, the last living remnant of the Trees of the Mordius Grove throve in the Eldwood. This tree, called the Great Oak, became a god to many. Others worshiped the darkest imaginings of the All Father, horrid memories, of which Narrheit was the greatest. Within the Empire there existed a strange mixture of good and evil, slavery and dominance, a plethora of powers feeding off the collective imaginings of man. For ever had it been so. From the earliest days of the worship of Mordius to the present, the gods waxed in strength the more men worshiped them. The rule of the Emperors of Aenoch was marked by Chaos and so it reigned in all of Erde.

The magnificence of the Empire is marked well in the annals of that land. Some Emperors ruled with a genuine concern for the welfare of their subjects, some ruled with malice in forethought, and some with indifference. But so great was the wealth of the Aenochian Empire in those early days, that the Emperors could squander it. They built magnificent cities and fortresses, roads crisscrossing the land, and walled towns and castles along their length. In general, there was peace. They waged sporadic wars with the tribes of orcs and beast-like hobgoblins, and fought an occasional rebellion. But overall the Emperor's rule went unchallenged.

During the reign of Marcus IV, the unbroken line of the Golden House became entwined with wizardry. Marcus styled himself a sorcerer to rival the Goblins of yore, and in truth, he waxed powerful beneath the sun and moon. With his black arts he cast an ever greater control over his lords and nobles, so much so that their own wealth became threatened. When they hinted at rebellion and threatened his person he smote their numbers and devastated their houses. The descendants of these lords remembered the days and weeks of slaughter well. They called it the Festival of Clowns, for the emperor's assassins covered themselves in masks before stalking their prey.

Marcus lived in fear ever after. He feared for his line and its extermination. To safe guard the inheritance of his people, he crafted a powerful spell. He cast upon his line a binding with the throne and the Cunae Mundus Usquam, the crown of his forefathers. And it was prophesied that only one which bore the Mark of the true house could rule in Aenoch. The mark was seen in Marcus' own grandchild, Owen, who later ruled as Owen IV. The Mark, or so the histories report, consists of a singular vine upon the back, whose tip ends in a point.

After three centuries of rule, the Empire of Aenoch came to an end. Nomads from the distant west settled upon the frontiers. These fierce tribes hounded the Empire with constant border wars. Worse still came from the Northmen in long ships. Filled with a rage of violence and lust for plunder, they began raiding the lands. These Northmen were ever more a plague for the twin peoples, even into and beyond the rule of the Winter's Dark. The Emperor expended great amounts of wealth to combat these foes, and in so doing, stripped his lands of troops. The people of Ethrum rose in revolt, casting off the shackles of the Emperor's rule. Before he could muster the strength to combat them, his nobles rose against him.

The Wars of Liberation caused much devastation on both sides of the straights. Imperial armies marched to and fro attempting to crush the rebellious subjects, and mercenary troops looted, plundering towns and villages. The land burned and her people were despoiled. At the height of the war the Tarvish leaders of the Ethrumanians lay siege to the great fortress city of Avignon. For many long months they starved the city, but when this proved fruitless, their commanders led bloody assault upon the walls, eventually breaching them and bringing the city down in flames. Much destruction fell upon the folk of Avignon. Hostages were taken from the wealthy, and a great host of lords and ladies were done to death for serving the Emperor in far off Al-Liosh.

After the city fell, Lord Tarvish looked to his own defense. His armies were spent and his coffers empty, so he turned to fortifying his position. His first order concerned the Bridge of Ursal. He ordered the ancient edifice destroyed so that the easy traffic of armies between the east and west would come to an end. For many months his masons and engineers worked upon the bridge, tearing out many of the supporting foundation stones until at last, that herald of the ancient world fell into the sea. After many long years of intermittent war, the Emperor Marcus Owen I, great grandson of Marcus IV, fell at the hands of an assassin's blade and the line passed into obscurity.

So ended the Empire of Aenoch.

The Age of Heroes

Even as the Empire fell new Kingdoms and Principalities rose to replace it. With the Emperor's crown lost in the Wars of Liberation, the throne in Al-Liosh remained empty. There was little left of the old divisions of the two tribes. The peoples of Ethrum and Aenoch had become, by those days, intermingled, so that only a few lines of pure blood remained. These were restricted to a few noble houses and to isolated groups and settlements. The old tongues, long suppressed by the Empire, passed into the memory of men, replaced by the Vulgate language, a singular common tongue spoken by all but the old aristocracy.

An age of magic dawned upon Erde. For the first time, Sorcerers rose to prominence, separate from the seats of power, and men were not ruled by Kings alone. The magic of the Old World lingered in dark places, dungeons and abandoned cities. Great artifacts surfaced and were lost again. Men mastered the spells of old, remade them, and cast them anew in different forms. These wizards and sorcerers gathered in guilds, secret enclaves from which they master-minded the world's currents. There were many such societies, only a few of which are named here. These men and women bent their minds to unraveling the magic of the world, searching for the Language of Creation and attempting to make greater and greater spells.

It was an age of warriors, heroism, and legend. Many tales speak of errant knights carving out kingdoms for themselves. Mercenary captains commanded armies of freebooters in great battles and acts of war. One such knight, Gerard by name, changed the course of history. He found a tongue of flame burning on a slab of stone. The flame, or so the tales relate, was the last spark of the Language of Creation and as such a powerful source of magic. He took this fire, placing it in a dish of silver and platinum, and bore it aloft amongst men. He called for the holy and the righteous to join him in a brotherhood of arms. Soon after, he founded the knightly Order of the Holy Defenders of the Flame.

This was the Age of Heroes, when men, elves and dwarves battled the evil remnants of the Old Empire, fought monsters of myth, fashioned weapons of overwhelming power, and strove with one another for dominance of the world. It was truly an age when the gods reigned supreme and heroes, like Aristobulus, Luther, and Daladon half-elven, ruled the day.

For two centuries these small Kingdoms of men ruled the lands of Erde. They wrestled for possession of land where the Emperors had fought for whole provinces. This division gave rise to a host of new entities, and the lesser races gained more prominence.

The Gnomes, wasted somewhat in power and numbers, remained in the east, protected by the walled towns of mayors and burghers. Their's proved to be a precarious life, for not all the folk loved them and many blamed them for financing a continual spate of wars fought between the Middle Kingdoms. Eventually, many of the clans left these enclaves and settled in the foothills south of the Grundliche Mountains. The Flintlock became the home of many clans, and in later years, their only refuge.

The Halflings, ever passed over by the Chroniclers, enter the annals of these days in a strange fashion. It is reported that in the year 614oy, the city of Avignon, only slightly recovered from the Wars, commissioned 42 wagons owned by the Halfling Mac Muddles. The unnamed court scribe, no doubt in the employ of the city exchequer, goes on to mention the employment of the said Halfling's whole family as drivers, porters, cooks, and craftsmen. They traveled the land in tight bands, family units bound together by race and language. The laagers of wagons served the Halflings in many capacities, as homes, shops, caravans and even, or so it is reported, as castles.

The Elves too made their appearance in the annals, though little is known about their history. They came to the world during the Third Great Goblin-Dwarf war and worshiped Wenafar the Faerie Queen. They lived secretive lives, always lingering on the borders of Fay and Erde. But increasingly, as the world unwound, the Elven folk grew curious and moved to Erde to dwell for a time. Many of their folk grew to love it, for the strangeness of the place was unlike anything in their experience. They lived in their own Kingdoms deep in the wilds, for many years avoiding the Empire's reach. But during the Wars of Liberation they found themselves at odds with the Emperor and many joined against him. A fierce people when roused, the Elves left a lasting mark on the men of the west and they were given lands to call their own.

Only one Elven Kingdom, however, is known to have existed. Ruled by Queen Adavia, the realm of Elean stood upon the edges of the Shelves of the Mist. Here the Elves lived in peace, being content with the wonders of those dark woods and deep valleys. But bands of elves settled elsewhere across both the lands of Ethrum and Aenoch. The most notable of which lived upon the edges of the wild north of Kayomar, home to the Elven Prince Lothian, father of Daladon Half-Elven, who later came to play a great role in the history of the world.

It is said of Dwarves that "water washes away a stone mark sooner than a Dwarf forgets." But even the Dwarves forgot, or at least, set aside the memories of the ancient wars and at long last rekindled their forges. In Norgorod-Kam, they opened their doors and welcomed the coming of strangers. Dagmar I ruled in the beginning and when he fell to stone, his son, Dagnir I continued the intercourse with other peoples. In the east, Grundliche Hohle opened its gates, King Angorn IV bringing the wealth of his folk to the world.

So it came to be that in the traffic of the world there were many races and peoples represented.

But evil has ever plagued the lands of Erde. And so it was during the Ages of Heroes. As is written, the mage Trigal, who served under the last Emperor in Al-Liosh as a court scribe, rose to power during the reign of Owen IV. In 449oy he founded the White Order, or as

In a rage Daladon cursed his people and damned them.

it came to be known, the Ice Wizard Guild. Here he trained men and women in the arts of sorcery. It seemed in those days that his motives were no different than any other of his kind. But later, during the Imperial Wars, his dark designs were unearthed. The White Order in fact sought the Paths of Umbra, an ancient spell of the Goblins, said to have been used by Ondluche when he broke the Wall of Worlds.

The Emperor spent no time condemning Trigal but threw him out of Al-Liosh, disbanded the order, and forbade any on pain of death to seek out or come to know the Paths of Umbra.

Trigal discarded his name and adopted one more fitting his person. He called himself Nulak-Kiz-Din, but in later years he was known by a different name, Mongroul, the Troll Lord. He continued his quest for the Paths long after the demise of the empire and finally met success in 676oy. Legends repute that Nulak found the spell buried in the deeps of none other than Gorthurag. Many, however, dispute this, for that land has long been lost, her gate buried under tons of collapsed stone. And it is known that the Dwarves of the old world did not command such magic.

Regardless of the spell's origins, the discovery of the Paths of Umbra gave Nulak great power in the workings of magi across Erde. He reconstituted the White Order and gathered about him a host of sorcerers and wizards. From the spell Nulak learned the makings of the world, of how the All Father had discarded many powerful memories when first he pounded the substance of the world from the Void. He learned too that many of these memories lived as powerful entities, bound to the Void for eternity. Gates existed into the multiverse, opened by the Great Goblin Ondluche, but none existed to the Void, and the Wall of the World stood still against the prying eyes of those creatures left beyond.

With this knowledge Nulak thought to himself that he could bring such a creature to the Erde and it would rival any of the gods of men. And he thought that it would be his to control. So came to the world another tragedy. With the power commanded by the White Order, Nulak cast himself into the Void questing for a host to bring home. He searched for many years until last he found a dark sliver of the All Father's nightmare. He opened its mind and prepared it for entry.

Nulak failed to understand that the creature he found was not a simple dark dream. Rather, it was the All Father's greatest terror. It was a nightmare, a horrid thought conjured in his youth, cast aside as soon as it rose to the surface. The black thought lay buried in his mind until the spells of Ondulche gave it freedom. It passed through the Maelstrom and into the Void. This nightmare lived, though never dreamed of Erde. When Nulak came to it, it pretended to be amazed and enthralled, and so secretly it bound the sorcerer to him.

When Nulak returned to Erde he brought the beginnings of an undescribable plague. He set to building great temples to garner the power of the world's people so that he could add the weight of it to the spell of the Paths. These temples became, in time, instrumental to the summoning of the dark.

Nulak set to making the casting of the Paths of Umbra a reality, and in so doing, alerted other mages far more cautious than he. Patrice

of the Wood lived a simple life in the Kellerwald forest far in the south, but near enough Al-Liosh to know of the White Order and much of its doings. Patrice was a powerful wizard and good man. He kept to himself, seeking to let the world unravel its own history. But the White Order alarmed him. He studied them and in this way learned of the Path of Umbra and the making of the incantation. He set out to stop them, gathering a band of sorcerers from across the lands of Ethrum and Aenoch to combat the White Order.

These were the very days that Luther the Paladin, called the Gallant, of the House Pendegrantz, rose in the west to be a great knight and eventually, King of all Kayomar. Riding at his side were a group of companions who the gods fated to ride the crest of history beyond the Winter Dark. With Luther rode Daladon half-elven, son of Lothian the Elf; Dagnir the Dwarf, grand nephew and eventual King of Norgorod-Kam; Aristobulus the White Mage; and others. Many of their boon companions died, victims of many adventures, lost now to the annals of time. But many more rose and remained as powerful men throughout the continent. The greatest of these, Robert Luther, Luther's son, became Kayomar's greatest King. Jaren the monk, founder of the Order of the Scintillant Dawn, penned the very prophecy that foretold the present age. And Aristobulus' apprentice, Rapscallion, who bore the mark of Emperors, succumbed to the designs and greed of the White Order.

To these and others Patrice looked, for ever did that wizard command the sight of the future. He saw in Luther the rising power of the sword Durendale, a great part of the magic of Corthain. In Daladon he saw more, for the March Lord, as he was known to some, would in years to come, lay with Wenafar, the Faerie Queen and sire a demi-god, Utumno. And he saw Aristobulus, who would become the greatest wizard of any time. Seeing these futures, Patrice brought them into his fold and Council, and made them his allies in the war with the White Order.

For years these men struggled, meeting tragedy and sorrow, overcoming obstacle to win unsung victories. The tales of their battles are legendary and defy the space of the chronicles. Luther battled dragons in dark caves, spouting flame and death. The White Mage matched spells with spells in a grim contest of sorcery which lit the very heavens. Daladon hewed giants like wheat to claim the last sapling of Mordius' grove. It was an age where innocence died, when Avenging Sword, Durendale came to the fore. These were days of action, days of struggle. An age of heroes.

Patrice's Council consisted of twelve wizards of like power. The most notable of these, those who come into the tales of our days, were Crisigrin, who in later years traveled the seas of time, Helius the Singing Fool, Ozanna the Black-hearted, and Sagramore, who through the curses of Nulak and the horned god, fathered the race of blood thieves, the vampires. These mages, their servants, and the Kings of Kayomar waged a ceaseless battle with Nulak and the White Order.

The war came to a head in 706oy when the apprentice turned mage, Rapscallion, knowing the truth of the Mark of Emperors, turned on his master, betrayed his friends, and sought out the counsel of Nulal-Kiz-Din. Nulak led him in the destruction of all the pretenders to the throne and the Cunae Mundus Usquam. Rapscallion gathered his armies and commenced the conquest of his Kingdom. War flamed across the lands of Aenoch.

In the chaos and terror of these days none could predict the outcome. War consumed the world and the power of the sorcerer Rapscallion and the White Order seemed unstoppable. In 718oy, Rapscallion, having conquered most of Aenoch, placed the Cunae Mundus Usquam upon his brow, proclaiming himself God Emperor of Aenoch and Lord of Ethrum. With these proclamations, he brought upon himself the wrath of the Council of Patrice and the Kings in the west, most notably Luther in his high towered halls of Du Guesillon.

It was in these years that the Elves began to quietly leave their homes. They gathered in a great meet at the feet of the Queen Adavia of Elean, and debated the merits of remaining to aid the humans and dwarves, or returning to fay. The loss of life seemed strange to them, for they still possessed longevity, whereas men did not. The Elves never understood the Judgment of Corthain and how it made men seek hurriedly for a vanity that they never attained. Prince Lothian sought most of all to leave the world, for he had quarreled bitterly with his half-human son and wished nothing more than to rid himself of the vestiges of memory. But no decisions were made, and they waited to see the outcome of certain wars.

As war rolled across the great straights, the remaining Kingdoms gathered in a Holy Alliance and plunged themselves on a mad crusade against the enemy. Luther had, by this time, abdicated his throne in favor of his son Robert Luther, and taken the Durendale Sword into the east in an attempt to slay the Sorcerer Nulak, or the Emperor Sebastian, whichever came near him. With him traveled his old companions, Aristobulus and Daladon. Their task proved fatal, and Aristobulus fell to a Demon Lord from the Abyss before they reached the east and Luther, that greatest of heroes, called by the gods, carried the Durendale from the plain into the Dreaming Sea, there to guard and hide it from the enemy.

Daladon Lothian returned to the west, determined to raise more armies and continue the war. He learned then that the Elves, choosing to depart, had been leaving Erde for many years. In a rage he cursed his people and damned them. Unknowingly, his curses left his own half brother, Meltowg Lothian, possessed of a driving

need to battle upon the plains of Erde. He left his father in the lands of Fay, returning by secret ways to the world at large, where he and a small band of Elves battled the evil for a thousand years and more, until he was mad with his lust for war and destroyed any and all who stood against his grim purpose, whatever that may be.

In truth, not all the Elves fled the world with the Queen. Her own daughter, Londea remained behind with an order of Elven warlords, the Lunar Knights. They fought on into the modern era, and few remained when the Winter Dark Wars began. Many others stayed behind, hidden in the deep forests. Most notable of these were Nigold, King of the Wood Elves of the Eldwood. But also, there were the others, some becoming corrupted by the victories of the dark. These evolved into the Twilight Elves, neither good nor evil, but possessed of great knowledge of sorcery.

The greatest blow to the forces of good came when Nulak stole away to Castle Kelsion in the far north where Patrice had come to reside. The duel of wizardry fought between them lasted for many days and weeks. It is written that the arcane duel the two fought lit the heavens of the north for hundreds of miles, shook the earth, and left scars that to this day can be seen in the vicinity of that place. In the end Patrice was thrown down. Nulak bound him in a piece of the Paths of Umbra and hurled him into the heavens where he resides still, or so it is said, as a comet Patrice, circling the world, as it came to be, every thirteen years.

The Emperor in these days began to fear the power of the Arch-Magi and he forged a blade of Iergild metal and imbued it with arcane powers. By secret ways he stole himself into Luther's old land of Pendegrantz where the Holy Flame lay and he bathed the blade in the Language of Creation. So great the heat of flame that the steel of the blade turned fiery red and Sebastian lay spells into the receptive metal. The magic mingled with the Language and bound the Spell of Unmaking with the blade, so that ever after the Emperor felt secure against the coming dark.

Without the White Mage and Patrice, the Council proved too weak to combat the White Order and in the end, one of their own number, Ozanna, betrayed them. They were overwhelmed. Those fated to be so were hidden away, to return and fight another day.

Daladon and Jaren alone, of all the great heroes of that day, stood in defiance. But tragedy struck them a final blow as the Half-Elven fell to a dragon in the south. Jaren bore his body back to his home in the Eldwood, laying it upon the ground at the feet of the Great Oak. There the tree consumed his body and soul, harboring it for another day and other battles. Jaren, the last of the last, returned to Robert Luther's side and bound himself to the fate of that greatest of Kings. At this time the Holy Alliance stood strong and the Lords of Kayomar and the other realms defied the Emperor and taunted him to come and battle. But all feared the power of the son of Luther and none would come forth.

So the world stood when at last Nulak-Kiz-Din broke the seals of the Paths of Umbra and summoned the Unklar, the horned god, to the plane of Erde.

The Last God Emperor and the Coming of the Dark

As the last breath of the Days before Days blew across the land the Emperor Sebastian Olivier I sat upon his throne with the Cradle of the World upon his brow. Behind him stood his councilor, the High Priestess, Nectanebo, servant of the goddess Imbrisuis. Before them both stood Nulak-Kiz-Din. Folds of sorcery wrapped the Arch-Magi, clothing him in power. He called upon this fountain of magic and lay the Incantations of the Paths of Umbra to summon the horror from the Void. Sebastian Oliver, last of the House of Aenoch, used vile sorcery learned from the Wizard Aristobulus, to aid him and Nectanebo lent her considerable weight to the spell's undertaking. The Paths of Umbra, a spell of Ondluche the Goblin's of old, split the Wall of the World, opening a gate to the beyond. And Unklar, wrapped in shrouds of the substance of creation, stepped into the world of Erde.

None could have foretold the true horror which Paths of Umbra would bring. Indeed, had Nulak known he would not have cast the spell, and had the Emperor known the fate which Unklar would deal him, he certainly would not have consented to the atrocity.

But as is told in the year 748oy the devil came to Erde and the long days of the Feast of Death began. The High Priest Nectanebo he slew upon sight, even before the spell fully completed its cycle. Sebastian, alarmed, drew forth his great sword, Discipero and commanded the beast to yield. It was the first and last time any mortal commanded Unklar in any tone. He slew the Emperor Sebastian and cast his broken body upon the daos. He cast aside Sebastian's sword and crown, and took his seat upon the throne of the God Emperors.

The Crown, the Cunae Mundus Usquam, the Cradle of the World, the one which had rode upon the brows of the Emperor's of Aenoch of old, fell to the earth. The ringing of its fall sounded like a singular bell, tolling the demise of the world. But the Emperor's chief constable, the Baron Harakon Petrovich, stole the iron banded crown and the sword of his master and fled the world to the hinterlands of the planes, where he hid both items from the prying eyes of the undeserving.

This great horned devil from the darkest imaginings of the All Father set to destroying the known world. Nulak became his mouth on Erde, and together they waged a war on the Middle Kingdoms. He fashioned the ungern, the children of the dark, from the substance of the Void, which he carried with him when summoned. He made them in the deeps of Al-Liosh, which was Aufstrag, and set them loose upon the world. He bound many people to him and made war upon all the lands.

But the Dark was named, Fell Unklar, and in his fear roused himself and fortified the Keep of Al-Liosh anew. Rending the earth with his great axe he clove huge rifts about the Imperial castle, destroying the city of Al-Liosh. With sorceries he created great pools of water and pestilence to cover the rent lands. And all of Aenoch between the rivers Udunilay and Uphrates was made a swamp of fell death. He destroyed the inner city, turning it into rubble. For miles about he ruined 3000 years of history. Then, lifting the ground on high, he made a true mountain of slag amidst tumbled buildings and set his high citadel atop. The fortress itself he fashioned in the shape of a tree thousands of feet high, a grim mockery of Wenafar and the Great Tree in the west. All this he surrounded with mighty buttresses and fell towers. And this abode he named anew, calling it Festung Aufstrag, the Citadel of Command. The ruins of Al-Liosh sprawled underneath Aufstrag and into the countryside around.

The Elves watched in horror from the land of Fay. Many became distraught and called for a return to Erde where they could stand or fall with the Holy Alliance. For these folk Erde held a special place, a true home that was not fashioned from the death of the All Father as the lands of Fay had been. The lords and ladies of Shindolay became embittered in the debate and sundered thereby. Many, remembering the words of Daladon Lothian, made to return to Erde but they found the plane barred to them by the will of Unklar. They focused upon the gates, making spells and war on the closed portals, ever seeking to return. So they remained for countless years, living in limbo, refusing to return to Shindolay. They called themselves the Fontenouq Elves, which mean, roughly, "the ones abandoned, or lost." These elves grew in knowledge, but also in bitterness, and they harbored hatreds for the dark one in Aufstrag, but also for their kin in Shindolay.

The Holy Alliance gathered what forces they could to resist the coming dark. They built fortresses, fortified Avignon anew, and lay in stores for a war they increasingly felt was hopeless. What peoples in the east still remained, fell quickly. Rumors of the slaughter spread to the west and people came to know fear. A wave of panic rolled over the people and many cast themselves into rivers or hid themselves away. They despaired, for truly none had believed that a return of the terrors of the world would ever come to pass. And many could not bear the face of evil which strode the plains.

A respite of sorts came to the folk of Ethrumania for Unklar first turned his attention to the gods. The other Powers saw the onslaught too late. Smug in their hidden worlds, safe in the fealty of thousands, they failed to realize the threat and evil of Unklar. For eleven brutal years he stalked out the gods, slaying them or casting them into chains. In this War of the Gods, some few escaped his wrath, Tefnut, Durendale, the Great Oak, but many fell and ceased to be. Narrheit alone, lord of chaos and evil, stood against the Unklar and they fought upon the rolling hills of the north. At the height of the battle Narrheit lifted his sword to cleave down the dark one, but Unklar turned the ground beneath him to ice and struck the earth a mighty blow. The ice crumbled, shattering into a thousand shards. One such shard gouged Narrheit's face and he staggered and fell into the newly formed glacier and was penned. So terrible the battle between these two gods that the lands about them became a wasteland, frozen now by Unklar's spells, a glacier stretching hundreds of miles. In later days it was named the Frozen Salt Flats, for a frost of ice forever remained and the soil of the place still bore salt from the sea that covered it in the Days before Days.

The horned god bound Narrheit and imprisoned him in a tower of brass. Around the tower he built a keep, and around the keep he built a city with walls interspersed with twenty towers. This the City of Seven contained Narrheit for a thousand years, though in truth the city never fully contained the chaos of that god. The City of Seven became a strange wicked place, where many things escaped the order of the world of Winter Dark. Old Lords of Law, and many others beside, traveled there from time to time, to hunt chaos and to relish that peculiar entertainment.

With the fall of the gods the folk of Erde thought all was lost. The Dwarves closed their Kingdoms to traffic. But for a few, the last of the Elves passed into Fay. The Gnomes and Halflings fled to forest deeps and hid themselves away. The Orcs, Hobgoblins and even those Eldritch Goblins who remained, joined Unklar in warring upon the men of the world. Many peoples in other lands flocked to Unklar's banners, seeing in them their respite. He welcomed them, melding them with his own force.

For 40 years Unklar waged his war against Erde and wherever he went the clouds of winter lingered ever after.

At the last, only the men of Ethrum held out. They stood against the dark for a great while, led by King Robert Luther, his family, and Jaren of the Order of the Scintillant Dawn. These last wars, which came to be known as the Catalyst Wars, were long and brutal and saw the extermination of the House of Pendegranze and the end of active resistance on Erde for a thousand years.

 he Catalyst Wars

In which the line of St. Luther was brought to an end and the light extinguished in the world. These Chronicles are drawn directly from those written by Mourilee Lothian Pendegrantz before she died, and recount this last great war in the world's defense. The names of ancient Kingdoms have been supplanted by the more recent political entities in order to better comprehend where the battles were fought.

761-763 The armies of the dark came across the Straights of Ursal and first lay siege to the fortress city of Avignon. For two years the Mayors of that noble town withstood the dark. Twice the Kings of the West attempted to break the siege but failed. The Holy Defenders of the Flame led the second attack and many of their number fell at the hands of the enemy, such that the Flame itself was almost extinguished. After two brutal years the town, starving and rife with diseases, opened her gates to the dark.

763-777 The next battles of the Catalyst War were fought in and around the lands of Angouleme. These were the borders of the free Kingdoms of Ethrum after the first onslaught of the Unklar in 748. The armies fought on the plains of Angouleme, the Gelderland, Sienna and Maine until at last the forces of the Free Peoples were thrown back and into Kayomar. Many of King Robert Luther's family fell in these battles. His elder sister, Vivian Brightleaf, fell at the side of her son, Owen Augustus, at the battle of Iaden Hill in 763. Another nephew, Vivian's second son, Robert Oralius, known the

world wide for his knightly virtue, fell in 783. The King's first born and heir, Talerein Uther, died at the battle of Crossed Fork in 777. Talerein, who slew a Red Dragon with the Achel Sword, fell during the last great charge of the Holy Defenders of the Flame. From those to the last the Defenders were few in number.

775 Nulak-Kiz-Din commanding an army of Ungern overwhelmed the lands of Angouleme and Sienna. He rose in the councils of the dark god, Unklar.

778 In this year Jaren the Wise spoke the language of prophecy. He predicted a long winter ahead for the world. Robert Luther spurned his council and told him to gird himself for war. He would never hear of such talk and demanded further that Jaren discover a way around the world's folly. Jaren began exploring the Maelstrom through study and contemplation.

789-790 The campaign continued with the last bastion of Law holding Kayomar against a pincer attack from north and south. In the south, Prince Erik Aristobolus Euryiance, commanding Kayomar's fleet, routed and destroyed the bulk of Unklar's navy (789). The Prince, though, falls in combat, mortally stricken by a great iron bolt thrown by the giant Herigold. The northern Marches are completely overrun (789-790). The mighty fortress of Pendelion held the enemy at bay. The first siege of Pendelion was broken in 790 by the King and his host of Knights.

Jaren, 85 years old, traveled a channel in time. He convinced a youthful Aristobulus, Luther and Daladon to strike one of the temples of Unklar and keep the god from arriving on the plane. The plan fails, but Jaren became obsessed with this quest. He returned, aged and more tired.

791 Unklar's troops regrouped and attack again in 791. They attacked with a massive army along the Great River through the Shelves of the Mist. Unbeknownst to the King, they held a large force in reserve north of Pendelion.

The King moved his host to the Shelves to counter the thrust of orc and ungern legions. In the Battle of Merrick Fords (791), the liege men of Maine turned on the King and joined Unklar. They fell upon the baggage train and encampments, slaughtering all they could find. The King, being outnumbered and surrounded, fought his way into the eastern marshes and there regrouped. The King's youngest sister, Merilee Lothian *(the Chronicler's own mother~Roland)*, was slain in the encampments.

Jaren again broke into the time stream, this time into the future to lay the seeds for his own survival, for he saw the end near and knew that no amount of aid could give the King his victory. My master begins penning the Books of Jaren.

792 Unklar's reserves were thrown against Pendelion. For nine months they laid siege to the city/fortress. The King tried twice to break the siege. The enemy at last stormed the city and conquered it. Another of the King's sisters fell in this, the second siege of Pendelion; the bodies of Gwenowin Lilly, and her children were stolen away and borne back to Du Guesillon by a magical weird of Jaren's crafting.

These twin victories opened central Kayomar to Unklar. Robert Luther fought a withdrawal, hoping for supernatural aid as promised to him by Jaren the Wise. For the next eight years Unklar's folk stormed castle and fort, rooting all the folk out of the valley, despoiling what they could. The people fought bravely, selling themselves dearly. Unklar's folk suffered losses so great that even today the mention of Kayomar and her King is a horrid thing to the Orcs and Ungern.

794 The prophecy comes to Jaren. He predicted the return of the White Mage and the sword Durendale. Robert Luther pondered upon these prophecies, wondering if Jaren's age had not finally caught up with him.

798 The King ordered a paladin of the order of the Holy Defenders of the Flame to take the sacred dish to safety. The knight, Jared of Hale, bore the dish and flame into the Rhodope Mountains. He hid it there beneath the roots of a great sentient tree.

799 At last Du Guesillon is surrounded and the siege begins. For almost two years Unklar's legions battered at the doors of the mighty fortress, but to no avail. The King laughed them from the walls and lead countless sorties into the fray, slaying much and more beyond. But at last Unklar himself came and unmade the walls. With a great crash they fell to the earth. The dark assailed the King in his the Tower of Hope, the last bastion. Some of the last to fall are in the House Pendegrantz. Jariel Galen, third son of Luther, fell on the steps of the tower at his brother's feet. Roger of Guis, Lord of the Defenders fell there too, as did the Ranger Volstagg. At last the King stood alone. He sallied forth to fight Unklar, and the two fought upon the courtyards of Du Guesilon. Even so outmatched, the King fought bravely to the end, so wounding Unklar, or so it is told, that that god evermore feared the House Pendegrantz. The King fell on the 28th day of Nochturn, 800, and the light went out in the world.

Jaren the Wise, Master of the Order of the Scintillant Dawn, stood alone. He could do little in the end but pen the Books of Jaren, wherein he foretold the fall of Unklar and how this might come about. Nulak-Kiz-Din came to him then, for Unklar could not enter the Tower of Hope. He took the monk in battle and carted him off to Al-Liosh, which was afterwards called Aufstrag and bound him there, reserving for him a particular hatred, though the reasons for this are lost to us. A curse of memory he placed upon the monk so that never more would he know what he wrote, or how he wrote the prophecies of the Winter Dark's eventual unmaking.

800 The Year of the Dark.

The Waning of the World

Mourilee Lothian Pendegrantz fled with many other refugees of Kayomar into the far distant west. The victory of Prince Erik Aristobulus Euryiance over Unklar's navy in 789oy left the command of the sea to the folk of Kayomar. They gathered what ships they could and in the company of Luther's bastard son, Morgeld, set sail for the Wall of the Worlds. For years they sailed, the journey a legendary trek fraught with countless horrors. The voyage sent them to the far edge of the world where they founded a colony.

Later, this colony became the Solarium Empire, the Empire of the Sun. Morgeld settled upon an Island, called the land of Bliss, where he lived out his immortal days in the company of similar warriors, bound in the ecstasies of pleasure and defeat. Here, he ruled with an iron fist, holding the Black Spear, Gorgothorium, in his grasp.

All the other peoples of Erde had fallen to the dark god Unklar and bore little hope. Myths arose around the Books of Jaren, saying that they held the hope of the world. It is also told that Jaren's time travels bound him to the Tower of Hope. An incarnation of his future self co-existed with his present, and in the past a schism in time emerged so that a specter of the monk is always seen in the Tower of Hope. These are the legends of the Tower and Jaren, who in our day became the Falkynjager.

Other legends came as well many originating in the Books of Jaren which have since been lost. They told stories of the Return of the sword Durendale, how Luther, father of the King, would carry it to slay the Unklar. Too, the Holy Flame would emerge from hiding and remake the world with the its language, removing the stains of Unklar. But more important was the blade Discerpo, Sebastian's sword. For it was told that within that steel the Emperor, no little sorcerer, cast the Spell of Unmaking. A horrid word, which if properly cast, would close the Paths of Umbra and seal Unklar in the Void once more.

In the last ten years of light, the Kingdom of Kayomar stood alone against Unklar and his vile folk. But, only the Great Tree avoided Unklar's touch for it hid in the deeps of the Eldwood, on the edge of the world. There, servants of the Oak under the spirit of the ranger lord Daladon, struggled through the long lonely years of the millennial dark.

So the Age of Heroes ended, so the light of the sun left the world and so began the Age of Winter Dark.

The Age of Winter Dark

Being an Account and History in brief of the Millennial Darkness, the Winter Dark; of the Wrapping of the World & the Binding of the Twin Sisters. As compiled by the Court Scribe of King William I of Angouleme, Leopold of Passou.

Unklar the Black settled within the Halls of Al-Liosh and made that place his fortress. In time of years the place became a cesspool of all things vile. Tunnels, great and small, fanned out beneath the halls into the rock of the world, towers and buttresses rose into the sky, and the fortress city sprawled out over the hills and along the river valleys.

In the beginning some resistance remained. Of the Dwarves, Grundliche Hohle and Norgorod-Kam held out for some time. Many other folk, in distant lands did as well, though their tales do not come into the telling. Unklar spent many years battling them, until at last Norgorod-Kam closed her gates, and he sacked Grundliche Hohle The fall of that Kingdom echoed in the world and from that day to this, the Dwarven Folk shudder at the loss, for the greater part of them the Lords of Unklar carted off to Aufstrag as slaves, many more they slew. Only a few fled into the hinterlands of the Grundliche Mountains.

As testament to all those who resisted him, Unklar took up the battered body of Jaren the Wise. The monk still lived, though his aged body could not have lasted long in the dungeons of that place. But Unklar gave of himself to the monk, breathing the breath of life into his lungs so that Jaren became immortal. He crucified him then, nailing his body above the gates of his citadel. There he hung for a thousand years, the slow trickle of his blood spilling upon the ground. Many came to see him, reveling in his suffering, and his blood became a drug to evil lords who thirsted for such things. But too, it was a holy sufferance. And it is told that one Leonidas, follower of the Scintillant Dawn, came to Jaren and took up some of the blood in a holy cup.

Unklar's power waxed great in the early days of his rule, and after the fall of Grundliche Hohle he set himself the task of reshaping the world. Foremost, he gathered together the gods of man and dwarf whom he had not slain. Some he bound to him, and they became his

Captain Kings and ruled Erde in his name. Most of these were the great devils, who in the after days fled to the hell. They proved to be an unruly lot and rose in rebellion against their master time and time again. The Lord of Sorrow was chief amongst these Captain Kings and commanded Unklar's hosts in battle, often against the other Kings.

Unklar did not restrict himself to the divine ordering of things. He set about creating a true Empire of men. He ordered roads built between the larger cities and fortress. He built castles along the way, to house his troop or to imprison his enemies. He awarded loyal men with land and serfs, appointed assessors to gage the wealth of his land, and marshaled legions of troops to guard it. Taxes, duties and tithes filled the coffers of his minions who eventually formed a powerful aristocracy. These ruling elites controlled the more mundane affairs of the world, paying the dark god respects and making him sacrifice.

Unklar pondered the world and his ownership of it. He thought upon the countless ages of imprisonment in the Void. Ever as powerful as the early gods, Corthain and Thorax, Unklar knew his substance. He knew of himself as a memory, a passing emotion of the All Father's, and therefore, unbound by the Language of Creation, nor restricted in his doings by the substance of the Void. He saw the work of the All Father and thought to himself that creation had gone astray. He thought too, that he would repair the damage done by folly and neglect, for ever did he see himself as the better part of the All Father. With this in mind he set to refashioning the whole of the World of Erde.

As is written, the world was flat, contained by the great fog of the Wall of the World. Erde stood as the center of creation. This Unklar could not abide. Beneath the world he found the bones of the All Father and within these the magic of creation. This Unklar stole and used for his own purpose. He took lust from the dead All Father and lit a great fire which burned evermore in the heavens above Erde. He wrapped the world around the skull of the All Father and chained it to the Fires of Heaven. Erde orbited the burning embers of the dead god, taunting the people of the world with a light they could not have. The dark of night haunted the folk of the world.

In defiance of Unklar, Frafnog the Great Dragon stole the heart of the All Father and gave it to the Faerie Queen. She hurled it into the heavens to mock Unklar's lust and to remind him that his rule would end and he raged against her and hated her everafter.

With his great might Unklar devoured the fog of the Wall of Worlds and blew it forth again as a breath of chill air. Great clouds settled far and wide across Erde, blanketing all in a world of Winter and Dark. The legends of those days tell of a great fog rising in the heavens, of the dampening of the light of the sun. The fog, they called the Shroud of Darkness or the Cold Mist for it brought a terrible cold. Sheets of snow and sleet blanketed the northern lands in ice, and much of the south as well. The Shroud hung over Erde for 800 years, and in time the warmth of the sun and the pure, unfiltered light of day, became legends to the people. They spoke of these things as if faerie tales.

The Winter Dark settled upon the land.

In defiance of Unklar, Frafnog the Great Dragon stole the heart of the All Father and gave it to the Faerie Queen. Unklar raged against her and hated her everafter.

It is said by some that the Twin Sisters, the All Father's moon and sun, never fell to Unklar, but rather fled into the Maelstrom. They were of the All Father's first creations and were possessed of wondrous power and defied him from beyond. Though they never fought Unklar, nor served the folk of Erde in the long struggle to overthrow the horned god, they did return after his defeat. Many accounts of great balls of fire hurling forth from Unklar's sun after he died and of a greater radiance coming from the moon. For this reason they are called by some few, the Twin Sisters, and are often confused with the gods of that same name.

Unklar surveyed his work and deemed it good, and sat upon his throne in Aufstrag and slept for a great many years. In truth, Unklar spent much of his power in recasting the Wall of the World. Forming the Shroud of Darkness took much of the magic he brought from the Void and never again was he what he had been.

The Elves, under their new King, Calphone, hid their realm with a magic of mist, not unlike the Shroud of Darkness.

When at last Unklar awoke, he found his vassals in a great war with one another. The Captain Kings, seeing nothing of their Lord for many years, warred upon one another for dominance of Erde. They fought battles upon the broad plains, within the skies, and under the ground. They placed huge armies of men, orc and ungern into the field, and they clashed in contests of arms.

A rage took Unklar and he flew forth from Aufstrag to force the fealty of his vassals once again. Men, great and small, flocked to his side, for none could resist him in those days. Nulak, always waiting in the wings, once more served as the voice of Unklar. The Arch-Magi's power waxed great. In dismay, the Captain Kings faltered and fell back. They feared him and cast themselves upon his mercy. He chastised them, binding them with ever greater spells, and forced them to do his bidding once more.

With the war finished and the fury of his vassals abated, Unklar turned his attention to the world of Erde. He pondered long and hard upon what shape he could fashion the world so that no one could flee him. He saw the Maelstrom and the multiverse. As he pondered these things, Inzae rose from the world beneath and fell upon Unklar. The Dragon goddess lamented the All Father's demise and she swore to unmake Unklar. But lo, his power was never greater than in those days, and the source of it was the All Father himself. And Inzae realized that Unklar knew the Language of Creation and that she could not unmake him. They wrestled in the heavens above Erde for many long weeks until at last Inzae quit the battle, returning again to her own world.

For his part Unklar knew not the origins of Inzae, but he realized that he could never overcome her as he had the other gods. He watched and waited for a great while until at last he understood that the world of Inzae resided on the underside of Erde. So, Unklar took up the All Father's bones and lent himself to bending the world, wrapping its form around the All Father's skull so that the corners met. He remade Erde around that of Inzae so that forever more the one lay within the other. In this way the Dragon goddess, Inzae, and her world, became prisoner within Erde.

And he spun Erde through the Maelstrom, making it turn around the sun. The moon, he captured, and bound it to the world, so that together, all three would spin through the heavens. As before, his tasks completed, Unklar returned to fell Aufstrag and slept, secure in his towers and halls of stone, weaker all the more.

As is told during these long years, the people of Erde could offer Unklar little resistance. Though in truth the powers that eventually challenged him began to surface in small ways. Aristobulus, long bound to a demon prince in the Abyss, adapted himself to the shadows and stole away into the deeper pits of the horrid plane. For many years he hid himself from prying eyes, a shadow of a shade. At last he learned to bend light and took form once more. In this way he returned to Erde to haunt the world of Unklar and to seek aid wherever he could.

The Order of the Holy Defenders of the Flame struggled on as well. Their Master, his name lost to history, took the Flame from its hiding place and moved it to the Tower of Hope in the ruins of Du Guesillon. There he hoped it would serve as a signal for Luther's return from the Dreaming Sea. A singular knight always stayed in the snow bound ruins of the castle to keep watch and to bear word when the Paladin should return. This vigil they kept for the full 6 centuries until his return was realized.

South, in the Eldwood, the Watchers in the Wood stayed true to the memory of Daladon and they battled the forces of Unklar's devising for many long years. Those march lords fought lonely battles against hopeless odds there in the dark of the world.

Unklar at last awoke to find the world of Erde blanketed in a cold dark sheet of snow and ice. He reveled in it and called to his minions to cease their squabbles, which they had begun again. In the pits of Aufstrag he carved out a forge. The size of it defied comprehension. It became a place of wicked experiments, tortures and craftings. The folk of Aufstrag named it Klarglich, that is "The Pit of Woe," for the suffering screams of the damned filled the place. Unklar first used Klarglich to create the Hounds of Darkness. These sulking beasts, birthed from the tortured bodies of faerie kin, possessed but one purpose, to root out the elves upon whatever plane they existed. Though the creatures failed, many dying in the process, they signaled of things to come.

Soon thereafter, as is recorded by the Elven Scrolls, the folk of Shindolay, that realm in the lands of Faerie, found an entrance to Erde and sent out the Quest Knights. These Lords had two purposes, to find Londea, the daughter of the Queen, and to locate the elves of Fontenouq. Though they hunted for many centuries, they failed in both tasks, many suffering death, many suffering a fate far worse. Only one returned, and he brought reports of evil and mayhem and of a world in strictest order.

In despair, Melius the Wise bared the gates of Faerie to all, forever closing out the possibility of any Fontenouq elves returning. He bound all in a portal, fashioned after one of the Brass Rings. Within it stood the gates of Faerie, Erde, and, unknown to Melius, Fontenouq. The ring he placed in a stone and set many knights and magic to guard it in the Castle of Spires, buried in the planes, but linked to Erde by the Twilight Wood.

It should be noted that the world under the Winter Dark was an ordered place. Despite the tyranny of the evil of Unklar, he rarely bothered the common folk. Indeed, he sometimes leant his assistance to them. It is recorded that when the Shroud of Darkness overwhelmed the plain that many men and animals succumbed to starvation as crops withered and died. Unklar saw that the death of so many men weakened him, as he throve on their worship. So he set to creating a host of resilient plants that could endure the cold and the lack of light. These crops became the main staple of food for the men of Erde.

There were cities, towns and villages as there had always been. People bought goods and sold them in common markets. The world existed under his evil even as it had under the Middle Kingdoms, and all the other realms that came before. The greatest difference was the rule of law and evil. None could move that were not watched. None could speak that were not heard. It was a land and a time, stagnant, in the grip of one tyrannical god.

It was then that Nulak-Kiz-Din found the Dwarf, Dolgan, son of Hirn, in the Grundliche Mountains. He was but a boy and could not long resist the Arch-Magi, who made him a slave. Dolgan was the last of the line of Angrod of old, Kings of Grundliche Hohle, and possessed great gift of forging and crafting. In time the Dwarf came before Unklar and the horned god knew him for what he was. He tried to force the Dwarf into servitude, but the son of Hirn would not yield. His blood came from the Language of Creation, and more, he was a Dwarf. This act of defiance earned him a name amongst many in the pits of Aufstrag. They called him Dolgan Furchtlos, which is the "undaunted." But Unklar named him differently, calling him Dolgan Ungekront, the "uncrowned." Unklar bound him to Klarglich then and bid him do what he would, so long as he fashioned weapons of war for the dark lords.

Wars uncountable were fought between and with the Captain Kings and ever and anon did Unklar spend himself to break them apart and ever did he leave vestiges of his power in hidden places.

In his later years, with the aid of the enslaved son of the last King of Grundliche Hohle, Unklar forged splinters of his own mind and made the Mogrl, great spirits of fire and ash. He fashioned twenty-four of the beasts and he set them to watching the world. But they took from him more power and thus diminished him even more.

In the latter days Aristobulus took himself to the City of Seven, the only place of chaos left upon Erde. There he founded the Mystic Enclave. Those magi he dedicated to unearthing the ancient Books of Jaren, locating Luther and the sword Durendale upon the Dreaming, and learning of the final fate of Daladon.

Unklar came to Dolgan at this time and bid him fashion a crown for the God Emperor of Erde. Dolgan, after 300 years of servitude to the forge, had become a Master in the craft of making. His knowledge included the natural skills of his people as learned from the

All Father in distant times, but too, it included the skills of Unklar, for often had the horned god aided Dolgan at the forge. And there in dark solitude Dolgan bent iron and shaped the greatest of his creations, a crown to meet the Dark One's lust for beauty, and he crafted the shape with magic held in the deeps themselves and released by the might of the Dark God. He named it the Krummervole, the "Crown of Sorrow." So perfect was this creation that the forge slave sought to keep it for himself but Unklar took up the crown and laughed. The Dwarf cursed him, and called him thief, for the Crown took his mind with the lust of greed. Upon his own brow Unklar sat the wondrous Crown and in his hand the Urtiel mace, "the hand of Judgment." So did Unklar rule the world.

In the 1003(md) year of his reign, which is the 1803oy by the old calendar, Unklar discovered the Dreaming Sea. And he became aware of Luther's presence. In fury he cast himself upon that wild expanse and fashioned warriors from his own dreaming. These, as Luther called them, "slivers of Unklar's imagining," traveled the dreamscape hunting the paladin. They fought on many occasions but the paladin proved too strong and killed them or drove them off. This creation weakened Unklar more than he knew, for when the Paladin, who had become master of the world's dreams fought the warriors upon the dreamscape, he came to know Unklar. The horned god's fears and weaknesses revealed at last, Luther resolved to return to Erde and take up the long abandoned war.

Luther watched from the Dreaming Sea, and he learned that Dolgan,

son of Hirn had gathered a host of slaves, Dwarves, Goblins and men, and led them in a revolt in the very pits of Grundliche Hohle. Many tales abound as to why Dolgan took up arms against his dark master. It is known that he had befriended an Eldritch Goblin, Agmaur, the very one who had sacked the Dwarven Kingdom of Grausumhart 3000 years before. And many believe that the two together rose in rebellion. Some others relate that Dolgan could not bare the stealing of the Krummervole by Unklar, and he therefore threw off his shackles. But the truth of it bore the likeness of no other tale.

Dolgan saw the Unicorn. Such a beautiful beast came into his chambers, brought to him for his use. The beast hardly passed for living and Dolgan, seeing its wonder and beauty, took pity on it. When it died, it gave Dolgan the right of its body and he used the horn and blood of the creature to fashion an ax to rival the Axe of the All Father. This fell weapon he named Havoc, "revenge."

In 1012md he made war on the dark, raising the slaves of the pit in rebellion. He and Agmaur gathered Goblins and Dwarves, men and orcs, and fought the troops of Unklar in the bowels of the earth. Untold was the suffering of the Trench Wars. The wicked battles fought in dark holes, down darker corridors, against an implacable enemy. Knives and hatchets ruled the day, primitive powder weapons left tunnels filled with mutilated corpses, smoke and ash. At last in the 1018th year of Unklar's reign, the Dwarves and other slaves broke free and fled to the mountains in the north.

During this chaos, as the horned god spent himself to unmake the damage Dolgan had done, Luther strode onto the plane. He came from the Dreaming Sea to the very gates of Aufstrag. He battled the guard for control of the wall and they fell back in fear of the sword and the Paladin returned. He cut Jaren from the wall and took him unto the Dreaming where he healed him. Then Luther and Jaren journeyed to the Isle of Wonder where Aesop the Mage had imprisoned Aristobulus. They freed their long time companion and slew Aesop, and traveled to the Eldwood to the grove of the Great Tree.

Unklar's power had waned and those survivors who had hidden themselves for many years gathered around the spirit of the Great Tree. The Watchers in the Wood, the Holy Defenders of the Flame, and others besides, gathered for war. Dolgan came, and with him Agmour the Goblin. They were joined by Nigold, the Elven King, and all his folk, who were a wonderment in those days, for as is told, they had remained when the greater part of the Elves fled the world.

Others joined this growing alliance. Daladon Half-Elven returned from the halls of the dead, and Albrecht the River King left the service of the dark, taking a host of knights with him. All these folk made war upon the dark and the winter, and in the 1019th year of Unklar's reign the Winter Dark Wars began.

he Winter Dark Wars

Here begins part of the tales and deeds of arms of those who fought in the Winter Dark Wars. A recounting of the rise of the Council of Light, the return of the Dwarves to Glory, and the fall of the Unklar and end of the Winter Dark.

1019md

As is written, the War commenced in the 1019th year of the reign of Unklar, styled "the Dark." A plethora of men and women gathered together under the leadership of Luther, Master of the Order of the Holy Defenders of the Flame, Aristobulus the White Mage, heir to the Council of Patrice, and Jaren the Wise, called the Falkynjager, for his lust for revenge consumed him in those early days. These and other Lords formed a secret gathering, the Council of Light, and made ready for war.

The first act of aggression came not from the Council however, but from the long suffering Elven Warrior, Prince Meltowg Lothian. Ever hounded by his brother's curse, Meltowg had fought the dark in many places. His body carried scars, his mind wounds, and many reported that a madness had long overcome him. But he did not care. He traveled with a company of mercenaries, mostly Elves of the Lunar Knights, and these men called themselves the Vale Knights.

Meltowg had long ago learned of the Castle of Spires where the portals to the Elven realms lay, and he had knowledge, gained from sorcery, of the elves of Fontenouq. He entreated Melius to open the gates to Shindolay and Fontenouq for the Dark was much weakened. But Melius refused and Meltowg and his company laid siege to the Castle. The kin slaying began as Elf slew Elf for possession of the portal. The siege lasted for a great while.

The early months of the war saw the Council gathering allies in the west. They traveled to the Solarium Empire to gather aid and knights for their battles. There they found many allies, chief amongst these, Luther's half demon bastard son, Prince Morgeld, who rallied to their cause. But all this activity brought the ire of Unklar down upon Solarium. He marshaled the Lord of Sorrow and bid him destroy the enemy in the west.

1020md

The One thousandth and twentieth year of the reign of the Dark saw the opening of the Gate of Thonor. The Lord of Sorrow managed the gate by using the ancient Rings of Brass of Dwarf make, which they had fashioned during the second Great Goblin-Dwarf war when the world was young. In this manner the host of the Lord of Sorrow issued forth into the Great Waste before the gates of the Valley of Light and the Empire of the Sun. The Empire was well guarded by natural terrain. In the west stood the sea, where Prince Morgeld, the Fell Knight, lived with his navy and army of immortal soldiers. High mountains in the north and south came together in a narrow defile, which offered the only egress to the Valley of the Empire. Here, a wide, deep river flowed upon the western banks of which were tall crenelated battlements. These walls stood boldly forth in defiance of the dark host, but siege was laid against it and war brought to the far west.

But Unklar knew of Morgeld and knew too his heritage. He sent forth a fleet of black ships, filled with foul orc and ungern soldiers, to hound the Son of Luther and retrieve the Black Spear. But being bold and fierce, the Prince, roused from his drugged stupor by Luther, gathered his Islander host and set his seven great ships to sea as if for war. The folk of Morgeld, the Immortals, were few in number but fierce in battle. These men or elves, all lords from the Age of Heroes, had cheated death in one fashion or the other. Armed and girded for war, they slipped from the Isle in a lust for battle. Terrance the Gnome, Lord of Illusion, lately joined of the Council, cast a great wind of wizardry to hide the fleet from the Dark. By such devious paths the Fell Knight came upon the Dark Fleet and broke it asunder and sent many Orcs and other folk of the craven Lords to their doom at the ocean's depths.

But some broke free and they laid siege to the Isle of Bliss which had been Morgeld's realm. They cast down its high towers. They set there a great Captain, and he ruled there for long ages and came to be known in after times as Trubsal, which is misery in the Vulgate tongue and his isle was named, Unglucksfall. And it is now known that this Captain was a Mogrl, forged from the hatred of Unklar when he was young.

The Fell Knight suffered as well, four of his mighty ships were lost forever to the water and one cut asunder and lost to him. So with lessened might he sailed south around the great continent and in the years twilight came to the Elorian Islands. There he built a castle, and this new home he named Letzen Bastei which, in the vulgate, is the "last bastion."

But the Council made secret war, hid themselves in the deeps of the city of City of Seven and reestablished the Mystic Enclave, those who worshiped the White Mage. There in the High Tower of Delight they uncovered the god Narrheit, and the Wizard made ally of him, bringing worship of that evil and malignant god back into the world. And Durendale revealed himself to the Paladins of the Flame, who still held out in the snows of Old Kayomar. So Luther of Old, lost on the Dreaming Sea for so many years, the King, returned again and the land rejoiced and even prospered in the knowledge of the ending of the Dark.

The Council, seeing that Solarium would hold her walls and that Morgeld defeated the enemies' fleet, retreated to planes beyond Erde to gather power in allies. Wondrous adventures they had, few of which come into the tale of these days. But Jaren the Undying was made anew and burned with the Spirit of Revenge, and fell to Worship the hawk god of Ethrum, Horus. And Jaren took a new name, given to him by the hosts of his enemies, the Falkenjager. Too, he took a wife, and a girl child came of the union, and she bore the mark of the House Golden which is the royal line of Aenoch of old.

Learning of the coming war, the druids of the Great Tree summoned the spirit of Daladon Lothian, "Halfelven," who returned from the bark of the Great Tree where he had lived for a thousand years. Daladon pondered long on what he must do. In this state Helius, the Singing Fool, who himself spent the Winter Dark years hounding Unklar's minions, came to him and bid him travel to Mount Monrudge where the goddess Wenafar lay bound by the machinations of Unklar. And the Halfelven assailed the mount of Monrudge to bring back the Queen of Fay.

Long and hard battles he waged upon the slope of the mountain, Helius ever at his side, until at last he broke through to the Queen. He found her in a wondrous grove of trees and swore to liberate her. She took him for awhile and released him back into the world. There, he fell, taken in the end by Mongroul Troll Lord, that is Nulak-Kiz-Din. He bore Daladon aloft, binding him to the throne of gods upon Mount Thangondrim, the very seat where the All Father sat pondering his creation in the Days before Days. Here, Malikor the Dragon, one of the first born of Unklar's lust, set to watching and tormenting the March Lord.

Unbeknownst to Daladon a child came from his brief union with Wenafar. Utumno, the Dreaming god, who after came to dwell upon the Dreaming Sea with St. Luther.

But the Elven hosts were still lost to the world upon their floating Isle, and they hid themselves by narrow paths in the skies above and looked upon the world in pity and horror and wondered if the time for their return had come.

1021md

Rumors circulated far and wide of the return of the Paladin and the Durendale Sword, and the White mage as well. The prophecies as foretold in the Books of Jaren had lingered in the minds of people great and small. Many prophets came forth shouting for war and the end of Winter's Dark. People spoke of the Great Tree blooming again, and discontent with the rule of Unklar's minions spread.

News of the binding of Daladon came to the Council, and they made travel to Mongroul's lands and assailed his minions. After a horrific duel in the air between the Dragon and the Mage, the Falkynjager flew into the combat and smote Malikor such a blow on the chest that his wings folded forever and he plummeted in ruin upon the high peak of Thangondrim. So great was the Dragon's fall that Thangondrim broke asunder, and that most ancient of mountains sundered. The quake drowned a host of Mongroul's trolls in rock and slag, ending their days forever. A great shuttering went through the world, and the hosts of Darkness were dismayed.

And behold the quest of the Halfelven was finished, and the world given back to the Queen taken an age ago, and the realm of Faerie at last set free. Bringing a host into the world's hidden places the Queen set the Twin Sister's afire and the heat of the sun burned and fought the Shroud of Winter in the heavens all about the world. But Unklar knew nothing of defeat, and he rose on high and gave battle with the Queen of Fay. Wenafar fled to Erde, in the twilight of Winter, and knew no recourse except to hide and hope. But nonetheless, the world was warmed by her coming and the Shroud weakened thereby.

Nulak-Kiz-Din, named now Mongroul by the wide world, stole from Aufstrag back to his lands where Thangondrim had stood under the eye of Malikor. And he knew dismay at the wreck and ruin of his land. But he fortified anew Turm Graugusse, which is the Iron Tower, and made the lands between the mountains a wicked desert of slag and horrid plague, and peopled it anew with hosts of evil intent. Taking on the shape of a Wolf, mighty and bold, he went into the east as if on a Great Hunt. And he searched for the Council and Durendale Sword. More though, he hunted for Aristobulus the White Mage, who, tis said, stole the days from time, hounded the Dark on its edge, and corrupted Law with his Chaos.

But the world changed around the Lords of Winter's Dark. The Dwarves of the Norgorod-Kam proclaimed themselves in the midst of the realms of Unklar and opened their Kingdoms as if for War. Their mighty and fell Lord, Dagmar III, bore the scepter of one of the Captain Kings, and the Axe which is the rightful possession of the Dwarf Lords. And the servants of Unklar fled from him and the whole of his mountains, but for the deeper places, were made clean, and the Dwarves knew much pride and rest in the days to come.

And in the far west the Solarium Empire drove back the Lord of Sorrow and made a great victory. But the cost was great and The Holy Council of the Empire entombed the fallen and dead of their realm. And ever did they look to the Western Seas in vain hope of securement for times were hard and hardy men few.

1022md

In the early spring Grundlich Hohle reopened and the Dwarf Lord, Dolgan, was crowned its King. He declared the Grundliche Mountains clear of the filth of Darkness and made war on the black tree of Aufstrag. And the Lord of the Marsh, Coburg, Unklar's chief lieutenant in the lands of Aenoch led 50,000 men, orcs and giants against the Dwarf Lord whose folk numbered in the ten's of hundreds only. As is known, only one road leads into the high mountains where the Dwarf Kingdom lies. The road, known as the Stone Way, was easily fortified by the Dwarves and they held this castle, named Castle Havok, against the enemy.

Early in the year, Morgan, Lord of Paladins, and a noble of Kayomar, engaged an Imperial Legion. They forced him into battle, driving him into the Shelves of the Mist with the greater part of his host which numbered 187 Paladins, 352 Knights, and 2000 footmen. They were hounded by the scourge of darkness, great packs of wolves and evil beasts. Despite this, the men and orcs of Unklar's Legions held their posts in fear for the coming of the Old King and the return of Kayomar, for they remembered well the battles of the Catalyst Wars and the losses they suffered in those days.

And UnKlar rose in rage and fell upon those of his Captain Kings who still lived. He deemed them incompetent for, even as he was assailed in his lands of Aenoch, so were they being hounded in their realms. They battled for their lives against their dark master, the result of which does not come into these tales.

At Midyear, Daladon Lothian arrived in the Eldwood, taking up the leadership of the Watchers in the Wood. His folk made ally with good King Nigold of the Wood Elves, and the Half-Elven at last came to the Sacred Grove to see the Great Tree with living eyes, which he had planted over a thousand years ago.

In fear of his master's rage, the Lord of Sorrow marshaled his folk once more for an attack on the Solarium Empire. They dammed the river and battered the walls, breaking them apart. But when his host made to move through the pass, a cleric, the High Priestess of Tefnut, who had these many years lay hidden in the river, broke the dam and the pent waters spilled out and across the armies of darkness. Despite this setback many came over the mountains and laid siege with great desolation to the city, towns and keeps beyond. Though in the end the Lord of Sorrow's folk fell back and beyond the walls which were fortified anew.

Men from the north, sailing in small dragon prowed ships, began raiding along the southern coasts of the Inner Sea. They caused a great deal of destruction and loss of life. The Imperial Governors called for aid from their Aufstrag's navy.

Lord Aziz, commander of the Imperial Legion in Kayomar, called for more troops. Indeed, the greater part of the Legions are fighting in far west, under the Lord of Sorrow and there are only a scant dozen or more legions remaining in the environs of Aufstrag. Troops are stripped from garrisons as far away as Angouleme to gather in the Province of Maine. Aziz moved to hunt out Morgan and destroy the Order of the Flame. He hoped to thereby draw out Luther and the Durendale Sword and slay him as well.

Being forwarned of Mongroul's coming, Aristobulus moved the whole of the Council to the reaches of Centauris, the city of the center, and hid them there away for Mongroul. For the mage knew Unklar's strength could not be surpassed, and nothing towards his unmaking would be gained as yet.

A great bloodletting occurred when the Vale Knights under Prince Meltowg Lothian stormed the Castle of Spires. The Prince bore aloft the blade Noxmoros, a sword of his own making. In the ensuing battle, all the folk of both companies were slain, the Vale Knights and the garrison. Meltowg, bleeding from a dozen wounds, becames enraged, ripping the Aurefex Mutatio, the Prism of Alteration, from Melius's hands, he killed the elven wizard with his great sword. All lay in misery and death, the keys to the three realms, soaked in elven blood.

And about this time many folk of the Mystic Enclave moved to the Rhodope Mountains and there, where in ages past Aristobulus had made a tower, they lifted it up again and fortified it, naming it anew, Turm Gewirr, "Tower of Chaos." But in after days it was named Turm Damon, "Tower of the Demon," for men came to fear the magi of the old world.

The people of Angouleme formed a council of various Burghers and town mayors. They appointed battle lords and hired mercenaries to defend them from the Northmen and the growing lawlessness of the provinces.

1023md

In the month of Erstdain, the Lord of Sorrow invaded the Valley of the Sun with all his host and in a great battle once more breached the walls and valleys and laid waste to it. He encamped his army in the valley of the sun, called by some Logn-Kor, and made ready to besiege the city. The Emperor-Paladin chose then to break the dikes which ever held back the sea and flooded the whole of the valley, and it is told that beyond 90,000 of Unklar's Lords, Knights and troops drowned in that great flood. But the Lord of Sorrow was not daunted and turning, he split open the earth creating a portal to hell. He fled from the wrath of his fell Lord, Unklar, and with him went the damned of Logn-Kor. Many speak of his act as one of treachery to his dark master. They speak of deals between the Lord of Sorrow and Jaren Falkynjager, but the truths of these tales is not known to the chronicles.

The Battle of Eadore and how Morgan, Master of the Order of the Holy Defenders of the Flame, tired of fleeing the enemy and met him in a contest of arms.

Morgan gave battle to an Imperial Legion on the heights of Eadore Ridge. With 2000 men-at-arms and 500 knights and paladins, he met the 5th legion on the 19th of Erstdain. The Legion of 16,000 men and Orcs, formed into three divisions, was led by Aziz personally and supported by many hundreds of skirmishers from other Provinces and a further 4000 horse. Upon the eastern slopes of the Shelves of the Mist, Morgan ordered his men to build a wall of dirt and stone atop Mt. Eadore, a long ridge. Aziz threw first troops, the 194th cohort, against the hilltop and it was utterly destroyed by arrow and pike, never drawing any but a little blood. Then a force of the 3rd cohort attacked along the flanks. The arrows of Morgan's folk were spent by this time and the orcs mounted the dirt wall. The ferocity of the defense of the men of Kayomar staggered the orcs, long used to ruling through fear and fear alone. By sword and axe they were thrown down from the wall so that they made little progress. By mid-day of the battle's second day they fell back in dismay. So great had been the discipline of the Knights and Sergeants of Kayomar that they suffered little and slew much. Upon the morning of the third day the last cohort of Aziz drew up at the hill's foot and waited. Morgan sallied forth in rage with his 500 Knights and Paladins at his flanks. Such was their charge that the 63rd cohort of 5000 men was utterly destroyed and put to flight. Aziz fled into the Gelderland with his 4000 horse and quit the field forever. The battle was ever after, called Morgan's Song.

Aziz's defeat spread disenchantment throughout the ranks of Unklar's Legions. In the central lands a quarrel broke out between the Commanders of the 32nd and 40th legions. Lord Pius of the 32nd sought to hold his men largely in reserve to the orcs of the 40th. The two Legions fought minor skirmishes throughout the remainder of the summer and winter.

The Burghers of Angouleme gathered under the tutelage of the Provincial Governor, William, and elected him as their spokesman to the Lords of Aufstrag and the feuding Commanders.

The Battle of Gokstad Deep

The ravages of the Northmen spread throughout the Inner Sea, and many raiders passed through the straights, some even attacked Avignon. The Admiral of the Imperial Fleet dispatched the whole of his remaining ships to travel into the northern waters and destroy the raiders' homes. Twenty-five vessels bore the 58th legion from Aachen into the north, sailing for Gokstad. Two months on the open sea brought them into the vicinity. The Northmen were forewarned of their coming, however, and had put 60 longboats into the water. They sailed to meet Imperials in open battle, lusting as they did and still do, for death in war. Never in the memory of men had a human fleet contested the seas with the ships of Unklar, and the captains were afraid. And the Northmen surrounded the larger vessels and disabled them with fire and axe, and so great was their lust for slaying, that they forgot all booty and with great waste burned the fleet into the depths. Making sacrifice to their grim gods they celebrated a great victory. And the 25 ships and all of the 58th Imperial Legion returned home never more.

The Council of Light found the home of Nurich II, the Fire Giant King, and penned him at the feet of Mount Tur. Here too was Ozanna the black, a member of the Council of Patrice, and Nurrich commanded him to kill Aristobulus. The two fight a duel arcane, but Ozanna had grown at the feet of Nulak, and ever did the Troll Lord mistrust him and retard his power and skill. Ozanna was little match for the Council and the White Mage, and Aristobulus slew him. The battle with the Fire Giants raged over hill and mountain, blood on both sides being spilt. Jaren the Falkynjager was horribly wounded, and Dolgan King's back broken. The siege ended when Daladon, using the power of the Great Tree, split the earth at the feet of Mount Tur slaying the Fire Giant King and many of his kin. This deed the giants have never forgotten, and because of it a war between the rangers of the wood and the giants has been fought from that day to this.

When Mount Tur split open a wondrous thing came to light. The mountain housed an ancient Dwarven realm, one buried in the morass of history. Roheisen Hohle, the Iron Halls, remained as one of the oldest Dwarven realms in all of Erde. There Dwarves lived, under their King Ondorog Helgostohl IX, a line unbroken since the beginning of recorded time. These Dwarves were few in number and cursed with the Stone Curse, an ancient malady which precluded them from traveling in the light of day. Despite this, they offered the Council and Dolgan King to the south what aid they could.

The death of Nurrich also released the village of Haven from servitude and its leader, Philip the Guileless, as well. He left Haven, preaching the dictums of a new religion. So it was that the worship of Demeter began.

In the year's closing days, Unklar was utterly besieged in his realms of Aufstrag, for rain began to fall, dampening the snow, and thunderstorms rolled across the swamps and marshes of the Gruasamland.

1024md

After the battle with the Fire Giant King, the Council retreated to the Eldwood to seek healing. They gathered forces arcane and minions to help them in their war against the dark.

As is written, Wenafar warmed the heat of the sun. Because of this, the Shroud of Darkness unraveled in the far kingdoms, and the ice in the southern seas began to melt and by years end the channels of old were free and the movement of ships great and small made all the easier thereby. The rivers of the land flowed deeper, freed from ice, and the workings of gods of old came to pass. Unklar felt the loss of his far scattered realms. Few of the Captain Kings paid him heed, still unrecovered from his rage. They hid in their own towers and awaited the outcome of the war with the Council.

With the breaking of the ice, the raids of the Northmen continued unabated and much slaughter and devastation came to the lands of Ethrum and Aenoch. They built small forts along the coasts. The rivers served as avenues for the raiders and the first of them arrived in Augsberg, traveling up the Olgdon River. They plundered several castles and killed a number of the men living there. The Northmen saw Unklar's clerics as evil men, and burned them wherever they could, as they do any who pay credence to the God of the Black Tower. They carted great mounds of booty back to the north. Lord Quin, Commander of the 18th Legion, sought to stop them and moved men from the Luneberg Plains to the mouth of the river and to other extremes, hoping to block the raiders. In this, he was fatally outdone for a large party of Northmen fell upon his scattered cohorts and in a series of rapid attacks, scattered them. The 18th, mostly inexperienced men and tribal orcs, disintegrated and Quin fell upon his own sword.

In the north, the new religion of Philip spread rapidly. It appealed to the farmers, artisans, the poor, and those oppressed by the tyranny of others. Its call was for strength of arms and hard work in the fields. Those who followed Demeter preached celebrations with feasts of wine and food. And the folk took up the beliefs of Philip the Guileless with hearty joy and happy militance. They built churches to the god Demeter and made sacrifice to him. By years end the religion spread into the reaches of Augsberg, entering the cities and towns there. Many servants of Philip traveled into the west to spread the word as well. These disciples moved from Avignon to Angouleme, and on to Sienne and even into Kayomar. Everywhere people recognized the thinning of the Shroud of Darkness and rejoiced.

Albrecht Commander of the 67th Legion and Lord of the Imperial Horse, served Unklar in the battles against the Dwarves of Havok Castle. During those frightful days, he diverted the greater part of his cavalry, useless in the mountains, to the Olgdon River, to guard against the northmen. Or so he said. But in truth, Albrecht had met with the Council and Dolgan King and they had struck a bargain. For a Kingdom on the river he turned on Unklar and brought with him 6000 heavy cavalry.

In the west, civil war between the followers of the Commanders Orkhan and Pius broke out. A brutal strife entailed the destruction of many men and orc. Pius needlessly sacrificed two solid battalions of ungern and hobgoblin troops in an assault on several castles. They were utterly destroyed. Orkhan fell soon after, slain in battle with a small retinue of knights. Pius utterly routed the folk of his 40th Legion. He settled them throughout the area of Maine and ruled there as their Lord. He would not seek council from Aufstrag in those days, heeding the word of Nulak only.

Kayomar suffered greatly in the aftermath of Eadore. With the withdrawal of Aziz, and Morgan too weak to stop them, bandits, unemployed mercenaries and other freebooters attacked and plundered many towns and villages. The folk of Luther and Morgan, tried to rally the people to little avail. Morgan tried to raise more men and turned to the Eldwood for aid from Good King Nigold.

News of the the Grand Fleet's defeat in the far west spread as Prince Morgeld, as is told, settled in the Elorian Isles.

The greatest of misdeeds came when Nulak-Kiz-Din bewitched the Council into retrieving for him the Pride of the Goblins, the spirit of the long dead Goblin King Ondluche. As is told in the histories, Dognur VII destroyed the body of Ondluche and cast it into the deeps of the sea. How it came to rest upon the shores of Aenoch none knew. But Nulak gained the artifact and sought to thereby win over many of the Goblins whom Dolgan King had in his employ, for as is told, many of those folk, all Eldritch Goblins, joined the Dwarf in the Trench Wars under Aufstrag.

1025md

The Council remained in their strongholds and made few overt movements against the enemy. But the enemy was dismayed and everywhere besieged.

From the dark side of the planes great hordes assailed Unklar on his throne. These lords of the abyss, long held in check by the horned god's bindings, rose against him. They brought the forces of chaos with them and many report that Narrheit himself had come to roost in Aufstrag. Great rumblings and quakes rocked the fortress and for five months it rained black rain above. Using his Urtiel to terrible effect, Unklar drove the lords of the abyss back to their realms, but the cost proved a great.

The Shroud of Darkness unraveled in distant parts so that Unklar was forced to withdraw it to the realms of Aenoch and Ethrum. As Spring came to the world at large, Unklar brooded in his halls.

The religion of Philip the Guileless spread throughout all the Augsberg and Aachen and down the Ursal Straights. The people built altars of stone, and carved the likeness of the horse god in symbols. They celebrated the world's coming Spring with wine, dance and great festivity. In truth the world began to bloom, even in Aenoch and Ethrum. Only where the powers of Unklar's minions remained strong was the Shroud thick enough to filter the warmth of the sun.

In places, the followers of Demeter threw off the yoke of the black clerics of Unklar and burned them at the stake. In many towns the magi were not distinguished from the priests and they too were cast into the flame. To Angouleme the word spread and Philip himself traveled even to Avignon. The daughter of William of Angouleme, Eleanor, converted to this new religion and she was brought to the love of the people thereby. And the words of the disciples of Philip spread to the borders of the Rhodope Mountains. And against this Fell Unklar could do little, so beset was he in his Keep. And the Troll Lord moved not, but waited and plotted, making dark allies in strange places.

In the west the folk of the Solarium Empire deemed their lands unlivable and the greater part of them departed for the east in ships and galleys. Some few remained behind, living in the city which escaped the flood.

And the Northmen came down the water ways of Ursal once more in ships with dragon-prows to sail across the Amber Sea. They plundered the outskirts of Avignon and ravaged the coasts of Angouleme, burning many cities, villages, and towns, carrying off many to slavery and death. Too, their plundering reached the Elorian Isles. In the east they arrived at Trier, but the Admiral of the Black Fleet did not put to sea, but fortified himself in his ports. And the

castles in the north to guard against any imperial armies that might threaten him.

William, the Imperial Governor and Count, was named Lord of the Lands of Angouleme by the Burghers and other Lords of those lands. Being a shrewd politician, he converted to the religion of Philip and Demeter. For this the common folk welcomed his rule and the people called him ever after, William the Good. He placed a great altar stone in the capital of those lands, which is Angouleme, and it became, in after years, a holy place of the temple of Demeter. William marshaled and fortified his people against Pius in the south and the Northmen raiders. He doled out land for those warriors willing to defend it.

In the waning days of the year, Albrecht, Commander of the 63rd Legion, moved his troops onto Olgdon River basin, there to manage the defense of that place against the depredations of the Northmen. Though now it is common knowledge that he did this more to create a bastion of power against Aufstrag than for any other reason.

Northmen plundered all the coasts far and wide, and as far inland as the rivers let them sail. A small party passed into the southern gulf but they are defeated and slain in a monstrous battle with ships of Morgeld's crafting.

Dolgan King returned to his realm and called for a great mustering of Dwarves. Refugees who had for years lived in mountain fastness flocked to the opened gates of Grunliche Hohle. Though it is told that a band of Northmen raided even here, slaying some forty Dwarves on the edge of the mountains by the sea.

Pius solidified his victory in Maine by fortifying his western Marches against Kayomar, and he strengthened the garrisons in towns and

1026md

In the early months of the year, the rain began to fall in the north, breaking the Winter's ice of the Inner Sea. A Mogrl, fell servant of Unklar, settled upon the coasts of the Grundliche Mountains and slew many Northmen. He carved a home in the stone, and built a great castle. In after years it was called only the Castle upon the Sea and was a horrid place of foul death and disease.

William called upon the Burghers of Angouleme to crown him Duke of all Angouleme, which was his homeland. The folk in other provinces followed his lead, and called upon their Burghers to grant them title to land and ancient rights, forgotten since the dawn of the Winter Dark. Albrecht fortified his castles along the River Olgdon. Pius consolidated his position in Maine.

The fleet of the Solarium Empire returned to Kayomar in these days, but they were not welcome and they sailed on, searching for a land to call their own. They split into two groups. One moved into the east. The other sailed back to the limits of Ethrumania and there they settled, building a city which they called Brindisium. There were many folk who lived in those lands, and they paid homage to the horned god. Emperor Moridain ordered their keeps stormed and towns burned. His Knights and men-at-arms reduced the lands and put many garrisons to death. The Emperor then declared a Crusade against all those who served the Dark, and they began clearing out all vestiges of the horned god's religion. In the Winter in a raid into of the enemies' strongholds, Moridain, was stricken with a poisoned arrow and died. His inheritance, the crown, went to his son, Raymond. Raymond was not a Knight, nor did he hold his father's love of the ancient world.

It was in these days that Kayomar consolidated. With threats arising in the north and east, Luther Pendegrantz, with much pageantry, was crowned as Palatine King of Kayomar. Representatives from King Dagmar III of the Norgorod-Kam, Dolgan I, King of Grundliche Hohle, and Daladon Lothian of the Eldwood, as well as Aristobolus, were all present.

Further east, across the straight of Ursal, in the forested hills of the Harz, a mercenary Knight, Baldwin, settled with his knights and their families. Recently displaced by the civil unrest of Pius's rule in Maine, these men and women searched for a new home, and they followed Baldwin for he claimed to have seen the Unicorn, a holy steed from legend and myth. In vain, he followed the beast, trying to see him once more. But the beast alluded him. In the high summer he established himself in the Harz. Through gallant force of arms he and his knights drove out the orcs and pacified the men of those dark wooded hills. By early Summer he began construction on a great castle at Aachen. In other places across the countryside he fortified the towns and garrisons. Later he declared the Order of the Knights of the Horn. His daughter Ephremere, the Wonder of the World, was with him.

The Council mustered and beneath the banner of the Durendale Sword attacked Unklar and his many minions in the fortress tree of Aufstrag. The battle was hard fought and lasted many days, but the Council failed once more, retreating from that place with scars that time cannot heal.

With the complete routing of his armies across the fields of the world, Unklar summoned his folk back to Aufstrag and closed the great gates. In a great weaving of sorcery he brought the Plague riders into the world. They scarred the land with plague, famine, war and death to the realms. Even the Paladins were hard pressed to stem the tide. The Elven folk suffered the least and the most, for the last of the children of the wild elves were born in those days and their souls were trapped forever in limbo.

Albrecht, Lord of the Oldgon, declared himself King of the Augsberg. His troops occupied all the castles along the length of that great river and held those lands in his name. He was called by men the "River King."

Late in the year the Dwarves of Grundlich Hohle launched a massive attack against the withdrawing legions which besieged Havok castle. They utterly routed the enemy. Well over 15,000 orcs and men were lost, the remnants fleeing into the Punj. The Dwarvin King, Dolgan, proclaimed himself Suzerain of the Flintlock. Also, he brought to the halls of Grunliche Hohle a Lore Drake, who, of old, served the Dwarves as historians and sages. She carried two eggs with her.

Agis I, nephew of the Emperor of Brindisium, arrived with his fleet off the coast of the Aachen. There he fortified a town on the coastline. He called his land Lakonia and his capital, Tegea.

In Kayomar, Lord Morgan gathered his knights and men-at-arms and attacked the Orcs in the Wilds. The war raged around the ancient castles of that place, neither side having victory or defeat. The Battle of Weather's gap drove the Orcs into their fortress of Ox and Morgan besieged that place. The Wood Elves, under Daladon Lothian and King Nigold, joined Morgan in his war on the Orcs.

The Shroud of Darkness over Ethrum began to disintegrate. Wenafar set great winds to blowing into the east. Her sorceries smashed into Festung Aufstrag and battered the towers there. Unklar strove to drive back the winds and nearly succeeded but other gods, Tefnut among them, threw their weight into the struggle. With great malice Unklar fell back to his halls, his Shroud of Darkness in tatters.

Many people celebrated the coming of Spring and the seasons turned once more in Erde. Many were distraught, for their lives had been without the unfiltered light of the sun. When it burned off the snows of Winter's Dark, they were amazed and scared. There was chaos in places and many despaired, but in the end, they saw the goodness of the world without the Shroud of Darkness.

By Winter's end the war on the dark and Aufstrag seemed won, for the horned god was everywhere beset by enemies and deserted by friends, and the world's Spring had begun after so long a winter.

1027md

The Council, under the command of Luther, attempted to muster the world's folk in alliance. The Nine Day War ended in failure for the free people were not yet strong enough to assail the Dark in his towers of Aufstrag.

Fantheous, the daughter of King Nigold, fell to the Troll Lord's possession. He took her to the Halls of his dark tower in the north. He hoped to break the alliance of men and elf and to do so, he bargained with Narrheit, giving him the child. In return Narrheit, gave Nulak-Kiz-Din the thirteen stones of Chaos. Narrheit hid Fantheus where he had hid the lost Paladin, Heiromyous, that is, upon the Bridge of Colors.

She was rescued later in the year by Daladon Lothian, though he knew it not. He saw only a helpless girl, whose mind had been stolen by Narrheit. He renamed the child Hope.

The Elven King Nigold returned to the Eldwood, broken in spirit. The Elves scattered across the world in search of Fantheous. Nigold left 3000 of his Elves at the siege of Ox, but told them to stay only so long as the fort held, no longer. This on the strength of the promises of the Council that they would rescue his daughter.

Embassies from Grundliche Holhe arrived at the Stone Dwarves' realm of Reheisen Hohle, Dolgan's brother at their lead. The 47 clans of the Gnomes of the Flintlock made an entreaty to the Dwarven King for alliance.

The Council of Light disappeared on the Dreaming Sea, there to combat the sorceries of Nulak-Kiz-Din. Morgeld, bewitched by the dark sorcerer, was made to slay his father, Luther. But Nulak's plot was foiled. Though, in truth, as it after became known, he but tested his enemies, learning in the combat their many strengths and weaknesses. These battles arcane with the Troll Lord kept the Council lost for nearly a year.

Baldwin, The Knight of the Horn, cemented his claims in the Harz. With gold from the Half-Elven he employed many Northmen as mercenaries and attacked the orcs in the Detmold and Heristat.

In the spring, King Albrecht moved his capital to Acre and there, remembering the spirit and not the failure of the Nine Days' War, mustered the flower of his people. The greater host, numbering 15,000 men and horse, crossed the Olgdon River into the Luneberg Plains. They drove back the Imperial legions and conquered the whole land. They came to the foot of the Red Hills. The whole of the Winter Kingdoms were threatened.

Duke William of Angouleme mustered his battle lords, knights and others, and made him their King. His own great castle of Angloume was named the capital of those lands. He began redistributing the wealth of the land to various of his knights and Lords and the city Burghers. So came to Erde the Kingdom of Angloume.

Late in the year Baldwin, with significant victories over the Orcs and lauded by his people, proclaimed himself King of Aachen. There was much celebration in his capital, Paderborn, which is also called Aachen. His lands included the Detmold, Heristat and the Harz Forests.

At year's end, Kain the Godless, Ducal Lord of the Abyss, came to Aufstrag to serve the Dark. Ever was the master of the Winter Dark a lawful creature but he knew that Chaos begets Chaos and he sought to put one of the greatest abyssal lords against his foes.

1028md

Even before the shades of winter passed, Kain mustered the better part of three legions and launched a massive attack against Albrecht in the Red Hills. Several small inconsequential battles were fought throughout the spring and into the summer, but at the battle of Aaronborg Albrecht suffered a defeat and drew back into Luneberg. Later in the year, at the Battle of Arc Bridge, Albrecht was thoroughly defeated and thrown back across the Olgdon River. There was great loss of life on both sides.

In the Detmold and Heristat, King Baldwin waged a guerilla war against the Orcs for the whole year. The North Men in his employ proved hard to control, especially when the Orcs were driven into their fortresses. His mercenaries grew restless with the Siege warfare, and began to desert, a problem that has ever plagued those folk and always served to great benefit of those who fought them. No aid came from the Council, who themselves were still embattled by the black mage, Nulak. Baldwin's army began to disintegrate, but in the end, the Northmen's love of the old Knight kept them in the field and at war.

The Commander of the Punj mustered forth the 19th Legion and, flanking Kain's, attacked in the Luneberg, and plunged into the Flintlock to engage the Dwarves and Gnomes before those peoples cemented an Alliance.

In the west, even as war unfolded across the plains of the east, Lord Morgan mustered his Knights, Paladins and men-at-arms. He levied the free peoples of the Shelves of the Mist, and used the remaining Elves of the Eldwood to storm the city-fortress of Ox. The city held for two months until Dagmar III, King of Norgorad-Kam, enjoined his folk to go to battle. Twelve thousand Dwarven shields marched from beneath the arches of that ancient realm, bearing siege equipment and other armaments. The battle waged for days and nights, and none could take the walls, but in the end, the Dwarves mined a section of the wall. When it collapsed, they poored into this "weathered gap" and held it against all attacks by the enemy until the hosts of men and Elf joined them. So great was the loss of life on all sides in this gap that the battle is named for it. But eventually, the flower of Kayomar and the Elves stormed the ramparts and Ox is thrown down. Morgan himself engaged Mudom, the Orc Lord, in battle and slew him. The whole of the orc host was laid waste and with them many ungern, legionnaires, lords, and knights of Unklar. The last of the orcs were driven and hounded into the wilds north of Kayomar.

The Council escaped the sorceries of Nulak-Kiz-Din and returned to the world and war.

They arrived in time to fight at the Battle of Gotzenburg in the Flintlock. Herein, Dolgan King and his Dwarfs held their own fortress, Gotzenburg, against the enemy for many months. The battle raged in and around the walls and ditches with a ferocity seen in few places. For the Dwarves and their Goblin allies were once servants to the Lords whom they now fought. The hatred on both sides caused a slaughter that would end without total devastation. But the Dwarves would not yield. At last, the Holy Knight Luther arrived and threw down the Emperor's Commander, Feodor Pakevitch, in singular combat. Though, for reasons lost to the histories, he did not slay the Commander, but banished him to his own lands. The Legion fell back in dismay, and the Dwarves sorely wasted, with numbers much diminished, could not pursue them.

Luther returned at last to his realm where he ruled only in name. He made truce between Morgan of Kayomar and Pius of Maine. Pius he named King there, being the provinces of Maine, Artois and the Lechfield. His son Aenor was recognized as heir by Luther. His capital he set at Chinon.

Aeronoush the Elven hero, found the clue to Fantheous's fate and knew thereby that Daladon held her in safety. He bid the Half-Elven to seek the Silver Pool. Here in the skeletal bowels of a long dead giant the truth of imprisonment would be found. The Half-Elven did so and learned that to cure her he must need possess the Truncheon of Hope. He brought this relic from the Nine Hells to his one House and bid the child, Hope, to drink of it. Fantheous was returned to the world. But, in the end, tragedy stalked the Half-Elven, though none knew at the time, for even while drinking at the Silver Pool he was made to love Fi-Deal the hopeless, the green witch and he brought her to his halls in the forest deeps.

Philip's disciples began the construction of a magnificent temple in old Avignon. They built it using the foundations of the Imperial Governor's Palace. Philip arrived, naming one Sixtus as Bishop of that Prelacy. They proceeded to organize the church in the central lands, founding a Prelacy in Angouleme, in Aachen, in the March of Zeitz, and in Albrecht's Kingdom of Augsberg. These are religious realms that possessed no real boundaries, but were rather areas for conversion of people.

Aristobulus the White Mage met Nulak-Kiz-Din upon the remaining Shrouds of Dark that still hung over the lands of Aenoch. They parlayed for a time, speaking of things that had gone in the days before the dark. Many questions were asked and answered, for neither bore the other ill will, each only seeing another sorcerer bent on guiding the world as they saw fit. In truth Aristobulus had risen in power to that of an equal to Nulak and both were Archmagi with little limits on their powers. This third encounter saw no battle but that of wits. The White Mage returned to the world assured of victory over Unklar and his minions.

1029md

Called "The Long Year." Herein are related the deaths of many Kings and the great battle of Olensk which broke the power of Unklar upon the plane .

In the early Spring, when the land was still cold, King Baldwin, old and beyond years, lay upon his bier to die. Daladon, being close to the old King took his daughter, Ephremere, under wing. He took her to deeps of the Detmold and there, like her father before her, she saw the Unicorn. Through his ensorcellements, the stallion bound itself to her line and the two lived on in her son, Baldwin II. They say that the Unicorn left the grove winter rose to the very gates of Baldwin's castle. He took him up and bore his everlasting spirit into the land of Fay, there to serve his beloved Faerie Queen forever and anon.

In the north, the Dwarves of Grundliche Hohle made peace with the 47 clans of Gnomes and the Flintlock was given over to them to hold in fealty. Jarl Thrushbeard, their chieftain, embraced Dolgan King. The King is called by the Gnomes, and indeed by the other Dwarves, by the name Aegold II. The two people celebrate their union at the Feast of Forty Seven.

After three years of absentee rule, King Palatine Luther I abdicated the throne of Kayomar in favor of his friend and Master of the Holy Defenders of the Flame, Morgan. Morgan's own wife crowned him, naming him King Morgan I. His first official act as King of

Kayomar bound his line to Luther evermore. In the lands which Luther's family owned, even before the Winter Dark, where Luther was a boy, Morgan established an order of clerics. They built a temple there to honor and worship the Paladin of the Dreaming Sea and the Durendale Sword. Morgan named it the Paladin's Grove and in after days, it became the holiest of shrines for the lords of law and good. The Grove encompassed 300 acres of wooded land surrounded on all sides by a low wall. The Druids of the Great Tree came to the grove at the behest of Daladon Lothian and planted there a crop of silver birch, said to be the offspring of the Trees of Mordius from the dawn of time. By years end the Holy Flame, in its dish of platinum, was placed in the altar chamber of the Temple where it sits to this day.

The tale of the Fall of Luther and his Return as the Confessor

After the Feasts of the Forty Seven, Dolgan King unmasked a mystery where Togglin, a Gnome from the north, revealed the whereabouts of the Pride of the Goblins. Dolgan summoned the Council and they struck to the outer planes where they embattled the High Priestess of the clerics of Unklar, Nectanebo XVIII, for possession of the Pride. Though in truth she bore it not, for it had passed into other hands.

She took the guise of a horrific spider, but Luther was not dismayed. In a furious battle the Durendale Sword broke in half, for the Paladin Luther failed to aid Daladon with the blade's might. Seeing his shame, Luther hurled himself upon the Priestess bearing only the broken half of the blade. In the ensuing battle the enraged Luther cast the Priestess down and she passed from the world forevermore, but not before she had poisoned the Paladin and he too fell and died. Luther ever loved the sea and so his friends consigned him there. And behold, the Eveningsong came and bore him and the Holy Sword to the Dreaming Sea and the Isle of Blight. The Paladin Lord was Dead.

But not in truth, for he was even then a god. On the Dreaming he labored upon his sorrows and troubles and grieved at the loss of the sword. In secret he took the shards to the Paladin's Grove, and there lay them on a stone within the temple. There they would lie, awaiting the next bearer. In grief Luther walked amidst the hills of his youth, though he recognized little from those happy days. Into his reflections came Corthain, the Justice Maker, that very god of old who had battled Thorax at the beginning of recorded history. Luther fell to his knees and the god breathed a bit of himself into the Paladin, reinvigorating him. Luther saw in this his own divinity and he wove for himself a Mantle to wear in humility. Imbued with the gifts of Corthain, the Justice Maker, this Mantle became the article of Confession which marked Luther's latter days in Erde. He became Luther the Confessor and when at last he mustered the strength to return to the world of men he returned as an angel of good, with the duty to cleanse men's souls.

Dagmar III fell in battle with the Giants at the gates of Norgorod-Kam. His son was crowned King of Norgorad-Kam, Dagmar IV.

Daladon Lothian grieved at the death of his long time friend and comrade in arms. He saw then the suffering of the homeless and the war torn people of Erde. He took a great part of his wealth and established a monastery in Kayomar. He took the good and kindly and placed them in charge of the Orders. They were made to build

She took the guise of a horrific spider and Luther hurled himself upon the Priestess bearing only the broken half of the blade. Though she passed from the world, Luther too, lay dead..

houses to aid the suffering. Abbot Edmund established the Rules and Orders of the Monastery. Those who joined the fledgling monastery adopted the name of Lothians and in time, they became clerics and monks. The first Lothian Houses filled with a small host of orphans. The early success of the monastery encouraged Edmund to establish many more.

In the east, the Eldritch Goblin Uandlich, took many of his kin from the service of Dolgan King and traveled into the deeps of ancient Ichlin-Yor. They retook the caverns and for the first time in thousands of years, Goblins strode the halls of Ichlin-Yor. They sought then their Queen, knowing not her fate, nor whereabouts.

Assassins overtook the Solarium Emperor, Raymond, murdering him in his own bed. The leading families of the Old Empire gathered then in a Senate to discuss what next should be done. Many argued that the Imperial line failed the people, and so they elected two Consuls to rule them. The Emperor's Paladins were disgraced and the Senate reorganized the army. They formed two legions of infantry and adopted the Eagle as the Imperial Insignia.

Their cousins in the city state of Tagea enfranchised over 5000 people who lived on the Isle called Lakonia and made them citizens of the city state. The city, besought by enemies on all sides, became heavily militarized. They constructed a great wall to defend themselves and all men were made to join the army. These Hoplites came to rule all the folk of Tagea, and they chose two Kings from their own numbers to lead them.

Daladon, Dolgan and Aristobulus stole into the depths of Aufstrag and tore the Krummervole from the throne of Unklar. In a rage the horned god fell upon them, rent the dwarf in twain and unmade the White Mage. Though Daladon escaped in a desperate plight to keep the Krummervole. Through the magic of Jaren Falkynjager, both the Mage and Dolgan returned to Erde, brought back from the Halls of the Dead. In truth their lives were no longer their own, for many folk worshiped them as gods and they were given greater roles than they themselves knew. For ever was it the law of creation that belief was as strong as reality.

Kain cared little for the Krummervole, nor even for Unklar himself, and in the Summer he crossed over the Olgdon River with two full Legions of Imperial troops.

Unklar's rage did not cease and he plundered the planes in search of the Half Elven and the Krummervole. The chaos caused by the loss of the Krummervole drove the remaining Lords of the Empire to guard themselves against the intrigues of Nulak-Kiz-Din. Civil War broke out in many places, particularly in the Punj.

In the planes Unklar fell upon Daladon and though he did not slay the March Lord, he broke his grip on the Krummervole so that it fell into the mists of time. And Unklar continued to search anon.

Jaren's daughter, named Pryzmira, she who bore the Mark of Emperors, turned nine-years-old and she called for a quest to reclaim the Cunae Mundus Usquam. Many enjoined with her and word spread through Erde that the line of the Emperors of old was revived. Many welcomed this, for they remembered the tales of Sebastian and his attempt to slay Unklar. Many others, however,

saw this as an evil thing, for it was the power of the Emperor which brought forth the horned god. The crown was at last retrieved, but only after the Council interceded. They found it in the crypt of Baron Harakon Petrovich, where too, lay the sword Discerpo.

Upon the fields of Augsberg, near the small village of Olensk, Albrecht met Duke Kain in battle.

Olensk

Upon the 4th of Trocken, 1029md, King Albrecht, the River King, marshaled the whole of the flower of Augsberg, with Dwarves from Grundliche Hohle and mercenaries from the north. They clashed with two of the dark god Unklar's Imperial Legions, commanded by the Duke Kain, near the village of Olensk. The armies drew up upon the gently rolling snow covered downs in the early morning hours. Albrecht's 9000 footmen, 4500 horse, 3000 dwarves and 4500 mercenaries were arrayed in a tight battle line, with the Dwarves under the Hero Oxleigh in reserve. Before him Kain commanded two Legions, the 11th and 33rd, about 27,000 men. The Imperial Legions were set in two great squares with light troops of skirmishers on their flanks. They stood thus for several hours, neither one willing to commit, but by mid-morning Kain grew impatient, unleashing the fury of Unklar's folk upon Albrecht.

Kain hurled the orcs of the 33rd against Albrecht's right flank. They soon broke through and ran headlong into the Dwarves. A gory contest of arms ensued. The Dwarves refused to yield against the overwhelming numbers. Here the orcs and dwarves wrestled and the bleeding of both armies began. For Kain used the orcs, not sparring their numbers. Albrecht's Royal Levies were drawn from the center and his mercenary horses were committed by days end. But these proved too few and too late and the Dwarves were at last driven back and with them the Royal Levies overwhelmed. By mid-afternoon the right flank collapsed. The orcs slaughtered the Dwarven wounded who lay behind their lines.

For the whole day the battle raged, the loss of life, immeasurable. But on the left the battle turned, the whole of Augsberg's cavalry charged, striking the lines of the 11th with a deafening impact and in a very short while the 11th legion was almost wholly overwhelmed. Their leader, the Sanjak Hamid, fell, grievously wounded. But too, Albrecht's youngest son, Frederick, was killed when an orc lance struck his breast. The heavily armored knights broke through the shattered legion.

The Dwarves, driven back, the Royal Levies slaughtered and the whole command in doubt, the army tittered on the brink of destruction. Not until the Dwarf Lord Oxleigh, Chief Lieutenant and Heir of Dolgan fell, did the tide turn. The Dwarves were driven into a frenzy and counterattacked, some 800 grouping together hurled themselves against the thousands of orcs who remained. The Dwarves fell, but their blood and honor blunted the orc charge. Not far from this melee the King's First Born, Albrecht II, cut off by the orcs, fell amidst a heap of bodies. And about his corpse his guard gathered, a mass of blood and flesh waging a merciless war, but they too were overwhelmed and destroyed.

Into this fray came the greatest of Kain's Captains, Korak. He shattered Albrecht's center and cut off the retreat of the Dwarves and the others from the right. The battle raged insanely around the village of Olensk. Korak himself drew up in the confused melee, the Dwarves in their lust to slay orcs, unknowingly cut him off, and the Vikings under young Fyorgyn, brought over from the left, hammered him. They carried his head to the halls of the dead. So fell Kain's second in command. With this the army became disheartened and for a moment stood confused and in doubt. Then the other of Kain's servants rallied them. There proved to be precious little time to regroup for into the melee the knights from the left flank, with Albrecht at their head, came about and plunged into the rear of Kain's battle line. Here the orc leader Arcoz was cut down and killed.

Kain's host staggered about, thrown into consternation. Leaderless they attacked in fitful groups about the field. Albrecht's knights rode to and fro crushing the foe until a chance blow from a great axe brought down Albrecht. He fell, wounded and bleeding. For a moment the battle hung in the balance, but the orc losses proved too great and they were without leaders on the field, they reeled and at last they began to flee. Albrecht's horse regrouped once more and pressed the retreating orcs. Across the bloody fields and rivers the orcs fled to there master, Kain. In the waning hours of the afternoon he rallied them and grouped them in troops of several thousand. They were brought into line in time to hear the rising tumult of the River King's folk. Albrecht's horse charged, led by his third son, Franz Conrad, thrice wounded. There rode the flower of Augsberg, all that remained of Albrecht's army. Against this, Kain's legionnaries fell like wheat to the scythe and the great part of them slaughtered in moments. Some unknown hero cut Kain's steed from under him and horribly wounded that grim captain. But he rallied his guard and fled the field to haunt other pastures and other places. The grim business of slaughter carried on into the night and the following day.

Albrecht pardoned no one and ordered all the prisoners slain and thrown in the river, so that the death toll of Imperial Troops ranged well above 21,000 men and orc, the rest having fled into the hinterlands. Two Legions were extinguished in their entirety. And the Dwarves too exacted a horrible revenge on all the orcs and goblins who lived. But their losses were great and their master dead, fully 1600 Dwarves died and 'went to Stone.' Throughout the night and following day their moans carried far and wide and they tore at their beards. In their grief they vowed to clip their beards, to burn a bald spot on their chins in memory of their fallen comrades, and they were called ever after the Bartigtot, the Deadbeards. But Albrecht's losses were great too, along with two of his sons, including his heir, 3400 of his troops died, a further 6000 were horribly wounded, thus, leaving the valiant King a bare 3000 able bodied warriors to guard his realm.

The Closing days of the Long Year

Kain, leaving the battlefield of Olensk, began marauding through the lands. In the winter he attacked Avignon and slew the Bishop Sixtus I.

The Council of Light, fully reconstituted, sought to ever press the grieving god in Aufstrag and drive evil from the land. They explored the Twilight Wood, seeking the memory of Meltowg Lothian. There they uncovered the mysteries of Utomno, Daladon's son by

Wenafar, and the paths of the Twilight Elves were revealed. Too, they discovered the Castle of Spires and they entered that fell place. The bodies of the dead from the kin-slaying remained as they had fallen, and Daladon found his brother, dead after all those long years at the hands of a High Elf of Shindolay. His grieving shook the world. The passing of his spirit, so bound to Erde, caused a great shudder to pass through the world. The Aurefex Mutatio, the Prism of Alterations, lay on the dais of Melius' making, stained in Elven blood. Daladon took it up and cast its spell of unmaking, opening the gates to the worlds of the Elves of Shindolay and Fontenouq. Daladon took up his brother's blade, Noxmoros ,and stood at the gates to Shindolay for he sought only to kill the Elves as they came through. But they did not come, taking council amongst themsevles as to whether they should return to Erde or not.

Only the Elves of Fontenouq came through the gate to their realm and they passed behind Daladon, neither knowing of the other's presence. Thus, some of the Elves came back into the world. They were filled with a great vengeance and sought to destroy the dark in his home, and they took up the war immediately.

Nulak entered the southern lands and there rallied support for the coming civil wars against those who would shirk his rule. By years' end, many Lords swore their loyalty to him, these included the lands of Ihlsa, Unduliland, Rleuland and the Hlobane. The men in the extreme south threw off his rule, granting the throne of Aenoch to young Pryzmira. She was crowned with the Cunae Mundus Usquam. The Empire was born again amidst the flames of civil war.

Dolgan's army, cleared of the threat of Kain, swept the Luneberg Plains free of the enemy and besieged them in their castle upon the Red Hills. After three long weeks of battle, Dolgan was forced from the field by armies from the Grossewald and the Punj.

1030md

One thousand Dwarves from Norgorod-Kam, as sent by King Dagmar IV, arrived in the Flintlock to aid Dolgan King. The Folk celebrated for many weeks upon the union of the kin, for as is told, no Dwarves of any Kingdoms had aided one another for 3000 years.

Nulak-Kiz-Din, fearing the coming light, cloaked himself in sorceries and vanished from the face of Erde for a time.

About this time, Innocent, a noble-born warrior from the Red Hills, rose to prominence over the men of the lands south of Aufstrag. His origins are lost to history, but it is known that he quickly gained control of the Imperial bureaucracy and with this controlled the pay of the army. In a brutal campaign he seized the control of Ihlsa. He was made Prince of those people and ruled them with an iron hand. He gained allies in Unduliland and Rleuland, and with them forged the Ring of the South, a network of alliances. By years' end he invaded the central province of Torrich and subjugated the local nobility. He declared his Principate from that city and called all his lands the United Kingdoms.

King Morgan I of Kayomar consecrated the Paladin Grove and the silver birch trees, Daladon's gift, they placed in the earth. Almost immediately they bloomed, their leaves turning a wonderful green.

Soon the grove became a place of pilgrimage and worship to both Luther and Durendale. Luther was Sainted by the rising clerics of Durendale for bearing the Holy Sword, this on the first day of Spring. He has forever after been known as St. Luther.

King Albrecht, hoping to replace his horrid losses of the previous two years, invited open colonization of the Luneberg plains, which he claimed for his own. In this Dolgan King gave his blessing, wishing for none of the land himself. Albrecht invited any and all to settle in those barren regions, promising them title to land and protection in return for feudal oaths. Many came and for a time, they held those plains against the east.

In the summer of that year, the Council of Light gathered together once more. There was much discord amongst the Lords, for Dolgan King and Jaren Falkynjager found themselves at odds, one with the other. While they bickered and argued the Lord Daladon returned to the Eldwood, called by the Great Tree, and there he learned of the return of Unklar to Aufstrag.

In a wave of terrible fear the horned god came to his dark throne. He called for the only servant whom he trusted, the Goblin, Erix, and together they contemplated revenge. The gods had tried but

failed to drive him from Erde. Wenafar and Durendale alone stood against him. But lo, they were too weak and he too strong. And it came to pass that he sought council on how best to destroy them. Erix told him to gird himself for battle, call his Mogrl to him, and go to war.

Aristobulus, following Daladon Lothian's lead, returned to Erde, and there pondered in deep places. He came even to Sagramore, his old friend, who now lived the horrible life of the undead.

Sagramore lived in a castle at the height of the world and there feasted on the luckless. Bent on an evil he could not control, he welcomed the visit of the Arch-Magi, for ever in the days of old had they been friends. Aristobulus talked long into the night and Sagramore gave over to him one of the Books of Jaren for it bore the words of prophecy.

As is told, Jaren Falkynjager knew nothing of the texts he wrote in the days of the waning of the world. A thousand years of torment on the walls of Aufstrag gave over to him a certain madness of memory so that he could not recall things from the old world, but for his great love of Robert Luther. But Aristobulus took the book Sagramore gave him and he read it through. It took many weeks for the mage to untangle the manifold prophecies and dreams of the author, but at last he came to the forging of Discerpo, the Emperor's own blade.

He learned how it had been bathed in the Holy Flame and how Sebastian remade it with incantations and spells. He knew then that the sword Discerpo could slay the dark god's mortal form and cast him back into the Void. He called his comrades and told them of his findings. And they sought the sword which they knew the Elf Setiva possessed, for they had given it over to her when she joined them in recovering the Cradle of the World, the Cunae Mundus Usquam. So he called the council to conclude their personal war, which was done with no decision.

Setiva, late of Shindolay, had redeemed herself in the eyes of many of the Council but for Daladon who ever hated the High Elves. They had given her that ancient blade in honor. Discerpo even then hung upon her battle gear. They bid her take it up and redeem her people in the acts of war and help them slay Unklar's mortal form.

On the last day of Spring, the Council took Agmaur the Goblin, comrade and friend to Dolgan King as their guide, and stole away to Aufstrag to make a hindrance upon the Dark Lord. There they found him, sprawled upon his throne in contemplation. Wrapped in the cold dark of his own soul they could see him plainly, great cloven hooves for feet, long clawed hands, and his brow crowned by black horns that stretched above him like the torrents of rage. He looked upon them and laughed.

Battle was met before the Throne of Unklar and the Council made grievous war upon him. Long and hard they struggled in arms. Luther, ever in the forefront, cloaked in his Mantle; Aristobulus veiled in arcane power, Daladon with fierce Noxmoros. Morgeld too fought at Luther's side, the Gorgothorium spear in hand. Dolgan held the Hammer of Angrod, the weapon of his forefathers, and Setiva stood by him with Discerpo. Only Jaren Falkynjager held back, for he awaited the coming of Nulak-Kiz-Din. That fell mage arrived soon after the battle was joined and Jaren fell upon him with the vengeance of a thousand years of suffering. Aristobulus too turned on the Arch-Magi for he knew that no magic of his would slay Unklar, only Discerpo. The Emperor Sebastian, "the Rapscallion," had forged Discerpo at the dawn of the Age of Winter Dark for only one reason, to slay a god. The Council was crushed beneath the strength of Unklar. Setiva, in the end, herself standing upon the brink of death, hew one great blow and clove a Horn of Darkness from Unklar's head, banishing him from the plane.

Unklar howled and saw the Emperor's hand in his death and cursed his memory, but all to no avail for he thundered into the Void, hapless for a time. Light and a true warmth spread across Erde. Nulak fled to hidden places and others of his minions were for a time dismayed. The Shroud of Darkness hung over Aufstrag and the Grausumland only.

And so ended the Age of Winter Dark and began the New Age and the world new peace of sorts. The folk of Demeter, knowing full well the victory won in Aufstrag, proclaimed the seven days of battle fought between the Council and Unklar a holy time, so that those days were celebrated ever after as the Feast of the Unmaking.

But behold Morgeld stole the broken horn of Unklar and brought it to his island in the twilight of the world.

Other crimes followed. In the high summer, the Mogrl gathered and made war upon the Council in dark revenge for their fallen god. They assailed Grundliche Hohle and the Ranger's Knot and tore the party apart. Luther, hard pressed by ErsteTot, the first born of the Mogrl, overcame him only with great effort and the aid of his allies. But the battle ended his days as a mortal on Erde and he returned to the Dreaming Sea. Dolgan took to retrieving his folk from Aufstrag and he too fell to one of the Mogrl, cast a broken King in the pits of Aufstrag once more. Setiva with the broken shards of Discerpo, fell in the Eldwood, another victim of the Mogrl. She fought at the side of Daladon, and in the end, was redeemed in his eyes. He took to the forest deeps once more, avoiding contact of man and Elf.

In the end Nulak took Aristobulus unaware and bound him with enchantments. He lay for many years until at last, making his way to freedom, came back to a world much threatened by the hordes of Aufstrag, this time led by the Undying Lord Coburg.

Dolgan, broken beyond doubt, became ensorcelled by the power of Fantheous, the Elf King's daughter, who kept him in the Eldwood for seven years.

The Council was forever sundered.

In the wake of their defeat, Paskevitch and his minions, one of which was a dark Mogrl, overran all the Flintlock and made war on the Hohle. They took Havok castle and renamed it Unklarglich. The Dwarves were besieged in their pits and the 1000 warriors sent over from Norgorod-Kam were driven into the high north. The Gnomes scattered and the Halflings as well.

So the year ended in victory and defeat. The long Winter's Dark ended at last, but the gods and heroes of man and elf and dwarf fell to the machinations of the enemy.

1031-1036md

The lands rejoiced at the news of the fall of Unklar, but war followed soon as they took up arms against each other.

In the south, Prince Innocent marshaled the remnants of the Empire under a sprawling Confederation of Kingdoms. A great civil war broke out between the remaining minions of Unklar in the environs of Aufstrag. In the north, Paskevitch declared himself King of the Punj and the Goblin Lord, Erix, moved many of his folk and others besides to the Grossewald Forest.

In the south, the Duchies and the city states of Outeremere combined in a loose confederation and united under the Imperial Crown of Pryzmira.

In Aufstrag itself, House Lord Coburg poisoned the swamps and sealed the gates.

The lands of Augsberg, recovered some from the wars, began to rebuild in those days, fortifying their borders against the east. A heavy traffic in goods began between the River King's folk and the Dwarves of Grundliche Hohle where Dolgan's seven year old son, Angrod II, ruled.

In the west, the lands of Ethrum settled into peace, from Angouleme to Kayomar. Only the Great Wall, built in earlier days by unknown hands, remained a stronghold of the enemy.

Daladon Lothian joined Queen Ephremere of Aachen in her war with the orcs of Iregaul. There the orcs had built a great monolithic fortress upon the heights of the Detmold near the lands of Eisenheim.

From their high walls they terrorized the surrounding lands. Their raiders burned, looted and pillaged the valleys around. Daladon and Ephremere gathered a host of arms and laid siege to the city for over a year, but in the end they failed to overcome it. As the folk of Aachen retreated, the orcs attacked their rear guard and Daladon once more wielded Noxmoros in a bloody contest of arms. He was joined then by a Visigoth Priestess, sister of King Theodohad from the north, Fyorgyn of the Two Hammers, who would later be Queen in Augsberg.

Twice again Queen Ephremere attempted to take horrid Iergaul but failed. In the end its walls were thrown down but the fortress deeps never fully cleared. It has since become an evil scar in the Detmold that only the most foolhardy dare to attack.

The Goblin Lords under Uandlich uses magic buried in the Goblin hordes of Ichlin-Yor to secretly free their queen, Oglatay. Nulak came to them and bore with him the Pride of the Goblins, a magic needed to revive her and remake her in her role as mother of Goblin kind. He let them use it for a time, only long enough to breath life back into the beastly woman, at which point she began to lay eggs once again.

When Nulak left the halls of Ichlin-Yor he traveled south to unknown destinations. Upon the road, Erix the Goblin ambushed him north of the Red Hills. Nulak discarded the iron bound chest which holds the Pride. Erix did not realize such, so that the Pride of the Goblins, that most ancient and powerful of artifacts was once more lost in the wide world. Rumors abound that a mad Gnome, who lives on the bones of fish alone, travels the rivers and ponds of the Red Hills using the box as a foot stool.

Many disputes were fought between the new Kingdoms of the world, even as they are today, but these were largely border disputes and the like. Only once more would the free peoples of the world unite under the tattered banners of the Council to battle the dark in the tree of Aufstrag. In the 1035[3h] year as the dark reckoned time, a great power arose in Aufstrag. Coburg the Undying Lord gathered great hosts of men, orc and ungern. He brought the Punj and the United Kingdoms under his sway and he made war on Augsberg. The Shroud of Darkness, never fully extinguished over Aufstrag, rose again and blanketed the land in cold snow and ice.

This so alarmed the gods and heroes of men and dwarf that they summoned Luther to the plane, who brought back many of the Council, including Dolgan the Forge God. The Confessor Knights rode forth from the Dreaming, proclaiming a Crusade against the Tower in the east and many flocked to their banners. Folk of all the free Kingdoms, including many elves of Fontenouq, dwarves of both realms, the gnomes and many halflings gathered in Augsberg for over a year. They numbered tens of thousands and were filled with the youth of a world reborn.

For months, men, dwarves, and elves gathered in the wilds of the Luneburg, and in the high summer of 1037md, the allied host crossed the Udunilay river to attack Aufstrag. But the Imperial forces had not been idle. They had gathered the flower of the empire and called on those dragons who still lived. Several of the foul Mogrl joined them, as did many wizards. The Battle of the Tree, or the Ten Day Battle, shook the world.

When the two armies met in battle the sound rang across the world. The great host of Aufstrag, marching forth under black banners, moved across the lands of Alpa where they met the combined might of the Kings and Lords of the Young Kingdoms. A great and terrible battle they fought there, for ten long days the forces of good and evil struck and repelled one another. The slaughter was without equal in the history of the world, since the Goblin-Dwarf wars of old. Many old soldiers of the Winter Dark Wars fell there. Morgan I, King of Kayomar, who abdicated his throne for the right to press home the final battle, died when a horde of Ungern slew his horse and he refused to leave its body. Albrecht the "River King," old beyond years, fought from the back of a horse to which he had to be tied. A spear took him down and he passed from the lands of the living. Queen Ephremere's daughter, Elisa, a battle lord tried and true from the countless sieges of Iergaul stormed the very gates of Aufstrag, but there, Coburg tore her helm from her head and clove her golden locks with his axe. Four of Luther's Confessor Knights died and countless other Paladins.

Aristobulus tore the enemy ranks apart with his spells, ever seeking the Arch-Magi Nulak. But the Troll Lord never came to the field of battle and for this reason the forces of Aufstrag could not in the end withstand the combined might of the Council and the Young Kingdoms. At the end of ten terrible days, the battle concluded with the route of the Lords of Aufstrag and the death of Coburg. Though in truth, Coburg returned to the halls of darkness as a wraith to rebuild his armies and power. Only the Hlobane, the Orcs of the Red Hills, retired in order, for their pride has always been their strength and they could not be sundered.

The Lords and Kings of the Young Kingdoms made some futile gestures against Aufstrag, but in truth their might and youth were spent, and they left the field carrying their wounded behind. In after days no family could claim to be free of loss from the Battle of the Tree.

The fields of the Alpa never recovered from the scourge of war and the whole land about Aufstrag turned into a desolate wasteland. So great was the carnage that men left their brothers on the field, elven souls sank into the morass, and even the dwarves' stout hearts failed to pull the fallen from the calamity of what became the Toten Fields.

In time, the earth swallowed up the dead and the land healed some little. But as is written the lands of the Toten Fields were everafter haunted places, plagued by the howls of the dead and damned. It is said that on warm days the goodly Princess Elisa can be seen calling for her lords and her father to come to her and find her still.

As the Winter Dark ended, Erde stood as at its creation.

The Young Kingdoms or The Long Days of the World

When the Battle of the Tree ended the shattered armies and soldiers of the victors returned to their homes. Some took to the sea where they fell victim to pirates and brigands. Most traveled by land in large caravans and troops, until months of hard travel brought them to their own lands. Some turned to brigandage themselves, and mercenary companies have been a problem in all the free lands ever since the war's conclusion.

In the void left by the fall of Aufstrag, the Young Kingdoms jostle for power across the land. Some, such as Kayomar, model themselves after the Middle Kingdoms of old, others develop anew. In the west, Angouleme and Maine dominated the lands Ethruman. In the east, vestiges of Unklar's empire remained, haunting vast stretches of the land, particularly in the south. The three realms, Augsberg and Eisenheim became particularly close when the sister of King Theodohad, Fyorgyn, married the crowned King of Augsberg in 1045. The two realms now live in peace and property.

In 1040md, a gathering of Princes and Nobles, the Electors, crowned the 30 year old Pryzmira Empress of Aenoch. They took the ancient crown of the House Golden, the Cunae Mundus Usquam, the "Cradle of the World," upon her head. And many bethought themselves, that the new age was truly dawned. But not all for within a few short years she vied for power with the United Kingdom of Innocent III as she still does today.

And new gods spawned new religions. The church of Demeter is the most powerful. The god of crops and labor is worshiped by most common folk, and everywhere throughout the realms, his churches are rising. Already have they grown powerful in the See of Avignon and at the court of Angouleme.

Some Dwarven kingdoms, most notably Norgorod-Kam, at last have recovered and trade with the peoples of the world. The Folk are not uncommon travelers on the road. The greater part of the High Elves remain in Faerie, but some have returned, and the gates in the Castle of Spires remain open. They live in wondrous palaces and brood upon the shame of their hiding. Those elves who remained and endured the Winter Dark, live in the wilds and have changed. The wood and twilight elves linger still in the forests and wilderness. Gnomes build towns and villages, seeking to claim a stake in the new world. And the laagers of the Halflings once more lumber down the highways of the world, though those people are much embittered in their persecution and have become warlike.

And yet the world bears the imprint of Unklar's thousand year rule. The roads and calendar, and the bureaucracies of his imperial rule all survive. Many of his servants still crawl the earth in search of vengeance and a way to bring back the dark age.

But distance of time removes the pain of his rule, and the horror of the Winter Dark is recalled by the very old.

And Erde is filled with promise of adventure and glory, of lost treasure and power arcane, and battle against dark things that linger in dark places. . . .

The Realm of Winter's Forge

Huzah! Winter Wars all won!
The Battles' Victories beneath the sun!
Winter's Dark , and Unklar's gone,
Slaves no more, Anon!

To Erde! To Erde! To Erde we go!
The Realm of Winter's Forge!
To Erde! To Erde! To Erde we go!
The Realm of Riches and War!

The Dwarves now enstoned,
In halls of Iron and Bone!
The Elves in ornate helm,
Return to Erde, Anon!

To Erde! To Erde! To Erde we go!
The Realm of Winter's Forge!
To Erde! To Erde! To Erde we go!
The Realm of Riches and War!

The men of old arise,
Sounds of war! Battle cries!
Kingdoms taken by storm,
Glory in arms, Anon!

To Erde! To Erde! To Erde we go!
The Realm of Winter's Forge!
To Erde! To Erde! To Erde we go!
The Realm of Riches and War!

Ungern! Slaves to evil war,
Crusade of death ever more!
Seeds of Winter's Dark,
Lust lost in greed, Anon!

To Erde! To Erde! To Erde we go!
The Realm of Winter's Forge!
To Erde! To Erde! To Erde we go!
The Realm of Riches and War!

Of the Cosmos and the Gods

An examination of Erde's place in the Cosmos – The Solar System, Inzae, The Maelstrom & Multiverse, A Sea of Dreams, The Void, from which all things Originate – Of how the days of men are reckoned & the Calendar – The Gods, other Divine persons & the Heroes of the Lands of Ursal.

And ye shall come upon a child
Whose hands are clothed in linen.
And ye shall know of a certainty
That these hands of linen are pure,
Unsullied by by earthly elements.
These virgin hands alone are kept
Clean of earthly turmoil for they alone
Must carry the Flame's holy Dish.
The Prophecy

Erde, the Maelstrom and the Cosmos

Of the Sun and Moon

"The dark of night haunted the folk of the world. In defiance of Unklar, Frafnog the Great Dragon stole the heart of the All Father and gave it to the Faerie Queen. She hurled it into the heavens to spite Unklar's lust and to remind him that his rule would end. When the Winter Dark ended, the light of the Sun flowed across the earth and the Moon traveled the night sky in silent mockery."
~Excerpts from the Histories

There are several aspects of the Cosmology of Erde. The solar system within which Erde lies, the Inner world of Inzae, the Maelstrom, the Multiverse, the Dreamscape and the Void. All but the Void were created by one, both or all of the All Father, Unklar and Inzae. Travel to and from the various planes is possible, though in some instances restricted as is explained below.

The Solar System: The solar system within which Erde lies consists of three planets. At the center of the system lies the sun, created when Unklar ignited the lust of the All Father and hurled it into the Maelstrom. He next bound Erde to that sun through that celestial body's own gravitational pull. There is a single moon which revolves around Erde. Two other planets, recognized by the astrologers of Erde, have come into the gravitational pull of the Sun. They are distant from Erde and are referred to, in the Vulgate, as Illus and Nuxus. These planets were created within the spiraling matter of the Maelstrom. Both are worshiped as gods in more primitive settings, such as The Great Northern Forest.

Inzae: Within the world of Erde lies the Inner world of Inzae. Inzae was formed by the goddess of the same name in the days before time. The world was bound inside Erde and created both from the Maelstrom and the Language of Creation. When Unklar attacked Inzae he bound her, and her world, within the world of Erde, binding it in infinite space so that it stood a part of but wholly separate from his own. Inzae, a brutal place, (*referernce the Death in the Treklent series of modules*), is much akin to Erde in that it is peopled by Dwarves, Elves, Orcs, men and so on.

Travel to Inzae is difficult but can be achieved via the magical Rings of Brass which the Dwarves fashioned during the Goblin Dwarf Wars. The Rings access winding staircases like tunnels which the Dwarves of Inzae constructed in order to return to Erde. In fashioning these tunnels the Dwarves tapped into the nexus of Inzae's creation and opened more gates to other planes of chaos and madness. Upon the steps of each tunnel are encrypted the whole of the Language of Creation. There are hundred of thousands of these tunnels and to master the language one would have to discover them all, for each tunnel possesses only a small section of the language.

The Maelstrom: Erde's solar system spins through the Maelstrom, that great cloud of matter which Inzae inadvertently created before time began. The spiraling chaos slowly consumes the Void, converting the substance of that plane into matter. Within the Maelstrom are a multitude of nebulae, stars, planets, comets and other cosmic bodies. These have formed both from the ever spinning matter of Inzae and residual magic left from the All Father's Language of Creation, sung before the Wall of Worlds was made. This whole Maelstrom constitutes the Universe. Whether or not life exists beyond Erde and Inzae is a matter for the sages and philosophers.

Movement through the Maelstrom is possible, though dangerous, through the use of magic. There are residual sounds of the original Language of Creation as sung by the All Father that linger within the Maelstrom as do certain powerful creatures created by him before time. Also, the chaos of Inzae still plays upon the ever expanding edges of the Maelstrom. Rumors abound that powerful Magi attempt to plunder the Maelstrom for bits and pieces of the language, but only two are known to have done so, Aristobulus and Patrice.

The Multiverse: Beyond the physical matter of the Maelstrom lie a great multitude of planes of existence. When the All Father died the knowledge of worlds beyond the Void, as learned from Inzae, spilled out into Erde. These dreams of other planes combined with the Language, and opened a host of gates and portals with the Wall of Words, to the other planes, Faerie, Hell, the Abyss and so on. Many creatures came to Erde via these doorways, peopling her as she is today. Though Unklar closed most of these portals, when he fell, they reopened and are once again used by the powerful, the lucky or the foolish.

Gates and portals abound through Erde which allow passage to these others planes. Some are well traveled, such as Faerie, but others are well hidden from the curious. Access can also be gained by Astral and Ethereal travel.

The Dreaming Sea: The Dreaming Sea (sometimes referred to as the Sea of Dreams or the Dreamscape) is a plane juxtaposing that of Erde. The sea is a watery plane of chaos, each drop a physical manifestation of a dream. These droplets of the dreams and nightmares of the living creatures of Erde, past, present and future, have accumulated over the millennia to form this great ocean. They are infinite in number, and the Dreaming Sea has no bottom. Few know of it, fewer still have traveled upon it, and fewer still have returned from the Dreaming with their sanity intact.

When the world of man, Elf, Dwarf, etc. is calm so is the sea, and when the world of Erde suffers the Sea becomes more tumultuous. These accumulated dreams are called the Dreamscape. Those with power can travel upon and through it.

In the Age of Heroes the gods chose Luther the Paladin, the lawful and good King of Kayomar, to rule the sea to bring order to its madness. This was before the coming of Unklar. Luther set sail in the magical boat, Evening-Swan, and sailed the timeless Sea of Dreams, mastering its currents and eddies, learning to seek out one amongst the infinite many and read that mind's dreams. He learned of the plight of Erde during the Age of Winter Dark and used the avenues afforded to him upon the Dreamscape to send thoughts of himself into the world, and during the long Winter's Dark, to maintain the fire of hope.

In time, Luther came to be known as the Dreaming Paladin, or Dreaming Knight. His presence upon the Sea calms it, even when the world of Erde is engulfed in war, famine or plague. St. Luther shares his domain with the god Utumno, Lord of Nightmares. The two bear no ill will toward one another. The latter being but the darker shade of the former. They are called collectively, The Dreaming Lords.

Regular travel upon the Dreaming Sea is impossible. Only two magical crafts are known to exist which can sail upon the Sea unimpeded. These are the ships Evening-Swan and Dream Horn. Powerful creatures have been known to summon the Dreaming Lords and bid them to port them onto the sea, and the Confessor Knights of St. Luther come and go at their master's will, but aside from these, travel upon the sea is unheard of.

When in either craft the Dreaming Sea is treated as an ocean in all respects. There are ocean currents (frequently driven by the force of collective wills), wind currents, storms (manifesting when gods dream) and all other climatological affects one would find on the open sea.

There are no random encounters upon the Dreaming Sea. Only a very few monsters have come to inhabit those dreaming deeps. The Dream Warriors of Unklar's Fashioning, the nightmarish Genug Dragon, and Utumno's Knightmares. If other creatures exist they have yet to be discovered.

There is no traditional night or day upon the Sea, regular time has no meaning. The plane exists in the collective unconscious of the world's dreaming. Travelers experience the cyclic daytime/nighttime of their own plane while upon the Sea, though perceptive travelers will realize there is no Sun or Moon. Frequently these daytime/nighttime cycles change as the circumstances dictate. Storms upon the Sea darken the seascape and experience an extreme amount of magical lightning.

(*For adventures in the Dreaming Sea refer to the module "The Malady of Kings."*)

The Void: The Void is an infinite expanse of space surrounding all things. The name, however, belies its nature, for in truth the Void is a vibrant if mysterious plane. There, great currents move through the emptiness like winds across the sea. The Maelstrom, ever growing, pushes against whatever matter exists in the "Great Empty." And some creatures, both those created by the All Father before he fashioned Erde, and those which existed apart from him move through the plane.

Travel to and from the Void can be achieved through various spells or psionic abilities. The Ethereal and Astral planes border the Void. Leaving it however is far more difficult than entering it, for many spells which work upon Erde fail altogether within the Void. Because of the nature of the Void it is impossible to die from lack of water, food or air. Tales of powerful magi floating in the infinite expanse of the Void, helpless for the lack of spells, are told in almost all of the Mage guilds of Erde.

Of Climate

Due to the lengthy period of glaciation brought on by the thousand year rule of Unklar, Erde is an extremely wet world. There are seven months of Spring and Autumn, three of Winter and two of Summer. It rains or snows much of the year.

The northern climes, those regions north of the Inner Sea, are cold almost the whole year long. A short spring allows some agriculture, and plant growth. The lands are stark, travel is difficult and dangerous. The people tend to live in long houses dug into the earth. These protect them from the wind and keep the heat in.

Further south a more temperate environment exists. From the Punj to Burnevitse and south to Fontenouq, northern Kayomar and upper lands of the United Kingdoms and all that lies between are lush lands. Plentiful amounts of rain and sunlight make for rich soil and good agricultural conditions. Houses with thatch and shingled roofs, castles and keeps all dot the lands here.

Upon the southern reaches of Ethrum and Aenoch the conditions are drier and warmer. The lands of Brindisium, southern Kayomar, Eloria, and Outremere all benefit from long warm periods. The architecture as well as agricultural development reflects this different temperature. Open houses, roofless in some parts of Eloria, verandas and broad columned porches dominate most of the wealthy establishments. Grapes and rye, both suited for a drier climate are grown in these lands.

Unklar The Horned God

The Calendar

Religion in the World of Erde

There are 367 days in a year. The year is divided into twelve months and one week of Celebration and Holiday, the Feast of the Unmaking. Each month has thirty days and the Feast seven. Though there are many local and religious holidays, the Feast of the Unmaking is celebrated universally throughout the Young Kingdoms as a time of thanksgiving for the destruction of Unklar.

Calendar reckoning: The standard calendar year is that of the Millennial Age (as begun by the Dark God Unklar). The current year is 1097md. There are, however, four calendars of reckoning, Dwarf, Elf, Olden Year and Millennial. All campaign dates are given in md.

Conversion chart:
Millennial Age (md): 1
Olden Year (oy):   800
Dwarf Year (df):   12188
Elven Year (ey)   3452

To arrive at the Olden Year, add 800 to the present md. For Dwarf year add 12188, and for Elven year 3452. A History will read: In 1029md (13217df; 1729oy; 4252ey) the Dwarves of Grundliche Hohle made peace with the 47 clans of Gnomes.

The twelve months of the year.	
Erstdain (First Month)	Spring
Regnerisch (Rain)	Spring
Lothian (named for the god Daladon)	Spring
Uthdain (named for the god Luther)	Spring
Feast of the Unmaking (7 days)	
Falkhyn (named for Jaren Falkynjager)	Summer (low)
Trocken (Hot)	Summer (high)
Frostig (End of heat)	Autumn
Erstfhroe (First Frost)	Autumn
Lexlicht (Last Light)	Autumn
Nochturn (Evening)	Winter
Winterdark	Winter
Arist (named for the god Aristobulus)	Winter

Deities are divine beingsof great power tied to the fabric of the mulitverse. No person in Erde denies belief in the gods, but individualized worship of the deities helps define existence and explain the mysteries of the universe.

Despite the control the Priests of Unklar maintained over the hearts and minds of the people for a thousand years, multifaceted religious worship flourishes across Erde. The Winter Dark Wars sparked the fire, and when the world was born anew, old and new religions emerged from the long dark. Some elder deities found new worshipers in the lands After Winter Dark, but many new deities arose to guide the of races of Erde.

In Erde, philosophy of life and codes of ethics are based upon prayer to more than one god. Very few, if any, worship a single deity. Instead, the people of Erde exhibit a healthy respect to most all powers aligned with their ethos. Some pray to those powers who can best aid them in time of need, and most invoke the names of various deities important to daily life in a hard world. Even priests and clerics of a specific deity might call upon a power similarly related to their own patron. For example, a cleric of St. Luther might call upon the light of Durendale if battling a vampire. Such situations are those that would generally unite followers of various deities against a single cause.

Certain deities, despite the versatile prayers of the people of Erde, have risen to prominence. These include Demeter, Wenafar, Durendale, Poseidon, and even still, Unklar. Also, while there are deities considered specific to nonhuman races, anyone may worship such powers just as a member of that race. It is also possible to become a cleric of a racial deity even if the cleric is not of the deity's race, but such is extremely rare if not unheard of.

Origins

Deities are divine beings bestowed great power by those that worship them. The deities of Erde can be classified into three groups based upon their origin: Eternals, Spirits, and Immortals.

Eternals: They existed before the All Father fashioned the Language of Creation, and as such, were slivers of his memory or emotion that he had discarded into the Void. Because they originate from a part of the All Father, the Eternals are not bound by the laws of creation. This makes them powerful beings. Many came to Erde before the Wall of Worlds, some when Ondluche slew the All Father. Unklar alone stepped onto the plane when the Paths of Umbra were opened. The Eternal deities are: All Father, Corthain, Thorax, Mordius, Narrheit, Poseidon, Wenafar, Unklar, Tefnut, and Toth.

Spirits: They originate from the substance of creation that was forged by the All Father or from a part of one of the Eternals. The worship of the Spirits rose to prominence due to the Eternals intercession into the lives of mortals. Corthain used the Language of Creation and fashioned Durendale from his own body. Oglotay owes her power to the manipulations of Thorax. The Spirits are: Durendale, Oglotay, the Twin Sisters, Aenouth, Athria, Burasil, Frafnog, Glorianna, Grotvedt, Imbrisius, Urnus Gregaria, Wulfad, Amenexl, Angrim, Krateus, Adrius & Zernius, and Rhealth.

Immortals: They arose After Winter Dark. Created entirely from the substance of Creation, these deities owe their power to their worship by mortals or by their acquisition of magic that lingered from the Days before Days. The Immortals are: Demeter, Aristobulus, Augustus, Daladon, Dolgan, Falkenjagger, Nuluk-kiz-din, St. Luther, and Utumno. A few heroes and villains border upon becoming Immortals, including Almuric, Kain, and Mithlon.

Powers and Spells

In addition to classification by origin, the deities can be grouped according to their level of power. The five levels of power are: Supreme, Greater, Lesser, Minor, and Heroes/Villains. The more powerful a deity, the more spheres of spells available to the deity's clerics. A deity's level of power greatly corresponds to the number of worshiper's that invoke their name, except for the supreme deities. The supreme deities maintain the fabric of the multiverse. Mortals play little part in their machinations, and they do not attempt to cultivate followers any longer.

Deity Descriptions

The most commonly worshiped deities are detailed below. Other deities do exist, including a few lesser deities and many minor ones. Indeed, whole pantheons of deities might be found in certain locales, such as those brooding gods who dwell in Asgard that are worshiped by the northerners.

Each deity's alignment is noted next to their name. Pronunciation of the deity's name is included in the description of the deity if warranted. The emphasized syllable is capitalized. The pronunciations indicated are consistent with American English.

Holy Symbols: Each deities' symbol is a stylized representation of that which is most holy to the convictions of the god in question. A cleric's holy symbol is a representational icon of spiritual significance that is typically worked into an item that can be used or carried. The most common holy symbols are icons that are hand-held or worn around the neck, and rods or staves bearing the icon at their top. A representative illustration of each deity's holy symbol appears next to their description.

Raiment: The more organized religions also place great value in the attire of their priests and clerics. Variations in raiment is sometimes used to indicate rank within the church. Clerics who wander the lands serving their deity often prefer certain armor or weapons. Preferred raiment, armor, and weapons relevant to each deity are discussed in their description.

Supreme Deities

Most consider these elder gods as beings of vast and unknown power whose tenets mean little in a hard world. Of the four supreme deities, two alone still thrive, Corthain and Thorax. Only enlightened and brave mortals worship them, although some deities of lesser power rose to their present state in service to one of these supreme deities. It is unknown as to whether other supreme deities exist beyond the Wall of Worlds.

All Father: In the beginning there was the All Father. He fashioned Erde from the Void, and set life into motion. There is no active worship of the All Father in Erde, but his name lives on with the Dwarves. They utilize the moniker "All Father" when designating the most wise and eldest counselor of a Dwarven kingdom.

Otherwise, most vestiges of the All Father are lost to time. The Dwarves recorded his existence in the Mammoth Scrolls, and some of the other major deities remember his presence. It is unknown whether those deities still give tribute to the All Father. Any being that accesses the Mammoth Scrolls might discover that the All Father is represented by a simple circle.

Corthain (L): Corthain (KŌR-thān) is the supreme deity of law, justice, goodness, and reason. He seeks revenge against his brother, Thorax, for the murder of their sister, Mordius. Upon her death, Corthain swore in her honor to forever maintain a balance of power among the gods. In upholding this conviction, Corthain has slain many gods and beings of extreme power whose names are now lost to time. For this, Corthain has garnered the titles Justice Maker, Slayer of Gods, and Shatterer of Worlds.

Enlightened beings of good and law worship Corthain, though their number is few. Other deities with connection to Corthain include Durendale Glorianna, and St. Luther. Corthain's relationship to the Holy Flame in Kayomar is unknown. Corthain's holy symbol is a spear with the head pointed down and the spear's other bladed end pointing up; a two-headed spear crosses through the center and arcs downward on either side. It represents Corthain's ultimate creed, "Justice, all things come to one." His favored weapon is a spear.

Thorax (C): Thorax (THÔR-aks) is the supreme deity embodying evil, chaos, and destruction. His arrogant malevolence knows no bounds, having slain his sister and corrupted a strain of the first-born Dwarves into the Eldritch Goblins. Extremely powerful (or foolish) and evil beings offer prayer to Thorax. Thorax's holy symbol is a stylized bull's head, representing his favored form in combat.

Mordius (N): Mordius (MÔR-dē-us) was the sister of Corthain and Thorax. Where Corthain embodied all that was good but strong, honorable but stern; where Thorax embodied all that was evil; Mordius embodied humanity and nature, the balance and beauty, enlightenment and journey. Thorax became so envious of his sister's enlightened beauty that it drove him mad, and he devilishly murdered her. In honor of his fallen sister, Corthain swore an oath to maintain a balance of power amongst the gods. Mordius' holy symbol is two entwined ovals with thin, crescent arcs to either side. The symbol represents the circular pattern of nature, and the converging and expanding paths of evolution.

Greater Deities

These are the most powerful gods who lord over Erde and define existence. They concern themselves with the state of the universe and Erde, and the place of their convictions within it. Some greater deities actually walk the plane, and, as in the case of Durendale, are active in shaping the history of the world. Churches to these deities are the largest and most powerful as well. All races worship the greater deities.

Demeter (NG): The most pervasive religion of the day is that of the humble deity Demeter (Də-Mġ-tər). Being the god of peace, nature, agriculture, home, and revelry, Demeter appeals to the common folk of Erde, including Gnomes and Halflings.

Demeter's followers trace their heritage to the town of Haven at the foot of the Dwarven realm of Roheisen Hohle. Phillip the Guileless arose there, speaking the praises of Demeter and converting the folk of the land. The religion spread rapidly from village to town, from town to city. Churches and monasteries sprang up and people flocked to Demeter's worship. Many of the current monarchs of the world worship Demeter, with most making it a state religion. Demeter's church has thus grown powerful and wealthy. The church's bishops, prelates, and abbots are always prominent figures in their local community, and regularly engage in its politics.

Demeter's holy symbol is a wagon wheel. Another common representation of Demeter is the rearing horse, and his followers pay great respect to that noble animal. While the priests in the upper echelons of the Church of Demeter display wealth in their dress, the warrior-priests and traveling priests wear more practical and common clothing. They favor weapons made of wood.

Durendle (LG): Corthain fashioned Durendale (DəR-in-dāl) from the muscle of his body and cast the god into Erde in the form of a sword. It is the god of law, order, goodness, and the sun, and it seeks to deal justice across the lands. Through it's servant, St. Luther, Durendale led the forces of good during the Winter Dark Wars. Though it's followers and churches do not number as many as those of the other greater deities, many call upon Durendale to combat evil for it is the power of pure good. Durendale is actively worshiped in the Kingdom of Kaymar at the shrine of the Holy Flame and the tomb of Saint Luther. (*Reference the DM's Handbook to Erde, Magic Items, for Durendale's powers when wielded by a mortal*).

Durendale's holy symbol is downward pointing representation of the sword with an upturned cross-guard. The cross-guard represents the chalice into which all matters are poured, and the blade represents the straight arrow of law and justice that funnels out. Durendale's clerics prefer armor of chain or plate. Those that become proficient with the sword achieve a place of rank and respect among their peers.

Narrheit (CE): Narrheit (NÄR-hīt) is the god of chaos, power, trickery, and wrath. His title is The Lord of Change. His favorite weapon is an ever-changing two-handed sword. Narrheit's evil mind is always alive with dark plots, and his ego drives him to ever seek more power. While his followers are dubbed foolhardy, many call upon their dark master for power and revenge. Some Twilight Elves and denizens of the deeps pay homage to Narrheit.

Narrheit's archenemy is Unklar, for the horned god bound him in chains in the High Tower in the City of Night. There, Unklar forced Narrheit to serve the whims of the great lords of the Winter Dark. Narrheit eventually manipulated the mage Aristobulus to loose his chains, and he escaped into the world again. A deadly competition still exists between Narrheit and the lesser deity Aristobulus, and their followers sometimes engage in battle as well.

Narrheit's holy symbol is four interlocking circles. This symbol mocks Mordius and the Earth, for chaos is all things and nothing escapes the Maelstrom.

Poseidon (CG): The King of the Gods and Lord of the Seas, Poseidon (Pu-SĪ-dun) is worshiped by sailors and all who wish safe passage on the seas of Erde. His churches are common in Tagea, Brindisium, and Eloria. Though rare, some high elves pay homage to Poseidon (see picture previous page).

Poseidon never fell to Unklar. He ruled the depths of the oceans where the horned god dare not go. He is deferred great respect and alliance by most all deities, particularly Wenafar, Tefnut, and Toth. The lesser deity Aristobulus marks Poseidon as his patron.

Poseidon is represented as an impersonal and unemotional deity. He doesn't brook flattery, and he can be impatient. If cause raises him to anger, however, his wrath is devastating. His holy symbol is an eight-armed octopus holding onto the edge of a ring.

Unklar (LE): The great evil of the horned god, Unklar (ŌŌN-klär), and his rule of Erde for a thousand years is well detailed in the Histories. He is the deity of command, evil, marshes and night. Although he weaves complicated plots and traps, he ultimately resorts to brute power to overwhelm his foes. Unklar's titles are many and include, The Horned One, Lord of Winter Dark, God of

Night, and The Marsh Lord. His order is balanced with evil and cruelty, and his will is unparalleled. Unklar wields Utriel, the Mace of Judgment.

Unklar's dark priests roam the world, seeking to summon him anew to return the Winter Dark to the world. Large gothic cathedrals to Unklar still tower over the Kingdom of Punj and the United Kingdoms, for the people there recall the order and progress of civilization that arose in the Age of Winter Dark. But in other parts of the world, Unklar's temples are hidden and his worship kept secret. The sorcerors and wizards in the Paths of Umbra worship Unklar, and the Ungern continue to do their master's bidding, long after the end of the Winter Dark Wars. While most humanoids pay Unklar sacrifice, the goblins loathe his name because of the years of slavery and torture they suffered at Unklar's hand.

Unklar's holy symbol is the crescent moon, typically displayed on a black field. It represents his bending of the flat world created by the All Father. The Justiciaries of Erde, Unklar's clerics, indicate their station by the orientation of the holy symbol pointed downward. Those warriors who are, or were, Legionnaires in Unklar's army, point the moon toward the left, while those in the Paths of Umbra point it right. Common worshipers point the moon upward, thus doubly representing that they worship the horned god. Clerics of Unklar prefer maces, morning stars, mauls, and the like as weapons.

Wenafar the Faerie Queen (N): An eternal goddess of infinite power, Wenafar (WIN-ā-fär) commands the elements and the fey, and watches over the animals and peoples of the forests. She if bound to the lesser deity Daladon and the Great Oak which he protects, and she interacts with the world through them. Wenafar and Daladon's son is Utumno, the Lord of Nightmares. She often allies herself with Poseidon.

Wenafar's worshipers are numerous and varied. All who live in Faerie call her Queen, and elves, whether high, wood, wild, or twilight, pay her homage. Forest dwellers, rangers, and druids give her worship, and the common folk of Erde who live away from civilization often offer her prayer. Gnomes and halflings typically incorporate worship of Wenafar into their religious ceremonies. She is also Queen of the elemental lords and those native to the elemental planes.

Other than her holy symbol, a lily, worship of Wenafar incorporates no recurring raiment, ceremony, or organized prayer. Typical display of the holy symbol is done with a wand or rod with a bulbous "seed" bottom leading toward a lily in full bloom.

Lesser Deities

These gods are generally associated with only a few specific spheres. The peoples of Erde call upon them in time of need as would be appropriate. Worship of the lesser deities varies from being widespread to very localized. The gods of Asgard that are not detailed below should be considered lesser deities.

The lesser deities include the primary racial deities. The race of their primary worshipers is indicated in a parenthetical following the deity's name.

Aenouth (High Elves) (LG): High Elves value qualities in their deities that are quite alien to most every other race. This holds true for Aenouth (Ā-näth), the androgynous High Elven deity of air, knowledge and magic. Aenouth's place in the elven cosmology has been indecipherable to outside races, and High Elves seldom openly worship or display any symbol relating to the deity. Supposition is that Aenouth is the keeper of the spirits of the Elves.

Aenouth's holy symbol is an elven rune of unknown meaning. As this symbol is not displayed outside of High Elven ceremonies dedicated to Aenouth, clerics of the deity utilize a glass vial containing air, or if possible a wisp of mist or fog, as their holy symbol to combat undead and cast spells.

Aristobulus (CG): (*reference picture, p. 143*) The patron deity of arcane magic, Aristobulus (ə-rist-Ō-bool-us) became immortal due to the knowledge he acquired in warring against Unklar during the long Age of Winter Dark as a member of the Council of Light. He came to understand the universe, gathered pieces of the Language of Creation, studied the Blood Runes, tested wits against Unklar and Narrheit, and traveled away from the dark path of the worship of Narrheit under the guidance of Poseidon.

Aristobulus commands powerful and destructive magic, and like his patron, his blood boils if he is angered. His nature is quite chaotic, giving him an uncanny ability to achieve success against all odds. He will sometimes be seen upon Erde, although such sightings are often incarnations of the Arch-magi from differing points in time before he rose to an immortal state. In most all cases, he appears as an old wizard, long of beard, with pale skin and an eye-patch over his left eye. He is loathed by his former patron and nemesis, Narrheit, with whom he often matches ego and wits. Aristobulus and his followers constantly work and war against Nuluk-Kiz-Din.

Aristobulus is mostly worshiped by sorcerors, wizards, and other arcane spell-casters, including a number of humanoids and intelligent beasts. Various demi-human races also incorporate his worship into their pantheons. The Dwarves call him Weisedrache (in the Vulgate, "White Dragon"), the counselor of the all-fathers. The Wild Elves pay homage to him in the form of a white eagle. The Halflings see him as a great white wolf, watching and protecting them from the black wolf, Nuluk-Kiz-Din. He typically appears in each of the pantheons of the Gnome clans as a wizened old sage. Aristobulus' holy symbol is an open eye upon crossed lightning bolts, and is used primarily by those who still follow the paths of the Mystic Enclave (*reference Guilds & Orders, p. 198*).

Athria (NG): Athria (ə-THRǵ-ə) is the goddess of maternity and continuation. Most all peoples, except elves, pay her homage, especially during Spring ceremonies and at the birth of a child. Her religion is thus widespread. It is said that Athria appears to each person as they die and removes all pain associated with the death. Her holy symbol is a rune representing the cycle of life from birth to death.

Augustus (LN): Augustus is a god of strength and war, and warriors in the various armies of the nations of Erde pray to him, especially before battle. His worshipers also include the wild Halflings, Dwarves, and Wild Elves. He is a master of all weapons, and his clerics often outfit themselves in heavy armors. His holy symbol is a two-headed eagle clutching a sword and spear. Augustus' clerics tatoo this symbol upon their body, and often incorporate it into their armor, helms, and shields.

Burasil (High Elves) (CG): Somewhat less alien than Aenouth, the High Elven god of war is Burasil (BYOOR-ə-sil). Like other High Elven deities, Burasil is androgynous in appearance. His fury is such that fire burns about him, and inflicts pain upon his enemies. One ancient elven tome records that Burasil became encased in fire at the return of the Fontenouq Elves to Erde. Burasil fights with flaming sword and dagger.

Worship of Burasil always involves fire. Upon achieving priesthood, his clerics receive their holy symbol, a gold ring upon which an actual flame always burns (acts as fire in all respects). Most non-elves avoid touching such a ring, and thieves do not covet it for the curses it might bring them. If a cleric of Burasil loses her ring, however, she must atone by successfully drinking from the Holy Flame. Burasil's connection to the Holy Flame is unknown.

Daladon Lothian (NG/CG): The Lord Protector of the Forest, Keeper of the Great Oak, Daladon Lothian (DAL-ə-dôn) walks the forests of Erde meeting evil with contempt, but always seeking to maintain a balance in the natural order of things. He maintains some command of all the elements, but particularly earth and air. Daladon is the consort of Wenafar and father of Utumno, and worship of those deities incorporates some prayer to Daladon as well. He always wields a great, two-handed sword.

Daladon's place in history is many, but as a member of the Council of Light, he cast Unklar from the plane. Also, his contempt for the High Elves that left Erde at the coming of the Dark is legendary. He cursed them and made them need to sleep, and thus dream, forever more.

Daladon is worshiped by rangers and druids, particularly those members of the Watchers in the Wood and the Order of the Oak, as well as by all denizens of the forests. To them, he appears as a stern elf with flowing copper hair, encased in plate armor and a living cloak of leaves. While High Elves pay him no heed as expected, most all Wood Elves, Wild Elves, and Half-Elves call upon him. Their image of Daladon is more rustic and wild, generally conforming to the typical dress of their culture. In some instances, he appears fully bearded. Many Halflings incorporate Daladon into their family pantheons in the form of a wild halfling with a flaming red mohawk, covered in tatoos, who slays giants with a single swing of his sword.

Daladon's holy symbol is a representation of the Great Oak with branches representing the two circles of life, Mordius and Wenafar. His clerics typically display the symbol on the end of a staff.

Dolgan (Dwarves) (CG): Dolgan (DŌL-gôn), son of Hirn, was born in Grundliche Hohle and took to the forge before he could walk. His skill surpassed all, and he is called the Forge King. As recounted elsewhere, Dolgan's mortal existence was one of varied sorrow and triumph. He is Dwarf through and through for his blood was crafted from the Language of Creation. For his role in defeating Unklar, Dolgan became a hero, a legend, and eventually, a god to his peopole and race.

In Dolgan do the Dwarves see the pinnacle of what they strive to be: a master of stone and metal, a mighty warrior strong of spirit, hearty of fortitude, and quick to action. For this, he is sometimes called Dolgan First-born. He commands the realms of the earth, knowledge, and war. He wields Havoc, a great axe and weapon of revenge that he forged in the pits of Aufstrag while a slave to Unklar. Dolgan's other followers include Gnomes, Halflings, warriors, and those who work with stone or metal. A representation of Havoc serves as his holy symbol.

Falkenjagger (LG): Jaren Falkenjagger (FÔLKIN-yā-gur) is the deity of law, revenge, thought, and planar travel. The foundations of his religion lie in that ancient pantheon of Ethrum gods that were once worshiped in the Kingdom of Kayomar, of which only Tefnut and Toth remain. 'Tis said that Falkenjagger is the reborn incarnation of that mythos' avenging god, Horus. With Tefnut and Toth, Falkenjagger heads a triumvirate whose worship overlaps one another. in the Judgement. This triumvirate is closely linked with St. Luther, and allied with Poseidon and Aristobulus. An enmity exists between Falkenjagger and Dolgan, but it is not one of open hostility.

Falkenjagger rose to immortality following the banishment of Unklar. He served Robert Luther and saw his king die at Unklar's hands, only to be captured himself and crucified above the gates of Aufstrag. There, Nuluk-Kiz-Din tortured him for one-thousand years. It was also there that the worship of Jaren Falkenjagger began, in the form of the Cult of the Hanging God.

Falkenjagger appears as a human, often dressed as a monk. Tattoos litter his body, and within his chest burns a glowing palm-sized jewel. In combat, he wears a great helm shaped like a hawk's head, and he commands gigantic hawk wings to spring from his back at will. Legend holds that Falkenjagger guards the Books of Toth in a floating city on the edge of Time.

His worshipers include all seeking revenge, those interested in planar travel, and paladins, warriors, and monks. His clerics prefer loose fitting raiment, but are not slow to don armor and wield mighty weapons in combat.

Frafnog (Dragons) (N): The Father of Dragons, Frafnog (fraf-NÄG) the great came into the world in the Days before Days. He knew the mind of the All Father and speaks the Language of Creation. Other than the Sentients, he is perhaps the oldest living creature upon Erde, for even now he nestles in the heart of the Kolkrab Mountains. He is worshiped by Dragons and dragon-kind, as well as by wizards, seers, Dwarves, Gnomes, and the Wild Elves. His holy symbol is a ring in the shape of a dragon.

Glorianna (LN): Corthain forged Glorianna (GLÔRg-ônə) from a sliver of his heart. She is the sister of Durendale. Unlike Durendale, however, Glorianna take the form of a beautiful woman in full armor who resembles Mordius. Militant in her quest to destroy chaos, Glorianna is the lesser deity of war, law, and destruction. She wields an exquisite magical longsword of holy power that rivals Durendale itself. There have been reports of such a sword appearing in the hand of a great champion of law just as they entered combat against powerful beings and beasts of Chaos.

Glorianna's clerics follow the example of their patron and seek to exterminate chaos and evil. They favor full body armor and will use any weapon. A great number of lawful warriors and paladins pray to Glorianna, as do all that seek to uphold law. Most races incorporate her worship into their religion in some form. Her holy symbol represents law and justice.

Grotvedt (Gnomes) (NG): Grotvedt (GRÄT-vedt) is unique among the gods for no people worship him directly. Each of the forty-seven Gnome clans in Erde worship a separate pantheon of clan elders that represent the valued traits of gnome culture. Grotvedt sits upon his throne and grants audience to the hundreds of Gnome deities of the clan pantheons, giving them counsel. A common Gnomish prayer is "May Grotvedt bless the Elders."

Gnomish history recounts that Grotvedt was a dwarf who led his clan above ground, where they evolved into Gnomes. They cultivated crops and established contact with other races. While there are no clerics of Grotvedt and thus no need of a holy symbol, his representation is found in Gnomish currency. Gold coins minted by the Gnomes bear a sickle and hammer,

representing the tools of economy and of defense of the clan which are the foundation of gnome society. These are the tools Grotvedt's clan carried with them always as they worked their fields and fought off encroaching invaders and beasts.

Imbrisius (CE): Imbrisius (M-brēz-əs) is the goddess of pain and death, and she is wholly evil. She takes joy in creating vile monsters and casting them into Erde to wreck havoc. She is the consort of Narrheit. Her worship involves dark rituals under the cloak of night. Her holy symbol is a tear drop, and for every level gained, the cleric adds another tear drop to his necklace, bracelet, armor, or staff. High priests wear leather masks.

Nuluk-Kiz-Din (LE) (Mongroul, Troll Lord): Nuluk-kiz-din (NŌŌ'əL-uk-kiz-den), predates the present age and the previous one. He rose to prominence in the Age of Heroes when he summoned Unklar to Erde via the Paths of Umbra to Erde. There are few followers of the dread diety. Most who do pay him homage are in fact adherents of Unklar who wish to bring the horned god back to the plane through Nuluk's sorcery. Their greatest strongholds are in the United Kingdoms, those lands where the wizard-priests of Unklar were long established. The exceptions to this are the Crna Ruk assassins who pay only Nuluk worship, and the trolls and other fell beasts of the Gottland and Moravan plains. Some wizards and sorcerers worhips Nulak for they find Aristobolus a distant deity.

Nuluk is sometimes called The Troll Lord by those who wish not to speak his name. He often takes the form of a huge black wolf and roams the lands keeping an eye on all his enemies. His holy symbol is the crescent moon of Unklar pointed downward, with five chimes hanging from it in the position of a wolf's paw pad. The dreaded tingling of the chimes heralds the coming of the Troll Lord.

Ogoltay (Goblins) (CE): Ogoltay (Ō'G'L-tā) is the Mother of Goblins. Ogoltay resides in Nogorondo and lays many eggs from which goblin warriors an drones, and once in a great while, an Eldritch Goblin, are born into the world. Ogoltay appears as a beastly goblin woman, and she is evil beyond measure. All goblins pray to her as their primary deity. Her clerics prefer the morning star and spiked ball and chain as weapons. Her holy symbol is a representation of herself.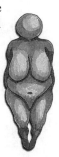

St. Luther (LG): Luther the Paladin, called the Gallant, of the House Pendegrantz, rose in the west to be a great knight and eventually King of Kayomar. His son was Robert Luther, Kayomar's greatest King. In Luther burned the magic of Corthain and the power of the Holy Flame, and he wielded the god Durendale with impunity and strength of will against evil in all its forms. With the Council of Light, he banished Unklar from the plane and ended the Age of Winter Dark. In later years, after he gave up Durendale, Luther cloaked himself in the righteousness of Corthain and became Luther the Confessor. In Kayomar, he became a saint.

St. Luther has many titles, including the Dreaming Paladin, Lord of Dreams, the Confessor, and the Gallant. He lords over the Dreaming Sea with Utumno, the Lord of Nightmares. It is in dreams that all who pray to St. Luther can most easily reach their patron. All races incorporate this incarnation of Luther into their pantheon in some form.

As the Confessor, St. Luther does service to Corthain, showing a side of justice that that supreme deity lost long ago – redemption. As the Gallant, St. Luther is a beacon of law and good for knights and paladins to follow. St. Luther's holy symbol represents Corthain's rules of law. The three swords stand for retribution, confession, and judgment, all intersecting upon the plane of goodness.

The Confessor Knights serve St. Luther upon the Dreaming Sea. More, they travel the land seeking to bring forgiveness through confession to the wanting (see Confessor Knights, p. 196).

The Paladin's Grove, or Palladium Grove

North and East of the Nordmark in Kayomar, between the Bergrucken Mountains and the Ardeen River lies the Paladin's Grove, the most sacred shrine in the western world. In 1029md King Morgan of Kayomar established the Grove in honor of St. Luther. He ordered a shrine built to serve the Holy Defenders of the Flame and dedicated to the worship of St. Luther and Durendale. For the site of the Shrine Morgan chose the ancient family holdings of Pendegrantz.

The Grove encompasses 300 acres of wooded land surrounded on all sides by a low wall. A temple building stands built in the center of the Grove along with a few smaller buildings for travelers to stay in and one villa for the King of Kayomar. The Holy Flame, in its dish of platinum, rests in the altar chamber of the Temple (*reference Magic Items, p. 225*). In further honor to the sainted knight the Druids of the Great Tree came to the grove at the behest of Daladon Lothian and planted there a crop of silver birch and elm, said to be the offspring of the Trees of Mordius from the dawn of time.

The temple honors St. Luther, promoting his worship as well as that of Durendale. It is a place where people come for peace and to learn of themselves by spiritually traveling the Dreaming Sea to learn from the Lord of Dreams what they may. Others come on pilgrimage to learn what truth the Holy Flame can reveal. Though all who approach the Flame must be bare of foot. It is said that the sword Durendale lies hidden in the grove. The grove is maintained by generous gifts from various Lords (*reference Cleves, p. 82*) and through donations.

It is the most holy ground for the Holy Defenders of the Flame.

The Twelve Orders of the Confessor Knights

Let it be known that all Confessor Knights are duty bound to follow the code set out below in the Twelve Orders of Confession. In all things a Knight must by his actions, his speech and his bearing keep himself in truth, honor and righteousness.

The Five Orders of the Contest of Arms

I   A Man's worth may not be determined by the contest of Arms alone.

II   A Man's worth is a man's honor. A Man's honor is a man's strength.

III   A Man's strength is determined by the strength of his faith, body and spirit.

IV   The spirit should be such that one is willing to die for the Oath of his faith.

V   Death in the service of Justice is an holy act.

The Three Orders of Induction

VI   A Man must deal in fairness with the High and the Low.

VII   A Man must always deal in Justice, Temperance and Wisdom.

VIII A Man must keep the deserving from harm, enrich the poor and aid the wounded.

The Two Orders of Negation

IX   One must not be selfish or vainglorious.

X   One must not covet the accolades of other men be they Kings or peasants.

The Two Orders of Conduct

XI   A Man may not possess more than may be carried upon the Knight's Horse or a Squire's back.

XII   Bounty gained from Acts of Justice must be delivered to the Halls of Justice, to alm houses or hospitals.

Tefnut (LG): Tefnut was a greater deity in a pantheon of gods worshiped in the lands that are now the Kingdom of Kayomar. Those gods vanished in history, with only Tefnut and Toth living on. Tefnut lords over the earth and its fresh waters, and he sometimes takes the form of a sleek water dragon. There is much respect between Tefnut and Poseidon, and they worked in tandem in guiding the forces of good against Unklar in the Winter Dark Wars.

Tefnut is still worshiped in some Kayomar locales, and also in regions near fresh waters. He is primarily worshiped in Brindisium, where the people pay homage to the triumvirate of Falkenjagger, Tefnut, and Toth. Tefnut's holy symbol is a circle with a horizontal line dissecting it. His clerics prefer bronze or bronze-colored armors and colorful garb.

Toth (N): Toth (TÄTH) is the second survivor, with Tefnut, of an ancient pantheon of gods that fell into decline. He wears three faces. As the overseer of the dead, he guides the souls of the deceased to their resting place without favor or disfavor. Toth also knows all things, perhaps even possessing memory of the birth of the All Father, but he is possessive of his knowledge and protects it always. Because of this supreme knowledge, Toth has perfect command of the Language of Creation and thus, magic. His understanding of the universe, and therefore his place within it, has resulted in his steadfast refusal to use the Language of Creation.

Legend holds that the Books of Thoth exist in a city on the edge of time, and any who find them may ask any three questions they desire which will be truthfully answered. The consequences of asking questions regarding the foundations of the universe, however, could be dire for any mortal who so dares. The origins of the Mammoth Scrolls may lie in the Books of Toth.

Toth's worship is typically individualized. Sages, wizards, seekers of knowledge, and those involved with the dead all pay homage to him in some way. Toth is always given worship by the devotees to the Falkenjagger, for Toth is that god's trusted advisor. Toth's holy symbol is a circle within a circle, representing the two worlds of man and god bound together.

Twin Sisters (N): The All-Father forged the Twin Sisters from his soul, and they were called the Maiden of Night and the Maiden of Light. They were first called the Twin Sisters by the dwarves, and the early kingdoms of men began worship of them. When Unklar remade the world as a mockery of that which the All-Father created, he reforged the Twin Sisters and bound them to their course as celestial bodies. When the Winter Dark came to end, the light of the Sun flowed across Erde and the Moon traveled the night sky in silent mockery.

The sisters are worshiped by astronomers, sages, soothsayers, and lovers of the sun and moon. Some of their clerics worship them in tandem, while others only worship one of the sisters. Their holy symbols are of course the sun and moon.

Urnus Gregaria (LN): Urnus Gregaria was once a mortal who achieved god status through a life of adventuring. He was a bard of the highest repute and specialized in string instruments. His journey through life carried him to many foreign lands and into contact with druids and wizards. He was renowned for his ability to craft magical staves. Through heroism in service to the Empire he was granted a noble title by the emperor in the city of Gaxmoor. Urnus therefore has a special connection to that city, and he considered it his home despite his preference to be on the move.

Concentrated worship of Urnus outside of Gaxmoor is uncommon. Bards and other travelers often pay him homage. His holy symbol is an imperial eagle.

Utumno (Twilight Elves) (N): Utumno (ə-TOOM-nō) is the son of Wenafar the Faerie Queen and Daladon Lothian. He is the darker shade of St. Luther, and together they lord over the Sea of Dreams as the Dreaming Lords. He is known as the Lord of Nightmares, and patron deity of dreams, travel, and the Twilight Elves.

He moves through the night in a misty form, and he wears an alien armor. He rides an otherwordly horse across the planes, and sails the his ship, Dream Horn, upon the Dreaming Sea.

The Twilight Elves revere him, and his other worshipers include lovers of the night and mages. All make prayer to him to keep nightmares away. His holy symbol is a square pegged between two crescents, representing the two faces of the Dreaming Sea and the two ships that sail upon it unimpeded, the Dream Horn and the Evening Swan.

Wulfad (Halflings) (CG): While Halflings, like Gnomes, worship family deities, they all recognize Wulfad (WOOLF-ad) as the father of the Halflings. Even those halflings touched by human civilization pay homage to Wulfad, although their ceremonies typically reflect a desire to return to life in the wilds. Representative  of Halfling traits, Wulfad is noble, just, and strong of will. He fights with a sword, but wears little armor besides his hide covered wooden shield emblazoned with his holy symbol, a rising sun. Halfling legend is that wherever the sun rises a halfling will be found.

Minor Deities

Every region or locale in the World of Erde will have house deities, racial deities, spirits, elemental powers, and infernal beings that the populace invoke or pray to. Below is a sampling of the various minor deities that populate the mythos of Erde.

Adrius/Zernius (LG): The origin of these twins is unknown, but their worship arose before the coming of the Dark and has outlasted it. Adrius is a god of strength, and Zernius a god of protection. They are worshiped by paladins, monks, and many common folk of noble and good heart. Their holy symbol is a representation of the themselves.

Amenexl (Dark Fey) (CN): This minor god originates in the realm of the dark fairies, and many of those fey call upon him in to aid in the weaving of dark spells and malevolent trickery. Amenexl (ämen-NEKS-ool) typically appears as a stunted, and pale skinned brownie, but like all faeries he changes form upon whim or as needed. Amenexl is especially interested in gaining possession of the Blood Runes. Outside of dark faeries and other planars, few on Erde worship him. His holy symbol is unknown.

Angrim the Black (Dwarves) (CE): Angrim the Black (ĀN-grim) rose to legend in the halls of Norgorad-Kam. One of that kingdom's greatest warriors, Angrim's ego and quest for power eventually overtook him. He fell under the spells of Narrheit and led a force of humanoids through secret tunnels to make war against his family and kin. Angrim overreached, however, and his army was slaughtered under the expert tactics employed by the dwarves in their own halls. Angrim's treachery coupled with Narrheit's influence drove Angrim to madness, and he now wanders the planes spreading making war and spreading chaos. Evil dwarves and those who dwell in the deeps pay him homage. His holy symbol is four black swords upon a beaten shield, their pommels touching and radiating out to represent the many directions of war and chaos.

Crateus (CE): Crateus (CRĀ-tē-us) strode Erde as an almost invincible anti-hero before the Age of Winter Dark. He was the first champion of Narrheit, and he wrecked nations with abandon. The wizard Zoas was also a protege of Narrheit and he saw Crateus as competition for his master's favor. He laid a trap for Crateus and imprisoned him within his own sword. The cursed sword still remains in Erde, and Crateus is ever seeking escape from his prison. The worship of Crateus is kept alive by those who deal in treachery and chaos. His holy symbol is a cracked helm.

Rhealth (NE): Now a minor god, Rhealth (RELTH) once lorded over the realm of the dead. He was cast out by the god Toth during the time of the Winter Dark. A few dark cults, necromancers, and the undead themselves pay him homage. His holy symbol is a sword from which ariseundead spirits.

Heroes/Villains

As with the minor deities, every locale has heroes and villains which have shaped them. A sampling of these is described below. Some persons worship such heroes and villains.

St. Almuric the Lion (LN): Almuric is the founder of the Covenant of the Lion. He was a noble warrior of great strength. The warriors of the Covenant of the Lion pay him homage.

Kain (CE): Duke Kain is an oddity in Erde. His origins are unknown, coming somewhere from the multiverse. For centuries Kain has struggled to carve himself a kingdom in the Abyss. In that respect, he rules a vast sprawling realm upon the abyssal planes from his great fortress-city of Altengrund. Kain is merciless, having no love for family, friend or foe. He rides a Nightmare, Sadowa, and in battle he carries the black-edged vorpal sword, Omdurman. It is said that he can only be killed while sleeping. Kain came to Erde in the service of Unklar, and has been known to travel the lands After Winter Dark for plunder and war. Those that lust for war and chaos sometimes call him patron. It is believed that demons in the abyss actively worship him.

Mithlon (Elves) (CG): This noble elf remained in Erde when most of his people left for Shindolay. He wandered Erde smiting evil in all its aspects. His humble deeds brooked respect from all the races of elves, and all that he aided. He was slain under the eaves of the forest which now bears his name. He is a patron deity of many elves, be they High, Wild, Wood, or Twilight, especially elven ronins.

Morgeld (LN/E): Morgeld is the half-demon bastard son of St. Luther. He is called the Black Prince and he rules in Eloria. His symbol is a black spear.

Setiva (Elves) (LG): Setiva became legend by striking the blow banishing Unklar from Erde with the sword Discerpo. Many High Elves look to her as a saint of redemption from their guilt for leaving the world in its darkest hour.

The Kingdoms of Erde

This being a Lexicon of all the Kingdoms, Realms & Countries of the Lands of Ursal, those lands of Aenoch & Ethrum - The Heraldry of various Lords of Import - Geneologies of Monarchies - The economy of the Lands cataloged.

Honorable reader, a note on the economies of the Realms. Each Kingdom is assigned an EC Rating, one through five. These are graphically represented as well. In short a rating of one, the scythe, equates to foodstuffs, clothing & local trade. Two, the barrel, equates to luxury items & raw materials, & short to medium distance trade. Three, the wagon, equates to processed goods and luxury items, & long distance trade. Four, the hammer, equates to speciality items & long distance trade. Five, the book, equates to magic items and like services. An even greater explanation of these ratings can be found on pages 200-201 and again on 252.

achen, the lands of

Here King Baldwin III rules. He sits upon the high backed chair of his fathers in Castle Aachen, upon the Edle River deep in the Harz foothills. Ever is the ruling house of Aachen recognized by its banner: two white and gold manned unicorns facing each other across a red war-board. Upon the shield is a single Winter Rose and two trees.

The Land, Its People and Its King: The lands of Aachen begin at the sea and the straights of Ursal. There, gently rolling, sparsely wooded hills and meadows of the Harz and Heristat stretch for well over a hundred miles, until they give way to the deep forests of the Detmold. By and large a conifer forest, this young wood shields a far more ancient patch of trees. This copse of old oak, standing at the forest's center, is a holy place for Druids and Rangers. It is the heart of the forest. It is where Ephremere saw the Unicorn (*see below*). The forest blankets the land almost to the Voralberg Mountains, which mark the eastern boundary of the Kingdom. In Aachen, fresh water abounds in the many streams, lakes and small rivers that cross the land before they tumble into the sea.

Baldwin III rules with a benevolent hand. He is a man in the prime of his life. A Knight of the Unicorn, he spent the better part of his youth questing for a glimpse of the creature. Though he never saw the beast, he longs for it still . He sits upon his wooden throne, thinking about what could have been. Aachen is a large, powerful castle filled with wonder and wealth, yet Baldwin spends little time there. He travels a great deal, dragging his royal household from one end of the Kingdom to the other, meeting out justice as he goes. Recently, Baldwin brought in a score of Dwarven coinsmiths and began minting his own coin. They craft silver pieces only but are well worth their weight.

Many small castles dot the landscape of Aachen, houses for the Barons, Knights and their families. Occasionally there are villages nearby, but for the most part the castles stand alone, overlooking a valley or along a river bank. Much of the land is farmed out to peasants for a fee, a payment due in kind or service. The lords of Aachen pay homage to Wenafar, though some few are followers of Demeter. Several castles of the Knights of Haven have recently been constructed here (*reference Guilds and Orders, p. 197*). There is a proud tradition of warfare among the nobility and they frequently call for tournaments which the King invariably provides.

The close ties established with the barbarian lands of Eisenhiem are the source of continual migrations of Northmen into Aachen. The proud and warlike traditions of those people intermingle with the subdued personality of the local populace. Disputes invariably break out, but for the most part the peasants accept the newcomers with little argument. This mixture of knights and barbarians enables Baldwin to field a formidable army. In battle he commands heavy cavalry, with his knights and barbarian infantry.

Aachen produces medicines, ivory from the Inner Sea, wood products from the Detmold, and horses. Also the tax on pilgrims makes up a large portion of local incomes. Wool production, however, provides the greatest source of revenue. The wool produced by the farmers finds its way to the small textile factories which pepper the towns and some of the villages. From there the finished product is brought to the markets of Avignon, Angouleme, the Hanse Cities and so on. The wealth generated due to the increased trade has brought general happiness and prosperity to the folk of Aachen. Of course, this wealth has brought bandits, Orcs and other undesirables to the countryside. They are aided by the often great distances between castles. Despite this, the people tend to be friendly and welcome travelers of all sorts into their local taverns.

Aachen is the only human land where worship of the goddess Wenafar is sanctified by the state. For this reason many believe the tales of Ephremere's glade and the winter rose. Adventurers come from far and wide seeking that hidden place and the power the rose petals are reputed to imbue.

The Manner of How the Kingdom Came to Be: In the waning days of Unklar's rule there rose to the fore a mercenary captain, Baldwin of Klun. Baldwin served Lord Pius in the west where he fought against the Holy Defenders and hunted the Elves of the Darkenfold and Eldwood Forests. Though not a cruel man, upon the field of war he showed little mercy. In the civil war between Pius and Orkhan (*reference Maine, p.* 110), Baldwin led Pius' troops at the battle of Redhill in 1024md, and was instrumental in Orkhan's defeat . After the battle, Pius entreated Baldwin to hunt down the fleeing Orkhan and kill him.

This Baldwin set out to do. He gathered his troops and crossed the river Saline and shortly overtook the hapless General. A short brutal fight ensued. Orkhan's guard either fell or fled, and the general cast himself upon Baldwin's mercy. Baldwin showed none, but rather returned to Pius with the General's head in a sack. Pius rewarded him with land and title in the newly forming Kingdom of Maine. Baldwin accepted these with no reservations (some claim that Baldwin's descendants still have rights to these properties).

In those days, men said that the Lord Knight Baldwin lived a life twice blessed. His wife, with her last breath, gave birth to his daughter, Ephremere, the Wonder of the World. Into this child the world surrendered all its strength, its wisdom, its beauty and people marveled at her. Then Baldwin saw the Unicorn.

Upon a field of deep green where men strove in mortal arms Baldwin saw the noble beast. The Knight's iron will, caste in bloody gore, crumbled at the sight of the wonderful creature. And in the pale blue eyes of the one horned stallion Baldwin's life changed forever. He looked about the field of carnage, where armored men slew one the other. Before his very eyes laid a calamity, a swirling mass of shattered lances, bright hued plates of steal, broken shields and riven helms. Men awash in the black of dirt mixed blood, while about their feet lay the churning earth, embraced the fallen and the dead. The pitiful cries of wounded men mingled with screams of rage and pain as those still able waged war without respite upon the field of green. And amidst all this, both a part of and apart from the world, stood the Unicorn. The noble beast looked upon Baldwin, snorted once and galloped away, passing with ethereal speed into the deep blue horizon.

Baldwin believed it a gift from the realm of Faerie sent to lead him away from the dark paths of war and slaughter. He lusted for a sight of the beast again, and he swore an oath to that affect. Though already an old man, Baldwin forsook his lands and deserted Lord Pius, taking with him his daughter, a small army of like minded men and their families. He wandered the lands of Ethrum and Aenoch in search of the legendary beast, but to no avail. In time, he and his folk settled in the Harz, a fertile land of rolling hills and deep forests. There he built the castle Aachen, upon a hill overlooking the Edle River.

All about him were lands where small villages and farmsteads, mainly sheep farmers, were the norm. Northmen had settled there along the coasts as well. Though they plundered some, many of these migrants seemed bent on settling the country and farming it.

In a surprisingly short time, Baldwin seized the Detmold and Heristat. The Imperial forces fled and in the dwindling days of 1027md, he proclaimed himself King of the lands of Aachen. The local peasants did not seem to care and the Northmen respected the King's prowess in battle and did not challenge his rule.

In Baldwin's failing years he was befriended by the Ranger Lord Daladon who himself waged a bitter war against the Dark. Daladon visited Baldwin often, for he loved the old man greatly and too, he knew of the Unicorn. He promised the old King that he would lend aid and guide his daughter, Ephremere, as much as he could.

Ephremere, innocent in those days, failed to see the signs of her father's death. She became enamored with the Ranger Lord and flattered herself that he loved her as well. Their's is a strange tale, but suffice it to say Daladon's heart another held, and he could not see Ephremere in any light but as the daughter of his friend. Seeing the danger which lay ahead for the young land of Aachen, whose King lay dying with no heir but a woman-born, Daladon sought council in the wood. At last he understood why the Unicorn presented himself before Baldwin. The mare Unklar slew many years ago and the stallion alone remained. The worlds of Fay and Erde hung ever in the balance. Daladon brought the young woman to the forest deeps and summoned the Unicorn. Through his ensorcellements the stallion bound itself to her line and the two lived on in her son, Baldwin II. Wherever they stood, the magical winter roses grew.

As the union came to completion, Baldwin breathed his last. The tales relate how many a man and woman saw Baldwin the day of his passing. He looked younger than ever he had before and he rode upon the back of the great stallion who moved like the wind. And the King laughed, they said. But whether these tales hold any truth none may now say.

With Baldwin's passing, Ephremere became Queen. She relied much on Daladon, for almost immediately her throne came under attack. The Orc Lords and Ungern Chieftains of Iergaul (*reference Zeitz, p.136*) came south plundering as they marched. They rolled over much of Eisenheim and into Aachen. King Theodahad raised his armies, and uniting with Ephremere, drove back the enemy. They lay siege to Iergaul but failed to break its walls.

The next decade played witness to the continued struggle between the city-state, the twin Kingdoms and others besides. Ephremere sent men to Olensk (*reference Augsberg, p.* 74) and afterward to the battles of the Luneberg Plains and the Great Tree where her only daughter, Elisa, fell at the hands of Coburg the Undying. Eventually she became a warrior queen of great renown and often led her Knights and many barbarian mercenaries from Eisenheim into battle.

Ephremere ruled a land of independent peasants, Northmen, and knights. She followed her father's example and dolled out much of the land to her loyal Knights, anointing them with titles of Baron and Lord. But she admonished them all to treat the people kindly and to molest them as little as possible. She passed several ordinances giving the peasants the right to move where they would and to buy land if they possessed the money. She also sanctified the worship of Wenefar, much to the joy of her nobles, for all but a few worshiped the Unicorn.

After her long reign ended she was laid to rest next to her father in the crypts below Aachen. A druid of the Order of the Oak (*reference Guilds & Orders, p. 199*) crowned her son Baldwin II . Already 50 years old, Baldwin did not rule for long. But in the short time he sat on the throne, he exempted all woven articles from taxes for five years. In so doing he bolstered the textile industry in Aachen which found ready markets for the finished products in the western Kingdoms of Ursal.

John, Baldwin's son, sat on the throne for only a few years and reigned over Aachen during a time of plenty and peace. He claimed that the Unicorn came to him in a dream and told him to seek the patch of winter rose where his grandmother had last seen the Unicorn. And so he passed into the Detmold forests upon a cold wintery night seeking the ancient oak trees of the forests' center. He vanished in the wood never to be seen again. The Druids crowned his son King Baldwin III.

Ec Rating III

OF HER KINGS
Baldwin I (1027md-1028md)
Ephremere (1028md-1070md)
Baldwin II (1070md-1079md)
John (1079md-1083md)
Baldwin III (1083md-present)

Angouleme (Kingdom of)

From the towers and halls of Angouleme-ot-Neider, King William III rules as his father's have since the fall of Unklar. The heraldry of that realm is well known to all. The red banner with a crowned ram rearing draws all eyes to the power of the King, whereas the plants of green holly, reveal the Monarch's love of peace. By divine right he rules both Lords and church, hence the wheel of Demeter, and the knightly horse.

Of that Land, Its King and Its People: Angouleme is a large land which extends from the gates of Avignon to the Great Wall of Ethrum. The northern border lies upon the Hanse River but in the south the border is more liquid, the King claiming much of the Elethian Wood for his own. The land is gentle on the traveler, generally flat, where small rivers and streams abound. In the western regions, small forests, outgrowths of the greater ones to the north and south, dot the landscape. Roads, dating from the Imperial era are still in fair shape. There are towns, several large cities and many castles across the wide Kingdom, offering the weary traveler warm drink, good food and refuge from the weather.

William III is a goodly man who has ruled for many years in Angouleme. His bulk, age and many old wounds allow him to sit a horse only with difficulty and he rarely takes up arms. Despairing the religious conflicts of his father (see below) he attempts to rule in an equitable fashion. Despite this he has thrice been drawn into wars with his Dukes and once with Avignon. To this affect he maintains a large host of Knights, and forces his feudal dues to be paid in a mixture of coin and service. He travels during the Spring, arriving unannounced at various estates and monasteries. In this way some of his feudal dues are taken in Kind, foodstuffs, lodging and the like.

William has no heir, and this worries him greatly, for there are many would be adherents, including the Count of Cleves. The Duke of Enois has recently sent Emissaries to Cleves in order to press that young count to take the throne for he hopes that Count Eurich, who pays homage to St. Luther, will not press him so hard to crush the religious Katherines (see below).

The Dukes, ensconced in their own lands, rule separate from the King. Enois in the Greenwood is home to the Katherines, that heretical sect of monks of Demeter who espouse that clerics should carry no wealth in the world. Many of the nobles, converts to the new religion, turn to the Lord of Capes, Conrad, for leadership. He treats with the Duke but to little affect and the religious disputes continue. Rumors of a crusade against the heretics abound, for it is known that William III is opposed to them. Aquaitaine, Blois, and the Limousine, all centrally located, are wealthy in foodstuffs. There, the traditions of the tournament are strong. Knights dominate the area, their great horses, lances with pennants, armor and so on set them apart from commoners and adventurers alike. These lords call for wars to the south, north and east more frequently than any other. Many of their younger sons have gone on the crusades called by the Empress of Outremere (*reference Outremere, p. 122*) Orange, braced as she is against the city state of Avignon, is a hotbed of rebellion and discontent. It is the Duke there who continually calls for the rights of the Bishop of Avignon over the Kingdom to be recognized. Karilia, Cleves and Sienna all maintain their independence as they have since the days of the Winter Dark.

Due to the efficient union of imperial bureaucracy, powerful merchant families and a wealthy peasantry in Angouleme prospers. A great deal of trade passes through the Kingdom. Many of the towns, though frequently walled are well off and able to field their own small armies. Merchants travel in large caravans, trading the local textile goods, sheep, cattle, horses, wood products, pottery, and grain for foreign iron, coal and worked steel. Angouleme is well known for the production of finely crafted armor. The merchant guilds are struggling to assert their power in the towns, and to do so they are attempting to control the trade routes. Thus, tensions are growing between the noble and mercantile classes.

In the west, the realm commands a deciding voice in the young kingdoms and is the major pillar of the Church of Demeter. The Bishop of Angouleme vies for control of the church with the Bishop of Avignon.

The greatest threat to travelers are robber barons and lordless knights who prey on the weak. The King attempts to quell these actions, but his realm is large. And though Angouleme fields an impressive array of mounted Knights in battle, often supported by a large peasant levy, it is difficult for the King to bring these folk to heel, for the land is large and in some places only sparsely populated.

A Governor Winter Dark Who Would Rule as King: During the age of the lands of the whole of the Ethrum and Aenoch were divided into provinces which reflected the realms as they existed in the days before. The Lands from the Hanse River to the the Massif and the Twilight Wood, were divided into nine provinces; Angouleme, Enois, Aquaitaine, Blois, Limousine, Orange, Karilia, Cleves and Sienna. The folk who lived there, a proud people, traced their lineage to the old aristocracy of the Ethrumanian Kingdoms, and as with their ancestors they reveled in war and tournament. To bring these folk to heel, Unklar appointed Governors to rule them and garrisoned cohorts within town and country.

Despite this the Knights proved difficult to govern and they rebelled continually. To overcome this, the Governors appointed them to administrative offices, exempted them from taxes and allowed them to employ small troops of retainers. To control these men further, a noble, usually the most influential, was appointed as Count of the Province. The counts, though locally powerful, ruled in name only, answering to the dictates of the Governor. In this way, the Governor's pacified the region by creating an aristocratic cast of bureaucrats who made their wealth through controlling the whole of the region's commerce.

When the Winter Dark Wars began, Unklar's generals stripped the central lands of Ethrum of their garrisons. The Lords of Aufstrag desperately needed experienced soldiers for the battles in the south and east (*reference Kayomar, p. 104*). The central lands they deemed safe from rebellion, and they did not fear the consequences of withdrawing so many soldiers. They did not count, however, on the raids of the Northmen and the ambitions of William, the ambitious Count of Angouleme.

William, an older man, bore three titles, given to him by the Lords of Aufstrag. A younger son of a minor bureaucrat, William joined the legions in around 1005md. He eventually attained the position of Horse Commander, at which point he retired to his home in Angouleme. There he married the only daughter of Philip, the Count of that province. Recognized for his loyal service, he soon attained the post of Governor of Angouleme and, when Philip and his only son died of a plague, William attained the title of Count as well. By the outset of the Winter Dark Wars, William served both posts as Governor and Count of Angouleme. This powerful position, unrivaled in the region by others soon attracted him a following of young knights, mostly men of military service.

When the Wars began, William watched carefully. The Imperial defeats in the Flintlock and in Kayomar coupled with the civil war in Maine cast him in the firm belief that the age of the horned god would soon be over. In 1023md he called his knights to arms and drove out the few Imperial garrisons left in the area and established himself within the halls of his Castle of Angouleme-ot-Neider.

His revolt spread rapidly to the other provinces. The Imperial Governors tried to rally the garrisons but those who remained could not be relied upon. With the Empire helpless in the provinces, the Imperial bureaucracy joined the revolt and the peasants shortly thereafter. William asserted himself over the other lords from the beginning. He commanded an impressive array of knights, ex-soldiers, lords and bureaucrats. Within a few short years, the provincial counts recognized William as their King, giving him rights over them for protection, guidance and leadership. In turn he invested each of the great lords with property and privilege. All joined but for Karilia, Cleves and Sienna.

As is elsewhere written, Philip the Guileless came to Angouleme during these days, bringing with him the worship of Demeter. The peasants and town Burghers embraced this new religion of hard work and reward so much so that almost the whole realm converted. William, a shrewd man, did not let this opportunity pass. He openly converted, embracing Philip upon the steps of his own Great Hall. By as early as 1025md, William ruled a vast region, overflowing with wealth. He attempted for a time to conquer the Hanse river basin though this ended in failure when those peoples formed the League of Hanse City States (*reference Hanse City States, p. 100*).

William proved a benevolent ruler, sitting on the throne for nigh on fifteen years. He strongly supported the erection of churches and monasteries. When he died his young son was crowned by the High Priest of Avignon, a close friend of William I, as William II, King

of Angouleme. William II ruled much as his father did. He enjoyed his pleasures in the quiet of his castle on the Neider.

William II allowed the various lords of his Kingdom to exercise an impressive amount of control and rules. For monied payments, he exchanged rights and privileges. Under his tender rule localism became the norm and the nobility became far more powerful than they had been before. The local rule of the churches of Demeter waxed powerful as well. Though in truth William cared little for all of this, for they paid dues in coin, which he used on horse and gambling houses in Avignon. There the King died, of a curse, it is said, laid upon an ancient Dwarven coin which he had won in a game of cards.

Philip William, his son, crowned once more by the Bishop of Avignon, stood in stark contrast to his father. A devout monk for much of his life, he left the cloth when he saw his father's kingdom slipping into ruin. As King he ruled far more firmly and the first true struggles between the lords and dukes began. Philip appointed his old master, the Monk Jared, as Bishop of Angouleme and took the power of appointing prelates from Avignon, investing it in his friend. In time, this proved a powerful tool to use against both lords and the bishop of Avignon.

He granted those churches who supported him tax exempt status, freeing them of feudal dues. They waxed in wealth and proved loyal servants of the crown, bending their own powers over the Burghers and peasants in the Kingdom to force the hands of the nobility to follow the King's will. Also, during those days, various religious sects sprang up across the kingdom, most particularly in the Duchy of Enois. There the Katharines shirked the rule of Bishops and monastic lords, calling for a simpler life for the clerics of Demeter. The Duke of Enois, a benevolent ruler, did little to quell the unrest so that in time most of his Duchy had converted to the new creed.

The religious/secular disputes erupted in war in 1060md when the Dukes rebelled and called to the Bishop of Avignon to grant the Kingdom to William Philip's son. The Bishop acquiesced and threw his own loyal guard into the fray. But William Philip commanded a powerful force of knights from his own realm and relied on many lesser nobles to aid him. The battles lasted for two years, during which time many seiges and small engagements took place. Much of the land was ravaged and the wars ended only with William Philip's death at the Battle of Hardon.

The Bishop of Angouleme preempted any action from his fellow cleric in Avignon when he crowned William III King of Angouleme in 1072md. This affront has left strained relations between the two realms, so much so that the Bishop of Avignon has begun offering some support to the Katharines.

Ec Rating III

OF HER KINGS
King William I (1027md-1042md)
King William II (1042md-1061md)
King Phillip William (1061md-1072md)
King William III (1072md-present)

Aufstrag (Festung Aufstrag, the Citadel of Command)

As in the days of old, the tower of Aufstrag has come under the rule of one. Coburg the Undying, Lord of the Tower, sits upon the Throne of the Horned God. Behind him, upon standards of samnite and violet silk, beams the silver crescent moon of Unklar.

Fell Unklar, brooding in fear, roused himself and fortified his Keep. Rending the earth with his great axe he cleaved huge rifts about the Imperial castle of old Aenoch, and with sorceries created great pools of water and pestilence to cover the rent lands. And all of Aenoch between the rivers Udunilay and Uphrates was made a swamp of fell death. Lifting the ground on high, a mountain of slag was built amidst the marshes and his high citadel set atop, surrounded by mighty buttresses and fell towers. And his new abode was named Festung Aufstrag, the citadel of Command.
~Leopold of Passou.

Of the Undying One and Festung Aufstrag: Aufstrag stands in the midst of the Grausamland, the Fell Swamp. The vast citadel, shaped vaguely like a gargantuan tree, towers over 3000 feet high. It dominates the horizon of the Grausamland for miles around. At the foot of the great tree lies its gate. Huge stone towers flank the iron doors, and upon the arch spanning the opening are the words, "Upon Bended Knee Know Thy Master." It was here that Jaren Falkynjager hung for a thousand years, and the imprint of his pain remains here still. These gates give entry to the greatest fortress in all the world.

Few tread near Aufstrag for evil still lurks here. Foul ghosts and devils, and other evils, are said to crawl its vast empty halls, living in a nightmare of the past. Rumor holds that several of the Mogrl still dwell in the deeps of the fortress, awaiting the return of their dark master.

The fortress is in fact a city with tunnels, halls, winding staircases, and ramps all serving as roads. Rooms serve as houses, mansions for the lordly, garrisons, depots, stables, taverns, and inns. It is powered by heat from the Klarglich pits, and watered by a network of fountains and waterways. All was built by the hands of Dwarven slaves. The towering complex is girded in parapets, walls, and battlements. Long causeways wind around its girth, allowing defenders to rush to any beleaguered section of the tower. Near the apex lies the great Throne of the Horned God. It is surrounded by walls of stone, with columns resembling shackled gods holding up a vaulted ceiling. From this high backed chair Unklar sat, ruling the world for a thousand years.

Aufstrag consists of four layers, which are accessed via a multitude of ramps, stairways, wells, ropes, ladders and chutes. The lower level, the Trenches, lies wholly beneath the earth. Above it are the Klarglich Pits. The Pits abut the trenches and rise the first 1000 feet of the citadel's height. The Halls of living quarters, garrisons, markets, granaries, inns and taverns, form the center of Aufstrag, roughly measuring 1500 feet in height. The Citadel makes up the final 700 feet, and contains the throne room, the treasuries, and halls for the Blood Guard, fierce Dwarven slayers who are forever held to Unklar's side and the treasure rooms.

Around all of these layers stand fortifications. Though the heights of Aufstrag are almost unassailable, they are guarded nonetheless. Walls and towers were built into the bast so that the defenders could rain death upon any who dared lay siege. Along the length of the Tree are windows and walkways, and these too are guarded by walls and battlements. Many of these entrances are now abandoned, though they remain as dark apertures to the Tree's interior.

The Trenches: Deep beneath the fortress tree of Aufstrag are the Trenches. They earned their name only recently after Dolgan and Agmour led the slaves of the city in rebellion. For six long years these tunnels (originally mines) served as a battleground for both sides. In the Trenches various tunnels, caverns, caves and rooms were fortified against each other, with one side frequently living within earshot of the other. The wicked nature of the war led to an infinite number of secret doors and passageways crisscrossing the already jumbled underground complex. A river flows underneath Aufstrag, and the combatants used it to flood or guard certain areas by digging canals and channeling water. These waterways and pools remain throughout the maze of tunnels.

The brutal war fought in the dark left thousands dead and it is not uncommon to find all manner of equipment and riches left in some forgotten hole. The complex is inviting to those who live under the earth, and a number of monsters have come to live in the Trenches. Adventurers frequently seek out the Trenches, but few return home. On occasion, old Dwarves can be found, returned after all these years to mourn their fallen and forgotten comrades.

Klarglich, "The Pit of Woe:" From the Trenches one can gain entrance to the Klarglich through any number of a thousand ramps, stairs, and causeways. The pits are huge, encompassing a dozen floors and thousands of square feet. They were the granaries of Aufstrag, the supply depots where was stored all the raw material required by the lords of the forge. Two score minor forges surround a great forge of Unklar's make. The great forge lies in a chamber at the heart of the Klarglich. It is beyond comprehension and is truly the pit of woe. There was forged much of the world's evil (*see below*). Cells and dungeons abut the forges as well, places where poor creatures of the world lived out their final days.

Travel in the Pit is easier than in the Trenches, for despite the structural damage done to the fortress during the Winter Dark Wars, many passageways, stairs, ramps, and rooms remain. Many creatures have come to roost here. They come over the battlements and through long unguarded windows, and many a bold thief finds his way into Aufstrag in this way. Rumors fly that a Mogrl has returned to the Pit, seeking memories of his horned father.

The Halls: This region of Aufstrag is in far greater disrepair than any other. It served as the heart of city in the days of Winter Dark, and contained markets, inns, taverns, and living quarters. When war came to these areas, though too high for easy assault, the lack of many fortifications proved easy entrances for the gods and their minions. They burst into Aufstrag here and great battles erupted between the gods and Unklar and his Mogrl. Upon the north face lies a huge hole exists, spanning 300 feet across. Some say a dragon tore the hole in the wall of the tree, while others say that Narrheit, the god of chaos, entered Aufstrag there.

The Halls are a wrecked ruin of their once opulent state, and they offer up many strange artifacts. The heart of the citadel contained a great deal of magic and the wizard-priests had many temples there. Rumors of untold wealth abound.

The Citadel: Towering high overhead are the upper levels of Aufstag, the Citadel. Within it are the throne room, the temple of Unklar, the schools of the magi, libraries, dozens of large mansions, two garrison chambers, and the treasuries. Other rooms and chambers also mark the Citadel, but these are simply mundane places such as kitchens and storage areas.

A great deal of activity lately has taken place in the Citadel for a new lords claims suzerainty there. Coburg the Undying, long time lieutenant of Unklar, has risen from the depths of Aufstrag and conquered the upper levels. His folk cleaned out much of the debris and are rebuilding the level quickly. Old tapestries hang again upon walls, carpets line the floors, and lanterns light the halls. Though much wealth has been lost, little of the mystique has and Coburg uses it to cow any would be usurpers.

Travel in the Citadel is impossible unless one uses one of the many secret doors that wind upwards through the fortress. Within the halls of the Citadel live Orcs, many of them from the Hlobane (*reference the United Kingdoms, p.* 134), that are fiercely loyal to Coburg who strive for the return of the horned god. Coburg also commands a host of Ungern and a large dragon, the latter of which he uses as a mount. It is said that a Morgl, one of the horned god's personal guards from yesteryear, made alliance with Coburg and resides in the throne room with him.

Coburg the Undying: Once Unklar's lieutenant and Commander of the House Guard, Coburg outlived his contemporaries. He rose to power sometime in the 8th century of Unklar's rule and has remained there ever since. He has died at least twice, the second time being at the Battle of the Tree, where he fell to St. Luther's sword. Both times Coburg rose from the dead in some unknown fashion. Coburg is a clever warrior with some ability at magic, but his greatest gifts are his charms with which he has wooed friend and foe alike. Coburg can be very cruel, but never so when it interferes with the business at hand. He rules from the throne room, though he never sits upon the Throne of the Horned God. He shares the space with one of the Morgl. Coburg dreams of greater conquests and of bringing those who worship the horned god back into the fold. To this end, he regularly sends emissaries to the Punj, United Kingdoms and Onwaltig.

The History of Aufstrag and the Winter Dark: When Unklar came to Erde he came to the great halls of Al-Liosh, the capital of Aenoch. From there he delivered evil into the world. As is written,

the horned god was not satisfied with the city of the god-emperors, and he set to remaking it. He destroyed the inner city, turning it into rubble. For miles about he ruined 3000 years of history.

Then, lifting the ground on high, he made a true mountain of slag amidst tumbled buildings and set his high citadel atop. The fortress he fashioned in the shape of a tree thousands of feet high, a grim mockery of Wenafar and the Great Tree in the west. He surrounded this with mighty buttresses and fell towers. And this abode he named anew, calling it Festung Aufstrag, the Citadel of Command. The ruins of Al-Liosh sprawled underneath Aufstrag and into the countryside around.

Upon the great gate he carved the words of welcome and there Nulak-Kiz-Din bound Jaren, Master of the Order of the Scintillant Dawn. Jaren's hands were nailed to the stone and his thighs as well. Nulak wove a mist of time around him so that he could not age, but would hang there suffering for all the long years of the world. In time of years the place became a cesspool of all things vile. Tunnels, great and small, fanned out beneath the Tree into the rock of the world. More towers and more buttresses rose into the sky, and the city sprawled out over the hills. Unklar filled Aufstrag with his legions and, in time, with tens of thousand of slaves. These were Dwarves and Goblins carted off from the mountains to the north and elsewhere, not the least of which was Dolgan King of Grundliche Hohle, though he was not yet king in those days. Unklar bid them to make his fortress stronger and to forge his armies weapons of war. He knew the power of old possessed by Dwarf and Goblin alike, and he exploited it.

Unklar moved the throne of the god-emperors to the heart of his own citadel and there remade it from the bones of the All Father. This throne he called the Throne of Unklar and from it he ruled Erde for a thousand years. He gave and he took.

In the pits of Aufstrag Unklar carved a huge forge. The size of it defied comprehension. Halls filled to overflowing with raw materials stolen from all across the world. He built a huge bellows so that he could forge the greatest of metals, and in time of years he did so. The forge became a place of wicked experiments, tortures and craftings. Many creatures found themselves carried into the deeps never to return. It was a black place of evil and death. The folk of Aufstrag named it Klarglich, that is "The Pit of Woe," for the suffering screams of the damned filled the place. Unklar first used Klarglich to create the Hounds of Darkness. These sulking beasts,

Ec Rating
I

birthed from the tortured bodies of faerie kin, possessed but one purpose, to root out the elves upon whatever plane they existed. Though the creatures failed, many dying in the process, they served as signals of things to come.

The pit doubly earned its name of woe when Unklar bid Dolgan to serve him in a new creation. He forged, with sorcery and magic and with spells crafted in a time before time, great beasts of the pit. He made them from his own twisted soul and from the stuff of dark places, and he gifted them with life. His face tore as if in childbirth, and his pain-filled cries brought forth an evil dark never seen before and never to be seen again. His agony was their life, and they were pure in malice with no thought but those of evil and madness and destruction. These beasts were terrible to behold and Dolgan knew fear only as when he wrestled with the horned god himself. Their coming was a weighty thing in the world, and Unklar named them Mogrl, and they were demons of horror. And the Mogrl rose one by one and lifted themselves from the halls and strode forth into the world. They were twenty four in number.

There were other things forged as well. The Ungern (*reference new Monsters, p. 242*) came from the Pits of Woe. All manner of armaments, huge cumbersome canon, muskets and hand bombs too. Also magic of indescribable power, the Krummelvole, Havocm, the axe of Dolgan King, and Nulak-kiz-din's Ring of Iron. For a thousand years the chutes of Aufstrag belched black soot into the air, and it hung there ever after.

The halls of Aufstrag grew in strength and size for hundreds of years. Minions came and died under the long rule of the horned god. When he slept, as at times he did, exhausted from his labors, his servants kept the fortress from falling into ruin. Four of the Mogrl were always with him and Nulak-Kiz-Din as well. In those days Coburg rose to the post of House Guard Commander, keeping the strongest and best trained of the soldiers of the world. Coburg's ruthless efficiency and cruelty stood him well in the council of the dark.

In 1012md a slave rebellion commenced in the lower halls. From whence it came few could say, but it is known that Dolgan and the Goblin Agmour led it. They made war on the dark, raising the slaves of the pit against their masters. They gathered Goblins and Dwarves, men and Orcs, and fought the troops of Unklar in the bowels of the earth. Untold was the suffering of the Trench Wars. The wicked battles were fought in dark holes, down darker corridors against an implacable enemy. Knives and hatchets ruled the day, and primitive powder weapons left tunnels filled with mutilated corpses, smoke an ash. Kin fought kin for Unklar's most loyal guard were the Blood Dwarves and they sought ever to kill those who sought freedom. Goblins too fought one another, for many loved Unklar and believed his was the only world in which they could live. The combatants dug trenches and tunnels in the deep places of the earth, holding them against one another until at last they would rush upon their foes trying to drive them out and back. The brutal warfare left thousands dead in the open holes and ditches between the various fortifications. At last, after six brutal years of warfare, in 1018md, the Dwarves and other slaves broke free, fleeing to the mountains in the north. The desolation of this rebellion was such that the fortress never fully recovered.

After the initial defeats in the Winter Dark Wars, Unklar refashioned the lands around Aufstrag. He destroyed the outer city, and with the Krummelvole churned the earth into great heaps and let the waters of the twin rivers Udunilay and Uphrates poor into the mangled ground. He created a swamp, the Grausamland, where the city once stood and it surrounded Aufstrag evermore.

When St. Luther began the Winter Dark Wars he allowed the old gods, those who survived, both good and evil, to rise again. Wenafar, Narrheit, Toth and others came to Erde and assailed Unklar in his vast Fortress. For years they battered at his wall and slew his minions but could never throw him down. Unklar, the horned god, was second only to the All Father of old and no power but his own could destroy him. In the end, they quit the field but not before the whole of the outer fortress lay in ruins.

As is told elsewhere, the Council of Light at last came to Unklar's great hall and made war upon him. St. Luther stood and fought the horned god for many hours with the others at his side. Not until Setiva, with the enchanted blade Discerpo fell upon him, was he defeated and cast from the plane. So great was the god's anguish at his defeat that his bellowing shook the whole of Aufstrag, bringing much of it to ruin. The echoes of the horned god's death cries carry there still, in the high places, nigh on upon the divine throne of the Horned God.

When the wars ended with Unklar driven from Erde, the halls of Aufstrag fell into decay. The Great Battle of the Tree did not see the armies of the west and north sack the grim fortress, but they slew most of its guard and left it empty for a great many years. It became a grim testament to a bygone age. Some Imperial generals ruled from Aufstrag for awhile without success. The foul place slowly sank into the mire of its own stench, until at last Coburg the Undying came again to its halls and made himself Lord of the Halls. (*reference above & the Toten Fields, p. 166*).

Of How the Mogrl were Made to be

Restless dreams came to those in the deep places, even to those who ever slaved upon the dark forge. Dreams born upon the nightmares of Unklar by the sainted Paladin, dreams of war and vengeance, of deeds great and terrible, and of death. And all this roused the horned god, and he came himself to deep Klarglich, the forge, the pit of woe. He bore with him a horrible intent and desire. His cloven hooves ground the stone of the forge to dust as he crept into the Hall where Dolgan, Dwarf King and slave, labored at tasks unnamed. So great was the power of Unklar that Dolgan's servants died in screaming madness or fled in terror, lost to the deep places under the world, for his visage they could not bare, as no mortal man can. The blood of Unklar's skin burned hotter by far than any flames of any forge and his eyes, terrible in evil, turned to Dolgan. His voice, deep with echoes of madness and memories rank and foul thundered forth: 'DOLGAN, MAKE TO YOUR BELLOWS AND DO AS I BID!'

The Dwarf and the Dark labored long and hard in that fell place. Klarglich doubly earned its name of woe for the horrors born of that making haunt the world even to this day. Unklar forged, with sorcery and magic, with spells crafted in a time before time, great Beasts of the Pit. The Mogrl. He made them from his own twisted soul and from the stuff of dark places in the world and he gifted them with life. He wove the Language of Creation into them, singing it through them as Dolgan pounded upon the flesh of life.

After many days the Dwarf staggered from the effort of the labor. The Language bore upon him, weighing him down with power no mortal could contain. He hovered on the brink of madness, screaming now in pain, then laughing hysterically, then at last sobbing with terror. But Unklar bore him aloft, keeping him from destroying himself. For the horned god needed the might of the King's hammer to forge and shape the life he created.

Unklar too hovered upon the brink of madness. Never had he used the Language of Creation for life alone, but always for manipulating what the All Father forged. In his lucid moments Dolgan could see the suffering of the horned god. The beast's face was torn with the effort of childbirth, and his pain-filled cries shook the caverns of Klarglich. He bellowed and growled, all the while his muscled chest corded knots of tension. Despite this, Unklar brought forth a dark never seen before, or would ever be seen again. His agony was their life, and they were pure in malice with no thoughts but thoughts of evil and madness and destruction.

It is said that Unklar himself spilled into life from the All Father's dreams. And not since the All Father spun those dreams in the darkness of the Void had such creatures come to be.

They were terrible to behold and Dolgan knew fear as he had when he wrestled with the black god himself. Their coming was a weighty thing in the world, and Unklar named them Mogrl, and they were demons of horror. And the Mogrl rose one by one and lifted themselves from the halls and strode forth into the world. They were four and twenty in number.

Unklar sagged in exhaustion and wandered from the hall muttering that a time of war had come to the world. Unklar rose high and laughed shaking the Krummervole in his mighty grasp so that it split the high roofs and walls of Mithgefuhl and turning he said, 'Dolgan. Make ready for war. The time of doom is at hand.'

Aufstrag and Environs

Key to Map	
I	Aufstrag
II	Fetid Heap
III	The Tangles
IV	The Great Fen
V	Gnostwood
VI	The Spires
VII	The Deeps
VIII	The Knuckled Swamps

Augsberg (Kingdom of)

Good King Aetherlred II, of the Cerdric line, rules all of the river country from his mighty castle of Eichstatt. The coat of arms of this house is well known to any and all of the whole of Aenochia. The simple green background is cut hard with a single diagonal blue strip.

Of the River Folk and Their King: The Kingdom of Augsberg stretches from the deep woods of the Aenochian Forest in the south to the rugged highlands of the Flintlock in the north; from the feet of the white capped Voralberg Mountains across the great river and into the Luneberg Plains. It encompasses most of the Olgdon River's length and many of her tributaries. The river is the lifeblood of the realm.

In general, Augsberg is a rural society. The great city of Eichstatt is an only exception to the many smaller towns, villages and farmsteads. The people are a contented lot, many of them ex-soldiers, or the children of refugees from the despoilment of Kain (*see below*). The soldiers till land they call their own, but the peasants live at the Kings will. There is no aristocratic class in Augsberg, only the King, the soldiers of his garrisons, the merchants and the farmers.

King Aethelred II is robust with a keen eye for women and horses. Unlike his father, he rebels at the administrative tasks of his realm, seeking to enjoy sport and food more than all else. The King excels at mounted combat while professing to being poorly trained when on foot. He rules through his ministers, attending to the business of state only when pressed. For this reason, under Aethelred's hand, the Kingdom of Augsberg is more loosely governed than at any time in its history.

Here, the knightly ideal never materialized as it did further west in Angouleme. Warfare in the neighboring Luneburg plains is a deadly business and there is little room for chivalry, particularly when it crosses the river into Augsberg. A heightened state of military preparedness exists, allowing King Aethelred II command of an impressive force of heavy and light cavalry with some auxiliary infantry. These are spread in small garrisons throughout the Kingdom and owe their loyalty to the King alone. They are paid in coin as well as land and are generally loyal to the Cedric Kings.

The merchants, always a powerful segment of society, work to influence crown councilors through their powerful guilds. They control tariffs, trade and the amount of traffic in and through the Kingdom. Their influence over the well sought for armaments from Grundliche Hohle is particularly telling, fees and bribes being necessary to gain a glance at the equipment. The Dwarves there are treated well (*reference below & Grundliche Hohle, p. 96*), and though aware of the price fixing by the merchants, do not seem to care. In general, the towns of Augsberg are controlled by these guilds and like minded associations.

This wealth has of course brought many a would-be thief. Muddles Inc. (*reference Guilds & Orders, p. 198*) is well established throughout the valley as are other thieve guilds. They ply their trade well, with an almost wilful abandon, and when caught lose little more than a finger or hand.

Augsberg farmers are an independent lot, producing a variety of goods. The Kingdom is wealthy in horse flesh and fish from the river. Small villages and steads abound throughout the realm where people farm the rich black earth and cut wood in the numerous forests. There are also many grape farms in the Voralberg Mountains, producing a locally famous wine. All these goods are traded for textiles from Aachen, armaments from Grundliche Hohle and other such wares. Augsberg is best known for her horses. Men pay as much as double the normal cost if they know the steed is from Augsberg (*reference New Monsters, p. 240*). Much wealth is derived from the taxing of merchant caravans passing through the kingdom as it controls all the northern passes over the Voralberg Mountains.

Despite all of this, Augsberg is a land of great opportunity. Much of the region is uninhabited, particularly in the Voralberg Mountains and south in the Aenochian Forest. The stains of war are only glossed over, and many an adventurer has carted off great stores of wealth uncovered in this greatest of lands.

A History of Tradition: During the latter days of Unklar's rule, discontent spread through the ranks of his people. The Troll Lord, Nulak-Kiz-Din ruled in the horned god's absence and many resented his harsh and altogether evil ways. At the outset of the Winter Dark Wars, Albrecht, Commander of the 67th Legion - the flower of the Imperial cavalry - secretly rebelled. He joined the Council of Light, pledging to break with Aufstrag and bring his men over. In turn, the Council promised him a Kingdom for he and his heirs.

Soon thereafter, Albrecht broke with Aufstrag during the battles with Grundliche Hohle, leaving Paskevitch (*reference the Punj, p. 124 & Grundliche Hohle, p. 96*) to fight the war alone. This act alone allowed the Dwarves and the Council to conquer the whole of the Flintlock.

In the subsequent wars with Aufstrag, he soon established himself along the length of the Olgdon River. He fortified the various fjords and bridges and built castles to guard them. He settled his own household, in the valley of Eichen and there constructed a great fortified castle, Eichenberg. At the age of 61, in 1026md, Albrecht Cedric declared himself King.

In these early years, his Kingdom forged a fast friendship with the Dwarf King Dolgan and his folk of Grundliche Hohle. The Dwarves, ever grateful for his rebellion, sent engineers and architects to aid the men in the construction of their castles and city. It proved a good beginning to an everlasting friendship.

For the next several years, Unklar's minions struggled to regain mastery of the battlefields of Erde. To aid them they summoned the demon lord Kain, Duke of Altengrund, and gave him command of their armies. Kain led three legions across the Luneberg plains threatening the west. In battle after battle the men of Augsberg, Dwarves from the Hohle, and men from Aachen and Eisenheim fell to his conquest. Kain fought a brutal war, burning the countryside behind him so that his men could not flee. Any who opposed him, he put to death.

In 1029md, Albrecht marshaled a great host of men and Dwarves. He met Kain at the village of Olensk and there King Albrecht fought and won the most decisive battle in the war against Unklar (*reference The Histories, p. 45*). With him stood three thousand Dwarves from the Hohle and several thousand men from Aachen and Eisenheim. The battle raged all the long day and into the night. The slaughter-filled struggle left thousands dead or maimed. In the end, all three Imperial legions were destroyed, and Kain was forced to flee the field. Albrecht's troops, however, did not suffer lightly. Albrecht II died while trying to rescue the beleaguered Dwarf Lord, Oxleigh, the trusted friend of Dolgan King (*reference Grundliche Hohle, p. 96*), who also died. Frederick, Albrecht's third son, died leading a cavalry charge. Franz Conrad, fourth born, lost an arm, but despite the wound drove Kain and his personal guard from the field of battle. A further nine thousand men were wounded or killed. The Dwarves suffered greatest of all. One thousand six hundred comrades died on the field, one in two that had fought there (*reference the Bartigtot, p. 196*). The friendship between the Dwarves and the men of Augsberg grew all the greater.

In the meantime Alfred, Albrecht's second born, led a troop of cavalry across the Olgdon River into the Luneberg to drive to heel all those who remained behind Kain. He crossed back over the Olgdon, leading his flying column south to harry the retreating armies of Kain to the dark forests beyond and even to the sea. He burned Kain's fleet and slaughtered the greater part of the refugees. Only General Kain and a few of his soldiers escaped the boy.

The old King, broken by his losses, would not leave the stricken Franz Conrad's side, for insanity had taken him. He brought his wounded son back to Eichenberg, hoping for a miracle. Though in truth, to look upon Kain can bring madness to the goodly folk of the world.

Alfred ruled by his father's side for the next decade. In 1032md, he converted to the worship of Demeter and took the cloak of a Knight of Haven. The religion gained a firm foothold in the Kingdom. Slowly the people of Augsberg recovered, but still they were forced to battle Vikings, Orcs and Ungern from Iergaul, goblins from the Flintlock and the horrors from the Luneberg Plains. As Albrecht grew in years, he divested power into his son.

Eventually Alfred married the sister of King Theodohad of Eisenheim, Thiodann Fyogryn, heroine and companion of Daladon. Together they had a son, Aetherlred. In 1046md, Franz Conrad died of his malady and King Albrecht slipped into a waking slumber; a madness of sorts. Franz, they buried in a hilltop cemetery deep in the Voralberg Mountains. St. Luther attended the funeral and blessed the grave. He planted a tree there from the Paladin's Grove (*reference Kayomar, p. 104 & The Holy Defenders of the Flame, p. 191*). Folk flocked to the grave, for they believed that the spirit of Franz lived on in the tree and could heal any ailment. The truth of this is unknown, for the tomb of Franz Conrad has been lost these many years.

Without resistance Alfred's men crowned him King. The Dwarves sent many gifts of gold and canon as did other monarchs besides. In 1051md, the River King, Albrecht I, died at age 88. The world groaned at his passing, for he truly had been the greatest monarch of his era.

Alfred ruled for many long years with Fyogryn at his side. He aided her in the management of Eisenhiem when their second born son became King there (*reference Eisenheim, p. 84*). The ties between the two peoples were strengthened thereby. They had many children and governed the land in peace. Trade between the Kingdoms of Grundliche Hohle and Augsberg flourished in those days. Wood, grains, beer and livestock moved north across the Flintlock and finished goods, armor and weaponry came from the Hohle. Trade with the far off Punj picked up as it did with the people further west.

Alfred maintained a great store of wealth, garnered it is said from Kain's abandoned treasure and loot. With this he paid his men out in gold, keeping the legions of his father intact. He placed them in garrisons along the length of the river. By supporting and taxing a strong merchant class, he paid for his army. A city grew up around Eichenberg during his long tenure, which the folk called Eichstatt.

After Alfred's demise, his son Aethelred was crowned in the old fortress of Eichenberg. He ruled for a long while and changed little of his father's policy. What he did change effected the army. He could no longer afford to pay them out of pocket, the upkeep in horse and gear, was simply too much. In order to waylay this, he cut the wages of the army and offered soldiers land for service. This in 1079md. Those who served in the garrisons were given land, both in Augsberg and beyond. He gave it to them in full right of ownership, they had but to pay a tax. Aethelred also began taxing the Churches of Demeter for they had grown in wealth and power. He exempted the Lothian (*reference Guilds & Orders, p. 197*) monks, however, out of respect for the memory of Daladon.

Aethelred died peacefully in his bed, his young son already confirmed as King Aetherlred II.

Ec Rating II

Avignon, the free City of

There are many powers in Avignon, but two stand above the rest: His Imminence, Bishop Honorius II and the Governor of the town, Milo Urner. The city has long been a pillar in Demeter's Church, and her heraldry reveals this. Upon an orange background stands forth a six spoked wheel at the top, beneath which are two crossed miters. These symbols harken to the city's loyalty to the Church. Below and centered is a round stylized shield framed in floral (peace), with two rearing green horses (strength and beauty) facing the shield. The city's motto is also there: "To every man his due." On the shield are three equally spaced gold keys representing the city itself.

Of the Nature of the World's Greatest City and Those Who Rule Her: Avignon is a huge town upon the western shores of the straights of Ursal, just north of the Lithanian River. Three separate sets of walls guard the city and divide it into distinct districts. The harbor houses so many vessels that it is called "the forest of Avignon." It too, is guarded by fortifications. Heavy chains reside just under the surface, attached to underwater pylons. They create channels through which only experienced captains can bring their ships. Almost every vessel requires a guide ship.

In the first district, that located in the southern part of the town, overlooking the river are the nobles, wealthy merchants, knights, priests, and the Bishop. Here the streets are cobbled, the houses made of stone and marble. It is clean and well patrolled by the city guard. In the second district are the merchants, guild houses and a host of houses where tradesmen and craftsmen dwell. It is far more crowded here. The houses are a mixture of old and new, jumbled together on narrow streets, some of which are cobbled, but most are not. The Captain of the Guard, Castus, lives in the second district and pays heed to the calls of his neighbors. In the third district, which surrounds the other two like a hedge, are the vast hordes of the working poor. They live in relative poverty and work hard to feed and care for their families. The streets are made of dirt and the houses are remnants of the old city. Many of the houses there, in whole neighborhoods, are still abandoned, giving testament to the size of Avignon in years past. They serve as refuges for desperate folk and are dangerous hives of bars, brothels, opium dens, etc.

Here are outlying districts as well. The port quarter of Avignon is larger than any in the world, being home to hundreds of ships great and small. The River district, along the north bank of the Lithanian, offers merchants easier access to markets than they would find in the city itself. There has recently been a petition from those permanent residents of the River district to be incorporated into the town. Upon the pylons of the ancient Ursal Bridge are small towns, built up around the barge way points (*reference Ursal Tal, p. 155*).

The present Bishop of Avignon, Honorius II, shares his rule with the city Governor Milo. The two are often at odds. The Governor remembers the days, under Honorius I, when his office held power. He commands a vast bureaucracy which controls of much of the city taxes and expenditures. The Bishop struggles to maintain the religious fervor which fed new life into the old city. His priests serve the masses and he commands four troops of religious soldiery, the Ussars. The two squabble continually and seek to outmaneuver each other in a paper war of rights. In general, the foreign population (which is very large), the merchants, and the guilds support the Governor. The bulk of the working populace and the sailors support the Bishop.

Recently, the Captain of the Guard, Castus, a Brindisium gladiator and mercenary, has risen to great popularity and causes both Bishop Honorius II and Governor Milo to look nervously in his direction. He commands respect in all four Ussar troops and has vast sources of outside income.

Honorius II also struggles to elevate the Prelacy of Avignon to that of the highest in the church. His greatest foe is the church, the King and various Bishops in Angouleme.

The city itself is a thriving community where anything can be had. Passing from district to district can be achieved with a few coins. Carriage services offer weary travelers transport to anywhere in town. The thieves guild, Muddles Inc., has its main den-hall in the second district, as do other groups and cults. Merchants sale wares of any description, armor, weaponry, clothes, wine, food and so on. Exotic monsters can be found in the slave pits as can human servants. The jumbled streets and tall thin houses make for a strange other worldly setting for the uninitiated. Within the walls of Avignon lies a world within a world.

This city of all cities is the central crux of the commercial world. Everything travels though Avignon. The tremendous wealth of the city is derived from its status rather than any strategic or military or economic power. It is the trade center between east and west, north and south. Avignon is, however, one of the few places in the world that magic can be bought. Eldritch spells and incantations, weapons and armor and so forth are available, if at a high price.

The History of Avignon: Avignon is perhaps the greatest city in all of Erde, its history stretching back to the dawn of the early Aenochians and Ethrumanians. In the Days Before Days, the Dwarves built a great bridge across the Straights of Ursal. They called this bridge Andstein (*reference Histories, The Rule of Man, p. 22*). There, upon the great span the two tribes of men came together to make peace, though as is told elsewhere, this did not last. In later years, after many wars, the Aenochian Emperors built a fortress on the western end of the bridge to safeguard their lands in Ethrum. Soon thereafter, the city began to grow around the fortress. They named the fortress Avignon after the Emperor's wife.

During the Wars of Liberation, the Tarvish Emperor-King of Ethrum ordered that the bridge be cast down and the city fortified against the east. The city expanded rapidly after that. During the Age of Heroes it became the hub through which all commerce flowed. The port expanded, the city grew beyond its walls and the Governors built new ones. Untold wealth poured into the city. Men of all kinds swelled the ranks of citizens, so in time the city became a metropolis where anything was possible.

All this prosperity ended when the armies of the horned god lay siege to the city. They broke the walls asunder and lay waste to much of the inner city. Under the Winter Dark, Avignon became a sprawling fortress complex. Concentric walls sprang up around the landward side of the city and sea walls on the bays of the Straights. Prosperity of sorts returned and the city thrived for a while, though it was only a shadow of its former self.

The city fell on hard times almost from the beginning of the Winter Dark Wars. The disasters which the Imperial fleet suffered at the hands of Morgeld (1020md) and at Gokstad (1023md) left the commercial shipping lanes open to the ravages of the Northmen. They raided everywhere, sinking ships at sea and in harbor. From Avignon to the Gottland trade came to standstill. The impact on Avignon proved disastrous. With no land to rely upon even for meager foodstuffs, the city fell victim to starvation. Riots followed in which many were killed and much of the city burned. In the waning days of the horned god's rule, the city fell into ruin once more, many citizens deserting to the west.

Philip the Guileless (*reference Divine Orders, p. 58*) passed through Avignon in 1024md, and stayed for many months spreading the word of Demeter to high and low. Those who remained were a pitiful sight, poor and bedraggled; deserted by all, they leapt at the new faith and the new hope. When Philip spoke, people flocked from all quarters of the city and they followed his word. They built churches and a monastery, dedicating both to the name of Philip. In turn, Philip appointed one of his disciples, Sixtus, to remain in Avignon and rebuild it.

Sixtus busied himself with organizing the merchants, gathering a small fleet of ships to begin fishing and rebuilding the inner city. He also established way points on the ancient pylons of the Ursal Bridge which served as hauling junctures for barges to cross the straights. This brought a wealth of goods from Aachen. All this activity encouraged commerce to some degree. In 1027md, William of Angouleme came to Sixtus seeking his aid in being crowned King. William knew that many of his folk had fallen under the spell of Philip and hoped that by securing the blessings of the High Priest that his seizure of power would be all the easier. Sixtus, with much fanfare, came to Angouleme-ot-Neider and crowned William King of Angouleme. The grateful Lord sent several caravans laden with foods and wine to the city and granted them a wide stretch of territory surrounding the walls. In a very short while, the city recovered enough to attract some few immigrants.

In 1028md, Philip the Guileless and Demeter's disciples began the construction of a magnificent church in Old Avignon. They built it upon the foundations of the Governor's Palace, and named Sixtus Bishop of that Prelacy. Sixtus used the position of the city to enrich the church, tithing barges and caravans that passed through. He rebuilt the cities' walls and towers, and soon thereafter, Avignon flourished as merchants, traders and all manner of people came to live within the safety of its impregnable walls.

Avignon saw the face of war only once during the Winter Dark Wars. In 1029md, smarting from his defeat at Olensk (*reference Augsberg, p. 74*) Kain, Duke of Altengrund, came to the great city. He saw that much of it remained in ruins and that it was not worth attacking. So he called upon the city fathers to pay him coin for his kindness in mercy. Sixtus came forward to speak with Kain, for he had it in his mind that he could lay enchantments on the fell creature and induce him to leave. But Kain saw through this spell and laughed. He slew Sixtus, leaving his headless body upon the ground. Kain left without his coin, but he took the head in its place.

The people of Avignon were horrified at the tragedy and took Sixtus' remains and lay them in the Church of Philip. His tomb became a holy place where pilgrims came to lay sacrifice in foodstuffs at his feet. More than one has claimed to be healed by the spirit of Sixtus. The clerics and monks of Avignon elected Pius I to the bishopric in Avignon. Pius ruled for many years and brought more wealth and prestige to the city. He crowned William II King in Angouleme, introduced grape farming in the land and granted tax relief to all those who owned a boat and brought trade into the city. This last spurred a host of ship captains to land cargo and sell it cheap to caravans and by 1059md the city was well on its way to mirroring its past glory.

Pius II, once elected to the Bishopric, ruled the Church in a far more careful manner. He maneuvered himself in various church councils to be recognized as the preeminent cleric of Demeter. This touched off a series of religious conflicts throughout the world of Demeter, which only ended with Pius' death. Pius II crowned Philip William King of Angouleme, the last time a Bishop of Avignon did this. He also instituted a draft which called for four troops of city guard to be established. The call went out, far and wide, for men of skill in the art of war, to come to Avignon and join the well paid Ussars, as the troops were dubbed. To allow people to distinguish each Ussar, one from the other, the various troops took on distinctive coloring in their uniforms.

Honorius I followed Pius in the Bishopric in 1076md. A very religious man, he disdained from worldly politics. He appointed a Governor to aid him in running the commercial affairs of the city. And he rarely interfered unless the tithing dropped off. Avignon prospered again, trade flowed into her harbors and out and a contented people grew larger than life.

Ec Rating
V

In 1090md, Honorius I died and his successor, Honorius II, took the Miter of Avignon.

Brindisium, Republic of

The Consulate and Senate of families rule in the city-empire of Brindisium. The coat-of-arms is inlaid upon a large rectangular shield. The shield is green, a blue stud dominating the center where eight straight black spokes fan out to the frame. Each corner has a small inset where the background is red, and within each inset is an graven image (see illustration).

A Land of Sharp Contrasts: The Brindisium peninsula is a featureless plain of sparse forest. The soil is not rich, but is home to a variety of wild grasses. Rainfall here is light, and the area is always warm as southerly trade winds blow inland from the Amber Sea. Near the isthmus the country breaks up, hills and gulches covered in scraggly trees being the norm. The Darkenfold lies to the immediate north, and strange creatures wander south into the plains from time to time. In the western part of the country the land is characterized by rolling hills.

The city of Brindisium is ruled by the Senate, which is in turn presided over by the Consulate. Only men who trace their heritage to the days before the dark are given citizenship. Recently, exceptions have been made for the voting population has dwindled markedly. The city controls the whole of the peninsula and isthmus. Only the borders of the Darkenfold stopped their early expansion. Those towns and villages conquered by Brindisium are little more that client states who have no rights to govern, but must answer to the dictates of the Consulate and Senate.

The city itself has been carefully laid out. The streets are all cobbled, and most of the houses are stone or, in some cases, marble. The populace is relatively well educated. A system of public schools joins a variety of other novelties, such as running water, warm bath houses, roads and gutteres in the streets, making Brindisium uniquely civilized. Most citizens, and even many slaves, speak more than one language and are able to write as well.

The most organized of all the Young Kingdoms, Brindisium sports good roads, large towns where citizens live in relative opulence and a large merchant class. Her people traffic in all manner of commerce and possess a sizable merchant fleet which trades with lands far and wide. Most of the traffic is diverted to the ports of Maine, as the two Kingdoms have come to equitable commercial arrangements (*see below*).

The Republic exports a great quantity of goods, but mostly marble from the quarries in the west, wine and fish. Both of these products are prized worldwide and can be found in markets as far away as Avignon. Even the Northmen Kingdom of Trondheim is known to have imported Brindisium wine, though in truth whether this meant

they looted it or paid for it none can say. Perhaps the most sophisticated of merchant peoples, they have outposts and trading stations throughout the world. They are tightly knit compared to the outside world. Their fleet is powerful, due to the expertise of her captains and nature of their craft.

The city is rife with corruption and intrigue. Families feud, and senators conduct secret wars against paladins who are forever trying to regain dominance. The Republic fields four legions of 4000 men apiece and can call upon many auxiliary troops.

The people there pay homage to the old gods, deities such as Toth and Tefnut, but also to family deities. There, the magic of clerics is common, but sorcery far less so. A small school for this craft has recently been established in the capital.

The Imperial Paladins are only a shadow of their former selves. Once the bodyguard of the Emperors, they now are outcast citizens who make a living the best they can. Holy men who follow Durendale they are often hermits or mendicant knights who help the downtrodden as well as they know how.

Their Long History and the Rise of the Republic: Brindisium traces her roots to the Age of Heroes. During the final days of the Catalyst Wars (771oy-800oy), as Kayomar faced defeat and Unklar stood triumphant, Mourilee Lothian Pendegranze fled with many other refugees of Kayomar into the far distant west. The victory of Prince Erik Aristobulus Euryiance over Unklar's navy in 789oy left the command of the sea to the folk of Kayomar. They gathered what ships they could, and in the company of Luther's bastard son, Morgeld, set sail for the Wall of the Worlds. For years they sailed, the journey a legendary trek fraught with countless horrors. The voyage sent them to the far edge of the world where they founded the Solarian colony. Morgeld settled upon an island, the so called, "Land of Bliss."

As Unklar's winter extended over all the world of Erde, only a few pockets of resistance held out against him. One of the most successful were the folk of the Solarian Colony. They built their home on a coastal valley beneath the shadows of the mountains. The valley was well guarded by natural terrain. In the west stood the sea, where Prince Morgeld, the Fell Knight, lived with his navy and army of immortal soldiers. High mountains in the north and south came together in a narrow defile, which offered the only egress to the Valley of the Empire. Here, a wide, deep river flowed upon the western banks which they fortified. They dammed the river and flooded the plain beyond. They built a great city and there constructed temples to the gods Toth, Tefnut and the Dreaming Paladin, Luther. It is said that Tefnut herself dwelt near the river in the pass and that the sun never set upon the Solarian.

Mourille passed her days amongst these people and died soon after the colony's founding. However, her line lived for many generations until at last the seed of it died out. These were the last of Luther's true descendants. Though even now, it is rumored, that some lived on, trekking across the great wildernesses of Erde in search of the unknown.

The folk of that proud land resisted Unklar even in exile. Eventually the Paladins of Kayomar established a Holy Council, and in conjunction with the High Priestess of Tefnut they founded the Solarium Empire, the Empire of the Sun, in the Valley of Light. The Master of the Order took the crown as Emperor and adopted the Eagle as his standard. They took the Imperial dignity for order, for tradition too, for the Tarvish Emperors of the past withstood the might of Aenoch and eventually won out their freedom. The Emperors continued to rule and to war against Unklar for a thousand years. The Solarium became powerful in wealth and magic, and it used this knowledge to fell intent. Unklar's minions never broke the wall of the pass but once.

The one thousand and twentieth year in the reign of the horned god saw the opening of the Gate of Thonor, a magical portal between Gottland and the Solarium. The minions of Unklar managed the gate by using the ancient Rings of Brass of Dwarf make (*reference The Histories, 2nd Goblin-Dwarf War, p.17*) In this manner the dark host issued forth into the Great Waste before the gates of the Valley of Light. The black hosts filled the flooded plain with refuse and hurled themselves across the river against the high crenelated battlements within the pass itself. These walls stood boldly forth in defiance of the dark host so that siege was laid against it and war brought to the far west.

The following year the Paladins drove back the black host for a time but the cost was great and the Holy Council of the Empire entombed the fallen and dead of their realm. In fear of their master's rage, the hosts drove against the walls once more. They dammed the river and battered the walls, breaking them apart. But when they made to move through the Pass, a cleric, the High Priestess of Tefnut, who had for many days lay hidden in the river, broke the dam and the pent waters spilled forth and across the armies of darkness. Despite this setback many came over the mountains and lay siege with great desolation to the city, towns and keeps beyond. Though in the end, his folk fell back and beyond the walls which were fortified anew.

The destruction proved too much, for the orcs and ungern had poisoned the very land. So the Holy Council, in 1025md, deemed their lands unlivable and the greater part of them departed for the east in ships and galleys. Some few remained behind, living on in the city which escaped the flood.

It took them only a year to return to their ancient homes, but they soon learned they were not welcome, for much had changed in the thousand years of Unklar's rule. The men and women of the Solarium had changed, now imperious and commanding, they drove off all allies. So they sailed on, searching for a land to call their own. They split into two bitterly opposed groups (*reference Tagea, p. 132*), one moving on into the east while the other sailed back to the limits of Ethrumania where they settled, and built the city of Brindisium.

There were many folk who lived in those lands, and they paid homage to the horned god. Emperor Moridain ordered their keeps stormed and towns burned. His Knights and men-at-arms reduced the lands and put many to death. The Emperor declared a Crusade against all those who served the Dark, and they began clearing out all vestiges of the horned god's religion. In the winter, late in the year while raiding one of the enemies' strongholds Moridain, stricken with a poisoned arrow, died. His inheritance, the crown, went to his son, Raymond. Raymond was not a Knight nor did he hold his father's love of the ancient world.

A great deal of squabbling commenced and before long assassins struck the Emperor Raymond down, murdering him in his own bed. The leading families of the Old Empire gathered then in a Senate to discuss what next should be done. Many argued that the Imperial line failed the people and so they elected two Consuls, each chosen from the leading families, to rule them. The Emperor's Paladins fell into disgrace, as did his religion. They bore the Eagle Standard still but retreated to the edges of the empire. The Senate reorganized the army which eventually attracted some of the Paladins. They formed two legions of infantry and adopted the iron shield, borne aloft on a staff, as the Imperial Insignia.

Brindisium began to thrive soon after the coup. Those folk, long used to suffering the torments of war and confinement, spread out. They enslaved the local populace, who went to work on their farms or in their mills. Crops of wheat and rye became staples of the small land holders, but the peninsula proved far more adaptable to livestock and in the northern hill country was grape and wine production. In the west they quarried marble. All of these industries have brought a great deal of wealth to the Brindisium.

In 1087md, a host of commercial treaties with the Kingdom of Maine were agreed upon by the Consulate. With newly opened trade routes, both Kingdoms flourished. This in turn attracted many pirates to the area, a problem which plagues Brindisium far more than Maine for the King's ships are better equipped for war.

In 1095md, Marcus Vipsanius Agrippa, Master of the IV Legion and once an Imperial Paladin, made a bid for the Imperial title. The whole of the IV Legion marched on the capital. In the ensuing battle, Agrippa was defeated by the Senate at the battle of Iliumagus. Agrippa was put to death along with his immediate family (though some rumors abound that he escaped) and many of his relations were sold into slavery. The Legion was disbanded and its Eagle Standard taken from it. The Legionnaries were given the choice of recanting or suffering a similar fate. Many died out of loyalty to their Master.

Ec Rating
II

> **OF HER CONSULS**
> Agius Grachi
> Crasusious Marcus

Burnevitse

The fiercely independent Hobgoblins pay homage to Vistenodge the Mad, who rules them from the squalid halls of Luxor, claiming to be a god-king. Their heraldry is a simple one; striking terror into the hearts of men in the central lands. Upon a red curved shield lies the black bull's head spitted on a stake. The bull, the symbol of the evil god Thorax, is a memory of dread for all the world of Erde.

The Lands of the Hobgoblins and Their God-King: The stark rocky precipices of the Bleached Hills give way, in the north and east, to a series of broad shallow valleys. The valleys are rich in soil and a deep grass covers the ground almost everywhere. In places this grass is shoulder high. Wild game and other animals abound, for water is plentiful and human and humanoid settlements few. Travel is difficult but not impossible. Though the old roads have washed away or been carted away and the countryside steep and largely uninhabited (but for nomadic bands of hobgoblins), the hardy adventurer will never want for food or water.

Vistenodge the god-king rules the hobgoblin Kells very loosely. Decades of warfare and centuries of tradition have lent that people a fierce tradition of tribal independence and they bend to his rule most reluctantly. The god-king, however is very wealthy. In his younger years he stumbled upon an Imperial treasure trove where some malcontent had stored tens of thousands of diamonds. This 'diamond mine' which Vistenodge claims to own is in fact nothing more than a huge horde of stolen goods. Vistenodge is a giant of a hobgoblin and very cunning. Though cruel, he will make deals in a heartbeat if it serves to increase his power.

The god-king is reputed to be from the world of Inzae. The stories relate that one the Dwarven Brass Rings (*reference Magic Items, p. *) lies buried in the Bleached Hills and Vistenodge, while in Inzae discovered that portal's secret entrance to Erde and took advantage of it. Whatever the rumors report, the god-king is indeed an unnatural hobgoblin.

Burnevitse is a conglomeration of independent Kells of Hobgoblins, loosely associated with the god-king. The area in which the hobgoblins live is broken and the many isolated valleys offer easy defense. Each valley or series of valleys has its own ruler. These too, rule loosely. Hobgoblins are nomadic in nature, moving from one encampment to the next seeking for fresh pasture for their cattle and sheep.

Culturally, the hobgoblins live in a very martial society with definite, inescapable class boundaries. The class system consists of the Vouts, the elite warriors, the U-Vouts, or common soldiery, and the Kells of workers; and the slaves. Women are separate and highly prized for they are very rare. Only the Vouts breed and they spawn hundreds of children. Slavery of all races, including their own, is very common.

They mainly farm dairy products, mine for ores and work wood and stone. The Kells are actively involved in the ore trade throughout the lands and they guard their merchants with great care. Hobgoblin engineers are known to ply their trade in surrounding kingdoms, particularly the Hanse City States and in the trading posts of Gottland. Hob stonework, highly skilled, has recently become a fashionable item in the Hanse.

This last is causing an ever increasing amount of friction with the troll bands of Gottland. Varucks, the Troll Lord, desiring to rebuild his land's ancient glory (*reference Gottland, p. 94*), claims the lands from the Mountains to the sea to the Tiefsich River. He continually threatens the trading posts and caravans which cross the river into his territory. This of course leads to reprisals from the god-king, who sends troops over the river to harry the giant trolls, even so far as attacking their fortress of Nacht within the Kleberock pass. In turn, trolls cross back over, carting off cattle, slaying hobgoblins and scattering encampments.

In fact, Vestinodge is looking for brave adventurers to go to Castle Nacht and slay the foul troll. In payment, he promises a coffer of diamonds, all cut, and worth a fortune. As yet, none have been brave enough, nor foolhardy enough, to take the god-king up on his offer. Though the Lady Lissza in Fiume pushes the offer to any and all who will listen to her.

Relations with the Hanse City States are very good (*reference Hanse Cities, p. 100*). Trade goods move via caravan to the coast where they are sold or traded for manufactured goods. They are then shipped on to the markets of the east. The diary products of the hobs are highly prized in the markets of Avignon and Aachen. Most of the caravans are small affairs, three and four wagons apiece and guarded by a dozen or so hobgoblins. The trading posts are all human establishments walled with wooden palisades to protect them from the occasionally marauding hobgoblin Kell.

A Past with Little History: In this far distant corner of the Empire, beyond the Great Wall of Ethrum, the frontier legions of hobgoblins and orcs found themselves isolated when war came. Kayomar to the south rose in arms and Angouleme and the other provinces to the east beyond the wall threw off the yoke of Imperial rule. The Legion commanders turned to Nulak in the Graugusse. The Arch-Magi, however, could not give them securement, for Aristobulus pressed him at every turn.

In 1021md, the Falkynjager slew the dragon Malikor, and the beast fell to earth, crashing against the slopes of Mount Thangondrim. Even in far off Burnevitse the earth shook so violently that houses collapsed. The hobgoblins grew restless and some mutinied and moved into the Bleached Hills. Loyal Orcs pursued them into that broken country. They hunted down the mutineers and killed them. This quelled the mutiny only for a short while. When word came of Kayomar's victory over Aziz at Eadore in 1024md, the hobgoblins grew even more restless and more slipped away into the hills. The most loyal troops were sent to the south to occupy the ring of forts and castles surrounding the massive burg of Ox (*reference Kayomar, p. 104*) leaving few reliable troops in the whole of Burnevitse and the Bleached Hills region.

Discipline began to break down further amongst the Hobgoblin troops. With few officers capable of keeping them sufficiently cowed, they began to break apart into separate tribal units, or Kells. No aid came from any quarter. The rebellions spread and the hob legions all but disintegrated. In 1028md, the fortress of Ox fell with much loss of life and the Orcs were broken. This shattered the thin veneer of discipline remaining in the north and the whole region collapsed into anarchy. Despairing for their lives, the human officers fled leaving their soldiery to their own devices.

The wars passed them by and the Empire forgot them. The legions developed into a broken patchwork of tribal units and Kells. They broke off from each other, fanning out into the wilderness areas, looking for food and land. The new age frightened them. The sun shone brighter than it ever had before and the hobs, for many long years, hid themselves from the light of day.

When at last they came out of hiding, the world was not the one their fathers knew. The proud towns and fortresses had fallen into ruin and the roads were crumbling vestiges of their former selves. Food proved scarce in those early years and the hobs competed fiercely for it. Too, knights from Kayomar and Angouleme came to the lands of the hobs to hunt them out. All this brought further chaos. Their proud status as Imperial Legionnaries was forgotten by all but a few, and the hobgoblin Kells began warring sporadically with one another.

Burnevitse, the Wilds to the south, and the Bleached Hills became dangerous places. The hobgoblins, becoming fiercely territorial, fought any and all who entered their country. Orcs too, descendants of the shattered combatants of Ox, wandered the forests in small tribal groups. Strange beasts, monsters and others besides came to the region to prey upon the weak or settle in deep quiet places far from the lances of heroes.

Kayomar to the south along with Angouleme and Maine encouraged the continuation of inter tribal warfare between the humanoids. A great deal of money flowed north, paying one group off against another.

This state of chaos remained until 1081md. The hobgoblin Vistenodge, of unnatural size and intelligence, unearthed a cache of treasure (the famed "diamond mines" of the Bleached Hills) and his standing in the tribe changed overnight. He used his wealth and cunning to overwhelm some of his neighbors and with the combined might of several Kells began subjugating others. Those who followed him were given stores of booty and loot; those who didn't were destroyed. As his power increased, more Kells came to him to offer their allegiance. In this way, Vistenodge forcibly united many of the hobgoblins. Within a very short while he sent the first armed forays into the surrounding lands, mostly into the settlements of the great Massif.

In 1085md, Vistenodge stumbled upon a great opportunity. A raiding party, lately returned from the Hanse Cities, bore with them a merchant's daughter, whom they intended to ransom. Brought before the grim Vistenodge the woman laughed. Vistenodge wondered at this, and resisting the urge to kill her, asked her where her foolish bravery came from. She returned the query, "When one such as I falls into the hands of such fools, then I deserve whatever death fate delivers me." The woman, Lissza Forth, the only child of a foundering merchant, was no fool. She saw the wealth of that squalid encampment. Cattle, grains, mounds of booty, and in the chieftains tent were diamonds and riches beyond anything she had ever seen. The two soon struck up a friendship, for Vistenodge, a clever beast, respected her boldness and intelligence. The land overflowed with wealth she told him: diamonds from the Bleached Hills as well as minerals and other ores. All these could be traded for finished goods and coin. The Hob's love of cattle produced a great plentitude of dairy products. This too, could be sold in markets upon the Hanse. Vistenodge took Lissza up on her offer, for far more clever than any of his race, he knew that true wealth lay in the Young Kingdoms, and through trade alone he could expand his power throughout the whole region.

Vistenodge sent agents to the Hanse Cities to open trade negotiations. The Hanse, whose shipping industry suffered for a host of reasons (*reference the Hanse City States, p. 100*), jumped at the opportunity. Within a few short months caravans began crossing the plains and the Great Wall, while ships began plying the waves of the inner sea. Small frontier ports sprang up all along the coasts of Gottland as merchants took full advantage of the new produce. The League quickly cornered the market of goods from Burnevitse and wealth once more flowed through the river valley. Lissza returned to Fiume and her father's house. Their wealth and power grew tremendously in a short time and eventually she took control of the family's concerns. The two, Lissza and Vistenodge, remained friends.

Wealth poured into Burnevitse. Armor and equipment arrived which allowed them to raid in strength. In time, they threatened all the neighboring lands. Vistenodge declared himself god-king of the world and set himself upon a throne of bones in the slag heap castle of Luxor.

Ec Rating I

(*reference the Hanse City States, p. 100*)

> OF HER LORD
> The God King Vistenodge

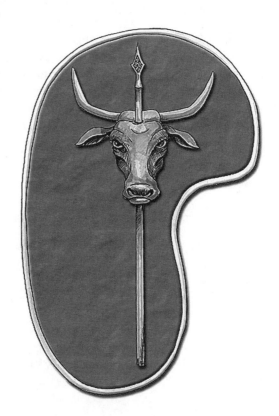

Cleves, Barony of

Not far from the ruins of the Great Wall of Ethrum, Count Eurich Gunshoff IV rules from the town of Olmutz. His coat of arms is easily distinguished, two blue chevron bands on a green background. In the lower field is a tower and in the middle field is a diamond with two wagons.

Of an Educated Lord and the Land He Rules: Cleves is nestled between the southern slopes of the Massif and the eastern flank of the Great Wall of Ethrum. The head waters of the Lithanian River begin here. The gently rolling countryside is rich in soil. There are few trees in the County and most of those, mainly hard wood and cypress trees, grow along the banks of the river. The villages are scattered and unwalled with houses of sod and grass roofs. Small keeps, the homes of the local nobility, are usually not far off. The only town of import is Olmutz, located further to the north.

Count Eurich Gunshoff IV comes from a long line of noble warriors. His demeanor, however, bears only a little resemblance to his ancestors. Slight of build, possessed of a keen intelligence , Eurich early on discovered his love for knowledge. He spent several years in the Hanse City State of Klagenfurt at the University. He excelled in philosophy and mathematics, surprising all of his professors. He wept openly upon his father's death for he loved his sire, and took the crown only reluctantly, trying to pass it on to his younger brother. His brother, Eric, would not take it, for he loved the life of adventure, and eventually left the County on a crusade in the distant east, to Outremere.

Eurich IV's mother, the aunt of King William of Angouleme, presses him to take the crown of that realm, a prospect the Count abhors. He realizes that, though his claim may be legitimate, taking it up would only bring war to both his County and the Kingdom. Even still, emissaries from the Duchy of Enois have arrived in Olmutz to discuss that very thing (*reference Angouleme, p. 68*).

The Count recently moved his seat of government from the castle Let-ot-Lithanian to the town of Olmutz where he has begun construction on a small university.

Like much of the western lands, knightly traditions are strong in Cleves. The local lords revel in tournament and war. The wealth brought to the country from cotton and mining allows them to build well fortified keeps. These are found in most areas and are almost always occupied by one or two knights and a handful of men-at-arms. Almost all the horses of the nobility are imported from Sienna. In war, Eurich can rely upon an impressive array of mounted cavalry.

Small villages of thatched houses are found throughout Cleves. The peasants farm a mixture of cotton, soy beans and barley. Along the

Massif are several small diamond mines and the villages there are a little more rugged. The peasants generally welcome strangers, particularly any knights of St. Luther. Every village has its own brew house and the taverns, though small, are inviting places.

Cleves is one of the few independently wealthy kingdoms in the world, its villages producing an abundance of food, its mines an abundance of wealth. It is one of the few areas in Erde where diamonds are found. Stonework and engineering, most on the University, account for much of the Count's expenditures.

Upon the Edge of History: During the age of Winter Dark the lands of the whole of the Ethrum and Aenoch were divided into provinces. These frequently reflected the realms as they existed in the days before. The Lands from the Hanse River to the Massif and the Twilight Wood Unklar's servants divided into nine provinces: Angouleme, Enois, Aquaitaine, Blois, Limousine, Orange, Karilia, Cleves and Sienna. The folk who lived there, high and low, carried their strong class identity into the new age. Many traced their lineage to the old aristocracy of the Ethrumanian Kingdoms, and as with their ancestors, they reveled in war and tournament. To bring these folk to heel, Unklar appointed Governors over them.

Despite this, the knights proved difficult to govern and they rebelled continually. To overcome this the Governors' appointed them to administrative offices, exempted them from taxes and allowed them to employ small troops of retainers. To control these men further, a noble, usually the most influential, was appointed as Count of the Province. The counts, though locally powerful, ruled in name only, answering to the dictates of the Governor. As time passed more nobles entered the government as administrators, always seeking an appointment to the County Seat. In this way the Governor's pacified the region by creating an aristocratic cast of bureaucrats who made their wealth through controlling the regional commerce. The nobles never forgot their heritage, however, nor did they lay aside their warlike tendencies. In time, many of the younger sons turned aside roles in the Imperial Governorships and joined the Legions instead.

When the Winter Dark Wars began, Unklar's generals stripped the central lands of Ethrum of their garrisons. The Lords of Aufstrag desperately needed experienced soldiers for the battles in the south and east in the Grundliche Mountains. The central lands they deemed safe from rebellion, so they did not fear the consequences of withdrawing so many soldiers.

In 1023md, when William of Angouleme declared his independence and set himself up as Count of Angouleme-ot-Neider, all of the other provinces followed suite (*reference Angouleme, p. 68*). Cleves was no exception. There, the same family had ruled under the local governors for over a century. The Gunshoff Counts possessed great wealth in land and castles. Count Eurich Gunshoff I held back during the initial days of the rebellion. This led the Imperial Governor, Menmtebno, to mistakenly think that Gunshoff remained loyal to the Empire. He sent orders to the Count to rally all his knights and attack William in his castle.

Though well placed to carry out such an attack, Gunshoff had no intention of doing so. He ordered that the Governor and his staff be placed in the castle of Haridon upon the edge of the Great Wall. He informed the Governor that it was for his own protection. The wizard priests of Unklar, always a large presence in Cleves due to its proximity to the Great Wall of Ethrum, bid Gunshoff to release the Governor and declare himself for Aufstrag or against it. In those days however, the Priests of Unklar were much weakened. Their master failed them, for in truth, Unklar could not answer their prayers in those days. He was pressed too hard and fought off the attacks of other gods and the Council. When Gunshoff learned of their weaknesses, he ordered the priests to be rounded up and confined with the Governor.

In 1024md, the Crna Ruk, paid by coin from the Governor, stole into the Count's castle of Let-ot-Lithanian. They slew him and his wife in their bed where they were found the following day. This proved a fatal mistake, for Gunshoff's son, Eurich II, took up his father's crown and sword and declared himself, by the Grace of Saint Luther, Count of Cleves, completely breaking with the Empire. He ordered his knights to go to Haridon and gather the priests, the Governor and all those within and put them within the inner Keep. Eurich forced them to carry their jewels and monies with them. "You may need these monies to buy your way into hell, for the light of day you shall never see again." Once done, masons came and sealed all the doors and windows with stone and mortar. There the unfortunates lay in suffering misery. For days their cries and shouts for aid carried across the walls and into the lands about. Many went mad with hunger or fear, tearing at their fellows. The dying agony of those responsible for the assassination sent a clear message to the Empire and all those who pretended overlordship of Cleves.

Eventually all those within starved to death and their bodies, some half eaten, lay strewn about in heaps and piles. Ever since, the Haridon has been a haunted place. Noone came to reclaim its walls and the castle fell into great ruin. Legends speak of ghosts and ghouls stalking the halls and the countryside about, looking for food while they call for aid from their dark master. And there it sits to this day, nigh upon the Great Wall, its walls crumbling, vines covering the whole of it. And the Inner Keep sealed with mortared bricks, is a brooding place, watching and waiting.

All these sufferings occurred around the 5th of Lezlicht, 1024md. The Howling Night, as the locals call it, became a holiday in Cleves. These locals, peasants mostly, gather in great halls dressed as ghouls, feasting and dancing the whole night.

When Eurich Gunshoff II proclaimed himself Count by the Grace of St. Luther he set himself apart from the rest of the rebelling provinces. There, the words of Phillip the Guileless carried the weight of gold. Whole towns and villages converted to the worship of Demeter. Knights too, and above all else King William of Angouleme himself did. Even as the religion spread into his own domain Eurich clung to the patronage of St. Luther. He built in the castle of Let-ot-Lithanian a temple to St. Luther, where he invested his knights and barons with land. Many of the warrior aristocrats viewed Luther as a god of war. If not completely on the mark, their

accolades proved good enough to attract the benefice of the Sainted one. Eurich and the whole of the knightly class bore testament to a collective vision where the Paladin god invested them all and their realm with his blessing.

The next four years were telling ones. Plenty of rain brought bountiful harvests and King William chose to allow the Count his freedom, dropping claims to overlordship, and the wars which raged all around them seemed never to come home to Cleves. The notion spread that for all this good will the folk of the County owed the blessings of St. Luther. Soon the worship of that god spread even to the peasants and merchants, who built small temples of rock to pay homage to the patron Saint. Though the word of Demeter spread to the County and some converted, it never caught on as it did in the more eastern provinces of the region.

Eurich II ruled Cleves for many years. He treated his people fairly, setting aside one day each week to hear their complaints. Any could come to him with any grievance and expect a fair hearing.

Eurich II inherited a sizable treasury from his father and with this he managed to rebuild many of the castles of the County which had, during the Winter Dark, fallen into ruin. He traveled the length and breadth of the country, staying for many months in one place or the other. But ever did he come back to his favorite castle, Let-ot-Lithanian, to must upon the world at large.

His Barons and Knights, never great in number, were, as they still are, fiercely loyal to their Lord.

Upon his death, Eurich II passed a donation of 100,000 golden crown to the Priests and Clerics of the Pallidium grove, for its continued maintenance. In turn, the Priests gave the Count's son a seedling from the Grove, one of the silver trees of Mordius. The tree they planted upon the heights overlooking the Count's favorite castle where his tomb lay. The tree took root deep in the ground and to this day, it is a holy place for all those who pay homage to the Sainted Paladin.

Eurich Gunshoff III reluctantly took his father's seat. His reign, shorter than his father's, was largely uneventful. He fought two short wars against Hobgoblins from the west and spent a small fortune repairing a section of the Great Wall. He is most noted for bringing cotton to the peasants. No one could say where he acquired the strange plant, though many speculated that he took it from the Hobgoblins, who were always dabblling in strange affairs. Regardless of its origin the plant thrived in the low country of Cleves and brought a great deal of revenue to high and low alike.

Upon his death Eurich III granted a benefice of 25,000 gold crown to the Grove and in turn the priests brought to his grave a small box of holy earth. His son, Eurich Gunshoff IV, lay him next to his father at Let-ot-Lithanian.

Ec Rating II

Of Her Counts
Eurich Gunshoff I (1009md-1024md)
Eurich Gunshoff II (1024md-1067md)
Eurich Gunshoff III (1067md-1080md)
Eurich Gunshoff IV (1080md-present)

Eisenheim, Kingdom of

In the large wooden halls of Lund, King Thorismund rules this land of Northmen. His simple heraldry, crossed spears on green with a longship underneath, mimics his origins.

Of Her King, His Land and His People: Eisenheim lies upon the sea, between the dark forests of the Detmold and the rugged peaks of the Flintlock. Gently rolling hills and shallow valleys are pockmarked by small wooded glades. Streams and riverlets crisscross the whole realm. The Kingdom gets a great deal of rain, as do all the lands of the region, and many sailors curse the ever present fog that lingers in the coastal waters.

King Thorismund is an older man who loves the sea. He leads raids occasionally, but for the most part takes his dragon ships into the fjords of the far north or through the isles of the Roheisen Straights. There he searches for the crown of his father and the Frost Giant axe lost at sea so many years ago (*see below*). Eisenheim commands a notable force of irregular infantry. In addition, they are some of the most skilled sailors of all Erde.

Close ties with Aachen and Augsberg continue to keep the peace in the region. When the Northmen of Eisenheim feel the need to raid, they do so in the west, in Ethrumania, sparing their neighbors. The Thanes of Eisenheim are powerful and wealthy and do not bow to the King in Lund. They meet in council frequently and argue any course the King may plot for the realm. There are some few castles here, but for the most part the Thanes live in great wooden halls with their peasants in villages all about. They welcome most travelers, particularly the warlike Knights of Haven, and give food and lodging freely. All travelers who take such hospitality can not help but notice the wealth in plunder from the west.

The Goths who make up Eisenheim have, for the most part, settled in peaceful farming communities throughout the rolling hills and valleys of the land. In large part due to the laws of Theodahad I and Fyorgyn, the settlers live in peace with the indigenous people (*see below*). There are no serfs in Eisenheim; any man or woman is free to go when and if they desire. It is a kingdom much like the Northern Kingdoms across the sea where women have an equal say in the rule of law. And those, like Fyorgyn of old, who bear weapons are welcome at the King's Council. For the most part crops that are grown are for local consumption and the manufacture of beer, the wealth of the peasants, comes from livestock. Small herds of sheep and cattle are in abundance.

Wealth here is dispersed and the kingdom produces little of its own for export. The iron that is mined in the Flintlock and foodstuffs dominate the economy. The sailors of Eisenheim make up much of the world's fleets and their raiding vessels can be found in all corners of the world. They are also very good traders.

The lands are not wholly tamed and the folk have not given up all their warlike traditions. On occasion, young Thanes gather small armies and take to the sea to raid the lands in the west. Too, due to the area's long history, old ruins of ages past, abandoned and forgotten, are continually being unearthed.

On Longships They Came: With wild hair and beards to match the ferocity of any Dwarf the Northmen descended upon the Lands of Ursal. For centuries the men and women of the wild north lived free of the rule of Unklar. They thrived in the Winter Dark, for they lived already in the frozen north, pulling their livelihoods from the sea. These people lived in tribes, many the direct descendants, or so it is written, of Dwarves from the Days before Days. Along the coast and in the hinterlands of the inner sea there existed several large tribes of note. Upon the eastern slopes of the Roheisen Mountains lived the Ostrogoths and upon the western slopes the Visigoths. {*Note: the name derives from ancient Dwarven, "gotha" being the word for tall. The Dwarves called men the Gotha fu, literally the "tall people". Those tribes local to Roheisen Hohle eventually adopted the name themselves*} Legends and songs of the Goth tribes relate tales of a time when man and Dwarf lived in peace and great concourse, though the halls of Roheisen Hohle had long been closed to the outside world until only recent memory (*reference Roheisen Hohle, p. 126*). The Ostrogoths and Visigoths were in turn divided up into several tribes.

These scattered tribes of Ostrogoths and Visigoths lived in the snow bound mountains and along the ice locked seas. With the onset of the Winter Dark Wars, the snow began to recede and the southern lands became lost in internecine war. For reasons that are not completely understood, the northerners suddenly exploded upon the lands of Ethrumania and Aenoch. Whether they sensed a weakened zeal in the Imperial Legions or they reacted to internal turmoil is not known, but what is understood is the terror they brought with them from the north.

With the likenesses of the gods and the dragon Inzae upon their ship prows, the Northmen rode the tides of the Inner Sea to war and slaughter. At first they raided small villages, burning coastal farm houses and thorpes. They sank fishing vessels and threw their captains into the sea. They initially carted off many slaves and a little plunder. But in the year 1019md, the Ostrogoth Angatyr led a bold raid against Toninburg, a town upon the northern shores of Angouleme. In Toninburg stood a temple to Unklar and many wealthy merchants who made their living off the trade of produce from the sea. Angatyr, with four ships carrying 30 Northmen apiece, attacked the town one early morn. The town, helpless against the onslaught, fell to Angatyr, who ordered it plundered and burned. The booty they carted back in gold, jewels and slaves amazed their fellows and galvanized the whole of the Northern tribes.

The Northmen built larger ships and filled them with eager warriors and by 1022md, the first large scale attacks took place all along the coasts of the Inner Sea. The Imperial response was rapid. They dispatched a fleet of galleys to destroy the barbarians. They sailed north to the sprawling city-encampment of Gokstad, intending to burn out the barbarians, but the Northmen set out in a host of long boats under King Thorismund the Great and met them at sea. In the ensuing battle, Thorismund destroyed the Imperial fleet and the entire 58th Legion with it. This victory opened the southern lands to further depredations and eventually to migrations. The raids also triggered the creation of several states, such as Angouleme and the Hanse City Federation.

In 1025md, Theodahad the Ostrogoth of the Amal clan, son of King Thuidemere, son of Thorismund the Great, gathered a host of Visigoths, some Ostrogoths and many freed slaves, then set forth to forge a kingdom in the wealthy south. His sister Fyorgyn joined him. They raided as far west as Avignon, but then turned north to the coasts of Aenoch. The sparsely populated lands north of the Detmold Forest offered the migrants a perfect home and they conquered the region in 1026md.

Along the coasts of the Inner Sea they forged the Kingdom of Eisenheim. Theodahad worked hard to integrate his folk with the indigenous people. The peasants who occupied the many scattered villages and thorpe of the area fled at first, but promises of safety and, eventually, hunger, brought them back. Theodahad forbid any of his warriors to molest them, but rather gave his soldiery control of land and villages, both to protect and tax. In this way a union of the two peoples came about and in time of years, they bore fruit in the semblance of a strong Kingdom.

Within two years Theodahad's folk became deeply involved in the Winter Dark Wars with many serving as mercenaries in the armies of Aachen and Augsberg. Theodahad led them, alongside those of King Albrecht, at the Battle of Olensk in 1029md. In the waning years of the Wars, the Northmen joined Aachen and Lord Daladon in their battles with the orcs of Iergaul in the Flintlock (*reference March of Zeitz, p. 136*). Here, Fyorgyn and Ephremere, Queen of Aachen, formed a lasting friendship with each other and with Daladon of the Council of Light.

The power of Eisenheim grew when Fyorgyn married Alfred, the son of King Albrecht of Augsberg. The marriage proved a long and fruitful one, and Fyorgyn bore Alfred many children. Her power as a priestess of Heimdal and her ferocity in war led this woman to, in time, lead her own people. Theodohad lived only long enough to see his sister married, for he died young, slain upon the walls of Iergaul by the Orc Afrix.

The thanes of Eisenheim crowned Fyorgyn's second son of her marriage to Alfred, Eurich, as their King. In truth, he was but a boy of two and his mother ruled in his stead. Fyorgyn ruled with a firm hand, dabbling in all aspects of the Kingdom. She continued the laws of integration started by her brother, as well as reaffirmed the alliances with the neighboring Kingdoms. When Eurich died at the age of nine, taken by disease, Fyorgyn, ever associated with the arcane doings of the god Daladon, quit the governing of her realm and retired to her lands in Augsberg. Her lands and castles she left to noone and they became wild places in the heart of Eisenheim, for few dared to explore them lest they bring down the wrath of the heroin Fyorgyn. Braga, Theodohad's son, a brash youth passed over by the Thanes, took the crown in a bloodless coup.

Braga ruled the Kingdom for over twenty years and his rule reflected that of his forefathers. A powerful man with a lust for war, he could not contain himself to the quiet life of a King in his hall. He reassembled the fleets of raiders and began plundering the shipping lanes and towns of the western coasts. He became the terror of his age and few could sail upon the Inner Sea that did not bring his raiders down upon them. Braga himself led forty vessels, some drawn from his cousins in the north in a raid on Avignon in 1071md. He carried a great war axe, taken, it is said from a Frost Giant King

in the Grundliche Mountains by Braga himself, and battered down the outer gates. They plundered the outskirts of the town but when the wealth of Avignon brought forth thousands of mercenaries Braga quit the attack and fled back to the east. Nevertheless, his ships were laden with booty. Braga died upon the sea when his ship went down in a storm off the isles of the Roheisen straights. He bore with him his Frost Giant's axe.

Theodahad II, Braga's son, took the throne upon his father's demise. Raised in the households of Aachen, Theodahad carried with him a hint of civilization. Curtailing the raids he spent his wealth and time on rebuilding the long neglected realm. Castles in the southern fashion, though made of wood and dirt ramparts, began to appear here and there. The Northmen began at last to employ horsemen, though this practice never caught on.

Theodahad ruled for fourteen uneventful years. The raids slackened and there was peace in the land. He died upon his throne, sitting in Council, with his eyes open to the world. Ever after, it has become a saying in Eisenheim, "With eyes open, we face the other side."

Neither of Theodahad's two wives bore children so upon his death, his brother, Thorismund took the throne. Named after his great ancestor, Thorismund brought some of the old world back to his people and to Eisenheim.

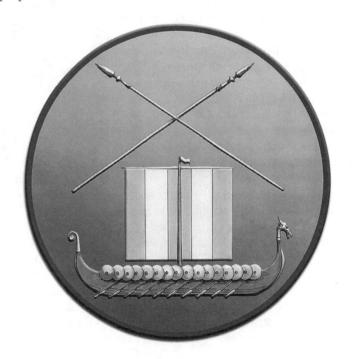

Ec Rating I

OF HER KINGS AND THANES
Theodahad (1027md-1040md)
Eurich son of Fyjorgan (1040md-1051md)
Braga (1051md-1076md)
Theodahad II (1076md-1090md)
Thorismund (1090md-present)

loria (Latzen Bastei "The Last Bastion")

Upon the windswept Isle from the halls of Elorisia Prince Morgeld of Nevermore, the Fell Knight, called the Demon Prince and Half Breed, St. Luther's son, rules from his throne of gold. His troop of Immortals bare his symbols in war. The midnight blue banner with the runes of chaos upon it foretell their loyalty, "In the name of Morgeld, Oh Our Prince."

The Land of That Place and Its People: The many scattered isles of Eloria lie off the coast of the Gelderland across the Straights of Ungara. The country here is much the same as it is on the mainland, with rolling hills of broken scrub oak and grassland. Some scattered forests dot the island, protected by edict of the Prince. Mythic monsters have settled here as the Prince styles the whole isle his menagerie. The lesser isles are rocky outcrops with little forest, but where large pastures of deep grass grow. They are particularly known for their rugged and fierce breed of wild panthers.

Prince Morgeld rules in the capital halls of Elorisia. He is a beautiful man, well groomed, tall, muscular and a little pale. He is charming and has a silver tongue. Morgeld rules the island as a tyrant. His word is law, and he uses the dreaded Crna Ruk to carry it out (*reference Guilds & Orders, p. 196*). Morgeld, as in the past, is very addicted to a variety of drugs and drink, much of which is imported. He loves pleasure overmuch and, or so the tales relate, treachery as well. He is the last member of the Old World who strives for mortal gains upon the plane of Erde.

None challenge Morgeld's rule for his Immortals, of which only 900 remain, are fiercely loyal to him and guard him well.

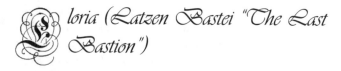

These mercenary knights, many of whom traveled with the Prince in the Age of Heroes, are all experienced warriors and battle mages. They go to war in outlandish decorated plate mail, with high helms and long shields. Though, as is common knowledge, many are addicted to the same pleasures of the flesh as their Master. To augment his forces, Morgeld, in times of need, hires mercenaries from the Gelderland.

The island itself has become fabulously wealthy. Elorisia has grown into a sprawling city that continually outgrows its walls. Jumbled houses and buildings crowd the narrow roads and alleys, making much of the city a dark forbidding place. There are no city officials, only the word of Morgeld. Because of this, much of the city is a dirty place, where little care is taken to maintain public works. Only in select neighborhoods, where the merchants live or the temples lie are facilities kept in good working order. Elsewhere it is up to the locals to do what they may.

Morgeld decreed that a whole district of Elorisia be set aside for religious worship. Only on temple grounds does he allow others to have a say in their own governance. The edicts of religious tolerance have given home to a host of religions. The greatest temple is the Rock of Poseidon. The High Priest of the King of Gods dwells there, for he is given much latitude by the Fell Knight. There are others besides, great and small. The only known temple of the Crna Ruk lies in Eloria. There, the assassins pay heed to the faceless master of their order. The temple district is set aside from the rest of the city.

This led to the quartering of the city into other districts; a merchants quarter, several for commoners and so on. The worst district of the city is the Break. There, all manner of ruffians gather; mercenaries, sailors, thieves and those down and out. Muddles Inc., always in competition with the Crna Ruk, set up house in the Break. The thieves grow fat on the wealth which flows through the city. Morgeld keeps little law in the city, and most everyone has small armies of retainers or guards to keep them safe.

Within the center of Elorisia lies the Imperial City and it is set aside by a great wall of granite and steel. Within are the palaces and places of pleasure for the Immortals and a select few princes and ambassadors allowed within this sacred place. Few enter and none leave this place who were not bidden. The palaces are beyond compare, for the Immortals are well versed in ancient and abyssal architectures and know well how to create beautiful things. Here too is the only place the edict forbidding the construction of roofs and covering is obeyed, for Morgeld believes the elements are the most ancient source of power and exposure to them the only path to knowledge and power. The rarest of flowering trees grows therein, for Morgeld is fond of beautiful things. The fell Prince himself sits upon his throne of ivory, perched above his columned courtyard beneath the open skies, buffeted by the winds and rains of all seasons, pondering his fate, his loyalties, and his needs.

Outside the city the rolling hills bear huge manors and spired castles. The people of Eloria are indolent and revel in the wealth which their master spreads around. As is told, many of these lords are powerful and have traveled with the demon prince for eons. Little is produced in Eloria other than debauchery. The immense wealth of the Prince is changing the commercial sea lanes in the south as he endeavors to control all seaborne trade. He has developed a primitive banking system which loans at tremendous rates (enforced by the Immortals). The Prince raises a great deal of revenue through taxing pilgrims. They have recently allied themselves with Tagea to reassert their power over the southern sea lanes.

From the Womb of the Abyss, Oh Prince: The history of the Isle of Eloria is one bound to the history of its Prince, Morgeld the bastard, for he rules there with his Immortals.

Centuries ago, during the Age of Heroes before the Millennial Dark, King Luther of Kayomar (*reference St. Luther, Divine Orders, p. 62*), waged continual war upon the Lords of the Abyss. Those fell creatures could not overcome his strength, nor that of his comrades the White Mage and Daladon. However, what they could not win by force they attempted to achieve by guile. In the heat of battle, Luther fell to the ensorcellements of the succubus Tetstiana. She bound him for a short while, hours only, but long enough to serve her purpose. Eighteen months later, Tetstiana gave birth to Luther's bastard son, naming him in the demon tongue, Peineger, that is in the Vulgate, "To bring Torment."

As a boy, Peineger bore the twin spirits of his father and mother. Law and chaos struggled within him, as did good and evil. At times Peineger waged war upon his father, but at others he fought by his side. When Luther, then King of Kayomar, learned of his identity, he wept bitter tears. He forgave the boy and bid him shed his demon name and take that of Morgeld, Luther's own father's middle name. The boy wept as well and embraced his father, taking the title of Prince aside that of Luther's legitimate child, Robert Luther. They lived for a time in peace with each other, but in the end the machinations of his mother drove Morgeld to war with his father once more. So they were sundered for many long years.

After the coming of Unklar, Morgeld withdrew to his fortresses in the Gelderland. He gathered a host of men, half demons and even some elves about him and they made to flee or fight. These ruffians came from all over, but mostly from the east in Al-Liosh. Their's was a desperate company of desperate men. Morgeld awaited the outcome and when the wars turned against the west and hope faded, he gathered his folk together, and with the black spear Gorgothorium in hand, made for the sea. They plundered on their march, gathering stores of wealth before they came to the port cities on the sea. They forced their way onto several ships and joined the exodus into the far west. He traveled for a time with a fleet of other refugees, but eventually broke with them and settled his people on a slag of volcanic rock on the Edge of Forever, the so called borders of the Wall of Worlds.

There, Morgeld styled himself the Prince of Nevermore, and also, Lord of the Isle of Bliss. He bid his folk to construct a great citadel. They slaved for years in the task as the Prince and his soldiery plundered the dying kingdoms of Erde and the Planes. They stole riches and arcane magic and bore it all to the island realm. They brought slaves, beasts and all other things they may need to survive. When at last the citadel stood complete it dominated the island and the oceans around. The great black hulk of it, carved from the rock itself, stood as a testament to its dark master. The burg was mighty in defense, so that none dared assail it. So it stood for over a thousand years.

Those years were hard on the Prince and his Immortals. Bound to Erde they could no longer plunder the planes for riches and booty, but instead found themselves slaves to time. For there, on the Edge of Forever, they did not age. Truly they were the Immortals. Morgeld slipped into a world of chaos and debauchery. He took drugs and much drink to ease the pain of his life's guilt, for in truth he always loved his father most and hated his mother for the chaos she wrought.

When the Wars began, the Council of Light came to Prince Morgeld to rally him to their cause. He welcomed his father and the company and swore to aid them in their battles with the horned god. In truth he rejoiced, for he had since grown tired of his life. The Immortals too rejoiced, for they ever loved war beyond all things.

But Unklar knew of Morgeld and he knew too his heritage. As is told elsewhere, he sent forth a fleet of black ships, filled with foul orc and ungern to hound the Son of Luther and retrieve the Black Spear, Gorgorthorium. But being bold and fierce, the Prince roused now from his drugged stupor, gathered the Immortals together and set to sea in seven great ships outfitted for war. The folk of Morgeld were few in number, but fierce in battle. These men and elves carried themselves in wild abandon, armed and girded for war in outlandish suits of mail. They slipped from the Isle in a lust for battle. By devious paths Morgeld, named anew, the Fell Knight, came upon the Dark Fleet.

At the Battle of Utland he broke the fleet asunder and sent many Orcs and other folk of that ilk to their doom in the 'deep quiet.' The Fell Knight suffered as well, two of his mighty ships were lost forever to the waters and a third cut asunder and lost to him. In after times, or so the tales relate, this third ship after many long adventures, came upon the island spires of ancient Dwarven homes which they believed were the remains of Alanti. But their tale does not come into Morgeld's evermore. So with lessened might he sailed south around the continent and in the year's twilight came to the Elorian Islands. There he built a castle, Elorisia, and this new home he named Letzen Bastei which is the "last bastion" in the Vulgate.

As is told some folk of the black fleet broke free of Morgeld's battle line and came to the Isle of Bliss. There they laid siege to the citadel, breaking its walls they plundered it, casting down its high towers. They set there a great Captain, and he ruled there for long ages and came to be known in after times as Trubsal, which is misery in the Vulgate, and his isle named Unglucksfall. It is now known that this Captain was a Mogrl (*reference New Monsters, p. 238*), forged from the hatred of Unklar when he was yet young.

Morgeld joined his father and the Council in the war against Unklar and led his Immortals many times against the minions of the horned god. Many tales relate of his adventures and struggles during those days and of his betrayal and forgiveness. Too, rumors speak of his bitter feud with King Alfred of Augsberg and how he slew him with the Black Spear, Gorgorthorium. In the end, his crime was greater than all others, for behold after the heroine Septiva felled Unklar, Morgeld stole the broken horn of Unklar and brought it to his island kingdom, enshrining it in the bowels of his own palace.

After the war the years passed without event with the Prince and his remaining Immortals slipped into their old lives of wild abandon, comfort and debauchery.

Ec Rating
IV

Of Her Master
Prince Morgeld the Fell Knight

Fontenouq, The Principalities of

The noble families of the scattered Principalities of Fontenouq rule their small estates independent of each other. They bare devices upon their shields and the crests' of their helms which carry little likeness to anything else in the world. They are known mostly for their high conical helms and elaborate armor.

Of The Lordly Elves and Their Lands: The lands of Fontenouq are wild, inhospitable places, consisting of rocky outcrops atop steep hills, whose slopes follow wild descents into ever darkening woods. In the valleys the trees and bramble grow close. They are fed by many small streams, pools and ponds. There are no roads here, only trails, and these seem to crisscross the country in no particular pattern. A plentiful amount of game is available for the wary hunter, but there are many predators, both magical and mundane.

The spired castles of the Fontenouq Elves dot the countryside. Though some went to great lengths to hide their towers in the dark deeps, others were content to build them heedless of who saw them. These high thin towers rise from forested hills or valleys like singular moments. They are out of place, these otherworldly towers, but even so seem to belong with the countryside. Often the trails leading to these forested palaces are difficult, if not impossible, to find and many a would be visitor has entered the forests never to return.

Those who do find themselves at the gates of one these palaces is likely to stay there. The Elves do not welcome visitors generally, though on occasion they will give refuge to those they feel deserve their aid; warriors and the like. They have no friends in the world and so do not worry themselves with being kind to strangers. Instead, they indulge in internal pursuits such as the study of philosophy, music and poetry. Even so, they retain a fierce nature and skill in armory, weapons and magic. Fontenouq is not adverse to gathering under arms to help the kingdoms of man and dwarf defend themselves against the evils of the world.

There is no commerce in Fontenouq and it is not a wealthy kingdom in the human sense, but the Elves there care for their own and produce some of the finest weaponry in the world. They are also known for their carving in wood, ivory and bone, wondrous magical tapestries and clothing.

Though the Elves do not traffic in worldly goods, the bold sorcerer or wizard can find a wealth of information arcane in any one of the Elven Princes' abodes. Sometimes they give this information freely, to aid those they feel are continuing the struggle against the minions of the horned god. Sometimes they seek payment, and this is always something to aid them in understanding the sins of their history (*see below*). It is said that certain Elven Princes' take in human apprentices and train them in the arts of the magi. For this reason alone many travel to Fontenouq, though in truth, few return.

The Elves of Fontenouq have no rulers. They live independently of each other, nestled in the foothills and forests of their adopted homeland, rarely leaving their abodes. For this reason their numbers are slowly declining. The young devote themselves to martial exploits, philosophy, or some other endeavor, rarely concerning themselves with propagating their race.

Occasionally some of the younger Fontenouq leave their palace castles to explore the wide world beyond. They are easily recognized by the weapons they bare, all long and thin, and the warlike attitude they possess.

The Sin of Their History: Of all the folk in the world the Elves of Fontneouq are the most melancholy. Their past is clouded with treachery, cowardice and guilt, for they abandoned the world of Erde when all others stood and fought against the tide of Darkness. For this crime the Elves have paid with their souls, turning from the carefree, noble born Fey of yesteryear to the personified avatars of war and vengeance.

Before the Age of Winter Dark, representatives of all the High Elves of Erde gathered in a great meeting before the feet of their Queen, Yaeondae of Elean to discuss the future of the world. One of their number, Carados Scotland, a wizard of great renown and a member the Council of Patrice, warned the Elven Lords of the coming of the Winter Dark. His master, Patrice of the Wood, possessed the gift of sight and saw the future of Erde. The elves debated long and hard upon what to do. In the end, heeding the Councils of Prince Lothian, they chose to leave the plane of Erde and return to Fay where their forefathers had come from many years ago. They could not understand the thoughts of mortal man, or their greed in land or conquest, and they wished to preserve themselves, for to them life is precious. They returned to Fay, to the ancient lands of Shindolay.

The Wood and Twilight Elves stayed behind as did some High Elves, for they loved the world of Erde most of all.

The true horror of Unklar's conquest unsettled many of the Elves as they watched it from the lands of Fay. They watched as Daladon Lothian, half-elven, cursed them with a vengeance. Too, they watched his brother Meltowg succumb to that curse and cast his life into the long fray. Many became distraught at the wars, the death and the destruction, and they called for the Princes to return them to Erde to aid the last King, Robert Luther, in his struggle against the horned god. But all to no avail.

As the debate grew bitter between the two halves, the folk of Shindolay were soon in open disagreement. Many, at last, under the leadership of Silithian "Moonbeam" turned on the Princes and the Queen. They armed themselves with magic spells, weapons and arcane knowledge and made as if to leave. The Queen's guard barred their passage, but Silithian drew his blade and slew a number of them. For the first time in the history of the Elven folk, Elf had slain Elf. But the rebellious Elves were undeterred and left the lands of Fay fully intending on going back to Erde to live or die by the sword.

Further tragedy and frustration greeted them. They found the portal to the world closed, for Unklar knew of them and others besides, for which reason he bound Erde in a ring of power. The Elves raged against the gates, but to no avail. They hurled themselves and their magic against them, but the gates would not yield. They knew that the blood of their kin lay upon their hands, so they could never return to Shindolay, though few, in truth desired it. Better to fight in limbo, they thought, than not fight at all. But they did not fight, rather they watched Unklar destroy the last resistance and damn the plain to a thousands years of law and evil.

So these immortals lived upon the gates for a thousand years. They called themselves the Fontenouq, that being, "the ones who are abandoned, or lost." They settled in limbo and built homes for themselves from what little magic they could glean from that horrible place. Their bitterness and rage increased. They blamed those in Shindolay for cursing them with cowardice. They hated the horned god and his minions. But most of all, they hated themselves for they sought honor in death and could not achieve even that. Hate consumed them.

But these Elves, the Fontenouq, made themselves ready for war. For a thousand years they made themselves ready.As is told elsewhere, the Elven sorcerer Melius fashioned a gate in the guise of the Prism of Alteration which opened portals to Erde, Shindolay and Fontenouq. He placed this gem in the Castle of Spires. When Daladon came to the Castle in the waning years of the Winter Dark Wars he found the garrison slaughtered, Melius dead and his own brother fallen upon the floor. It became obvious to him that Meltowg Lothian had made war upon these Elves, his kin, and slain them in order to open the gates. It took Daladon not a moment to finish the job his brother had begun and he opened the gates to Fay. As with Melius, he did not realize that a portal to Fontenouq lay in the Prism, but thought it only a gate to Shindolay. He set himself there, to watch any who might come through, so that he might slay them. In this manner he missed the passing of the Fontenouq back into the world.

When the gate opened before them, the Fontenouq rose in arms almost immediately. Silithian, tired and old, took the lead; his son Sathonos, born in the limbo, led the army. They passed into the world, mounted upon thin, long legged beasts of arcane origins. Their conical helms and long shields set them apart, as did their thin, light but sturdy spears and swords. They were a grim lot, men and women armed and accoutered for war.

The passing of the host shook the earth and all fled before them. They rode from beneath the eves of the Twilight Wood in lusting rage for war. They crossed over the straights of Ursal into the east and enjoined themselves in any battle they could. They fought at Iergaul upon the Luneberg, and even in the end at the very gates of Aufstrag upon the Toten Fields. The enemy fled from the terrible face of them, only the most hardy daring to stand against them. They brought ruin and devastation upon all the forces of the horned god who remained. Many of their folk died in these wild years, Silithian being one of them. He fell to the axe of a Morgl. But many more lived on.

When at last the wars ended, these folk found themselves strangers in a land that did not welcome them. Few knew anything of Elves and drove them out. Those who did remembered well the desertions in the face of the enemy so many years ago. So the Fontenouq traveled though the world of men, seeking redemption.

They eventually settled in the forested hills south of the Twilight Wood. The lands were little occupied by man, Dwarf, Orc or Ungern and made as good a home as any. There the Elves settled, mostly in family groups and built for themselves wondrous homes. They used the magic gleaned from the limbo, some say the very Language of Creation, to fashion substance from nothing. They surrounded themselves with books, art and music. They talked philosophy with each other, debating the sins of their history, and studied the world of magic, exploring boundaries few dared to cross.

In time of years these Princely Warlords became as removed from the world of men, even as they had been in the days of limbo. They closed their gates and settled back in their silks and ivory towers to nurture the comfort of their guilt. They could never shake this guilt, knowing as they did, that they quit the war too early, and that they joined the war too late. Eventually they removed themselves from each other. Each family remained in his own castle, coming out to visit only once in a great while.

Burasil the Elven God of War

Ec Rating
I & V

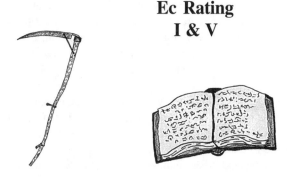

Gaxmoor, The Lost City.

Upon the ridges of the Massif stands the Lost City. There, no single lord claims rule, but rather, a host of mercenaries, bandits, and monsters vie for power within the crumbling walls of the once proud city.

Of the Nature of the City: The fasts of the Massif are littered with hidden valleys and dark caves. Iron and copper abound in its southern reaches, but especially valued is its silver and emeralds. In the north of the Massif are diamonds, the largest known the world over and many a battle is waged over these precious deposits. But there too are found irons and copper. The rock is difficult to work and only engineers of phenomenal ability and the giants know how to unmake and remake it. This is the selfsame rock that was transported north and used in the building of The Wall Ancient, or the Wall Ethrum.

Within the Massif are the gently sloping plains of Illithrumia. These are well fed grasslands, moist with all the flow from the Massif and very fertile. For the most part, the plains are open and clear with deep flowing bright green grasses offering fantastic vistas. Along the edge of the Massif are copses of Aspen and some towering dark green firs while within the plains proper are small beech and oak glades, lakes, ponds, rivers, streams, and swamps. Into this quiet setting of small villages and farmsteads the powers of Narrheit have thrust the ancient city of Gaxmoor.

Gaxmoor has only recently returned to Erde (*see below*). It lies ensconced along the rim of a great mesa, within an ancient river valley, upon the western slopes of the Massif. At first glance it seems a devastated city, but close investigation reveals a set of solid double walls surrounding the city, with inner walls towering over the outer. Beyond these lie towers, gates and buildings of an altogether alien style. The architecture is old, harking back to the days of the Aenochian Emperors.

The city is peopled by all manner of folk. Descendants of the original inhabitants, speaking pure Aenochian, struggle to survive against the invading armies of Narrheit. Only a few now hold out against the tyranny of that evil god. The Shapely Siren Brothel is one such place, its marble walls having long held at bay the raving hordes. There, a score of humans under Sheila the Madam struggle on. A band of Sobekki, under their leader Hsithra, have taken up residence under the great canal which traverses the city. Others beyond these struggle to survive as well.

In truth, the very armies which they fight against, and the hosts of mercenaries they employ, war with each other as much as they do the Aenochians. The whole city is rife with intrigue and war. The Orcs of the Red Axe clan dominates much of the city, but Hobgoblins, gargoyles and other creatures haunt the now crumbling ruins and largely deserted streets of the once greatest of all cities.

Gaxmoor's secrets are in the hands of diabolical beings and the assorted vermin they brought with them. Finding no one common foe to battle, the assorted leader's selfish desires and the splits within the mercenary groups caused their armies to feud amongst themselves. Even so, the bands of humanoids and evil creatures that now plague the area are causing great harm to the lands of Cleves and the peoples who dwell upon the banks of Lake Orion. The Count of Cleves, Eurich Gunshoff IV, has put out a general call for help. With the pressures threatening those proud folk, particularly the squabbles with Angouleme, the pleas for assistance must now be taken up by brave and bold adventurers of all classes. This is especially necessary due to the decimated Border Companies and the state of losses amongst the troops throughout the country. Much treasure lies hidden within the ruined city, and the lost knowledge of Urnus Gregaria may be able to help offset the rising power of Narrheit in the lands of the Ethrum.

Groups of Note.

Bone Crusher Clan (Vegg): This clan of Hobgoblins is under new leadership since the attack on Gaxmoor. The old chief was killed in the assault. Vegg, his second in command, is now the chief. Vegg dresses in colorful scarves and pilfered finery. He is more interested in celebrating his new status than anything else. He is a hedonist in the extreme and pays little attention to organizing the clan. He spends most of his time in the harem or drinking ale. The Bone Crusher clan will react more slowly to attacks and have relatively low morale when faced with a determined foe.

Gnolls (Harrg and Clasch): The gnolls are spilt into two main groups. The body guard of Harecules and Harrg's Band. The larger group is in the palace with Harecules. They are his shock troops and resent their lowly position. But they obey Harecules nonetheless for fear of him. The other group is lead by Harrg and Clasch. Harrg is an experienced warrior and good leader. His band suffered heavy losses in the attack from the Governor's wizard.

Harecules: Harecules is a trusted servant of Naarheit. His mother is the deamoness, Tracassa and his father is the Ogre Magi, Saburo Sato. He was the original commander of the humanoid armies which attacked Gasmoor. He quickly lost control of his cohorts when he began searching for the Staff of Urnus Gregaria. He still commands a sizable army in the Citadel, accompanied everywhere by his two demons and Ettin.

Red Axe Clan: This is a veteran war band from the Red Axe Tribe. Their leader is a crafty warrior named Grond . He runs his war band like a well-disciplined military unit. They actively patrol their area and keep guard at all times. They react to an attack quickly and use their resources wisely. The Shaman will focus spells on the strongest fighter and use his wand to keep enemy wizards busy. Grond is in the city to get treasure and fame so that he can go back and challenge the Tribe leader. He is not opposed to working with the PCs to obtain his goals. If they were to happen to die in the process though he wouldn't be too upset.

Tracassa the Daemoness: Tracassa is the mother of Harecules and one time consort of Saburo Sato. She seeks to gain the Staff of Urnus Gregaria.

Cities From the Past: The magnificence of the Empire is marked well in the annals of that land. During the early days of man, as the Aenochian Empire expanded, many of this sort of walled city dotted her frontier, and the wealth of Erde flowed into imperial coffers. Some Emperors ruled with a genuine concern for the welfare of their subjects, some ruled with malice in forethought, some with indifference. But so great the wealth of the Aenochian Empire in those early days that the Emperors could squander it. They built magnificent cities and fortresses, and roads crisscrossed the land, walled towns and castles marking their lengths.

In general there was peace. The Empire waged sporadic wars with the tribes of Orcs and beast like Hobgoblins, and fought an occasional rebellion, but overall the Emperor's rule went unchallenged. And as the Aenochians conquered the lands of Ethrum they constructed great fortress cities to both guard their caravans and pacify the conquered peoples.

Gaxmoor was such a city. Lying upon the frontiers of the Empire, north of Kayomar, the fortress city dominated the western approaches to the Empire. The city rapidly became a haven for travelers crossing from the Empire into the wilds. It served as the home of the followers of the deity Urnus Gregaria (*reference Divine Orders, p. 63*), and as such it received many of that deity's special blessings. Not known as a god who worried or greatly cared about large standing structures or huge temples dedicated to his worship, Urnus Gregaria loved the city for its hospitality and games. Thus rest and diversion were offered to weary travelers before they continued their search of exotic goods and treasures.

After three centuries of rule, the Empire of Aenoch came to an end. Nomads from the distant west settled upon the frontiers. These fierce tribes hounded the borders with constant war. Worse ravagers came from the north as men in long ships, filled with a rage of violence and a lust for plunder, began pillaging the lands. These Northmen were ever after a plague for the twin peoples, even into and beyond the rule of the Winter's Dark. The Emperor expended great amounts of wealth to combat these foes and in so doing, stripped his lands of troops. The people of Ethrum rose in revolt, casting off the shackles of the Emperor's rule. Before the Emperor could muster the strength to combat them, his own nobles rose against him.

The Wars of Liberation caused much devastation on both sides of the straights. Imperial armies marched to and fro attempting to crush the rebellious subjects, and mercenary troops looted and plundered towns and villages. The land burned and her people were despoiled.

At the height of the war, the Tarvish leaders of the Ethrumanians laid siege to the great fortress city of Avignon. For many long months they starved the city, but when this proved fruitless, their commanders led bloody assault upon the walls, eventually breaching them and bringing the city down in flames. Much destruction then fell upon the folk of Avignon. Hostages were taken from the wealthy, soldiers looted, and a great host of lords and ladies were done to death for serving the Emperor in far off Al-Liosh.

Eventually, the alliances of the many enemies, dissension of her conquered subjects, and a final conflict with the Tarvish Emperors weakened the once-mighty empire and resulted in the destruction of both. Barbarism spread, and the stone of the old border cities became quarries for the small villages that sprung up from the remnants of the former metropolises. The lack of any safe communication with the East spelled the doom for the remaining border outposts of the vanquished empires.

As fire, sword and ultimately magic overtook the rest of the Aenochian Empire, the mighty patron of Gaxmoor decided that his city must be saved. He accomplished this by removing Gaxmoor from its position in Erde, casting it into a pocket universe where time ran slow. There it was to remain until such time as Gregaria's priests felt it safe to recall Gaxmoor to Erde.

Ages came and went, kingdoms rose and fell, yet Gaxmoor remained oblivious. In time of years, as is told in the Histories, Unklar conquered the world and the long days of Winter's Dark settled upon Erde. Even so, Gaxmoor hung in the world between worlds, between the sands of time. But when Unklar fell in the Winter Dark Wars, the world, born anew, came under the guiding hands of other powers, some far more sinister than the horned god.

The powers of Chaos, though, took a stronger hold on the world than the Lord of Traveling expected, and over the centuries the methods of recalling the city fell into the hands of the followers of the selfish and malign Narrheit (*reference Divine Orders, p. 58*), an entity of darkest Evil. It was thus Narrheit's adherents that returned Gaxmoor to Erde, for the foul purposes of their master.

It was servants of this demonic entity who brought the city back in an untimely manner. The Ogre Magi Saburo Sato, wove a great spell of Naarheit's keeping and knocked the staff from the diorama, bringing the city hurtling back to Erde. There, his son, Harecules the Cambion, accompanied by his mother, Tracassa, had gathered a great army of humanoids and mercenaries to take the ancient town, in hopes of loot and magic and most of all, the magical Staff of Urnus Gregaria.

When Gaxmoor returned, surprise took all the parties concerned. As the hordes of humanoids and assorted villainous mercenaries of the dreaded Lord of Chaos fell upon the city, they discovered it was no burgeoning treasure house. Instead they discovered that it was already in disrepair and only sparsely occupied, its citizens were falling into barbarism. After some considerable slaughter, the place was "pacified" and became a haven again, this time for Evil!

Ec Rating I

elderland

Here there are no Kings or Princes. No man rules that does not carry a sword. No one man rules that cannot defend himself and his land. The standards that are recognizable are those of the Orcs. The Ulgars have blood washed shields with chains upon the surface. The Othines disdain the use of shields, mounting totems upon poles. They have a saying in the Gelderland, a greeting of sorts. "Are you equal to it?" one will say. "Slowly. Slowly." is the response.*

On the Nature of that Blasted Plain: The Gelderland is a fierce country of broken hills, where rocky outcrops covered in sparse trees overlook deep gulches. One is easily lost in the steep, winding valleys. Thick bramble and forest grow in these refreshingly cool 'downs' as the locals refer to them. There is an abundance of water as well, the melting snows of the Winter Dark having left many pools, ponds and small streams. But often these streams run to muck filled bogs and peat swamps. There, strange creatures are known to dwell. One hill top looks much the same as the next and only the most skilled of Rangers know the land well.

The Gelderland attracts all manner of adventurer. In the years before the Winter Dark the land served the Emperor Kings of Ethrum, and the ruins of those people dot the country side. Rumors of fabulous wealth, buried in deep dungeons and forgotten tombs abound. The Ethrumanians built huge cathedrals, decorating their interiors with gold and silver. The lucky hunter can still find such ruins and earn renown and wealth for himself as he may desire. Though many eldritch creatures, who lived out the Winter Dark in these deep ruins, dwell there still. The Gelderland is a hard land of high adventure and many who enter its borders are lost therein.

The country is sparsely populated and most of those people who do dwell in the Gelderland do so on the coast. Here, the greatest towns are owned by the Tageans, chief of which is the walled berg Icanthos. They vie for control of the sea lanes with the Kingdoms of Maine and Eloria. The Tageans govern the towns loosely, taking full advantage of the independent nature of the settlers in their ongoing maritime struggle with Maine. Icanthos is, consequently, a rough town with several powerful thieve's guilds and a small click of Crna Ruk (*reference Guilds and Orders, p. 196*). Followers of the Paths of Umbra live in Icanthos as well, seeking refuge from the witch hunts further north. The streets are paved, though sometimes in timber carted in from the hinterlands, and the houses tend to be two story affairs with high conical roofs. A great deal of coal is burnt for fuel, imported by ship from Norgorod-Kam, and the city is forever stained in black soot.

Other towns lie upon the coast, most notable of which is Taggenbrun, where the local lords sponsor arena combat in the Cleaver pits. These violent battles are always fought to the death and attract all manner of ruffian.

A few hardy folk have settled in the hinterlands, carving homes for themselves from the rock of the hills. These small villages are always wild, have little contact with the outside world and are peopled by stout folk. They traffic with the Halfling Gypsies, trading iron and wood for finished product.

The Gelderland Halflings are numerous as those folk are counted and are particularly warlike. Their wagons are large affairs, small fortresses really, and are always pulled by some beast of heavy burden. The Halflings speak a cant few can understand and are as quick to kill and rob a traveler as offer him food and drink. As with all those people they carry the bitterness of being hunted for sport in the Age of Winter Dark deep in their minds and forever seek to destroy all vestiges of the horned god's rule. They are battle hardened, competent fighters and dangerous enemies. They pay heed to no gods but their own and Narrheit, calling upon that dread lord of chaos for aid against the perfidy of fools. Once upon an occasion the various families gather to discuss the affairs of trade, the orcs and to swap brides and grooms. Borin, a warrior of fierce pride, commands respect in the whole of the Gelderland. And the female Waldrada is unsurpassed in the whole country in the use of the iron shod mace. The Halflings are possessed of wealth in salt, sheep and peat, all of which are gathered from unknown sources in the hinterland.

Of particular note to the region are the Orcs. In the Gelderland there exist some dozen smaller tribes and two very large ones, the Ulgars and Othines.

The smaller tribes are all nomadic, moving where they can get the most plunder. They are fierce in combat, always fighting in orderly bands. They bare the remnants of the weaponry of the Legions (*see below*), heavy cuirasses, long shields, thick swords and spears. They wield composite bows with deadly accuracy. All in all, they are a fierce people.

Of All the Tribes the Greatest Are the Ulgars: These Orcs dwell in wood and dirt forts in the rugged back country bordering Fontenouq. The Anjak (Orc title for Commander) of the tribe is the huge Orc, Unk Oakbone. Their capitol they have named Orgstall, a bastardization of Aufstrag, placing it deep in the Gelderland, high upon a hill. The reddish glow of Orgstall's fire pits can be seen upon clear nights for miles around. During the day a pallid cloud of smoke always hangs over the dreaded place. A large wooden complex in the valley below the fortress serves the Orcs as a temple to Unklar. Their shamans never mastered the Paths of Umbra and for this reason they have brought many humans to their kingdom. These men lead them in the worship of the horned god. As with many of their ilk, the wizard priests search the arcane worlds for a spell powerful enough to bring back their beloved lord.

The Ulgar territory stretches from Maine to the very doorsteps of the Elven principalities. These Orcs traffic in slaves and stolen booty from Maine, carrying them to the coasts to sell in the slave pits of Icanthos. An Elven slave is an almost priceless commodity, but nearly impossible to get, for the Orcs are well aware that whenever one of their number attacks the Elves that those folk, normally so scattered and self involved, gather in a great concourse and come down on the orcs with a vengeance. Equally dangerous and almost as valuable are attacks on the Halfling wagons.

The Orcs content themselves with raids into the west and the north. It is not uncommon to see the Ulgar Chain-Shield upon adventuring Orcs all over the western world. They speak the Vulgate well and communicate with many men and Dwarves. It is not unknown for these folk to leave the tribe entirely and try their hands at other ventures both economic and warlike.

In war, Unk can call thousands of well armed and accoutered Orcs from their scattered strongholds, though he has not done this for many a year.

Almost as Great Are the Othines: The Totem Orcs. Led by their dual Chieftains, Mordun and Grauschvoll, the Othines control the central valleys of the Gelderlands. Much as their cousins the Ulgars, the Othines live in wood and stone forts, though these are generally built deep in the valleys. They are well known for eating flesh raw, so that travelers are never warned by cook fires or smoke of an Othine encampment, but stumble upon them to their dread and demise.

The Totem Orcs are religious creatures and very superstitious. They believe, as the shamans have taught them, that Unklar still resides in Aufstrag and the world of men and Elf is nothing but an elaborate illusion cast by their dread master to test them. For this reason they are most fearless in battle, fearing the rage of their god more than death upon the field. Any who defy the word or image of Unklar, in thought or deed, is brutally killed.

These Orcs traffic in mostly foodstuffs, furs and what metals they can cut from the surface of their rocky world. Much like their cousins in the north, the Orthine are skilled bowyer/fletchers and their arrows are some of the finest made in the world. They trade these goods for finished armor and weapons from the Halflings, who they see as immune to the illusions of Unklar for they live much as they had a hundred years ago.

Despite its relative proximity to the sea borne trade routes, the Gelderland continues to languish as a backwater amidst the Young Kingdoms. Its people are poor, living near subsistence level. It is a place where slavery is rife. The large fishing fleet is nearly defunct. Much internal wealth is derived from mercenary bands that ply their skills to Kings and Princes. The crafty trader can come away with abundant supplies of peat, sheep and salt, all commodities which the Halflings possess. The Gelderland's wealth is almost purely in lost plunder of forgotten ages.

There is Little of a Coherent History: In days of old three powerful Dukes and an unknown number of Barons and lesser lords ruled the region, paying homage to the Emperor Kings of Ethrum. During the Imperial Wars, the Aenochians invaded the Gelderland and despoiled much of its wealth. The region barely had time to recover during the Age of Heroes when Unklar's minions despoiled it again, burning many of its fortress and towns to ash. Here the first battles of the Catalyst Wars took place and some of St. Luther's kin, his brother most notably, perished. Prince Morgeld, St. Luther's

bastard son, plundered the land as well. The wealth of magic and gold lost in the deep is untold, but many surmise it to be surpassed only by the spoils of Aufstrag herself.

With the rise of Unklar, the trade routes shifted north to Angouleme and what remained of the region's prosperity declined rapidly. It became a refuge for criminals and those who sought to escape the horror of Unklar's rule. Orc tribes settled in the land, the Ulgars and Othines being the most notable. Many a young Orc found service in the legions of the horned god and returned to their homes, after many years of service, as battle hardened veterans. In a world ruled by law, however, the Gelderland remained lawless.

During the Winter Dark wars, many refugees fled from disastrous campaigns in Kayomar. Aziz led his 4000 men into the wilds of the Gelderland and many Orcs and Ungern followed suit. It is said of Aziz that he died soon after he arrived in the Gelderland. His troop took up residence in the ruins of an abandoned town, where they stayed for a few weeks. Their activities unearthed some horrid creatures of the undead and all but a few of these proud horsemen died. Those who lived fled to the north, but few would ever speak of what horror beneath had been unearthed. Aziz, hounded from the world by the Knights of the Flame, was at last lost to the world.

After the Winter Dark Wars, Kayomar, exhausted from nineteen years of almost continual war, failed to muster the strength to reclaim their ancient heritage. Those Kings became embroiled in sporadic warfare to their north and south and left the Gelderland to its fate.

*This is actually an Albanian proverb.

Ec Rating
I

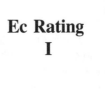

ottland-Ne, "the land without gods"

In the far north upon a hill of slag Lord Varucks, sits upon "the Elephants Back" in Castle Nacht. He rules a land of troll, foul beast and orc. There is no standard here, for he bares none, only totems and poles displaying their grisly conquest.

Of the Lands of the Trolls: The Gottland is a broken land of stark hills with little vegetation. To the north and west it borders the Shadow Mountains, in the east the Inner Sea and the south the Ington River (or Deep Flow in the Vulgate). It is best known for the bitterly cold winds which blow off the mountains and through the Kleberock Pass. The wind is forever whistling as it coils through the clefts and rocks, mimicking the sounds of the dead. This horrible whistling has given birth to the legends of the walking dead, where those who suffered from the depredations of the Wizard Mongroul Nulak and the Troll Lords are forced to wander the land as the damned. Strange solitary trees dot the countryside, almost always dead, with scant branches and no leaves. Despite this they remain firmly rooted to the ground (*see below for the nature of the Gottland Trees*). The Gottland is a forsaken land where little grows, but monsters abound.

Travel in the Gottland is difficult for there are no roads for wagons or beasts, but rather broken trails winding through the twisted rock, scrubb brush and broken country. The Trolls from Nacht hound travelers as do various Orc and Hobgoblin bandits. It is as inhospitable a place as the world has ever known.

Though the Troll Lord Varucks rules from the "Elephants Back" and lays claim to the whole country he has direct control of little beyond Castle Nacht and the valleys to the south. Even the Kleberock Pass is a wild place. This huge Troll (*reference Monsters of Erde, p. 242*) is slow to act, but clever. He uses the threats of pretended power to cajole the unwary into doing his bidding. He wields two large hammers in combat, calling them by their names, Var and Ucks. Varucks commands a powerful but small troop of trolls in battle. When needed, he forces local tribes to give warriors and material to raise a sizable, if disorganized, army of orcs and hobgoblins.

But even these foul folk need goods, and at times, the very brave or desperate bring caravans into the region. Recently, the Hanse Cities have established trading posts along the coasts in their growing trade with the Hobgoblin King of Burnevitse. This has led to some pitched battles with the inhabitants of the Gottland as the humans and southern Hobgoblins strive to defend their growing trade and the northern Humanoids seek to plunder it.

This trade has brought to the country even more disreputable characters. The owners of the trading posts exercize little control over the inhabitants, letting them do as they please so long as the ships sail on time. This, of course, has attracted hosts of would be adventurers, thieves, bandits, ruffians, explorers and any other breed of man which seek to leave the perfumed comforts of civilization behind them. The towns are rough affairs where only the strongest survive.

Within the interior the scattered humanoid tribes are mostly migratory. They feed off of livestock, cattle mostly, and a tough breed of sheep. They are forced to move from one place after the next, for the grazing is sparse. These groups tend to be small and possessed of little wealth. Their greatest sport are the Cleaver Pits. Once in awhile, the smaller bands gather together, dig pits here and there and throw in contestants which fight to the death. These are not unlike the Cleaver Pits in the Gelderland far to the south. In times of turmoil these Orcs and Hobgoblins turn to the Troll Lords in castle Nacht for protection, for the memory of the wizard lingers in the hearts and minds of these people.

In the far west country, upon the slopes of the Shadow Mountains and around the headwaters of the Ington River, the Olgrack Orcs rule from their fortress of Rackenburg. Their Chief is a thin, wiry Orc by the name of Uranoch Scatterskull. His name derives from the split in his skull which is ever visible and forever dribbling puss and blood. Uranoch is very intelligent and rules his Orcs by threatening, pleading and cajoling them. They resist the Troll Lords whenever possible.

In this thankless place on the edge of the world nothing is produced other than terror and slavery. The creatures there are self sufficient, depending on fishing and farming. The Orcs mine gold from the Mountains and have recently begun carting it to the coast for trade of arms. The one thing that brings the wary merchant are the flowers found around the roots of the "Gottland Trees." They are reputed to have great healing powers and to be the source of the troll's regenerative powers.

The Trees of the Gottland: Lonely things, these dead husks stand with feet firmly rooted to the ground. Folks say that these are none other than the souls of dead Trolls. As is common knowledge, Trolls do not die like mortals, but live on until their life's evil deeds weigh them down, planting them to the ground. The most ancient of Trolls, though they speak, cannot move for the weight of their own evil deeds. Many argue that trolls are in fact the spirits of evil tress that walked the world in the Days before Days. The Trolls, the tales relate, are really the manifestations of the souls of those evil trees and when a Troll dies, the twisted tree's souls rise to feed upon the corpse, to grow again into the trees of yesteryear. Around the base of the "Gottland Trees" grow small patches of violet flowers, and when pulped into a mush and used as a salve they can heal minor wounds (1d4).

Upon Those Hills, even Trolls Feared to Tread: Early in the age of Winter's Dark, Nulak-Kiz-Din, called Mongroul and The Troll Lord, established his great spired tower, Graugusse, in the Moravan Plains. These plains lay beyond the Shadow Mountains and were, as they still are today, accessible by crossing an overland trail which led into the heart of his domain, the Kleberock, a pass of broken country. In those days, when Unklar slept much, his minions warred one with the other, so much so that they built towers and walls against each other. So Mongroul built a wall to guard his own tower. He summoned a great Troll Lord, Hasryck, to his side and bid him to gather a host of his fellows to encamp upon the southern end of the Kleberock and block egress to the Moravan Plains beyond.

Mongroul's voice, laced with spells, captured the mind of Hasryck and that troll set about doing the wizard's bidding. He took mounds of gold into the Shadow mountains to bribe others from their holes and come to the Kleberock. The trolls who gathered there served the gold of Hasryck if they did not serve the Troll himself. Hasryck chastised the gathered Trolls from on high, castigating them, calling them mules and the like trying to force them into building a castle upon the footsteps of the pass. Trolls abhor work of any kind, and they refused, but instead convinced Hasryck to gather slaves for the labor. They entreated him to lead them to the stone giant halls where they could "bind those fools as slaves." Hasryck smiled, for this was his intent all the while.

The Trolls gathered themselves for war, entering the mountains beneath clouds of snow. They came upon the giants in one of their many caverns. Hasryck bid them to quit the dark recesses of their holes, "Come with us dear giants, bind yourselves to us and serve the Trolls of the Kleberock. If you do this you will know only happiness and contentment, for we shall allow you to build halls of stone for us." Unmoved at this speech, the giants laughed at the Trolls and threw rocks at them. The war which ensued shook the mountain to its core. The giants hurled boulders the size of houses onto the heads of the Trolls. The Trolls in turn, threw spears and axes at the giants. Many giants fell to horrible wounds, but too, the Trolls could not stand against the rocks from above.

In the end a great wolf came upon the field and bid Hasryck to cease his attacks on the cave entrance and wait for the giants to come forth. The wolf, of course, was Mongroul and in this guise he stole into the cave. Once the dread wizard entrenched himself there he summoned arcane magic and unleashed them upon the giants. They fled from him, for those giants bore superstition like a shield, tumbling out of the cave in wild abandon. The Trolls pounced upon them, bound them in chains, hauling them soon thereafter down the mountain and into slavery.

Hasyrick ordered the giants to build a castle for the Trolls. They set about this task reluctantly. But they gathered slabs of rock and piled them on high, shaping them at the Troll Lord's direction. It took them many years, but in time a fortress of jagged rock took shape at the very mouth of the Kleberock. They called it the fortress of Nacht. There, Hasryck ensconced himself, declaring himself "Keeper of the Graugusse," a title seldom heard in these days, but one still dear to the Trolls. Other Orcs and Hobgoblins settled in the surrounding country, building villages and squalid moats and bailey castles. The Gottland, "the land without gods," served as the gateway to this realm and reflected the evil of its dark master.

So Hasyrick ruled the Kleberock for many hundreds of years until he fell in battle with a Mammoth of such proportions that a single tread could break boulders to dust. From the northern glaciers it wandered into the fields south of the castle. Hasryck made to attack the beast, for such a trophy could not be passed over. The fatal contest did not last long. The beast trampled Hasryick, gored him with its great tusk, and finally tore the unfortunate Troll asunder. The beast Hasryck's guard killed, though not before many more Troll kin fell, and its corpse they hauled back to the slag castle.

There, another Troll Lord rose in Hasyrick's place. Rodzek by name, he took the corpse of the mammoth to the great hall, where he ordered all to feast upon it. He then took the bones and built a monstrous chair, upon which, he declared, "All Trolls who rule the Kleberock must sit here, upon the elephant's back." The Trolls rejoiced by drinking great quantities of beer. Rodzek ruled in the Kleberock until the Winter Dark Wars.

None dared assail the Trolls or their fortress of Nacht until Mongroul's tower fell in ruin. When the lords of the west gave battle to Malikor the dragon upon the heights of Thangondrim Mountain, it ended in disaster for the Arch-magi. As is written "So great was the Dragon's fall that Thangondrim broke asunder and that most ancient of mountains cast down. The quake drowned a host of Mongroul's Trolls in rock and slag and ended their days forever. A great shuttering went through the world and the hosts of Darkness were everywhere dismayed and hid themselves for a time." (*reference Moravain Plains, p. 112*) By these acts and others, the power of the mage passed from the north and the Trolls of the Kleberock found themselves without guidance.

A hero born of Gnome blood came to castle Nacht soon after the Winter Dark Wars concluded. Olaf Tryggvason sought to treat the Troll Lord with death for crimes against his own clan years in the past. By stealth he avoided the guards, coming to Rodzek's hall by secret ways. He called out to the Troll, bidding him come down from the "Elephant's Back" and give him justice. "But you are not but a little thing, Gnome. How can I give you any justice." Olaf swore at him to come down, "You will give me justice or I'll pay the passage!" Olaf smote the troll a blow on the foot which roused him to anger. But even before Rodzek could lift his great bulk from the chair, Olaf struck him again with his hammer, cracking the bones in his knee. Rodzek toppled to the ground where Olaf Tryggvason slew him with repeated blows of his mighty hammer.

The Trolls of Nacht scattered at the death of their lord and for many years the place remained a wild, dangerous country and it stood abandoned by folk. Only recently has some order returned. The Troll Lord Varucks, harking back to his younger years when he served Hasyrick, has reentered castle Nacht and conquered much of the region from the Kleberock pass to the Ington River, (called "Deep Flow" in the Vulgate) in the south. He bound Trolls, Orcs and Hobgoblins to him and so they rule in the Gottland, creatures of ill intent and dangerous evil.

Ec Rating I

Varucks Rules
From the Elephant's Back

Grundliche Hohle

In the undermountain Kingdom, with the Hammer of Fundin in hand, the Dwarven King Angrod II rules an ancient people and ancient realm.

Of the Dwarf King and His Halls of Stone: Grundliche Hohle lies within the deeps of Mount Orn. The Mountain itself towers 14000 feet high. It stands out of the Grundliche Range in both height and girth, from the thin precipice of its peak to the jumbled boulders at its base. The country surrounding Mount Orn is nearly impassable. High ridges, steep cliffs, deep crevices, fields of boulders and so on block any pathways trough the mountains. Access to the mountain kingdom is gained via a pass that leads into a broad valley. Towering at one end of the valley is the Great Mountain and the massive entry doors to the Kingdom. These gargantuan stone doors have never been breached by any force, save Unklar. A village of Gnomes and Halflings, Trelleborg, lies near the pass upon the eastern slopes of the escarpment.

Grundliche Hohle dominates the southern Grundliche Mountains. The wide valley which leads to the mountain kingdom is populated by Gnomes, Halflings, Dwarves, and humans. Trelleborg's houses and streets climb up the slopes of the valley wall. There, stairs, wooden and stone, ramble in a haphazard fashion from one spot to the next. The buildings are mostly of wood imported from the south and roofed with slate shingles. This last product the Gnomes are particularly skilled in fashioning, and they export the commodity as far south as Outremere. Trelleborg is always bustling with activity. The Gnomes manage the caravans that carry goods over the mountains. They frequently employ dour faced Halflings to guide them. Trelleborg is famous for its taverns, of which there are over thirty. The town itself is home to about 2000 people, but many more swell its hotels, halfway houses and inns during the trade season.

Angrod King, II, is a young beardling, born during the battle of the Dens. He only recently reached maturity. Angrod is stout, thin for one of his kind, with a full blue tinted beard. He is rarely seen without the Hammer Fundin, the sacred artifact of Kings. His mother, Thorva, who ran the Kingdom for many years (*see below*), stands by his side in council and court. He defers to her often, but rarely in public. Despite this, Angrod is beginning to "get the taste of iron," as the Dwarves are want to say, longing for the glory days of the past.

This energy displayed by the young King has stirred up the Dwarves of the Hohle. The taverns, inns, and market squares are filled with gossip about impending campaigns. Despite this, business goes on as usual in the Hohle. Gnome wagons, pulled by large oxen, ramble through the iron gates, down or up ramps carting goods to various markets throughout the Kingdom. Travelers come and go, bearing goods and news from the southern lands. The best beer in all of the Young Kingdoms originates in Grundliche Hohle and this alone draws people from far and wide.

Grundliche Hohle thrives on trade with the west, particularly with Augsburg, trading armaments for food and wood. Wagons lumber into the valley, their contents auctioned to the highest bidder, and then hauled into the Mountain. In turn, the Dwarves take orders for special made armor or weaponry, which is given to smiths in the deeps. They fashion black powder canon and muskets in the deeps, but only a few of the smiths have mastered this, and they are expensive beyond any common man's means. They also mine silver and other ores.

Recently a delegation from the Punj arrived with letters of introduction for Angrod. They seek to open trade with the Dwarves, but the memory of past battles is recent for the Dwarves and no answers have been given.

All of this awards Grundliche Hohle a wide cultural diversity and makes the realm a lively place. Many come here to winter, for it is generally safe in the valley and the folk are friendly. But even beyond that, the mountains to the north and the Flintlock to the south are filled with riches and adventure. This attracts small armies of adventurers who settle in Trelleborg or the Hohle itself (for even there there are inns with rooms specifically designed for men), using the valley as a base for their operations. Too, many come in hopes of glory and service to one of the elder lines of Erde.

Despite Angrod's youth, the Kingdom's voice is powerful in the councils of men. Thorva's word alone carries great weight in the politics of her world.

A Past Buried in the Mountain Roots: As other Dwarven Holds fell in the Goblin Wars or were lost in time, those of Grundliche Hohle, or Deep Halls in the tongues of men, delved ever deeper. Ruled by the kin of old King Fund, they plundered the deep places of the earth for their forges and made mighty things of great renown. Human Kingdoms came and went, yet the Dwarves took little heed. But in time the folk of Fund fell in number, and Angrod and his people took the mantle of Grundliche Hohle. When the Unklar came, King Angrod's offspring, old now and bitter, closed his halls and buried them deep under mountain and stone. The people under the mountain fell and declined. But at the last the Dark One came and unearthed them and made great war upon them. He unmade the doors and opened the deeps and slew the whole of Angrod's kin but a few.

The Dwarves were fierce yet and hearty, and though they fled into the surrounding mountains, they swore vengeance and eternal hatred to all of the Dark One's Folk. Here in the high wastes was Dolgan born and raised by his father Hirn, a distant child of King Fund's second son who too was named Fund. Dolgan took to the forge before he could walk, and as a child his skill surpassed all. The Wise Ones took notice and spoke of the prophecy of his birth and doom, that he must be the Forge of the Sword and in time remake the Halls of Grundliche Hohle.

Rumor of this came to the Dark and ever fearful he plotted to take the yearling Dwarf, to bend him to his ill purpose or slay him outright. By guile and sorcery, Dolgan, a child still by Dwarf reckoning, was taken to the grim holes beneath The Dark One's Halls and lost.

So by evil ways Dolgan, son of Hirn, with some few companions and friends of his youth were stolen from the terrible heights of the Grundliche Mountains. His brother, Margnan, younger by some few years, was with him and left the bright light of hills for the dark ways of the Underworld. Goblins and Orcs most foul carried them to the pits of Aufstrag, that fell city which Dolgan later called Mithgefuhl, which is the Land of Pity in the ancient Dwarf.

In time the Dwarf came before Unklar and the horned god knew him for what he was. He tried to force the Dwarf into servitude, but the son of Hirn would not yield. His blood came from the Language of Creation, and more, he was a Dwarf. This act of defiance earned him a name amongst many in the pits of Aufstrag. They called him Dolgan Furchtlos, which is the "undaunted." But Unklar named him differently, calling him Dolgan Ungekront, the "uncrowned." Unklar bound him to Klarglich then and bid him do what he would so long as he fashioned weapons of war for the dark lords.

There he worked at the dark forge, Klarglich, and fashioned all manner of war machine. And so it was for years without count that Dolgan worked as a slave to the forge. But too, as the tales recount, the forge was his great love, for his hands and heart were made to the craft, and only his mind bent towards war and revenge. So he worked and grew in skill, and in time of years far surpassing all those of reckoning he was made Master of armaments and the fashioning of fortifications of Aufstrag. He came to know every hole and fissure of those caverns. He aided in the construction of Aufstrag, and stood by the bellows fanning Unklar's fire of hatred which gave birth to the Mogrl. Too, he fashioned the Krummelvole a wonder for all the world (*reference Magic Items, p. 226*).

In time of years, Dolgan sought to throw off the yoke of Unklar and for this he gathered a host of slaves, Dwarves, Goblins and men and led them in a revolt in the very pits where they served. Many tales abound about why Dolgan took up arms against his dark master. It is known that he had befriended an Eldritch Goblin, Agmaur, the very one who had sacked the Dwarven Kingdom of Grausumhart 3000 years before. And many believe that the two together rose in rebellion. Some others relate that Dolgan could not bare the stealing of the Krummelvole by Unklar and he therefore threw off his shackles. But the truth of it bore the likeness of no other tale. Dolgan saw the Unicorn (*reference Aachen, p. 66*). Such a beautiful beast came into his chambers and was brought to him for his use. The beast hardly passed for living and Dolgan, seeing its wonder and beauty, took pity on it. When it died, it gave Dolgan the right of its body and he used the horn and blood of the creature to fashion an ax to rival all others. This fell weapon he named Havoc, that is, "revenge."

In 1012md, he dreamed of St. Luther, and he made war on the Dark, raising the slaves of the pit in rebellion. He and Agmaur gathered Goblins and Dwarves, men and Orcs, and fought the troops of Unklar in the bowels of the earth. Untold was the suffering of the Trench Wars. The wicked battles were fought in dark holes, down darker corridors against an implacable enemy. Knives and hatchets ruled the day, while primitive powder weapons left tunnels filled with mutilated corpses, smoke and ash. At last in the 1018th year of

Unklar's reign, the Dwarves and other slaves broke free and fought their way to the mountains in the north. They bore the scars of that place ever after.

Dolgan joined the Council of Light soon thereafter, striking up a friendship with Albrecht of Augsberg. With their aid they cleared the deeps of Grundliche Hohle of Unklar's filth. Once done, Dolgan sent out messengers to gather his scattered folk.

In the early spring of 1022md, Grundliche Hohle reopened and the Dwarf Lord Dolgan crowned as its King. He declared all the Grundliche Mountains clear of the filth of Unklar and made war on the black tree of Aufstrag. And the Lord of the Marsh, Coburg, Unklar's chief lieutenant in the lands of Aenoch led 50,000 men, orcs and giants against the Dwarf Lord whose folk numbered in the ten's of hundreds only. As is known, only one road leads into the high mountains where the Dwarf Kingdom lies. The road, known as the Stone Way, was easily fortified by the Dwarves and called Havok, which they held against the enemy for many months.

In this they were aided by Albrecht Commander of two legions of Unklar's men. He bargained with the Council and the Dwarves. If he held his forces back, they would support his future claims to a Kingdom. In truth, Albrecht tired of Unklar's rule, descended from an ancient line of Aenochian nobility and he leapt at the opportunity to overthrow the horned god's rule. Due to Albrecht's constant delays, the full siege of Havok did not commence until 1026md. Even then Albrecht quit the field taking the better part of his men with him (*reference Augsberg, p. 74*).

Feodor Paskevitch, who commanded the other legions, cursed Albrecht, and moved his great army into the Flintlock and threw them against the castle. But in the space of years provided by Albrecht, the Dwarves had gathered in great strength. They came from the mountains and hills, singly or in small groups, answering Dolgan King's call to arms. So Paskevitch faced an army of thousands instead of the hundreds he expected. The battle lasted for many months, but Paskevitch could not break the walls. At years end, his food stores exhausted, he ordered the legions to withdraw.

The Dwarves launched a massive attack against the withdrawing troops. Panic spread and the enemy ranks began breaking apart. The Dwarves utterly routed Paskevitch's men. Well over 15,000 orcs and men were lost, the remnants fleeing into the Punj. Dolgan King proclaimed himself Suzerain of the Flnitlock. Also in those days, he brought to the halls of Grundliche Hohle an Emerald Dragon, who, of old, served the Dwarves as historian and sage. She carried two eggs with her. They were gifts from St. Luther for battles hard fought and won.

Early the following year, before the snows had melted, the Dwarves came forth in full battle array. They fell upon the rear of

Paskevitch's retreating armies, throwing them into disarray. A great slaughter commenced as the men fled to the east to escape the avenging Dwarven Shields. But lo, in these Battles of the Flintlock, the Dwarves unmade the legions, killing them without mercy. The valley's they filled with the dead and dying and the rivers ran with blood so much that the retreat turned into a route. All that saved the legionnaires from ultimate destruction were the Kobold dens.

There upon the edge of the Flintlock lay a great hive of Kobolds and their minions. As the Dwarves passed over, they came forth and a great battle commenced. The Dwarves fell to slaughtering them, entering their deep holes and hidden places. Kobolds are wickedly intelligent creatures and having full knowledge of the layout of the twisting tunnels gave them a great advantage. The Battle of Dens (1027md) took place over many months and Dwarves and Kobolds fell in deep places beneath the earth, unsung victims to the desolation of war. But the Dwarves won out in the end, driving all but a few to earth.

By the onset of Winter, the Dwarves settled in Gotzenburg, a great hilltop fortress in the Flintlock which they secured for defense. This proved a propitious move, for far quicker than any expected Paskevitch recovered his legions (*reference Punj, p. 124*), and in concourse with Duke Kain, attacked the Dwarves once more. The council came forth to aid Dolgan, arriving in time to fight at the First Battle of Gotzenburg. Herein the Dwarfs held the fortress Gotzenburg against the enemy for many months. The battle raged in and around the walls and ditches with a ferocity seen in few places, for the Dwarves and their Goblin allies were once servants to the Lords whom they now fought. The hatred on both sides caused a slaughter that would end only with total devastation. Aristobulus arrived and cast his potent magic upon the field, strengthening the walls and driving many men to madness. The Dwarves would not yield. At last, the Holy Knight Luther arrived and threw down the Emperor's Commander, Feodor Pakevitch, in singular combat. Though, for reasons lost to the histories, he did not slay the Commander, but banished him to his own lands. The legion fell back in dismay, and the Dwarves sorely wasted with numbers much diminished, could not pursue them.

The Dwarves had no time to recover from their long battles, for as is told elsewhere, in the spring of 1029md, Duke Kain crossed the Luneberg with three legions. King Albrecht marshaled all the men he could and called for Dolgan King to aid him with any Dwarves available. Dolgan combed his exhausted cohorts for volunteers. So great was the love the Dwarves bore for the noble men of Augsberg, that 3000 Shields marched to the summons. They marched under the leadership of Oxleigh, trusted friend, lieutenant and heir to Dolgan King.

Albrecht met Kain at the village of Olensk and there King Albrecht fought and won the most decisive battle in the war against Unklar (*reference Augsberg, p. 74*). The battle raged all the long day and into the night. The slaughtering struggle left thousands dead and maimed. The Dwarves stood upon the right flank and absorbed casualties the whole long day. In the early afternoon, Kain's legions succeeded in driving a wedge between the men in the center and the Dwarves. Reluctantly, Oxleigh ordered his Shields to fall back. The Orcs, who had failed to move the Dwarves all morning, rejoiced, pressing home the attack with greater vigor. Many Dwarven

wounded lay behind the enemy lines, these suffering death at the hands of miscreant Orcs. Oxleigh himself fell in a horrific duel with a host of Orcs, the screaming frenzy of their attacks overwhelmed the Dwarven Lord so that, despite slaying scores of them, he was pulled asunder. When Albrecht II fell in an attempt to rescue the Dwarf, a great groan escaped those Dwarven Shields who still stood. Eight hundred gathered in a wedge of iron and steel. They fell upon the hosts of Orcs with reckless abandon. In dismay the Orcs fell back, the slaughter of them soaking the earth in a morass of blood. Though the Dwarves fought all the long day, their troops were shattered, and unable to act coherently.

In the end all three Imperial legions were destroyed and Kain forced to flee the field. Though the men of Augsberg suffered greatly, the King himself losing three sons, the Dwarves suffered the greatest of all. One thousand and six hundred Shields 'turned to stone' on the field, one in two that had fought there (*reference the Bartigtot, p. 196*), and countless others were wounded. Only 77 survived the battle standing, and all these bore wounds of one sort or the other. Throughout the night and following day their moans carried far and wide and they tore at their beards. In their grief they vowed to clip their beards, to burn a bald spot on their chins in memory of their fallen comrades and they are called ever after the Bartigtot, the Deadbeards. The friendship between the Dwarves and the men of Augsberg grew all the greater.

In 1029md, shortly after Olensk, the King linked up with the army at Havok Castle. He stood upon the battlements to watch his weary troops passed by. An early snow had fallen, filling the mountains with a grey hue and covering all in wispy clouds of dark. Gray clouds greeted the army as it returned.

The sight of the army numbed the King. From the Halls of Grundliche Hohle, in the year 1026md, marched an army of proud Dwarven Shields, well armed and equipped. Their beards were long, their weapons sharp and armor strong and they were ready for battle and war. They shone in the sun like gems on the mountain.

Three years of battle had taken its toll. Below, on the Road, marched columns of sullen Dwarves. Battered and torn, many without a full complement of weapons, they stomped in lengthy troops up the mountain track. Some pulled carts loaded with wounded, maimed and the dead. Others lead or carried yet more wounded. And still others carried yet more dead. Upon their backs were worn and empty packs. Their armor was rent and torn, rusted and in shambles. Pole arms had been turned into litter poles and other weapons piled in carts and on ponies, for the snows were already deep and the tired host exhausted and hungry for relief.

As they passed the King, he saw their faces, grim and gray, hollow with vacant stares. These were the veterans of countless battles. They had left comrades all over the eastern plains, from Olensk to the Punj. Their boots were worn through, some marching with rags wrapped around swollen feet. The army shrunk against the back drop of jagged peaks and gray snow, their struggles seeming ant-like as they pushed into their mountain homes.

Yet still they marched in some order. Battalions were marked out by standards and officers, some dating back to the far off pits of Aufstrag, led them on. They saluted the King as they marched by and cheered, but the cheer was quickly lost in the whipping winds of snow. At last the battered column passed. The last unit was the oldest. The 1st Auger Battalion of 500. The King saw that its numbers were reduced by over half. The battered remnants brought up the rear and with them were the emissaries of Albrecht, Lord and King of Augsberg.

The King joined the march and suffered the hardships of the last eight day trek through the Grundliche Mountains until at last they came to the Great Halls of Grundliche Hohle. There the combined citizens came out to meet them. Women, children, the elderly; almost 17,000 folk gathered along the ridges and in the valleys to watch the army's return.

Watching from the High Pass which lead into the wide valley below, the King saw the stretched column of Shields coiling across the plain past the lake and to the escarpment. Like a dirty trail through the snow they tramped on and on. There, the people began to merge with the troops, looking for loved ones, comrades, fathers and brothers, sons and nephews. Slowly the valley filled with an echo of rolling wind; a mournful sound of ghostly wailing. And it came to him, the wails, rolling past him, over him and filling the whole snow rent sky ... the moans of grieving kin folk filled the world of Dolgan King, for surely did more than 3000 of his kin fall in the south lands and the Folk cried out at their loss. And Grundliche Hohle came home again.

They brought with them many refugees, most notable being the Gnomes. The Gnome Jarl (in the vulgate, "Chieftain") Bronstead, of the Vulsgard Clan entreated the Dwarves for safe harbor in the valley in the shadow of Grundliche Hohle. Dolgan King granted this so that they built a village upon the eastern slopes of the valley. With them came many Halflings.

Soon thereafter, as is written, Paskevitch delivered the single greatest defeat that the western alliances suffered. In 1030md, at the second Battle of Gotzenburg his men stormed the Dwarven fortress and threw them down. The Dwarves fought on in many small pitched battles. But in truth they had never recovered the losses of Olensk and were made to suffer thereby. In battle after battle, the Dwarves were routed from the heights of the Flintlock and by year's end driven into the Mountains. There the disciplined legions dealt the Dwarves another humiliating defeat. In a stunning coup, the impregnable fortress Havok fell to Paskevitch. 'Tis said that Goblin sorcery opened the gates of that place and let the men in, but none can now say for the castle is lost to all. Renamed castle Unklarglich, it has become a place of dreaded evil. They say that a Mogrl from Aufstrag settled there, hungry for vengeance against Dolgan King.

When the wars ended, Dolgan yielded his thrown to his infant son, Angrod II. The battle weary Dwarf took his war to the enemy on others planes and his tale passes from these (*reference Divine Orders, p. 60*). Thorva, Dolgan's wife who won great renown on many battlefields, took over the rule of Grundliche Hohle.

In the long years of peace after those dark days, the Hohle recovered much of its spent strength. Thorva ruled conservatively. She spent lavishly on rebuilding the Dwarven halls. She gave aid to the Vulsgard Gnomes in constructing the town of Trelleborg which came to dominate the caravan traffic from the valley. Together the

Gnomes and Dwarves built a new road which led north and west of the horrors of Unklarglich. In time, trade with Augsberg and other Kingdoms increased. The demand for Dwarven goods, mostly armor, arms, and beer increased. Food and lumber came north.

In 1097md, Angrod, now 60, came to maturity and took the reigns of the Kingdom from his mother.

Ec Rating IV

Of Her Kings
Dolgan I
Angrod II

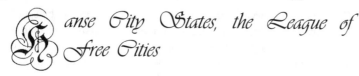

Hanse City States, the League of Free Cities

In Fiume, representatives of the League meet to discuss the affairs of their various city states. Presently, Master Darwin of Klagenfurt serves the League as Chancellor. The League members all have their own heraldry. The most recognized are those of Fiume, crenelated battlement on black and red; Arbel, one yellow chevron and three vertical black bands on a sanguine background; and Capidstria, white shield with two green strips and the mermaid, her sea captains pay homage to upon every voyage.

Of the Cities and Their Burghers: The broad slow moving Hanse River winds its way parallel to the coast, running almost the length of the Angouleme Plateau. The soil along the river banks is rich and the river itself full of fish. The coast here, unlike elsewhere on the Inner Sea, affords many small inlets and bays. All these factors have made the Hanse basin one of the wealthiest and most crowded in all of Erde. There, walled towns and villages are generously placed on coast and river where harbors are filled with vessels great and small, unloading and loading trade goods from all over the world. Each town looks much like its neighbor. The quays upon the sea, where men load and unload ships, give way to crooked, often narrow, streets. These wind through wood and stone buildings and houses, most three and four stories high, all jumbled together within the narrow confines of the walled towns. Shops, warehouses, bars, brothels, slave blocks, market squares and Cleaver Pits are sprinkled throughout the cities where trading in all manner of goods goes on. The towns are old and at night reflect the darker side of the merchants world.

The city states are powerful, independent and ruled by commercial oligarchies representing the trading guilds. The greater cities, Fiume, Capidistria, and Arbel, dominate the sparsely forested grasslands militarily and commercially. The constant shifting of political and commercial alliances have made the region a hot bed of small wars and the home to hosts of mercenaries as the guilds vie for commercial control. Many folk find refuge in the Hanse area, for money buys freedom and security.

No one city dominates the rest, and the town Burghers govern loosely when they govern at all. Order is kept here by city guards, which essentially serve as the local military. These are always commanded by mercenaries. These professional soldiers are often members of the Cult of the Sword (*reference Guilds and Orders, p. 197*), and follow the creed of that order. They are loyal to whomsoever pays them regularly and treat their men well. These Captains are usually difficult to bribe, for their creed calls for "honor to be given to the gold already spent." Though of course, when the amount is high enough, they can be bought.

The town fathers meet, usually in secret, to discuss tariffs, gate dues, trade deals, etc. etc. They pass city ordinances to keep the peace. However, a certain lawlessness exists here for these same Burghers are well aware that they need strong and bold men to lead their caravans and undertake whatever missions they deem necessary. They are a monied class, very jealous of their wealth and power. They frequently use assassins against would be usurpers or

members of their own guilds who push the limits of personal power. Within the Hanse League there is a constant underground economic war being conducted.

These industrious people create goods for sale around the world. The towns possess very fine craftsman in woodworking, leather, book bindings and so on. They produce weapons, armor, wood goods, pottery, wagons, copper goods, etc. Known for its art community, the Hanse city states produce a wide variety of fine artworks, statues, books, scrolls and frescoes. All manner of goods move through the port towns: ivory, bone, sealskin, furs, fish, cheeses from Burnevitse, and gold from the Gottland.

Fiume: This city, where the Hanse Congress League gathers once every two years, is home to the Chancellor of the League. It is the greatest of the city states and commands an army of several thousand mercenaries. Three families vie for power in Fiume. The  Forth's, who control most of the external trade, are led by the Lady Lissza, who in years past opened the trade with the hobgoblins (*reference Burnevitse, p. 80*). The house of Timothy Ferris, who dabbles in everything from diamonds to slaves. And the old Dwarf Angrim the Mad. All three are bitterly opposed to each other. They and other merchants meet regularly to conduct city affairs and make certain that the mercenary Captain Eomar is always paid and his men cared for.

Capidistria: Slightly smaller than Fiume, this city is dominated by the trade Guilds; the Weavers, Fish Mongers, Stone Cutters and so forth. The constant squabbling between the various guilds and families earns Capidistria the reputation as the most deadly city in the world. Muddles Inc, the Crna Ruk and the Paths of Umbra are all active there.

Arbel: A smaller city at the mouth of the Hanse river, this city is far better organized than any other city state in the League. The Bennett clan controls most of the city. These folk made their wealth decades ago and have retained much of it. The master of the family, David, has recently begun importing a great deal of stone and artisans in order to build a town hall and a palace for himself. The boost in spending draws folk from far and wide.

Klagenfurt: A small town nestled at the headwaters of the river, Klagenfurt is best known for its University. There, people come from far and wide to study under the Masters of Theology, Arcana and History. Mayor Peter Weinmeister rules the small town as he has for many years. Rumors of experiments leading to an outbreak of lycanthropy have yet to be disproved.

In all, the League is rich in adventure and opportunity, at least for those bold enough to risk their lives to achieve it. Merchants and mercenaries run the whole region and pay hard coin for information, service, and unearthed arcaña.

A League of Commercial Defense: For all the long years of Unklar's rule, the Hanse River served as a highway for soldiers and goods moving from east to west. Its proximity to the sea allowed movement of goods from Aufstrag to Gottland and Graugusse to be particularly easy and this garnered the attention of Mongroul Troll Lord, Nulak-Kiz-Din (*reference Moravan Plains, p. 112 & Divine Orders, p. 61*). That fell wizard showered the cities of the region with gifts and made certain that the laws of Unklar's world did not strangle their commercial concerns.

This Imperial benevolence lent much to the growth of the cities under the Winter Dark. The merchants grew wealthy and a class of Burghers soon controlled the whole region. Their power, at its zenith, surpassed that of the local legion commanders and what ministers of Aufstrag tentatively ruled the districts. The Winter Dark Wars brought all this to an end.

Three great calamities struck the city states, one after the other, which led to the immediate reduction of their power and influence.

The first occurred when the war broke out. When Kayomar rebelled against Unklar, Mongroul sent great hosts of men and material to the southern lands. The troop traffic along the Hanse, so prevalent before dried up almost immediately. Garrisons, stripped of their soldiers, remained empty. Many artisans and craftsmen left the region for the south, looking for more lucrative returns on their services, for soldiers always need new equipment and repairs to the old. Trade too shifted with them. The Legion in Gottland moved south and the Hobgoblins of the Burnevitse, lacking leadership, splintered into various tribes and began warring one with the other.

The Burghers hardly had time to adjust to these changes when the second calamity struck. Though the tale is best told elsewhere, Mongroul's tower of Graugusse sat upon the very feet of Mount Thangondrim. Upon that mountain he foolishly bound Daladon Lothian, Lord of the Wood and Protector of the Great Tree. When his allies assailed the Mountain to free him the dragon Malikor rose to destroy them. The battle brought down Mongroul's tower in ruins. What trade remained from the east to the northwest came to a sudden end.

About this time, the third calamity struck. The Northmen plundered the town of Toninburg, a small city near the mouth of the Hanse river. The ease of the victory brought down twenty years of pirating raids, burnings, looting and led to a great host of the people of the Hanse Cities being carted off to slavery.

As the Empire proved unable to defend all its many parts against the depredations of chaos, many turned to defending themselves. The Hanse Cities were no exception. They enforced men, and sometimes women, into local militias. They began building walls around their towns and hired mercenary captains and troops to fight off the ravages of the Northmen. When the lords of Angouleme (*reference Angouleme, p. 68*) rebelled against Unklar, the fiercely independent cities along the Hanse River followed suit.

The struggle which ensued was not fought against Unklar's legions, but rather against the newly anointed King in Angouleme. King William strove to include all the lands from the Twilight Wood to the sea under his rule and to this end sent first emissaries, and then troops, into the river valley. The smaller towns fell to William with hardly a struggle. Seeing this, Fiume called a congress of the remaining free cities and in 1029md they formed a defensive league against both William and the Northmen. Many of the Burghers were still possessed of great wealth and they spent it willingly on mercenaries, and of these there were plenty.

Men flocked to the Hanse; some ex-legionnaries, some soldiers passed over in the victorious south, many just displaced thugs looking for easy pay. The rough and tumble bands which gathered fought furiously against William and the Knights. Ever an indecisive man, William fought on for only a little while longer and then pulled his armies back across the river, a border which divides the two peoples to this day.

At the war's conclusion, the many Burghers and guild masters of the various towns and cities gathered once more in Fiume to discuss their collective future. In long, often heated debates, they set down the future of the League. They determined to maintain independent armies that would, in times of regional difficulties, be joined together under a joint command. However, they expanded the League to include commercial interests. All member cities would maintain favorable tariff and custom duties to other member cities. They also established free right of passage along the whole length of the Hanse river to all merchants who belonged to city guilds. The delegates appointed a Chancellor to oversee all of these varied activities, an office renewable every two years or whenever the Congress of Cities met and decided upon a new Chancellor.

In the early years after Unklar's fall the League struggled with northern raiders, greatly reduced trade and the ascending star of the city state of Avignon (*reference Avignon, p. 76*). However, in 1085md, events took a decidedly favorable turn. The Hobgoblin lands of Burnevitse, long embroiled in internal conflict, at last combined under the firm rulership of the Hob warlord Vistenodge (*reference Burnevitse, p. 80*). Far more clever than any of his race, he sought to expand his influence into the Young Kingdoms (and thereby his power) through trade. The land flowed with wealth, "diamonds" from the Bleached Hills, minerals and other ores. The Hob's love of cattle produced a great plentitude of dairy products.

Vistenodge sent agents to the Hanse cities to open trade negotiations. The Hanse jumped at the opportunity. Within a few short months, caravans began crossing the plains and the Great Wall, and ships began plying the waves of the inner sea. Small frontier ports sprang up all along the coasts of Gottland as merchants took full advantage of the new produce. The League quickly cornered the market of goods from Burnevitse and wealth once more flowed through the river valley.

With their new found wealth they bought their way into Northern holds and have since then come to dominate the commerce on the Inner Sea and much of the straights.

**Ec Rating
III**

Karilia, County of

Count Josef Olbrich retains control of Karilia from the great fortress of Khemi, where he sits upon the Dragon Throne. His coat of arms is respected far and wide. Upon an azure blue background, two towers represent the fortitude of his people. The connecting rampart symbolizes unity of mind and the stylized dragon between them harkens back to Josef's grandfather's heroic battle with a dragon (*see below*). The wreath pays homage to the god Demeter.

Of Her Lord and People: Karilia is a land of gently rolling hills, where deep grass gives way to cropland. There are streams a-plenty and copses of trees here and there. Small villages dot the landscape, often looked over by the watchful knights in their castles of stone. The castles are generally small affairs and the villages too, with mud and waddle walls and thatched roofs. There are plenty of small taverns however, whose proprietors offer travelers space on the dirty floors.

Joseph Olbrich rules in Karilia. A young man filled with the legends of his forefathers, Josef fiercely defends even the slightest insult to his honor. He pays homage to Utumno and has dedicated several temples to this lord of dreams.

There, as elsewhere, the knightly tradition is upheld through tournament and war. Castles and fortified townships dominate the County. The fierce spirit of independence in Karilia is supported by close relations with the County of Sienna. Intermittent warfare with the Kingdoms of Angouleme and Maine offer employment to the local knights, as well as to all manner of adventurers. Much of the wealth of the lords of Karilia comes from ransoms and plunder. As with their Lord, many of the nobles pay homage to Utumno.

The peasantry are generally contented and the Lord's rule there is lax. It is not unheard of for peasants to rise above their station in service to a noble and earn the title to a piece of land. There is some movement to reverse this trend, to make the rule of the nobles more in tune with those of Angouleme, but the peasants resist it as much as the Count. In general, Karilian peasants take advantage of the rich flat lands, producing crops of wheat, barley and oats. A great deal of timber is logged and exported to Avignon. The local folk are known far and wide for the taste of their brew.

Bordering the Twilight Wood in the west and the Gelderland in the south, Karilia is victim to many strange occurrences. Travel at night can be dangerous and it often behooves those who find themselves on the road too late to fall upon the kindness of castle wardens.

As the worship of Demeter spreads, many churches great and small are springing up across the land. They are generally poor, relying on locals to aid them in the creation and maintenance of the churches.

Upon the Tide of History: Karilia rose from obscurity. As with the other provinces in this region, Karilia gained her independence when the Imperial garrisons withdrew to the fortified cities. Even as the provinces of Angouleme moved slowly but certainly to a bloodless revolution, Karilia moved violently into the maelstrom of war and rebellion.

The Imperial Governor of the province, Actaneb, a priest of Unklar, settled in that land as an acolyte. No mean intellect, Actaneb mistakenly thought he understood the rule of law. He applied his with a harsh, unforgiving attitude. Whereas many folk living under the yoke of Unklar knew at least the vestiges of prosperity, the people of Karilia did not. Actaneb taxed them heavily and spent the money on lavish residences and temples to the horned god. When war came to the west and the power of Aufstrag waned, Actaneb fell back on his own resources. He employed an army of mercenaries and hired assassins of the Crna Ruk (*reference Guilds and Orders, p. 196*) to kill those who opposed him.

He also dabbled in sorcery. Actaneb became obsessed with death and sought to waylay the day that he would breathe his last. To this affect he sought ways of transmuting his soul into another host. The dread experiments which he performed on people pulled from the local environs fed the hatred of the people he ruled.

Events came to a head in 1025md. Actaneb's servants kidnapped the son of a powerful knight, a one time legionnaire, who went by the name Mattahius of Olbrich. Mattahius was not a man to be trifled with, but too late did Actaneb discover that he had tortured and slain the man's first born son. Mattahius gathered an army of men about him, ex-legionnaires, mercenaries, bandits and others who would join him and openly rebelled against Actaneb. They sought but failed to attain the aid of the Council of Light, for in those days the Council struggled with their own folk fighting a secret war against the dark.

Mattahius campaigned throughout the fall and winter until he forced Actaneb's army into battle. Upon the beaches of the Amber Sea the two small armies met in combat. The mercenaries fought for a short time but could not long stand against Mattahius. Many were done to death and thrown into the sea. The rest fled to the north and south, seeking refuge in distant parts. Mattahius turned his attention to Actaneb himself.

By early summer he caught up with the Governor, besieging him in the halls of fortress Iliador upon the edge of the sea. Several weeks passed before Mattahius mined the walls and broke into the castle. A great slaughter followed and none were spared. Mattahius did not restrain his men, but rather let them plunder and serve the evil its just do. Actaneb, in terror of being tortured, threw himself from the high towers of that place. Mattahius abandoned that terrible castle of death and suffering. It is said that even those who sought to plunder its wealth could not do so for fear of the undead. It is also said that Actaneb did not die when he fell from the tower, but lived on to haunt the castle as a dread spirit of terrible evil.

The war ended as soon as it had begun. No support came from the legions in the north or east and Mattahius found himself in control of the whole province. The men who served him proclaimed him their Lord and sought for him to take a crown. The folk of Karilia welcomed the rule of the man who had slain Actaneb.

In 1027md, when the Lords of the north crowned William King of Angouleme, Mattahius sought to join his lands to those of the northern monarch. In return for the security offered by Angouleme, Mattahius swore an oath of fealty to King William. In turn, William invested him with the County of Karilia and placed him high in the councils of the land.

This arrangement worked for awhile. Count Mattahius enjoyed the comfort of security offered by his King. His lands sat astride the east-west trade routes, for in those days Avignon stood as a ruined fortress only. Troops fleeing the east crossed his land continually, pillaging all the while. Many small battles were fought in which Mattahius proved himself a competent general and hardy soldier. Augsburg's victory in the east (*reference Augsberg, Olensk, p. 74*) shattered the ability of the Empire to maintain any control in the west and left many loyal to Aufstrag without recourse but to fight their way into the Young Kingdoms. Battle followed battle, particularly in Karilia.

Many men of great renown earned their spurs in service to the Count. Lord Charles Galveston, an errant knight of unknown origins, first gained the recognition of the Council by slaying a great Ungern battle lord here (*for further reference to Lord Galveston, see the module "A Lion in the Ropes"*). The Elven Prince Meltowg, half brother to Daladon Lothian, respected the Count so much that they campaigned together frequently.

Mattahius lived to see the end of the Winter Dark, and fought in the final battles of the Toten Fields, but he died when a vengeful member of the Crna Ruk, still remembering the death of Actaneb, shot him with a poisoned arrow.

Francis, Mattahius' younger brother, took the reigns of power. This did not sit well with William II of Angouleme, however, who sought to give the County to his own nephew. The King sent the Dukes of Mousine and Orange south to represent his case. They claimed that William had not promised to invest any but Mattahius with the County of Karilia and therefore Francis should yield to the King's nephew. To this, Francis replied with these stern words: "My Lords, I thank thee for your kind representations of the monarch of Angouleme. But I would have you bring him word of my displeasure at his claims so that he may know I reject them utterly. And, my Lords, you have but two days to clear my lands or I will have you drawn and quartered and your entrails fed to the fish." They fled north to bring news of the disaster to the King.

Francis' act of rebellion benefitted from two simultaneous events. The first occasioned a religious rebellion in Angouleme. In that Kingdom, as in no other, the worship of Demeter had taken a firm hold. There were many doctrinal disputes between the early priests, not the least of which was who controlled the Church, the King of Angouleme or the Bishop in Avignon, a city that had grown rapidly after the fall of Aufstrag. Rebellion and war spread throughout Angouleme, keeping the King from responding to Francis' insult (*reference Angouleme, p. 68*).

The second occasion marked Francis as one of the greatest heroes of his day. An ancient blue worm descended upon the County. It terrorized the whole region from the Twilight Wood to the sea. Francis armored himself with plate and shield, took up the lance of his father and rode to give battle to the creature. Upon the way he met an elf who befriended him, saying that he was an old friend of Meltowg and wished to return the kindness which Mattahius always showed the Elves. He gave over a sword that he claimed St. Luther bore in combat against the dragons of another era. With the dragon slayer at his side, Francis rode to war.

He met the dragon beneath the eves of the Twilight Wood and there they fought a horrible dual. The air thundered such that the calamity of the battle could be heard for miles around. They felled trees and shook the earth in that contest of arms, but in the end the dragon slayer took the life of the beast leaving Francis the victor. The Count payed homage to Utumno, the dark god of dreams, and left that place where, it is said, the bones of the dragon lay still.

Francis placed the dragon's hide upon the floor before his throne and mounted the beasts four great paws upon the throne itself. Ever after has that throne been called the Dragon Throne. Francis added the dragon to his families' coat of arms.

Francis ruled for a short while after the battle, but eventually died of his wounds. His son, Francis Mattahius, took the Dragon Throne and the sword, ruling as his father had for many long years. Under his rule, the County became the feudal realm it is to this day and the worship of Demeter spread to many of the common folk, though Francis Mattahius worshiped Utumno, a practice that grew common amongst the nobles of Karilia. When he died in 1091md, his son Josef, a thick strapping youth, took the Dragon Throne.

Ec Rating

I

OF HER LORDS AND COUNTS
Mattahius of Olbrich (1027md-1046md)
Francis of Olbrich (1046md-1062md)
Francis Mattahius Olbrich (1062md-1091md)
Josef Olbrich (1091md-present)

ayomar, (Kingdom of)

Here, the Great King Eadore rules from the ancient and hallowed halls of the world's greatest castle, Du Guesillon. The sword and axe crossed over a four quadrant field signals to all the coat-of-arms of that noble house. The weapons represent the rule of law and strength in battle. In the upper left and lower right quadrants, the black and red checker board reflects the colors of old Kayomar. In the lower left and upper right quadrants, the white and red checker board represent that of the house of Luther of Pendegranze. Set just above and between the head of the axe and the pommel of the sword lies the golden crown of royalty.

Of Her King, The Lands and Her People: Kayomar extends from The Wilds in the north to the sea and the Eldwood in the south and from the Ardeen River in the east to the Rhodope Mountains in the west. This vast land of rolling countryside is a fertile plain where four major and countless minor rivers flow in their tumbling courses to the Danau (pronounced Dan-ow) River before spilling out to the sea. The people live in towns and villages spread thinly across the wide country. Though roads connect many of these establishments, the land is simply too vast for it all to be included. Hence, there are great empty stretches of grassland where herds of buffalo and wild cattle roam. Only in the south do the plains give way to more dramatic terrain, the stark highlands of the Bergrucken Mountains, the Eldwood and Darkenfold forests and the Shelves of the Mist. The south is more populous too. There the knights live in their castles and homes of stone.

The Great King Eadore, descendent of Morgan, is a boy of fourteen. He assumed the throne at the age of four. Because of his youth, he is the first king to rule Kayomar who is not a paladin. His father's sudden death (*see below*) did not prepare the Kingdom for a regency, so his mother, Debera, assumed the post. She has ruled the kingdom for ten years with the aid of a few select advisors, one a wizard of the Mystic Enclave, Em-Ian. The boy is on the verge of maturity, reached at age fifteen in Kayomar, and is completely unsure of how to approach his reign, for the families of Kayomar are once again clamoring for rights.

There are eighteen noble families in Kayomar who trace their lineage back to the Age of Heroes. These Lords and Ladies fought the horned god, in one capacity or another, for the entirety of the Millennial Dark. Many of them were, and still are, Holy Defenders of the Flame, though the practice is dying. They believe that their blood is as blue as the Kings, and they are right. They rule vast estates which, for the most part, are held as ancestral domains, meaning that they cannot be retaken by the King unless they commit acts of high treason or no male issue exists to assume the title. These are the Barons of Kayomar, and they carry such names as the Baron Erlangen, the Baron Gerhard of Sinsich, Baron Unstruut, and the Baron Landshut. These families field small armies of retainers, knights and even paladins. They continue to maintain the rights which their forefathers had before, and even some besides.

These priviledges include the right to tax, lay tolls on roads, bridges and ferries within their lands, supply mercenary soldiers to meet the King's levy (as opposed to reporting themselves or sending knights), maintain small private armies and establish religious houses which do not owe fealty to the King in Du Guesillon. This last has been a source of great revenue for the families, for these monasteries, which till the land or raise livestock, owe their dues to the Barons who sponsor them.

In his turn the King has sole rights to mint coins and this, above all things, has allowed him to maintain financial control of his realm. These "marks" of gold and silver are prized by merchants for they are never debased and always pure and worth their weight. He also exercises the right to collect dues in monies, kind or service, call the Kingdom to arms, and make peace beyond the borders of the realm. Furthermore, he is the final arbiter in all disputes, high or low.

The King rules alongside a council of nobles, which consists of the representatives of the eighteen families, the High Priest of the Grove, the Bishop of Demeter (also located in Du Guesillon) and the Master of the Holy Defenders. Laws must be approved by the council before enacted, though if the King does not wish an act to become a law, it is thrown out.

In war, Eadore commands the Holy Defenders of the Flame (*reference Guilds and Orders, p. 191*), raises feudal levies (each Knight must serve for 60 days a year, each Baron for 30 days and also send a pre-determined number of knights), and accepts the mercenaries which the older families supply in place of regular levies. Eadore commands an impressive cavalry of 400 Holy Defenders and 2000 heavy and light horse. The ranks are flushed out by some 8500 men-at-arms and mercenaries. He can, if need be, raise several thousands of crossbowmen and archers. In pressing needs he can raise money to hire his own mercenaries.

Kayomar is synonymous with knightly virtues and the rule of law and order. Many castles, large and small, overlook the countryside where small villages abound. The land is rich in soil and produces crops of wheat and barley. The people lead a simple, prosperous life, content in the protection their lords offer them. These simple folk farm the land, raise cattle and pigs, travel little and speak of the far eastern lands in vague terms. They are a religious folk and pay homage to their Saints (Luther and Vivienne) and call upon the protection of the Paladin's Grove more often than not The region is well known for its taverns and drink. Due to its proximity to the Wilds, however, the Darkenfold in particular, Kayomar's borders are constantly threatened by creatures of evil intent.

Though the worship of Demeter is common, most of Kayomar pays homage to Durendale, Saint Luther and the Paladins of the Dreaming, the Confessor Knights. Kayomar is defended by two relics: the Holy Flame (*reference Magic Items, p. 225)* and the Durendale (*reference Magic Items, p. 220)*, a holy sword. The former, said to be a spark of the All Father's Soul, burns in a sacred dish within the temple complex of the Paladin's Grove. The latter, though its whereabouts are unknown, is so bound to the Grove that most believe it to be buried under the monument of St. Luther (*reference Divine Orders, p.62*).

Kayomar produces notable quantities of wool, beers of great renown, and serves as the granary of the southern world. It supplies the Gelderland, Maine, Eloria, Norgorad-Kam, Sienne, Twilight Elves and Fontenouq with foodstuffs. Most of the external trade passes through Maine. Craftworks of metal from the western part of the kingdom and gold mines from the shelves region also bring great wealth to the realm.

Kayomar is ancient and as such offers the adventurers plenty of opportunity to explore lost ruins, forests and mountains. Wealth abounds within the many deserted castles and ruins, particularly on the borders of the Wilds in the Nordmark where the rule of the Great King is less than total.

The History of Kayomar: Kayomar's past encompasses several thousand years. Even at the beginning of man's recorded history, kings ruled there. The tribe of Ethrum traced its origins to the valleys of Kayomar. And the Tarvish Emperors, who fought so long against Al-Liosh and the Aenochians, ruled their lands from spired castles along the Ardeen River. Once in a while, after a flood or storm, the ancient ruins of buildings or dungeons crop up, reminding people of just how old the land is. The history of that land, however, at least so far as the modern world is concerned, begins during the Age of Heroes.

In the Age of Heroes, Luther reigned as King in Kayomar and at his side stood Vivienne, his Queen. For sixteen glorious years they reigned together and forged a realm of peace, prosperity and power. The holy sword, the Durendale, shined over the land. In countless battles against the evil of the world he prevailed. But always over the light of his reign stood the moment that was his Queen. At the height of his reign, war came, once more from the east, this time upon the horns of Unklar.

As war rolled across the great straights, the remaining Kingdoms gathered in a Holy Alliance and plunged themselves on a mad crusade against the enemy. Luther had, by this time, abdicated his throne in favor of his son Robert Luther, and taken the Durendale Sword into the east in an attempt to slay the Sorcerer Nulak, or the Emperor Sebastian, whichever came near him. With him traveled his old companions, Aristobulus and Daladon. Their task proved fatal, and Aristobulus fell to a Demon Lord from the Abyss even before they reached the east and Luther, that greatest of heroes, called by the gods, carried the Durendale from the plain into the Dreaming Sea, there to guard and hide it from the enemy.

He left in 639oy aboard his ship, the Evening Swan, while all thought he would soon return. But Vivienne knew better, and she knew that she would never see her love in life again. He had cast himself out onto the Dreaming. The Queen died and was buried in the family tombs on the Freiden Anhohe only three years later (*reference The Malady of Kings adventure module*).

The Knights of Kayomar and King Robert Luther continued the war against Unklar.

The Catalyst Wars (*reference The History of Erde, Catalyst Wars, p. 29*) saw the overthrow of the Kingdom of Kayomar and the fall of Robert Luther. For 39 years the King waged his war against the Dark in the east. The songs of his deeds ring true even today, and he is accounted the greatest hero of all the world. At last, in 798oy, Unklar besieged Du Guesillon. For almost two years Unklar's legions battered at the doors of that mighty fortress, but to no avail. The King laughed them from the walls and lead countless sorties into the fray and slew many and more of the evil god's minions.

But at last Unklar came and unmade the walls and assailed the King in the Tower of Hope. The King came forth to face the dark god. "Your crown of horn has no meaning here! Now, get thee from this place!" With that he struck Unklar a blow upon his helm so great that it split the iron, and drew blood. The blow sent the horned god falling from the high wall where he crashed into the ground with a mighty clap. Robert Luther's laughter frightened the Orc hosts such that they broke and ran from that land in complete terror. But Unklar lifted himself from the ground to come against Robert Luther once more. This time the horned god came as a ball of furious hatred. He pounded the walls with his mighty fists and tore the gates asunder. In a voice akin to graveled iron the god spoke, "I have unmade the world. So I shall unmake you." He fell upon Robert Luther with all the might of his grim power. His spells wove a deadly mist from the Language of Creation, binding the King in a maelstrom of swirling ash. Robert Luther struck one last blow, taking a great splinter from one of Uklar's horns. Unklar cursed and gored him with his twisted horns. So the King, Robert Luther, on the 28th day of Nochturn, 800oy, died and his body fell to the earth. The light went out in the world.

Some of the last to fall were in the House of Pendegrantz. Jariel Galen (third son of Luther) fell on the steps of the tower next to his brother's body. Jaren the Monk fell too, in the tower, struck by the mage Nulak-Kiz-Din. Unklar's minions sacked Du Guesillon and left the castle in ruins. They left behind the Holy Flame (*reference Magic Items, p. 225*) however, for that sacred artifact the paladins carefully hid with spells within spells.

Those who survived the war fled into hiding. Many slipped beneath the eves of the Eldwood and the Darkenfold Forests. Others took to the Shelves of the Mist, and many had no place to go but lingered in the Wilds to face the coming winter. The refugees survived largely due to the protection of their patron, Luther (*St. Luther, reference Divine Orders, p. 62*). He came to them in their dreams, breathing life into the struggles. He gave them hope for the future. Too, he planted secret strengths in the people of Kayomar, so that in their dreams they were heroes born and bred.

During the long Millennial Dark, the Holy Defenders of the Flame fought on. They made Du Guesillon a holy place, where they came to pray and ask for aid from there gods, Durendale and Luther. The dish remained in the ruins of the castle and a paladin made to watch over it at all times. The order shrank to a few dozen knights, for the lives of these paladins was hard, and they had no lords. The older warriors recruited younger ones from those who they deemed worthy, trained them, and taught them the law of good. They went out into the cold world of Winter to fight lonely battles against impossible odds. Countless and nameless were the heroes of those dark days, but ever did they struggle on in their war against the dark. These few brave men held the order together, waiting for the time when their King and Lord would return from the Sea of Dreams.

In these days the only place the knights could find succor lay in the Eldwood. There, the Wood Elf Kings never bent beneath the weight of Unklar, for none could assail the magic of that place. As is told elsewhere, Great Trees from the Days Before Days still wandered that ancient forest. But too, the Watcher in the Wood, a ranger order, founded by Daladon Lothian defended it with bow and spear. The Holy Defenders forged a deep bond with the folk of the Eldwood (*reference Eldwood, p. 141*).

When, in 1019md, Luther came to the paladins baring the sword Durendale, he gathered them for war, bidding them to collect their strength. He threw himself upon the sea of Dreams. From there he cast himself into the dreams of those who slumbered still and in this way many awoke thirsting for war.

Morgan, Master of the Holy Defenders, called to his knights and paladins to gather at Du Guesillon. They unearthed the Holy Flame and, holding it aloft, they traveled the land gathering those who would fight the enemy. Men and women armed themselves, joining him in droves. Even those who did not join Morgan fought. Unklar's minions were often stoned by villagers who too dreamed the dreams of Luther. The Orcs fled their holds and Lord Aziz, from fear of the legends of Luther, called to his Masters for aid.

At first Morgan's troop fought small battles, harrying the enemy's caravans, burning outposts or killing guards. Aziz did not move against them until their depredations became such that his revenues declined. With troops from across the Ardeen he attacked Morgan. He pursued him into the Shelves of the Mist where he suffered a minor defeat. At the battle of Two Creeks, a troop of mounted paladins annihilated several dozen giants and hundreds of his own mounted men. And so the war was fought. Aziz hounded Morgan but could not bring him to heel. Morgan slew many of Aziz's troops but could not master his overwhelming numbers.

As the war spread elsewhere, Kayomar became a drain on the Imperial Legions. Experienced cohorts were pulled from the lands of Maine and the Gelderland and sent to fight for Aziz in the south. At last Nulak-Kiz-Din came to Aziz and told him to press Morgan into battle, or be killed as a traitor.

Early in 1022md, Aziz's Imperial Legion came upon Morgan on the banks of the river Hume. They forced Morgan into battle, driving him into the Shelves of the Mist with the greater part of his host, which numbered 187 paladins, 352 knights, and 2000 footmen.

There, they were hounded by the scourge of darkness, great packs of wolves and evil beasts. Despite this, the men and Orcs of Unklar's Legions held their posts in fear for the coming of the Old King and the return of Kayomar for they remembered well the battles of the Catalyst Wars.

Lord Aziz called for more troops. Though the greater part of the Legions were now fighting in the far west under the dark host and only a scant dozen or more legions remained in the lands of Aenoch and Ethrum, Nulak chose to reinforce Aziz once again. Troops were stripped from garrisons as far away as Angouleme and sent to Kayomar. At last in 1023md, his cadres swollen with troops, Aziz moved to draw out Morgan and destroy the Order of the Flame. Nulak hoped the battle would draw out Luther and the Durendale Sword so that he could put an end to the paladin.

Morgan gave battle to an Imperial Legion on the heights of Eadore Ridge. With 2000 men-at-arms and 500 knights and paladins, they met the 5th legion on the 19th of Erstdain. A legion of 16,000 men and Orcs, formed into three cohorts, was led by Aziz personally and supported by many hundreds of skirmishers from other Provinces, as well as a further 4000 horse. Upon the eastern slopes of the Shelves of the Mist, Morgan ordered his men to build a wall of dirt and stone atop Mt. Eadore, and there they awaited the enemy. Aziz first threw troops of the 194th cohort against the hill top and it was utterly destroyed by arrow and pike, never drawing any but a little blood. Then a force of the third cohort attacked along the flanks. The arrows of Morgan's folk were spent by this time, and Orcs mounted the dirt wall. The ferocity of the defense of the men of Kayomar staggered the Orcs, long used to ruling through fear and fear alone. By sword and axe they were thrown down from the wall so that they made little progress. By mid-afternoon of the battle's second day they fell back in dismay. So great had been the discipline of the Knights and Sergeants of Kayomar that they suffered little and slew much. Upon the morning of the third day the last cohort of Aziz drew up at the hill's foot and waited. Morgan sallied forth in rage with his 500 knights and paladins at his side. Such was their charge that the 63rd cohort of 5000 men was utterly destroyed and put to flight. Aziz fled, not stopping until he crossed Maine and into the Gelderland. He took with him his 4000 horse and quit the field forever. The battle bore two names ever after; some called it Morgan's Song, but to most it was simply the Battle of Eadore!

Aziz's defeat spread disenchantment throughout the ranks of Unklar's legions. And soon all of Kayomar threw off the yoke of Unklar's rule. When the Shroud of Darkness began to fade and the people once more felt the light of day they rejoiced in Kayomar, singing songs to the dark's demise. But one more great battle would be fought before the lands were freed of the ilk of Unklar.

Lord Morgan once more gathered his knights and men-at-arms and attacked the Orcs in the Wilds. The war raged around the ancient castles of that place, neither side having victory nor defeat. The Battle of Weather's Gap drove the Orcs into their fortress of Ox and Morgan besieged that place. The Wood Elves, under Daladon Lothian and King Nigold, joined Morgan in his war on the Orcs. But not until the Dwarves of Norgorod-Kam came down from the Brass Halls were they able to overthrow the Orcs there (*reference Norgorod-Kam, p. 116*).

In this same year Luther took the crown of Kayomar upon his brow. The people rejoiced for the dawning of the new age. He rebuilt Du Guesillon and lay the Dish of the Holy Flame in the high Tower of Hope, haunted still by the shattered spirit of the Jaren Falkynjager (*reference Divine Orders, p. 60*), and where two of his son's had fallen so many years ago.

Luther's reign did not outlast the Wars. Luther fought many battles in the east and came home seldom. He loved the war against the evil eversomuch and would not quit the field. After three years of absentee rule, King Luther I abdicated the throne of Kayomar in favor of his friend and the Master of the Holy Defenders of the Flame, Morgan. Morgan's own wife crowned him, naming him King Morgan I. Luther retained the title of Palatine King of Kayomar, reserving his right to assume the throne if ever the need should present itself. He then returned to the wars and later to the Dreaming Sea.

Morgan's first official act as King of Kayomar bound his line to Luther evermore. In the lands which Luther's family owned, even before the Winter Dark when Luther was a boy, Morgan established an order of clerics. They built a temple there to honor and worship the Paladin of the Dreaming Sea and the Durendale Sword. Morgan named it the Morgan Paladin's Grove, in afterdays, it became the holiest of shrines for the lords of law and good. The Grove encom- passed 300 acres of wooded land sur- rounded on all sides by a low wall. The Dru- ids of the Great Tree came to the grove at the behest of

Daladon Lothian and planted there a crop of silver birch, said to be the offspring of the Trees of Mordius from the dawn of time. By years end, the Holy Flame in its dish of platinum was placed in the altar chamber of the Temple where it sits to this day. (*For further information on the Grove and the Holy Defenders of the Flame, reference Divine Orders, p. 62 & Guilds & Orders, p. 191*).

In the years which followed, Morgan attempted to establish a feudal hierarchy in Kayomar. However, due to the predominance of the other aristocratic families, he failed to seize complete control of the Kingdom. Of the ancient houses of Kayomar, few had survived, but those that did strove to exercise the same rights they believed they held under the previous Kings of Kayomar. Morgan wearied of these continual disputes with the nobles. At one moment he was heard to remark, "I now understand Unklar's reluctance to live in this land, so headstrong are these folk, that they are ungovernable."

In 1045md, Morgan abdicated the throne to his son, and traveled with the crusading knights to Aufstrag in secret. There he flung himself against the enemy with reckless abandon, causing much havoc in their ranks before he fell. It is said that his trusted horse,

wounded beyond healing, gave out beneath him and he would not leave it. Fighting over its dying screams he held off a horde of Ungern until at last he too succumbed to a multitude of wounds.

When the Wars at last ground to a halt, the Kingdom settled into a long peace. Morgan's son ruled for 40 long years. So prosperous was his tenure that folks called him the Great King, even before he died. His reign is viewed as the Golden Age of Kayomar for there were few wars or disturbances and the realm flourished. Towns grew, trade increased and artists and poets flocked to the courts of the Great King. Morgan II built roads throughout the realm. He also ordered that a University be established in the city of Du Guesillon, giving it an institution which produced philosophers, wizards and theologians of high repute.

Morgan II did not choose to interfere with the spread of the religion of Demeter. It took on in some areas, mainly in the north near the Wilds. There, people built churches and called to the god of common folk for aid. But in truth, with the Paladin Kings on the throne of Kayomar, the people had no need of new gods or new ways of life.

Morgan II's, son Luther II, followed in his father's stead. The title of Great King remained, attached now to the throne. This paladin possessed of amazing abilities did not rule the Kingdom for long. While on campaign in the Wilds, hunting a giant troll, he fell afoul of a devil from the hells. They fought long and hard in that desolate place. But even as Luther II's men came to his aid, he fell to the creature's axe. The other paladins fell upon the devil with a lust not seen since the days of the Winter Wars and slew him soon thereafter. The body of the noble King they bore back to Du Guesillon and lay it with his forefathers.

Luther II was Morgan's youngest son. His wife bore only one child, and this late in their marriage. She gave birth to a boy in 1079md. They gave him the name Eadore, after the famous battle which his great grandfather had won. This young child of four assumed the throne as the Great King Eadore.

Ec Rating
III & V

OF HER KINGS & LORDS
Palatine King St. Luther I 1026-1029 (House Pendegrantz)
King Morgan I 1029-1045 (House Dawin)
King Morgan II 1045-85
King Luther II 1085-1087
King Eadore 1087-present

uneberg Plains

Where none rule the empty spaces. Only the cities of Magdeburg and Unspt claim any rights, and they the heraldry of evil. In Magdeburg, a red banner with gold depicts a black double headed eagle (Duke Kain's very own). In Unspt, a dark blue banner carries a black wolf.

The Geography of a Wasteland: A vast savannah of rolling hills and wild grass, the Luneberg is home to a host of abandoned castles, ruined towns, and dungeons. The land itself is much recovered from the depredations of war. Wild grasses mixed with wheat grow everywhere; waist deep in some places. Many of the small streams, lakes and ponds are cleaned of Kain's poison, which has allowed animals to return. Wild cattle, deer and elk, wolves, coyotes and the like are common now in the Luneberg. Seeds carried on the winds from the Grossewald forest have given life to small copses of trees which grow here and there.

In consequence, the country has become a wild place, refuge to a host of all manner of folk. Hermits take advantage of the solitude of open spaces. Mystics come to find the lost powers of a passed age. Pilgrims of Demeter come to see the land to convert people who are too wild to care for the gods. Brigands, wild Orcs and evil creatures live here as well, for there is no law but the sword. Of course these folk bring the wrath of errant Paladins and knights, or even bounty hunters who come seeking to slay evil, or cash in on their worth. The Luneberg Plains are wild lands.

Only two cities thrive here; Magdeburg and Unspt. Both places are dirty, disreputable townships, where small winding streets and old, dilapidated buildings are jumbled together, crammed behind ancient crumbling walls. They are ruled by the local mayors and the city guard, who are controlled by the thieves' guilds.

Magdeburg is the greater of the two. Located in the southern plains near the Red Hills, Magdeburg sports a thick wooden and stone wall, with scores of stone houses and paved streets, considered the inner city. Here, Mayor the Lord, Enternich, rules. A mercenary by trade, he settled in the town after overstaying his welcome in the Rhuneland.

Through muscle he has taken control of most of the burg, but continues to vie for control with the Thieves Pit, a motley collection of rouges, brigands, prostitutes and thieves. The Thieves Pit exists "beyond the walls" as the outer town is called. Here, the town quality declines rapidly. Built upon the ruins of the old city, rickety houses of wood and slate jumble in a cacophony of architectural noise. Dirt streets, hardly more than alleys, snake and twist between buildings which sport shops, taverns, opium dens and brothels. Magdeburg is a dangerous place where weapons are borne openly. The city guard has authority only in the inner city. "Beyond the walls" belongs to the Thieves Pit.

Despite the fact that Unspt survived the wars, it is smaller than its southern neighbor. However, its location beneath the eastern eaves of the Grossewald Forest gives Unspt a far most interesting population. Burghermeister Mark, "the Sandy," rules there. He is wickedly clever and cherishes solving riddles and games. His network of spies are augmented by two hill giants that serve him as guards. He controls the town only loosely, allowing the thieves' guilds wide latitude in running the Cleaver Pits, gambling houses, and brothels. (Note: there is no real thieves guild in Unspt, but rather a collection of several factions who constantly war with one another for possession of the city streets). He cares little for others' beliefs, but himself follows the religion of Demeter and has built the only church to that god in the whole wide region. Unspt attracts many people, Orcs, Gob-

lins and other hu-manoids, Halfling, Gnomes and Dwarves as well. They come here for supplies, which Mark imports from the Rhuneland and sells at inflated prices, of sport or drink. The Cleaver Pits, as else-where, are popular venues of entertain-ment. Combatants are thrown in and made to fight to the death. Mark has added his own touch of flavor to the games. If one wishes to challenge him to a contest of riddles or puzzles, they may. He is undefeated and many would be intellects' bones have fed the local dogs. Like Magdeburg, the town of Unspt possesses narrow winding streets and old rickety houses. Built upon the slopes of several hills, these lanes tend to be steep and in the winter are downright treacherous. The houses are built into the sides of cliffs, on top of them, and in the Halfling quarter underneath them.

Some of the best horses in the world are raised in the Luneberg, but are very difficult to obtain because many are wild and the rest are closely guarded and valued very highly.

The Luneberg is an area rich for plunder. The scattered ruins of old cities, towns, castles and dungeons are said to be filled with forgotten riches. The armies of Kain are known to have lost a great deal of their wealth after the defeat at Olensk (*see below and reference Augsberg, p. 74*) and rumors of a fabulous treasure laid in an abandoned crypt of the old world bring many a would be adventurer to the Luneberg.

The Long History of Death: The Luneberg Plains, much as their neighbors to the north in the Rhuneland, served as the heart of the Imperial domains under the rule of Unklar. There, the gifts of the horned god in the early days of his reign enriched the whole of humanity. With the Language of Creation he wove new life into the frozen tundra. He gave to the people of those lands a wealth of plants to grow, so that his frozen world of ice and snow would not starve. Ever since, the soil there produced abundant crops, full and rich to eat.

The sages remind us that Unklar did not do this out of kindness for the madness of starvation which his winters brought to Erde. Rather, he did it from necessity, for the strengths of gods are forever bound in the strengths of those who worship them.

But during the age of the Winter Dark, the people of the Luneberg grew fat upon the trade of foodstuffs. Towns were erected throughout the plains, from the Olgdon River to the Grossewald

Forest. Farmers tilled the earth, planted and grew crops which were carted all over the wide world. The western provinces of Aenoch particularly relied upon the Luneberg produce, for much of their wealth was spent elsewhere. All this brought wealth to the area which attracted an ever greater number of folk. Things were conducted with a greater order here than in the Rhuneland. The Lord of Magdeburg, leader of the greatest of towns, often offered guidance to the lesser townships; a kindness they returned.

The people lived thus for many hundreds of years. Families grew old and passed into oblivion while new ones rose. As in the Rhuneland a class of urban knights established themselves in most of the towns. Retired mercenaries who bought shares in the towns gained a vested interest, so they stayed and settled. They, of course, brought their sons and daughters up in service to the towns. A kindly competition, which rarely ended in violence, grew up between the various city states. The inhabitants enjoyed sport far more than war. Tournaments were common between knightly families and towns.

All this changed when the Winter Dark Wars began. Even from the outset, war came to the Luneberg. In 1012md, the Dwarves and Goblin slaves rebelled in the pits of Aufstrag and their battles spilled out into the fields around Aufstrag. When they broke free, they passed over the Luneberg, many looting as they went. The House Legions under Lord Coburg, Master of Aufstrag, pursued them and, unused to the world at large, they too (Ungern mostly) attacked the local populace.

Later the war carried to the Flintlock, the Rhuneland and Augsberg. This last Kingdom brought war to the Luneberg plains. Formed in 1026md under the overlordship of Albrecht, the River King, Augsberg's men crossed the Olgdon River into the Luneberg, conquering vast stretches of it. Augsberg, always poor in grains, desperately needed food for their vast herds of cattle and horses. Aside from that, Albrecht wished to consolidate as much land under his banners as he could. In 1026md, shortly after he was crowned King, Albrecht lay siege to the city of Magdeburg.

The battle did not last long. Albrecht himself, an ex-legionnaire general (*reference Augsberg, p. 74*), knew the city and its weaknesses well. Many of the towns in the Luneberg, wishing to avoid destruction, called the River King their Lord. This brought the attention of Lord Coburg once more. With the wizardry of Nulak-Kiz-Din behind him he hurled his Ungern soldiery against Albrecht. The horsemen of Augsberg could not stand against the horrid beasts of Unklar, for they were strange to them. The King fell back in disarray, recrossing the river. Before he went he strengthened the garrisons of many of the larger towns.

Coburg gave each town a chance to surrender or suffer destruction. Some few held against him. These he overwhelmed by siege and true to his word the towns were sacked and burned and many folk done to death. After the towns Lijana and Druna suffered thus, the other towns opened their gates and lay down their arms. Magdeberg alone withstood the Master of Aufstrag and he wasted many of his troops against those high walls. He quit the field late in the year of 1027md. But as he left to return to Aufstrag he ravaged the country.

The following year the whole series of tragic events re-occurred. Augsberg stretched out across the river, conquering towns and bringing the whole country into his realm. Coburg retaliated by burning towns and villages, uprooting crops and carting wagons of booty to the deep halls of the Great Tree of the east. Coburg himself had lost the confidence of his dark master and did not bring with him the powers of the Arch-Magi.

Unklar sought to turn the tide against the west and summoned the Demon General Kain, called the Godless (or more appropriately the Duke of Altengrund) to command his legions. Kain's power lay in his evil and he laughed at Coburg for his kindness to the people of the Luneberg. "Do they say to you, little man, 'We shall close our gates against you?' If this is so, you should tell them that Kain is coming and he shall lay waste to the whole of this country." His words bore more than the hint of truth. He gathered together three legions of men, taking them mostly from the south. He also brought over from the lands of chaos a troop of demon kind and all these were made to cross into the Luneberg. He sent the word forward, "All those who do not lie down in the roads before my chariot will be put to the sword."

He came to the town of Dobrich first. Here a contingent of Dwarves from Grundliche Hohle, men from Augsberg and several magi of the Mystic Enclave strengthened the garrison. Kain drew up his armies in front of the town for three days. They had no siege equipment or articles to break the walls, so the Dwarves laughed at him and called them cur. Upon the evening of the third day Kain unleashed his sorcery and broke the gates asunder in a great ball of fire. His was an eldritch power that few could resist, even the magic of an engineer's stone could not bare it. When the gates fell wide the Dwarves and men of Augsberg threw themselves into the gap and fought a great fight. But the legions came on in countless numbers, and with grapples and ladders they breached the walls in scores of places. Kain at last joined the contest, bringing ruin upon the head of the Defenders with his black sword, Omdurman.

The town fell within hours and the whole of the populace was put to the sword. This brutal affair Kain repeated time and again. He sent his legions across the whole of the Luneberg, burning towns and villages and houses, carting off loot and enslaving or destroying the people. He ordered the roads behind him destroyed, the waters and wells poisoned, trees to be cut down and the whole region utterly destroyed. When at last he crossed the Olgdon River to meet defeat at the Battle of Olensk, little remained of the once prosperous Luneberg towns. Even noble Magdeburg lie in ruins.

The suffering of that country did not stop there. For even after Kain's defeat, war came to the Luneberg. The Dwarf King Dolgan led many soldats and horsemen of Aachen and Augsberg into the wastes to root out the few small garrisons that still dwelt there. When at last they withdrew, only Unspt stood, though it too had suffered repeatedly. So the Luneberg stood for many years, a blasted wasteland. After the wars, few ventured into the Luneberg, leaving it to the ghosts of the dead.

Ec Rating
I

The proud King Louis III (pronounced with an 's') rules the whole of Maine from his palace fortress of Chinon. The realm's coat of arms is a simple one representing the three kingdoms under one crown. A tri-colored shield rides in the middle of a red background, the upper division dominating the two lower. The upper partition is yellow with three crowns upon it and a coiled blue dragon beneath. The stylized lion upon blue is in the lower right partition. And the lower left has a red raven on green.

Of Her people and King: Despite numerous border wars with the Dwarves of Norgorad-Kam and disputes with Kayomar, the Kingdom of Maine flourishes. Sandwiched between the Ardeen River in the west and the Saline in the east and with the Begrucken Mountains in the north, the people of Maine are well protected by natural frontiers. The monarchy is well established, King Louis III being an able and crafty ruler. Despite the disputes over his inheritance with Kayomar (*see below*) he controls Maine with power and money. The lords, descendants of legionnaries from the Winter Dark era, have been generally supportive, for he allows them a great deal of autonomy. The King is not adverse to rewarding loyal service with patents of nobility and land.

The aristocracy is well placed in Maine, the Lechfield and Artois, living in castles or fortified palaces and paying out land for military service. They are not especially warlike, preferring to spend their wealth on pleasures. It is not uncommon for the Lords and Ladies of Maine to own slaves or for the Lords to have harems of wives. It is reported that some of the northern Ladies who own land in their own right possess harems of husbands. The knightly class has settled into Maine as it has in most of the west.

Maine is the greatest regional maritime power, only Eloria comes close to her. The early support given to the merchant class by Pius (*see below*) has allowed these folk to thrive, especially in the south upon the peninsula. All merchants pay a docking fee and a tenth in duty to the royal house, but beyond this they are left to their own devices. They traffic in wheat and maize from Brindisium; coal, copper and iron from Norgorad-Kam; and horses, gold and cereals from Kayomar. The greatest export is wine. Maine is well known for producing cheeses, fine wools, silver and other metals from the Massiff, as well as a large fishing fleet.

The peasant class is generally divided into segments. The greater number of them are tied to the land they farm and pay homage to the nobility or King. The others are the sons and daughters of retired soldiers who were given land by Pius for loyal service to the crown. These men, generally a little better off than their counterparts, are forced to continually defend their rights and privileges. The vast

majority of these people worship Demeter and support the ever growing class of priests that threaten to overtake the Kingdom. They produce a variety of crops, mostly cereals. But Maine is best known for its fine grape, and taverns selling all manner of wines dot the country.

Rumors still abound about the treasure horde of Aziz (*see below*) and many hearty adventurer comes to Maine to seek it out. The Kingdom also serves as a way point for those bold enough to cross the Saline River into the Gelderland, and as such, there are always mercenaries, freebooters and adventurers drifting about her towns, villages and lingering in the ports. The thief guild, Muddles Inc, is well established in the merchant class and they continually battle the assassins of the Crna Ruk for control of the night.

A Land Born of Strife, the Kingdom of Maine: The Lords of Maine long ago mastered the arts of war and diplomacy. When Lord Morgan, Master of the Holy Defenders of the Flame (*reference THe Histories, p. 38*), defeated the Imperial Legions at the Battle of Eadore the military might of Unklar dissolved in the far west. What remained were two legions commanded separately by Generals Pius and Orkhan. They ruled the Lechfield, Maine and Artois. Aside from their own soldiers, both Generals regularly employed assassin priests of the Crna Ruk (*reference Guilds and Orders, p. 196*).

As is told elsewhere, General Aziz's defeat at Eadore spread disenchantment throughout the ranks of Unklar's legions. Living upon the borders of the dreaded Kayomar, where memory of the Catalyst Wars lingered, the servants of Unklar feared that land as a place anathema to them. When Aziz fled his post to the east he rode his 4000 horse straight through the Lechfield and on into the Gelderland.

A quarrel soon broke out between Pius and Orkhan, though what they fought over is anyone's guess. Some rumors abound that they fought over the treasure of Aziz which many believed (*and was proved, see below*) he abandoned in the Lechfield. But it is known that Orkhan wished to attack Kayomar and destroy Morgan, a thing Pius thought foolish at best, hopeless at worst. The argument came to blows when Pius refused to attack. Quarrels broke out everywhere between the servants of the two generals and soon the whole of land was fortified.

In 1023md, the two legions fought minor skirmishes throughout the summer and fall. By winter, Pius, tiring of the fruitless battles and desiring to shift his allegiance, made open war upon Orkhan. By spring of 1024md, a full fledged civil war ensued. The brutal strife entailed the destruction of many men and Orc. Pius, at one point, needlessly sacrificed two solid cohorts of Ungern and Hobgoblin troops in an assault on several castles. After that, all the humanoids in his ranks fled for fear of him.

Dwarves from Norgorod-Kam inadvertently sparked the final battle. In several brutally fought campaigns they drove Orkhan from his mountain castles and forced him to move south. Caught between the hammer and the anvil he sought battle. In the late summer, on the fourth day of Trocken, Pius utterly defeated Orkhan at the Battle of Redhill. The defeated general fled the field only to be slain crossing over into the Gelderland by the mercenary knight, Baldwin of Klun (*reference Aachen, p. 66*).

Pius, realized that the Winter Dark Wars were no where near finished and that the power of Unklar, though greatly reduced, still reigned paramount, stepped out of the fray to await the outcome. He settled his folk throughout the area of Maine, the Lechfield and Artois and ruled there as a petty tyrant. He solidified his power by fortifying the western Marches against Kayomar and strengthening the garrisons in towns and castles in the north. He never sought the council of Aufstrag, but in those days, would heed the word of Nulak only.

For four long years he ruled the three provinces, gaining power and wealth. During the civil war, unrest had spread throughout the whole area. Legion commanders ruled as minor warlords and the guilds controlled towns and commerce. Pius moved quickly to quell the strife. He quietly drove out the remaining humanoids and broke the power of the legion commanders by dispersing the cohorts. He fortified castles and gave them to his most loyal men. He ruled by duplicity and strength, but also he ruled by the power of the Crna Ruk. Many men and women who pretended to power disappeared, victims, it is believed, of assassins.

In 1028md, Pius gained the recognition of the Palatine King, St. Luther of Kayomar. Luther returned at last to his realm where he ruled only in name. He needed the power of Kayomar for his continued wars in the far east, and so made a truce between Morgan of Kayomar and Pius. For pledges of loyalty and peace, Luther named Pius King of Maine, Artois and the Lechfield. Luther recognized Pius' son, Aenor, as the rightful heir to the Tripartite Kingdom. Many contend that this peculiar incident gave the Kings of Kayomar the right to crown the Kings of Maine. These early disputes were further clouded when Pius retired to his fortress of Chinon, crowning himself with much pageantry. That the Kings of Maine owe their crown and homage to the Kings in Kayomar is disputed to this day.

Pius, though personally cruel, ruled benevolently. The lands of Maine, never wealthy, waxed much under his guiding hand. He moved quickly to quell the border disputes with the Dwarves of Norgorod-Kam and to establish a maritime trade for Maine. He gave generous license to the merchants and ship captains who lived along the coastal region and upon the peninsula. The budding trade between Brindisium and Kayomar and the far east was soon passing through the commercial shipping lanes of Maine.

King Pius reigned for twelve years and died quietly in his bed, surrounded by his harem. Aenor, barely at maturity, assumed the dignity of his father's crown, but not his rule. He inherited his father's sense of cruelty but not his judgement. His reign was long and wicked. He moved the royal household to the city of Ethenael on the coast. He loved the sport of the gladiators and imported architects and masons to build an arena, the greatest in the western world. He peopled his reign with sycophants and his government proved both corrupt and inept. The power his father spent a lifetime building eroded as nobles, priests and commoners alike struggled against his oppressive rule.

As the worship of Demeter spread throughout the region King Aenor attempted to quash it. It is said that he paid homage to dark Narrheit, the Lord of Chaos, and as such could not bare the sight of those pious folk. Many died on the gallows, hung or quartered for their religious beliefs. This did little to impede the spread of the religion however as many nobles, particularly in the north of the country, converted.

Aenor's rule ended only when his brother, a convert of Demeter, slew him and took the throne. He crowned himself, Pius II. A terrible civil war followed in which the north fought the south, each raiding and plundering one the other's lands. Pius did not rule long, but succumbed to a fatal illness, dying after only three years of rule. The nobles and merchant houses gathered in a great concourse upon the death of Pius II and chose to leave off the religious disputes which fragmented the realm. The throne they gave to Aenor's young son, Louis, who, as tradition bespoke, crowned himself King of the Tripartite Kingdom.

Peace became the rule of the day during Louis' reign. He proved a good man, but a mortal one. After only eight years on the throne he died. His son took the dignity, crowning himself King Louis II.

Louis II did much to repair the remaining scars of the civil war. His luck in discovering part of the treasure of Aziz strengthened his hand in the politics of the day. He used his wealth as leverage, buying off nobles, priests and merchants. He also reacquainted his people with the Crna Ruk, using the assassins where money failed. The feudal nobility and the monarchy became firmly entrenched during these years, maintaining control of the merchant guilds (and subsequent thieve's guilds).

When Louis died, he ordained that his son Louis III take the crown. But Kayomar threatened war. King Luther II, desiring to break the control Maine had over the seas demanded that Louis come to Du Guesillon to be lawfully crowned. War brewed along the Ardeen •Rriver. Skirmishers from both sides crossed the river, investing castles and sacking towns. Before the dispute could evolve into full scale war, King Luther II died. His sudden death left a boy on the throne of Kayomar, and the hostilities were quickly called off. Louis crowned himself King of Maine as his fathers had done before him.

Ec Rating III

Of Her Kings
King Pius 1028md-1040md
King Aenor 1040md-1058md
Ling Pius II the White 1058md-1061md
King Louis I 1061md-1069md
King Louis II 1069md-1087md
King Louis III 1087md-present

Moravan Plains

There are no lords here, for the lord of the Moravan passed from the world 67 years ago. For here, Nulak-Kiz-Din, the Troll Lord, Mongroul, ruled for 600 years. All that remains of his rule is the poisoned wasteland and The Graugusse, the Grey Tower.

Upon the Nature of a Desolate Realm: The Moravan Plaines are deserts of dried broken slate. A glacier of ice covered the lands in the Winter Dark and before that a great inner sea. All that remains are a series of plateaus which give way, one after the other, until they reach the Great Northern Forest. The cliffs between each plateau are steep, jagged and difficult to climb. The skies above the Moravan are poisoned with the fumes from the Grey Tower, and in the dark and barren soil little of worth grows.

The dark stain of Nulak's magic remains on the Moravan Plains. For too many years his experiments went on, unmolested in the Grey Tower. The Arch-Magi is gone and has never, or so it is believed, returned to his home. Much of what he worked upon in the early days remains where he left it.

Graugusse's abandoned halls watch over the wild wastes of the Moravan. The whole complex consists of two towers, one smaller than the other, connected by a thin bridge. A score of out buildings gave homes to guards, masons, smiths, and other servants of the evil Mage.

The smaller tower, the Schestusse, the "sister tower," is only 100 feet tall and very thin; 60 feet at the base, and barely 20 feet in diameter at the top. Within is a narrow staircase which winds up the whole length of the tower, giving egress to the upper chamber. In Nulak's day the powerful gargoyles guarded the tower against intrusion. Upon the very top of the Schestusse is a small room; the upper chamber. A single door which opens out to the narrow walkway takes one to a thin bridge, spanning the distance between the two towers. It is the only known entrance to the greater tower. Though rumors of secret doors abound, none have yet come to light.

The main tower, the Augusse, "the tower of the eye" is roughly 250 feet tall, and some 120 feet wide at the base. It maintains this width for the first 200 feet, at which point it narrows drastically. There is no entrance at the base, only one from the Schestusse. Within are a host of chambers, halls, bedrooms, kitchens and all other manner of rooms one can imagine. The top of the tower narrows into a winding staircase which takes one to the pinnacle of the whole complex. There, a door leads to a thin walk of stone which arches out above the whole complex. It is 40 feet in length and has no supports, seemingly hanging in the air. There, upon the slightly widened end, Nulak-Kiz-Din stood to contemplate the world. How the span survived the fall of Malikor none can say (*see below*). Beneath the tower a massive Dungeon stretches out in miles of tunnels, rooms, pits and cells. Nulak conducted the most horrid of his arcane experiments beneath the earth, venting the remains through small flutes which stretched up to the plains above.

Both towers suffered horribly from the fall of the Dragon Malikor, but neither collapsed. The stones are magical in nature, for Nulak bound the souls of his victims in the rock of that place and made it so that they clung together with spells and magic. However, the main tower is split and the bridge is no longer secure in it moorings.

The tower purportedly holds vast treasures in gold and magic and attracts all manner of adventurers. Few return, and those who do report terrors beyond imagining.

The plains themselves are home to bands of vicious Trolls, several small Orc tribes, and other evil creatures. Most of these feed off of each other or hunt game in the Northern Forests. Travel is difficult in the Moravan, for there are no roads and water is sparse.

Thangondrim still stands upon the northern reaches of the Shadow Mountains. Better than half of it collapsed when the Dragon fell at its roots. All about it, huge boulders lay strewn upon the ground and in the midst of all this debris lies the body of Malikor. In all the years since the battle with the White Mage and the Falkynjager the body has not suffered any rot. Legends repute that the longevity of the creatures flesh is due to lingering sounds of the All Father's voice, for here he sat in the days of old, forever speaking the Language of Creation. What treasures and magic this fallen beast holds within him only the bold will learn.

The History of the Plains and Tower: Graugusse, the Grey Tower, dominates the Moravan plains. From those dark halls the Arch-Magi Nulak-Kiz-Din ruled a vast network of holdings, including the Shadow Mountains and Gottland. During the Winter Dark, the Troll Lord's evil power attracted all manner of fell beasts, Orcs, and Trolls to the Moravan. He ruled there for 600 years.

Though his tale is another one (*reference Divine Orders, p. 61*), it should be noted that Nulak served the Emperor of Aenoch long before the coming of Unklar. In those days the Empire held sway over a vast land, from the Rodope Mountains in the west to Al-Liosh (Aufstrag) in the east. Magi openly wandered the world, vying with one another for power over the arcane. Nulak was such a mage. An evil man, he sought dark routes to his goals and to do this he needed a place secluded from other men. He chose to build his tower in the Moravan Plains. He enlisted Trolls, paying them in coin, to gather slaves and construct the edifice. They used grey stones quarried in the Shadow Mountains to build it.

The tower itself stood within sight of Mount Thangonodrim, "the throne of the sky." There, in the Days before Days, the All Father sat and watched the world of his creation unfold. But now, the glories of the past were gone, and the lonely mountain watched the evil of the Arch-Magi fashion a dark house from grey stone.

At first the tower was a modest affair. A hundred feet in height with a wall and a few outbuildings. But in time, as Nulak's power grew so did the tower. As its master added to it the tower grew, new construction covering the old. A network of dungeons were added, as well as battlements and a second tower several hundred feet away. More buildings and walls followed. Nulak could not pacify the lands around so he laced the building stones with magic, the spells giving them some protection against siege.

There, in the Grey Tower, Nulak discovered the Paths of Umbra, those deadly incantations which summoned the horned god to the world of Erde, which eventually brought about the Winter Dark. When Unklar came to the world he forced Nulak to attend him, and not for many dozens of years did the wizard return to his tower. Though it had not suffered plundering, it had fallen into disrepair. He rebuilt it, peopling it this time, with slaves, servants and the wizard's who followed the Paths (*reference Guilds & Orders, p. 198*). The tower now consisted of three consecutive towers, one built atop the other, all resting on a massive foundation. It stood well over 200 feet high. More battlements were added and the smaller sister tower rebuilt as well. A bridge spanned the heights from the top of the lesser tower to midway up the greater.

The whole tower fortress stood upon the flat plains like a great grey monster. From this fortress tower, Nulak sent forth plagues of spells. These, in time, enabled him to bring the whole of the Moravan to ground. The Orcs and Trolls who lived there took to worshiping him as a god. Nulak, ever a vain man, reveled in the adulation. He extended his rule beyond the Kleberock, the great pass through the Shadow Mountains, to Gottland and beyond. In those days, when Unklar slept much, his minions warred one with the other, so much so they built towers and walls against each other. So Mongroul built a wall to guard his own tower. He summoned a great Troll Lord, Hasryck, to his side and bid him gather a host of his fellows to encamp upon the southern end of the Kleberock and block egress to the Moravan Plains beyond.

Though the tale of Hasryck the Troll is told elsewhere (*reference Gottland, p. 94*),

suffice it to say that the castle Nacht was built upon the southern end of the Kleberock. There, no armies could pass, but they had permission from that dread creature.

The Mage ruled those lands for many hundreds of years. In the Graugusse, he labored over his dark sorceries, ever striving to twist the world to his own dark imaginings. Laboratories the size of Great Halls held tables and shelves which bore tens of thousands of vials, decanters, and jugs. Spell components in small boxes, pouches, sacks and boxes were piled everywhere. Huge fire pits cooked strange concoctions, dungeons held those unfortunate enough

to fall into the Arch-Magi's hands. The tower itself, laced with eldritch sorceries, seemed to be a living thing. There were runes carved into every block of stone, though what they said few could discern. Aristobulus the White came here once and retold how the runes were spells which bound spirits into the stone and wove them together. In this way the tower could not suffer destruction but through some great calamity.

Such a calamity came on sudden to the Graugusse. During the early days of the wars, Nulak-Kiz-Din captured Daladon of the Eldwood (*reference Divine Orders, p. 60*) as he fled the heights of Monrudge. He bore Daladon aloft, binding him to the throne of gods upon Mount Thangondrim, the very seat where the All Father sat pondering his creation in the Days before Days. Here, Malikor the Dragon, one of the first born of Unklar's lust, set to watching the Marcher Lord.

This brought forth Aristobulus the White, ever Nulak's nemesis, and the demi-god Jaren Falkynjager, he who had been bound upon the walls of Aufstrag for a thousand years. They set about freeing the Marcher Lord but brought the Dragon down upon them. The battle which followed shook the heavens, so that rocks fell from the skies. The dragon carpeted the skies in acidic flames and the mage hurled lightening upon its crest. In the end, the Falkynjager smote the beast a massive blow upon its chest so that its heart exploded and Malikor tumbled to the earth in flaming death. When he struck the ground he shook Mount Thangondrim to its roots and broke the mountain in half.

The collapsing wall of stone crushed an army of Trolls and wasted the land for miles around. The earth shook so that the Graugusse sank into the earth. The massive stress upon the stone split the tower and the span between the two towers slipped its moorings. Though the Graugusse did not fall it became an unstable place.

Nulak never had recourse to repair the towers for the wars took him and he found himself battling the White Mage at every turn. The Arch-Magi's complete disappearance in 1030md left the Moravan empty and leaderless. In his absence, the Moravan soon reverted to a wild country where local tribes of Orcs vied for power with Trolls and Giants.

Ec Rating I

Ngorondoro, Ichlin Yor

In the rough cut deeps of the earth, The Eldritch Goblin Lord, Uandlich rules his folk with an iron fist. Upon the poles of iron and brass the likeness of the Goblin Queen signals to all that the Goblins thrive in Erde once more, in the deeps of Ngorondoro.

Of Uandlich and His Goblin Realm: Ngorondoro is a deep, wide underground kingdom. Here hundreds of miles of ancient caves, tunnels, staircases, ramps and houses are carved from the rock. A great river flows through the deeps and the ruins of many canals fan out from its length like spider webs. Old dams and debris clog canals and river alike, flooding whole areas of the dungeon deeps. Most of the realm is deserted, jumbled ruins and crumbling walls piled hither and yon. Monsters, great and small, stalk the deeps preying off the unwary. Travel is difficult, but not impossible.

Ngorondoro is a foul place of ancient evil and vile sorcery. Uandlich the Goblin King controls only a small portion of the vast underdeep. There he hordes his kin and they guard the Goblin Queen, Oglotay (*reference Divine Orders, p. 60*) as she lays eggs for their future. Uandlich holds court at the feet of a glittering water fall, a marvel the Goblins reconstructed. He is served by close to 400 Eldritch Goblins (*reference New Monsters, p. 234*) and several thousands of the drones which continually hatch.

Though the Goblins have peace with the Dwarves, they are ever an evil race and their fell deeds are etched in the stones of history. Few are allowed access to the deeps of this, the only Goblin realm, and much of it remains a mystery. Many Goblins would unmake the alliance with the Dwarves, chief amongst these are the brothers, Ixius and Sonixius, both Eldritch Goblins. In time of war, Uandlich commands an army of several hundred Eldritch Goblins and several thousand drone Goblin warriors.

Occasionally they come forth to trade with the Dwarves or the men of the Punj. They produce large quantities of platinum and gold. But more than that are the exotic components for spells. As is told, the Goblins brought sorcery into the world and they mastered it long before any others. For this reason their knowledge and skills are always sought after by the wizards of the world, in particular those who follow the Paths of Umbra. Much of the gained wealth goes into the water parks of the underground, for these the Goblins ever lust to be remade as they were in the ages long past.

The rest of the caverns remain abandoned. They are dark and travel is hard as many of the old roads and tunnels are partially collapsed. Since the snows of the Winter Dark have melted, many smaller cave entrances and doors have come to light so that egress to the underground Kingdom is rather easy. Surviving within is not. Many creatures have fled into the deeps over the centuries, many more since the fall of Unklar. The Goblins stalk the lower halls and few survive capture, though the very clever may buy their freedom from the Goblin King.

The ancient Goblin water parks were destroyed long ago (*see below*) but near the huge opening where the river first flows into the caverns, debris and damming material have created a large, deep lake. It is said that beneath this lake lies a gate to the other worlds, but whether true or not is unknown for within the waters a great Dragon has taken up residence.

Of Goblins Returned: The Goblin Kingdom of Ngorondoro rose from the ashes of history in the midst of the Winter Dark Wars. Built upon the ruins of the ancient Goblin home of Ichlin-Yor its very halls are steep in the history of ages past.

When the god Thorax first twisted the Goblins from the substance of the world he gave them such loathing for the light of day that they hid themselves in the deep places of the earth. One of the greatest of these holes were the caves of Ichlin-Yor, the caves "where light dies." (Note: 'Ichu' is the Goblin word for death. When the suffix 'lin' is added, it changes the meaning. 'Ichlin' mean to die. The suffix "lun" changes the word to mean undead. King Ichlun, King of the Undead. 'Yor' is the word for light.) The Goblins took up residence here before the first Goblin-Dwarf wars. They mined the caves for wealth, carving their homes out of rock.

In truth, Ichlin-Yor was a place of great beauty. The Goblins love water, flowing water most of all, and spend much of their energies creating artificial falls, with dams, locks and breaks aplenty. Ichlin-Yor sported a large underground river which flowed through its lower caverns. The Goblins constructed a series of canals which branched off the river, and dug a whole series of caverns beneath it, creating water falls, pools and underground lakes. They stocked these waters with fish, newt and salamander and there, for many years, lived out their lives in solitude.

The Goblins of course are malignant creatures, possessed of a great desire to destroy the Dwarves. And so in time they came to the Dwarves in war. The Great Goblin-Dwarf Wars are told elsewhere and need only be mentioned here as they concern the fate of these caves. In the first Goblin-Dwarf war, the Dwarves of Grundliche Hohle broke into the upper halls and laid waste to them. Many a Goblin fell, but most retreated to the depths and the Dwarves did not possess the strength to pursue them. The halls the Goblins rebuilt during the long reign of King Ichlun. Centuries later, during the Stone Wars, an army of Dwarves led by Angrim broke the gates and plundered the whole realm. Goblins died in droves, only a few surviving, fleeing to the very deeps. The Dwarves destroyed many dams, flooding vast regions, and they filled the canals, with rock. When they left, the caverns were a crumbled ruin and so they sat for thousands of years.

During the Age of Heroes a band of adventurers uncovered a door which led to these unimaginable deeps. They stole some of the riches in the upper chambers and fled to the south with tales of their plunder. This sent word of the caverns far and wide, eventually attracting the attention of an Eldritch Goblin, Uandlich. He explored the mountains, found the door and to his amazement the old holes of Ichlin-Yor. He had no time to gather a band of Goblins for the dawn of Unklar's Age began and he, as with so many of his kindred, found himself a slave in the Pits of Aufstrag.

The last of the Eldritch Goblins found themselves bound in servitude to Unklar with Dolgan and the dwarves of Grundliche Hohle. Slavery knows no hatred but for the master and in time the Goblins and Dwarves worked together. Agmaur the Goblin, the same who destroyed Grausumhart and slew the Dwarf King Rotterkin X during the Stone Wars, became one of Dolgan's closest friends. Together, in 1012md they rose against their masters, fighting the bitter battles of the Trench Wars for six long years.

When at last they broke out into the world the Dwarves returned to Grundliche Hohle and there reopened that ancient place. The Goblins traveled with them, for they had no homes of their own and found that the Young Kingdoms bore them little welcome. Uandlich kept his secret for a great while until at last, embittered by the wars he called upon Dolgan King.

As the Dwarves recount the tale:

Into the halls came the Goblin Warband, seventeen strong. They were a hearty troop with grim face and a hungry look. Outfitted for war with shields of iron, wicked swords and curved daggers they stood before the Dwarven King. Some few he recognized, but the Goblin troops had grown since the days of the Trench Wars.

This warband's leader, one Uandlich, a Goblin powerful in his own right and held to be a blood in the brotherhood of Agmaur, Dolgan King knew well. He had fought alongside him in many a tunnel beneath the halls of Aufstrag. A ferocious cut throat and warrior Uandlich made a name for himself on both sides of the battlefield. Twice he pulled Dolgan's fat from the fire.

The Dwarf Thanes gathered around as Uandlich stepped forward. The Goblin Chief did not lower his shield but rather spoke around it in a defiant manner.

"Lord, King of Dwarves, I, Uandlich seek your audience." He waited and when the King gave a nod for him to continue he spoke thus: *"For many years the Goblin folk have labored at your side. We have plotted and planned for you, stole in the night and slain foul Orc or human at your heed and call. We watch your borders for you and let none trespass that your will does not allow. For these things we have nothing.*

"You and yours have rebuilt the great Under Mountains of Grundliche Hohle and covered its walls in wealth and filled its halls with mirth and food. Yet my folk have nothing.

"You rest in comfort care of your children and your beards grow long and soft with the comfort of these great holds. Yet my folk have nothing.

"Agmaur is dead at his own folly and Argorat owes you his blood for trail brothers in the high mountains and the rescue of his son Uel. But I, Uandlich and my folk cannot wait for his fawning to end and come to seek a boon and reward from the mightiest of Dwarven Kings.

"We want not gold or silver. We want a hole to call our own. So this I ask of you: north of here in the high Grundliche lies an old Fortress and mountain deep with halls called by my folk the Ichlin-Yor. It is long abandoned now but for a few ghosts and howls of the dead.

"We, I, would ask you for the right to take up abode in this place of Ichlin-Yor and call it home."

To this entreaty Dolgan King wept, for he loved his Goblin allies and he granted a great wealth of gold, silver, iron and tool, lumber and other supplies so that they might make a home for themselves. And the goblins under Uandlich retook the caves of Ichlin-Yor. This was the year 1029md.

Some 400 Goblins entered the halls to rebuild their homes. They found the place in utter ruin and learned too quickly that many fell creatures had taken up residence in the twisted dark depths. Some of the Goblins perished, but in a few years they reclaimed the lower halls. Some of them remembered the halls as they were so long ago and they strove to rebuild the dams and remake their beloved water falls. They labored in the dark for many years.

In time Uandlich uncovered ancient magic which led them to the rescue of their Queen. A feat which they did through many adventures and loss of life. They brought ancient Oglotay back to the deeps of their Kingdom where Uandlich made her Queen once more. Nulak-Kiz-Din came to them then, baring with him the Pride of the Goblins (*reference Magic Items, p. 229*), a magic needed to revive her and remake her in her role as mother of Goblin kind. He let them use it for a time, only long enough to breath life back into the beastly woman, at which point she began to lay eggs once more.

When Nulak left the halls of Ichlin-Yor he traveled south to unknown destinations. Upon the road, Erix the Goblin, who served Unklar as the most trusted of lieutenants, ambushed the Wizard north of the Red Hills. Nulak discarded the iron bound chest to battle the Goblin for Erix was possessed of great power and bore the Horn of Breaking (*reference Magic Items, p. 225*). Erix did not realize what the iron trunk held, so that the Pride of the Goblins, that most ancient and powerful of artifacts was once more lost in the wide world. Rumors abound that a mad Gnome, who lives on the bones of fish alone, travels the rivers and ponds of the Red Hills using the box as a foot stool.

But in Ichlin-Yor, renamed Ngorondoro, Uandlich ruled as King, Oglotay lay eggs once more and drone Goblin warriors and workers came into the world. Once in a great while, a Goblin of Eldritch power came again into the world, hatched from one of the beastly woman's eggs. In this way the Goblins returned from the depths of history and once more play an active role in the world of Erde.

> **OF THEIR KING AND DREAD QUEEN**
> Uandlich and the goddess Oglotay

Ec Rating II & IV

Norgorod-Kam, The Brass Halls

Upon the Iergild throne sits King Dagmar IV, Lord of the Brass Halls. As with all the Dwarves of Erde a totemic pole serves as heraldry. The totem of Norgorod-Kam is a brass pole at the top of which are two hammers extending out in a T-shape. Upon each hammer are the symbols of the Twin sisters, the moon and the sun. All the totems, disks, and placards, are gold; one disk with the name of the father of the house, one disk with the present King, further disks representing units, professions, etc.

But the world changed and the Dwarves of the Bergrucken proclaimed themselves in the midst of the realms of Unklar and opened their Kingdom's deeps as if for War. Their mighty and fell King, Dagmar III, bore the sceptre of the King of Crazeul and the Axe which is the rightful possession of the Dwarf Lords. And the servants of Unklar fled from him and the whole of the Bergrucken, but for the deeper places, were made as if clean, and Dwarves knew much pride and rest in the days to come.

~Leopold of Passou

Of That Bearded King and the Folk: The Bergrucken, or Saddleback in the Vulgate, are an ancient chain of mountains. They do not aspire to the heights of other mountain chains, such as the Grundliche or Rodope, but what they lack in height they make up for in sheer ruggedness. Deep narrow canyons are surrounded by loose shale and rock. Swift flowing rivers, channeled into these gulches are known to carry the unwary to a rapid watery death. Winding trails, ridges, and escarpments lead one into a maze of ancient brown rock of broken wild country. Aside from certain monsters only the Dwarves live here, patrolling the heights that have been their home for a millennia.

King Dagmar IV rules in his golden halls and commands a powerful army of Dwarven Shields. Norgorod-Kam has never in its long history fallen to an enemy and the opulence of its throne room mirrors the wealth of the whole kingdom. The king sits upon the Iergild throne, arguably the oldest and most valuable throne in all the world. He is much like his father, a little large in the gut, filled with mirth and friendly, though fierce when roused. In battle he bares the Axe of the All Father, that greatest of Dwarven blades.

Aside from the occasional dispute with the Kingdom of Maine, the Dwarves of Norgorod-Kam dwell in peace with their neighbors. Kayomar and the Dwarves have a warm relationship, trading food for worked goods. Whenever a child is born into the royal family of Du Guesillon Dagmar King sends gifts of gold, worked artifacts and the like. The Dwarves guard the mountain passes with regular patrols. This is particularly true in the north for the Hobgoblins of Burnevitse have recently begun raiding in these areas. Too, the city of Gaxmoor, long removed from the world of Erde has returned of late and rumors report the vile god Narrheit has overwhelmed the place.

The Dwarves trade manufactured goods for raw materials. They are well known for fine craftsmanship, particularly where musical instruments are concerned. A harp of Norgorod-Kam is generally worth five times its normal value. The lute, pan flutes and others carry similar value. Beyond these the Dwarves fashion armaments and weapons. Beer for the Brass Halls is in great demand as well, and it is not uncommon to see large wagons lumbering down from the mountains piled high with barrel after barrel of beer. But the greatest export for the Dwarves is coal. From all over the Bergrucken Mountains they mine the black gold and sell it in markets from Maine to the Hanse City States. Mostly the Dwarves bring in lumber, food, wine and wool from Brindisium.

The Dwarves keep the roads over the Bergrucken safe for travel and welcome folk in their halls of stone. The Doors Impregnable are open and travelers come and go at will. There are taverns and Inns built for men and Elves. There are markets, concert halls, libraries and the like inviting merchants and scholars to explore them. All this is within the first few layers of the doors. The throne room is in the high vaults, and it is said that the Dwarven skill in shaping rock allows those within to see the world without, but those who clamber over the rocky precipices would never know that they walked upon a Dwarven world.

The taverns are famous for their fine beer and good music. They draw all manner of patrons to the kingdom. Songs of the old Kingdoms are very much in style, and Dwarven bards are commonly seen reciting tales of the ancient days. They speak mostly of the Lillian Way and its disappearance. There are rumors that the King will pay a great sum in worked Iergild and coin for those brave enough to explore the abandoned mines at the root of the Kingdom for that long lost highway.

A History Like None Other: The first mention of Norgorod-Kam comes during the rule of the Goblin King Ichlun during the early days of the Dwarves. There, the Dwarven smiths first unearthed the long lost passages to Inzae, the world within Erde. They fashioned wondrous spells which made traversing the space between the two worlds possible, and they followed them to the center of the world. From there they found tunnels that led back to Erde and more importantly, to the other Dwarf Hohles, where their kinsmen lay in hiding. They took many years to understand the workings of Inzae and Erde but when they did they set to forging the Brass Rings. These magical devices allowed the Folk to travel from one point in Erde to another (*reference The Histories, p. 17*). With this magic the Dwarves gathered great hosts of their kinsmen in one place and made war on the Goblins. As is told elsewhere, the Dwarf Lords overthrew the Goblin King and the wars went on.

These rings forged of brass earned the Kingdom the name, Halls of Brass. The king the folk called the Brass King, though in truth, iron flowed in their veins and they sat upon a magical throne made of pure Iergild metal.

After this the Kingdom fell into the mists of time and history, only the famous Mammoth Scrolls relating her day to day affairs. What little that is known the historians glean from the many songs and poems which the Dwarves love to retell. They fought in the many and long Goblin-Dwarf wars. Thousands of young beardling Shields marched to war under the brass pole, never to return. It is known that, in later years as other Dwarven Kingdoms fell into decay, that Norgorod-Kam prospered. Her halls did not suffer the ravages of the Stone Wars and her Kings ruled in an unbroken line from those days to these. They tunneled deep into the earth, making mansions fashioned of stone. Great arching hallways, bridges and roads led one through the well lit Kingdom to various places, houses, markets, smithshops and so on.

The greatest of their works they fashioned during the age of the Aenochians. As the story relates the Empress Rachel Lilly loved shoes very much. As with today, the Dwarves of the Brass Halls were possessed of many skills in fashioning art. They wove magic into their crafts creating instruments, jewelry, books, tapestries and clothing sought the world over. The Empress came to the King of the Brass Halls and begged him to fashion for her the most beautiful pair of shoes ever devised by man or Dwarf. That Empress, the Dwarves loved over much, for she, unlike many of her kin, laughed often and always made great efforts in complementing the Dwarves in the halls of Al-Liosh. And for this reason the Dwarf King heartily agreed to her request. (Of course the vast fortune she spent may also have had something to do with it). So the King set his best smiths and magi to crafting the shoes and when completed gave them to her in her palace in southern Kayomar.

The Empress, or so it is told, wept at the sight of them for their beauty was almost too much to bare. In gratitude she awarded the Dwarves all the revenue of the traffic which passed through or over the Bergrucken.

When she died she requested that her body be buried in the Brass Halls with the shoes upon her feet. This the Dwarves agreed to do. They took her to the roots of Norgorod-Kam and built for her a great crypt. There her body lay from that day to this.

In later years the Dwarves built a great tunnel which stretched underneath the mountains from east to west. They fashioned it of inlaid brass and placed two huge gates upon each end and named the highway The Lillian Way. They taxed the caravans coming underneath the city, vexing the Lords of Gaxmoor for stealing revenue. Though both entrances to the Lillian way have been lost, it is said in song and poem that to find it, is to find the Crypt of the Empress Rachel Lilly and those shoes of wondrous beauty.

So the Dwarves of the Brass Halls loved and labored. Their fame as craftsmen of artifacts of power and beauty spread the world over. When war came from the east under the banners of the horned god, the Dwarves came forth in whole troops. Cast in iron shod boots, with armor, shields and helms they soon proved that at the arts of war they excelled as well. They drove back the enemy time and again, only retreating to their mountain fastness when the Catalyst War ended all hope of the Kingdoms of men stealing victory from the jaws of defeat. The Dwarves fought on for two centuries, but when word came to them of the sacking of Grundliche Hohle, their King,

Dungror ordered the halls shut and bound. He set to making iron doors to hold the pits against the coming of the horned god. He collapsed the lower tunnels, burying the doors to the Lillian Way forevermore. Dungror set to fashioning chains from the Iergild iron and bound the gates in this substance. They called them the Doors Impregnable. In this way Unklar was denied entry to Norgorod-Kam for even that fell lord could not unmake what the All Father had made (*reference Iergild metal, Magic Items, p. 226*).

The Dwarves of Norgorod-Kam survived the Millennial Dark hidden in the fastness of their mountain kingdom. They lived in safety and as always before prospered, making their homes grander and mined the earth for ever more riches. The numbers of the Folk waxed in those dark days, and as is related, they alone of all the people of Erde thrived and grew stronger.

When war came, the Dwarves unleashed the pent up fury of centuries and delivered stunning defeats upon the enemy. Dagmar III led them, young and filled with the lust to see the sun and the moon unhindered. He ordered the Doors Impregnable open and marched forth with an army cased in iron and steel. The King bore the scepter of one of Unklar's Captain Kings, and the Axe which is the rightful possession of the Dwarf Lords. And the servants of Unklar fled from him and the whole of his mountains, but for the deeper places. The mountains were made clean, and the Dwarves knew much pride and rest in the days to come.

In an amazingly short time they cleared the Bergrucken and the Norlling of the enemy, even coming to the shores of Lake Orion. They harried the armies of Lord Orkhan in Maine and at the last joined King Morgan of Kayomar at the battle of Ox. Dwarven courage opened the Gap in the walls of that massive city fortress and held it against waves of Orcs, until reinforcements could come.

When Dagmar III fell, slain by a fire giant in the Norlling, the world moaned. He held the iron blood of his ancient forefathers and many grieved. The King of Kayomar alone sent 5000 bars of gold to decorate his tomb in the deep halls of Norgorad-Kam.

OF THE DWARVEN KINGS
Dagmar III
Dagmar IV

Ec Rating III & V

Northern Kingdoms

Countless are the Thanes and Chieftains who rule the northern wastes. But of them all, three stand out. The Kings of Haltland, Holmgald, and Trondheim. They carry no standards, nor coat of arms, but all the folk in the wide world know well their totems and dragon ships, the bear, the wolf, the elk. All are symbols of the barbarian north.

Of Those Three Realms and Others Besides: The northlands are wild places, where steep mountains rise from the wastes of the sea. The rugged coast hides many coves and harbors where small, cold beaches end in sharp cliff faces. In a few places, the fjords and the hills are not so steep and offer man and beast refuge from the winds of the Inner Sea and the cold of the northern mountains. There, giants stalk the land, beside huge cave bears and lions with teeth as long as daggers. It is an harsh land, dangerous to the bold, deadly to the unwary. The land is cold, winter lingering into spring. Snow drifts on land and ice caps at sea make the land an inhospitable place to those unused to the biting cold.

All along the northern coasts of the Inner Sea men have carved out homes for themselves. They bare little likeness to the civilized folk of the Young Kingdoms, for they dress in furs and carry little armor but shields and helms. They worship wild gods, hunt bears for sport and pay little heed to magic or sorcery. Many farm what arable land exists in the northern latitudes, others hunt and many more make their living by pulling fish from the sea. They hunt whales for oil, and walruses for ivory. But no matter their occupation, they love war and battle, and do not fear the death such a life brings. The Thanes of the tribes bring terror to the Young Kingdoms in wooden ships of simple sail.

There are many small tribes and several lesser ones along the coastline and in the bays of the north. They rule small kingdoms of villages and towns, and field armies of dozens of men only. They raid the coasts in the south in three or four ships, but despite the small numbers, or because of them, they bring a great deal of destruction. The Lothian Monasteries (*reference Guilds & Orders, p. 197.*) have recently suffered from these raids, proving to many that the reach of the forest god Daladon does not extend to the depths of the Inner Sea.

Trade with the Northmen is sporadic. However, some bold shipping captains from the Hanse Cities do travel the Inner Sea seeking those things only found in the north, or found cheaply in the north: Carved ivory, iron, loot, bone, wood, bear skins, pelts of beaver and fish. The Northmen jealously guard their hunting grounds where they whale for the feared Leviathan beasts (sperm whales) for their delicate meat and oil that is sold at extremely high prices throughout the known world.

Of all the many scattered tribes of the Northmen, three have risen which are greater than the rest and rival many of the Young Kingdoms in wealth and power.

Haltland: Here King Odovakar rules from the Great Hall, Borgundullum. There lies one of the more prominent barbarian kingdoms of Ostrogoths. Haltland lies in the mountains of the far northern climates. Several tribes of Ostrogoths make up this loose confederation. Their King is chosen by a test of arms and rules until challenged and slain. The Ostrogoths are a fierce tribal people who glory in battle and war. They live communally in great stone and thatch halls nestled in the bays and estuaries of their land. Travelers are welcome but must endure feasts that last days, tests of arms that often run deadly and other dangers of the flesh. The Haltlanders are forever warring on their neighbors and crossing the Inner Sea to plunder and ravage the Young Kingdoms.

Holmgald: King Thorismund IV towers over his land in the Great Halls of Gokstad. Holmgald is the sister Kingdom of Haltland. Just before the Winter Dark Wars Thorismund the Conqueror united the Visigoth tribes, some of the Ostrogoths and Tervengi under the Amal clan. The Amals still dominate this frozen kingdom. Much like the Ostrogoths, the Visigoths revel in raiding and war. They are not adverse to plundering the coasts of their foundling kingdom, Eisenheim (*reference Eisenheim, p. 84*). Like their neighbors, the people of Holmgald gather in small villages and great halls and are famous for their seamanship.

Trondheim: Here lies the home of Thane Karl the Bear, called such for as the tales relate, with his hands alone he strangled and pummeled the life from a Cave Bear. He rules from Aggersholm on the sea. Trondheim as with all the north, benefitted from the battle of Gokstad (*see below*), and is home to the powerful Gruetungi and Alanni tribes. These wild northmen, like their cousins to the west, live off of plunder gathered in the southern lands. The Gruetungi are usually at war with their immediate neighbors, the Visigoths, in Haltland. Karl makes his home in the Great Hall of Trondelag in the city of Aggersholm. Trondheim is home to many strange travelers, for it alone serves as a gateway to the Frozen Salt Flats (*reference Terrain, p. 161*) where, it is said, the battles between the gods Unklar and Narrheit occurred.

They Carried No Fear for the Dark of the Deep Quiet: For centuries the men and women of the wild north lived free of the rule of Unklar. They thrived in the Winter Dark, for they lived already in the frozen north, pulling their livelihoods from the sea. They saw the coming shroud of Darkness as the breath of the world and wondered when Ragnarok did not come. These people lived in tribes, many the direct descendants, or so it is written, of Dwarves from the Days before Days. They lived their lives apart from the history of men, concerning themselves only with the immediate and the distant; that being the road to the afterlife. The harsh life of the northern mountains made them a sturdy folk and the livelihood they pulled from the sea made them mariners without equal.

They lived in tribes and bands, all along the mountainous coast and in the hinterlands as well. They bore names which reflected animal totems; the Alanni (those like the bears), Amals (the whalemen), Gruetungi (wolves on rock), and so forth. They fought each other on occasion but mostly they fought the Frost and Stone Giants who forever terrorized them.

In time some tribes rose above the others. Upon the eastern slopes of the Roheisen Mountains Thane, Thorismund of the Amal clan, conquered many of the tribes and bound them under his rule. These Ostrogoths, so called for they lived on the eastern slopes of the Roheisen Mountain, vied for control of the islands of the straights with the Visigoths, who lived further east. {Note: the name "Goth" derives from ancient Dwarven, "gotha" being the word for tall. The Dwarves called men the Gotha fu, literally the "tall people." It is a name which the Northmen adopted only after the Winter Dark Wars} Legends and songs of the Goth tribes relate tales of a time when man and Dwarf lived in peace and great concourse, though the halls of Roheisen Hohle had long been closed to the outside world until only recent memory (*reference Roheisen Hohle, p. 128*).

With the outset of the Winter Dark Wars, the snow began to recede and the southern lands became lost in internecine war. For reasons that are not completely understood, the northerners suddenly exploded upon the lands of Ethrum and Aenoch. Whether they sensed a weakened zeal in the Imperial Legions or they reacted to internal turmoil is not known, but what is known is the terror they brought with them from the north.

With the likenesses of the gods and the Dragon Inzae upon their ship prows, the Northmen rode the tides of the Inner Sea to war and slaughter. At first they raided small villages, burning coastal farm houses and thorpe. They sank fishing vessels and threw their captains into the sea. They carted off many slaves at first and little plunder. But in the year 1019md, the Ostrogoth Angatyr led a bold raid against Toninburg, a town upon the northern shores of Angouleme. In Toninburg stood a temple to Unklar and many wealthy merchants made their living off the trade of produce from the sea. Angatyr, leading four ships filled with 30 men apiece, attacked the town upon an early cold morn. The ease of the victory caught Angatyr and the town by surprise. The town, helpless against the onslaught, fell to Angatyr who ordered it plundered and burned. The booty they carted back in gold, jewels and slaves amazed their fellows and galvanized the whole of the Northern tribes.

The Northmen built larger ships and filled them with eager warriors and by 1022md, the first large scale attacks took place all along the coasts of the Inner Sea. The raids picked up and the raiders became bolder, attacking down the coastline to Freiburg and beyond. The people there clamored for protection, calling to the powers in Aufstrag. The Imperial response was rapid. They dispatched a fleet of galleys to destroy the barbarians. They came from Iergaul, Avignon and other cities, sailing north to the sprawling city-encampment of Gokstad, intending to burn out the barbarians.

Twenty five vessels bore the 58th legion from Aachen into the north, sailing for Gokstad. Two months on the open sea brought them into the vicinity of that town. But the Northmen set out in a host of long boats under King Thorismund and met them at sea. They sailed to meet the Imperials in open battle, lusting as they did and still do, for death in war. Never in the memory of man had a human fleet contested the seas with the ships of Unklar. The captains were afraid, not knowing what to do. But the Northmen did know, and in packs they surrounded the larger vessels and disabled them with fire and axe. So great was their lust for slaying that they forgot all booty and with great waste burned the fleet into the depths. Making sacrifice to their grim gods they celebrated a great victory. And the 25 ships and all of the 58th Imperial Legion returned home never no more.

This victory opened the southern lands to further depredations and eventually to migrations. The raids also triggered the creation of such states as Angouleme and the Hanse City Federation.

As is written, when the ice began to break asunder, and the Shroud of Darkness parted, the raids of the Northmen continued unabated and much slaughter and devastation came to the lands of Ethrum and Aenoch. They built small forts along the coasts. The rivers served as avenues for the raiders and the first of them arrived in Augsberg, traveling up the Olgdon River in 1027md. They plundered several castles and killed a number of the men living there. The Northmen saw Unklar's clerics as evil men and burned them wherever they could find them as they do any who pay credence to the god of the Black Tower. They carted great mounds of booty back to the north.

Lord Quin, Commander of the 18th Legion, sought to stop them and moved a great host of men from the Luneberg Plains to the mouth of the Olgdon river and to other extremes, hoping to block the raiders. In this he was fatally outdone for a large party of Northmen fell upon his scattered cohorts and in a series of rapid attacks scattered them. The 18th, mostly inexperienced men and tribal orcs, disintegrated and Quin fell upon his own sword.

And the Northmen come down the water ways of Ursal once more and with ships of dragon prows they sailed across the Amber Sea. They plundered the outskirts of Avignon and ravaged the coasts of Angouleme, burning many cities, villages, and towns and carrying off many to slavery and death. Too, their plundering reached the Elorian Isles. In the east they arrived at Trier. The Admiral of the Black Fleet did not put to sea, but fortified himself in his ports. And the Northmen plundered all the coasts of the Amber and Inner Seas and as far inland as the rivers let them sail. A small party passed into the southern gulf but they were defeated and all slain in battle with ships of Morgeld's crafting.

The raids slackened with time but the Northmen gather in ships still, pray to their gods and cut the waves of the sea intent on plunder and war.

Ec Rating II

Fyorgyn

Onwaltig, the Orc realm, The Crusp

From the back of his horse the Sanjak Mordinang, "The Voice of Unklar" rules a populace of warriors. In Xarteris, his capital, he piles the collected loot of his marauding armies. The broad banner of that land hangs from a staff and pole. The cloth is stained black with a crescent moon, and upon the cross pole hanging from short chains are horns, horns, horns.

Of Onwaltig's Lords and People: The archipelago of Onwaltig consists of three large islands and a dozen smaller ones. The waters here are treacherous for those who do not know the lanes. Rocks jut up from the ocean floor to just below the surface, easily placed to tear a gaping wound in a ship's hull. The water is always choppy and unpredictable. Upon the islands themselves are rich pastures for grazing or farming. These give way to gently rolling hills that tumble down to low sea cliffs and broad beaches. Orc villages abound, particularly on the main southern island. There are few trees upon the wind swept isles of Onwaltig.

Mordinang the Orc is Anjak in Onwaltig. He dwells in a large temple fortress just on the outside of the town of Xarteris. From there he commands his legions, bares witness to the priests and speaks law as the "Voice of Unklar." It is Mordinang's greatest dream to bring back the horned god, and to this end he employs wizard-priests to seek out their master and bring him back. He gives them monies and plunders the world for whatever components they may need. Many an Orc adventurer has left the island lands in quest for some exotic leaf or something similar, only to die upon some lost trail. Mordinang is a small Orc, but skilled in combat. He holds his position through a mixture of cunning and cruelty.

The Anjaks of Onwaltig command with absolute authority. They watch the island, and all that comes and goes, through a series of small towers perched along the coastline. These vary in distance from one another, but are always within sight of the watch fires, for this is how each tower communicates. Generally the towers have eight to ten occupants and a few slaves to keep them. There are regular patrols as well, for the Orcs live in constant fear of an attack by one of the Kingdoms to the north or west.

The wizard-priests of the Paths of Umbra dwell in the Xarteris practicing their craft openly, as they can do nowhere else but for the Pung and the United Kingdoms. They bend their time to seek the answers to the riddles of Unklar's disappearance. They are a powerful sect in the Orc society, all the more surprising since they are all humans. Rumors abound that the Arch-Magi Nulak-Kiz-Din resides here, plotting alongside the orcs for the return of Unklar.

The Orcs live in villages, usually surrounded by ramparts of wood and dirt. Their houses and other buildings tend to be made of sod or, in some cases, wood imported from the mainland with great difficulty. They farm for subsistence for the most part, however, several farmers grow large crops of barley and rye to brew beer. Large herds of cattle supply them with enough food and leather to meet all their needs. Especially important to the coastal areas are the pearls from the sea and dried fish foods. Inland, a wealth of food, wood and spices support the Orcs and their armies. Few will openly trade with Onwaltig, but merchants from the Hanse City States and Eloria come here on occasion.

Onwaltig is a dangerous place to travel and few interlopers are permitted. The tales of vast treasures which were carted here after the war, abound, however, and attract all manner of thieves and erstwhile adventurers.

The Anjak Mordinang commands four thousand heavy orc infantry, and several hundred wolf riders. They have a dozen large warships, and numerous troops of light infantry.

The other islands are much like the main one, though not as crowded nor as well guarded.

Of the History of Onwaltig: During the days of the Winter Dark many Orcs served Unklar in his legions. They fought loyally in almost every campaign from Al-Liosh to the Solarium Empire. Quickly, the battle captains of the horned god learned that singly or in small groups the Orcs could not be relied upon, but when permitted to fight in large units, they achieved amazing feats of arms. They possessed, as they still do today, a penchant for organization and mass battle tactics. Heavy casualties only added fuel to their rage upon the battlefield, so long as large numbers of them remained. For these reasons the Orcs served the mighty Unklar well, for many hundreds of years.

For their part, the Orcs loved their dark master, if such creatures can know love. He conquered a world and laid it at their feet. More, he conquered a world which, for centuries, hounded the Orcs in their every cave and fortress. He showered them with lands, property and rank. Even their own cruel gods failed them in these things. But Unklar did not and to him they pledged themselves. And they ruled in Erde for a thousand years.

In heavy armor, plate, and shield, with axes, cudgels and iron shod hammers the Orcs of the Winter Dark terrorized all with whom they came in contact. Their stamping feet, martial songs and lusty howls for war became common place in the towns and villages of the horned god's empire. People fled from them, for of all the cruel servants of Aufstrag, these possessed the meanest of natures. They tortured and pillaged when they needed supplies. They forced common folk into work camps. The Orcs carted others off to the slave pits, the mines, or the galleys, many of these poor souls never seen, nor heard from again.

During the Age of Winter Dark the Orcs earned the greatest hatred from all the demi-humans and men as well. The Halflings most of all hated the Orcs, for those poor gypsy folk could do little to fend off the iron banded legions, in the early years at least. Later, after the Halflings scattered into the deep woods, living in smaller family groups, they learned to fight all the minions of Unklar. But in truth, they relished destroying Orcs.

The Orcs' greatest weakness lay in Kayomar and under the dark eves of the Eldwood. There, in the closing days of the Catalyst Wars, King Robert Luther, leading his paladins and knights, fought for so long, so hard, destroying thousands, that the Orcs believed he possessed the soul of some undead god. Ever a superstitious lot, the Orcs feared him as an unconquerable spirit, an avatar of their own destruction. During the final siege of Du Guesillon, the King struck Unklar a blow upon his helm so great that it split the iron helm drawing blood. The blow sent the horned god falling from the high wall where he crashed into the ground with a mighty clap. Robert Luther's laughter frightened the Orc hosts such that they broke and ran from that land in complete terror.

To this day the name of Kayomar is whispered amongst the Orcs in fear, and the name of Robert Luther never mentioned but as the foulest of curses.

When the Winter Dark Wars began the Orcs fought with a ferocious zeal. Never in their wildest imaginings would they have thought that anything but victory would be theirs. With wild abandon they plunged headlong into battles. They fought the Dwarves in the Flintlock and Grundliche Hohle. Their iron shod boots tramped over the Luneberg Plains, Augsberg, Aachen and Karilia. They fought in Maine against the rebellious Pius. And a host of them even dared dread Kayomar in the Battle of Weather's Gap and the siege of Ox. More than this they fought upon the walls of the Solarium, finally destroying that distant land. And many thousands perished at the hands of Morgeld in far off seas.

The Orcs served with zeal and loyalty, but their commanders could not master the enemy. They did not understand it but their god could not aid them, so in the end, despite their cruelties, their hatreds, their love for one-sided war, the Orcs and their dark master were thrown down. Defeat after defeat destroyed the integrity of the legions, so that many of the soldiers deserted, seeking more lucrative, and perhaps less dangerous, employment. The Orcs, their numbers shattered drifted into hiding. They took to the deeper forests, the Darkenfold, the Grossewald and rugged mountains and wilderness, seeking safer grounds from the ever present lust for revenge of which the men and their allies seemed to possess an unending flow.

Many priests of Unklar joined the Orcs, for their religion made them hated enemies of most men and to remain in their temples invited certain death by burning. The wizard-priests first suggested to some of the Orc chieftains that they, the Orcs, should carve out a kingdom for themselves before their enemies utterly destroyed them.

An Anjak (the Orc title for Commander) by the name of Issa took the wizard-priests seriously. He listened to them for a great while, until at last, he thought he understood the message of Unklar. A rather intelligent Orc, possessed of many skills, Issa applied himself to unraveling the mystery of where they should found such a Kingdom.

In a very short while he decided upon the island of Onwaltig. Isolated, yet near the land, this island could house a host of his fellows and give them a safe harbor within which to recover their numbers and power.

Issa called upon the wizard-priest to send messages to others of their kind, to the shamans of the Orcs and so forth. He bid them tell the Orcs that in Onwaltig they could find succor from their many enemies. Issa himself led a small army of Orcs, warriors mostly, but many females as well to the island realm. They passed, after many hardships and adventures, over the Red Hills and into the Aenochian Forest. There, they built river boats and set off down the wide Olgdon until at last they came to the sea. Next, they sailed their cumbersome river craft out into the waters of the ocean, though Issa carefully steered a path parallel to the coastline. In 1043md he abandoned the coast, cutting across the Lagon Straights, to come at last to the island of Onwaltig.

Issa built a camp from which he organized the construction of the Orc Kingdom. The Orcs set about fortifying the island with monstrous slag heap castles and numerous underground warrens. Town and village sprang up across the fertile plain, particularly as more Orc refugees arrived. They came on ships, rickety boats, canoes even. In all this the wizard-priests gave instruction, guidance and rekindled the Orc lust for their master in Aufstrag.

Issa used the old Imperial chain of command to ensure the survival of the country. He divided the warriors into cohorts, the number of which increased with every influx of fresh bodies. He established a small fleet as well by taking the best of the ships which came to Onwaltig for himself and his marines. Within a few short years the Orcs were pirating along the coasts and north to Tagea. No folk in those days possessed the strength or the will to dislodge the Orcs. So they were left to their own devices.

By the time of Issa's death in 1060md, the island had become well fortified and structured into a highly caste society. Those who followed the long rule of Issa could never master the efficiency of his rule, but they did maintain his power.

Later attempts at dislodging the Orcs proved futile and were soon abandoned. The Tageans attempted on several occasions, but only led the Orcs to occupy the two islands north of Onwaltig.

Ec   **Rating**
II

OF HER MASTER
The Anjak Mordinang

Outremere, The Far Kingdoms, The New Empire

In wondrous Ascalon her Imperial Highness the Empress of Aenoch, First of Al-Lios, the lady Pryzmira, sits upon the throne of her ancestors. The heraldry of the Empire reflects the political complexity of its makeup. The hawk harkens to the ancient heraldry of the House Golden. In its claws are the red and white rose of the old realms of Aenoch and Ethrum. The sword he bears is holy Discepro, the blade forged by Sebastian in the days of old. The bulls flank and support the Golden hawk with their backs, even as the followers of Demeter and the church in Outremere support the Empress. Five heraldic shields represent the Duchies of the realm, and two banners represent each of the city states. Woven throughout the background are snaking daggers, the birth right of the House, the Mark of the Emperor Marcus IV. And above it all the Cunae Mundus Usquam, the Cradle of the World with the jewel of god, the Eye of Thorax.

We have thrown off the yoke of one autocrat, we will not except the yoke of another. Know that we Free Cities of Outremere have signed a pact to elect the Empress to her throne. She has been in contact with us, as you very well know, for several years and we had some inclination of you coming from her.

Desmond of Ascalon to Jaren Falkynjager of the Council

The Empress & her Empire: Outremere, a name given to the lands by those coming and going from the west, is rather small in comparison to the greater Kingdoms elsewhere. It constitutes the whole of the isle of Ionus, much of the Kellerwald Forest on the east bank of the Udunilay, the coasts and some of the hinterlands beyond. The rolling hills and plains are rich in black earth and where the land is not cultivated a deep prairie grass grows. The Kellerwald is a deep, dark forest, where strange creatures abound. Too close to the Grausamland to be safe, it is more wild than civilized.

In 1097md, Pryzmira celebrated her 57th year as Empress of Outremere. She is old, 87, and the last of the rulers who emerged from the Winter Dark Wars. She has seen the world born in war and remake itself in its aftermath The venerable old woman is much beloved by her people. Whole generations have grown to maturity while she has sat upon the throne of Aenoch. Many view her person as the Empire, dreading the day of her demise. For her part Pryzmira has long since laid aside the heavy hand of rule and takes a less than active role in the administration of her realm. She struggles with increasing the commercial power of Ascalon in the markets owned by the Electors. Her military power is much greater now, due to the frontier conquests of so many crusader knights. They swear fealty to her alone, a fealty she gladly accepts.

In truth, her one great goal is to see her daughter, Neratite, crowned Empress, but to do this she must gain at least four votes from the seven Electors. To increase her bargaining position, in 1095md she called for another crusade.

The Empress of Aenoch is elected to the throne by the seven Electors. These Electors are lords of the towns and provinces of the region and are the Dukes of Dundador, Ascalon, Aesperdi, Thuringia, and Westlichia, and the Magistrate of the city of Trier and the Bishop of Heimstadt. It is these lords that Empress Pryzmira seeks to influence, garnering their votes for her daughter's dignity.

Crusader conquests bring mixed blessings to the Electors. On the one hand they enjoy an increase in trade of goods to the crusaders and the newly conquered frontiers. On the other hand these conquerors swear fealty to the Empress and she gains their dues in monies, kind and service (*see below*). This increases the might and the bargaining power of the Imperial House. So the Electors bend their wits and fortunes to restrict the acquisition of new land and hold back the crusaders.

The people of Outremer live in small towns or one of the few cities in the area, such as Trier. The lands about are dangerous, due to the proximity to Aufstrag, and most of the towns are walled. Most farm steads are as well, or, at the very least, easily defended. The worship of Demeter is strong here; churches and monasteries abound. In general the people are devout. The Empress struggles with maintaining the worship of the elder gods in the face of the church of Demeter.

The wealth of the Empire derives from the silk trade and from several spices culled from the sea. The silk trade is slowly slipping from their hands as it is now being transported directly west as the waters are becoming increasingly more dangerous due to pirates from the United Kingdoms and Eloria. They still control the sea spices and sell at ever higher prices in the far west. They are also well known for their luxury items, silver work and statuary. Another and more recent source of wealth has been the church. Taxation on pilgrims and protection services are growing in leaps and bounds. In turn great quantities of food and livestock are imported, for the land around is too dangerous to farm.

The Crusade, which the Empress has recently re-instituted, brings hosts of young hopefuls to the Empire on every boat. The docks and quays overflow with men and women seeking glory and fortune. What they conquer is theirs, they have but to swear fealty to the old Empress and she will grant them title to the land. This attracts all manner of people to the cities and towns, making them dangerous places where thieves and rogues stalk the unwary. The Church of Demeter supports her in this crusade, continually calling for the brave to travel to the New Empire to war upon the enemy.

Outremere promises high adventure and quick wealth. The political and religious unrest cause constant feuds between the seven Electors and the Empress, between the old and new gods. The added threat of pirates from the United Kingdoms only stirs the tumultuous waters. A continuous call for crusaders to rid the lands to the north of wild orcs and remnants of the horrors of Aufstrag make Outremere a beacon for would be glory hunters. And of course the Imperial promise that "what one conquers, one keeps, what one keeps one swears homage for" only draws more adventurers, for land, after all, is power.

The Long Reign of Tradition and the Making of an Empire: The history of the early empire as told elsewhere relates the story of the Mark of the House Golden, the line of the Emperors of Aenoch. Any child born of this line bore a birth mark of a snaking vine with a needled point. In the year 1010md a slave of Aufstag gave birth to such a child. The tales relate how Jaren of the Order of the Scintillant Dawn, suffered a thousand years of torment in the pits and upon the walls of Aufstrag. At times he lay at rest in dark dungeons, Nulak, his ever present tormentor worried lest the spirit of a his play toy be destroyed. He let the monk heal, with copious amounts of food and drink.

A slave woman in the pits with Jaren served him during these times. Eventually the two became enamored with each other. The end result was the birth of their child, whom they named after the old Ethrumanian goddess, Pryzmira. Jaren entreated his paramour to flee the pits, knowing that Nulak, if ever he got wind of the child would make them all suffer and encouraged her to flee during chaos of the Trench Wars (*reference the Histories, p. 34-35*).

In time Jaren escaped dark Aufstrag and joined the Dwarf and others in the Winter Dark Wars. He sought out the halflings and brought his love and his daughter to safety upon the Isle of Dreams. There, while not at war, he raised Pryzmira as a priestess of Toth. When he shaved her head for the induction he found the Mark of the House Golden and was amazed, that ancient brand which the Emperor Marcus IV gave over to his descendants. Pryzmira stood as heir to the Imperial throne of Aenoch. In a few short years she came of age and when she learned of her heritage she declared she would seek her throne.

The Winter Dark Wars raged across Erde for two decades. Everywhere men waited to see which way the wars would go, but after Olensk it seemed obvious. Pryzmira knew she had but to find the right allies to support her claim. She soon found them, or they her, in the lands south and east of Aufstrag in the Kellerwald. The provinces and cities of Heimstadt, Trier, Dundador, Ascalon, Aesperdi, Thuringia, and Westlichia had lived under the shadow of Aufstrag for a thousand years. They grew wealthy through control of the overseas trade routes and they suffered little from the hand of Unklar. In consequence, a powerful, educated merchant class came to rule these cities. When war came to the Empire, these lords and Burghers banded together in a loose confederation and prepared to rebel.

In those days, much as it is today, the merchants of that region employed a small host of house wizards, sages and the like. They did this mostly to learn of weather and bandits, but on an occasion one would surface with the true powers of a magi. Such a one came to the Lords of the seven cities and claimed that a new Empress waited upon the Dreaming Sea for a call from her people to come to Aenoch and rule again. They sent their prayers to the Lord of Dreams and bid him bring her to them. This St. Luther did at her request.

Pryzmira, last daughter of the House of the Old Empire of Aenoch, came to them and promised the wealth and power of the Council if they would support her claim to the ancient lineage. She bore the Mark and they believed her. They agreed to league with Pryzmira under the stipulation that each of the seven lands, the provinces of Aesperdi, Eichstatt, Kourland, Thuringia and Westlichia and the city states of Heimstadt and Trier, be given the rights to elect the Empress and her heirs to the throne. In turn, she demanded that their borders be permanently fixed, that they give her the city of Ascalon to rule from, and that they grant her wide privileges of taxation and expansion.

In 1030md, the provinces and cities declared themselves against Aufstrag and invited Pryzmira to rule them. Aufstrag had no strength left to combat this final blow to her prestige, so the rebellion went unchallenged. Pryzmira refused to be crowned without the Cunae Mundus Usquam, so her father, Jaren Falkhynjager gathered his

companions of the Council, and they tore the crown from the undead hands of the Lich Baron Harakon Petrovich, that servant of the Emperor Sebastian who had held it in safe keeping lo these many years. At last in 1040md, the Electors crowned the 30 year old Pryzmira Empress of Aenoch, by placing the Cunae Mundus Usquam, the "Cradle of the World," upon her head.

In short the constitutions drawn up were these: The military and mercantile alliance of the cities and provinces of Outremere granted their support and elected Pryzmira Empress after she conceded the following: 1. Pryzmira recognized the territorial rights of the League members and agreed to the investiture of Ducal authority for each territory with subsequent rights given to the Lord, including justice, maintenance of troops, and taxation. 2. Pryzmira recognized the rights of the City Burghers and Lords to choose the successor from their own number to each Ducal throne. 3. Pryzmira agreed to support the League militarily, maintaining the League's mercantile rights. 4. Pryzmira agreed to support a general free trade throughout the League 5. Pryzmira agreed to maintain an army from her own expenses to act as protection of the League and "Empire." She agreed that the Imperial army would not be used but for extreme purposes within the territories of the League itself. However the members agree to supply 500 well equipped men-at-arms in support of the Imperial Army for a period of 40 days each year or in the advent of no troops being available to supply monies to hire mercenaries.

In turn the League bestowed the crown of Aenoch upon Pryzmira's brow and installed her as their new Empress. They gave her lands surrounding the city of Ascalon to support her household. In Ascalon a castle and tower were built for her at the League's expense. Furthermore, she was given all rights of taxation upon the roads and rivers and sea ports (this last only upon non-League members). At last the Imperial House gained sole rights to the minting of coins and the status and conquest of territory they left to the Empress's judgement.

In this manner Pryzmira came to rule the New Empire, though in truth hers was but a shadow of her ancestors power. Though for many years she strove to combat the Dukes and gain leverage over them. This led to many internal conflicts and the slow evolution of a complicated feudal system. Pryzmira introduced the cult of Toth to the realm to vie for the souls of the common men. Only a few converted, and mostly those possessed of great wealth.

As she grew older the Empress mollified her demands and rarely struggled with her Dukes. She turned instead to conquering new land and in this vain called to the west for a crusade, promising land and wealth. The summons generated wide enthusiasm in the west and hosts of men came to carve holdings for themselves. Though the coming years saw many victories and some expansion, the Empire failed to expand much beyond its original borders. The worship of Demeter, however, came with the crusaders. Before long the seven lands became powerful supporters of the new religion only adding to the complexity of the highly charged politics of the realm.

Ec Rating III & V

| **OF HER RULERS** |
| Empress Prymira |
| The Seven Electors |

Punj, the Kingdom of

The present King, Feodor III, rules here from the halls of Ivangorod. The standard of this vile Kingdom still pays tribute to the god Unklar, a large black eagle on a white background, beneath whose claws are two cannon pointing out with other weaponry on the field beneath. A castle sits upon the eagle's right and Unklar's silver crescent moon is emblazoned above the eagle's left.

Of Her King and People: Feodor III, equal in stature to both his father and grandfather, rules the Punj with an iron fist. Unlike his forefathers he is a religious man, paying heed to the priests of Unklar and their prophets. He styles himself a religious warlord and openly calls for the return of the orderly rule of Unklar. Feodor III relies upon the High Priestess as his chief servant. The King is a cruel man, and his court a dangerous place. Hhere, intrigue abounds, as scions of the noble houses vie for power with merchants, thieves' guilds and priests.

The wizard priests of Unklar, personified in the Cult of the Paths of Umbra, pay heed to their dark god and their temples are in every major city. The High Priestess styles herself Nectanebo XIX, after the great priestess of Unklar's day. Despite this, they do not inflict evil upon the populace as in the days of old. But rather concern themselves with the business of the King and exploring the vastness of the outer planes in search of a spell to bring back the horned god.

The countryside is ruled by a nobility of ancient linage. These families command the King's Cohorts and rule the serfs as they see fit; some corrupt, others less so. Orc lords and even a few Eldritch Goblins, once a powerful contingent in the Imperial legions, remain in Punj, and serve the King and his offices. Punj wars upon her southern neighbors, but more often her energies are spent staving off barbarian attacks from the north and east. They still maintain the militaristic traditions of their fathers. As in the past a great deal of their wealth comes from the plunder they take from raids upon their neighbors. Most of the world's slave traffic originates in the Punj, as barbarians from the steppes are captured and sold as galley slaves and farm hands.

The Punj is a country of small deep forests, valleys and a rolling prairie. The serfs cultivate vast stretches of the region, growing an assortment of crops. Rye and wheat dominate the agricultural production, but lesser crops of barley and sugar beets are grown as well. The realm flourishes in trade, most of the traffic passing over the Flintlock in well guarded caravans to the west, where it is sold in the markets of Augsberg, Eisenheim and as far away as Avignon. Horses are the most valuable import, coming mostly from Augsberg. Of late, many of the merchants and nobles have begun trading with the Dwarves of Grundliche Hohle. This has met with mixed success, for the Dwarven memory is long and the loss of Havok Castle remembered (*see below*).

The Punj is a civilized land. Her people, nobles and merchants prefer to live in large walled cities, assigning the management of their estates to trusted foremen (usually soldiers). Though some are beginning to adopt the western habit of moving out into the countryside to manage their own affairs. In this manner small palaces and castles are becoming prolific across the whole Kingdom. In the cities, the streets are generally paved and the walls in good repair and heavily guarded. These towns are the last vestiges of Unklar's world and are orderly on the surface. The thief guilds own the night, many in service to the Umbra, but they pay a heavy price in gold to city officials for this privilege.

Many products are still grown in the Punj, nuts of many types, rare spices, fruits and so forth. The nuts travel to the farthest corners of the world and beyond so highly are they prized. A pound of spice may bring as much as 10gp.

The borders on the unknown east offer the bold a chance for glory and adventure.

The Punj Owes Its Very Existence to Unklar: When the horned god ruled the world of Erde he commanded vast legions of men. These experienced soldiers formed the nucleus of his rule. But as with any army of man or god, there are soldiers who command the fear of other soldiers. Such were the men of the Punj. Here, the lands bordered the wild Grundliche Mountains where the Dwarves of Grundliche Hohle waged a continuous war against the towers of Aufstrag. To crush them, Unklar strengthened the Punj with money and power, so that in time the men of those towns and villages became wealthy in the service of Unklar. They waxed powerful under the tutelage of the Winter Dark and became the greatest of the horned god's legionnaires.

During the Winter Dark Wars two legions held the Flintlock and the Punj against the Northmen, the rebel legions of Augsberg and the Dwarves. Eventually they were driven out. At the first Battle of Gotzenburg, 1028md, Paskevitch met and fell at the hands of Luther, Lord of Dreams, though the Paladin spared the Commander for reasons untold in the histories. Paskevitch fell back to the fortified towns and castles of the Punj. Defeated and disheartened, these men were all but forgotten in the continuing struggle. When The Council of Light banished Unklar from the world, the Winter Dark Wars at last seemed to be over.

But Paskevitch repaid Luther's mercy with continued war. In an amazingly short time he regrouped his scattered Legions, reformed them and made an attack on Flintlock. Many refugees from Aufstrag, Orcs and Ungern, joined him and several Eldritch Goblins as well. With their sorcery and his armies of men and orc he returned the war to the Council.

As is written Paskevitch delivered the single greatest defeat that the western alliances suffered. In 1030md, at the second Battle of Gotzenburg, his men stormed the Dwarven fortress and threw them down. The Dwarves fought on in many small pitched battles. But in truth they had never recovered the losses of Olensk (*reference Grundliche Hohle, p. 96*) and were made to suffer thereby. In battle after battle the Dwarves were routed from the heights of the Flintlock and by year's end driven into the mountains. There the disciplined legions dealt the Dwarves another humiliating defeat. In a stunning coup the impregnable fortress, Havok, fell to Paskevitch. 'Tis said that Goblin sorcery opened the gates of that place and let the men in, but none can now say for the castle is lost to all. Renamed castle Unklarglich, it has become a place of dread evil. They say that a Morgl from Aufstrag settled there, hungry for vengeance against Dolgan King.

Paskevitch, with Dwarven rule in the Flintlock ended and his western borders free, turned to reforming the scattered townships and cities. There, local nobles began asserting themselves in the absence of direction from Aufstrag. The consummate soldier, Paskevitch conquered the townships and reorganized them along military lines. Any who resisted him went to the gallows. Very rapidly he consolidated his power over the whole vast region. Though in truth, the Rhuneland threw off his rule after only a few years (*reference Rhuneland, p. 126*) Using the priests of Unklar he raised himself to the throne of the Punj where he ruled until his death in 1051md.

Mikhail Paskevitch, cousin of Feodor, assumed the crown upon the old warrior's death. He too knew little outside the life of a legionnaire. Born in a military camp, he grew up with little else and he spent the better part of his young life on campaign in the Winter Dark Wars. His proved to be an orderly, if harsh, rule. Mikhail, never kind, always dealt equally with his people, high and low. Under his guiding hand the remnants of the old legions were reformed. Their maintenance proved burdensome to the realm, and in order to alleviate this problem King Mikhail divided the old cohorts into smaller troops and dispersed them across the realm. The troops were segregated, the Orcs and Ungern, being put in cohorts of their own.

Always a wealthy province of Unklar's Empire, the Punj found adjustment to the new world difficult. They struggled against the growing chaos of particularism. It is for this reason that the folk of the Punj adapted well to the leadership of the House of Paskevitch. They were harsh task masters but they maintained the orderly world set down by the horned god. Too, they brought wealth in plunder and trade back to the lands and her people.

In the eighth year of his reign King Mikhail died battling raiders from the north. He is remembered as a great King by the folk of the Punj, his dying words entreating his lieutenants to keep his Uncle's Kingdom intact and safe from the "corruption in chaos which comes from the lands of the west."

Mikhail had no children and his fall ended the short lived Paskevitch dynasty. Feodor Godunov, the commander of King Mikhail's Horse Guard, took power in Ivangorod. Only a few challenged him but the scattered armies remained loyal to the name Feodor and so it was that the Godunov's came to power in the Punj.

Under the Godunovs, the Punj increasingly developed along the lines of the other realms of Erde. During his short reign Feodor II re-fortified the capital-fortress of Ivangorod. In order to maintain the cost of the cohorts he strengthened the hands of the nobles against the peasants and merchants, giving them rights to lands and property above and beyond what his predecessors had dared to do. The people groaned a little, but food remained plentiful and the power of the King untouchable.

Feodor II met his end at the Hittendain Forde in the Flintlock. The Lindesfarne clan of Gnomes refused to pay tribute and their Thane fell upon Feodor at a feast. He slew Feodore with a great hammer. For this the Lindesfarne clan was all but exterminated and to this day Gnomes enter the Punj with the greatest of care for their lives.

Feodor's son, Yuri, took the throne and during his long reign solidified the realm of the Punj as a great power. He further strengthened the privileges of the nobility and established their further loyalty to the Crown by liberally granting many of them commands in the cohorts. Many of these lords used these posts to further strengthen their regional power. Some were Orcs and a few Ungern, they ruled as any lords of the Punj. Yuri counteracted this by granting more rights of trade to the merchants so that they too would be loyal to him. In the ever increasingly complicated politics of the Punj, Yuri played one side off the other.

In the final years of his reign, King Yuri reformed the cohorts once more. He ordered the old brigandine breast plates discarded, and in their place the men were outfitted with chain shirts, long conical shields, basinets, scimitars and spears. Each regional commander was ordered to train one in every three of his men as horsemen (all the humanoids were exempted from this service). The House Guard, long mounted, was similarly attired and under Yuri it became common practice to hire mercenary soldiers to both fill the ranks and command the troops. He ensured their loyalty with generous payments of gold.

Yuri continued the tradition of his forefathers by dying in battle. In the latter years of his reign the powers of Aufstrag came under the rule of Coburg the Undying. He sought to bring back Unklar and in preparation for this began an attempt to reform the eastern lands where worship of the horned god remained common. Yuri rebuked Coburg and war followed. Coburg's power, still untested, proved no match for the martial spirit of the cohorts of Punj. Yuri led the army against the minions of the Undying one and destroyed them to a man at Crossed Plains. However, Yuri fell in the maelstrom, his body being brought back upon his own horse.

The priests of Unklar celebrated the victory and mourned the death by crowning the King's son as Feodor III.

Ec Rating III

OF THE PUNJ KINGS
Feodor Paskevitch 1031md-1051md
Mikhail 1051md-1058md
Feodor II Godunov 1058md-1064md
Yuri 1064md-1087md
Feodor III 1087md-present

Rhuneland

The Imperial Governors are gone and there are no Kings or Princes here; only towns. These powerful burgs possess high walls and are ruled by Mayors, Councils or Lordly families. Their Standards are too many to count and reflect the power of each city individually, the families who run them, the guilds who own them, the knights who defend them and so on.

The Character of the Merchants and Their Towns: The Rhuneland lies between the Olgdon and Ondavar Rivers. The Undunilay River runs through the region's center. These great rivers, smaller to be sure in these northern climes, and their tributaries water the flat rolling plains that lie between the Grundliche Mountains and the Grossewald Forest. Much of it is grassland, where a mixture of wild wheat and prairie grass grows. Old abandoned farms, stone shadows of their former selves, dot the countryside.

The Rhuneland is a wild place, where a dozen or so towns compete with one another for trade and farmland. Merchant families, guilds, peasant communes and a breed of urban knights are caught up in the ongoing struggle. The years of war long ago led the towns to erect walls with parapets and towers around them, and very few citizens dare to live in the open. This, coupled with an increase in the east/west trade, has brought a great deal of brigandage to the countryside. Orcs and Ungern from the Grossewald Forest and Hobgoblins from the mountains all stalk the open, unguarded country. Giants even, from time to time, come down from the north, hunting for easy prey.

The towns themselves are rough places. Taverns and brothels mingle with shops and markets on all the major streets. Out from the main thoroughfares people live in small houses, crowded on narrow streets. Mostly wooden affairs, these buildings are hazardous for a variety of reasons. Fires are common; thieves more so. It can be very dangerous to walk the streets unarmed at night and sometimes even during the day. The knights control the town guards, usually their own retainers, and are, as often as not, the city's only law. The various Mayors, Burghers and Guildsmen spend much of their time and money hiring rogues to do ill jobs against their competition. Sometimes against people in other towns, but more often against their neighbors.

Almost anything of an illicit nature can be found in the Rhuneland. Opium and lotus dens abound, most of them controlled by that guild of guilds, Muddles Inc. (*reference Guilds & Orders, p. 198*). Brothels and slave pits are common as well. The sport of Cleaver has even found its way into the towns. These small arenas, where two armed combatants are thrown against each other in a fight to the death, attract a great many gamblers.

The towns wage constant warfare against each other. They hire mercenaries to attack their neighbors, despoil the land and kill the farmers. This has led many farmers to form small communes. They till the land under the watchful eyes of the town guards, but at night retire to small walled burgs. Those who tend the cattle herds generally bring them into walled enclosures each night, or at the very least, up near the town's walls. Strangers are rarely welcome unless they bring plenty of coin. The farmers grow rye and some wheat.

Halfling Gypsies come to the Rhuneland all the time. Their wagon fortresses offer them an easy defense against marauding bandits. They thrive on the desperation of the townsmen and guilds.

The regions greatest export is leather, and this mostly to the Punj and the Dwarves of Grunliche Hohle. This has led the leather guilds to dominate in many of the towns.

The Red March lies within the Rhuneland's borders (*reference the Fantastic Adventure Module*). Some of the towns of note are Gorlice, Laibach, Celtje (pronounced with a 'K'), and Oroanograd.

Once Upon a Time, the Bread Basket of Erde: The vast sprawling Rhuneland, as well as the Luneberg Plains, served as the heart of the Imperial domains under the rule of Unklar. Here, the gifts of Unklar in the early days of his reign enriched the whole of humanity. With the Language of Creation, he wove new life into the frozen tundra. He gave to the people of those lands a wealth of plants to grow so that his frozen world of ice and snow would not starve. Ever since, the soil there produces abundant crops, full and rich to eat.

The sages remind us that Unklar did not do this out of kindness for the madness of starvation which his winters brought to Erde. Rather it came from necessity, for the strengths of gods are forever bound in the strengths of those who worship them.

During the age of the Winter Dark, the Rhuneland throve. Towns were erected along the banks of the great rivers, in the plains and upon the slopes of the mountains. They tilled the earth, planting and growing foodstuffs which were carted all over the wide world. The Punj to the east relied upon the foodstuff to feed their armies. Aufstrag's host of slaves could not have lived but for the Rhuneland. All this brought wealth to the area, which attracted an ever greater number of folk. The towns swelled with men and women whose whole concern was the buying, selling and transporting of produce. The farmers in their small villages grew the goods and the merchants used them to fill their purses.

They lived thus for many hundreds of years. Families grew old and passed into oblivion, while new ones arose. A fierce competition existed between various houses and towns. Mercenaries from all over were hired to defend caravans, to collect customs and to intimidate farmers. In time, a class of urban knight became prevalent there. Retired mercenaries who bought shares in the towns gained a vested interest, so they stayed and settled. They of course, brought their sons up in the service of various towns and grew wealthy in its defense as well as through the exploitation of the villages and farmers. In the latter years of the rule of Aufstrag, conditions became so bad that peasants and farmers built stone walls around their houses and barns. Often towns paid for these to help protect them and their produce from marauding bandits.

In all, the Rhuneland suffered greatly from the continual fighting of its masters. But the powers in Aufstrag turned a blind eye to the whole affair, so long as the food kept flowing to the legions.

During the Winter Dark Wars the region miraculously escaped despoilment. The battles shifted south to the unfortunate Luneberg Plains. The towns there were utterly destroyed, farmers put to flight or death and the whole area turned into a wasteland (*reference Luneberg Plains, p. 108*). But here, only the Dwarves threatened the security of the towns. They found themselves at war in the Flintlock more than in the plains, fighting the Master's of Punj for control of that great corridor to the west.

The Rhuneland did suffer however, for the Empire used up its vast wealth financing the war. The Commanders of the Punj garrisons marched through the towns continually on their way to the Flintlock. They quartered troops, procured food and equipment without pay and, most telling of all, robbed the region of most of its draft animals. These last they needed to pull wagons of supplies with them and to haul their great siege engines into the mountains.

When, in 1028md, the Dwarves defeated the Lord Commander Paskevitch at the first Battle of Gotzenburg, the retreating legions plundered their way across the Rhuneland. They ransomed merchants, impressed hundreds into the army and, in some cases, they looted the smaller villages often putting their inhabitants to death. When Paskevitch regrouped and attacked the Flintlock again in 1030md, much the same occurred as before. Grain was taken, livestock and equipment as well, and they paid for nothing.

The priests of Unklar encouraged the towns to give over their wealth to the legions to support the holy war they waged against the evil of chaos. Many turned against them then, welcoming the missionaries of Demeter who preached a better world under the new found sun.

The fall of Unklar led to rebellion and civil war throughout the Rhuneland as various towns and wealthy merchants vied for power. For a short while the King of the Punj, Feodor Paskevitch, exercised rule over the region, but his troops were too few and the towns too rebellious. By 1038md, he pulled out leaving the area to its own devices.

The region sunk into a long morass of internecine warfare of which it has only recently begun to recover. At first, the towns relied upon their own knights, long accustomed to defending the various burgs, to protect them. But the wars were brutal and the knights too few, so they hired mercenaries to fight their battles. All this warfare horribly disrupted the harvests, which had barely recovered from the depredations of the Winter Dark Wars. Trade dwindled until at last it dried up. With little money coming in, whole towns were soon bankrupt, unable to pay the many bands of mercenaries which now resided throughout the countryside.

These mercenaries began robbing their would-be masters, burning and pillaging the towns. This led, for a time, to mob rule. The guilds of various towns, acting in unison, drove out the mercenaries in one painstaking campaign after another. The slaughter on both sides was horrible and reflected the horrors which her sister lands in the south, the Luneberg, had suffered during the Winter Dark Wars.

At last, after many years, a certain equilibrium came to the Rhuneland, though not enough wealth remained to attract the soldiers of fortune. The guilds and merchants, desperate to reopen commercial trade with their neighbors, lay aside their internal squabbling and attempted to rebuild. And farmers returned, albeit in far lesser numbers, to the homesteads.

The Rhuneland prospered for a time, particularly during the reign of King Yuri in the Punj. He spent vast fortunes on reequipping his cohorts, and bought whole herds of horses from the western Kingdoms. Though his own folk guarded the transport of the animals, they had to pass through the various towns of the Rhuneland where they paid dearly for fodder and water rights. Eventually the export of grains to feed the horses of the Punj became a major source of income, as did worked leather goods for the cohorts. The slave traffic, mostly from the east, found ready markets in the Rhuneland.

Though towns suffered financial setbacks during the 1080's, due to bad harvests and giant raids from the mountains, they recovered quickly by shifting their focus to livestock grazing. Cattle farming became the norm and the leather guilds soon dominated the economy.

Ec Rating II

Roheisen Hohle, The Iron Kingdom & The Silver Halls

Here the venerable King Ondorog Helgostohl XIV rules from the Iron Rock. At such times these rare Dwarves are seen in the wide world, they bare the iron totemic pole of their people. At the apex of the pole a fan of thinly wrought iron blades extends to the heavens. Upon each blade are the names of great smiths. Beneath the blades are totems made of iron mixed with gold and platinum. The top disk bares the name of the Hohle's First Father. The second disk holds that of the King, the third depicts the Hohle's All Father, and all succeeding disks represent units, professions, etc.

Of the Mountain Fastness and Its Dying People: Roheisen Hohle, beneath Mount Tur, is the oldest of the existing Dwarf Hohles. Carved from the very rock of Mount Tur, the city kingdom sprawls out like a spider's web. The inner city is as old as any Dwarf structure. Little space is wasted here; halls border houses underneath bridges which span the roads to other homes and buildings. All of this carved from the heart of the mountain. But here, unlike most Dwarven Hohles, the tunnels fan out from the inner city, plunging into unspeakable depths, and driving outward as well, some beneath the straights of Roheisen. These holes and forgotten places were carved long ago, and have long since been abandoned by the Stone Dwarves.

The King is a large, very old Dwarf. He enjoys his drink overly much, determined, or so he says: "to spoil my last days on Erde with beer for blood in my veins and stone for skin on my bones!" He welcomes strangers as a novelty and guides them on tours of the abandoned halls of Roheisen.

The Dwarves here are not plentiful. Only several thousands occupy this vast city. They are anachronisms of the old world. They look different from the Dwarves which walk the south lands. They are thick boned with broad nose and lips. They hear and see in the Dark better than any but for the Eldritch Goblins. More than this, they suffer the Stone Curse (*see below*).

These last people of the ancient Folk do not trifle with wealth, for the combined masses of gold and silver within Roheisen defies description. They live life as they desire. Millennia of eating fish captured in the depths, and living off the peculiar molds and underground fauna that Dwarves have always eaten has given way to a plentiful amount of food imported from the southern lands, mostly from Grundliche Hohle. The Dwarves pay for these staples in coin or magic and in this manner some of the older world's arcana has come back into circulation. They also mine precious stones from the deeps, and to this day the trader comes to the iron doors seeking these rarest of rare treasures.

The Dwarves work hand in hand with their cousins in the Grundliche Mountains. They traffic in goods from one land to the other. Rumors report that both people are striving to dig a tunnel connecting the two mountain fastnesses. But more than the southern Dwarves, the Roheisen Dwarves love the Halflings. For these folk, in their large wagons, lumber up and around the coasts through Trondheim and Haltland to trade with the Folk of Mount Tur. On occasion they offer passage to the Stone Dwarves, for as is told, these poor souls cannot suffer the light of day upon their skin (*see below*). They travel within the wagons, secure in the knowledge that the Halflings will keep them safe and eventually return them home.

Many people lusting for knowledge, wealth or pure adventure come to Roheisen Hohle. The King readily grants permission to explore the lower halls. Any who do so must of course bring their findings to him, give over to him anything of particular value to the Dwarves, and pay a tax. The rest they may keep with his blessing. Many dark and strange creatures linger in the lower halls, having long since taken advantage of their abandonment.

Of Haven: The town of Haven, where Philip the Guileless first spoke of the coming of Demeter lies at the foot of Mount Tur. It served the Lords of Aufstrag as a penal colony during the Age of Winter's Dark. Though much damaged in the battles with the Fire Giant King, Haven quickly rebounded, serving as it did, and still does, as the greatest destination of pilgrims in all of Erde (*for more information on Haven, reference Divine Orders, p. 58*). The Stone Dwarves are on good terms with the town and its fathers.

A History Buried in the Depths of Time: Even before the Goblin-Dwarf wars, Roheisen Hohle stood out amongst Dwarven homes. There, in those days of yore, the Dwarves mined great stores of metal and these they fashioned into all manner of goods. The Kingdom's Under Father, Helgostohl, strove to carve a wonderful city from beneath the earth. He began by fashioning a throne from a huge block of iron, and this Iron Rock became the center of the all the happenings in Roheisen ever after. In time, the city grew large underground. The tunnels were like highways, bridges spanned the gulfs and arches carried roads from one height to the next. Thousands of Dwarves went about their daily tasks, crafting and mining, all in the well lit chambers of the underdark. Here, a city flourished, wholly underground.

In time, during the Goblin-Dwarf wars, an All Father placed one of the Brass Rings in the depths of Roheisen and the Kingdom became a great forge where were built all manner of articles of war. The depths they plundered for every scrap of iron they could to make themselves and their cousins invincible to the Goblins. As is told elsewhere, the wars raged across the planes and mountains of Erde for thousands of years and many a Hohle the Goblins plundered. Though on at least two occasions the Goblins lay seige to Roheisen Hohle, they never took the mountain city. During the second long siege, they managed to breach the underhalls but to no avail, for the Dwarves slaughtered them in great numbers and cast their dead from the heights.

In the 89th century, as Dwarves reckon time, during the height of these wars and after the second siege, King Helgostohl IX closed the gates to Roheisen Hohle and sealed all entrances to Mount Tur with magic of his own crafting. The King reasoned that their Hohle lay too close to the Goblin Kingdoms in the Grundliche Mountains and therefore suffered too much from the Goblin despoilment. Also, he reasoned, they had the Ring of Brass and could come and go as they chose and aid their cousins in the never ending wars.

This they did for some great many years, until at last a flaw in the great Ring caused it to crack. The King ordered his smiths to mend it and open the portals to the other Dwarven realms. This they failed to do though they labored upon it for many long years. At last King Ondorog II, the grandson of Helgostohl IX, commanded that they desist and that the gates to the valley be opened. But too many years had passed and the spells of the old King were forgotten. Try as they might they could not break the seals. Such were the magics of that previous monarch that the Dwarves were bound within Mount Tur, unable even to mine their way out.

In truth this did not perturb them over much. The Kingdom lived in peace and had not known such comfortable days since the early years before the Great Wars. To this end, the Dwarves lived out their days apart from the world above. They were ruled by the kings of the line of Helgostohl, called the Under Fathers. They mined deeper into the world of Erde and fashioned wondrous works of art and sculpture. They unearthed a vein of silver and with it decorated many walls and arches. It caused a peculiar affect. It reflected the light of torches and lanterns, casting a glittering array of light in front of any who traveled the halls. In this manner the Dwarves of that place took to calling their home the Silver Halls of Roheisen.

The years underground greatly diminished the folk of Roheisen Hohle. The light of day became as a legend to these people and as more of the elder Dwarves passed into stone they forgot their histories. Legends of ancient battles were told to children as fairy tales. They forgot their way in the dark deeps of the world. For a great while their population remained constant, even growing some. But when the Plague of Stone came into the halls, all changed. For a Dwarf the Stone Curse is a great calamity. It is an incurable ailment of the skin. Only Dwarves are subject to it, though some say that the Goblins also, fall to the curse. Its origins are not of the natural order but rather the mystical. Some say breathing the dust of magic crafting brings it on, others say lengthy exposure to the dark of the underworld is the cause. Still others report that the Stone Curse is nothing less than a corruption of the Language of Creation; a corruption of that magic which formed the world and which can never be overcome, even as creation may not be unmade.

Whatever its origins, the Stone Curse is a horrible disease, for it binds its victim to the dark. If a light much brighter than a torch brushes the skin, then that very skin is turned to stone. The pain of the transformation is excruciating, and the stone-skin must be cut off from the whole flesh. Those afflicted cannot even look at torch light or their eyes meld to rock, in which case they soon die. If the light of day should touch any part of the diseased then the unfortunate himself turns to stone. How the curse spread from one to another has always been a mystery. There is no cure for it, no magic poultice nor spell has ever had any affect.

This curse bound the Dwarves to an even darker world. Only with the greatest of care could they fashion things, as is always the want of Dwarves, for the light of the forge enacted the curse. They took to avoiding one another, few ever wed or mated, and fewer still brought offspring into the world. Soon, despair took them. They felt imprisoned in their underground world. They could not leave and those free of the curse knew that eventually they too would succumb. All attempts to combat the curse failed as they have to this day.

In time of years the once great Kingdom of Roheisen Hohle declined, becoming a shadow of its former self. Her Kings ruled an embittered people and the people cared not whether they lived or died. The world forgot about them. Those Dwarves who mastered the histories of their folk wrote the Kingdom off as one of the many which disappeared in the Goblin-Dwarf wars and even its locale they forgot. So the Dwarves of Roheisen lived, forgotten beneath the steps of Mount Tur, for thousands of years. And the world changed above them.

In the early years of the Winter Dark Wars the Council of Light pursued the Fire Giant King across the island straights to the very foot of Mount Tur. In the battle Daladon threw down the Fire Giant King, but his spell broke a great rift into the mountainside, uncovering halls of silver. The Council stood in amazement and set about exploring this lost world. They entered the caverns, exploring the deeps. They were greeted by heavily armed, pale skinned Dwarves of an otherworldly nature. Dolgan King of Grundliche Hohle stood at the Council's fore and talked with King Ondorog Helgostohl XIV. The two brother monarchs wept bitter tears for the discovery, and Dolgan pulled upon his beard at news of the horrid Stone Curse.

During the Winter Dark Wars, King Ondorog Helgostohl XIV made alliances with Dolgan and some of the Gnomes. Men styled the Dwarves of Roheisen Hohle the "Stone Dwarves." And though they did not come out of their kingdom to fight, they made weapons of war for their cousins and allies. Only once did the Stone Dwarves participate in battle, and that in the closing days of the war. Few could match them underground and a small troop of them, bound in cloth and moved in heavy wagons traveled to the Great Tree, entering its depths to fight a war against the creatures crawling underneath that horrid place. Tragedy befell these noble souls for they came even to ancient Klarglich, the forge of Dolgan when he served as Unklar's slave (*reference Grundliche Hohle, p. 96*), and the fires of that place ignited, casting them in a pale ball of light. One and all they were turned to stone, some only partially so, and their screams carried long into the hard places of that hard world.

To this day, the Stone Dwarves struggle with the Curse, trying to find a cure to the dreadful disease. They travel in huge iron bound wagons, drawn by fierce bears and mastered by Halflings who have endeared themselves to the Dwarves for the two peoples have had equal sufferings in the world.

Ec Rating III

WHO RULES FROM THE IRON ROCK
Helgostohl XIV

Sienna, the County

From Capua Count Jean-ot-Artemai rules the scattered lands of Sienna. Her coat-of-arms is easy to distinguish. A shield divided into four quadrants where the upper right and lower left quadrants are aqua blue with a white band going through each separately. The upper left and lower right quadrants are black with three Redbud leaves in each.

Of the Peculiar Nature of the Count and His Land: The small County of Sienna stretches from the eastern slopes of the Massif to the Elithian Wood. The land here is dry, an extension of the broken country to the west. Only in the shades of the Elithian does the soil improve, where water is plentiful in the guise of lakes and pools. Otherwise the traveler is greeted with a broken hill country, where scrub and prairie grass eke out a living from the sparse elements.

Count Jean-ot-Artemai rules from behind closed doors. When first endorsed by the Gathering of Forty, he toured the County, accepting oaths of fealty and re-affirming various lords in their lands. He traveled the land a great deal in the early years, but in 1090md, this abruptly stopped. He met his council in the late afternoons, and then only in the Great Hall of his palace where the doors and windows were shut. This struck many as odd, but few thought anything of it until he built the tower of Artemai. This tall dark edifice, set in the center of Capua, he surrounded with a high wall and gardens of thorns. The Count ruled Sienna from the tower with "stones for windows," or so the people called it.

His pale complexion, dabblings in sorcery and habit of working only at night lead many to believe that the Count has in fact given himself over to the undead. They fear him and only the bravest come to see him in his halls, where it is said, "his gaze is such that it can freeze the hearts of men." Disappearances of late, in the villages and towns, and once in awhile in the castles, have convinced people that Jean, in fact, is a Necuratul, or a Vampire. To make matters worse, wolves have come to settle in the country.

Jean rules through the Governor, Kenneth, who he trusts to keep the peace. Kenneth of O'nesbou, controls most of the trade and markets. He does this in the name of the Count, who owns the whole enterprise. Kenneth, a cleric of Demeter, feels for the poor and is seen traveling the countryside healing the sick and offering aid as well as he can.

As with her neighbors, Sienna thrives on the knightly tradition, and small castles and fortified towns dot the countryside. These are not as elaborate as their northern neighbors, for the country is poor and frequently are made of dirt and wood structures only. The Lords themselves depend upon the Count for employment. They frequently enter his service in the old Imperial posts which still exist (*see below*). The nobles are beginning to chafe at the dark nature of their Count and speak of his habits in hushed tones. Count Jean has not called a Gathering of the Forty in many years and this only causes more discontent. They do, however, jealously guard the privileges bestowed upon them by the previous count.

There are many small villages in Sienna where people make their daily bread through hard work and toil. The land is poor for crops and difficult to till, but the people are tied to it and may not leave by order of the Count. The peasants are a sullen lot, poor compared to their neighbors. They too wonder at the peculiar habits of their lord, and the fact that people disappear with little trace only adds to their worries. They are unfriendly and suspicious to strangers.

The region is known for its excellent warhorses, and raising and selling them is considered an honorable profession. The Count however, controls the herds, allowing only those loyal lords to utilize his stock for their own gain. The country produces little else.

A Land of Fierce People and Long History: During the age of Winter Dark, the lands of the whole of the Ethrum and Aenoch were divided into provinces. These frequently reflected the realms as they existed in the days before. The Lands from the Hanse River to the Massif and the Twilight Wood Unklar's servants divided into nine provinces: Angouleme, Enois, Aquaitaine, Blois, Limousine, Orange, Karilia, Cleves and Sienna. The folk who lived there, high and low, carried their strong class identity into the new age. Many traced their lineage to the old aristocracy of the Kingdoms of Ethrum, and as with their ancestors, they reveled in war and tournament. To bring these folk to heel, Unklar appointed Governors over them.

Despite this, the knights proved difficult to govern and they rebelled continually. To overcome this, the Governors appointed them to administrative offices, exempted them from taxes and allowed them to employ small troops of retainers. To control these men further, a noble, usually the most influential, was appointed as Count of the Province. The counts, though locally powerful, ruled in name only, answering to the dictates of the Governor. As time passed, more nobles entered the government as administrators, always seeking for appointment to the County Seat. In this way the Governor's pacified the region by creating an aristocratic caste of bureaucrats who made their wealth through controlling the region's commerce. The nobles never forgot their heritage, however, nor did they lay aside their warlike tendencies. In time many of the younger sons turned aside roles in the Imperial Governorships, but joined the Legions instead.

When the Winter Dark Wars began, Unklar's generals stripped the central lands of Ethrum of their garrisons. The Lords of Aufstrag desperately needed experienced soldiers for the battles in the south and east in the Grundliche Mountains. The central lands they deemed safe from rebellion so did not fear the consequences of withdrawing so many soldiers.

As with Cleves to the north and west, Sienna broke with the Empire slowly. When William of Angouleme spread rebellion throughout the northern provinces, the Count of Sienna did nothing. He offered hopes for a bright future and marshaled his men, but could not be induced to go to war. After William took the crown of Angouleme, the Governor of Sienna, Jerald of Ier and Count Etienne of Sienna sent emissaries, dutifully offered their congratulations and promised to meet with the King and discuss future arrangements. The Count of Sienna had no intention of surrendering what little power he had to the King and entreated the Governor to hand over the treasury to him so that he might hire mercenaries to stave any attack. The Governor, a weak man, horribly addicted to the pleasures of the flesh, acquiesced without any argument. So Etienne set about acquiring men, arms, armor and horses. The latter were furnished to him by a merchant from the Olgdon River region Augsberg. There they bred the best horses known in Erde and the Count paid for them all. In this way he inadvertently created what would, in time, become his realm's chief source of income.

The local aristocracy flocked to Sienna's banner. He promised them copious amount of gold for their loyalty. When, in 1026md, they gathered at the Count's castle, he dutifully paid them and they in their turn swore oaths of fealty to him. The meeting, called The Gathering of the Forty, became a tradition in Sienna, where the lords of the country reaffirmed their loyalty to the ruling Count and the Count granted them gifts and land.

In 1028md, King William once more sent emissaries to Sienna to press his claims of overlordship. These were rejected and the Count threatened war. Embroiled in conflicts in the Hanse City States and quarreling with Karilia and Cleves, William did not feel strong enough to press his claims. They were dutifully laid aside and in exchange for a sizeable gift, William dropped them altogether.

So the Count settled his House in the Governor's palace at Capua, the largest town in the region. Etienne never forgot his friend the Governor, and continued to endorse his position. Jerald lived out his days in the palace, drinking and frolicking. The Count also allowed those Imperial officials who swore oaths of loyalty to remain in their posts. In this way, he continued the efficient rule of the whole County by relying upon the bureaucracy already in place. The post of Governor he also renewed, even after Jerald died (of excessive drink), a practice which has continued to this day. This has created the interesting conglomeration of old Imperial government along side a feudal administration supported and endorsed by the occasional Gatherings of Forty.

Etienne died without issue in 1039md. A cousin, Hugh, endorsed by the Forty, took control of the County. Hugh soon learned that the Imperial treasure which Etienne relied upon for years was all but gone. In seeking a solution to the financial problems he knew he would soon face he stumbled across the idea of breeding the famous Olgdonberg horse which Etienne imported so many years previous. He immediately set about purchasing as many of the horses, particularly mares, that his lords would allow.

He bred the horses with great success. Within a few short years he established a market for their sale, primarily Destriers, in Capua.

People came from far and wide to purchase them. The horse, Sienna Olgdonbergs, are prized amongst the lords of Angouleme, Cleves and Maine.

During these years, the religion of Demeter spread throughout the country. Churches and a number of monasteries sprang up across the land. Even small villages spent their frugal earnings on churches, made mostly of wood.

Hugh I died a wealthy man. His young son, Hugh II, took the crown. Hugh II's passion for horses was only surpassed by his passion for the tourney. He sponsored events on the day of his accession and many more afterwards. He instituted the tradition of tourney's at the Gathering of the Forty. But this life led to his early demise. In 1053md, during a joust, a knight called Jaques Ali-Ance struck the Count such a blow that it broke his neck, killing him instantly. His body they lay next to his father's in the Crypt outside Capua.

Jeanne Charles, a distant relative, took the crown. The first Gathering of the Forty endorsed his candidacy and he ruled the County for many years thereafter. He supported the Bishop of Avignon during that Ecclesiastic's disputes with the King of Angouleme in 1060md. This led to resentment at the court of Angouleme-ot-Neider, a sentiment which has carried over to the modern era.

During Jeanne's reign, the County of Sienna suffered severe economics woes. The trade routes shifted further north, forcing many merchants out of business. Only the lucrative horse trade survived wholly intact, and this, of course, lay in the hands of the Count. A long series of droughts struck the country in the 1070's, devastating crop production. With starvation rampant peasants began to uproot and travel north and south, where they hoped, greener pastures could be found.

This exodus alarmed Charles and he forbid peasants to leave their homes unless they paid a tithe to him. This of course led to social unrest and some minor rebellions, often led by clerics of Demeter. The nobles put these down with a ferocity which surprised all. Even the King in far off Kayomar, Morgan II, called the blood baths inhumane and threatened to go to war against the Count. Threats from distant quarters aside, Charles continued the oppressive measures, dividing the country even further.

In 1084md Charles took his last breath and his cousin Jean took the crown. Jean, a clever man, dabbled in sorcery in his castle at Artemai. The Lords of the land endorsed him at the Gathering of the Forty. He appointed a Cleric of Demeter, Kenneth of O'nesbou, as Governor to aid him administer the land.

Ec Rating II

Of the Counts in that place
Etienne (1017md-1039md)
Hugh (1039md-1053md)
Hugh II (1053md-1057md)
Jeanne Charles (1057md-1084md)
Jean-ot-Artemai (1084md-present)

Tagea, the Ocean god's folk

In Tagea, two Kings rule. King Leonidas the soldiery, and King Demosthenes the city and populace. They carry long, black and red shields in battle and these are decorated with a gold circle in the center, from which eight spears radiate.

The Land of Two Kings: The islands of Tagea consist of eight larger isles and dozens of smaller ones. Gentle hills and slopes dominate the isles' topography. Wild grass, mingled with brush, cover the islands, making them prime grazing land. A few small wooden glens grow here and there, usually around a small lake of which there are plenty. There is some wild game here, but mostly birds, cranes, geese, ducks and the like. The country is not difficult to negotiate, making travel easy. The smaller isles have few people living on them, a colony or two at best, and attract religious hermits, retired veterans and so forth. Those, in other words, who enjoy a repast of solitude.

The Tageans are ruled by two kings who each serve for one year. The kings are elected by the warrior citizens, the hoplites, heralded as some of the best warriors in the world. Tagea is unusual in that any race may vote in choosing the king. So long as he or she resides in Tagea for more than a year, is productive in some capacity and is willing to defend the city by force of arms or by spell

The present kings are Leonidas and Demosthenese. Leonidas is a young man who earned his reputation as a warrior fighting under King Araxia. He is headstrong and seeks to push the powers of Tagea even further onto the mainland. In this respect he is looking south to the delta of the Olgdon River. He has sent word to Avignon for experienced explorers to chart the area for his navy. Demosthenes is older and more conservative, wishing to strip the mainland colonies of their wealth and quit them. They have had recent battles with both the men of Aachen and the Orcs of Onwaltig.

The rest of the population, those who make their living wholly by farming, craftsmanship, sailing, etc. have no voice in government. They are generally taxed heavily to support the hoplite armies and the navy. The governments in the colonies are roughly the same, supporting Tagea with light infantry and auxiliary troops.

Much of Tagea's wealth comes from fishing and trade. For this reason they keep a large navy with several dozen ships of varying sizes. They are good seaman, and few but the Northmen can match them on the open sea.

The Tageans dwell in sprawling open air villas and revel in building great colonnaded temples to the ocean god Poseidon. They are generally an open, friendly people who do not fear outsiders, but welcome them. A strong military tradition feeds into their national confidence. The taverns of Tagea, generally a clean and orderly city, are well known for their wine and food.

The Tageans produce little beyond fish foods, armor and the famed Tagean Hound (*reference Monsters, p. 241*). There is some whale killing that garners much oil and is sold abroad. For the most part, the Tageans have grown wealthy by forcing themselves upon the sea lanes of the world and taking them over, though this has recently changed. The Hanse City States in the north and Maine in the south have pushed the Tageans out. To counteract this they have established a loose alliance with Eloria. Together they are attempting to regain control of all south-ern seaborne traffic.

Legends relate of how one of the Tagean Isles, it is unknown which, is actually the isle of Ibernia. There, in ages past, Arnulf the monk hid the Grail of Jaren One Hand, the Falkynjager, from the minions of Unklar. The shrine is said to be in a place, "where silent water falls, two streams join." What this means is anybody's guess, but it is certain that those fortunate enough to unmask the riddle will find the Grail of Jaren One Hand (*reference Magic Items, p. 224*).

A History of the Island Kingdom: Tagea's history is bound with that of Brindisium, and as the story is told elsewhere, those twin peoples trace their roots to the Age of Heroes. During the final days of the Catalyst Wars (771oy-800oy) as Kayomar faced defeat and Unklar stood triumphant, Mourilee Lothian Pendegranze fled with many other refugees of Kayomar into the far distant west. The victory of Prince Erik Aristobulus Euryiance over Unklar's navy in 789oy left the command of the sea to the folk of Kayomar. They gathered what ships they could and in the company of Luther's bastard son Morgeld, set sail for the Wall of the Worlds. For years they sailed, the journey a legendary trek fraught with countless horrors. The voyage sent them to the far edge of the world where they founded the Solarian Colony. Morgeld settled upon an Island, called the Land of Bliss (*reference Eloria, p. 86*).

As Unklar's winter extended over all the world of Erde, only a few pockets of resistance held out against him. One of the most successful were the folk of the Solarian Colony. They built their home on a coastal valley beneath the shadows of the mountains. The valley was well guarded by natural terrain. High mountains in the north and south came together in a narrow defile, which offered the only egress to the Valley of the Empire. There, a wide, deep river flowed upon the western banks, which they fortified. They dammed the river and flooded the plain beyond. They built a great city and there constructed temples to the gods Toth, Tefnut and the Dreaming Paladin, Luther. It is said, that Tefnut herself dwelt in the river in the pass and that the sun never set upon the Solarian.

Mourille passed her days amongst these people and died soon after the colony's founding. However, her line lived for many generations, until at last the seed of it died out. These were the last of Luther's true descendants. Though even now, it is rumored, that some lived on, trekking across the great wildernesses of Erde, in search of the unknown.

The folk of that proud land resisted Unklar even in exile. Eventually the Paladins of Kayomar established a Holy Council and in conjunction with the High Priestess of Tefnut they founded the

Solarium Empire, the Empire of the Sun, in the Valley of Light. The Master of the Order took the crown as Emperor and adopted the Eagle as his standard. They did this for order, and for tradition too, for the Tarvish Emperors of the past withstood the might of Aenoch and eventually won out their freedom. The Emperors continued to rule and to war against Unklar for a thousand years. The Solarium became powerful in wealth and magic, and it used this knowledge to fell intent. As is told, Unklar's minions never broke the wall of the pass but for once.

In 1020md, when the dark hosts came to the walls of the Solarium once more, they were held back by the heroics of a small company of men. Professional soldiers defended the walls. They lived, drank, ate and slept within earshot of the walls and gates. When the hordes came forward, throwing grapnels and ladders against the heights, this company of men, led by their Captain, Tagea, threw them off time and again. The horrific slaughter lasted for many days until at last the Orcs could take it no more and retreated. The whole realm celebrated the victory. They took to calling the company of men the Tageans.

The following year, despite thousands of deaths, the Orcs at last penetrated the valley. Though they did not breach the walls, they managed to come over the mountains. They lay siege to the whole county, burning villages and farmsteads, sacking castles and putting all they could to death. The Tageans rallied. After a bitter march, they cut their way across the valley to the great city itself. There the Captain admonished the Imperial Paladins as cowards, "Why did you not come to aid us in our hour of need? It is true that the blood of the old world flows not in your veins!" This act forever set the two peoples apart.

The destruction of the valley proved too much, for the Orcs and Ungern had poisoned the very land. So the Holy Council, in 1025md, deemed their lands unlivable and the greater part of them departed for the east in ships and galleys. The Tageans went with them. Some few remained behind, living on in the city, which escaped the flood.

It took them only a year to return to their ancient homes, but they soon learned they were not welcome, for much had changed in the thousand years of Unklar's rule. The men and women of the Solarium had changed, now imperious and commanding, and they drove off all allies. So they sailed on searching for a land to call their own. Tagea at last grew tired of the Paladins and broke with them. They demanded the ships be returned and realizing that his would mean their being abandoned upon the shores of the Gelderland, Tagea refused. In the evening's early hours he weighed anchor and sailed for the north and west.

They traveled for a time until they came to the islands south of the lands of Aachen. Tagea set foot upon the larger isle to explore it for water and food. He came across a small band of druids who payed homage to Wenafar. Their leader, Cornelius, promised them riches in food if Tagea would but slay a beastly creature that stalked the island's hinterlands. Tagea agreed to this for he knew that his people were desperate for a home. He set a trap for the creature in the island's hinterlands by placing a dead cow in a pit. Tagea waited patiently for it to come. It did not take long. Half man, half bear, the shambling monster fell upon the proffered bait, devouring it with a rage of hunger. Tagea leapt forward with his men in tow and stabbed the creature repeatedly. The lycanthrope threw off their attacks with ease, falling upon them and rending them asunder. Tagea, a large man by most accounts, grabbed the beast up in his massive arms to crush the life from him. The lycanthrope fought fiercely, clawing great gobbets of flesh from Tagea's backside, until at last the two collapsed to the ground, dead.

The surviving men carried the body down the slopes to the beaches. As word spread, the Tageans came forth from their ships much distraught. They buried the hero upon a slope overlooking the sea. There they wept at his passing, calling for the gods to carry his soul into the other worlds. Now leaderless, the Tageans gathered in a concourse to discuss what next to do. After long debates it was decided to stay upon the isle and build a city there. So they did. They entreated the druids to join them and together they built their homes upon the sea. They named the city after their beloved Captain, Tagea.

They built a Temple to Poseidon upon the grave of Tagea overlooking the sea. Later in 1043md, the architect Pylus began construction on the Great Temple of Poseidon. Made purely of marble this huge edifice sprawled over the hillside. Within were gardens, statues, and temple grounds all overlooking the sea, a forum large enough to hold all the Tagean citizens, quarters for priest, visitors and so on. Pylus rebuilt the tomb of Tagea, placing his body in a marble sarcophagus overlooking the forum.

The Tageans established a republican form of government where the people elected two Kings, one to rule the army and the colonies, and the other to rule the navy and the home city. Only those men and woman who fought could vote. Every year the Cadre of Warriors gathers in the Temple of Poseidon to choose the new Kings.

After the Winter Dark Wars, the Tageans prospered. Sitting astride the trade routes, Tagea soon became a favorite stopping place for merchants and fisherman. They conquered the neighboring isles and colonized them. Though in truth there were few people there to conquer, and those that were gave themselves over freely. The colonies farmed and tended herds of sheep. The Tageans became famous for a breed of dog which they sold to only select people for a very high price. The animal, a Tagean hound, could communicate telepathically with its master: in images, smells and tastes.

A fiercely militaristic society, the Tageans soon found themselves in demand as mercenaries in the surrounding states. In 1092md, their King Araxia, conquered the southern Heristat from Aachen. The wars were short and brutal, ending with the Tageans ensconced in walled towns along the coast. They grew wealthy on ship borne trade and established close ties with Eloria, whose Immortal Prince held a special place for his one time neighbors (*reference Eloria, p. 86*). Their immediate neighbors in the Kingdom of Onwaltig trouble them, for the orcs there are skilled sailors who pirate ships of all nations (*reference Onwaltig, p. 120*).

Ec Rating II

United Kingdoms, the Princepate

Fom the city of Torrich, Prince Innocent III rules a polyglot Realm. The red banner with golden chalice heralds the Prince, but other heraldry is as recognizable. The blue and white crosshatching with manticore of Ihlsa. The blue crossed white shield with crescent moons of Unduliland and the blue crosshatch over white with bear and wolf of Rleuland. There are others, too numerous to catalog, which represent the Principate

Of the Prince, the Kingdoms and Their People: The lands of the United Kingdoms encompass the Rleuland, the sea towns of Ilhsa, Unduliland, the city of Torrich and the Hlobane. These lands (*covered individually below*) stretch from the Kellerwald Forest in the east to the Kolkrab Mountains in the west; from the Red Hills in the north to the Amber Sea in the south. People here tend to live in large villages and towns, mostly along the sea. The land is not rich in soil, but supports many wild and domesticated animals. The old Imperial roads have slipped into decay, as have many of the outlying settlements. For this reason alone strange beasts slip down from the highlands, finding easy prey in man and beast.

The ruling Prince, Innocent III, is beautiful above all men. His youthful appearance resembles that of his father and grandfather so much that rumors abound of his origins. Some say that he is the same man, an undead creature, who changes his guise and name to stave off suspicions. The Prince holds tentative control over his many realms through magic and assassination. In the latter, he utilizes the skills of the assassin guild, Crna Ruk, the Black Hand. He rules from the large sea town of Torrich, a well ordered town of cobbled streets and stone houses with shingled roofs. Strangers are always looked upon suspiciously but the many pirates who find a warm welcome there make moving through the town easier.

Humans dominate the United Kingdoms and the old imperial bureaucracy holds it together. Constant warfare has led to the country being fortified. Towns are walled, except for in the Rleuland, and few villages survive without defensive protection. Strong towers dot the landscape. Whereas in the west gallant knights battle one another for glory as much as for land, here, war is much more deadly. Honor and nobility rarely enter a contest of arms, making warfare vicious.

Rleuland: The Rleuland stretches between the eves of the Kellerwald along the coast to the peninsula. The country is largely flat. Gentle low hills and almost unnoticeable ridges are found in the south, and in the far north, in the country of the Hlobane, are featureless hills. Under the eves of the Kellerwald, the ground becomes a little more rich and the grass thicker. The people there live in small villages and towns, raising livestock and the like. There are few castles in the Rleuland, that practice never having penetrated the country. The lords prefer to live in palaces or walled villas. Most abandon their holdings in the country altogether, choosing to live in Torrich or one of the larger towns of the coast.

The poorest of the United Kingdoms, the Rleuland never attracted the priests of Unklar. Consequently, the peasants are less inclined than their neighbors to the worship of the horned god. They revolted against the Prince in the early days of his reign (*see below*) seeking to align themselves with the Empress of Aenoch. The brutal repression has led the locals to shirk the rule from Torrich; they hide food, do not pay taxes when they can get away with it and offer solace to almost anyone in the country. The local priests, who dwell in every town, try to control the populace through fear. They have done little but alienate it.

Unduliland: The Kingdom of Unduliland derives its vast wealth from salt and silver, both mined in the Kolbkab Mountains. The locals live, much as their neighbors to the east, in villages and towns. Though unlike the Rleuland, many of these are walled. Large herds of cattle graze the land, but these are owned entirely by the lords. The peasants live in complete poverty, subject to the whims of their masters. Where the old lords ruled with reason, the new rule with fear. Many of the locals are carted off into slavery in the salt and silver mines.

Temples to Unklar abound throughout the Unduliland. The wizard-priests of Unklar rule hand in glove with the lords and serve Prince Innocent III unquestionably. Travel here is dangerous for those not initiated into the Paths of Umbra, though the lure of wealth in magic, possessed in the temples, draws many thieves from far and wide. Rumors abound that Muddles, Inc. has even managed to infiltrate the priesthood.

Ihlsa: The crowded Sea Towns along the Bay of Massoll are loosely organized under the banner of Ihlsa. The main towns are Nochi, Raveen and Caphyrna. Stone walls predating the current era surround most of the towns, but the inhabitants live in large wooden houses, characterized by small rooms and many corridors. All are jumbled together, built one on top of the next. The town Governors tax the people for walled space so the houses tend to have as many windows as their struts will support. The harbors are home to few merchant ships and many pirates. They raid the coastal lanes of Outremere. Recently, pearl diving in the Bay has increased the wealth of the townships. In general the Sea Towns are flthy disorganized affairs. (*Reference the adventure setting, Heart of Glass*).

Hlobane: The Nation of the Hlobane live in and around the Red Hills. They are numerous and powerful and still hold to the old ways of the horned god. Their shamans worship him and their warriors fight under his banner. They are a prideful people for they alone survived the catastrophe of the Toten Fields. Their units never broke, but withdrew in order. They live in townships with large dirt parapets surrounding them. Travel here is dangerous for any but the servants of the horned god .

The History of Southern Aenochia: Under Unklar's long rule, the lands south of Aufstrag served him well. Their service to the lords of that great city predated even the horned god's coming. Here, the folk worshiped the Aenochain Emperors of Al-Liosh as gods. Many of the aristocracy of these lands served the priesthood which eventually gave its aid to Emperor Sebastian and Nulak-Kiz-Din in summoning Unklar. When the face of the Emperors changed and Unklar came to roost in the capital halls of Al-Liosh, they did not turn away, but rather took him as the heir to their own god-emperors.

Nulak always relied upon the south to supply the Paths of Umbra with the wizard-priests the cult so desperately needed. Many temples were built upon the holy places of the god-emperors and they worshiped Unklar and his minions. In time of years the wizard-priests came to dominate all the lands between the sea, the Grossewald, the Kolkab Mountains and the Kellerwald. They built temples, schools, guild houses, all of which were geared toward the lord of Aufstrag. For many centuries these lands served as the breeding ground for the dark worship of Unklar.

When war came, they took up arms and the wizard priests strove to join their might to that of the other minions of Unklar. But they soon found that their close connections to Unklar hindered them as much as they helped. For when the gods assailed Unklar in his high tower, they tore his attention away from those who needed him most. Their prayers went unheeded and their power over Erde waned.

Despite this, they fought on. They served the legions as best they could, adhering to the dictates of the dark priestess Nectanebo. The schools were stripped of young wizards to fight the ever rising numbers of enemy. Many marched off to war, though few returned again to their homes.

Amazingly the lands south of Aufstrag never suffered the ravages of war. They served as recruiting grounds and gave over vast treasure troves of wealth to finance campaigns, fashion armor, supply armies and so forth, but the war never came home to them. Their loyalty remained undaunted even after the fall of the horned god himself.

With Unklar's demise the ruling priesthood retreated into seclusion. Rumors spread throughout the region that a woman had come who bore the Mark of Kings. The men east of the Kellerwald declared for her, promising her the Imperial crown of her forefathers. As with the horned god, these folk saw the new Empress as the legitimate heir to the god-emperor's throne, with their traditions and legends supporting this. But they did not have the opportunity to pay homage to the Empress, for civil war overwhelmed the region.

In 1036md, a man arrived in Torrich calling himself Prince Innocent. He claimed to be the heir to Unklar's reign. The Prince marshaled the demoralized priesthood behind him when he revealed to them sacred rituals known only to the higher priests. He entreated with them to jettison their beliefs in prayer and dedicate themselves to sorcery. Many did this, but others repudiated him, calling once more for the horned god to return. With these sorcerers he slew many of that dark brotherhood, and drove the rest into hiding.

With the wealth of the temples at his command, he paid off the four cohorts of troops in the large port city of Torrich. He also hired a host of mercenaries. In 1038md, when his preparations were complete, he launched a brutal campaign south into the Rleuland. The lords there resisted only a little but the people rose in rebellion

anticipating the return of the old line of Aenoch. Prince Innocent crushed the rebellion in a few short months. Villages were burned, newly erected temples to the Empress were torn down and many people put to the sword. In a very short time the whole of the Rleuland recognized Prince Innocent as their suzerain.

Along the eastern shores of the Inner Lakes lay the towns of Ihlsa. Few of them bore walls of any description and Innocent's conquest in the winter of '38 proved easy. Rumors of the destruction in the south aided him tremendously. Next he crossed the lakes and attacked Unduliland. Here, the lords resisted him. They rose peasant levies, calling on them to support the Empress who rumor reported had arrived in Ascalon to the east (*reference Outremere, p. 122*). In 1039md, however, Innocent overwhelmed the region. His gold bought allies in the great Orc nation of Hlobane. These Orcs, living in the Red Hills, came down upon the Unduliland in droves, burning and pillaging as they moved south. Little remained when Innocent entered the area. The rest of the region fell to him with relative ease.

Innocent called the lords and burghers together in 1040md, forced them into a federation and crowned himself Prince of the United Kingdoms. Ihlsa, parts of Unduliland, Rleuland, the orc nation of Hlobane, and a dozen cities entered into a pact with the Prince. He established the rule of the Principate in the city of Torrich.

The Prince's rule was further cemented when he re-established the Imperial bureaucracy. This highly efficient state organ, disrupted during the civil war, returned to the old system of managing the excise rolls, taxes, the movement of persons, livestock and goods and all the other mundane affairs of state with little fanfare. For millennia they had kept the rule of the horned god an efficient one, and they now turned their energies to supporting their new master, the Prince.

During the next twenty years, Prince Innocent ruled the United Kingdoms. He crushed several rebellions of peasants in the Rleuland and lost portions of the Unduliland to civil war, but otherwise his rule continued unabated until his death in 1060md. His son and successor, whom the Prince had kept in seclusion in the priesthood, bore a striking resemblance to his father. He took the crown as Prince Innocent II.

The early years of his reign were marked by an expansion of trade. The ship captains found that the merchants of Outremere had long since established the necessary contacts, built a large merchant fleet and plied the oceans with goods. Their frustration led them into piracy. They began raiding the shipping lanes, impressing sailors and hauling the goods back to Torrich or other towns along the coast. This eventually led to retaliation from Outremere. A continual naval war along the coast continues to this day.

In 1080md, Prince Innocent II died. His son too had been secluded in the temples of Unklar in Torrich. And much like his father, Innocent III bore a striking resemblance to his predecessors.

Ec Rating II

THE PRINCES
Prince Innocent I
Prince Innocent II
Prince Innocent III

Zeitz, the March

Upon these coastal plains there are no Kings or Princes, but rather a hardy folk who rule themselves. All that is but for Iergaul, that dread remnant of Unklar's rule. Here, the Ungern rule under their dread chieftain, Mithruck. They march to war under a host of banners for the Ungern divide themselves into clans, though in Iergaul they pay homage to the crescent moon by topping all their lances with that dread shape of Unklar's rule.

The Coast, Its people and Iergaul: The March of Zeitz consists of a broad coastal plain stretching several hundred miles along the northern escarpments of the Grundliche Mountains. The area is breathtakingly beautiful. Gently sloping hills tumble down to the sea, dropping off suddenly into rocky coves or small, secluded, sandy beaches. Small streams and rivers run off the highlands, through narrow gulches to spill into the sea's churning waters. Here, the waters of the Inner Sea are choppy for a whole range of craggy islands stretch across those deep waters to the Roheisen Mountains in the far north. Behind it all, the stark granite world of the Grundliche Mountains with their long ridges and white capped peaks overlook the country, like tired old men.

The March attracts wild adventurers, desperate fugitives and erstwhile wizards. The locals war and intrigue against each other and raid the lands to the south. There are several powerful castles of the Knights of Haven, sitting astride the main north-south road, only adding to the confusion in the region.

The March has little to offer the civilized folk of the world. There are towns and one city, but all of these are rough frontier communities. The people build their homes out of thick timbers and rock, using thatch to cover them. Sturdy yet primitive buildings, they serve the people as small forts within the larger walled communities. Only the more wealthy towns have stone walls, most having wooden palisades. Within, the people are a dour lot. Men mingle freely with Dwarves, Orcs, Ungern and other races. They care not who someone is; only that someone avoid nosing about. They are brigands, warriors, bandits and adventurers mostly.

Some, however, are pilgrims, arriving on foot from the southlands. These stout souls seek spiritual aid from the town of Haven which sits upon the far shores of the Inner Sea (*reference Divine Orders, Demeter, p. 58*). For the most part they are poor men and women, but a few nobles come along, though they rarely travel without guards of one type or the other.

The Knights of Haven (*reference Guilds & Orders, p. 197*) are a continual presence in the March, serving the pilgrims as guides and guards. They have a few large castles, mostly on the coast, where importing lumber is relatively easy. But in the hinterlands they live in small moat and bailey castles. As singular knights, or in pairs, with a dozen or so men-at-arms, they offer refuge to any folk of Demeter. Food and housing is given freely, though it is common custom to offer goods or coin in turn.

In the March these knights, even the lesser ones, are rarely molested by the local populace. To do so may bring scores of them to the countryside where they put all malcontents to the sword, regardless of who the original perpetrator was. This is not to say, of course, that their lives are sacrosanct. Many knights die upon the highlands. They fight lonely battles and die lonelier deaths, slain by creatures of eldritch evil and power.

Iergaul: The only city in all of the March is the dreaded town of Iergaul. High walls with towers interspersed along its whole length make the city look the part of an impregnable fortress. Its history (*see below*), well known to the locals in legend and song, only adds to the mystic. But the truth is different. The walls are old and cracked in many places. The once impenetrable gates are gone as are many of the towers. Though the cobbles remain, many of the streets have been torn up. Stone buildings great and small lay in ruin, though some still sport shingled roofs. The city is a wrecked ruin, a shadow of its former self. Though, as many have recently learned, it is not uninhabitable.

Many strange creatures call Iergaul home. Even as Haven serves the pilgrims of Demeter so does Iergaul serve those who pay homage to the horned god. Wizard priests of the Paths of Umbra (*reference Guilds & Orders, p. 198*) live in the underhalls where they plot to bring their long banished master back to the world. Recently an Ungern Lord, Mithruck, has arrived in the city. With him came several hundred of his own folk. He claims to rule the whole city, styling himself "Lord Under Unklar." But he no more rules the whole place than does the horned god himself.

Many adventurers are lured to the city for within its halls are reputed to be many lost treasure troves, hidden away in secret where the crusaders of years past could not find them. But, too, there is glory to be had, for slaying the folk of Unklar is always a credit to ones' name.

The History of the March & Iergaul: During Unklar's long reign the northern barbarians never fell to his conquering armies. When the Shroud of Darkness came the barbarians thought only the great Fenris wolf had come to Erde, blanketing the world in his breath. On more than one occasion the horned god or his servants sought to subdue the barbarians. To this end they built a fortress city upon the sea, one which could hold great stores of goods, horses, men and other necessities of war. This fortress they named Iergaul and peopled it with a host of Unklar's folk.

The first expedition sent several legions marching around the Inner Sea and against the barbarian tribes of what is today Trondheim. Early successes led the legions to plunge deeper into the wild north. There they attracted more tribes of these wild Northmen. And though these battle lusty folk always fought one another, they banded together for the glory of the war with the southerners. The campaign ground to a halt in the frozen north. The barbarians chipped away at the legions until at last they began to disintegrate. Their Commanders withdrew the legions to the south.

Many more expeditions followed and, they too, ended poorly. The barbarians loved war, rarely shrinking from a fight. Eventually the legionnaires established a few colonies upon the islands south of Mount Tur (*reference Roheisen Hohle, Haven, p. 128*), but these were eventually abandoned.

Iergaul meanwhile grew into a large sprawling port city. Much of it remained within the walls, but whole districts sprang up in the direct environs. It attracted all manner of folk during the Winter Dark. Here, men could find work as carpenters, metalsmiths, blacksmiths, sailors, boatsmen and other besides. If all else failed, then as mercenaries they tramped into the distant north to fight the ever present barbarians hordes.

During the Winter Dark Wars the region languished from neglect. The Dwarves closed the passes through the Grundliche Mountains so that only a few could manage to cross over to Iergaul or the lands around. Worse came when the Northmen arrived in their ships, girded for war. They raided the outlying communities, burning and pillaging. The threat became such that a great concourse of ships gathered in Iergaul, and in 1022md when the main fleet sailed from Avignon intent upon the barbarians' destruction, they joined it. They never returned to the city, for as is told elsewhere, they perished at the battle of Gokstad (*reference Eisenheim, p. 84 & The Northern Kingdoms, p. 118*). For the first time in many centuries the folk of Zeitz knew fear. The raiders came more frequently and the Northmen became more bold. Larger towns fell to the raiders. Those that did not die, fled to the hinterlands or found themselves slaves in distant northern climbs.

Thrown upon their own resources, the region quickly desolved into a host of small cities and townships. They fortified their homes; walls with parapets sprang up as if overnight. Those who did not defend themselves soon perished. The lords of Iergaul rebuilt the walls with huge fortified towers interspersed along its whole length. They turned away many who came to the gates pleading for aid, but only the strong were allowed entry. It soon became a desperate place filled with fierce men, Orc and Ungern.

The Zeitz continued to suffer. The Imperial cohorts that remained deserted the country in 1026md. They plundered the whole country on their march to the south. In some instances they ransomed whole towns with threats of destruction. But for the most part, they burned and pillaged, taking what they wanted. Early the following year these same cohorts, little more than a disorganized mob, came over the western mountains to Eisenheim. Marching on to the Detmold in new born Aachen they fell afoul of Baldwin and his knights. There they perished but for a few.

These desertions only served to embitter those who remained. Once a proud and powerful land the March slipped into the obscurity of a backwater. The land soon became the home of many deserters, bandits, homeless knights, adventurers and other riffraff. The towns took on a decidedly different character. Gone were the days of Imperial order, replaced by ramshackle communities ran by strong men and thugs.

The barbarians' raids continued, only abating a few years after the fall of Aufstrag. The coves and bays of the coastal region served the barbarians well and many settled there, building small fortified enclaves from which to continue their raids. Within a few years of the Winter Dark Wars, the March broke apart into a dozen walled towns and an equal number of Northmen settlements. Iergaul, for a time, lorded over the region. Internecine war consumed the towns and settlements and the March became a chaotic place, dangerous to all.

The greatest of these battles took place in the early years following the banishment of Unklar. In the 1020's md the lords of Iergaul, seeking to enjoin themselves to the victories of the King of the Punj (*reference Punj, p. 124*) sent great waves of Orc and Ungern south and west into Eisenheim. There, they overwhelmed the Northmen settlers, driving all before them into Aachen and the Detmold eventually. All of this brought the god Daladon to the northern wastes. He brought with him a host of rangers mounted on griffins and Wood Elves from the Eldwood. Together they joined Queen Ephremere in campaign against the Orcs of Iergual. For almost the whole year of 1031md Daladon remained in the north. He fought two great battles against the Orcs. One at the River Rot-tor and the other at Utual. Here Daladon was hard pressed to keep the forces of the Queen together. He met the warrior cleric Fyorgyn, the Visigoth sister of King Theodohad from the Eisenheim. In early 1032md, Daladon and Ephremere lay siege to Iergaul. But they could not break its walls and after many months of futile combat they quit the field.

Early the following year the Orcs again raided into the south, reaching Aachen where they burned farmsteads and small villages. And, as before, Daladon joined Ephremere in a campaign to destroy them. They fought a series of battles, at the River Rot-Tor and the Fortress of Utual. This last place remains a wrecked ruin, haunted by the ghosts of the dead. They came at last to Iergaul and surrounded it. The siege lasted longer this time and the Ranger god fell upon the Orcs in a rage, but as before, they could not break the walls and the Orcs taunted them so that Daladon became mad with a lust to destroy the city and all who dwelt therein.

To this end he attacked Iergaul time and again. Thrice more he brought armies to the north, battering its walls. In 1040md King Theodohad of Eisenheim, stormed the gates of the great fortress, but made it no further, and died there a heroes' death. It would not yield, for that mighty place bore great magic, and the ice of the Winter Dark lay in its very stones. At last in 1043md, Daladon rousted out the long disbanded Council of Light. St. Luther called a crusade against Iergaul and many knights and adventurers came to the far north to lay waste to the March and break Iergaul at last. With the armies came Queen Fyorgyn and troops of Eisenheim and Augsberg. Dwarves also came, and they brought cannons with them as well. Many Elves of Fontenouq joined the siege, girded in strange armaments. The great host gathered upon the green hills before Iergaul and called for those lords to step down and quit that place.

The Orc warlord, Ustuf, stood forth, laughing and taunting the knights and gods before him. "Do not think you are greater than you are. You are not but low born curs. By trickery you slew our dread Lord Unklar while he slept in his great halls. But we do not sleep! We are vigilant and unafraid of you. For ten years you have battered at these walls, to no avail. For ten years we have carted off your people to our slave pits without fear of you. So get you from this place, return to your chattel houses in the south and await us like good little slaves. We are your dread foe!"

Daladon returned, "Ustuf! Beware, for I have brought a new battering ram." Then the wizard and Arch-Magi, Aristobulus came forth, steeped in Eldritch sorcery. He rode a gold hued charger and from its back called down the powers that only he and Nulak could command. A great howling wind thundered from the skies, battering the gates, even as Aristobulus hurled waves of fire and acid into the cacophony of magic. The doors, rent from their moorings, flew back crushing many an Orc, and the walls cracked, great pieces of them falling away. Daladon led the army forward then, filling the breech with iron and steel, blood, bone and flesh. He slew Ustuf upon the walls and many more besides. All day and night the battle raged until at last the town lay in ruin, a burning wreck of what it once had been.

But this war touched off more and the battles between the Marcher Lords, towns and other inhabitants continued, unabated for many long years.

Into this maelstrom of brigandage came the Pilgrims of Demeter. Within the foothills of Roheisen Hohle, across the Inner Sea, lay the town of Haven. There, Philip the Guileless had been born, lived and preached the religion of his god. Too, he retired there for some few years. In consequence, the town became a place of pilgrimage which drew many people of all walks of life. Though some crossed the sea, such voyages were costly, and many sought more direct, if longer, routes. This invariably brought them through the March of Zeitz. They trekked up through far western passes of the Grundliche

Mountains, coming down into the coastal plains seeking transport across the sea, or to continue their journey around the ocean through the dangerous lands of Trondheim. Small bribes bought them safe journeys or put them on fishing boats to island hop across the sea.

Though some brought troops of guards and others traveled in large bands, many more fell victim to the ravages of the Brigands of the March. They robbed and extorted from them, sold some into slavery, and others they killed. All of this eventually gave birth to the Knights of Haven (*reference Guilds & Orders, p. 197*), an order of paladins and cavaliers dedicated to protecting the pilgrims. They built small castles along the pilgrim's routes, giving them safe haven from the depredations of the brigands. They manned these castles with two or three knights and a dozen or so men-at-arms. In 1078md the first of them arrived in the March itself, where they remain still, adding to the constant warfare which plagues the region.

Ec Rating I

Notes on the Geographies

Varied maps of the Lands of Ursal – The Northwest – Southwest – Northcentral – Southcentral – Northeast – Southeast – An accounting of peculiar terrain, the inhabitants, & History – Major Oceans & Seas, Rivers, Lakes & Swamps, Mountain Ranges, Hills, Forests and Plains.

All about the Unicorn the world glittered & the snow light sparkled beneath the starry sky. Every move it made was a sound distinct. About its hooves blue sprouts sprung and winter roses blossomed. Blue stems sprouting white petals grew and crawled across the ground. The magic of the Unicorn was beyond any in the world. Cries of innocence echoed in its eyes. In his mind's eye Daladon saw Fedalea, his love, kneeling at a forest pool in a dress of green. Her hand skates the water. She weeps silently. There are leaves in her hair, decorations of the forest children & about her the weight of the world's sorrow, death the suffering of the drowned, and he feels her weight and wonders. And the Long Winter has given way to a new Spring.

The Tale of Ephremere & the Unicorn

THE NORTH WEST

Bleached Hills

These are a range of low hills and shallow valleys that rest on the north edge of The Wilds. This tumbling range is distinguished by its height and composition. The hills in the northern wilds have been ground down by time so that they are little more than lumps on the ground. Where the Bleached Hills begin the range has not suffered the vicissitudes of time so poorly as their brothers. In this region, the sandstone base is capped by a white limestone that has resisted the erosions of time and gives the region its name. Narrow valleys and steep cliffs predominate, while many waterways course through them to tumble out into the River Teifsich. The limestone has also given rise to many caves and caverns, both natural and unnatural. Some of these caverns stretch for miles into the earth and the dwarves, in all their long years, have yet to manage the deepest or widest of them. Much of the hills are forested in thick oaks and sturdy hickory but there are glades atop many of the rises and in many a vale. There, tall, thin grasses grow throughout the summer attracting all manner of herbivores.

The Bleached Hills were the farthest extent of Nuak-Kiz-Din's kingdom and power and a countless number of men and beast fell in the glades and forests. So many battles and so many deaths occurred in these tumbling downs, that the dead often lay unburied, forgotten monuments to the cruelty of the age. Skeletal arms, legs, skulls and ribs, pinioned through with spears and swords, tangled in the forest growth, remain to be seen. Many folk, those of a more morbid nature, claim this is the origin of the region's name.

The Coal Range

Commonly, this reference is to a range of hills north of the Bergrucken. More precisely, though, this is an outcropping found along the entire outer rim of the Massif. Here coal is found in abundance and mined from one end of the Massif to the next. These are generally low hills, worn by water and time, revealing large expanses of "black gold." Along the east rim the coal is mined by Humans, Gnomes, and even a few Dwarves down on their luck. The Halflings apparently will not stoop to such endeavors. In the western portions of the Massif the miners are human, locally referred to as coal burners. These are a mean folk, for slavery is what keeps them there. The coal is sold throughout the neighboring kingdoms of Maine, Angouleme, Sienna, Kayomar, Burnvetsi and the Gelderland.

The hills are sprightly forested in the pitiful loblolly pine. In the east they are shallow, rounded hills with shallow valleys and lazy streams. In the west, the hills are larger, a little more fierce, but still worn by water and time. They have resisted though and so the land is full of deep gulches, rocky precipices, narrow winding paths, and steep cliffs. This, mixed in with an abundance of bad weather, makes travel alone difficult. This is further hampered in the east by wandering bands of wickedly intelligent Kobolds, who clamber out of their wretched pits and caves to raid surrounding communities, merchants and travelers.

The Great Northern Forest

Few have traveled this far north and fewer still have bothered to tell about it. For this forest is far to the north of the world and no peoples have cared to explore or plunder its fasts. Even Nulak-Kiz-Din, during the height of his power concerned himself little with these lands. Even to this day, only wild Orcs tread beneath its black trees.

But this is known, the Great Northern Forest is a hilly land where huge magnificent conifers grow thick with firs that tower to the heavens. It is said that the boles of these trees are sometimes the size of small houses and that their tips touch the clouds in the sky above. The bark is dark, nearly black, and thick as the hide of a dragon. They produce tremendous cones, some even the size of a man's head. And the needles of these conifers are a dark blue green that shimmer at the sun's setting. The land about is cluttered with them, and travel becomes an arduous task even for the road weary and those who call the forest home.

The trees shroud the land in a gentle evening light during the brightest days and a pitch black in the dark nights. Undergrowth is thick in those spots where the sun might shine its bright light. Great leafy plants and thorny berry bushes abound. But this ponderous forest breaks on occasion to open glades, both small and large. Lakes, ponds, streams and rivers abound, all running with that gray cold water from the wintry north.

Wonderful and terrifying beasts roam this land. Large hairy elephants with twisting tusks longer than a giant's spear, elk larger than the warhorses of Sienna, wolves whose shoulders reach the height of a man and with jaws strong enough to shatter the bones of giant in a single bite. These, and other beasts of gigantic stature and others of strange design are housed within this forest.

Yet, some men attempt to dwell here. The wildest and hardiest of men, for they have to brave the long harsh winters without the shelter of house and home. As it is rumored, they live in caves and small huts, and they must brave and outwit the terrifying beasts of this forest. They must also fare with the giants that stalk the land. And these giants are the most terrifying of all the forest's denizens. They too are wild and little inclined to creating anything other than havoc and food, and it is believed that Elves make their most delicate dish.

It has been said that the eldest of the Faerie live within the night of this forest. These are they that sprung from the mind of the All Father after his unmaking, and they are the most eerie and primitive of the All Father's beautiful thoughts. They are from his base being and are said to mouth his will, still in these, the long days of the world.

The Ington River

This foul mess flows from that heap called the Shadow Mountains. Its origin is unknown, but many surmise it flows from the bottom of that stinking hole wherein resides Nulak-Kiz-Din. This lumbering giant of a river winds its way through the Shadow Mountains, passing many a foul hole and den, collecting refuse as it goes. When it spills into the plains of Gottland, it winds its way through that blasted landscape collecting much of that region's runoff. It is a stinking river and the water runs muddy and foul. Even the flow of the Teifsich River is not enough to dilute this mess. It dumps its impurities into the Drab Sinks near the Inner Sea.

Nothing but the grossest and meanest of creatures live in the river. Yet, the Orcs, Ungern, Hobgoblins and others live close to its banks, fishing out dead animals and muck dwellers for food. They fear not the seasonal flooding, and have houses and towns built behind great river walls or upon high stilts.

The Kleberock Pass

This pass lies between the north end of the Shadow Mountains and the west end of the Hollmgrads. It is a very low valley cut all the way through these two mountain ranges. It offers the safest - at least most level - passage from the Moravan Plains to Gottland. The wide valley was created when the world was young and travelers needed less arduous paths to move through. The valley is wide and was once verdant with all manner of flowering vines and trees. But these have long since been cut from the land as Nulak-Kiz-Din and his forces claimed the region. They blasted the valley so that now little grows there other than pain and suffering. Towers and fortresses are sprinkled throughout the valley floor as tribes of Troll or Orcs move back and forth battling for supremacy. Many slaves work the land for food and it is a horrible fate to befall any of those who are cast into slavery in this land.

Mithlon Eaves

This forest lies nestled in the shadow of the Rhodope Mountains. The forest was named for Mithlon, the High Elf, who died fighting off the incursions of both Goblins and Orcs. He failed and the forest was nearly overrun. So mean those battles, with no quarter given nor taken, that revenge and unsettled spirits still wander the nights in this wood. Many believe the spirit of Mithlon lives on, wandering the forest, seeking revenge upon those evil folk who find their way into the wood. With the passing of the Winter Dark, the wild Elves have come out of hiding, for in truth, they survived many of the world's degradations by hiding themselves away and sundering themselves from the remainder of the world. Living with them are many of their fey cousins and kindred once thought lost to the world.

The forest itself is a wonder to behold. The trees are tall and lithe with a yellow and red bark and deep green leaves. The leaves are small, fluttering in the delicate winds that whip off the Rhodope, constantly twittering with each other, retelling tales of the days before the Winter Dark and remembering the deaths of all the Elves who ever fought beneath its eaves. If one listens carefully one might eventually understand them, for these trees ever want the world to remember valiant Mithlon and the hosts who died at his side.

The Shadow Mountains

This is a dire place, a dreadful place, one full of foreboding and evil. They are called the Shadow Mountains for the shadow of Unklar once resided there, that cruel and maleficent one, Nulak-Kiz-Din. Though usually only referring to the western heap, this range of cragged volcanic peaks stretches from the Rhodope Mountains to the Inner Sea. Though in truth they are an extension of the Rhodope and share many of its characteristics. The mountains are treacherous for they stretch high into the sky and contain many tall peaks. They are young mountains and angry. Volcanoes abound and erupt white ash and molten lava that dumps and steams into the valleys and defiles throughout. They are ragged and tough, though easing at the eastern ends. Many passes trace up into the Shadow Mountains for there are Orcs and Ungern innumerable, the retainers of Nulak-Kiz-Din. Their castles, fortresses and palaces rival the volcanos in the production of filth and greasy smoke as they harness the deep fires to make there many weapons of war. Underground cities abound as the Orcs delve ever deeper into the earth seeking precious stones and rare minerals. Tunnels upon tunnels, and mazes of circuitous paths make up this pock-marked place.

The hills in the northern wilds have been ground down by time so that they are little more than lumps on the ground. Where the Bleached hills begin the range has not suffered the vicissitudes of time so poorly as their brothers.

Sorgon River (Slag)

A broad shallow river originating in the Shadow Mountains. It winds its way across northern Gottland until it spills into the Inner Sea. It is generally filthy as many Orcs and Trolls make their home upon its banks.

Teifsich River

The river begins far up in the Rhodope Mountains as a mere trickle. It flows down the mountains into the Mithlon Eaves. There, it gathers force from numerous feeder streams becoming ever greater until it finally spills into the Ington River. The waters are clean and pure, unsullied by the trappings of too many inhabitants. Fish are boundless in this river, attracting bear, eagle and other animals that find these fish a tasty morsel. The savannah to the east of the Mithlon Eaves slopes evenly and steeply to Gottland. These low hills give the river strength as it pours its water through open grasslands. The channel is narrow and rather straight as rivers go. It is also famous for its one most peculiar inhabitant, the blue skinned trolls, bent and disfigured from spending too many nights in dank caverns along the river's edge. These creatures are neither evil nor good, but simply try to survive in a land growing none too friendly.

Turm Gewir

And about this time many folk of the Mystic Enclave moved to the Rhodope Mountains and there, where in ages past Aristobulus had made a tower, they lifted it up again and fortified it, naming it anew, Turm Gewirr, "Tower of Chaos." But in after days it was named Turm Damon, "Tower of the Demon," for men came to fear the magi of the old world. ~ The Histories

During the Age of Heroes the mage Aristobulus built himself a great tower of stone. Through his sorcery he fortified it, making it virtually impregnable. It stood within the mountain fastness of the Rhodope Range, where two passes met in a deep wide valley. This valley was surround by high cliffs and jagged peaks and the passes, both narrow and treacherous, were easy to defend. Within the valley itself there stood a deep cool glacier lake with a small island in its center. Upon this island the Mage erected his tower.

It stood tall and possessed a double set of walls. He peopled it with mercenary Dwarves, in order to hold the passes, the walls and the gates. They spent many years building an underground network for the mage and maintaining the tower. From this high perch the mage surveyed the whole wide world and wondered when war came.

With the mage's passing the tower fell into disuse, only a few were bold enough to occupy its spaces and these held Aristobulus to be a god. Even before the Winter Dark Wars the Mystic Enclave came to be and held up the master's visage as the salvation of the world. To this end they rebuilt the tower and called in Turm Gewirr.

But alas it too fell into ruin when a great Mogrl came upon it from the air. He made war on the stone, tearing down much of the walls and buildings so that they lay in ruin. He slaughtered many of those within, for none possessed the strength to withstand him. And he hunted for the hated Magi. But he could not find the White Mage and he raged at his failure, taking his great hammer he smote the tower so that it cracked and pieces fell to the earth.

The tower has stood empty ever since, a haunted place of empty promises and eldritch power, for much of the Mage's sorcery lies there still. And some say that the Mogrl settled into the tower deeps to await the return of Aristobulus the White Mage, and they named it anew, calling it Turm Damon. But for the truth of these tales, none may say.

The Wilds

Beneath the Bleached Hills and far from the settled lands of Kayomar are The Wilds, a large untrammeled forest in the middle of Ethrumania. This forest is a mixture of pines and hardwoods. The northern tracks are thickly covered in tall aged pines. The forest floor is littered with their dying husks. In the south are large hardwoods, beech, oak, elm, hickory, locust, and the like. The lands roll with gentle and wooded hills and are cut by many clear flowing steams and creeks. Small ponds and lakes are fed by deep clear springs. The headwaters of the Ardeen River is found within this wood but none have yet found their exact location.

Little is known of this vast stretch of forest but a few hardy men of Kayomar have moved to its southern edges and begun to explore its depths. "There are creatures out there let me tell you, wild wolves the size of a horse, boars as big as elephants, snakes that can eat a man in one bit. There too are Dragons and giants, cruel trolls and others besides. But we brave these lands for the Elk are plentiful and the trees strong. Here we are far from the prying eyes of those taxing Lords of Kayomar which I fear even more than the Dragon." So say the men of The Wilds.

Aristobulus Lord of the Arcane

The Southwest

Brindisium

Soup Marsh

Darkenfold

Upper Danau

Islands of Helliwell

The Shelves of the Mist

The Kingdom of

Nordmark

The Wilds

Danau

Eldwood

River

Kayomar

Sudmark

Pu Guesillon

Paladin's Grove

Ardeen River

Norgorad Kam

Bergrucken Mountains

The Bay of Lothien

Augur Banks

The Kingdom of Maine

Chinon

Saline River

Ethenael

Chion

1 Inch = 150 miles

Southwestern Map

Ardeen River

Another of the massive rivers in central Ethrumania. The headwaters are known to be in The Wilds to the north of Maine and Kayomar, but no one knows exactly where. There is even a rumor of great reward to that soul who can find the headwaters, for its source is said to be a magical glade much sought after by wizards. The river collects runoff from the Bergrucken Range and the plains to its immediate west. It is a healthy, though muddy river, home to many fishes and water fowl. It flows rather steadily in its course, changing its banks only rarely and usually after great floods. It narrows in only one place, at the southern tip of the Bergrucken Mountains where it manages to cut a path through those low hills. As it dumps into the Amber Sea, it loses its strength and spreads out into a vast swampy, though not uninhabitable, region with many courses and breaks.

Its upper reaches are sparsely inhabited but its lower end is thickly peopled. Even the mouth of the river, in the swamps, has its villages and towns. It is generally pleasant and peaceful there. Its immense size makes war between Kayomar and Maine difficult, but not impossible. It is bridged in many places, and fjords are found in abundance to the north.

Bergrucken

Commonly referred to as the Saddleback Range, at least by those in Kayomar and Maine, these mountains stand like a long, thin, impenetrable wall between those two countries. The Dwarves of Norgorad-Kam refer to this as their home and refuse to name it anything other than Bergrucken. The range runs north to south, like a spill of rumbling rocks coming off the Massif. They are not tall mountains, though they are fairly rough. Travel is arduous over this range as one moves up and down through deep valleys and over steep passes. It is enough to weary a giant. The valleys are forested in dark evergreens and run with clear mountain waters. The heights are home to large white and gray mountain goats, huge elk, vicious cougars, and soaring eagles.

The Dwarves patrol these mountains constantly and it is not uncommon to find a patrol on a pass taxing passers-by, merchants, and travelers, which invariably causes friction with their human neighbors to the south and west. Nevertheless, it persists.

There are several passes, and most are safe. It is rumored that the Dwarves have a secret method of traveling across this range. A great road beneath the mountains, hidden from the likes of man, allows them quick movement to and fro. There are also the occasional bandits, as the Dwarves cannot be everywhere at once, and the merchants who make their way over these hills are fat and wealthy. Even Ogres live in these hills, but they are shy and scared, making their way out in the cover of darkness. Rumors abound of great abandoned mines, old palaces, tombs and the like. Most are proved to be nothing more than rumors but, if truth be known, many Ungern and others fled to rugged hills after Unklar's fall and his captains were ever want to build palaces in high places.

Danau River

This mighty river collects the runoff from the southern Rhodopes and the plains of far western Ethrumania. It begins small far to the north of Kayomar, collecting both water and power as it courses south. It bends and turns in great arcs through the plains of Kayomar changing its course constantly. The cities and towns of men may feel the encroachments of this mighty river and watch as it abandons them to move its course miles away. This has created a number of peculiarly placed towns in the river's flood plain. Docks sit far from the river awaiting its return while great sea walls are built in other places to stem off the corrosive effects of the stream. There is a constant war between men and the river. The flood plain is fertile and that is what attracts settlers. The earth is dark and loamy, smells good and grows thick harvests of grain and barley. Plentiful is the food in this region and good too. The river flows through the Soup Marsh and maintains its course to the sea.

During the rainy season and late spring the river is at its worst. It floods its banks in quick order, spilling into the lands about and covering many hundreds of square miles beneath several feet of water. Fish thrive in it and offer great sustenance for the people of Kayomar, but it also brings things from those high mountains. Water weirds and nymphs come down every spring to gather the dead and entice wise men into deep pools.

Darkenfold

The Darkenfold Forest stretches from the plains of Kayomar in the east several hundred miles to the doorsteps of the unexplored Rhodope Mountains in the west. In the south, the Great Soup Marsh hems in the ancient trees, but the forest continues in ceaseless growth from there to the far off Shelves of the Mist in the distant north. The Darkenfold marks the beginning of the Wild Lands.

The edges of the forest are hemmed in by long lean oaks. These young trees' leafy green branches hang to the ground to mingle with the thick tangled thorns and bushes growing in the rich black soil. Travel here is not easy due to the thick bramble which oft times overgrows the few existing paths. The tangled growth at the forest edge makes entry to the forest arduous and maintains the dark, deep mysteries within.

Beyond the tangle lies the old wood. Here, giant oaks heavy with foliage mark the heart of the forest. These peculiar trees are native only to the Darkenfold and give it its name. The mature trees are covered in greyish black bark that absorbs light. A campfire's light, for instance, will not flicker off the tree but rather it vanishes into the bark, as if the trees drink the light. At night the forest is dark beyond imagining and darkvision is effectively halved.

These great trees tower above moss covered ground, their leafy canopies blotting out the light of the sun. However, grassy knolls, open meadows and slow running brooks pocket the forest deeps and break the sinister visage cast by the old trees. Here, where the sun shines, lilies and other wild flowers bloom. At night the light of the moon and stars spills through, and when the evening is still, the faerie come out to dance and sing and play.

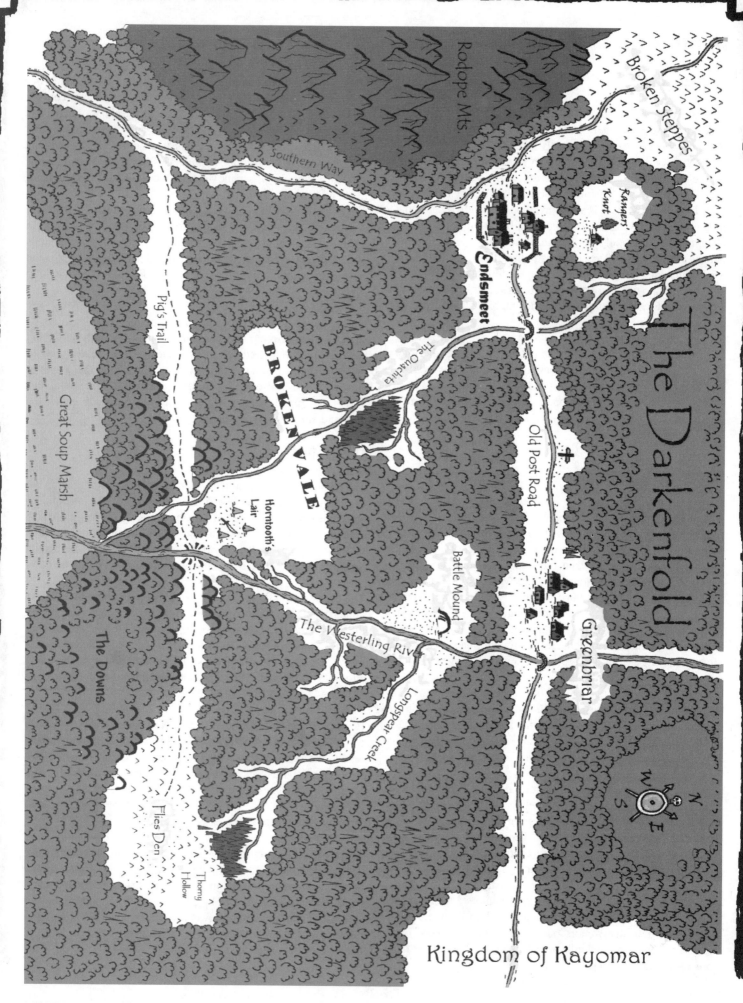

The Darkenfold

Rodope Mts.

Broken Steppes

Southern Way

Rangers' Knot

Endsmeet

Pig's Trail

BROKEN VALE

The Ouachita

Old Post Road

Great Soup Marsh

Horntooth's Lair

Battle Mound

Greenbriar

The Westerling Riv

Longspear Creek

The Downs

Flies Den

Thorny Hollow

Kingdom of Kayomar

Two main roads cut through the forest. The larger of the two, the Old Post Road, meanders through the upper reaches, suddenly veers north and emerges in the Broken Steppes. The Southern Way, a spur of the Old Post Road, is overgrown and weeded with small trees and is slowly vanishing back into the depths of the Darkenfold. Both roads are vestiges of the Age of Winter's Dark, when the Empire of the horned god stretched even to these distant reaches.

Few men venture into the Darkenfold. Those who do are a hardy lot with stout axes and stouter wills. Some settle in the few clearings or along the old roads, and build strong wooden houses beneath the dark trees and along the meadow tracks. 'Tis unknown what motivates them. Whether some crime or want of justice has driven them, or whether they desire a piece of earth far away from the civilized world, they find a dangerous home in the Darkenfold.

Where the Old Post Road and Southern Way meet lies the small village of Ends Meet. The remnants of an old stone wall surround the village. The wall is in ruins and in a few places rises above three feet. A small inn and trading post, the Cockleburr Inn and Tavern, encompass the pride and joy of the slightly suspicious, but overall friendly villagers who number about three hundred. Another village resides under the folds of the wood, Greenbriar. Smaller than Ends Meet, sporting only a tavern, the Long House, Greenbriar sits astride the Westerling River. The fifty or so hearty souls who inhabit Greenbriar are a friendly, if cautious, bunch. The size of the village makes them far more vulnerable than their neighbors in Ends Meet, and thus more watchful.

A small band of dedicated Rangers have taken on the onerous task of protecting the forest and the folk who reside there. They call themselves the "Rangers of the Knot" for they meet in a glade wherein two ancient trees have wrapped their boles around each other. Only recently has the Druidic Council recognized the rangers. The Council promised to deliver them a sapling offspring of the Great Oak to heal the Darkenfold.

The rest of the vast forest provides hunting ground for those creatures whose motives and concerns are little bent towards the good of men. Evil goblins band together and roam the forest. The most notorious of these foul goblins have taken up residence in a thicket of bramble and trees to the south called Broken Vale. Their leader, Horntooth, is intelligently wicked and merciless.

The Eldwood (see Map, p. 149)

Of all the forests in the world, the Eldwood is the eldest. Natural barriers have protected the forest from most incursions. To the east and south lies the sea, where towering, rocky bluffs divide the forest and ocean. Only small inlets, many of them hidden from the sea, and rocky beaches dot the coast, leaving little room for any would-be settlers. To the south lies a range of wild mountains inhabited by strange monsters. No one claims this inhospitable track of land, and only a few dour faced dwarves have settled there. To the west and south lies the Great Soup Marsh, a lowland collection of fetid, disease ridden bogs.

It is only to the north that the Eldwood is exposed to the ravages of man and dwarf, of orc and giant. But even there the Eldwood is protected, for the Kingdom of Kayomar, the most powerful realm in the west, stands constant guard. Her knights and cavaliers have long held the ravages of the world at bay. And her Kings long ago made peace with the Elven lords, so that the Eldwood's trees are not harvested by the men of Kayomar. All of this serves to make the forest the natural home of elf, druid and ranger.

Before the coming of the dark the Druids gathered in the Eldwood and planted a sapling there. The little tree was a gift from the Faerie Queen. In time it grew to become the Great Oak, father of all trees, and legend in its own right. The Eldwood survived the degradations of the Winter Dark and the rule of Unklar for over a thousand years, and the elves which people its more distant reaches never fled nor succumbed to his dark designs. During the Winter Dark Wars, the elves, chided by Daladon half-elven, joined the Lords of Kayomar and fought against Unklar, driving him from the southern lands. After the wars the forest came to know a peace it had not known since its earliest days. Daladon, a demi-god by some reckoning, dwells here, as do his flights of griffon riders and marches of rangers, the Watchers in the Wood. King Nigold rules the wood elves as he has done for time without count. And the druids meet still, gathering under their master, The High Druid, in their hidden glades to watch over the forest and their charge, the Great Oak.

The Eldwood is an old growth forest, consisting mostly of oak trees, though this is slowly changing. The forest is usually divided into three parts. In the Vulgate tongue, the outer forest is called the Rimwald (the forest rim), the old boundary the Festungwald (the wall), and the heart of the forest the Eldwald (the old forest).

In the Rimwald, travel is easy. There are many paths wandering through the open trees and a number of small human settlements are sprinkled throughout. Along its northern reaches the forest gives way to pine trees. Where the Soup Marsh lies, small forest oaks give way to wild trees and swamp grass. In the east, the great oaks of the forest's heart look down from high bluffs. And in the north, the forest has changed, if only in recent years. An ever growing number of silver maple and birch trees are expanding the size and slowly changing the composition of the forest.

Passing deeper into the forest the traveler encounters a great tangle of underbrush, younger trees, and wild animals, the Festungwald (festung being an old dwarf word, literally translated "fortress"). This marks the border of the old forest and the natural wall that ranger, druid and elf planted to keep the minions of the dark lord at bay. It also marks the old boundary of the Kingdom of Kayomar, and is now in some dispute between those who dwell within the forest and the King. In the Festugnwald, which averages in places 15 miles thick, travel is very difficult. The tangled brush, vines and thick growing trees all lend to an inhospitable maze. In places, when the Festung was planted, the rangers took advantage of the old fortification of Kayomar, so that dungeons, abandoned castles and old ruins are not uncommon.

Within the deep woodland lies the old forest, the Eldwald. Ancient oaks stand like monumental buildings. The boles of these massive trees line the forest like pillars of stone, and are capped by arching branches and leafy canopies. The trees are wide spaced, allowing easy passage across the vaulted forest floor. Beneath lies a land of ancient mystery. Deep pools in hidden places feed cold streams that trickle through lost valleys. Glades of wondrous beauty hide the homes of dryads and faerie. The wood elves of Nigold hunt here in small bands, and eldritch monsters from the world's dawn stalk the forest deeps. 'Tis said that the trees themselves come alive, and when the moon waxes that the eldest of them lift their tired roots from the ground and gather in a great meet to sing lamentations of their lost world, for they alone, of all the world's denizens, remember the Days before Days when the trees alone ruled.

There is but one road, The Old Post Road, which traverses the length of the Eldwood. It was constructed ages ago and stretches from the eastern borders by the sea, through the Eldwood and on into the Darkenfold forest. From there it goes into the far west, to the Rhodope Mountains. The ranger order, The Watchers in the Wood, led by the Half-Elven Ranger Lord and High Druid, Daladon Orcbane, guard the road and keep it in good shape. There are no villages on the road, but near the forest center there is a large open meadow called by the folk of that forest, The Open. Here the forest lords, elf, druid or ranger gather to meet one another or other folk who seek their aid or council. Travel on the road is at a normal pace, and it offers the only easy access through the forest.

Rhodope Mountains

This sprawling mountain range stretches from the Inner Sea in the North to the Amber Sea in the south. It is impossible to describe the entire breadth and range of these mountains in fewer than a volume. But this shall have to do. These are the truest mountains in all the known world. They are young and tumultuous, volcanoes sprout on many peaks spewing and belching forth fire and brimstone. Their smoke can, on occasion, be seen as far away as Burnvitse and Kayomar, and oft the mountains are called the Smokeys or the Smoking Giants. The tallest peaks stretch up into the sky nearly 40,000 feet, where no man can live. They are covered in perpetual snow and glaciers. Storms rise fast and angry at these heights, often catching those brave enough to battle them by complete surprise. These mountains have jagged peaks, tumbling boulder fields, narrow canyons, steep cliffs, and razor sharp ridges. Mountains of slate, ash, granite, and all the stones known to man can be found within. There is a constant rumbling and groaning of the earth as numerous quakes send boulders the size of ships crashing into the valleys below.

Few passes exist through these mountains and fewer still are the souls brave enough to attempt a crossing. It is not known what lies on the far side of the Rhodope for none have returned to tell the tale. The heights are commanded by giants who reside in the clouds, the glaciers by the giants who resemble them. Dragons are known to roost here in the old lava tubes and empty cones. There are other creatures beside, creatures from the Days before Days, creatures never tamed by time, by Unklar, by magic, nor by man. Aristobulus makes his home here, or at least he did during the Winter Dark Wars. His sprawling tower, Turm Gewirr, "Tower of Chaos," stands like a spire of granite upon the western faces, looking down across the Shelves of the Mist. It juts into the air almost 250 feet and is built into the very face of the mountain. There are no doors or windows, or obvious means of entry. Rumors abound that Aristobulus employed an army of Dwarves to build a network of secret passages and mazes beneath the tower to allow only those with some acumen

egress to his studies. He peopled the maze with strange denizens, eldritch creatures summoned from the Maelstrom. Arcane spells, traps and the maze itself serve to waylay those who would attempt to enter the tower. Many have tried, few have ever returned, earning the place its new name, Turm Damon, "Tower of the Demon."

All this is what brings the foolhardy to the Rhodope Mountains. For there are wonderful treasures, heaps of gold and silver, mountains of gems, artifacts of old, and magics unknown. These attract adventuring warriors and the curious mages as well as the most renowned of thieves to test their abilities.

Saline River

Lake Orion dumps over the Massif at the Thorgrim Falls. From here the waters course fast and plentiful to the Amber Sea. This is the Saline River and it passes through the Kingdom of Maine. The river dispenses its glory along its entire path as it brings with it fertile silts and sands from the Massif. The entire river valley is very rich and much grows here. The river valley itself is prone to flooding. During the rainy season, its waters overflow the banks and cover the lands for many miles around beneath cold fresh water. For this reason, few live along the river's banks but are perched some miles away on the hills and rises above. There, the inhabitants grow the most fantastic grape in all the known world. The people also know how to enjoy the river's bounty and celebrate yearly in revelries and wine festivals.

The Shelves of the Mist

These hills are a mixture of gentle swells coming off the southern tip of the Rhodope Mountains, and large escarpments overlooking perilous cliffs. Worn rough by volcanic activity and leveled by tremendous winter runoff and scoured by the winds from the vast plains to the west the Shelves of the Mist offer a vast array of tumultuous terrain. The entire region is sparsely forested in blunted oaks and towering pines. The land is hot from underground lava pools that threaten eruptions. Geysers dot the landscape, steaming pools litter the escarpment, the rivers run warm and the creeks hot. Falls and cataracts abound along the escarpment edges. Steam flows from the earth in these spots. Mixing the warm waters and cool airs creates a veritable curtain of mist over all these lands.

This is a veritable menagerie of the most fantastic creatures of Erde. Both good and evil dwell and constantly war with one another among these misty heights. The fortresses of ancient giants, the eyries of hypogriffs, the caves of troglodytes and the towers of mages can all be found perched amongst the peaks, crevices, plateaus, escarpments and valleys of this land. Even the falls hide perilous forts and nasty caverns. One must travel with great care in this misty land.

Too, the Shelves are a magical place. The very rock thinks arcane thoughts and many a mage spends a lifetime trying to decipher the messages and powers of this land. What draws them most are the rumors of gates and passages to other worlds and the lands beyond. 'Tis even said that these hills harbor the gates of Vakhund, and one of the Rings of Brass (*reference Magic Items, p. *), those doorways to other worlds.

Greenwood

...e a well tended and safe forest, watched over by the masters of
...and, its trees grew to great heights thick with long blue green
...les. The Greenwood became a special preserve during the
...r Dark for the tall trees, once cut, remained slightly pliant,
...g excellent masts for the ships that floated the world round.
...e lords of the land tended this forest well, cleared its land and
...ed a vast farm for trees. But times have changed and the
...rs have died. The forest is coming into its own as it has freed
...from the yoke of human control. The forest floor is coming
...with mosses and lichens, the animals are returning, as are the
...of the wood. Its paths are growing over and its endless rows
...es are slowly returning to their chaotic eruptions and
...ions. For now, no one rules this land. War is made upon its
...d the trees remain uncut in the forest's center. Some say the
...as finally come alive, others that it is doomed without the aid

Hollmgrads

...low range of mountains that creep out of the great northern
...nd edge up to the Inner Sea. The mountains are thickly
...in evergreen. Winter lasts throughout much of the year and
...fall at any time. In the short summers many creeks and
...f frigid water wash through frosty vales and across cool
...The mountains are not high and are gently sloped, having
...ed raw by the glaciation during the Winter Dark.

...tures of the north dwell here, sea lions, musk oxen, white
...ves and snow deer. Though an apparently uninhabitable
...ose who know its secrets, it is bountiful and full of
...inter is the only enemy for it is truly a cold place. Frozen
...the Inner Sea mix with the chilly storms of the north in
...e sky dumping great big flakes of snow or cold rains in
...The men of Holmgald call this place home, and many
...this land seeking fabled creatures, snowbeasts and
...ns.

...thrim

...dding forest. Though its beauty is only rivaled by the
...t is not a safe place for travelers." From a letter to the
...ignon.

...k and mysterious beech befriend one another in this
...Glorious and young is this forest, bound not by
...s and endless wars, these trees have grown to their
...somed handsomely under Erde's sun. The beech are
...and stretch straight to the sky as if they were
...ows ready to be let. Their nutty brown and white
...paper by the Twilight Elves, for the trees themselves
...certain wisdom to those that use them. The oaks are
...y tower so high in the air as to make one giddy, their
...e Dwarfing even the giant kin. These are truly the

...nd thickens and opens occasionally onto brightly
...h its boughs though, the air is clean, yet chilly and

rarely sunny. Dark green mosses and yellow lichens abound, strings
of clinging vines droop to the ground from the lowest branches. The
forest can be difficult to travel though. The husks of long dead trees
litter the ground like skeletons in a graveyard, further impeding
movement. And within the dark shadows and thick undergrowth
dwell all manner of nefarious creatures of Fay, having hid there in
times past, they brought with them the most unseemly part of their
being and plane.

The Inner Sea

The Inner Sea is a deadly place. Constant struggles occur between
the Hanse City States and the raiders from Holmgald, Haltland,
Trondheim, and Gottland. These fierce naval battles rage during the
early spring and throughout the winter as the more civilized nations
to the south try to stop those fierce icebound raiders from the north.
They battle over the goods that crisscross the sea, for the Hanse
Cities have grown exceedingly wealthy and the men of the north
exceedingly envious.

The sea itself is in constant turmoil. Buffeted by cold winds from the
Hollmgrads and warmer winds from Ethrumania, storms are a
constant fair. The waves, never great in height, are numerous and
constant, and only sturdy ships survive crossings of this lake.
Beneath the surface of these waters are great whales and massive
serpents. Water dragons and other monsters of the deep swim to the
surface to catch a tasty morsel on many an occasion. "Ever have
they been and ever shall they remain," claim the sailors who ply
those waters.

The depths of the ocean have not been fathomed. Somewhere
beneath is a city of dead ships crowded with the ghosts of sailors and
merchants. On those rare occasions, when the moon is right, and the
night sky cloudless, these dead are said to rise from the deeps and
return to the homes from which they came, trying to drag loved ones
to the lonely depths they now call home.

The Soup Marsh

This lowland marsh is fed by the Danau River and the seas from
Brindisium Bay. It is a shallow boggy marsh with a truly foul stench.
The salt waters from the bay mix in stagnant pools, and mud bars
create an odor that can be smelled as far as the edges of the
Darkenfold and some even say along the coasts of Brindisium. The
eastern half of the swamp supports little plant life and no large trees.
Thick tall reeds are mixed with a bushy, tangled, and knotty shrub
that grows out of the briny water. The western half of the swamp is
a mixture of large stretches of foul water, creeping with crocodiles,
lizards, and birds, both large and small, of the most beautiful hues in
all the known world. Trees too grow here, tall majestic cypress that
stretch hundreds of feet into the sky and which grow in large clumps
as well as individually. The waters of the swamp flow with the ebb
and neap of the sea and the flows of the Danau River.

Generally considered impassible, the river men and bargemen of
Kayomar know the route the Danau follows through these swamps.
But it is a shifting riverbed and its secrets are well kept, giving great
power to those who travel through the swamp. Otherwise, the
swamp is a horrible place, impossible to pass or navigate, a cesspool
of disease and death. It would be avoided by all if it weren't for the
constant rumor of mysterious towers hidden deep in the muck and
murk that house eldritch treasures and ancient magics of Dwarven
craft and construct.

The Wilds

Beneath the Bleached Hills and far from the settled lands of
Kayomar are The Wilds, a large untrammeled forest in the middle of
Ethrumania. This forest is a mixture of pines and hardwoods. The
northern tracks are thickly covered in tall aged pines. The forest
floor is littered with their dying husks. In the south are large
hardwoods, beech, oak, elm, hickory, locust, and the like. The lands
roll with gentle and wooded hills and are cut by many clear flowing
steams and creeks. Small ponds and lakes are fed by deep clear
springs. The headwaters of the Ardeen River is found within this
wood but none have yet found their exact location.

Little is known of this vast stretch of forest but a few hardy men of
Kayomar have moved to its southern edges and begun to explore its
depths. "There are creatures out there let me tell you, wild wolves
the size of a horse, boars as big as elephants, snakes that can eat a
man in one bit. There too are Dragons and giants, cruel trolls and
others besides. But we brave these lands for the Elk are plentiful and
the trees strong. Here we are far from the prying eyes of those taxing
Lords of Kayomar which I fear even more than the Dragon." So say
the men of the Wilds.

The North-Central Map

1 inch = 150 miles

The Detmold

This vast forest stretches along the western flanks of the Voralberg Mountains. In places thick and others thin, great conifers provide a blanket of light green across the lands of Eisenheim and Aachen. During the years of the Winter Dark this forest supplied the Empire with timber for its many fleets that crossed the Inner Sea and beyond. Fortresses and villages sprouted up throughout its depths as the ever increasing need for timber demanded a heavy price upon this once pristine wood. Times have changed though and the forest has been left to its own devices for many years. Travelers making their way into this grand wood note the many Imperial roads fallen into disrepair and the abandoned fortresses and villages that dot hillocks and dales alike. There are those who remained though, men who have carved small principalities out of remnants of the Empire's once mighty lands.

The forest itself is a mishmash of magnificent conifers and stunted hardwoods that clump around the region's natural springs and sprout thickly on the tops of hills. They cover this hilly land from the foothills of the Voralberg Mountains to the interior of Aachen where the forest gives way to a vast open savannah. It is a well watered forest with many rivers and streams coursing their way through its innumerable dales. It is a serene place, quiet with anticipation of the days to come. It is said that the Faerie have returned to the trees to care for their wounded spirits and that the nymph tend to the workings of the waters.

Lost within the forest's interior is the Glade of the Unicorn. There, at the heart of the Detmold lies a copse of hardwood trees which date back, or so legends recount, to the Days before Days. It is there that the god Daladon gave Ephremere over to the Unicorn. The sacred and powerful Winter Roses grow within the Glade.

Elithian Wood

This forest once stretched from the Straits of Ursal in the East to the Massif in the south and to the Inner Sea in the orth. The forest's trees are numbered amongst the strongest conifers in the world. Their strength is ideal for shipmaking, their pliability ideal for the construction of bows and lances, and their numbers feed the need for fuel and building materials in the burgeoning populations of Angouleme, Avignon, The Hanse Cities, Cleves, Sienne, and Karilia. It has shrunk since the days of old.

Great portions of the forest are well manicured by woodsmen in the employ of the various kingdoms that work its vast interior. In these sections, the trees grow tall and straight and are oft found in straight rows, piled up by the diligent woodsmen. It is illegal to hunt or reside in many areas, the woodsman strictly enforcing the laws. There are, however, many folk who make a living chopping the trees and cutting them into usable timber. Barges of all sorts ply these waters supplying the woodsman and transporting timber back to the cities beyond.

Yet, despite this, there are portions that have avoide[...] of progress. There are lonely spots tucked away [...] have defied the axe. There, the splendor of the old [...] found. Massive are the trees. Though by far no[...] world, they are the broadest. Five men linking [...] encircle the boles of these trees. They grow [...] taking the time the All Father gave them, unawar[...] upon their doorstep. They do not crowd arou[...] give each other space so that their limbs stre[...] boles, as much to cover a farm house and barr[...] and rivers which run pure as spring's day from[...] the thirst of the behemoths.

Much rumor has been spread about this fores[...] midst, the ancient trees still guard their gr[...] portions difficult to enter, and the ground i[...] those who trespass too deeply into its [...] Whatever the case may be, there are port[...] enter and oft upon a starry night, unwary [...] the likes of this world and meld into the [...] sublime trees.

The Great Wall of Ethrum

The wall is several hundred miles long[...] and width. The average width is 100 [...] about 200. A broad road mounts mu[...] castles built upon its height. Barrac[...] dors to connect them, run throughou[...]

In the early days of man the people o[...] for mastery of the lands of Ursal, t[...] and west of the Ursal Straights. Th[...] of the world so that only the Tarvis[...] against them.

During the great battles, called t[...] perors saw that they could not [...] flected upon how best to defend [...] they fortified the fjords and brid[...] and Ardeen. They did likewise [...] tains. There they constructed [...] the rolling lands of Angoulem[...] ing armies so there they set to [...] neers and laborers worked for [...] all the while the Tarvish Em[...] hold back the Aenochians. [...] Aenochians crossed the Ber[...] valleys beyond.

The wall stood for many [...] sometimes abandoned. S[...] home to whole peoples [...] tunnels, dungeons and m[...] it suffered neglect and th[...] tire sections falling into [...] has become an attracti[...] forts and castles are rep[...] and wonders of the old[...]

The ancient and beautiful Shelves of the Mist.

The Soup Marsh

This lowland marsh is fed by the Danau River and the seas from Brindisium Bay. It is a shallow boggy marsh with a truly foul stench. The salt waters from the bay mix in stagnant pools, and mud bars create an odor that can be smelled as far as the edges of the Darkenfold and some even say along the coasts of Brindisium. The eastern half of the swamp supports little plant life and no large trees. Thick tall reeds are mixed with a bushy, tangled, and knotty shrub that grows out of the briny water. The western half of the swamp is a mixture of large stretches of foul water, creeping with crocodiles, lizards, and birds, both large and small, of the most beautiful hues in all the known world. Trees too grow here, tall majestic cypress that stretch hundreds of feet into the sky and which grow in large clumps as well as individually. The waters of the swamp flow with the ebb and neap of the sea and the flows of the Danau River.

Generally considered impassible, the river men and bargemen of Kayomar know the route the Danau follows through these swamps. But it is a shifting riverbed and its secrets are well kept, giving great power to those who travel through the swamp. Otherwise, the swamp is a horrible place, impossible to pass or navigate, a cesspool of disease and death. It would be avoided by all if it weren't for the constant rumor of mysterious towers hidden deep in the muck and murk that house eldritch treasures and ancient magics of Dwarven craft and construct.

The Wilds

Beneath the Bleached Hills and far from the settled lands of Kayomar are The Wilds, a large untrammeled forest in the middle of Ethrumania. This forest is a mixture of pines and hardwoods. The northern tracks are thickly covered in tall aged pines. The forest floor is littered with their dying husks. In the south are large hardwoods, beech, oak, elm, hickory, locust, and the like. The lands roll with gentle and wooded hills and are cut by many clear flowing steams and creeks. Small ponds and lakes are fed by deep clear springs. The headwaters of the Ardeen River is found within this wood but none have yet found their exact location.

Little is known of this vast stretch of forest but a few hardy men of Kayomar have moved to its southern edges and begun to explore its depths. "There are creatures out there let me tell you, wild wolves the size of a horse, boars as big as elephants, snakes that can eat a man in one bit. There too are Dragons and giants, cruel trolls and others besides. But we brave these lands for the Elk are plentiful and the trees strong. Here we are far from the prying eyes of those taxing Lords of Kayomar which I fear even more than the Dragon." So say the men of the Wilds.

The North-Central Map

1 inch = 150 miles

Uncharted Wilderness

Broken Fingers

The Massif of Orion

Illirim Wood

The Great Wall of Ethrum

Cleves

Greenwood

Capsidastria

Flame

Hanse Cities

The Inner Sea

Mt. Anisagar

Holmsteads

Mount Norling

Lake Orion

Twilightwood

Sienna

Eilithian Wood

Karilia

Eilithian River

The Kingdom of Angouleme

Hanse

River

Arbel

Straights

Avignon

The Sea of Shataf

Tagea

Ursal

of

Eisenheim

Holmgald

Heristat

Harz

Aachen

Detmold

Gulf of Glenmeer

Rebeken Straights

Voralberg Mnts

North-Central Map

The Detmold

This vast forest stretches along the western flanks of the Voralberg Mountains. In places thick and others thin, great conifers provide a blanket of light green across the lands of Eisenheim and Aachen. During the years of the Winter Dark this forest supplied the Empire with timber for its many fleets that crossed the Inner Sea and beyond. Fortresses and villages sprouted up throughout its depths as the ever increasing need for timber demanded a heavy price upon this once pristine wood. Times have changed though and the forest has been left to its own devices for many years. Travelers making their way into this grand wood note the many Imperial roads fallen into disrepair and the abandoned fortresses and villages that dot hillocks and dales alike. There are those who remained though, men who have carved small principalities out of remnants of the Empire's once mighty lands.

The forest itself is a mishmash of magnificent conifers and stunted hardwoods that clump around the region's natural springs and sprout thickly on the tops of hills. They cover this hilly land from the foothills of the Voralberg Mountains to the interior of Aachen where the forest gives way to a vast open savannah. It is a well watered forest with many rivers and streams coursing their way through its innumerable dales. It is a serene place, quiet with anticipation of the days to come. It is said that the Faerie have returned to the trees to care for their wounded spirits and that the nymph tend to the workings of the waters.

Lost within the forest's interior is the Glade of the Unicorn. There, at the heart of the Detmold lies a copse of hardwood trees which date back, or so legends recount, to the Days before Days. It is there that the god Daladon gave Ephremere over to the Unicorn. The sacred and powerful Winter Roses grow within the Glade.

Elithian Wood

This forest once stretched from the Straits of Ursal in the East to the Massif in the south and to the Inner Sea in the orth. The forest's trees are numbered amongst the strongest conifers in the world. Their strength is ideal for shipmaking, their pliability ideal for the construction of bows and lances, and their numbers feed the need for fuel and building materials in the burgeoning populations of Angouleme, Avignon, The Hanse Cities, Cleves, Sienne, and Karilia. It has shrunk since the days of old.

Great portions of the forest are well manicured by woodsmen in the employ of the various kingdoms that work its vast interior. In these sections, the trees grow tall and straight and are oft found in straight rows, piled up by the diligent woodsmen. It is illegal to hunt or reside in many areas, the woodsman strictly enforcing the laws. There are, however, many folk who make a living chopping the trees and cutting them into usable timber. Barges of all sorts ply these waters supplying the woodsman and transporting timber back to the cities beyond.

Yet, despite this, there are portions that have avoided the destruction of progress. There are lonely spots tucked away in this wood that have defied the axe. There, the splendor of the old wood can still be found. Massive are the trees. Though by far not the tallest in the world, they are the broadest. Five men linking arms could hardly encircle the boles of these trees. They grow lazily into the sky, taking the time the All Father gave them, unaware that dooms tramps upon their doorstep. They do not crowd around one another, but give each other space so that their limbs stretch far outside their boles, as much to cover a farm house and barn. The many springs and rivers which run pure as spring's day from deep aquifers quench the thirst of the behemoths.

Much rumor has been spread about this forest. Giants lumber in its midst, the ancient trees still guard their groves, the faerie make portions difficult to enter, and the ground itself is said to consume those who trespass too deeply into its ever-shrinking bounds. Whatever the case may be, there are portions no woodsman will enter and oft upon a starry night, unwary travelers disappear from the likes of this world and meld into the dark eaves of those most sublime trees.

The Great Wall of Ethrum

The wall is several hundred miles long, and ranges in both height and width. The average width is 100 feet and the average height about 200. A broad road mounts much of it, with many forts and castles built upon its height. Barracks and dungeons, with corridors to connect them, run throughout the complex structure.

In the early days of man the people of Ethrum and Aenoch struggled for mastery of the lands of Ursal, those being the lands to the east and west of the Ursal Straights. The Aenochians conquered much of the world so that only the Tarvish Emperors remained to struggle against them.

During the great battles, called the Isles of Mark, the Tarvish Emperors saw that they could not master the Aenochians, so they reflected upon how best to defend their homeland of Kayomar. First, they fortified the fjords and bridges which crossed the rivers Saline and Ardeen. They did likewise throughout the Bergrucken Mountains. There they constructed mighty fortresses. But in the north, the rolling lands of Angouleme offered easy access for any invading armies so there they set to building a great wall. Artisans, engineers and laborers worked for many long years building the edifice, all the while the Tarvish Emperors spent their strength in blood to hold back the Aenochians. In the end it proved to no avail, for the Aenochians crossed the Bergrucken instead and plundered the rich valleys beyond.

The wall stood for many hundreds of years, sometimes occupied, sometimes abandoned. So great is its size, that the wall became home to whole peoples of all races. Soon it became laced with tunnels, dungeons and more fortifications. During the Winter Dark it suffered neglect and the harsh climate did much to reduce it, entire sections falling into ruin. But since those days the Great Wall has become an attractive place for adventurers, for its chambers, forts and castles are reputed to be full to overflowing with treasures and wonders of the old world.

The Greenwood

Once a well tended and safe forest, watched over by the masters of the land, its trees grew to great heights thick with long blue green needles. The Greenwood became a special preserve during the Winter Dark for the tall trees, once cut, remained slightly pliant, making excellent masts for the ships that floated the world round. So the lords of the land tended this forest well, cleared its land and created a vast farm for trees. But times have changed and the masters have died. The forest is coming into its own as it has freed itself from the yoke of human control. The forest floor is coming alive with mosses and lichens, the animals are returning, as are the spirits of the wood. Its paths are growing over and its endless rows of trees are slowly returning to their chaotic eruptions and collections. For now, no one rules this land. War is made upon its soils and the trees remain uncut in the forest's center. Some say the forest was finally come alive, others that it is doomed without the aid of man.

The Hollmgrads

This is a low range of mountains that creep out of the great northern wastes and edge up to the Inner Sea. The mountains are thickly forested in evergreen. Winter lasts throughout much of the year and snow can fall at any time. In the short summers many creeks and streams of frigid water wash through frosty vales and across cool plateaus. The mountains are not high and are gently sloped, having been scraped raw by the glaciation during the Winter Dark.

Many creatures of the north dwell here, sea lions, musk oxen, white bears, wolves and snow deer. Though an apparently uninhabitable land, to those who know its secrets, it is bountiful and full of promise. Winter is the only enemy for it is truly a cold place. Frozen winds from the Inner Sea mix with the chilly storms of the north in a battle in the sky dumping great big flakes of snow or cold rains in their wake. The men of Holmgald call this place home, and many wander into this land seeking fabled creatures, snowbeasts and white dragons.

Forest Illithrim

"What a forbidding forest. Though its beauty is only rivaled by the Darkenfold, it is not a safe place for travelers." From a letter to the Bishop of Avignon.

The mighty oak and mysterious beech befriend one another in this tangled wood. Glorious and young is this forest, bound not by ancient hatreds and endless wars, these trees have grown to their fullest and blossomed handsomely under Erde's sun. The beech are a nutty brown and stretch straight to the sky as if they were tremendous arrows ready to be let. Their nutty brown and white bark is used for paper by the Twilight Elves, for the trees themselves seem to impart a certain wisdom to those that use them. The oaks are gargantuan. They tower so high in the air as to make one giddy, their boles are massive Dwarfing even the giant kin. These are truly the oaks of oak.

The forest thins and thickens and opens occasionally onto brightly lit glades. Beneath its boughs though, the air is clean, yet chilly and rarely sunny. Dark green mosses and yellow lichens abound, strings of clinging vines droop to the ground from the lowest branches. The forest can be difficult to travel though. The husks of long dead trees litter the ground like skeletons in a graveyard, further impeding movement. And within the dark shadows and thick undergrowth dwell all manner of nefarious creatures of Fay, having hid there in times past, they brought with them the most unseemly part of their being and plane.

The Inner Sea

The Inner Sea is a deadly place. Constant struggles occur between the Hanse City States and the raiders from Holmgald, Haltland, Trondheim, and Gottland. These fierce naval battles rage during the early spring and throughout the winter as the more civilized nations to the south try to stop those fierce icebound raiders from the north. They battle over the goods that crisscross the sea, for the Hanse Cities have grown exceedingly wealthy and the men of the north exceedingly envious.

The sea itself is in constant turmoil. Buffeted by cold winds from the Hollmgrads and warmer winds from Ethrumania, storms are a constant fair. The waves, never great in height, are numerous and constant, and only sturdy ships survive crossings of this lake. Beneath the surface of these waters are great whales and massive serpents. Water dragons and other monsters of the deep swim to the surface to catch a tasty morsel on many an occasion. "Ever have they been and ever shall they remain," claim the sailors who ply those waters.

The depths of the ocean have not been fathomed. Somewhere beneath is a city of dead ships crowded with the ghosts of sailors and merchants. On those rare occasions, when the moon is right, and the night sky cloudless, these dead are said to rise from the deeps and return to the homes from which they came, trying to drag loved ones to the lonely depths they now call home.

The Lithanian River

The fabled Lithanian River, is often called the River of Wood. The Lithanian traces its circuitous path through the Elithian Wood. It is a broad and lumbering river fed by many creeks, streams, small rivers, and innumerable springs. The waters usually run deep, clear and clean. The Lithanian spills into the Straights of Ursal near the city of Avignon. The river is well traveled. From within the forest come the many thousands of logs floating to the sawmills scattered all along the lower banks of the Lithanian. Barge traffic also makes its way up and down this river, bringing supplies to the many bands of woodsmen in the Elithian and farmers along its lower banks.

The Massif

Thrusting out of the vast plains and gentle hills of Ethrumania are the jagged spires and crumbling cliff faces of the Massif. It is rumored in the halls of the learned that this tremendous bubble in Erde's crust was created in a weak spot when Unklar first bent the world. Others claim that this is where Inzae tried in vain to break through the crust of the world to gain entry to Erde. Still others, of a peculiarly modern bent, claim that a great eruption of earth and fire rent this hole in the land. Whatever its origin, the Massif is a peculiar and fantastic phenomenon in Erde.

Gigantic spires and cliffs of dark gray and black rock circle a lush valley in which reside Lake Orion and the forest Ilithrim. This ring of steep cliffs, sharp ridges, and ragged gorges stretches for many hundreds of miles in a large circle broken in only one spot, that at the Falls of Thorgrim. The cliffs are steeper on the east end and rather lazy at the far western edges. There are traces, paths, and a few well known and not so well known passes that crisscross the ridge. Most wind along precarious routes that edge narrow ridges and look over long drops into deep gorges.

The fasts of the Massif are littered with hidden valleys and dark caves. Iron and copper abound in its southern reaches, but especially valued is its silver and emeralds. In the north of the Massif are diamonds, the largest known the world over and many a battle is waged over these precious deposits. But there too are found irons and copper. The rock is difficult to work and only engineers of phenomenal ability and the giants of yore know how to unmake and remake it. This is the selfsame rock that was transported north and used in the building of The Wall Ancient or the Great Wall of Ethrum (*reference Terrain, p. 145*).

Within the Massif are the gently sloping plains of Illithrumia. These are well fed grasslands, moist with all the flow from the Massif and very fertile. For the most part, the plains are open and clear with deep flowing bright green grasses offering fantastic vistas. Along the edge of the Massif are copses of aspen and some towering dark green firs, while within the plains proper are small beech and oak glades, lakes, ponds, rivers, streams, and swamps.

The area is home to an abundance of wildlife. The famed long-horned antelope, the lumbering gold-bear, large brown furry bovine, and graceful elk predominate. There are also dreadful creatures that pasture in this fertile plain, the massive and hulking rhinodon, wolves of notorious bent, and scaly lizards crawling in the muck and mire near the swampier shores edging Lake Orion.

Mount Norlling

This is a series of tumbling time-worn mountains of sandstone and granite. It abuts the Massif but has no relation to it. Geographers and others wonder at its origins as it has no logical place in the region. But those less encumbered by modern thinking hint at its origins. They are those that still commune with the land's spirit and Mount Norlling's origins rests, it seems, in the mists of time and rumors of rumors may lead one to believe it was the mighty throne upon which the All father rested to survey his original creation. Others claim this is not so, they believe it is the remnant of the First Mountain of the Dwarf Kings.

Mount Norlling is not a single mountain as the name suggests. Rather, it is a series of ridges and peaks. These mountains have been worn smooth with the passage of years and its structure is neither very high nor strenuous. It is a gentle mountain. With few natural caverns and open accessible valleys, the Mount has never been used as a hiding for those less than estimable denizens of Erde, rather it has attracted giants of a not altogether evil bent who enjoy its peaceful valleys and easily worked stone. But, lest travelers grow less wary in these lands, be aware that it is also home to one of the most viscous of all living things, the Dragon.

Lake Orion

This lake is deep and cold. Its icy blue waters lap gently upon grassy shores for much of the year, but during winter the lake's character changes. It seems the gods of Lake Orion detest the cold and make war upon Unklar's season, giving rise to furious and frothy waves. It is perhaps the All Father's will that lives on in these icy depths or mayhap it is Unkalar's most ancient enemies who hid themselves in its frigid depths during the long Winter Dark that make the water so angry. But this is of only passing concern to those fisher folk that crowd the lake's northern end, for none even dare venture onto it during the winter.

Thousands of streams and small rivers pour down madly through the Massif before gently coursing their way through the plains to fill this lake. The mouths of the largest of the streams and rivers are murky and filled with reeds as high as a tree, and quagmires choke the only lands not covered in water. The lake empties out in one spot. At its southern tip a fast flowing river winds south through the low spot in the Massif. Here, the water careens through twelve foaming cataracts called the Falls of Thorgrim.

What beasts must live in the depths of the Lake keep mostly to themselves and rarely bother the land-bound inhabitants. But it is known that things do live in those waters, things that come aground occasionally, things that pull fishing vessels down in its depths.

night air like fingers of death and the tree's scabrous bark resemble the diseased of hell. The peculiar leaves, dark fleshy with white veins, absorb the light of the moon growing thick and long, lingering overhead as an headman's axe. In the forest heights, at the top of the canopy, are great leafy vines that droop and sway from limb to limb, clinging to branches and bole alike, blocking the light of the sun, such that the forest is locked in a perpetual twilight.

The land is home to Unklar's dreams and it is said that Utumno, the Dreaming God, wanders paths of his own making in these woods. All manner of fell beast reside here making residence in the many caves, crevices, nooks, and crannies off the slopes of the Massif. Fear treads this wood in the likeness of those souls who never crossed over. Many who die here are forever imprisoned in the nightmares of Unklar and must spend their eternal rest in this drab place. The Twilight Elves also walk this wood. These are the offspring of the high elves who chose to remain in the world rather than leave with the coming of Unklar. They are perverted though and unlike their kindred, for they fought alone beneath these eaves and learned to distrust men, Dwarves, and other Elves. They are as evil as they are good and are still locked in war with Unklar.

Sea of Shenal

When the cool waters of the Inner Sea spill through the Straits of Ursal they collide with those warm currents from the Amber Ocean creating the turbulent waters of what fisher-folk call the Sea of Shenal. There, fisherman from Avignon and Freiberg ply their trade. The waters are generally deep and cool, but closer to the surface, broad streams of warm currents draw hosts of fish. These are gathered in nets and stored in "Ice Houses," special holds kept cold by the ship-mage, usually a fledgling wizard with spells of ice and cold. It's a dangerous job, one that pays well, but one where many men and women lose their lives.

The Straits of Ursal

The straights connect the Inner Sea with the southern oceans. It also divides Aenochia from Ethrumania. The straights are fairly narrow, and with good winds a stout ship can cross in a few days. Generally, the Straights are friendly to those who traverse the waters, but on occasion it becomes fierce and stormy as the two seas collide and collapse in a maelstrom of wretched weather. During these times the winds toss the sea about in such a fury that the waves are as tall as a castle's walls. The winds whip up such a horrible froth that sails and masts can easily be ripped from their holdings. These storms seem to sprout and grow in little time and with little warning. Poseidon, many say, fights the connecting of these two continents as they creep ever towards one another. His war against the lands creates this tumultuous seascape.

For this reason, the great Ursal Bridge was constructed. But it is claimed that Poseidon did not like the bridge and helped in its destruction. And ever since he has populated these waters with creatures of ill intent to ensure that none rebuilds the edifice. There are further claims of a Kingdom beneath the waters. One in which great Lords of the seas gather to make war upon those who would close the gap between the Inner and Outer oceans.

The Twilight Wood

Twilight Woods

The Twilight Woods hunker along the eastern edge of the Massif like a wolf ready to pounce. It was once connected to the Elithian Wood and marked its southern terminus, but during the Winter Dark that great forest was sundered into three parts, this being the southernmost. And during that time this forest, once a rare and wonderful place evolved anew into something altogether different. There, the mind of Unklar warped and wove its black dreams into reality so that the elms and oaks, with twisted branches, grasp the

Ursal Tal

This bridge was constructed in the Days before Days. Men called this bridge simply The Ursal Bridge, but its true name resides with the Dwarves, who called it Andstein. (There is no direct translation for this word in the Vulgate tongue. "And" means to bind through an oath. "Stein" means stone. Literally the stone bind. It probably held significance as a stone creation which bound the early Dwarf Kingdoms together as would an oath.)

The bridge stretched across the Straights of Ursal from Aenochia to Ethrum. Its mighty stones rested upon tremendous pylons of granite. The bridge offered travel from Ethrum to Aenochia for many a millennia and cities grew upon its sides untill it too became a city, covered from one end to the other. As many as ten wagon abreast could cross the Ursal Tal completely unaware of the ravaging winds and rains outside.

But time, who beats everything down, eventually wore into the bridge. During the Imperial Wars, the bridge was worn with disrepair, the cities had long since been abandoned, and the pylons were cracking. It took little work for the Tarvish Emperors to destroy the bridge and prevent the eastern armies passage into thier realms of Ethrum.

The pylons still remain. They thrust from the frothy waters of the straights a hundred feet into the air. They are wide and long. Many small communities live upon them, serving as havens for bandits, thieves and even fishermen in times of need. This last remnant of the Days before Days continues to plod forward and fight the erosions of time and man.

Voralberg Mountains

The Voralbergs are a huge, towering range of mountains that stretch many hundreds of miles north and south. Volcanos are active in the roof of this chain but are not a constant occurrence. The peaks are high enough to have glaciers tucked between them and are covered in snow the year round. Deep troughs and narrow defiles and crumbling ridges make up the bulk of the mountains. Its upper reaches are bare except in the south where the range is more broad and vast. Upland plateaus can be found there, and are famous for their colorful summer flowers. The lower portions are covered in all manner of tree depending on the elevation. Crooked creeks and streams pour off the mountain in abundance feeding the lands to the east and west with fresh water.

No kingdom claims this range and it is an inhospitable place. It is peopled sparingly with a few Dwarves and Gnomes, some knights, and a few claiming royal lineage. These are found along the major passes of the mountains. These places are fairly safe but do see their fair share of banditry and raids from the more nefarious of the mountain's inhabitants. Outside those passes though, the mountains are dangerous. Many foul creatures wander the lands. Though not cruel by nature, the giants here are indifferent and care little for the ways of man, orc, elf, goblin, dwarf or any other creatures that walk or crawl across the earth. There are also great fabled beasts here, flying lions, three headed lizards and the like. For centuries untold they have been raiding merchants and traders who dared pass this range. And what went into their coffers never ever came out. So the mountains attract a great many adventurers, some successful and others not.

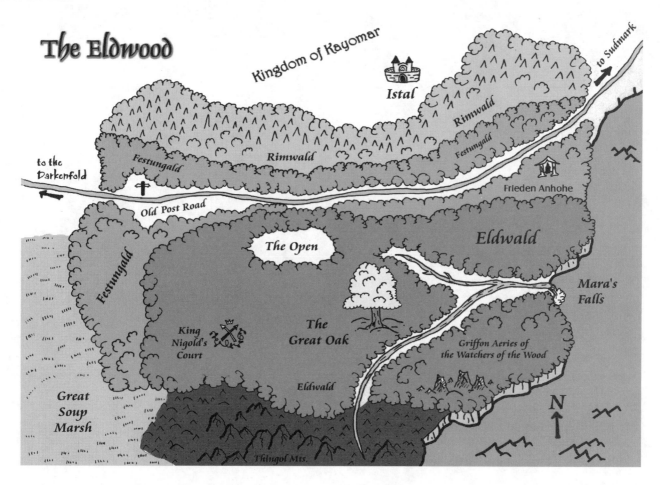

South-Central Map

The Amber Sea

Saline River

Eire Castle

Crel-et

Fontenouq

The Gelderland

Othines

Ulgars

Icantjos

Frieburg

Twilightwood

Eloria

Straits of Ungara

Onwaltig

Taigea

Laigon Straits

Mount Hayden

Rolkrab Range

Illumbrian Plains/Coasts

Voralberg Mnts.

Aenoch Valley

1 Inch = 150 miles

SOUTH-CENTRAL MAP

Aenoch Valley

This deep and ancient valley rests in the nook of the Red Hills and the Voralberg Mountains. It houses the Aenochian Forest. The Mundus and Olgdon Rivers flow through it before cutting a path through the mountains to the Amber Sea. The valley's rim is sparsely forested and covered in great sandstone boulders while its central region is covered by the consuming Aenochian Forest. The southern uplands of the valley are wild and untamed, with roots stretching into the ancient past.

The Amber Sea

Few dare brave the waters of the great southern ocean, and none know what lies beyond them. Some are drawn to the waters though. In these unfathomable depths one can catch and kill the great whales. The oils, skin, meats, and bones are valued highly throughout the world and in a good year can make a man wealthy enough to live in Avignon in style for the remainder of his days. But it is a daunting place. The heat of the days can be unbearable. Months may pass without a single drop of rain coming from the sky or a cloud to break the sun's heat. In moments though, storms brew into a frothy mess with waves reaching as tall as a great oak. Ships are sundered when cracked by these waves, and sink to the bottom of the sea. There are also tales of great serpents wrapping themselves around the largest of vessels and dragging them to the oceans floor. Other tales relate that furious monsters, with many tentacles wrap themselves tightly about a ship, flinging everyone overboard and leaving the ship to flounder upon a listless sea. The tales of the Amber Sea are too numerous to relate in such a small tome but are replete with underwater kingdoms, floating islands, and ghostly ships.

The Deeps

The Deeps are a small stretch of Ocean located several hundred miles off the southern coasts of Eloria. They are distinguished by their unusually calm seas. There are rarely storms of any significance and the waves hardly crest over two or three feet. The water is cool, even on the surface, and has little in the way of fish. Though whale pods are seen frequently, particularly Sperm Whales. They dive into the deep ocean hunting giant squid and other beasts. What strange occurrence causes this stretch of water to be so calm is unknown, though many speculate that in ancient days, when the Dwarves ruled Erde that here lay their most wondrous Kingdom, the realm of Alanti. They say that it is the magic of these Dwarves which causes the sea to slumber and the whales to play. And in truth the water here is tremendously deep.

Illumbrian Plains/Coast

This area of poorly watered lands extends from the Kolkrab Mounains in the West to the Red Hills in the north, and to the edges of the Kellerwald in the east. To the south lies the Illumbrian Coast. The plains are dry, receiving little runoff from the mountains and even less rainfall than those heights to the north and west. What little

water does fall pours into the region's many lakes and ponds, keeping them full and clear. The lands are gentle and generally flat, only rising slightly as one travels north away from the plains. The plains support a hardy prairie grass that withstands both the heat and dry of summer, as well as tall and narrow poplars.

The coastal region is stark and bare, but coves, bays and inlets hide beautiful and secluded retreats protected from the harsh seas of winter and cooled by the Amber Sea's lazy summer winds. These areas are highly prized by the more reclusive of the United Kingdoms, and home to some of the most powerful personages, both villainous and otherwise.

The Kolkrab Mountains

The tall spires of the Kolkrabs dominate southern Aenocia. They overlook a lush valley to the north and the Amber Sea to the south. These are gorgeous mountains with tall, thin, white capped peaks, whisping gentle snows and cool breezes off into the lands at their feet. Few trees grow here, most that do are tall deciduous trees that root deep and drink from underground waterways. They are lonely trees, kept company only by large black ravens. The mountains hold gold and silver in their roots, as well as gems and others precious things. Much has been taken from the mountains and it has given without regret for it was always a friendly place and remembers the

Mount Hayden where sleeps the Dragon

Days before Days and the goodness in the world then. Its valleys are gentle and its streams fresh with life.

But things are changing. For a thousand years the mountains suffered the yoke of Unklar and many a shaft was driven straight to its heart. Much was plundered and taken without return. Now the place is growing wary of strangers and fearful of miners as its life is being drained. The greed in the West is creating a rush for these lands and mines begin to drop deep. Giants and others are coming to the mountain's defense and are beginning to guard it well. It is said that Frafnog, that most ancient of Dragons, dwells in the Kolkrab and that his presence alone gives the range an almost supernatural life.

Mount Hayden

In days of yore a young peasant from the Rleuland traveled along the Illumbrian coasts seeking the wisdom of the Dragon Frafnog. Legends told that the ancient worm lived within a deep cave upon the spire of the highest mountain in the Kolkrabs. Whether true or not, the young man never returned and the locals named the mountain after him. Ever since Mount Hayden has drawn wanderers and hermits who seek its ancient wisdom. Stark and terrible the 9,000 foot mountain looks out over the shipping lanes along the coasts. Its stark cliffs and endless trails claim many a would be adventurer.

Nicoleigh Hills

These stark hills were once the hunting grounds of the royal houses of ancient Aenoch. Deep forests of oak and maple covered the hills, where streams ran deep and fast. Many folk eventually flocked there, settling there to earn a living off the nobles and their gold. But eventually constant hunting depleted the land of game, and the settlers destroyed much of the forests. In the waning days of the Empire, the Empress Nicole Leigh declared the lands her own domain and drove the many people who lived there from the hills. She destroyed towns, tore apart dams and attempted to reforest the area. She forbid hunting and the harvesting of trees in a vain attempt to restore the land to its past glory. In this she was only partly successful. Though civil war interrupted her endeavors, and she fell to an assassin's dagger in the very hills she loved, her efforts served the forest to some degree. Today, the water in the many streams and creaks runs clean and pure. Copses of forests grow here and there, slowly spreading across the now stark mounds. But in many places the land is rugged and broken, soil erosion leaving it unpalatable for much growth. Some few folk, those whose ancestors were allowed to remain, live off the land and remember and care for it. A druidic people, they worship the trees and sky and other natural spirits. Some monsters too have settled there, but these are ancient and they are friendly, as often as not. But few now remember the Empress who lent an Empire to save a forest.

Straits of Ligon

These straits lie between Onwaltig and the mainland. It is a bountiful area. The sea is fed fresh water in huge amounts, and with it comes nutrients to feed the teeming hordes of fish that live here. During spring, however, the area can be dangerous. The waters from the Olgdon come in such great heaves as to cause tumult in the ocean. The weather also becomes perilous as storms from the south whip the shallow waters up into a terrible fury.

The straits are sometimes called the Dragon Straights. Legend speaks of a great beast of a dragon living in the Kolkrab Range whose mate died in battle with a great hero from Avignon in the waters of the straights. On frosty clear nights when the sky burns bright with what seems to be gouts of flame, one can see a dragon come to mourn the loss of his mate. Woe to any who finds himself at sea when it arrives, for this dragon seeks revenge and will exact a terrible toll upon all those it can. Some variances on the legend say that this dragon is none other than Frafnog himself, but these are only tales and the night has been dark for many years.

Straits of Ungara

This is a very shallow and rocky passing between Eloria and the mainland. Many shipmasters refuse to cut this course, taking the southerly and safer route around Eloria. But those in a hurry, trying to escape pursuers, or just foolhardy, will try to wind their way through the straights. There are a few shipmasters who know these waters. The men of Eloria are said to pass them with ease as can the Tageans. It is also related that one of the palaces of Prince Morgeld sits on a rocky precipice overlooking the straights. This, more than anything else, is enough to keep travelers away, for he does not take kindly to ships that refuse to pay him heed and quickly dispatches those he can.

Voralberg Mountains

The Voralbergs are a huge, towering range of mountains that stretch many hundreds of miles north and south. Volcanos are active in the roof of this chain but are not a constant occurrence. The peaks are high enough to have glaciers tucked between them and are covered in snow the year round. Deep troughs and narrow defiles and crumbling ridges make up the bulk of the mountains. Its upper reaches are bare except in the south where the range is more broad and vast. Upland plateaus can be found there, and are famous for their colorful summer flowers. The lower portions are covered in all manner of tree depending on the elevation. Crooked creeks and streams pour off the mountain in abundance feeding the lands to the east and west with fresh water.

No kingdom claims this range and it is an inhospitable place. It is peopled sparingly with a few Dwarves and Gnomes, some knights, and a few claiming royal lineage. These are found along the major passes of the mountains. These places are fairly safe but do see their fair share of banditry and raids from the more nefarious of the mountain's inhabitants. Outside those passes though, the mountains are dangerous. Many foul creatures wander the lands. Though not cruel by nature, the giants here are indifferent and care little for the ways of man, orc, elf, goblin, dwarf or any other creatures that walk or crawl across the earth. There are also great fabled beasts here, flying lions, three headed lizards and the like. For centuries untold they have been raiding merchants and traders who dared pass this range. And what went into their coffers never ever came out. So the mountains attract a great many adventurers, some successful and others not.

A Life at Sea

Though in ages past the Dwarves of Alanti first put ships to sea, few now sail the oceans of Erde but for men and Orcs. Many make their living by pulling fish from the depths, others traffic goods, and still others pirate those who make an honest living of work on the sea. In the Lands of Ursal the Northmen, Tageans and Elorians are the most skilled, but others sail as well. Merchants from all over cart all manner of goods across the water. The wine ships which sail from Maine and Brindisium travel as far north as Avignon, that great trading hub. And pirates from Ilhsa (*reference the United Kingdoms, p. 134*) and Onwaltig terrorize the southern shipping lanes.

Recently crusaders from the west have begun to outfit their own ships and cross the sea in route to Outremere. They bare banners and shields depicting the spoked wheel of Demeter, or the symbols of Toth and the Empress (*reference Outremere, p. 122*). They sometimes raid along the way, punishing any and all they feel deserve it, particularly the pirates of Ihlsa.

Few ships which cross the deep water do so unarmed. Compliments of mercenaries are almost always on board. Depending on the size of the ship these can number in the hundreds. Some ship captains have even gone to the expense of buying small canon and mounting them deck. These primitive imports from the Punj lob shot across the water to tear gapping holes in ships and men.

There are a variety of ship types, from river barges to frigates. Many of the more primitive ships, the trireme and pentacontors are outfitted with sails and oars. Though many nations, such as the Hanse and Avignon have merchant fleets nicely outfitted with sail and tack. These large two and three masted galleys have as many as three decks, crews of hundreds and can stay at sea for many months. They are rare and expensive.

Only the ships of Eloria break the tradition of all ship building. These huge monstrosities date from the days when the Prince lived in the distant west. They have seven decks, three large masts, and hundreds of sails. The largest, *The Fell Knight*, measures 700 feet on the gun deck and nearly 100 feet abeam. They float by means both natural and magical. Only a few of these ships remain in the harbors of Elorisia and they are prized by the Prince above all his possessions (*reference Eloria, p. 86*).

The most unusual of ships are the fishing vessels of the Inner Sea. After the fall of Unklar many wizards of Umbra found themselves without a master. Stricken with poverty and frequently homeless many wandered as mendicants for a great while. It was the wizard Timerwin Burns who broke the mold. During the Winter Dark he had learned that flesh could be frozen and brought to life again. And so being a crafty man and able wizard he offered his services to the ship captain, Kenneth, of the *Neely*. "You take what you can from the sea, fill your hull with it and I will keep it cold and fresh. When we return to land we can sell it as new." Kenneth took him up on the offer and the two set off. The wizard spent much of his time in the hull laying sorceries of cold upon the fish brought aboard. Soon thereafter they returned from the sea with a hull full of frozen tuna. Thus, the commercial fishing industry was born.

Soon many ships, great and small plied the waters of the Inner Sea, fishing and crabbing, and all bore ice wizards aboard who, like Timerwin, kept the catch frozen for the market.

The payoff is generally very good and many make a living for a year by working for a few months. It is a dangerous life, for the waters there are turbulent, and many ship captains are reckless in their drive to bring in a great haul. (The *Neely* itself was lost at sea. After four years of sailing it crossed into the deep water of the Inner Sea alongside the vessel *Patty's Pride* when a storm overtook them. The *Neely* was never seen again. Though rumors abound that Kenneth and Timerwin live still, running a brothel and bar in the far northern town of Trondheim.)

The Deep Quiet

Travel upon the sea is dangerous and many sailors depart safe harbors never to return. Poor ships, pirates, Orc raiders, and monsters from the deep cause much loss of life. But far greater than these are the waters themselves. Storms, particularly in the spring and autumn, whip the already restless waters into a fury which only the most experienced or lucky can long survive.

All sailors pray and sacrifice to Poseidon, asking for his good graces, for the Lord of the Sea is a harsh task master and unforgiving. He has been known to rise from the depths and destroy ships which have offered offense. So sailors call to him before they sail and sacrifice to him upon their safe return.

Of those many who never see land again, but who fall overboard or whose ships slip beneath the tireless waves the folk of Erde have a saying. They call it the "Deep Quiet," for at the bottom of the sea there are no worries or work; nothing to hound a man but the silence of the depths. "He has gone to the Deep Quiet," is a common expression. Or "May the Deep Quiet keep you," is told to a departed friend. Sometimes it is used as a curse. But no matter the manner, it always refers to a death at sea.

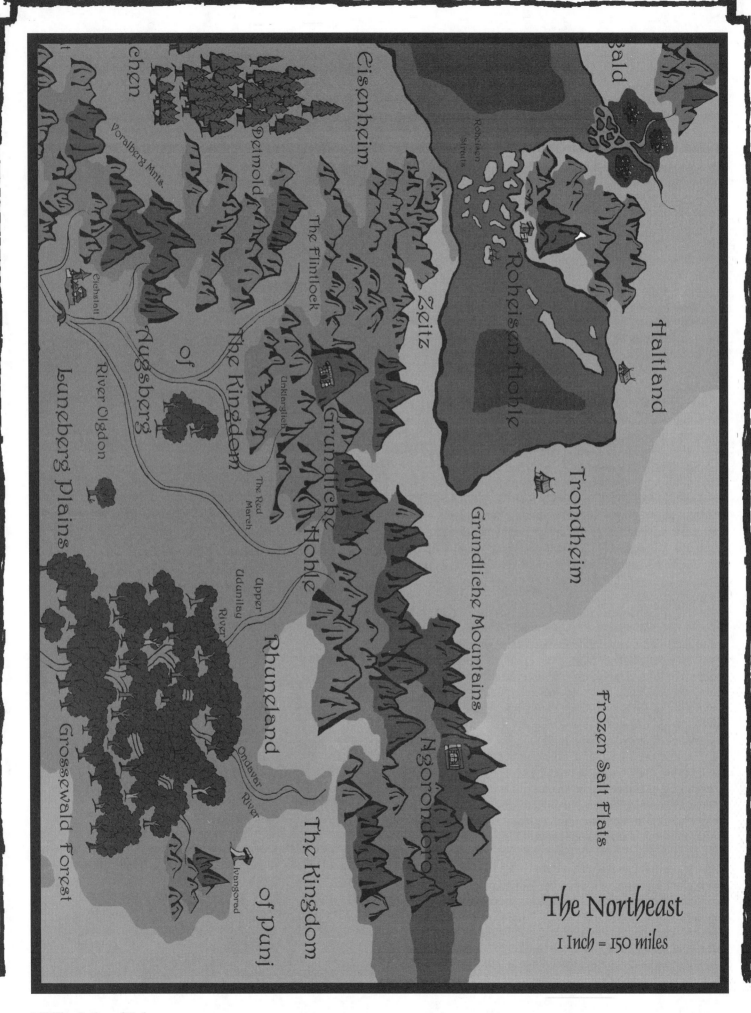

Northeastern Map

The Detmold

This vast forest stretches along the western flanks of the Voralberg Mountains. In places thick and others thin, great conifers provide a blanket of light green across the lands of Eisenheim and Aachen. During the years of the Winter Dark this forest supplied the Empire with timber for its many fleets that crossed the Inner Sea and beyond. Fortresses and villages sprouted up throughout its depths as the ever increasing need for timber demanded a heavy price upon this once pristine wood. Times have changed though and the forest has been left to its own devices for many years. Travelers making their way into this grand wood note the many Imperial roads fallen into disrepair and the abandoned fortresses and villages that dot hillocks and dales alike. There are those who remained though, men who have carved small principalities out of remnants of the Empire's once mighty lands.

The forest itself is a mishmash of magnificent conifers and stunted hardwoods that clump around the region's natural springs and sprout thickly on the tops of hills. They cover this hilly land from the foothills of the Voralberg Mountains to the interior of Aachen where the forest gives way to a vast open savannah. It is a well watered forest with many rivers and streams coursing their way through its innumerable vales. It is a serene place, quiet with anticipation of the days to come. It is said that the Faerie have returned to the trees to care for their wounded spirits and that the nymph tend to the workings of the waters.

Lost within the forest's interior is the Glade of the Unicorn. There, at the heart of the Detmold lies a copse of hardwood trees which date back, or so legends recount, to the Days before Days. It is there that the god Daladon gave Ephremere over to the Unicorn. The sacred and powerful Winter Roses grow within the Glade.

The Flintlock

The Flintlocks are a western spur of the Grundliche Mountains. They are high in the eastern ends and lower in the western reaches. The mountains and hills are jagged and steep to low and rolling. Water is plentiful, rolling off both to the east and to the west in small streams and rivulets. The northern reaches are stark and scoured by winds from the Inner Sea. To the south there are finely wooded areas with many red cedars and tall thin pines. Throughout the whole there are steep and shallow valleys, long narrow ridges and massive boulder fields, generously spread amongst the low peaks and rounded mountains. The snows fall heavy and thick during winter, blanketing the entire region in a perpetually white drift.

The hills and valleys, cliffs and peaks are dotted with fortresses, mines, caves, houses, farmsteads and the like. Many are abandoned but some are still held by Gnomes who live here in great numbers. These cousins to the Dwarves were once part of the kingdom extending from Grundliche Hohle. But no more, the wars with the Punj left the region out of the Mountain Kingdom's territory and the Gnomes call themselves kings of their own now, ruled by the Clan Thanes. There are 47 clans that reside here. Stout and harsh, the gnomes patrol the mountains incessantly, scouring the landscape of any and all unwelcome intruders. Many foul creatures keep them busy, for without the aid of the Grundliche Dwarves, the Gnomes face enemies they never had to battle before. The place is becoming positively dangerous to travel through, as more and more creatures of ill intent make there way to these lands. Gotzenburg Keep, long a Dwarf stronghold, is held by Orcs now. They hold to the old ways, are fiercely organized and ruled by the Anjak (Orc King), Rwin of Ateck, a large burly Orc with an eye for human slaves.

Frozen Salt Flats

The land is frozen in the north of the world. Unklar's freezing grip and icy breath are still felt in this fell region. Once a great and open savanna covered in dark warm grasses and thick black firs stretched across the northern reaches of Erde. Battle with Unklar left its mark upon this land though, blasting every living thing from it and blanketing it in a glacier of tremendous proportions. Miles thick, the glacier sits ponderously upon the land, its icy fingers stretching ever more gently into the south during the coldest of years and retreating during warm ones. The glacier itself is salty, attesting to the freezing temperatures in this region. The glacier is split and uneven, cragged in places, but smooth in others. Snow heaps and furls over the peaks, while shallow salty lakes amass atop the glacier during the summer melt. In its crevasse and splits and amongst its thrusting sections and razor sharp jags are innumerable shifting caves of ice.

What little lives in this land is most terrifying, for only Unklar's minions could survive in such an inhospitable place. But tales speak of massive white bears with long shaggy hair and teeth the size of small daggers, of slim six legged lizards with brilliant white scales that glimmer in the moonlight, and other fell beasts. Some brave souls do make their way to these lands, for into them fled the last remnants of Unklar's people after he was cast down and they brought with them great wealth. Wealth that has long since disappeared into the caverns and palaces of ice beneath the frosty wasteland.

Grossewald

This is an old forest. Its birth stretches back to the dawn of time and it has grown, inexorably, ever since. The trees are neither massive nor awe inspiring in their beauty, but they are hardy as the goblins who reside, to this day, beneath their eaves. They are as gnarled and knuckled as a pit fighter with thick gray and ochre barks, with bent and twisting limbs creeping towards the earth. They are green trees whose broad lobed leaves never brown or yellow with the season, but withstand the encroachments of age and time perhaps without dignity, but with great fortitude. These peculiar abilities allowed the forest to thrive during the Winter Dark. The forest is friendly to sun, allowing it to shine hither and yon into verdant green glades.

The forest spreads wide, dominating central Aenochia. The great rivers Udunilay and Ordavar flow mightily beneath the limbs of these trees. There, within the forest, creatures never seem to die, for 'tis told that Eldritch Goblins, the sorcerers of old, still move about in freedom. All manner of beast is found within; the remains of the All Father's imaginings, as well as those cast aside by Unklar. After the reign of that unholy lord, many a minion fled into these

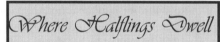
Where Halflings Dwell

uncharted wildernesses, biding their time in dark anticipation for his return. Along its frontiers, though, dwell clans upon clans of Halflings, the only untainted ones in all Erde willing to brave both the forest and its horrible minions. They are led by the battle lord, Witterkind, he who bares a Font of Narrheit upon his belt (*reference Magic Items, p. 221-223*). These stout folk live both in laagers of wagons and villages built into the hills, valleys and forests.

Grundliche Mountains

The white capped burgs of northern Aenochia dominate the northern end of Erde. They are the tallest mountains in the world. Some peaks are high enough that the clouds rest far beneath them. The mountains are both beautiful and horrible. Sharp spired peaks, with white tips, cross the horizon like the spears of the armies of eldritch demons. They tower over and above one another in an endless fashion. At these heights on a clear day the entire world can be seen bending off in every direction. From there the peaks descend perilously to deep troughs and great upland plateaus covered knee deep in snow the year long. Furious weather whips at these heights, dumping snow and blasting chill winds hundreds of miles per hour. Nothing lives here except the mightiest of beast and gods of old. 'Tis said, that somewhere in the sky bound peaks lies the battlefield where the Council first fought Unklar, and the remnants of their shattered weaponry lies there still.

Further down the mountains are narrow canyons carved by immense glaciers, sharp ridges, fields of boulder, mountains of slate, granite precipices and many other wonders besides. Even further down one comes to the trees and streams and rivers and valleys and dales and low plateaus. All rough and tumble, shaken by the quakes that still rumble and groan at the top of the world. Madly, the landscape slips and falls to the plains below and only then does it release its grasp upon the world.

Here live the famed Dwarves of Grundliche Hohle. Powerful and strong beyond compare, these dwarves have fought from the beginning of time to keep their grip on this land. They hold this perilous land dear and few tread where they live without permission. But the mountains are vast and untamable. Goblins also live here, in Ngorondoro. They strive, as do the Dwarves, for control of the mountains. There are great beasts, giants who reside at the roof of the world and care not for the happenings of man. Massive hulking beastmen who wander the upland plateaus are there. Dragons may also be found and fearsome tigers and cougars out of times past make this place their home. The beasts that stalk these mountains, like the land, are innumerable.

It is the immense wealth that brings everyone. The mountains are full of gold, silver, gems, jewels, and other ores of great value. The mountains have been home to folk for many thousands of years and many chambers and halls were built in days of yore. Much has been abandoned. The countless wars have left vast underground tracks empty of Goblin and Dwarf.

Upon the southern stretches of the mountains very near to Grundliche Hohle lies dread Unklarglich. Like a moment of darkness the castle of the Mogrl stands as a testament to the age of Winter Dark. The ever watchful beast within scans the mountains and the valleys, looking for any of the Council brave enough to challenge him. He is a dread master of the dark and only the foolish dare try him.

Only foul and powerful creatures dwell here now. Beware to those who dare travel these paths for all are your enemy. Interlopers are treated poorly by Dwarf and Goblin. Also be warned, Dolgan, the mastersmith, hammered out many a foul creature of immense power that now wander these halls.

Olgdon River

The greatest of the eastern rivers, the Olgdon flows from its headwaters in the Grundliche Mountains near, as tradition has it, the resting place of the first Dwarven king of Grundliche Hohle. It collects the waters from the Grundliche and Voralberg Mountains, as well as from the eastern plains and the Red Hills. It is truly a massive river, a ponderous giant that swells and buckles in its course. The river is nearly 3000 feet wide by the time it reaches the middle of the Luneburg Plains. From thence it only becomes wider. It is impassible except by barge or boat or the only two bridges that span its breadth in southern Augsburg. Fish and waterfowl abound in the marshes and pools along its banks, as well as clams, crawfish and freshwater shrimp. It offers great bounty to those who fish its murky waters. The river is well traveled with barges and commercial traffic and in some places even crowded.

It is not a perilous river by any means, it sits so lazy and flows so easy, but it has dangers. The river is large enough and deep enough to offer home and refuge to many creatures. Some of these are evil and cruel minions of Unklar who hid themselves in the deep murky waters. They tend to linger around towns and cities and rear their ugly heads in the most surprising ways. Hags too, live along the reedy river's edges with small tribes of cruelly misshapen men, water trolls and the like.

Ondavar River

Fed by the snows, glaciers, rivers, streams and springs of the Grundliche Mountains, this river flows fast and furious into Aenochia. It is a turbulent river, only calming as it approaches the northern reaches of the Grossewald. Through this forest it flows unevenly until emptying into the Udunilay River. It is home to blue and yellow trout. Halflings have gathered in small villages along its banks fishing for these tasty fish. It is also home to boundless number of beaver whose skins are traded as far away as Avignon. But there are mean beasts here also, creatures who have crawled out of the depths of time and live submerged in its waters, attacking lone travelers and unwary fishermen.

The Red March

The Red March comprises that region around the Rilthwood. It refers to a wilderness area that is claimed by no king, but is distinct for its stone mounds and friendly thickets. The land is fresh, the ground fertile, the winters mild, and the trees abundant. What distinguishes this land most though are its people. Hospitable beyond words, these sturdy farmers offer house and home to stranger and friend alike. It is a safe respite for those weary of the world and its dangers. Hearty food, heady ales, and comfortable feathery beds at a cheap price offer havens for many travelers and at a very reasonable price. The population is sparse though, and its plentiful waters and open paths attract all manner of creature, both fell and wild. Monsters situate their dens in the crooks, crevices and crannies of the land making passers-by and travelers their occasional prey. It is home to some very famous monsters, such as the giant Skullgrinder and his band of surly burglars, the Fallowmouth Serpent, the crazed Rendweird, and Palatine the wayward bard, who sings horrible songs with a breath that smells like a swamp and with the voice of an ogre. So famed are some of the monsters that the inhabitants would be loathe to see them go. But hardy adventurers and the like always manage their way into this land in search of easy loot and clean living.

Rilthwood

These slender, stark white trees rise high above the numerous ponds and streams like spires of bone. In the fall, the normally shiny bright green leaves of the Rilthwood trees turn a brilliant red. When viewed from the Grundliche Mountains to the east, the trees appear to be columns of white coated and red helmed giants marching across the landscape. The ponds there shimmer like mirrors in the sunlight, reflecting the subtly shifting colors of the Rilthwood. They are icy clear and one can see into these deep holes. If one looks carefully, very carefully and patiently one may witness the picture of the Rilthwood's past, for the ponds remember everything but are careful about divulging its secrets.

This wood is valued in the courts of princes and kings. When carved by skillful hands it is as if it were ivory. The armies of Grundliche Hohle haft many an axe with this white wood, and wizards claim it is inherently magical and makes for the best staves and wands, while seers value its waters, claiming it holds the memories of the All Father. Warily must one tread here, for the Halflings guard this land, while interloping mages and woodsman steel its magical bounty.

Udunilay River

A mighty river, perhaps the most fearful of all rivers upon Erde, the Udunilay begins high up Mount Undillay deep in the Grundliche Mountains near the Hohle of the same name. It is believed the water flows from the eye of the All Father so clean and pure is its beginning. It tumbles and careens over falls and mountains, fed by an ever increasing number of streams, until it dumps a mighty gush of water onto the broad plains of Aenochia. From thence it flows through the Grossewald, the Graussemland, and the Kellerwald before arriving at the Amber Sea. It is fed by the Undovar and the Uphrates, making the river as broad as a league. So powerful its flow, the Graussemland could not absorb it, though Unklar bent much of his will towards taming it. It is called the River of Eternal Life, for, like many things in this part of the world, it seems indomitable and endless.

Rot-Tor

This river tumbles madly out of the Grundliche Mountains in the north to the Inner Sea. The lands it cuts through are hilly and forested. The river has driven great crevices in the land and fills broad shallow glades. It grows to tremendous sizes during spring as the mountain snows fill it to flooding, causing the massive river to careen down the mountains. It winds its way through narrow defiles and over tall cliffs creating frothy waterfalls. It is impassible during spring except at well guarded crossings.

Voralberg Mountains

The Voralbergs are a huge, towering range of mountains that stretch many hundreds of miles north and south. Volcanos are active in the roof of this chain but are not a constant occurrence. The peaks are high enough to have glaciers tucked between them and are covered in snow the year round. Deep troughs and narrow defiles and crumbling ridges make up the bulk of the mountains. Its upper reaches are bare except in the south where the range is more broad and vast. Upland plateaus can be found there, and are famous for their colorful summer flowers. The lower portions are covered in all manner of tree depending on the elevation. Crooked creeks and streams pour off the mountain in abundance feeding the lands to the east and west with fresh water.

No kingdom claims this range and it is an inhospitable place. It is peopled sparingly with a few Dwarves and Gnomes, some knights, and a few claiming royal lineage. These are found along the major passes of the mountains. These places are fairly safe but do see their fair share of banditry and raids from the more nefarious of the mountain's inhabitants. Outside those passes though, the mountains are dangerous. Many foul creatures wander the lands. Though not cruel by nature, the giants here are indifferent and care little for the ways of man, orc, elf, goblin, dwarf or any other creatures that walk or crawl across the earth. There are also great fabled beasts here, flying lions, three headed lizards and the like. For centuries untold they have been raiding merchants and traders who dared pass this range. And what went into their coffers never ever came out. So the mountains attract a great many adventurers, some successful and others not.

The World of Erde

1" is 75 miles

The Southeast

1 Inch = 150 miles

Southeastern Map

Aenochian Forest

This is a dense forest that fills much of the Aenoch Valley. The forest proper is noted for its tremendous Birch trees. These are massive affairs with a black bark and dark green leaves as a result of the waters of the Nostian River. Trees there are clustered together choking out much of the undergrowth, except along creek banks and river sides. Lichens and mosses cling to the trunks of trees, and hang in long streamers from the tree's thick boughs. The forest grows evermore to the south, reaching its fingers up through the southern Aenoch valley to the base of the Red Hills. The Mundus River flows leisurely through the center of the forest before meeting up with the River Olgdon near the forest's eastern reaches.

But the Olgdon is well traveled by Augsburgian barges, ships, and traders while several outposts are even located along the river and under the eves of the forbidding forest. Ancient cemeteries housing the restless dead and long buried temples, castles and palaces are rumored to abound within this forest, for the forest was the ancestral land of the House Golden, the old Imperial family. Many believe these ghosts haunt the forest still. It is even said that the tomb of the last Aenochian King lies somewhere within, hiding the riches and magic of his folk.

Fromia River

This muddy river tumbles out of the northern Red Hills into the Aenoch Valley and thence into the Mundus River. It is a muddy affair that courses down steep valleys and over precarious falls, pulling dirt, soil, and clays along with it. The upper courses of the river and its many feeder creeks attract prospectors of all kinds as it is rumored that out of this region of the Red Hills come its only precious metal - silver. Though, in truth, it must be said that few Dwarves or Gnomes ever bother with the region, indicating the lack of veracity behind this claim.

Grausamland

This is the most horrible place in all Erde. It is so putrid that it defies any words devised by man, elf, or dwarf. Only the words of the All Father can do this pestilence justice. It is a mire of stinking, fetid, rotting, swamps. Unklar created this grotesque bog to protect his precious Aufstrag. He drained waters from the Uphrates and Undillay rivers into deep holes and innumerable underground passages filling the lands about with stagnating water. He devised hulking trees to grow out of this waterlogged land. These are tall trees that reach to the stars many hundreds of feet overhead. The roots are like gnarled beasts that grow in long spines out of the muck. From it branches, both high and low hang curtains of green moss and drapes of yellow lichen. The branches on high leaf out into narrow and thin green needles as thick as a wasp swarm blotting out all sunlight and moonlight. The swamps are dark, ever, ever pitch dark. The ground swells and bubbles, burping forth and spewing sulphurous odors and red muds. The land is virtually all under several inches of water and abounds in sink holes, holes, mud pits, quicksands, and slimy pits that suck down anything that happen to step upon them. Huge skeletal remains of long dead trees crowd the lower reaches as time and water wear them to nothing. The stench from this place is so overwhelming that it can easily kill a man of lesser make and can be smelled for dozens of miles in every direction from its borders.

This place is crowded with denizens of one's nightmares. Unklar's breath can still be smelled and the life he gave to so many a foul creature still persists in these swamps. And these are cruel creatures and wretched creatures. Their make is impossible to describe as they came in so many shapes and terrible forms. Most were hidden from the eyes of the world and left to find their way in these swamps and stop any would be interlopers. There are great bats that drink blood, lizards that breathe mud, snakes that fly, and others besides. Dragons are said to be here, Ungern in great numbers, orcs and goblins from old.

What would bring a man here. Treasure! Treasure unlike any in the world. The plunder from a thousand years is stored in deep holes and massive treasuries in these swamps. Arcane magics are too found and weapons from the wars at the beginning of time for Unklar was a hoarder of all things. The swamp also rests upon the ruins of Al-Liosh and all the treasure contained therein. When entering this land take heed to guard your waking dreams for fear attracts the worst of the beasts.

The Grausamland, a mire of stinking, fetid, rotting swamps. A horrible place to all.

The Kellerwald

Another of the great forests of old. A seemingly harmless and innocuous place, these fantastic beech, birch, oak, and hickory grow straight and tall. They are leafy and healthy trees. They rest upon fertile earth worn level by the tide of years. One might travel for miles through these wood without stumbling, so level is the ground. The trees are broad in areas and thick in others. The beech and birch groves are truly wonderful to behold. A veritable sea of brown and gray papery barks stretch in endless parades before the eyes. In fall the region explodes in colors only the All Father could have imagined. Yellows and reds of every hue celebrate the end of summer and await the long winter. From on high in the Red Hills one can see the Kellerwald during the fall and it is as if some great fire were raging along the coasts of Outremere and up to the borders of that foul heap, Grausamland.

The forest is a fairly safe place as the trees have never known the unbridled hatred of man nor even of Unklar. It does not act kindly to those who strip it and treat it poorly, so the Goblins, Orcs and other foul creatures make their homes elsewhere. But it is home to those who do care for it. Home to creatures that, though friendly to trees, are not so disposed to the races of man, Elf, and Dwarf.

Mundus River

The Mundus flows through the heart of the Aenochian Forest. It is possessed of tremendous currents, eddies and underwater whirlpools, largely fed by the fury of the two mountain streams which feed the river, the Fromia and the Nostian. Little is known about the Mundus, though some hold that it was a holy place to the ancient Aenochian Emperors and because of this hides vast troves of magic and treasure.

Nostian River

The twin rivers of the Fromia, these rivers twist and turn through the northern slopes of the Red Hills, crashing through valleys and cascading down cliffs and through narrow canyons. It carries the Red Hill's black clay and thus runs dark before emptying into the Mundus River. The dark waters have given rise to many myths and legends concerning the evil origin of the river and its nature. These legends have kept away all but the most fearless or foul of heart and little is truly known about the river.

The Red Hills

The Red Hills are part of the southern chain of the Antiquian Mountains. In the south they rise gradually out of the Illumbrian Plains. These hills and valleys undulate for many miles, increasing in height and depth the further into the mountains one travels. The northern reaches of the mountains become steeper though are not topped with the jagged peaks and steep cliffs found throughout much of the Antiquian Mountains. The upper slopes are sparsely forested with a mixture of aspen and stunted junipers while wispy grasses grow over much of the remainder.

The southern slopes are usually dry, being washed only by gentle winter rains and summer showers. During the winter, the runoff forms small creeks and streams that pour down into the plains to the south filling its many lakes and ponds. These rains have also cut into the deep red and black clays that form the lower slopes of the mountains. These clays are highly prized for making pottery and many a village depends on their export and processing for their livelihood. The upper reaches are poorly explored and little used, but the grasses do offer summer fodder for small herds of bovine, elk, deer and other undulates.

The spine of the Red Hills is found along its northern extremes. Here, the waters pour suddenly into the Aenoch Valley. The runoff here has created deep valleys and steep cliffs where only the hardiest of trees can gain foothold. During winter, many of the creeks pour over rough falls into cascading valleys before dumping their muddy waters into the Fromia and Nostian Rivers.

The Toten Fields (Fields of the Dead)

The Fields of Alpa were once fertile lands where folk lived out their lives in the relative peace of the Winter Dark. Villages and farmsteads dotted the landscape, and so close were they to the great tree that few molested them even during the height of the Winter Dark Wars. This changed in 1037md when the final battle between the dark and the Young Kingdoms was fought.

For months, humans, Dwarves, and Elves gathered in the wilds of the Luneburg, and in the high summer of 1037md, the allied host crossed the Udunilay River to attack Aufstrag. But the Imperial forces had not been idle. They had gathered the flower of the empire and called on those dragons who still lived. Several of the foul Mogrl joined them, as did many wizards. The Battle of the Tree shook the world to its foundations and left the whole land about Aufstrag a desolate wasteland. So great was the carnage that men left their brothers on the field, and even the Dwarves' stout hearts failed to pull the fallen from the calamity and ruin of the war.

In time, the place became a stinking morass of silted pools and poisoned earth. The magic which the magi wielded over those lands blasted the earth beyond healing, charging the very air with arcane power. Even the druids failed to break the horror which hung over the fields of Alpa.

In time the earth swallowed up the dead and the land healed some little. But as is written the lands of the Toten Fields were ever after haunted places, plagued by the howls of the dead and damned. It is said that on warm days the goodly Princess Elisa (*reference Aachen, p. 66*) can be seen calling for her lords and her father to come to her and find her. Untold wealth and magic lies buried in the Toten Fields, sunk deep into the earth, but the ghosts of the fallen wander the hills calling out their pain. Necromancers thus frequent the land in search of the power of the dead.

The only thing of value in the whole land is a small worm that, when cooked right, produces the finest silks in the world. But its cooking and the raising of the worms is a closely guarded secret. A yard of the silk can easily sell for 20gp in Angouleme. Reputed to be used only by the horned god himself in times past, the silk is now available only rarely, for few brave the wasteland to cull it from the stricken earth.

The Fields of Alpa were once fertile lands. But as is written the lands of the Toten Fields, as they are now called, were ever after haunted places, plagued by the howls of the dead and damned.

OF KNIGHTS AND THEIR HABITS

Mark le Graf of Ageineau rode north along the river road. He fled the shattered remains of the Count Philip of Valatois's army and with him rode his brother, Jean Louis. The battle for the town of Pedlow ended in disaster. Count Philip played the fool and wasted his 300 Knights by sending them out on a marauding campaign where the left the lands of Pedlow in a burnt ruin. With a few score Knights and several thousand footman he held the town at bay, or so he thought. In the absence of the Knights, the Burghers felt strong enough to attack Philip and so they did. They mustered out their men at arms and assembled them in the open spaces before the walled town.

Philip assembled his men. The footmen were deployed in three lengthy ranks and the score or so Knights who remained took a position in front of them.

The battle was short and brutal. The two armies met in the fields before Pedlow and the Count's Knights carved a bloody path into the Burgher ranks. They were too few however, and soon they found themselves cut off and surrounded, too far from their own footmen. When Philip's banner went down his army disintegrated and those who could bolted, those who could not, died. Though Philip carved through the mass and made good his own escape most of his men were lost. When word of the defeat spread, the band of marauding Knights found themselves leaderless in an altogether hostile region and they too left the region with haste. So it was that Count Philip of Valatois' army was destroyed.

Mark le Graf and Jean fought alongside their Lord the Count in those last desperate moments. When they charged they plowed through the men of Pedlow with ease and those sons of merchants fell beneath the brother's mighty steeds. But soon they too were driven back and found themselves hopelessly cut off from the Count and surrounded by a veritable host of halberds, staffs and iron poles. The churning mass of metal and flesh, a confused melee where the shouts of the living mingled with the painful cries of the dying. All heavy armor and great iron helms the two men could see little of the battle beyond so they strove only to break free from the melee, to regroup and to charge again.

Jean first broke from the mass and steered his horse up a long slope to the left of walled Pedlow and Mark le Graf followed shortly after. The two turned their battle mounts around preparing to launch themselves into the mass once more. The valley, however, was covered in the fallen and their Lord's banner was nowhere to be seen. Some few Knights fought on in the midst of the Burgher's army but most had vanished beneath the tide of human flesh. The foot soldiers were fleeing and a host of the enemy even now charged up the hill toward them.

"How now Mark? What to do?"

"Philip is gone, dead no doubt and our part finished, we must to our own lives lest we too fall on this godforsaken field at the hands of these merchant folk!" His shouts echoed his actions for he turned his horse and rode hard along the ridge, heading for the camp beyond. Jean followed suit.

They rode into the encampment which the folk of Pedlow had begun to invest and stopped only long enough to grab some little equipment, that which was readily available, and then made good their escape.

For a day and night the two brothers rode north away from both their own lands and those of the Count. With each league they passed they moved further into hostile territory. The fiercely independent Hanse city states were continually at war with the Lords of Angouleme and two Knights, alone in this land, were welcome prey to the locals. A captured Knight brought a princely sum in ransom and the promise of wealth outweighed the dangers of the capture.

By the following morning the brothers drew up in a ravine near the Hanse river and made a small encampment. There, exhausted and hungry, they broke fast, tended their steeds, cleaned their armor and oiled their blades.

"I don't know how you do it Mark, cleaning your own gear and tending your own horse. Its uncouth and does not become a Knight. Whatever in the world possessed you to become a Knight of Haven I'll never know."

"I was moved for the sake of pity for those less than able. Anyway, what became of Franz, your groomsmen? Did he make good his escape, or nay?"

"Poor Franz. He was a good soul. I saw him last riding abreast of me and he struck those men of Pedlow in the first charge. Methinks he fell though, for I saw his horse go down and men with halberds all around. Damn him for playing axes with those folk!" Jean's laughter echoed a little loss for he and Franz had known one another a long while.

"More besides your Franz fell yesterday. Sir Grisham went down, I know, as did the lords of Sone and Buke. And for all we know his Lordship the Count fell as well, for his banner was lost."

"Aye, not a good outcome at all, yesterday's scrabble." Jean paused and looked around. The day promised to be a brilliant one. The sky above shone a light blue with hardly a wisp of cloud. Birds chirped in the tall grass and the river flowed along as quiet as a winter's eve. "Where to now, good brother? Did you not just cross these lands last year to get back to Angouleme?"

"Aye, that I did. One of my Order is welcome as often as not in these parts and I thought mayhap I could learn a bit about these folk by traveling their roads."

"So did you?"

"I came over from Zeitz and crossed the Straits. From there along this very road to Pedlow and then south to the low cities. Beyond there of course to Angouleme. We are, by my remembrances a bare days ride from the village of Beaumont, a dangerous place for us."

"Seems a long ride, how near home?"

"I think that we might be able to ride back through the Hanse city states, but your colors will give you away as one of Philip's men, and even if they don't, the folk about will take their revenge on you nonetheless. I think we should consider going east. There are wars in Zeitz, booty for all and there is always need for one of my folk. There are many Houses of Haven there who have too few knights and too many enemies. Or we can even go on to Augsburg where the Good King Albrecht lives."

"Hmm, seems a long trip to make. But what do I care? Let us rest some this morning and ride in the afternoon. Then we can bring ourselves to the Straits, cross over and come into your north country and maybe into Augsburg itself." He settled back then, resting his head on a tuft of grass. He was silent for awhile and listened to Mark rub his horse down and then make his afternoon prayers. At last when Mark too had settled down he spoke, "Isn't the Zeitz a wild land, unsettled by men of nature?"

Mark mused for a moment. "I'd say so. Many robber Knights have gone to that country and taken up homes in the abandoned castles of the Old Empire. They prey on those merchants and pilgrims who must travel over that land. We'll no doubt have to be on our guard."

Not many days hence, the two sat upon their horses upon a rise overlooking the Straits. Jean's green and yellow surcoat, cleaned in river water after the battle, barely covered the breast plate and didn't cover at all the arm and leg greaves. His chain shirt was easy to spy under his plate and a painted shield hung upon his horse's tack. A great sword, belted at his side and a large axe hanging on his saddle marked him well as a Knight of some skill. Beside him Mark sat, his own black surcoat with the golden sepulcher emblazoned on its front was similarly dressed. Though a heavy staff with ball and chain was draped over the saddle. Both men rode with lances, Mark's with a green and yellow pennant, resting in the saddle cusp. So began the adventures of Mark le Graf and Jean Louis of Ageineau.

**Requires the use of the Dungeons & Dragons® Player's Handbook,
Third Edition, published by Wizards of the Coast.®**

Search for a Lost City

by Gary Gygax

a prelude to

*A d20 System adventure set in the World of Erde, After Winter Dark,
for 4-8 characters of no more than eight combined experience levels.*

The world of Erde is large, and contains many strange and unexpected things. Thus it was not astonishing to you when you heard of an exotic city suddenly appearing where no such place had been before. Following the old axiom of, "Believe none of what you hear, half of what you see," you....

INTRODUCTION FOR THE DM

This is a short and direct adventure module for a player group of four to eight, as noted. As it is a lead-in to a far larger adventure, character level is to be kept low. If your group consists of only two, then characters of multi-class are in order. Again, level in each class should remain low, 2nd in one, 1st in the other, six levels in all. With three players, characters should be multi-class again, all three with two classes of first level.

Now to the meat of things: The premise for the adventure is that the team has just met, or at least just determined to find out if there is anything to the tales of something strange going on in the area, a city appearing from nowhere. The party has been traveling towards the reported locale of the incident, and when the action starts, the sun is westering. They must find a place to encamp for the night.

As you read through the module in preparation for running the adventure, note that text to be read aloud to the players is given in **_bold italics_**. As DM you have carte blanch to add to, shorten, and otherwise revise such text as suits you, the players, and the situation at hand. At the indicated points in the adventure, however, some information must be supplied to the players. More rather than less is recommended, as long as you don't reveal too much, or go beyond what the characters' skills and senses and intellect would otherwise tell them.

Now proceed with your familiarization of the contents of this module. When you begin the adventure, pick up from this point.

PLAYERS' INTRODUCTION

It feels good to be traveling with the small band of which each of you are a part. You are all young, full of vigor, and what you lack in experience you, more than make up for in enthusiasm!

Of course you don't believe the rumors you've heard in the last few days: Tall tales of a golden city, a magical castle with walls of solid jasper, an ivory palace agleam with precious gems. While obviously fabulous, such stories' smoke indicates there is a fire somewhere not too far distant . . . .

Speaking of smoke, you have seen several columns of it on the horizon this very afternoon. The tall plumes somewhere in the distance were greasy black at first, then changed to gray-white, and now have been blown by breezes to tatters and gone from the darkening sky. The only smoke you see now is a little column rising from beyond a nearby ridge. Evening has come, and the road ahead is devoid of habitation.

You need a place to camp for the coming night as there are heavy clouds gathering on the horizon, signifying a storm. Perhaps the tree-lined ridge will do. There too you will likely be able to see the fire from whence the smoke rises. A snug cottage would be a much preferable place to spend the night if a downpour is in the offing. While sleeping under the stars has its charms, hard ground and insects detract from the experience a bit, but rain makes it quite unendurable. Besides, the thought of a good supper cooked by an apple-cheeked farm wife sets your mouth to salivating. The fare available in your packs may be nourishing, but it is drab.

With an exchange of glances, your whole party hastens to the right, up the shallow rise, and into the scattered trees. From the crest of the ridge you see that your hopes were not vain. Before you, in a dell, lie a house, barn, and various sheds and coops at perhaps 60 yards distance. Surely this is the steading of a rather prosperous farmer and his family. Without hesitation your party sets forth as one, moving down and out of the copse, heading happily for the farmer's well-kept cottage.

The westering sun makes an angry maroon in the layers of clouds into which it sinks to a muffled end of the day.

ADVENTURE EVENTS

Much of what follows is linear—perforce. As this module is to introduce the characters to far larger things, it is absolutely necessary that certain events occur. Once those events have occurred, though, the players are on their own as to what actions they perform. Thus, this is by no means a scripted play. Rather, it is the prelude to a grand and epic adventure. How well the characters succeed here will have considerable impact on their subsequent activities as they explore, discover the City of Gaxmoor, and face the many perils around and in that place.

Scene I: Trovard's Farmstead

Maps needed: Cottage and Farm Buildings Layout, and Cottage Map

Of course the party of adventurers is spotted as soon as they leave the trees, and the assembled family in the cottage react swiftly:

As you approach to within about 20 yards of the stone and timber cottage the door slams shut, windows and shutters bang closed, and from loops in the front door and the two windows facing protrude what looks a lot like the business ends of crossbows. At the same time as you see that, someone calls out from inside in a deep masculine voice:

"That's far enough, you lot! If you're bandits and thieves, get away or else. If you are honest travelers, lay down your weapons and come five paces closer. I'll count to three, then we'll let loose, so do one thing or the other now!

At this point begin counting aloud, with about two second's time between each number:

"One… Two… Three!"

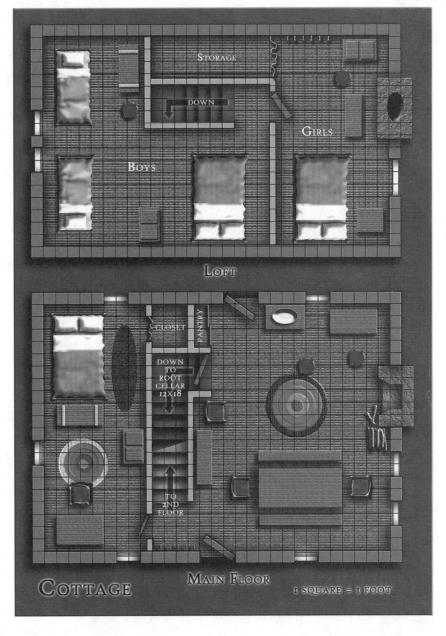

A. If the party runs back where they came from, they are likely really green. Speak to them as an advisor, ask them to analyze their reaction, and perhaps reconsider approaching the farmstead again, this time with weapons sheathed, and clearly not in aggressive manner. Advise them to have their characters drop their arms and shields at the place they were first hailed, then walk on with arms raised.

B. Should the team decide to begin a fight, they will suffer three automatic hits from bolts from two heavy and one light crossbow—these being braced and well-aimed. One bolt each for three characters. If combat continues, see the stats for Trovard and his family – his wife, Elmira, and their six children: four boys (Dorvoc, Brivard, Pront, and Edvard), and two girls (Jenta and Lossi).

This fighting will likely be rather hopeless for the party unless magic is used to overcome the defenders. This leaves two potential scenarios:

#1: The party retreats and stops attacking. If they retire to the Barn to heal their wounds, then move on to Act II with the assumption that while the beleaguered family is watching the barn, they are surprised by the gnolls who creep up undetected and break into the rear of the cottage.

#2: The party succeeds in defeating Trovard and his family, break in, and proceed to loot, and make themselves at home for the night. In this event the main force of the gnolls (see Act II below) fall upon them. Two gnolls will enter the front and back doors simultaneously, their scouts having seen the fight. The

odds are that the party will be slain. Too bad. They were foolish to attack a farm family when they were themselves seeking brigands and like miscreants to fight and destroy.

C. If the party immediately divests itself of their arms, then as they step closer to the cottage read aloud:

A sharp command comes from inside the door: "That's far enough. Stand in a line, shoulder to shoulder. You won't be harmed if you are not yourselves meaning harm."

As you comply, the front door opens, and a man with a heavy crossbow steps out, moving quickly to the side to allow a woman behind him with a smaller crossbow to help cover you. The man is large, square-shouldered, and dressed in work clothes. His wife is also middle-aged, as weathered as he, clearly a hard-working farm couple. There are still crossbows aimed at you from the windows flanking the door, so these folks are taking no chances. After careful appraisal of your group, the man lowers his weapon a trifle, and speaks:

"Who are you and what do you want?"

When the players have their characters give their names and reason for being in the area, continue:

"Well this is good news! Welcome to out steading. I be Trovard," he says with a slight smile, and crossbow now pointed at the ground. "That's my wife Elmira…. Yinglings, you come on out and greet our visitors—Dorvoc and Brivard don't point your crossbows at 'em neither." Trovard gestures. "Been reports of humanoid raider the last couple of days, and we're missing three heifers from the north pasture. Sorry to be so inhospitable at first, but a man's got to be careful. Come on inside. We's just fixin' to have supper, and wife will put on some extra right away." As the woman named Elmira hastens to do just that, the big farmer leads you into the cottage.

As a few drops of rain begin to patter onto the ground, Trovard's two older sons gather up your weapons, hasten to bring them into the house. They murmur apologies for getting any wet, wiping the water spots away with the hems of their smocks.

> **Trovard, Human War2:** CR 1; Medium (5 ft. 7 in. tall); HD 2d8; hp 10; Init +0; Spd 30 ft; AC 10; Att +2 melee (1d4 dagger) or +2 ranged (1d10 heavy crossbow); AL N; Fort +3, Ref +0, Will +2; Str 11, Dex 10, Con 11, Int 9, Wis 11, Cha 9. *Skills*: Handle Animal +4, Intimidate +2, Ride +2, Swim +2; *Feats*: Iron Will.
>
> **Elmira, female Human War1:** CR 1/2; Medium (5 ft. 5 in. tall); HD 1d8+1; hp 5; Init +0; Spd 30 ft; AC 10; Att +1 melee (1d4 club) or +1 ranged (1d8 light crossbow); AL N; Fort +5, Ref +0, Will +2; Str 10, Dex 11, Con 13, Int 10, Wis 10, Cha 11. *Skills*: Climb +2, Handle Animal +2, Ride +2, Swim +2; *Feats*: Endurance.
>
> **Brivard, male Human War1:** CR 1/2; Medium (5 ft. 6 in. tall); HD 1d8; hp 4; Init +1 (Dex); Spd 30 ft; AC 11; Att +1 melee (1d4 machette) or +2 ranged (1d8 light crossbow); AL NG; Fort +2, Ref +1, Will +0; Str 11, Dex 12, Con 9, Int 9, Wis 9, Cha 10. *Skills*: Handle Animal +4, Jump +4, Ride +1, Swim +1; *Feats*: Skill Focus (Jump).
>
> **Dorvoc, male Human War1:** CR 1/2; Medium (5 ft. 9 in. tall); HD 1d8; hp 5; Init +4 (Imp. Init.); Spd 30 ft; AC 10; Att +1 melee (1d8 shortspear); AL N; Fort +1, Ref +0, Will +1; Str 11, Dex 11, Con 11, Int 10, Wis 12, Cha 11. *Skills*: Climb +1, Handle Animal +2, Intimidate +1, Jump +1, Ride +1, Swim +2; *Feats*: Imp. Init..

Their father beams approval. "Good lads. Put 'em on the floor by the coat hooks. Trovard looks at your party with a grin. "Them swords and all will get in the way of setting in comfort to sup," he says. "They'll be handy, though, if'n you need to arm quickly." You note as you enter the cottage that they are just to the right of the front door, easily taken u. Satisfied, you agree.

Trovard is anxious to please, obviously. He commands,"You there, Jenta and Lossi, say 'hello', then help your ma get vittles prepared. Stop gawking, Pront, Edvard—help your older brothers move the work table so's you kids can eat there. Guests sit at the trestle table with your ma and I."

How glad you are that you made friends with this family. Outside the wind is howling, darkness is near total, as a great thunderstorm breaks overhead. The beating of rain in sheets can be heard between thunderclaps. That's soon forgotten in the warm light of fire and lamp in the cottage. The chatter and laughter of the young children, the smell of good food cooking, make it seem you are back home again . . . .

The interior of the house is well enough illustrated as to furnishings, so you should have no trouble describing it to players whose characters are visually examining their surroundings.

Trovard asks each character his (or her) name, shakes hands and has his two older sons do likewise. Elmira nods to each as do the other children of this fine couple.

The children are healthy and friendly. The youngsters are eager and bright eyed. All are of a robust sort, good-looking peasants, somewhat heavy and coarse, but well-mannered. As the food is prepared and the table set, the older girl, Jenta, will attempt to flirt with the male character with the highest charisma. This is innocent, of course. Similarly, if there is a female character with a charisma over 12, both the young men, Dorvoc and Brivard, will attempt gallantries. Edvard, fascinated by the toughest looking fighter, will state that when he grows up he's going to be a sell-sword. That will bring embarrassment to his parents who will hush him, ask pardon from the "offended."

Make the players feel their characters are at home in the farmer's cottage, almost like family or long lost friends. After you've done that, read aloud:

By light of fire and lamp you eat a jolly meal. Trovard has brought up a small keg of hard cider from his cellar. All face a little shrine, and after a brief thanks to the gods for the day and the meal about to be enjoyed, the farmer pours the cider and a bustling begins. His wife, Elmira, with daughters Jenta and Lossi, serve big bowls of stew. There is a great loaf of fresh bread on the table, sausage and several cheeses. Then comes a salad of fresh greens and garden vegetables and for dessert, berries covered with cream so thick you nearly need to spoon it from the pitcher.

After seeing that you have all ceased eating, Trovard belches in satisfaction. At that signal, the younger children come to clear the board, and the big farmer smiles and speaks to you:

"My apologies for the plain food. Had we known we were to have such fine guests 'Mira would have prepared a ham or maybe chicken… Well, nothing to be done about that, eh?" Trovard laughs, pours more cider for those with empty mugs. With pipe filled and fuming, smoke wreathing his head, the farmer asks about your party, where you come from and what you hope to do in these parts. As he does so the rest of his family draws unobtrusively nearer to hear what each of you have to say. Strangers are a great rarity in these parts, of course, tales of far-away places, and news, a precious commodity.

As DM query each player's character at this point. Engage in as realistic a conversation as possible, taking the roles of Trovard, Elmira, and the six children as opportunity arises. When this roleplay has been sufficiently done (the players or you tiring of it), end the conversation by reading aloud:

"Ach! Such a poor host I am being. Forgive me, sirs. It is well past bedtime, eh? You have much travel and adventure awaiting, and we have our work. T he morrow comes early this time of year, so to sleep!"

As he says that, Trovard looks a bit uncomfortable. "Errr... Again, pardon, but there is no place for you brave folk here. We fill this cottage to overflowing, but there's plenty of room in the barn—soft hay and straw to sleep on rather than a hard floor. Come, I'll get you settled in." So saying, the big farmer lights a lantern with a splint set aflame from the dying embers in the fireplace. He opens the rear door, and waits while you collect your arms from in front.

"Looks like the rain has let up," he says. Then the farmer lights a lantern, shows you to the barn just a little distance from his dwelling.

Inside, he lights a lantern hanging from a hook in the barn, bids you a good night's rest, and departs. It is relatively late, after 10 o'clock certainly, perhaps near to midnight!

If the party wants rations, the farmer supplies them with up to a total of 12 days good foodstuffs, all that's readily on hand, at the lowest rate for such supplies (36 sp).

Cottage Contents: If a thorough search is made of the family and the place, in addition to the crossbows (1 heavy and 2 light) with 30 bolts for each, there will be discovered a boar spear (short spear), a hatchet, a machete (corn knife), a large cleaver, one dagger, and four knives. There is sufficient food and drink in the place to feed eight people a full week. Other than a handful each of silver and copper pieces (3d6 each), there is no wealth. Trovard has buried some gold pieces (4d8), but he will never reveal the location (in the pig barn, buried under the hard clay floor in the exact middle of the place).

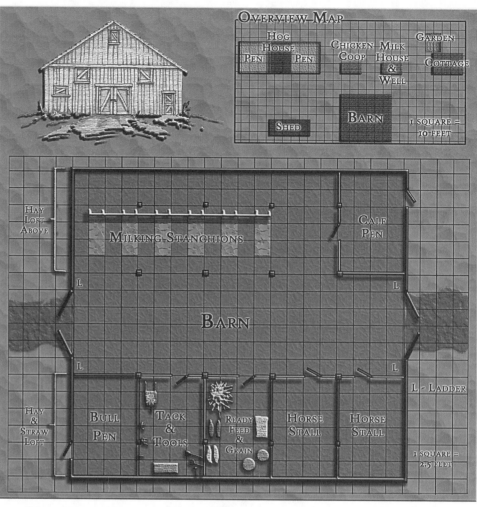

Scene II: The Barn

Maps needed: The Barn Map

This place is 45 feet wide, 50 feet long. It is built on a stone foundation, constructed above of thick timbers and sturdy plank siding. A glance at Map #4 shows the interior layout, except the loft areas to either side. The barns' middle 15 feet running lengthwise is open to the roof. To either side are long, open haylofts, 50 feel long, 15 feet wide.

You aren't surprised to see that the barn is far bigger than Trovard's dwelling. From the left hand far corner of the place comes a bellowing, a thud, and the barn shakes slightly. The area there, walled with strong boards, is certainly a bull pen, and Trovard must have a huge bull. That noise causes the four calves in the pen immediately to your right to get up and move around uneasily. At the same time, you hear restless stomping of hooves and a whicker. To your left are large stalls in which a pair of massive

draft horses are stabled. This farm family is prosperous indeed!

There are six cows in their stanchions asleep standing, ready for tomorrow's milking. The air in the barn is redolent with the rich smells of animals and their excrement. This is not repellant, certainly, but . . . .

You are all tired from a long day, a big meal, and the heady hard cider. Remembering Trovard's directions, you slide wooden bars into iron brackets so as to secure both ends of the barn against intrusion. A quick check of the upper and lower parts of the outside door to the calf pen shows them both secured by strong wooden bolts. In all, the barn is a fairly secure place. The thought of soft hay up in the loft, well above the dung, and ventilated by cross-draft from open haymow doors has strong appeal. What will your party do now? There are ladders fixed to the wall on either hand, leading to the lofts right and left, beckoning you to rest. A great peal of thunder and the sound of renewed downpour comes at this moment. Truly a good night to be indoors in a dry and comfortable place.

Notable barn contents:

Horse stalls: Halter and lead rope by each.

Ready Feed & Grain room: A small pile of excellent fresh hay for the calves, two barrels each of whole grain and grain meal.

Rager, bull: CR 2; Large Animal; HD 4d8+12; hp 28; Init +0; Spd 40 ft; AC 13 (-1 size, +4 natural); Att +8 melee (1d8+8 butt); Face 5 ft. by 10 ft./5 ft.; SA stampede; SQ scent; AL N; Fort +7, Ref +4, Will +2; Str 20, Dex 10, Con 16, Int 2, Wis 11, Cha 4. *Skills*: Listen +8, Spot +5.

Tack & Tools room: Two manure forks, two pitch forks, six coils of rope, four baskets, 24 empty jute sacks, six wooden pails, two barn shovels, four brooms, and harnesses and collars for the horses. There is a gallon crick full of a sort of tongue oil for softening and maintaining leather. There is a three-gallon earthenware jug that is two-thirds full of lamp oil (kerosene). If the two oils are mixed 2:1, the result will be a somewhat viscous liquid that will burn like alchemical fire, flaming for three rounds when it is set alight by the flame of something at least as hot as a candle. There are six bottles of one-pint capacity that have horse liniment in them. A wooden box holds rags for wiping down the horses. There is little else of interest herein.

Bull pen: The Dutch door has upper and lower latches. Someone has painted "Rager" in crude letters on the upper half of the door. The upper half of the door can be opened easily, and the bull will come and look out, snort angrily, toss its long and sharp horns. Anyone watching will see it is an ill-tempered and fero-cious brute, but such a person will also be 90% likely to note the large ring in his nose. Beside the door hangs a yard-long billet with a clip attached to its end by a heavy staple. It is the lead for the bull, of course. Attach the clip to the nose ring, and the bull is relatively docile and manageable. To get the animal to hold still for having the lead hooked to its nose ring, someone needs to hand-feed the animal some of the fine hay or grain.

Getting the lead onto the bull will take only two rounds' time after the upper part of the door is opened, and he thrusts his head out, assuming hay or grain is hand fed. Feeding grain in a bucket precludes the attachment of the lead handle for three rounds' time, after which the bull will lift his nose. Immediate attachment at this juncture can be done with ease. Otherwise the nose-in-the-bucket routine repeats.

Again, this is a linear point in the adventure, and the characters are meant to bed down for the night. If one or two stand watch, no matter. No skill will allow them to be alerted to what is coming. At about 3:30 AM, the following will occur:

First, there are two near-simultaneous crashes from the direction of the cottage. No thunderclaps these noises. A scouting band of 24 gnolls have come up with great stealth, and used a pair of logs to batter down both of the cottage doors. Sixteen of the humanoids are engaged in the attack there; eight have moved to the barn, four at each end.

Second, any character on watch will note that there are four gnolls approaching the barn doors at either end. At the sound of the cottage doors being smashed open, the gnolls give out evil laughs and derisive hoots. They are careless as they come up, assuming nothing but animals are quartered inside the building (proceed to Scene III).

Scene III: Attackers Outside!

Maps needed: Barn

Alerted by the cacophony of crashes, howls, screams, horrid laughter, and other noises coming from Trovard's cottage, your party knows that something very bad is happening. The rain has just stopped; only a few listless drops still fall. The night is still very dark, but at least vision is no longer obscured by sheets of wind-driven rain. What will you do?

Those characters with metal armor must immediately see to putting it on. Those not so engaged should be looking out from whatever vantage point they can, seeking to determine what is happening.

The cottage cannot be seen clearly even with darkvision, but any character with that ability, or simply keen eyesight will detect tall and ugly humanoids approaching the barn:

Facing the Cottage
At the end of the barn nearest the house, four gnolls are approaching the big double doors, growling in mirth, eager for slaughter of the animals inside. They proceed as follows:

Rounds 1 through 10: After being spotted it will be five rounds' time before they reach the doors, and

five more while they test them and the doors to the calf pen, finding them locked.

Rounds 11 through 25: After five more rounds of tugging and gnollish cursing, they will gather by the main doors, confer and then call out towards the house (asking for some of their companions to bring the battering rams to them). This takes 10 more rounds. So two and a half minutes of time has already elapsed.

Rounds 26 through 100: Four more gnolls will come up with the log after five minutes' additional time has passed. Organizing and breaking down the barn doors here will require two full minutes.

Round 101: The 10 gnolls will enter the barn after 10 minutes have passed since they were seen approaching.

Note that if the characters do not see the gnolls, they will still act according to the details above. Start counting time 10 rounds after the noise from the cottage is heard. This group will ignore noise from the far end of the barn, assuming that it is generated by their companions enjoying their sport.

Gnolls (4): CR 1; Medium Humanoid; HD 2d8+2; hp 11; Init +0; Spd 20 ft; AC 15 (+1 natural, +4 scale mail); Att +3 melee (1d8+2 axes and swords); SQ darkvision; AL CE; Fort +4, Ref +0, Will +0; Str 15, Dex 10, Con 13, Int 8, Wis 11, Cha 8. *Skills*: Listen +3, Spot +3; *Feats*: Power Attack. Possessions: Battle axe or sword, scale mail, 1d6 sp each.

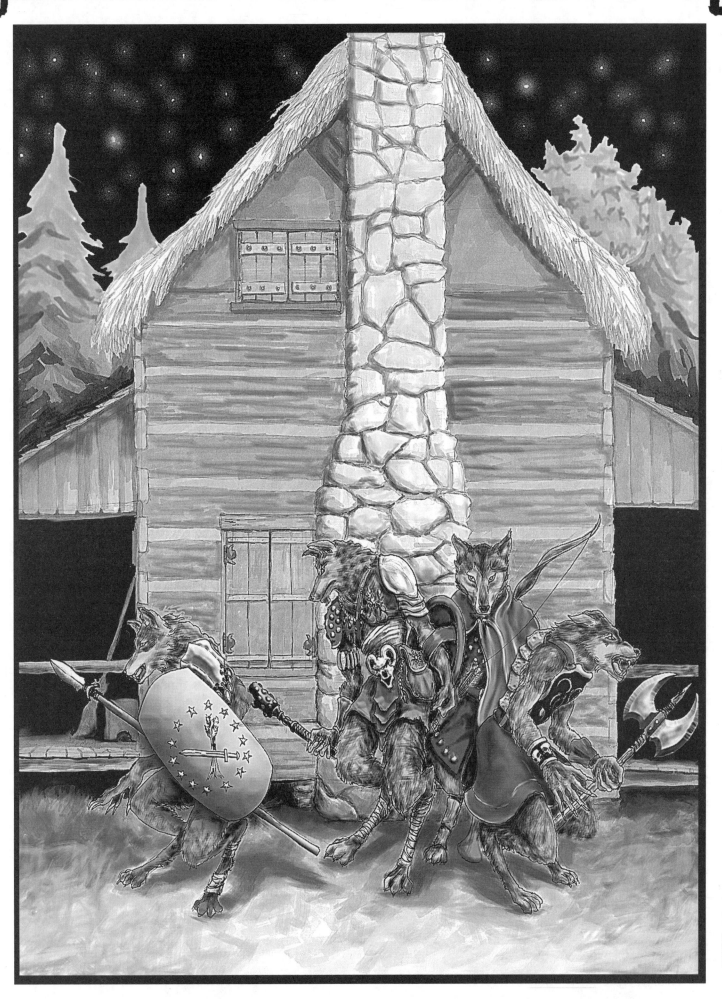

Back of Barn

At the far end of the barn, another four gnolls can be seen approaching at a loping trot.

Rounds 1 through 15: After being spotted, it will be eight rounds' time before they reach the doors, seven more while they test them and the doors to the bull pen, finding them locked.

Rounds 16 through 20: A large gnoll with a great axe shouts and screams at the other three. He points to the door to the bull pen.

Rounds 21 through 25: The three other gnolls scream back, the leader brandishes his weapon, and his subordinates cringe.

Rounds 26 through 30: The chastened gnolls mill around a bit, are then led by the larger one to the bell pen's outer door.

Rounds 31 through 40: The leader speaks braggingly to the others, shakes his axe at them, spits on his hands, and readies to show them how things are done. He is actually hesitant because of the bellowing from the bull inside, but he is determined to demonstrate just how tough he is.

Rounds 41 through 45: The gnoll leader smites the bull pan door with strong blows of his axe.

Round 46: The door and inner bars are sufficiently splintered so as to be opened easily…

In the midst of this confusion and commotion, read aloud:

It is clear now that there is a large band of humanoid raiders, gnolls by the sounds, and they make their appearance. They have certainly broken into the cottage. Poor Trovard and his wonderful family are dead…you hope! There's nothing you can do for them now. To attempt to rescue them would be futile; you know that you would all die in the trying. The barn is surrounded by a few gnolls now, but more will come when their fellows discover still more humans are holed up in the place. The choices you have are limited.

The animals inside with you are all wild-eyed and nervous. The horses are rearing, evidently reacting to the stink of the gnolls. Only the bull seems unafraid. Not to say he's quiet though. The presence of the humanoids seems to have made him more ferocious than ever. His bellowings are loud, butting of the barn posts frequent. It seems "Rager" isn't at all intimidated by gnolls . . . .

If that isn't sufficient spoon-feeding for the players to get the idea, you might throw a few more hints. Of course their only hope is to exit the barn at the far end. Doing that through the big doors will alert the four gnolls, the leader and three others, so that a melee will ensue.

Sergeant, Rgr1/Gnoll 1: CR 2; Medium Humanoid; HD (1d10+2) + (2d8+2); hp 18; Init +0; Spd 20 ft; AC 15 (+1 natural, +4 studded leather (+1)); Att +6 melee (1d12+3 greataxe); SA favored enemy humanoid (elves, +1); SQ darkvision; AL CE; Fort +6, Ref +0, Will +0; Str 15, Dex 10, Con 13, Int 8, Wis 11, Cha 8. *Skills*: Hide +3, Listen +3, Move Silently +3, Spot +3, Swim +3, Wilderness Lore +3; *Feats*: Power Attack, Track. Possessions: *Masterwork greataxe*, 2d4 gp, 2d6 sp, *Potion of Cure Light Wounds*, *+1 studded leather armor, Translation Medallion.*

Translation Medallion: *A bronze medallion showing a sage-like figure. It is a magical device that was used for conversing with "barbarians." It enables the wearer to both understand and speak the Imperial tongue, and it translates other speech to Imperial.*

Gnolls (3): CR 1; Medium Humanoid; HD 2d8+2; hp 11; Init +0; Spd 20 ft; AC 15 (+1 natural, +4 scale mail); Att +3 melee (1d8+2 axes and swords); SQ darkvision; AL CE; Fort +4, Ref +0, Will +0; Str 15, Dex 10, Con 13, Int 8, Wis 11, Cha 8. *Skills*: Listen +3, Spot +3; *Feats*: Power Attack. Possessions: Battle axe or sword, scale mail, 1d6 sp each.

Remaining Gnolls

Captain, Sor2/Gnoll 1: CR 2; Medium Humanoid; HD (2d4+2) + (2d8+2); hp 17; Init +1; Spd 30 ft; AC 14 (+1 natural, +1 Dex, +2 shield); Att +4 melee (1d6+2 light mace); SA spells; SQ darkvision; AL CE; Fort +4, Ref +1, Will +3; Str 15, Dex 12, Con 13, Int 11, Wis 11, Cha 13. *Skills*: Alchemy +4, Concentration +3, Listen +3, Spellcraft +2, Spot +3, ; *Feats*: Power Attack, Shield proficiency. Possessions: *Potion of Cure Light Wounds, +1 small wooden shield*, light mace, Gaxmoor banner, 2d6 gp, 2d6 sp.

Spells (6/5): 0 – *Ray of Frost (x2), Dancing Lights, Ghost Sound (x2), Mage Hand*; 1st – *Hypnotisim (x2), Spider Climb (x3)*.

Arcane spell failure: 15%

Note: The gnoll leader is wearing a colorful sash. If this is examined, it will be seen to be a flag with the words, "GAXMOOR, Imperator Governor" on it.

Sergeant, Rgr1/Gnoll 1: CR 2; Medium Humanoid; HD (1d10+2) + (2d8+2); hp 18; Init +0; Spd 20 ft; AC 14 (+1 natural, +3 studded leather); Att +3 melee (1d6 shortsword) or +2 ranged (2d6 greatbow); SA favored enemy humanoid (gnomes, +1); SQ darkvision; AL CE; Fort +6, Ref +0, Will +0; Str 15, Dex 10, Con 13, Int 8, Wis 11, Cha 8. *Skills*: Hide +3, Listen +3, Move Silently +3, Spot +3, Swim +3, Wilderness Lore +3; *Feats*: Power Attack, Track. Possessions: *Greatbow*, 10 arrows, studded leather, shortsword, 2d4 gp, 2d6 sp.

Gnolls (14): CR 1; Medium Humanoid; HD 2d8+2; hp 11; Init +0; Spd 20 ft; AC 15 (+1 natural, +4 scale mail); Att +3 melee (1d8+2 axes and swords) or +1 ranged (1d6 shortbow); SQ darkvision; AL CE; Fort +4, Ref +0, Will +0; Str 15, Dex 10, Con 13, Int 8, Wis 11, Cha 8. *Skills*: Listen +3, Spot +3; *Feats*: Power Attack. Possessions: Battle axe or sword, shortbow, 8 arrows, scale mail, 1d6 sp each.

The optimum tactic for the party is put the bull on the lead, gather in his pen, and as the gnolls break down the door, release the lead. "Rager" will come charging out through the partially broken door, getting a surprise attack on the gnolls. The characters can issue forth immediately without fear of attack, they having initiative in assaulting the startled humanoids not otherwise engaged with the bull.

When all four gnolls are dead, the party can make its escape with ease, assuming that fewer than 101 rounds of time have passed.

If the characters remain inside the barn and attempt to defend from there, the remaining gnolls in the band will come up and shoot flaming arrows into the building from all sides. It will catch fire and burn. In this case, getting out will be perilous. Each character will need to succeed in a Saving Throw against Fortitude at DC 16 or suffer incidental damage from fire, heat, and burning timbers falling each round spent inside the barn once it is aflame (10 rounds' time). Failure incurs 1d4 damage. Exiting the place will also expose the PCs to missile fire, followed by close combat as gnolls rush up to fight them.

The draft horses can be managed as steeds if a character or characters with riding skill place halters on them. These animals will carry two large humans each on their backs without being unduly burdened. Of course, this load will mean only trotting speed.

Scene IV: Exacting Retribution

Map needed: Area Overview

It is likely that the party will escape to the north. Following the rutted farm track to the hedgerow there, they will then probably follow the western hedgerow north, continue in that direction into the north meadow and on to the little ridge. At this point, assuming that the players have managed to extract their characters from the situation in shape to cause a little trouble for the gnoll raiders, then another bit of adventure can be managed. A little encouragement might be necessary. Something along these lines might serve in such case:

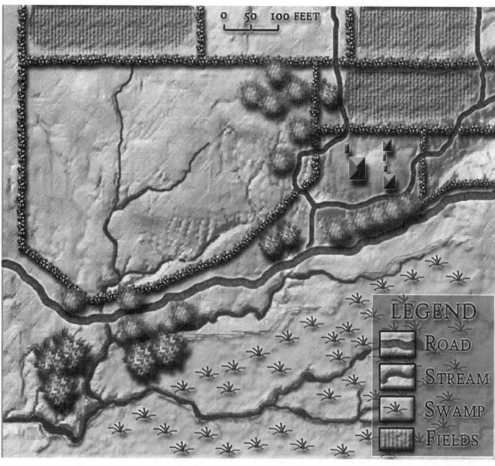

As you reach a long hill, pause a moment to look back at the conflagration, the burning cottage, outbuildings, and once-fine barn, there is something akin to real hatred stirring inside you. There are nearly a score of gnolls prancing and whooping around the flames, but what's that?

Dark shadows are moving rapidly in your direction. Several of the humanoids are running stooped over, both to sniff for your scent and to make themselves less noticeable.

From here you have clear aim at these monsters, they being about 250 feet distant and moving towards you at a steady pace, quite unaware that your party has halted, is not fleeing in panic.

The gnolls are only 150 feet distant now. The sky behind them is paling, and you can see them plainly in silhouette. There are five pursuers, a bigger one in the lead, four others trailing after. It is time to flee or fight.

The humanoids will close to 50 feet distance in two rounds' time, coming on unhesitatingly, sure of their prey. Unless two or fewer are left alive, the gnolls will then close to melee combat on the following round, *charging*.

If the PCs stand and fight, they will get up to three rounds of unanswered missile and/or spell attacks against the gnolls. Then hand-to-hand fighting occurs.

Epilogue:

As you leave the ruined farmstead, thoughts of Trovard and his family fill your minds. Their fate will haunt you for many months to come. So too will your hatred for the vile creatures who wrought their deaths, the destruction of so peaceful and pleasant a farm. There is no blame troubling your minds. Clearly you all did what you could. A handful against a great pack of gnolls is a hopeless contest, and you made those creatures pay dearly for their gristly amusement.

With some pride, but more determination to exact greater revenge from such raiders as those, you head away, looking for the rumored place from whence such monsters spring. The Lost City, a place called "Gaxmoor" perhaps, that has reappeared . . .

The Player's Handbook

Herein the player must find all the particulars of life in the Lands of Ursal. Notes on the Races and Languages – New Classess, Orders & Guilds – The Monies & Economies – Weapons & Armaments – New & Varied Equipments – And Spells, both Wizardly & Priestly.

And it is known that there are many peoples of many races who speak many tongues. They are warlike and carry many weapons & armaments not borne by other nations or peoples.

Lord Payne-Walloway

CHAPTER 1: RACES & LANGUAGES

Race is the foundation of every character. The race you choose to construct your character upon will affect both game play and role play. Remember, however, that race is only one aspect of every adventurer. Every individual person within a racial group is unique, and you should not feel limited by the descriptions of each race that follow or that are found in the *Player's Handbook*.

Although high elves are a typical race in most fantasy worlds, in the World of Erde they are a separate and distinct character class. The High Elf character class appears in Chapter 2.

RACIAL CHARACTERISTICS

To a large extent, the player character races in Erde are greatly similar to those described in the *Player's Handbook*. Any rule changes or important background information specific to a race are detailed in each race's description. Otherwise, reference should be made to the *Player's Handbook* for such details as personality, relations, and names.

The most significant changes to each race are beginning languages, bonus languages, height and weight ranges, minimum starting age, and maximum age. Each race's beginning languages and available bonus languages are listed in the racial description. More details, however, on these characteristics, as well as the changes in height, weight, and age, follow the racial descriptions.

Finally, religion differs from that described in the *Player's Handbook*. A summary is provided below regarding each race's religion, but reference should be made to the preceding *Cosmology* section (*reference Divine Orders, pg. 56*) and to the table detailing each deity's domains and typical worshipers in Chapter 4, Spells, for a more comprehensive description.

HUMANS

Humans are the primary race populating Erde. They are an adaptable and tough lot. The description and game rules on humans as detailed in the *Player's Handbook* remain unchanged.

Languages: Humans speak Vulgate (the common tongue). Their bonus languages are: Aenochian, Dwarven, Elven (Wild or Wood), Ethrum, Gnomish, Goblin, Halfling, Hobgoblin, Orc, and Ungern

DWARVES

Dwarves are called the "first-born" for they were the first people to walk the face of Erde. They were forged from the All-Father's anger and will, and those emotions are reflected in the Dwarves' legendary determination and hardy constitution. Although they once populated all the lands and even plied the high seas, the dwarven population has dwindled. Dwarves group themselves in kingdoms, not clans. Dwarven kingdoms are now found only within the protective confines of mountains. The remaining Dwarven kingdoms are Grundliche Hohle, Roheisen Hohle, and Norgorad-Kam. More details on the Dwarves can be found in the descriptions of those kingdoms.

Religion: The major Dwarven god is Dolgan, the Forge King. Dwarves also pay homage to the greater deities and various forefathers and heroes of their kingdoms.

Languages: Dwarves speak Dwarven and Vulgate. Their bonus languages are: Aenochian, Ethrum, Gnomish, Goblin, Hobgoblin, Kobold, Orc.

Names: In addition to the description in the *Player's Handbook*, Dwarves tend toward names comprised of one or two syllables. Surnames are uncommon, and only Dwarves of importance in the kingdom or of great achievement will have a second name, usually in the form of a title, such as Arack the Axe or Tundol, Priestess of the Brass Halls. Sometimes a dwarf will be given a descriptive moniker, such as Dagnier Firebeard.

Traits: Other than the additional skills that follow, Dwarven racial traits do not differ from those described in the *Player's Handbook*.

Skills: Dwarves have a sixth sense about stonework that has arisen from their long history of living underground. Thus, player character dwarves possess the following racial skills.

Craft: All Dwarves learn a Craft skill as they grow to adulthood. The character may pick one craft skill of 2 ranks, subject to the DM's approval.

Literacy: All Dwarves begin play with 1 rank in Dwarven.

ELVES

There are four types of elves in the World of Erde – High Elves, Twilight Elves, Wild Elves, and Wood Elves. The racial description of Elves in the *Player's Handbook* is generally applicable to each type of Elf in Erde. Differences in background and game rules are detailed in their individual descriptions below.

High Elves

High elf is a unique character class in the World of Erde as detailed in Chapter 2.

Twilight Elves

The Twilight Elves are the offspring of the High Elve who chose to remain in the world rather than leave with the coming of Unklar. Unlike the Wild Elves, they chose to remain isolationist. Their homeland is the Twilight Forest, that place where Unklar warped and wove black dreams into the elms and oaks, twisting them and covering them in scabrous bark. The forest canopy is composed of great leafy vines, blocking the light of the sun such that the forest is locked in a perpetual twilight. During the Winter Dark Wars, the Twilight Elves lived in their dark wood and fought alone. This led to a extreme distrust of the other races, particularly Humans, Dwarves, and other Elves.

Personality: The Twilight Elves have lost their connection to the Realm of Faerie. They tend to be quite serious, with mirth reserved for holidays among their own kind and for intimate relations.

Physical Description: Twilight Elves are the smallest of all the elves, standing between 4 to 5 feet tall on average. Their skin tends to a deep brown, with hair being almost any color. Most compelling are their eyes, which are typically violet, blue, or orange. They have no facial hair or body hair. Their ears are longer than other elven races. They dress in typical elvish clothing, but have a particular affinity for metallic colored tunics and jewelry.

Relations: Twilight Elves are rarely found outside of the Twilight Forest or other dark woods in which they have settled. They generally distrust all races.

Alignment: They are as evil as they are good, but most all are chaotic.

Religion: The patron deity of the Twilight Elves is Utumno, the Lord of Nightmares. Evidence suggests that they also worship various forest deities unique to the Twilight Forest.

Languages: Twilight Elves speak Elven (Twilight dialect), Sylvan, and Vulgate. Their bonus languages are: Aenochian, Dwarven, Elven (Shindolay High Elven, Wild, Wood), Ethrum, Gnomish, Goblin, Ungern.

Names: The name given a Twilight Elf at birth remains unchanged upon reaching adulthood. Twilight Elves do not make use of surnames. Such usage would be considered a reverence for the High Elves who abandoned the world in its time of need.

Adventurers: Twilight Elf adventurers are extremely rare. Those that do take up the sword and road are more likely to display a willingness to reforge alliances with the other peoples of the world. Doing so, however, is understandingly difficult given the race's history. If an outsider gains the loyalty of a Twilight Elf, it will be as strong as that given by any Dwarf.

Traits: The racial traits of Twilight Elves differ as follows.

Abilities: +1 Dex, +1 Int, -2 Con.

Weapon proficiencies: Proficient with either longsword, shortsword, scimitar, or rapier; and shortbow or composite shortbow. Other favored weapons include blowguns, javelins, sianghams, hand axes, and shurikens.

Wilderness Lore: All Twilight Elves begin play with 2 ranks in the Wilderness Lore skill.

Favored Class: Wizard. Magic runs deep in their blood, making them excellent wizards.

Literacy: Twilight Elves begin play with 1 rank in Elven (Twilight) and Vulgate.

Wild Elves

Wild Elves also descend from the High Elves. They chose to spread across the lands during the Age of Winter Dark, fighting Unklar's forces whenever and wherever they could. In doing so, they developed trust with the other peoples of the world, especially the halflings and barbarians living at the fringes of civilization. Aspects of halfling and barbarian culture help form the foundation of Wild Elf tribal society (which greatly resembles that of the plains and woodland Native Americans). Very few remnants of high elven culture remains among the Wild Elves.

Personality: Wild Elves value honor and great deeds. They have an affinity for the land, preferring the wind in their hair as they ride across the plains or the eves of the forest. The customs and habits of each tribe varies as much as human personality.

Physical Description: Wild Elves stand and weigh as typical among elves, but their skin tends toward deep tan to light brown. They are dark-haired, with eyes ranging from deep green to hazel. They have no facial hair, but they do have light body hair. Their ears resemble that of a Half-elf. Dress tends toward simple leather and hide clothing, decorated with natural stains and inks. Wild Elf features are more rough than fine.

Relations: Wild Elves relate well to Humans, Halflings, and Wood Elves, and they will generally trust a people until wronged by them. Once wronged, they are a fierce enemy. Wild Elves respect for individualism, however, can lead to friends among enemies.

Alignment: Wild Elves value individuality and freedom. They are typically chaotic good.

Religion: Wild Elves pay homage to Wenafar and Daladon Lothian, along with many animal and nature spirits typically thought to be the last remnants of the religion of Mordius.

Languages: Wild Elves speak Elven (Wild), Halfling, and Vulgate. Their bonus languages are: Dwarven, Gnomish, Goblin, Orc, Sylvan, and Ungern.

Names: Wild Elves have only one name. These greatly resemble the family names of their high elven ancestors, but are more likely to reference the lands in which they live, animals, and the elements.

Adventurers: Wild Elves take up adventure to explore the world. Most of all, they seek to test themselves, hoping to achieve great individual accomplishments.

Traits: The racial traits of Twilight Elves differ as follows.

Abilities: +1 Str, +1 Con, -2 Cha.

Weapon proficiencies: Proficient with spear; and shortbow, longbow, composite shortbow, or composite longbow.

Wilderness Lore: All Wild Elves begin play with 2 ranks in the Wilderness Lore skill.

Favored Class: Barbarian.

Literacy: Wild Elves begin play with 1 rank in Elven (Wild).

Wood Elves

Wood Elves originate in the Realm of Faerie. When the All Father's mind was splintered, the Realm of the Fey became part of the multiverse. For a brief time, the Faerie Queen allowed open travel between her realm and Erde. In those days, some fey passed into Erde, never to return to their homeland. Over many generations, those fey became Wood Elves. Thus, the Wood Elves are a sister race to the High Elves, rather than their descendants.

Personality: Wood Elves are reclusive and secretive, though not isolationist. They are the natural protectors of the forests and its inhabitants. They can exhibit the extremes of elvenkind's typical personality. When at war, they are deadly with sword and bow. And when at play, their singing and dancing delights the heavens.

Physical Description: Wood Elves are the largest elven race, with some equaling humans in proportion. Their skin ranges from fair to pink, and their hair shades blonde to brown. Eyes are rarely anything other than deep green or blue. Unlike other elves, some elder Wood Elf males develop facial hair. All have light body hair. Dress tends toward leather mixed with simple clothing and cloaks in the hues of the forest. They tend to generally exhibit a stern and serious expression that is then often betrayed by a bright smile.

Relations: Wood Elves prefer the company of forest creatures and fey, and generally relate well to Wild Elves and Halflings. They generally stick to their own affairs, but always rally to the cause of good when civilized lands are threatened by evil. In those times, they even gladly stand with Dwarves, who they typically consider boorish.

Alignment: Wood Elves value the natural order of the universe. Thus, they tend toward a shade of neutrality with neutral, neutral good, and chaotic neutral being the most prevalent alignment.

Wood Elven Lands: The description in the *Player's Handbook* aptly describes Wood Elven society except for one major difference. Wood Elves consider the entire clan to be the family unit. Little emphasis or importance is placed upon the biologic parents or siblings of a wood elf. Instead, the familial clan raises newborn Wood Elves, and each individual is groomed for a few particular roles in the clan. Which of these roles is eventually chosen is left to the individual, but once chosen, it becomes a life's commitment. Each individual declares their chosen role upon reaching adulthood.

Religion: Wood Elves revere Wenafar above all.

Languages: Wood Elves speak Elven (Wood), Sylvan, and Vulgate. Their bonus languages are: Aenochian, Dwarven, Elven (Fontenouq or Shindolay High Elven, Twilight, Wild), Ethrum, Gnomish, Goblin, Halfling, Hobgoblin, Kobold, Orc, Troll, and Ungern.

Names: Wood Elf names, chosen upon reaching adulthood, reflect their role in society. Some meaning is quite often lost when translated to the common tongue.

The number of names can greatly vary. Some choose more than one name upon reaching adulthood, while others add names as they progress in life. Additional names may reflect deeds accomplished, or simply nicknames. Some maintain only their adult name over the course of their life.

Adventurers: While it would seem likely that few Wood Elves would become adventurers because of the roles individual Wood Elves are nurtured to follow in their clan, they are in fact the most prevalent adventurers of all the elven races. Indeed, each clan particularly nurtures some of their children for a life outside the clan and forest. In this way, the Wood Elves stay current with the happenings of the world and train ambassadors who can more easily deal with other peoples. Those brave enough to choose such a life are held in great esteem and honor among all Wood Elf clans.

This is not to say that all Wood Elf adventurers spend their lives cultivating political allies and gathering information. Again, to the contrary, the Wood Elves believe that freely wandering the world, following your individual road best cultivates each elf's talents. Thus, Wood Elf adventurers may live a life of high adventure for decades, until such time as they are needed by their clan. At that time, those who have achieved great station in the outside lands honorably serve as ambassadors of all Wood Elves, not just their own clan.

Traits: The racial traits of Wood Elves differ as follows.
Abilities: +2 Dex, -1 Con, -1 Cha.
Weapon proficiencies: Proficient with either longsword or shortsword; and any type of bow. Other favored weapons include hand axes and spears.
Wilderness Lore: All Wood Elves begin play with 2 ranks in the Wilderness Lore skill.
Favored Class: Ranger.

Literacy: All Wood Elves begin play with   1   rank   in Elven (Wood).

GNOMES

Gnomes are an offshoot of the dwarven family tree. They are the third oldest of the peoples of Erde, coming after the dwarves and goblins. Somewhere in their history, the Gnomes became distinctly different from their dwarven cousins. They lived largely above ground, and became smaller in stature. They are very adaptive to new terrains and environments.

The gnomish population suffered greatly during the Age of Winter Dark. Tolerated, they lived on the fringes of society and established a soon-to-be thriving trade with the powers of the dark. This adaptation led to Gnomish society evolving into tightknit clans. Eventually, the strongest clans settled in the Grundliche Mountains and the Flintlock, and made war upon the Dark. The Gnomish clans now number forty-seven, and they are spreading to other regions.

Physical Description: The only difference in Erde Gnomes is that their height ranges from 3 1/2 to a little over 4 1/2 feet tall, and they weigh 70-90 lb. on the average.

Relations: Gnomes get along well with Dwarves and Halflings, and engage in a large amount of trade with Humans. They have little contact with Elves. Some damage was done to the reputation of Gnomes during the Winter Dark because of their trade relationship with the imperial forces. Most of the damage has been repaired, but some Dwarves and the Human nations in the west are a little suspicious, wondering if gnomish intent merely follows the golden coin.

Alignment: Gnomes tend toward good, with neutral good being the most prevalent alignment.

Religion: Gnomes worship a series of family and clan elders. A gnome would say, "I call upon my father's father, Terrence Bootstrap, to watch over me and my kin." The clan is the society and the great leaders of the clan's past comprise its pantheon. Thus, there are forty-seven different Gnome pantheons. Over the elders of the pantheons sits Grotvedt, the father of the Gnomes.

Languages: Gnomes speak Dwarven, Gnomish, Halfling, and Vulgate. Their bonus languages are: Aenochian, Ethrum, Goblin, Kobold, and Ungern. Gnomes retain their *speak with animals* ability.

Traits: The racial traits of Gnomes differ as follows.
Vision: Gnomes have both low-light vision and darkvision (60 feet).
Profession: All Gnomes learn a Profession skill as they grow to adulthood. The character may pick one Profession skill of 2 ranks, subject to the DM's approval.
Literacy: Gnomes begin play with 1 rank in Gnomish and Vulgate.

HALF-ELVES (and HALF-FAERIES)

Half-Elves do not differ from the description in the *Player's Handbook*, except that their physical description varies depending on whether they are the offspring of a High, Twilight, Wild, or Wood elf. Half-Elves can also be offspring of an Elf and a Faerie. Half-Faeries are extremely rare, resulting from a liaison between a Human and a Faerie. Half-Faeries look like humans but will generally have one characteristic to set them apart, be it small horns, oddly colored hair or skin, or even vestigial wings.

Religion: A Half-Elf's religion is generally dependant upon their background, and is not limited to any particular deities.

Languages: Half-Elves speak Elven (dialect fitting the character's background) and Vulgate. Their bonus languages are: Aenochian, Dwarven, Elven (Wild, Wood), Ethrum, Gnomish, Goblin, Halfling, Hobgoblin, Orc, and Ungern.

Half-Faeries speak Sylvan, Elven (High), and Vulgate. Their bonus languages are: Elven (Fontenouq or Shindolay High Elven, Twilight, Wild).

Literacy: Half-Elves and Half-Faeries begin play with one rank in either Elven or Vulgate.

HALF-ORCS

Half-orcs do not greatly differ from their description in the *Player's Handbook*. Half-Orc adventurers, however, are extremely rare.

Religion: Depending upon their alignment and background, Half-Orcs might follow any deity.

Languages: Half-orcs speak Vulgate and Orc. Their bonus languages are: Goblin, Halfling, Ungern.

Racial Traits: Differ as follows:
Abilities: +2 Str, +1 Con, -1 Int, -2 Cha
Favored Class: Fighter

HALFLINGS

The Halfling race is considered to be slowly dwindling into eventual extinction. During the Age of Winter Dark, those Halflings that were not already part of western Human society came to know rough and constantly threatened lives. The Halflings could find found no refuge anywhere. They survived by living in the forest deeps, spending their time defending themselves when not seeking shelter and sustenance. Indeed, the hunting of Halflings became a a favorite sport among Unklar's noblity. In time, the constant struggles bred a fierce warrior race well practiced in the arts of war and magic.

Halflings of Erde

To survive, Halfling society organized around small family groups of a dozen to a score. The family unit was led by a patriarch and matriarch, and was composed of their children, siblings, and cousins. If a family grew too large, it would split. These nomadic families occasionally would meet, exchange news, trade goods, and arrange marriages. In this way, the Halflings spread all across the lands. Today, two widely different Halfling cultures now exist. Some Halflings rejoined civilized society, while others enjoyed the wild, nomadic life developed over a millenia.

Those family units that eventually rejoined human society became servants and laborers. Some became likewise in Dwarven, Gnomish, or Wild Elf communities. Some took to organizing guilds dedicated to thievery. Other than the differences physical description, age, and Halfling racial traits as detailed below, the civilized Halflings of Erde generally fit the description given in the *Player's Handbook*.

Most Halflings, however, continued to live a nomadic life. To a large extent, this Halfling culture combines aspects of the Wild Elf and Barbarian societies. The details that follow describe the nomadic Halflings of Erde.

Personality: Halflings display a quick and deadly ferocity in combat, that is only heightened by intelligent battlefield tactics and strategy. They prefer hit and run tactics, rarely facing any foe one-on-one. They greatly love their entire family unit, but accept that death is a part of nature. They do not fear magic, and in fact, some Halflings become powerful druids and sorcerers.

Unlike their civilized cousins, they eat and drink only what is needed for sustenance, ever knowing that the next day might be one in which no food will be available. In general, they tend to conserve goods and to use them to their fullest extent, never being wasteful. Wealth is generally considered property of the family, not any individual. Halflings rarely own anything that cannot be carried on themselves or their mounts, which tend to be large wolves or great cats.

Physical Description: Larger than their civilized cousins, nomadic Halflings average 3 1/2 to 4 1/2 feet tall and weigh 50-70 lbs. Their skin is tanned, and their eyes are typically brown or black, but sometimes green. They wear their dark hair long, sometimes in braids or tails. Facial hair is very rare. They tend toward light dress of simple and practical design, and prefer not to wear footwear.

Relations: Halflings engage trade and are on good relation with the Gnomes, Wild Elves, and some barbarian tribes. They have some contact with Wood Elves as well. They avoid Human settlements unless otherwise necessary. They stick to their own affairs.

Alignment: Halflings tend toward some aspect of neutrality.

Halfling Lands: Halflings define nomadism. They roam the world, mining a region of its resources and protection before moving on. They sometimes follow in the wake of armies, barbarians, and other large groups, salvaging what is left behind.

Religion: Nomadic Halflings primarily worship Wulfad and other family deities. Some human religions have become family deities recast through Halfling perspective. These include Demeter, Wenafar, Augustus, Daladon Lothian, Glorianna, St. Luther, and particularly, Falkenjagger. Some even incorporate Frafnog. All Halflings seek eternal happiness in the Misty Brookshire.

Languages: Halflings speak Halfling and Vulgate. Their bonus languages are: Aenochian, Dwarven, Elven (Wild or Wood), Ethrum, Gnomish, Goblin, Hobgoblin, Kobold, Orc, Sylvan, and Ungern.

Names: Halfling names tend to those described in the *Player's Handbook*.

Adventurers: Halfling adventurers born in a nomadic family tend to creations of circumstance. They might be the sole survivor of a decimated family, an escaped slave, or an outcast. Some Halfling magic-users must simply leave their families to seek out knowledge and to develop their craft.

Traits: The racial traits of nomadic Halflings differ as follows.
Wilderness Lore: All nomadic Halflings begin play with 1 rank in Animal Empathy, Handle Animal, and Wilderness Lore.
Favored Class: Barbarian, Fighter, and Ranger.
Literacy: All Halflings begin play with 1 rank in Halfling.

HEIGHT AND WEIGHT

A player may choose his character's height and weight based upon the chart below. The base ranges below are simply guidelines for the average height and weight based on a character's race. The base ranges are for either a man or woman.

Table 1-1: HEIGHT AND WEIGHT

A player may choose his character's height and weight based upon the chart below. The base ranges below are simply guidelines for the average height and weight based on a character's race. The base ranges are for either a man or woman.

Race	Height Range	Weight Range
Dwarf	3' 10" to 5' 2"	140-180 lb.
Elf,		
High	4' 2" to 6' 0"	100-135 lb.
Twilight	4' 0" to 5' 6"	90-115 lb.
Wild	4' 4" to 5' 8"	100-125 lb.
Wood	4' 8" to 6' 6"	110-165 lb.
Gnome	3' 6" to 4' 8"	70-90 lb.
Half-elf	4' 2" to 6' 2"	90-175 lb.
Half-faerie	3' 4" to 5' 4"	70-110 lb.
Half-orc	4' 10" to 6' 5"	120-180 lb.
Halfling	3' 0" to 4' 6"	45-70 lb.
Human	4' 8" to 6' 8"	100-200 lb.

AGE

A character's minimum starting age is indicated on the chart below. A player may always elect a starting age higher than the mandatory minimum.

Table 1-2: Starting Age

A character's minimum starting age is indicated on the chart below. A player may always elect a starting age higher than the mandatory minimum.

Race	Adulthood	Barbarian, Cleric Fighter, Rogue Sorcerer	Paladin Ranger	Bard, Monk Wizard
Dwarf	150	+4d6	+7d6	+10d6
Elf,				
High	200	+7d6	+9d6	+12d6
Twilight	100	+4d6	+6d6	+8d6
Wild	40	+3d6	+5d6	+8d6
Wood	60	+4d6	+6d6	+8d6
Gnome	30	+3d6	+4d6	+6d6
Half-elf	20	+1d6	+2d6	+3d6
Half-orc	13	+1d4	+1d6	+2d6
Halfling	16	+1d4	+1d6	+2d6
Human	15	+1d4	+1d6	+2d6

Table 1-3: Aging

Race	Middle Age	Old	Venerable	Maximum
Dwarf	300	450	600	+2d% years
Elf,				
High	500	750	1000	+3d% years
Twilight	200	300	400	+2d% years
Wild	100	150	200	+1d% years
Wood	150	225	300	+1d% years
Gnome	75	112	150	+3d20 years
Half-elf	62	93	125	+3d20 years
Half-faerie	100	150	200	+1d% years
Half-orc	30	45	60	+1d10 years
Halfling	40	60	80	+2d20 years
Human	35	53	70	+2d20 years

Aging Effects: Aging effects are cumulative.
Middle age: -1 Str, Con, and Dex; +1 Int, Wis, and Cha
Old age: -2 Str, Con, and Dex; +1 Int, Wis, and Cha
Venerable: -3 Str, Con, and Dex; +1 Int, Wis, and Cha

RACE AND LANGUAGES

All beginning characters speak the common tongue, Vulgate. A character also begins play knowing how to speak additional languages depending upon the character's race. The descriptions of each race detail a character's starting languages.

Intelligence bonus: A beginning character with an Intelligence score of 12 or higher begins play with additional languages that he can speak. The player chooses his bonus languages from the list contained in each race's description. A character possessing an Intelligence modifier greater than the number of bonus languages listed in his race's description does not begin play with any additional bonus languages. Instead, the character may learn additional languages over time if the opportunity presents itself as he explores the World of Erde. If a character's Intelligence score modifier increases due to aging or magic, he gains additional bonus language slots at that time.

Class-related languages: Clerics, druids, and wizards can still choose bonus languages not detailed in their racial description as found in the *Player's Handbook*.

Literacy: Characters cannot read and write any languages she speaks unless it is noted in her race's description. For a character to learn to read and write a language she speaks, she must learn 1 rank in the skill Literacy for that language. Not all races begin play with a Literacy skill, even in their own tongue.

New Skill:
Literacy (Int; Trained Only)

You can read and write a language that you speak. Each additional rank gained indicates one step closer to scholarship in a language.

Check: A character with 1 rank can read and write as an average person. No check is needed unless a character attempts to read or write beyond his skill level.

DC	Task
–	Read or write with average ability; comprehend simple metaphors
5	Ability to write fiction/technical writing
10	Persuasive writing ability; comprehend complex writings
20	Excellent writing and comprehension abilities
30	Comprehend arcane writings; mimic other's writing style with flair
50	Shakespeare

LANGUAGES OF ERDE

Most of the languages of Erde find their origins in the ancient Dwarf language. This is true for modern Dwarf, Goblin, Gnome, Halfling, and Human languages apart from the Holy and Runic tongues. Knowledge in one, however, does not necessarily mean knowledge in them all for there are racial, socio-historical, and cultural characteristics which mark each language as unique. The languages spoken by Elves, humanoids, and Ungern do not originate in ancient Dwarven and are altogether different.

Besides those languages detailed below, the following languages listed under the Speak Language skill in the *Player's Handbook* also exist: Abyssal, Aquan, Auran, Celestial, Draconic, Druidic, Gnoll, Ignan, Infernal, Sylvan, Terran, and Undercommon.

Aenochian, "Old Imperial." This was the dominant language during the age of the Empire of Aenoch. It is a complicated and difficult language to learn. It is now spoken mostly by the aristocracy of the east, the Punj, the United Kingdom, and Augsberg. The Orcs of Onwaltig, and the Hlobane Nation (reference the United Kingdoms) speak it as well. The cult of the Paths of Umbra uses the language in their everyday speech. It evolved from the Runic Tongue.

The Language of Creation This is the language which the All Father used to spin the magic of his being into the World of Erde. It is a powerful language, and being the greatest source of magic serves as the root for the magic tongue. Mastery of it is impossible. The goddess of the inner world, Inzae, could not understand it when the All Father tried to teach it to her. He wrote it for her in the Obsidian Book. The Sentients learned it in the Days before Days, as did Frafnog.

Few of the Dwarves of old managed to comprehend it, and even when they did, it was a collective endeavor. Eventually the Greater Dwarves of Inzae wrote it down, scribing its magic upon the tubes they constructed between the worlds, the Rings of Brass, and later, in the Mammoth Scrolls. 'Tis said that Nulak-Kiz-Din mastered some of the Language when he discovered The Paths of Umbra, and that Daladon used its power to bind the Unicorn to the Ephremere, Queen of Aachen. Aristobulus, too, understands some small bits of the Language.

Any spell, written or spoken, represents a small portion of the Language. "Nothing so much as a singular drop of water in the Amber Sea," or so the Mage Patrice used to teach his students, in reference to their individual spells when compared to the overall Language. To master it, a nearly impossible task, would bring the wielder infinite power.

Dwarven. The language of the Dwarves is the base root of all Human, Goblin, Gnome and Halfling tongues. This is the reason that many place names seem similar to ancient Dwarven. It is a simple language based around solid descriptions. For example, in describing a decisive person, a Dwarf would say, "His mind is as certain as stone." These types of language constructs make Dwarven extremely verbose. Many Dwarves, most famously Dolgan, are long-winded, even when speaking other languages because they translate from Dwarf into the other tongue. An advantage lies in the language's structure, allowing most non-Dwarves to master it within a few short years of study. The language becomes complicated only when discussion turns to forge craft – 43 words exist for types of hammers alone. Dwarven is spoken in the Dwarven Hohles, and by Goblins, Gnomes and Halflings.

Elven. The Elven languages distinctly involve a great deal of body language. The Elves communicate not only by speech, but through emotive expressions which manifest in the way they stand and sit, their facial expressions, and so on. Learning the elven languages is extremely difficult, taking years of practice.

The Age of Winter Dark exaggerated the differences in the Elven races. The Twilight, Wild Elves, and Wood Elves remained on Erde, while the High Elves left the world and were split into two factions. All Elves speak dialects derived from High Elven. An elf from one race can achieve a basic understanding of the dialect of the other elven races, but true mastery is difficult to achieve because the emotive expressions dramatically changed among each elven race during that time. The dialects of the Wild, Wood and Twilight Elves are the most compatible.

The Elven languages are broken into five distinct dialects: High Elven (Fontenouq), High Elven (Shindolay), Twilight, Wild, and Wood. These developed according to the manner in which each race was forced to survive during the Millennial Dark.

Fontenouq High Elves: Their lust for war has given the Fontenouq Elves a militaristic world view. Their language is sharp and clear, with few references to things beyond the physical plane. Sentences tend to be short and to the point. Much of the speech has to do with war and violence. The Fontenouq are philosophers as well, however, and their speech also reflects it.

Shindolay High Elves: The High Elves of Shindolay speak this sing-song language which remains the root of most all the elven dialects.

Twilight: The Twilight Wood, a place which thrived during the Winter Dark, did so by feeding off of the light of the moon. The Twilight Elves adapted to the peculiar nature of the forest, and their language reflects it. The tone is quiet, almost secretive. They identify things and places through metaphor as much as through nouns. A close relation to the god Utumno has led to many peculiar references to the dreamscape within the metaphors employed in the language.

Wild Elf: These Elves remained upon Erde during the Winter Dark, migrating from one area to the next. The Wild Elf dialect is a smooth flowing, high pitched language. Their sentences are frequently laced with double meanings, for they lived in the open during the Dark and were hunted far and wide.

Wood Elf: Like the Wild Elves, these elves hid themselves in deep forests and combated the Winter Dark. The Wood Elf tongue is thickly accented, almost guttural, and is the most difficult for other Elves to comprehend.

Ethrum, also called "Kayomarese," or simply the "Western Tongue." This was and still remains the dominate language in the west. The decedents of the tribe of Ethrum have maintained their native tongue quite well over the centuries, even during the Winter Dark. It is associated with the struggle against the Aenochians, and also against Unklar. Ethrum is the common tongue in Kayomar, Eloria and Maine. It is the only tongue which the aristocracy of those two lands speak or write in. Like Aenochian the language is a complicated one, and difficult to learn. It evolved from the Runic Tongue.

Gnomish. This language is very much like Dwarven, its mother tongue. The main difference between Gnomish and Dwarven is that the Gnomish language has an expanded vocabulary concerning economics, similar to that in Dwarven concerning forge craft. It is one of the oldest tongues.

Goblin. Much like the Goblins themselves, this language is a twisted representation of the Dwarven tongue. Where Dwarven is easy to learn, Goblin is difficult. Sentences are convoluted, filled with many phrases and pauses that are seemingly pointless. The language is not, however, for Goblins are by nature devious and their language is as well. The Goblin language is used to force a person to respond and to thereby expose their own emotive desires. For this reason, Dwarves, who understand Goblins very well, are frequently found sitting motionless for hours while Goblins ramble on, speaking only when they are certain the Goblin has finished his speech.

Halfling. The Halfling tongue also derives from Dwarven, but it has aspects that make it wholly different from any other language. Few speak this language, however, for Halflings are not much accounted for. Gnomes speak Halfling because they engage in regular trade with them.

Holy Tongue, "the Words of Law." This is the language of the Holy Defenders of the Flame, the Confessor Knights, and the priests of Durendale and St. Luther. The language evolved over a long period of time, and involved emotive responses and intuition in its development. Only those of good alignment can learn the tongue as complete understanding comes from "realizing the good," as some scholars are want to say.

Humanoid Languages. Orcs, Hobgoblins, Trolls, Kobolds, and other humanoids speak their own languages which are generally unique to each individual race. Humanoids descended from the same race, or which often co-mingle will also often share bits and pieces of language.

Runic Tongue. This language predates most of the wars of Aenoch and Ethrum, coming from, or so scholars assert, the Age of the God Emperors. It is exceedingly complex and few on Erde can speak it with any fluency. The priests and wizards of the old gods are adept at the language, and frequently use it as their holy tongue. Those who are fluent can generally understand and speak both Ethrum and Aenochian.

Thieves' Cant. The language of thieves is spoken worldwide by almost every thief and guild. It allows one to communicate, even to an enemy, without giving oneself away. It involves hand gestures as well as key words with double meanings. Regional differences do exist.

Ungern. The Ungern speak their own tongue, reflecting the origins of their race. It derives from Old Aenochian, but Unklar's knowledge of the Language of Creation gave the tongue a hidden power the other languages of Erde do not possess. The language is guttural and very difficult to learn, requiring a minimum intelligence score of 16 to master it.

Vulgate, the Common Tongue. This is the common tongue of men. Merchants use it in their daily discourse for it is spoken all over the world. Most peasants speak it as well. It originated in the early days of the Aenochian empire and is a bastardized version of Ethrum and Aenochian. During the Age of Winter's Dark, the Imperial bureaucracy adopted the tongue to better integrate the rule of Unklar with the common folk, and for this reason, it became the most pervasive language in Erde. Most of the Young Kingdoms, from Eisenheim to Cleves, speak Vulgate in courtly circles.

Toth

God of Knowledge, Past, Present & Future

CHAPTER 2: CLASSES, ORDERS, & GUILDS

CHARACTER CLASSES

HIGH ELF

The High Elves of Erde are a melancholy race whose past is clouded by guilt for abandoning the world in its darkest hour (*reference Fontenouq, pages 88-89*). Unlike their ancient ancestors and kin, the High Elves have turned from carefree spirits into brooding philosophers, content to indulge themselves in the pursuit of music, poetry, and other art. Their independent lives have led to a slowly declining population, with little concern among the young for propagation.

Even so, the High Elves retain the fierce nature that developed in their return to the world, and the skill in armory, weapons, and magic that they have always possessed. Occasionally, some of the younger High Elves leave their family's castles to explore the world. Most are driven by guilt to redeem their family's name, if not their entire race. They are easily recognized by the make of their weapons and armor, their warlike attitude, and the sorceries they employ in combat.

Adventures: High Elves wander Erde seeking redemption for their families and their race. How pronounced their guilt is depends upon each individual High Elf, but it remains at the core of their adventuring motivation. Like paladins, they seek to do good in the world and to battle evil.

Background: High Elves will either trace their ancestry to those High Elves that remained in Erde and did not pass on to Fay, to Shindolay, or to Fontenouq.

High Elves that remained in Erde, and their descendants, wander the world as Ronin, righting wrongs, making war upon evil, and upholding good. They are noble and honorable. Having discarded the trappings of their ancestry during the long, hard Winter Dark, each individual chooses different armor and weapons and manner of dress as befits their own mind. They are quite humble.

High Elves descending from Shindolay tend to be more colorful in dress. They prefer to employ spell over sword, but when arming themselves, they utilize light to medium armors, bows, and swords. They most closely resemble their ancient forefathers, and some see them as arrogant. Still, good remains in their heart, and they will stand back-to-back with any that would eradicate evil.

High Elves of Fontenouq ancestry leave the safety of their family's towers, and their books, art and music. Instead of talking philosophy and debating the sins of history, they seek to live in the present and honor the memory of their ancient forefathers, those proud elven warriors that combated evil before their descendants fled the world. They typically arm themselves in conical helms and long shields, and wield light but sturdy swords and spears from the backs of their long-legged horses.

Other Classes: High Elves are the silent, dependable warriors that an adventuring party needs for a stable foundation. Their combination of martial skill and wizardry can be invaluable, especially in parties with few members. They relate well to clerics, rangers, monks, paladins, and wizards. They sometimes clash with bards and rogues, but realize that the skills they possess are often necessary in the battle between good and evil. They see sorcerers as undisciplined.

Racial Characteristics: The racial characteristics for High Elves is as follows.

Physical Description: High Elves average 4 1/2 to 5 1/2 feet in height, but some stand 6 feet. They weigh between 100 to 135 lbs. Their skin is fair, their hair is light, and their eyes bright. They have no facial hair or body hair. They move with grace and purpose, no motion being wasted.

Relations: High Elves are often strangers in a strange land. They can relate to most any race, but it typically takes time to develop trust and respect.

Religion: Many deities populate the pantheon of the High Elves. Two of these are Aenouth and Burasil. All high-elven deities seem quite alien to most every other race for the High Elves seem to revere qualities that are not easily definable in human terms. High Elves also pay homage to Wenafar, and the heroes Setiva and Mithlon.

Languages: High Elves speak Elven (Shindolay or Fontenouq), Aenochian, Dwarven, Ethrum, and Goblin. Their bonus languages are: Draconic, Gnomish, Halfling, Runic Tongue, Sylvan, Ungern, and Vulgate.

Names: Naming is as described for Elves in the Player's Handbook. Family names for Fontenouq high elves will tend to carry connotations of war.

Traits: The racial traits of High Elves differ from those described in the *Player's Handbook* as follows.

Abilities: +1 Dex, +1 Int, -2 Con, -1 Cha. High elves weakened constitutions are a result of the curse laid upon them by Daladon Lothian. The lowered charisma flows from the general mistrust all races secret against them for abandoning Erde at the coming of Unklar.

Weapon proficiencies: Proficient with either longsword or shortsword.

Literacy: High Elves begin play with 2 ranks in Elven (Fontenouq or Shindolay), and 1 rank in Aenochian, Dwarven, and Ethrum.

GAME RULE INFORMATION

High elves have the following game statistics.

Abilities: Intelligence determines how powerful a spell-caster a High Elf becomes, how many spells the High Elf can cast per day, and how hard those spells are to resist. High scores in Strength, Dexterity, and Constitution are helpful to a High Elf's adventuring career.

Alignment: Any good.

Hit Die: d8.

Starting Gold: 5d4 x 10.

Class Skills

The High Elf's class skills (and key ability for each skill) are Alchemy (Int), Concentration (Con), Hide (Dex), Knowledge (all skills, taken individually) (Int), Listen (Wis), Move Silently (Dex), Ride (Dex), Speak Language (Int), Spellcraft (Int), and Spot (Wis).

Skill Points at 1st level: (2 + Int modifier) x 4.

Skill Points at Each Additional Level: 2 + Int modifier.

Class Features

All of the following are class features of the High Elf.

Weapon and Armor Proficiency: A High Elf is proficient in the use of all simple and martial weapons, all armor, and shields. Normal armor penalties for skill checks apply.

Spells: A High Elf casts arcane spells without needing to memorize them from a spellbook. Table 2-1: The High Elf shows the number of spells per day that a High Elf may cast, which is improved by the bonus spells granted by the Intelligence modifier, if any. A High Elf cannot use a higher-level spell slot to cast a lower-level spell.

A High Elf begins play knowing three 0-level spells and one 1st-level spell of your choice. You choose the spells from the sorcerer and wizard spell list in the *Player's Handbook*. At each level, a High Elf gains one or more new spells according to Table 2-2: High Elf Spells Known. As with sorcerers, these spells can be chosen from the sorcerer and wizard spell list, or, if a spell is not on that list, learned from another source such as a spellbook.

To learn or cast a spell, a High Elf must possess an Intelligence score of at least 10 + the spell's level. In addition, a high elf receives bonus spells based on Intelligence. The Difficulty Class for saving throws against a High Elf's spell is 10 + the spell's level + the high elf's Intelligence modifier.

Arcane Spell Failure Reduction: High Elves know how to wear armor effectively and how to minimize the interference it might cause to their spells. Thus, a High Elf has a less difficult time casting arcane spells while wearing armor. The Arcane Spell Failure percentage of any armor is reduced by 15% when worn by a High Elf.

High Elf Starting Package

Armor: Studded Leather +3 AC, speed 30 ft., 20 lb., armor check penalty -1, arcane spell failure 0%.

Weapons: Longsword (1d8, crit 19-20/x2, 4 lb., Med. slashing); Longspear (1d8, crit x3, 9 lb., Large piercing).

Skill Selection: Pick a number of skills equal to 2 + Int modifier.

Table 2-2: High Elf Spells Known

Level	\- Spells Known \-									
	0	1	2	3	4	5	6	7	8	9
1	3	2	—	—	—	—	—	—	—	—
2	4	2	—	—	—	—	—	—	—	—
3	5	3	—	—	—	—	—	—	—	—
4	5	3	2	—	—	—	—	—	—	—
5	6	4	2	—	—	—	—	—	—	—
6	6	4	3	2	—	—	—	—	—	—
7	6	4	3	2	—	—	—	—	—	—
8	6	4	4	3	2	—	—	—	—	—
9	6	4	4	3	2	—	—	—	—	—
10	6	4	4	4	3	2	—	—	—	—
11	6	4	4	4	3	2	—	—	—	—
12	6	4	4	4	4	3	2	—	—	—
13	6	4	4	4	4	3	2	—	—	—
14	6	4	4	4	4	4	3	2	—	—
15	6	4	4	4	4	4	3	2	—	—
16	6	4	4	4	4	4	4	3	2	—
17	6	4	4	4	4	4	4	3	2	—
18	6	4	4	4	4	4	4	4	3	2
19	6	4	4	4	4	4	4	4	3	2
20	6	4	4	4	4	4	4	4	4	3

Table 2-1: The High Elf

Level	Base Attack Bonus	Fort Save	Ref Save	Will Save	Special	Spells per Day									
						0	1	2	3	4	5	6	7	8	9
1	+0	+0	+0	+2	Spell Failure Reduction	2	1	—	—	—	—	—	—	—	—
2	+1	+0	+0	+3		3	1	—	—	—	—	—	—	—	—
3	+2	+1	+1	+3		3	2	—	—	—	—	—	—	—	—
4	+3	+1	+1	+4		3	2	1	—	—	—	—	—	—	—
5	+3	+1	+1	+4		4	3	2	—	—	—	—	—	—	—
6	+4	+2	+2	+5		4	3	2	1	—	—	—	—	—	—
7	+5	+2	+2	+5		4	3	3	2	—	—	—	—	—	—
8	+6/+1	+2	+2	+6		4	4	3	2	1	—	—	—	—	—
9	+6/+1	+3	+3	+6		4	4	3	3	2	—	—	—	—	—
10	+7/+2	+3	+3	+7		4	4	4	3	2	1	—	—	—	—
11	+8/+3	+3	+3	+7		4	4	4	3	3	2	—	—	—	—
12	+9/+4	+4	+4	+8		4	4	4	4	3	2	1	—	—	—
13	+9/+4	+4	+4	+8		4	4	4	4	3	3	2	—	—	—
14	+10/+5	+4	+4	+9		4	4	4	4	4	3	2	1	—	—
15	+11/+6/+1	+5	+5	+9		4	4	4	4	4	3	3	2	—	—
16	+12/+7/+2	+5	+5	+10		4	4	4	4	4	4	3	2	1	—
17	+12/+7/+2	+5	+5	+10		4	4	4	4	4	4	3	3	2	—
18	+13/+8/+3	+6	+6	+11		4	4	4	4	4	4	4	3	2	1
19	+14/+9/+4	+6	+6	+11		4	4	4	4	4	4	4	3	3	2
20	+15/+10/+5	+6	+6	+12		4	4	4	4	4	4	4	4	3	3

Skill	Ranks	Ability	Armor
Hide	4	Dex	
Concentration	4	Con	
Ride	4	Dex	
Listen	4	Wis	
Move Silently	4	Dex	
Spot	4	Wis	
Spellcraft	4	Int	
Knowledge (arcana)	4	Int	
Alchemy	4	Int	

Feat: Dodge if Dex is 13+. Improved Initiative otherwise.

Spells Known: 0-level: *Resistance, Dancing Lights, Detect Magic*; 1st level: *Ray of Enfeeblement*.

Gear: Backpack with waterskin, one day's trail rations, bedroll, sack, three torches, and flint and steel. Spell component pouch.

Gold: 2d4 gp.

PRESTIGE CLASSES

HOLY DEFENDER OF THE FLAME

In the Age of Heroes, a knight, Gerard of Kayomar, changed the course of history. He found a tongue of flame burning on a slab of stone. The flame, or so the tales relate, was the last spark of the Language of Creation and as such a powerful source of magic. He took this fire, placing it in a dish of silver and platinum, and bore it aloft amongst humankind He called for the holy and the righteous to join him in a brotherhood of arms. Soon after, he founded the knightly order of the Holy Defenders of the Flame.

The order throve for many years but achieved its apogee under the guidance of Luther Pendegrantz. As King of Kayomar, he combined the might of the crown with that of the order and settled an Age of Peace that lasted 30 years upon his lands.

During the long years of the Winter Dark, the order was forced to hide in the hills and forests of Ethrum, yet it lived on. Their Master, his name lost to history, took the Flame from its hiding place and moved it to the Tower of Hope in the ruins of Du Guesillon. There he hoped it would serve as a signal for Luther's return from the Dreaming Sea. A singular knight always stayed in the snow bound ruins of the castle to keep watch, and to bear word when the Paladin should return. This vigil they kept for the full six centuries until Luther's return was realized.

When the Winter Dark Wars began, the Master at that time, Morgan of Dawin, called his knights together and they, first of all the peoples of Erde, rose in rebellion against the horned god. They distinguished themselves on many fields but none greater than the battle of Eadore where 500 knights and 2000 men-at-arms destroyed a legion of sixteen thousand. Morgan once more reunited the crown of Kayomar with that of the Master of the Order when Luther of the Dreaming surrendered the throne to him.

The Paladin's Grove, or Palladium Grove

The most holy shrine of the Order is found in the Pallidium Grove. Once the family lands of St. Luther, it holds the greatest relics of the order, including the Holy Flame and sometimes, the sword Durendale.

The Grove lies north and east of the Nordmark in Kayomar, between the Bergrucken Mountains and the Ardeen River. In 1029md,

St. Luther

King Morgan of Kayomar established the Grove in honor of St. Luther. He ordered a shrine built to serve both the Holy Defenders of the Flame and one dedicated to the worship of St. Luther and Durendale. For the site of the shrine Morgan chose the ancient family holdings of Pendegrantz.

The Grove encompasses 300 acres of wooded land surrounded on all sides by a low wall. A temple building stands in the center of it, along with a few smaller buildings for travelers to stay in and one villa for the King of Kayomar. The Holy Flame, in its dish of platinum, rests in the altar chamber of the Temple (*reference Magic Items, p. 225*). In further honor of St. Luther, the Druids of the Order of the Oak came to the grove at the behest of Daladon Lothian and planted there a crop of silver birch and elm, said to be the offspring of the Trees of Mordius from the dawn of time.

The temple honors St. Luther, promoting his worship as well as that of Durendale. It is a place where people come for peace and to learn of themselves by spiritually traveling the Dreaming Sea, learning what they may from the Lord of Dreams. Others come on pilgrimage to learn what truth the Holy Flame can reveal. All who approach the Flame must be bare of foot. It is said that the sword Durendale lies hidden in the grove.

The grove is maintained by generous gifts from various Lords (*reference Cleves, p. 82*) and through donations. The Protectors of the Flame (reference Orders and Guilds), maintain the grove and serve the Holy Defenders.

Becoming a Holy Defender

The Holy Defenders are the beacon of the western world. The order attracts many a young noble into its ranks. Only the most honorable and good find a home.

Paladins: Paladins may begin play as members of the order of the Holy Defenders of the Flame (not the prestige class). Those that meet the requirements of the prestige class and enter it may continue to multi-class and advance as a paladin.

Other characters: All characters, including paladins, must meet the requirements detailed below to become a Holy Defender of the Flame.

Hit Die: 1d10

Requirements

To become a Holy Defender of the Flame, a character must fulfill all the following criteria.

Alignment: Lawful Good
Deity: St. Luther or Durendale
Base Attack Bonus: +6
Knowledge (religion): 2 ranks.
Ride: 2 ranks.
Special: Must be sponsored by current member of the order.

Class Skills

The Holy Defender' class skills are: Concentration (Con), Craft (Int), Diplomacy (Cha), Handle Animal (Cha), Heal (Wis), Knowledge (religion) (Int), Ride (Dex), Speak Language (Holy Tongue) (None).

Class Features

All of the Following are class features of the Holy Defender of the Flame prestige class.

Weapon and Armor Proficiency: Holy Defenders are proficient with all simple and martial weapons, and with all types of armor and shields. Armor check penalties do apply.

Flare: At 1st level, a Holy Defender may cast *Flare* once per day.

Holy Sight: Holy Defenders possess a Spell Resistance of 15 versus spells that attempt to affect sight, such as *Blindness*.

Spells: Beginning at 1st level, a Holy Defender gains the ability to cast divine spells. To cast a spell, the character must possess a Wisdom score of at least 10 + the spell's level. Saving throws against these spells have a DC of 10 + spell level + Wisdom modifier. Bonus spells are based on Wisdom. If a Holy Defender gains 0 spells per day, they may only cast their bonus spells for that spell level. Spells are prepared and cast as a cleric. Spontaneous casting to substitute a cure spell in place of a prepared spell is not allowed.

Produce Flame: At 3rd level, a Holy Defender may cast *Produce Flame* once per day.

Smite Evil: At 4th level, a Holy Defender gains the Smite Evil ability as a paladin.

True Strike: Beginning at 6th level, a Holy Defender can cast *True Strike* once per day.

Holy Word: At 8th level, the ability to cast *Holy Word* once per week is gained.

Holy Aura: Finally, at 10th level, a Holy Defender can cast *Holy Aura* once per week.

Holy Defender of the Flame Spell List

Holy Defenders choose spells from the Paladin spells list.

The Knight's Code

A Holy Defender of the Flame who ceases to be lawful good, or who violates the code of conduct of his order loses all class features and spells. They also may not progress any further as a Holy Defender. Abilities will be regained if the Holy Defender atones for her violations (reference the *atonement* spell in the *Player's Handbook*).

Table 2-3: Holy Defender of the Flame

Class Level	Base Attack Bonus	Fort Save	Ref Save	Will Save	Special	Spells per Day			
						1	2	3	4
1st	+1	+2	+0	+0	Flare, Holy Sight	0	–	–	–
2nd	+2	+3	+0	+0		1	–	–	–
3rd	+3	+3	+1	+1	Produce Flame	1	0	–	–
4th	+4	+4	+1	+1	Smite Evil	1	1	–	–
5th	+5	+4	+1	+1		1	1	0	–
6th	+6	+5	+2	+2	True Strike	1	1	1	–
7th	+7	+5	+2	+2		2	1	1	0
8th	+8	+6	+2	+2	Holy Word	2	1	1	1
9th	+9	+6	+3	+3		2	2	1	1
10th	+10	+7	+3	+3	Holy Aura	2	2	2	1

Skill Points at Each Level: 2 + Int modifier.

PRIMAL DRUID

Unlike the more recognized priests of nature, the druidism of the Primal Druids is less a religion than it is a culture and belief system. Primal Druids respect and fear nature, but do not worship it. They view themselves not as a race separate and removed from nature as many humans do, but as creatures from and part of nature.

The natural world is not known for sympathy, democracy, or tolerance. The strong, quick, and cunning rule. They fee on or subjugate the weak, slow, and dumb. Primal Druids are much in tune with this philosophy. They are not cruel or evil, but instead strive to live by the laws of the wild, which are few in number and of which the most important is survival. It is the natural order that species become extinct as more fit species come along, and the Primal Druids seek to ensure that they have a place within nature.

Primal Druids respect nature and defend their territory, but they are not fanatical conservationists. Nature is a force of power beyond any person's imagination. It does not need defenders. Indeed, nature performs more self-destructive acts against itself than people will ever do. Droughts occur, followed by fires started by lightning which burn hundreds of square miles. Volcanoes, earthquakes, tornadoes, and hurricanes all wreak havoc upon the world.

Primal Druids provide an interesting alternative to the druid class, especially for those non-druid characters who develop an affinity for nature and its order. It is rare for druids to become primal druids, but some turn to the Primal Druid belief system.

Hit Die: 1d8

Requirements

To become a Primal Druid, a character must fulfill all the following criteria.

Race: Human, Wild Elf, or Halfling.
Alignment: Neutral.
Base Attack Bonus: +6.
Handle Animal: 2 ranks.
Knowledge (nature): 4 ranks.
Wilderness Lore: 2 ranks.

Class Skills

The Primal Druid's class skills are: Animal Empathy (Cha, exclusive skill), Concentration (Con), Craft (Int), Handle Animal (Cha), Heal (Wis), Intimidate (Cha), Intuit Direction (Wis), Knowledge (nature) (Int), Profession (Wis), Scry (Int, exclusive skill), Spellcraft (Int), Swim (Str), and Wilderness Lore (Wis).

Skill Points at Each Level: 4 + Int modifier.

Class Features

All of the Following are class features of the Holy Defender of the Flame prestige class.

Weapon and Armor Proficiency: Primal Druids are proficient with the following weapons: battle axe, blowgun, club, dagger, dart, gauntlet, halfspear, handaxe, javelin, light hammer, longbow, longspear, quarterstaff, shortbow, shortspear, shortsword, and sling. These weapons must be made from natural materials such as wood, stone, and natural ores (copper, iron, tin, silver) that have not been altered from their natural state (heated to a molten state/alloyed). They are proficient with light and medium armors but are prohibited from wearing metal armor other than studded leather and ring mail (again, the metal must be natural ores). Shields and helmet may be used but they must be only wooden.

Spells: Primal Druids gain their spell casting ability from the spirits that exist within all things. By establishing dominance over these spirits and bending them to their will, they channel power into spells. They do not do this in an overly destructive or wasteful manner, but as necessity demands.

Beginning at 1st level, a Primal Druid gains the ability to cast a number of divine spells. Primal Druids need not prepare their spells, but they are limited to casting a certain number of spells per day which is improved by bonus spells, if any. To cast a divine spell, the Primal Druid must have a Wisdom score of at least 10 + the spell's level. A Primal Druid with a Wisdom of 10 or lower cannot cast these spells. Primal Druids receive bonus divine spells based on Wisdom, and saving throws against their divine spells have a DC of 10 + spell level + the Primal Druid's Wisdom modifier.

Nature Sense: At 1st level, the Primal Druid gains this ability as detailed in the druid class.

Woodland Stride: At 1st level, the Primal Druid gains this ability as detailed in the druid class.

Speak Sylvan: By 2nd level, a Primal Druid has learned the Sylvan language from interaction with the forest spirits.

Spell Dominance: Dominance underscores the Primal Druid's belief system, even dominance over their fellow druids. A Primal Druid may attempt to assert a temporary spell dominance over another Primal Druid. The targeted druid's must be of an equal or lower level, and must be in visual distance.

To attempt spell dominance over the target, the Primal Druid makes an opposed check against his opponent. Both druids roll a d20 and add their Wisdom and Charisma modifiers. If the Primal Druid's resultant score is 6 or higher than the targeted druid, then he has established dominance over the target.

Success means that the Primal Druid has tapped into the spirits controlled by the target druid and dominated them. The Primal Druid then gains takes away one spell slot from the target druid on a temporary basis, and may use it to cast a spell. The stolen slot may be any level slot possessed by the target druid. The stolen spell must be cast within one hour's time.

If a natural 20 was rolled on the opposed check and it was successful, then the dominance achieved was so great that the Primal Druid gain's one day's time to cast the stolen spell. A natural 1 indicates that dominance may not be attempted again over that same target druid until one week has passed.

Speak Terran: By 3rd level, a Primal Druid has learned the Terran language from interaction with the earth spirits.

Trackless Step: At 3rd level, a Primal Druid gains this ability as detailed in the druid class.

Area Dominance: Similar to spell dominance, area dominance allows a Primal Druid to attempt to assert control over the spirits in a specific region. The targeted area or region will be a zone that is 1 mile in diameter.

To attempt area dominance, the Primal Druid makes a Will saving throw against the area's spirit level: Low (DC 10), Medium (DC 20), or High (DC 30). The DM assigns the area's spirit level. Success results in the druid gaining bonus spells depending on the area's spirit level: Low (+1 each in level one to level three spells), Medium (+1 each in level one to level 5 spells), or High (+1 each in level one to level seven spells). The bonus spells may be cast as long as the druid is in the region, but the duration is one day's time.

If a natural 20 is rolled, then the Primal Druid has achieved permanent dominance over that region and the bonus spells are gained anytime the druid is in the region (but they may not be accessed more than once per day). A natural 1 indicates that dominance may not be attempted again over the same region until the Primal Druid has gained another level.

Speak Auran: By 4th level, a Primal Druid has learned the Auran language from interaction with the air spirits.

Speak Ignan: By 5th level, a Primal Druid has learned the Ignan language from interaction with the fire spirits.

Assume Animal Form: At 6th level, the Primal Druid gains this ability. It mirrors a typical druid's Wild Shape ability except that the Primal Druid can only take the shape of an animal (or dire animal) by wrapping himself in the skin of the animal which he alone has slain. As stated in the *polymorph self* spell description, the Primal Druid regains hit points as if he or she has rested for a day. There is no risk of the standard penalty for being disoriented while in the animal form. The Primal Druid may only take the shape of Tiny, Small, Medium, and Large animals (or dire animals). The Primal Druid can use this ability more times per day at 8th, and 10th level, as noted.

Nature's Barrier: At 7th level, Primal Druids gain a Spell Resistance of 20 versus any spell listed in the following Cleric Domain spell lists: Air, Animal, Earth, Fire, and Water.

Primal Druid Spell List

Primal Druids choose spells from the following list.

0: *Create Water, Detect Poison, Flare, Guidance, Know Direction, Purify Food and Drink, Resistance, Virtue.*

1st: *Calm Animal, Cause Fear, Detect Animals (no plants), Detect Snares and Pits, Endure Elements, Evan's Minor Guardianship, Goodberry, Invisibility to Animals, Obscuring Mist, Summon Nature's Ally I.*

2nd: *Animal Messenger, Charm Animal, Delay Poison, Hold Animals, Hold Person, Loki's Spasm, Produce Flame, Resist Elements, Soften Earth and Stone, Speak with Animals, Summon Nature's Ally II.*

3rd: *Continual Flame, Dominate Animal, Neutralize Poison, Protection from Elements, Spike Growth, Stone Shape, Summon Nature's Ally III, Water Breathing, Water Walk.*

4th: *Air Walk, Control Water, Flame Strike, Repel Vermin, Sleet Storm, Spike Stones, Summon Nature's Ally IV.*

5th: *Animal Growth, Commune with Nature, Control Winds, Ice Storm, Summon Nature's Ally V, Transmute Mud to Rock, Transmute Rock to Mud, Wall of Fire.*

6th: *Find the Path, Fire Seeds, Stone Tell, Summon Nature's Ally VI, Wall of Stone, Wind Walk.*

7th: *Animal Shapes, Control Weather, Fire Storm, Summon Nature's Ally VII, Whirlwind.*

Table 2-5: Primal Druid Spells Per Day

Level	0	1	2	3	4	5	6	7
1	3	2	–	–	–	–	–	–
2	4	2	1	–	–	–	–	–
3	4	3	2	–	–	–	–	–
4	5	3	2	1	–	–	–	–
5	5	4	3	2	1	–	–	–
6	5	4	3	2	2	1	–	–
7	6	5	4	3	2	2	1	–
8	6	5	4	3	3	2	2	1
9	6	6	5	4	3	3	2	2
10	6	6	5	4	4	3	3	2

Ex-Primal Druids

A Primal Druid who ceases to revere nature or who changes to a prohibited alignment loses all spells and class features and cannot gain levels as a Primal Druid until she atones.

Table 2-4: Primal Druid

Level	Base Attack Bonus	Fort Save	Ref Save	Will Save	Special
1	+1	+2	+0	+2	Nature Sense, Woodland Stride
2	+2	+3	+0	+3	Speak Sylvan, Spell Dominance
3	+3	+3	+1	+3	Speak Terran, Trackless Step
4	+4	+4	+1	+4	Area Dominance, Speak Auran
5	+5	+4	+1	+4	Animal Intimidation, Speak Ignan
6	+6	+5	+2	+5	Assume Animal Form (1/day)
7	+7	+5	+2	+5	Nature's Barrier
8	+8	+6	+2	+6	Assume Animal Form (3/day)
9	+9	+6	+3	+6	
10	+10	+7	+3	+7	Assume Animal Form (6/day)

WATCHERS IN THE WOOD

This guild of rangers is dedicated to the worship of the Great Oak and bound to protect the forests of Erde. The order is perhaps the oldest of associations in Erde, being founded even before the Age of Heroes. Its greatest member, Daladon Lothian, rose to prominence during the Age of Winter Dark. Though he himself fell afoul of Nulak-Kiz-Din, the Guild struggled on throughout the long years of the horned god's rule. They lived in hiding, particularly in the Eldwood and the Darkenfold. Though their numbers were never very great, they came to play a major role in the wars in the west.

Daladon Lothian once more assumed leadership of the guild when he returned in 1019md. He led it for many decades and expanded its power across the Lands of Ursal. He planted Watchers and druids from the Order of the Oak in all the forests of the world. There, they enlisted the aid of the Fey and initiated others into the guild.

Today the guild is extremely strong and widespread. Reputed to be the best rangers in the world, the Watchers find close allies in a variety of states, particularly Aachen and Kayomar. In the former, where the Winter Rose grows, the rangers are treated with the utmost respect.

Their guildhall, the Ranger's Knot, is in the Eldwood. There the towering oaks of yesteryear hold the houses and lofts of the rangers in their high branches. Though Daladon left the guild leadership years ago, all in the guild pay him homage.

The main task of the Watchers is to aid the Order of the Oak in safeguarding the Great Oak. But, they continue to keep the forests of the world safe from the depredations of evil.

Hit Die: 1d10

Requirements

To become a Watcher in the Wood, a character must fulfill all the following criteria.

Class: Ranger
Base Attack Bonus: +5
Knowledge (religion): 2 ranks.
Special: The Watchers keep a close eye on rangers operating in the lands who show the potential to become a member of the order. Only those invited and who pass a test of strength, mind, and will may become a Watcher in the Wood.

Class Skills

A Watcher in the Wood is still a ranger. Skills are gained as normal under the ranger class.

Class Features

All of the Following are class features of the Watcher in the Wood prestige class.

Weapon and Armor Proficiency: As a ranger.
Continuing Advancement: Rangers that become a Watcher in the Wood continue to advance as rangers without paying the cost of any additional experience points. In other words, the abilities gained as a Watcher in the Wood are simply additional special abilities earned as the ranger advances in levels. Thus, a ranger character becoming a Watcher is not considered multiclassed.

Nature Sense: At 5th level, the ranger gains this ability as detailed in the druid class.

Speak Druidic: By 6th level, a Watcher has been taught the Druidic language by the Order of the Oak.

Woodland Stride: At 7th level, the ranger gains this ability as detailed in the druid class.

Trackless Step: At 9th level, the ranger gains this ability as detailed in the druid class.

Venom Immunity: At 11th level, the ranger gains this ability as detailed in the druid class.

Wall of Thorns: At 13th level, the ranger gains the ability to cast *Wall of Thorns* once per day.

Liveoak: At 15th level, the ranger gains the ability to cast *Liveoak* once per month.

Changestaff: At 17th level, the ranger gains the ability to cast *Changestaff* once per week.

Word of Recall: At 19th level, the ranger gains the ability to cast *Word of Recall* once per week. Can only recall to the Ranger's Knot.

Table 2-6: Watcher in the Wood

Ranger Level	Additional Special
5th	Nature Sense
6th	Speak Druidic
7th	Woodland Stride
8th	
9th	Trackless Step
10th	
11th	Venom Immunity
12th	
13th	Wall of Thorns
14th	
15th	Liveoak
16th	
17th	Changestaff
18th	
19th	Word of Recall
20th	

Watcher in the Wood Spell List

Watchers in the Wood are still rangers so they gain spells as detailed in the ranger class, and choose spells from the ranger spells list.

GUILDS & ORDERS

Asylum, The
The Asylum is one of the largest thief and assassin guilds in the lands. It is based in Avignon, and its name also refers to the district of that city which is its base of operations. The Asylum has its hands in all of Avignon's affairs. Gaining membership in The Asylum takes some time. Prospective members generally join one of the many sub-guilds to prove their loyalty and worth to the organization.

Bartigot
An order of Dwarves who survived the Battle of Olensk in 1029md. They are marked by a clipped chin beard. These Dwarves are largely homeless, the survivors having never returned to Grundliche Hohle. They are fierce brotherhood, intensely loyal to soldier and to any others who fought at Olensk. They numbe Most Bartigot are Dwarven Defenders (reference *D* classes).

Crna Ruk (The Black Hand)
An order of Assassins (reference *DMG* prestige classes) founded by Nulak-Kiz-Din in the early years of the Winter Dark. The Crna Ruk rose to great prominence as their master gained power. After the fall of the horned god, they attempted to bolster the power of the mage, but in so doing brought the wrath of Coburg the Undying down upon them (*reference Aufstrag, p 70*). Coburg put many of them to death.

Recently, their order has grown again, attracting many followers of Nulak. They form small independent units in towns and cities, paying homage to priest-assassins of their dark god. They are highly secretive, murderous, and altogether evil. They mark their kills with a tattoo of a black hand. Their main guild hall is said to be in the Punj. Some Crna Ruk are Cleric/Assassins or Shadowdancers.

A subsect of the Crna Ruk are the Black Slayers. The Black Slayers are composed of Blackguards dedicated to the service of Nuluk-Kiz-Din.

Confessor Knights
History: At the height of the Winter Dark Wars, in the year 1028md, St. Luther broke the blade Durendale upon the crown of the High Priestess Nectanebo. The blow ended her days forever, and she passed from the world. But in her death she also slew Luther, driving him back to the Dreaming Sea.

There he labored upon his sorrows and grieved at the loss of Durendale, the shards of which he took to the Paladin's Grove for safekeeping to await the coming of the next bearer of the sword. He wove himself a Mantle to wear in humility. Imbued with the gifts of Corthain, this Mantle became the article of Confession which marked Luther's latter days in Erde. He became Luther the Confessor, and when at last he mustered the strength to return to the world of men, he returned as an agent of good with the duty to cleanse souls.

In that year, 1029md, he founded an order of knights to bid his heed and serve the world in a similar fashion. They were chosen from the most lawful and honorable of men, be they peasant or lord, and were dubbed Knights by St. Luther. They were given mantles of azure blue to mark their station and rank. These great cloaks were pinned around their shoulders with clasp symbols of Law and Good.

Armored in plates of steel upon great destriers with lances and swords, these Knights left the Isle of Blight and the Sea of Dreams to explore the world and confess the deeds of men, whether they be good or ill. They numbered thirty-two in their beginning, but four fell in the intervening years. The order has grown little since then, for to join it one must gain the attention of St. Luther and be given residence upon the Dreaming Sea, a thing the Paladin Lord is little inclined to do.

The Ceremony: When Luther summons one to the Dreaming to become a Confessor, he bids them leave their worldly possessions behind, taking with them only the cloth upon their backs. They are told to lay in state for four days and contemplate the sins of their lives. Each must fast during this time, eating only a crust a bread in the morning and three droughts of water in the morning, noon, and evening.

When they feel their minds are open to Confession, they call to the Brothers in Arms for transport to St. Luther. They cast themselves before him, and await his Confession. When he deems they are ready, he holds them aloft and Confesses them. If they live through the experience, they are deemed able to bear the burden of men's souls. The inductee is returned to his cell to prepare himself for the test of arms.

For a month they will languish so, as armor and arms are made for them. When this is done, they are placed in their mail and brought to the clearing in the courtyard. There Luther knights them with his blade, and the Brothers in Arms place the azure mantle upon their shoulders. Once a Knights of Confession, the power of Confession flows into them, and it may be used over man, woman, or monster.

Power of Confession: Confession involves seeing into the hearts of mortals to understand them and their sins. No Knight will involuntarily confess anyone. The creature being confessed must ask the Confessor Knight to do so.

Confession is an aspect of role playing that should not be controlled by a dice roll. The DM should use her best judgment in determining the outcome of a confession. A successful confession redeems the confessed mortal of their sins, renewing their life in a way important to them individually. Those that fail confession are typically struck dead or insane, unable to handle the power of Corthain's justice.

When confessing, a Confessor Knight gains the following spell-like abilities, all operating simultaneously (cast as 15th level cleric): *1st – Command, Detect Chaos/Evil/Law/Good, Remove Fear; 2nd – Augury, Calm Emotions; 4th – Discern Lie, Tongues; 5th – Atonement, Commune (with recipient), Mark of Justice, True Seeing.* No Knight may confess anyone of a level greater than themselves.

Covenant of the Lion

Almuric the Lion founded the knightly order in 1051md in Angouleme. The Covenant primarily consists of noble sons and daughters dedicated to knightly virtues. Many of the nobles of Angouleme, Sienna, Cleves and Karilia are either members or are associated with the order. Master Charles of Sifford is the present guild leader. He has close ties to the King of Angouleme. The order has no affiliation to organized religion, though most of its members pay homage to St. Almuric. All of its members strive to earn the "Order of the Mane," a privilege given only to the bravest knight who achieve glory through arms.

Cult of the Sword

This mercenary order was founded soon after the Winter Dark Wars by Tiberious Claudious, after his master Agrippa failed to over-throw the ruling Consuls of the Republic of Brindisium. Tiberious and the other survivors were driven into exile. Tiberious harkened to his ancestors for guidance, and received a vision of Augustus, a great warrior from the Age of Heroes. It was his sword, now an heirloom, that Tiberious carried in battle. In the vision, Tiberious saw the disparity in wealth between those who fought for Kings and the Kings themselves.

Tiberious began to work toward founding a order of unaffiliated warriors and mercenaries, loosely bound together and following a simple code. The Cult of the Sword was born. The movement spread far and wide, and most who carry blades under its cause wear the tattoo of the Cult, a simple gladius sword on the upper left forearm with the name Tiberious Augustus stenciled around it.

The Code of the Cult is simple – members identify themselves to one another and state who they are fighting against. Any member who finds his opponent to be a member of the Cult can refuse to fight him for any reason without los-ing honor or face. In some places, particularly in the Gelderland towns and the cleaver pits there, the Cult is very powerful and its members control who lives and who dies.

Flintlockers

The Flintlockers are a loose band of Gnomes, Dwarves, and a few Halflings and hu-mans who are proficient in the Flintlock musket. In many cases they make up the backbone of the Gnome Clans' war parties. They have no guilds or leaders, but come together frequently for contests or "shoots." To become a Flintlocker requires a 15 Dex. Flintlockers gain a +2 bonus to attack rolls when using their musket.

Imperial Paladins (The Lost Brigades)

A once great order that served the Solarian Emperors, they are now a shadow of their former selves. Indeed, the Master of the Order was always the Emperor of Solarian. When revolution overcame the newly founded Empire of Brindisium, the Emperors were over-thrown and many of the paladins slain. Those that remained or escaped took to a wandering life.

Today they are mostly holy men who follow Durendale, or more often hermits or mendicant knights who help the downtrodden as best they can. For this reason they are frequently given safe haven by local towns or villages. Any member of the order must be a direct descendant of the old Kayomese gentry. They often have close ties to the nobility of Kayomar. Though they have no leader, the family of Aneisa and the descendants of the last Emperor, Raymond, still lay claim to the Imperial dignity. They are based largely in the hinter lands of Brindisium.

Knights of Haven

This order was founded in the latter days of the Winter Dark Wars. As the worship of Demeter spread throughout the lands, pilgrims began to flock to the town of Haven. The distant locale of the town, upon the slopes of Mount Tur across the Inner Sea, made the jour-ney arduous. Pilgrims had to cross the pirate infested seas or travel overland through Zeitz and Trondheim. So many pil-grims were lost on the road that a knight, Francis the Blessed, founded a clerical military order of hospitalers to protect them.

The Knights of Haven attracted many young converts of Demeter and soon became a stalwart pillar in the religion of that god. Through the patronage of the Church of Avignon and the Kingdom of Augsberg, the Knights were able to found a host of castles along the roads of pilgrimage.

Today the knights are a large, if scattered, order. Many of their castles are occupied by only three to four knights, and a dozen sergeants or attendants. Many of the knights travel sin-gularly, protecting those in need. The order relies upon the individual's own ethics and honor to maintain its strict and disciplined code. Their largest castles, most notably the Hafunich, are in the March of Zeitz. The present guild mas-ter is Eurich von Mager-Falkenheim of Aachen.

Knights of Wizardry

This guild in Outremere is dedicated to the study of magic, particularly its use in war. Sorcerers and wizards make up this order, and they have built a network of sages, alchemists, and loremasters to aid their studies.

Lothian Clerics

In the latter days of the Winter Dark Wars, Daladon Lothian saw the suffering of the homeless and war-torn people of Erde. He took a great part of his wealth and established a monastery in Kayomar. He peopled it with the good of heart and instructed them to aid those in need.

Abbot Edmund, the first Abbot, established the Rules and Or-ders of the Monastery. Those who join the fledgling monastery adopted the name of Lothian and in time, they become clerics, monks, and loremasters. The first Lothian Houses filled with a small host of orphans. The early success of the monastery encouraged Edmund to establish many more, and monasteries now spread across Ethrum and Aenoch. In some regions, particularly Kayomar, the orders are very powerful. They pay homage to the Faerie Queen as well as Daladon.

Lunar Knights

When the Elves chose to flee Erde to Shindolay, some remained to fight the evil that they knew was coming to the world. The Lunar Knights, a tight band of elven warriors, cavaliers, clerics, and wizards, was one such group. Very organized, these capable knights fought the minions of Unklar for the whole of the Winter Dark. They survived by constantly moving. Their most prestigious member was Londea, daughter of the Elven Queen.

Though the order is greatly diminished, it still attracts new members from amongst the Elves of Fontenouq or even those who continue to come from Shindolay. They have the patronage of Wenafar the Faerie Queen. The Lunar Knights are distinguished by their silver cloaks. These magical vestments, awarded to all members, allow the wearer to hide in the shadows (*Cloaks of Elvenkind*). A character must have a 15 Wis to become a Lunar Knight. Arcane Archers are found in this knighthood.

Mystic Enclave

A wizard guild founded by Aristobulus in 694md to serve his causes. It is no longer active.

Muddles Inc.

Muddles Inc., a varied shipping and wholesale company, fronts for one of the most notorious and profitable thieves guilds in Erde. Founded by the siblings, Mac and Susie, the Muddles family still controls this ever-expanding organization.

Muddles Inc. has five major guildhalls, all controlled by Halflings. The Muddles family sits at the head of the organization, and administers and maintains power over all of the guildhalls. It personally oversees the Avignon operation. It is headed by Mac Muddles the VIIIth, a calculating, highly intelligent master thief with ironclad control over the organization, who is very protective of his family's interests.

The Shortstride family oversees the Frieburg guild, one of the most profitable because of the open spirit of the city. The current master is Quigley, who enjoys rubbing shoulders with the upper-class of the city, especially when it leads to acquisitions for his ever-growing jewel collection.

The Frizzyfoots direct the Eichstatt guild in Augsberg, and have sunk most of their garnered wealth into a series of very profitable and legitimate bakeries. They are quite recognizable, having been blessed with genes causing them to be, on average, a full 6 inches shorter than the normal Halfling. The head of the family is Harlo, a wiry scrapper that stands a full 18 inches tall.

The Capidistria in the Hanse Cities guild is headed by MacKenzie Lumpkin. MacKenzie is the daughter of Mac Muddles, who married into the Lumpkin family. After Exeter Lumpkin, her father-in-law, and Ely, her husband, were assassinated in the Three-pit Guild War, MacKenzie assumed the mantle as family head. Some of the Lumpkin family work against her, resentful that she is only Lumpkin by marriage. But MacKenzie bends her father's ear and employs many of his tactics to maintain strong control over the Lumpkin clan. Chappy Lumpkin, Exeter's brother, stands behind MacKenzie and dissuades rebellion among the resentful of his family.

The fifth family, the Harrigrays, reigns over Rhuneland. This family is uniquely headed by brothers, Christian and Dotnevets. They are the youngest of the families and are fighting a major battle for control of the underbelly of Rhunland. They run the opiuim and lotus dens in those scattered cities.

Nulak-Kiz-Din Master of the Paths

A sixth family, the Griffiners, once ran a guildhall in the Sea Towns of Ihlsa. The family was wiped out during a guildwar with the Freetraders and Nachtkriechen.

Race is not a limitation to membership in Muddles Inc. Indeed, all manner of races, including some humanoids, serve in the various guildhalls, or as freelance operatives and contacts. Only Halflings, however, can be "made" a part of the five families.

Paths of Umbra

The members of this order are called "Umbrians." The "Paths" reflect a dual meaning. On the one hand the, they are a series of spells and magical incantations which Nulak-Kiz-Din mastered and used to summon the horned god, Unklar, to the world of Erde. Later, they became indicative of the wizard-priests of Unklar and Nulak, for it was said that a wizard-priest who served either of the two must first follow the Path of Umbra to know his dark lord.

Today, as the spells themselves are reputedly lost in the deep treasure labyrinths of Aufstrag, the "Paths" refer to the guild of wizard-priests who serve the memory of the horned god and worship Nulak. Since the Winter Dark Wars, the guild has broken apart into many smaller units. Only in the United Kingdoms and Punj does it exercise any real power. There it rules at the right hand of Prince Innocent and frequently works with the Crna Ruk. In other lands, the order has gone underground, building temples in old dungeons or abandoned castles. There are some who have entered Avignon and built secret places under the streets of the old city.

Those who follow the Paths of Umbra are altogether evil, seeking the destruction of the new world and a return to the order of the Winter Dark. They forever seek the Blood Runes, those incantations which allow one to travel time, in order to bring back the horned god and the "Age of Eternal White."

Members of this order include lawful evil sorcerers, wizards, clerics, or multi-classed combinations of such. Their possess masterful knowledge of cold-based spells, and receive +2 on saving throws against them. They are sometimes referred to as the "Ice Wizards."

Order of the Oak

This Order consists of Human and Elven druids, rangers, and arcane archers dedicated to the preservation and protection of the Great Oak in the Eldwood. There, the Great Oak towers over the forest, the last of the true Sentients of the All Father's original trees. The Oak is ageless, and worshiped as a god by many in the forest. It speaks only to those it deems worthy, and usually only to the deity Daladon.

The Order is very small, numbering in the hundreds only. Though the most them live in the Eldwood, they have adherents in forests all across the Lands of Ursal, keeping a watch on magical glades. These include the Detmold, where the Winter Roses bloom, and the Paladin's Grove, where the Silver Elm grow. They are very secretive, possessing no guildhalls and no allegiances to any prince. They are closely associated with the Watchers in the Wood, and pay homage to the deity Daladon. They are loosely aligned with the Wood Elves of King Nigold.

Members of the Order carry wooden staves or wands made from fallen branches of the Great Oak. All members of the Order gain the following abilities, usable once per day: *know direction, speak with animals,* and *speak with plants (Sentients only).*

Protectors of the Flame

The Protectors of the Flame maintain the Palladium Grove, the holy resting place of the Holy Flame and Durendale (reference Holy Defenders of the Flame above). They support and serve the Holy Defenders of the Flame. Clerics, fighters, rangers, druids, monks, wizards, and loremasters make up their number, although membership is open to all those good of heart that would serve the Holy Flame. Some of the Protectors go on to become Holy Defenders.

Rat's Den

This is the head guild of a loosely based organization of thieves guilds spread across the United Kingdoms. The heads of each thieves guild meet once a year in the Rats Den, which is moved to a new location every year.

Star Watchers

Rangers that pay homage to the star Patrice comprise this order. There is no real organization or leader of the order. Rather, the loose affiliation of rangers wander Erde doing good and fighting evil, sometimes meeting up to do so. They wear star shaped brooches upon their cloaks, and will come to the aid of any in their order if asked.

Vale Knights

Meltowg Lothian led an order of mercenaries during the Winter Dark. They were comprised of fierce elves and humans, and they waged a tireless and brutal war against the enemy. They were destroyed in the Battle for the Castle of Spires in 1022md when Meltowg attempted to open the gates to the Three Realms. The Vale Knights succeeded in overthrowing the castle, but were all slain but for one elf, Elysian of the Red March.

Elysian left the castle, stricken with grief for his fallen master. For many years Elysian remained in hiding, but eventually he gathered a small following of elves and others who sought his wisdom, dating as it did, from the days before the Winter Dark. He reestablished The Vale Knights under his guidance. Though the order is very small, it thrives throughout all the Lands of Ursal.

Vale Knights swear no oath, only paying homage to the memory of Metowg Lothian and the sword Noxmurus, which Meltowg wielded in his final battle. When combating the remaining minions of the horned god (Crna Ruk assassins, Ungern, Mogrl, Umbra wizard-priests, etc.), Vale Knights' morale and ire are raised such that they gain a +1 to melee damage, and +1 temporary hit points.

CHAPTER 3: EQUIPMENT & ECONOMY

COINS AND MONEY

During the Winter Dark the standard monetary unit was the "Gold Imperial." The coins were carefully minted and were as uniform as the coin presses could make them. Millions of these coins were produced.

With the end of the Winter Dark, there was an explosion of local coinage which eventually debased and eroded international trade. Only one country minted coins which were as precisely measured as the Gold Imperial, Kayomar. The "Kayoish Mark," or gold piece, rapidly became the single most valuable coin of the day. Merchants refused to take anything other than the Mark or the Imperial, still in use, and soon thereafter the two coins came to dominate economic transactions.

Many other countries have continued to mint their own coin, but they also adhere to the standard set by the Imperial and the Mark. These generic coins are called generally called "Crowns." A Mark, Imperial or Crown are all roughly the same value, one gold piece.

Coin value and weight is as detailed in the *Player's Handbook*.

Table 3-1: Nomenclature of the Coins

Base Metal	Kayomar, Imperial, or Other name
Platinum piece:	White Mark, Gulder
Gold piece:	Mark, Imperial, Crown
Electrum piece:	½ Mark (only coined in Kayomar)
Silver piece:	10th Mark, Shilling
Copper piece:	Penny, Pence

THE ECONOMY OF ERDE

The Economy of Erde is well developed. The thousand year reign of the horned god, Unklar, established an orderly world with both land and sea trade routes that were monitored and managed by the efficient imperial bureaucracy. When Unklar's reign ended much of the efficiency was lost, but nevertheless, the Young Kingdoms adopted some of the commercial sophistication that developed in the Age of the Winter Dark.

Most work in Erde is done by free men, however, slavery is common in the east and along the southern coasts of both the Ethrumanian and Aenochian land masses. Erde is in a pre-industrial stage with craftsman producing the goods. Trade is generally shifting from the southern climes to the more northerly ones. The countries in the north such as the Hanse City States, Avignon, and Aachen, are changing the nature of commerce by producing large quantities of manufactured or luxury items.

Each country in Erde is assigned a tier of trade/commercial development indicating the state of its economy and industry, whether it engages in long distance trade, and average taxation. Icons located in each country's information table indicate its economic tier. The tiers range from one to five, with each tiers being cumulative. Thus, the descriptions of tiers one to four would be applicable to a tier four country.

Tier One: foodstuffs, clothing, and essentials; local trade.

For the most part, trade within the countries of Erde consists of local trade of bare essentials such as foodstuffs, clothing, simple furnishings, and tools. Much of the trade occurs as barter, being confined to a local level. Virtually every country is capable of feeding and clothing itself. Taxes are paid in commodities, not money. Most peasants thus pay their taxes in livestock, bales of hay, or sacks of foodstuffs.

In Tier One areas, adventurers will find simple weapons, light armors, leather helms, wood shields, adventuring gear costing 5 gp or less, and mounts costing 30 gp or less.

Tier Two: luxury items and raw industrial material; short to medium distance trade.

Merchants and middlemen become involved in the long distance trade of industrial goods. The industrial goods making up the bulk of the second tier of trade includes timber, metals (iron, copper, tin), oils, coal, salt, and barley and wheat. It also includes slaves in those regions where it is not outlawed. The trade routes for these items are usually short, with several rare exceptions, due to the high cost of transportation and its necessary substructure of armies for protection, buildings for storage, and general infrastructure. Industrial goods are subject to moderate taxation, with traders typically paying in coin or barter.

In Tier Two areas, adventurers will find simple weapons, light to medium armors, wood helms and shields, adventuring gear costing 10 gp or less, and mounts costing 75 gp or less.

Tier Three: processed goods and luxury items; long distance trade.

The next tier is luxury items, and their trade generates the greatest wealth for the coffers of the importing and exporting countries. Luxury items include spices and fine cloths such as silk, wool, cotton, and linen, rare food stuffs (fruits), wines, beers, and finished goods such as weapons, furniture, rope, and fittings for ships. Because these items are relatively easy to transport compared to raw industrial goods, the return on investment is po-

tentially high. Hence, these items are traded across the known world and merchants brave dangerous lands to gather them. The high profit margins induce high taxation. The taxing authorities, however, will typically accept payment by barter as they are always in need of many of the tier three processed goods.

In Tier Three areas, adventurers will find martial, exotic, and renaissance weapons costing 100 gp or less, medium to heavy armors, steel helms and shields, adventuring gear costing 100 gp or less, mounts costing 200 gp or less, and special and superior items costing 150 gp or less.

Tier Four: speciality & rare items; long distance trade.

Tier four encompasses speciality and rare items such as artwork, gold, finely smithed goods, tapestries, rare animals, books and paper, and large items such as ships, wagons, or elaborate stonework. These valuable items fetch quite a sum, usually being made to order. Vast sums of wealth may be exchanged for these items, and of course, begat high taxation. Taxes on these items are almost exclusively paid in coin.

In Tier Four areas, adventurers will find all weapons, armors, gear, mounts, special items, and siege weapons.

Tier Five: magic items & services.

The final tier includes those countries where the traffic of magic items and specialty services occurs. Specialty services include divinations, healing, resurrections, and other magical spells, or the practice of sages. Although the sale of magic items or specialty services might occur on an infrequent basis in tier two to tier four countries, only in tier five countries will be found an active marketplace dedicated such trade. Magic items sales attract high taxation. Specialty services are taxed moderately, but religious specialty services, such as healing, are not taxed at all.

Frafnog, The Great Worm, First Born, Father of the Dragons

NEW WEAPONS

Below are detailed new weapons available in the World of Erde. Also, if a weapon appearing in Chapter 7 of the *Player's Handbook* has been altered or its description somehow changed, you will find it listed here and described again. Otherwise, all weapons detailed in the *Player's Handbook*, and the siege weapons and asian weapons in the *DMG* are available in the World of Erde.

For more details on weapon types and categories, as well as weapon qualities such as cost and damage, reference the *Player's Handbook*.

Table 3-2: Weapons

Weapon	Cost	Damage	Critical	Range Increment	Weight	Type*
Simple Weapons – Melee						
Medium-size						
Club, spiked	–	1d6	19-20/x2	–	4 lb.	(B/P)
Large						
Maul	18 gp	2d6	x2	–	20 lb.	(B)
Martial Weapons – Melee						
Medium-size						
Ball and Chain	12 gp	1d8	x2	–	10 lb.	(B)
Ball and Chain, spiked	14 gp	2d4	x2	–	12 lb.	(B/P)
Broadsword	20 gp	2d4	19-20/x2	–	6 lb.	(S)
Hammer, gnome hooked (Crowbill)	20 gp	1d6/1d4	x3/x4	–	6 lb.	(B&P)
Large						
Ball and Chain, two-handed	18 gp	1d10	x2	–	18 lb.	(B/P)
Greathammer	15 gp	1d12	x2	–	20 lb.	(B)
Exotic Weapons – Ranged						
Large-size						
Great Bow	150 gp	2d8	x3	150 ft.	6 lb.	(P)
Arrows (10)	3 gp	–	–	–	5 lb.	–
Great Crossbow w/Cranequin	100 gp	1d12	19-20/x2	160 ft.	12 lb.	(P)
Bolts (10)	5 gp	–	–	–	2 lb.	–

Siege Engines

Item	Cost	Damage	Critical	Range Increment	Crew
Trebuchet	1,100 gp	7d6	--	300 ft.	5

Special and Superior Items	Cost
Mighty great bow	
+1 Str bonus	250 gp
+2 Str bonus	400 gp
+3 Str bonus	550 gp
+4 Str bonus	700 gp
+5 Str bonus	850 gp
+6 Str bonus	1000 gp

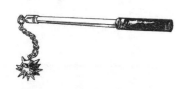

Renaissance Weapons (Firearms) – Ranged**

Weapon	Cost	Damage	Critical	Range Increment	Weight	Type
Small						
Pistol	250 gp	1d10	x3	50 ft.	3 lb.	(P)
Barrel, replacement	150 gp				2 lb.	
Bullets, pistol (10)	3 gp				2 lb.	
Firing mechanism	75 gp					
Gun Powder, horn (10 shots)	35 gp				2 lb.	
Gun Powder, barrel (30 shots)	120 gp				6 lb.	
Stock, wooden	25 gp				1 lb.	
Medium-size						
Musket	500 gp	1d12	x3	150 ft.	10 lb.	(P)
Barrel, replacement	350 gp				8 lb.	
Bullets, rifle (10)	3 gp				2 lb.	
Firing mechanism	100 gp					
Gun Powder, horn (10 shots)	35 gp				2 lb.	
Gun Powder, barrel (30 shots)	120 gp				6 lb.	
Stock, wooden	50 gp				2 lb.	
Large-size						
Cannon, 12 lb.	1000 gp	5d10†	x4	150 ft.	300 lb.	(P)
Cannon, 60 lb.	2500 gp	8d10†	x4	150 ft.	800 lb.	(P)
Cannon, 120 lb.	5000 gp	10d10†	x4	200 ft.	1500 lb.	(P)
Cannon, swivel gun (1 lb)	750 gp	3d10†	x4	200 ft.	100 lb.	(P)
Cannon Balls, 1 lb.	5 gp				1 lb.	
Cannon Balls, 12 lb.	20 gp				12 lb.	
Cannon Balls, 60 lb.	40 gp				60 lb.	
Cannon Balls, 120 lb.	60 gp				120 lb.	
Gun Powder, keg to 12 lb. (5 sh)	120 gp				6 lb.	
Gun Powder, keg to 120 lb. (5 sh)	150 gp				10 lb.	

Renaissance Grenadelike Weapons ***

Weapon	Cost	Damage	Blast Radius	Range Increment	Weight
Grenade	50 gp	3d6 (1d6)	10 ft. to 20 ft.	10 ft.	1 lb.

** Exotic Weapon Proficiency (Renaissance) gains a creature proficiency with all Renaissance weapons; otherwise, a -4 penalty is assessed against all attack rolls.
*** No proficiency is required to use Renaissance Grenadelike weapons.
† Damage indicated corresponds to a direct hit. Those within the 10 feet blast radius suffer the damage indicated. Damage from the explosion is reduced by 2d10 at 10 to 20 feet, and by 1d10 at 20-30 feet (ex. A 120 lb. cannon scores 10d10 on a direct hit, 8d10 from 10-20 feet, and 6d10 at 20-30 feet). Swivel guns do no damage beyond a 20 feet blast radius. A miss requires a roll for deviation.
‡ Grenades deal 3d6 damage in a 10 feet blast radius, and 1d6 from 15 to 20 feet. A miss requires a roll for deviation.

** Exotic Weapon Proficiency (Renaissance) gains a creature proficiency with all Renaissance weapons; otherwise, a -4 penalty is assessed against all attack rolls.
*** No proficiency is required to use Renaissance Grenadelike weapons.

† Damage indicated corresponds to a direct hit. Those within the 10 feet blast radius suffer the damage indicated. Damage from the explosion is reduced by 2d10 at 10 to 20 feet, and by 1d10 at 20-30 feet (ex. A 120 lb. cannon scores 10d10 on a direct hit, 8d10 from 10-20 feet, and 6d10 at 20-30 feet). Swivel guns do no damage beyond a 20 feet blast radius. A miss requires a roll for deviation.

‡ Grenades deal 3d6 damage in a 10 feet blast radius, and 1d6 from 15 to 20 feet. A miss requires a roll for deviation.

Weapon Descriptions

Ball and Chain: The ball and chain resembles a mace with a length of chain, at least 1 foot, between the handle and metal ball.

Ball and Chain, spiked: A ball and chain with spikes on it like a morning star. The spiked ball and chain includes the Binnol (short handle with long chain and spiked ball), and the Goupilon (handle with three chains bearing small spiked balls).

Ball and Chain, two-handed: The staff section on this ball and chain is about three feet in length, thus requiring two hands to wield. Otherwise, it is a ball and chain with or without spikes.

Broadsword: A heavy, thick sword.

Cannon: Cannons range in size depending upon the ball they hurl, from 1 lb. to 120 lbs. Other than the swivel gun, all cannons must be maneuvered into firing position. It takes one full round to change the firing position of a cannon. It takes a movement action to rotate a swivel gun. Damage indicated corresponds to a direct hit. Swivel guns do not damage beyond 20 feet blast radius. A minimum range of 1/2 the range increment is required, except for the Swivel Gun.

Club, spiked: Same as club, but cannot be thrown.

Great Bow: A gigantic bow, sometimes referred to as a "Gnoll Bow." Its arrows are often the length of a human's arm. A character needs at least two hands and a Strength of 15 to employ this weapon. It cannot be used while mounted. Great Bows fire one arrow per round.

Greathammer: A massive, two-handed hammer.

Grenade: These were popularized during the "Trenches Campaign", fought beneath Aufstrag. Grenades require no proficiency to use. A grenade must be lit before being thrown. This requires a standard action. Grenades explode upon impact. A direct hit indicates it has struck the intended target, and it additionally deal the same damage to all within the blast radius. A miss necessitates a roll to determine the grenades landing spot, with all creatures in the blast radius taking damage unless a Reflex Save (DC 20) is made for half damage. A critical miss indicates that the grenade explodes upon the thrower who suffers 3d6 damage.

Gunpowder: While gunpowder burns (with an ounce consuming itself in 1 round and illuminating as much as a sunrod) or even explodes in the right conditions, it is chiefly used to propel a bullet out of the barrel of a pistol or a rifle, or it is formed into a grenade. An ounce of gunpowder is needed to propel a bullet. Gunpowder is sold in small kegs (15-pound capacity and 20 pounds total weight, 250 gp each) and in water-resistant powder horns (2- pound capacity and total weight, 35 gp for a full powder horn). If gunpowder gets wet, it cannot be used to fire a bullet.

Hammer, Gnome Hooked (Crowbill): Although created by the Gnomes, the design of this hammer has become popular in human lands. They call it the Crowbill. It is a double weapon. A creature using a double weapon in one hand, such as a human using a gnome hooked hammer, can't use it as a double weapon. The hammer's blunt head is a bludgeoning weapon that deals 1d6 points of damage (X3 crit). Its hook is a piercing weapon that deals 1d4 points of damage (X4 crit). Either head can be used as the primary weapon head. The other head is the off-hand weapon.

Mace, Heavy or Light: Maces consist of a stick of wood or metal crowned with a metal ball or flanged design. It does not have spikes (see Morning Star).

Maul: A maul is a very large, two-handed mace.

Mighty Composite Great bow, Longbow, or Shortbow: A mighty bow is a composite bow made with an especially heavy pull to allow a strong archer to take advantage of an above-average Strength. The mighty bow allows a character to add his or her Strength bonus to damage up to the maximum bonus listed.

Morning Star, Heavy or Light: Morning stars are an offshoot of the mace. They consist of a spiked ball atop a metal or wooden handle.

Musket: The musket holds a single shot and requires a standard action to reload.

Pistol: This pistol holds a single shot and requires a standard action to reload.

Trebuchet: Similar to a catapult, the trebuchet is a large engine that launches projectiles through force gained from counterweights as opposed to twisted cordage. It has a much greater range and can fire heavier missiles with greater accuracy than a catapult. Operation of the trebuchet is identical to that of a large catapult, but the the crew member making the Profession (siege engineer) check does so at DC 22.

NEW ARMOR

As with the new weapons, the new armors detailed below are in addition to those found in the *Player's Handbook*. If an armor has been altered or its description somehow changed, you will find it listed here and described again. For more details on armor qualities, donning armor, and descriptions, reference the *Player's Handbook*.

Helmets

Helmets add extra protection to the head, and help prevent subdual damage. If variant combat rules are being used that allow for called shots or damage to specific areas, or instant kills, the DM also should allow helmets to decrease the chance for them or lessen their effect as detailed below.

Helmet AC Bonus: A helmet's AC bonus does not stack with any bonus received from wearing armor or using a shield. Rather, it applies to the head's AC only. Head AC is calculated as follows:

Head AC = 10 + Helmet AC bonus + Dex bonus + size modifier + all other modifiers

Helmets and Subdual Damage: Some attacks deal subdual damage. They can be inflicted with hands, feet, or even weapons (see *Core Rulebook I*, chapter 8). Subdual damage is not "real" damage. Instead, when a character's subdual damage equals his current hit points, the character is staggered, and when it exceeds current hit points, he goes unconscious.

Subdual Damage Reduction: Helmets reduce the amount of subdual damage suffered. The subdual damage reduction number indicated for each helmet type in the armor table below is the amount of hit points the wearer ignores from certain blows causing subdual damage.

Type: This indicates the type of attack for which a helmet's subdual damage reduction applies: Bludgeoning (B), Slashing (S), or Piercing (P).

Called shots: Some DMs allow "called shots," aiming an attack at a specific body part of an opponent. Called shots suffer an attack penalty ranging from -4 to -10, depending upon the difficulty and circumstances involved. The DM is the arbiter in this regard.

Called shot attack rolls must achieve or exceed an opponent's Head AC in order to hit.

Damage to Specific Areas: If a DM allows called shots, then the variant damage to specific area rules should be used as well (*see Core Rulebook II*, chapter 3).

Instant Kills: If instant kills are allowed, then a Helmet's AC bonus stacks with any bonus received from wearing armor or using a shield on the instant kill roll only (see *Core Rulebook II*, chapter 3).

Armor Descriptions

Caps (Leather, Wood, Steel): Simple protective head coverings. Caps are typically rounded and fit close to the head. They are held in place by leather straps that buckle under the chin. Some caps have ornamentation or ridges. Steel caps usually have a padding underneath to help cushion blows.

Great Helmet: Large, heavy head coverings that are basically blocks of hollowed steel with eyeholes. Great helms can inhibit the wearer's range of vision and ability to breathe.

Great Helmet, visored: Great helms with visors built in to help increase the wearer's field of vision and breathing when needed.

Helmet: Rigid protective head coverings. Unlike caps, helmets come in a wide variety of shapes and sizes. All, however, provide more protection than a cap, and often have nose and cheek guards attached to them.

Leather Coat: A long coat made from tough but flexible leather (not hardened leather as with normal leather armor). A leather coat should be considered leather armor for purposes of Getting Into and Out of Armor.

Ring Mail: A suit of leather armor with large metal rings sewn onto it. Ring mails should be considered as chainmail for purposes of Getting Into and Out of Armor.

Wooden or Steel: Wooden and steel shields offer the same basic protection, though they respond differently to special attacks (such as warp wood and heat metal).

Table 3-3: Armor

Armor	Cost	Armor Bonus	Max Dex	Check Penalty	Speed (30ft)	Speed (20ft)	Weight	Spell Failure
Light armor								
Leather Coat	7 gp	+1	+7	0	30 ft.	20 ft.	8 lb.	10%
Ring Mail	25 gp	+3	+5	-1	30 ft.	20 ft.	20 lb.	15%

Helmets

Armor	Cost	Armor Bonus†	Weight	Spell Failure	Subdual Damage Reduction	Type
Cap, Leather	5 sp	+2	1/2 lb.	0%	1	S/P
Cap, Wood	1 gp	+3	1 lb.	0%	2	S/P
Cap, Steel	5 gp	+5	5 lb.	0%	2	S/P
Helmet	9 gp	+7	7 lb.	5%	3	S/P
Great Helm	15 gp	+8	10 lb.	15%	5	B/S/P
Great Helm, visored	20 gp	+8	10 lb.	10%	5	B/S/P

† Helmets AC bonus only applies to the head's armor class.

CHAPTER 4: SPELLS

This chapter presents forty new spells specific to the World of Erde. These first appear in class specific and domain spell lists that supplement those found in the *PH*, including the spell list for the High Elf class. The chapter also includes three new domains and a reference table showing each deity, their domains, and their typical worshipers. The chapter concludes with the spell descriptions in alphabetical order by spell name.

Deities and Domains Table

Supreme Deities	Domains
All-father (dead)	All domains
Corthain	Confession, Fire, Good, Law, Strength, Sun, War
Mordius (dead)	Air, Animal, Earth, Healing, Knowledge, Plant, Protection, Water
Thorax	Chaos, Command, Death, Destruction, Evil, Magic, Trickery

Greater Deities

Demeter	Good, Healing, Earth, Protection
Durendale	Good, Law, Strength, Sun
Narrheit	Chaos, Destruction, Magic, Trickery
Poseidon	Air, Knowledge, Travel, Water
Unklar	Command, Evil, Law, War
Wenafar	Animal, Earth, Plant, Fire

Lesser Deities

Aenouth (Elf)	Air, Knowledge, Magic
Aristobulus	Destruction, Luck, Magic
Athria	Good, Healing, Protection
Augustus	Command, Strength, War
Burasil	Fire, Strength, War
Daladon	Air, Earth, Plant
Dolgan	Earth, Knowledge, War
Falkenjagger	Destruction, Law, Travel
Frafnog	Command, Fire, Magic
Glorianna	Destruction, Law, War
Grotvedt	Earth, Luck, Protection
Imbrisius	Chaos, Death, Evil
Nuluk-kiz-din	Animal, Evil, Magic
Ogoltay	Destruction, Evil, Trickery
St. Luther	Confession, Dream, Good
Tefnut	Earth, Travel, Water
Toth	Death, Knowledge, Magic
Twin Sisters	Air, Earth, Sun
Urnus Gregaria	Knowledge, Magic, Travel
Utumno	Dream, Travel, Trickery
Wulfad	Animal, Command, Sun

Minor Deities

Adrius/Zernius	Strength, Protection
Amenexl	Trickery (only)
Angrim the Black	Chaos, War
Crateus	Chaos, Destruction
Rhealth	Death, Evil

Heroes/Villains

Almuric the Lion	Strength
Kain	War
Mithlon	Good
MorgeldCommand	
SetivaSun	

NEW BARD SPELLS

1ST-LEVEL BARD SPELLS
Map Minion. Minor elemental that maps.

2ND-LEVEL BARD SPELLS
Cloudy Memory. Subject loses 1d4+1 Int for 1 hr/level.
Commanding Presence. Subject gains 1d4+1 Cha for 1 hr/level.
Debilitate. Subject loses 1d4+1 Str for 1 hr./level.
Hypothermia. Target suffers -4 to initiative.
Perfect Recollection. Subject gains 1d4+1 Int for 1 hr/level.
Repulsive Presence. Subject loses 1d4+1 Cha for 1 hr/level.
Worm's Grace. Subject loses 1d4+1 Dex for 1 hr/level.

3RD-LEVEL BARD SPELLS
Illusory Guard Dog. Creates illusion of ferocious dog.
Wall Walk. Walk on walls as if they were level.

4TH-LEVEL BARD SPELLS
Heimdal's Eyes and Ears. Confers enhanced vision and hearing.

NEW CLERIC SPELLS

1ST-LEVEL CLERIC SPELLS
Consecrate Weapon. Confers attack bonus on cleric's weapon.
Evan's Minor Guardianship. Summons animal guardian to watch over sleeping caster.
Hand of Vengeance. Grants attack bonus to natural weaponry attacks.
Map Minion. Minor elemental that maps.
Ordain. Sanctifies an item or place.

2ND-LEVEL CLERIC SPELLS
Commanding Presence. Subject gains 1d4+1 Cha for 1 hr/level.
Debilitate. Subject loses 1d4+1 Str for 1 hr./level.
Divine Wisdom. Subject gains 1d4+1 Wis for 1 hr/level.
Exhaust. Subject loses 1d4+1 Con for 1 hr/level.
Loki's Spasm. Localized earthquake knock down opponents.
Loss of Hope. Subject loses 1d4+1 Wis for 1 hr/level.
Repulsive Presence. Subject loses 1d4+1 Cha for 1 hr/level.

3RD-LEVEL CLERIC SPELLS
Heimdal's Eyes and Ears. Confers enhanced vision and hearing.
Holy Water Rain. Inflicts 2d4 damage to undead.
Tree Walk. Move through trees as if on ground.

4TH-LEVEL CLERIC SPELLS
Cloak of Righteousness. Creates shining rainment, blinding opponents and encouraging allies.
Holy Radiance. Allows multiple Turning checks against same creature.

5TH-LEVEL CLERIC SPELLS
Brothers in Arms. Allies exchange hit points and Str between themselves.
Frost Giant's Fist. One unarmed attack at 29 Str.

7TH-LEVEL CLERIC SPELLS
Counter-magic. Negates enemy's magic attack or AC bonuses.
Vigor of the Paladin. Combat allowed to -6 hit points.

NEW CLERIC DOMAINS AND SPELLS

COMMAND DOMAIN
Deities: Augustus, Frafnog, Morgeld, Thorax, Unklar, Wulfad
Granted Power: Can cast Command once per day.
Command Domain Spells
1 Charm Person.
2 Enthrall.
3 Suggestion.
4 Emotion.
5 Dominate Person.
6 Mass Suggestion.
7 Power Word, Stun.
8 Trap the Soul.
9 Imprisonment.

CONFESSION DOMAIN
Deities: Corthain, St. Luther
Granted Power: Can cast Zone of Truth once per day.
Confession Domain Spells
1 Divine Power.
2 Augury.
3 Prayer.
4 Holy Sword.
5 Atonement.
6 Geas/Quest.
7 Holy Word.
8 Holy Aura.
9 Miracle.

DREAM DOMAIN
Deities: St. Luther, Utumno
Granted Power: Can cast Obscuring Mist once per day.
Dream Domain Spells
1 Evan's Minor Guardianship. Summons animal guardian to watch over sleeping caster.
2 Sleep.
3 Clairaudience/Clairvoyance.
4 Dimensional Anchor.
5 Dream.
6 Legend Lore.
7 Limited Wish.
8 Maze.
9 Timestop.

EARTH DOMAIN
1 Loki's Spasm. Localized earthquake knock down opponents.

GOOD DOMAIN
4 Cloak of Righteousness. Creates shining rainment, blinding opponents and encouraging allies.
4 Holy Radiance. Allows multiple Turning checks against same creature.
6 Vigor of the Paladin. Combat allowed to -6 hit points.

PLANT DOMAIN
1 Shapero's Buckler of Thorns. Creates a shield for use by caster.
3 Tree Walk. Move through trees as if on ground.

LAW DOMAIN
6 Vigor of the Paladin. Combat allowed to -6 hit points.

STRENGTH DOMAIN
5 Brothers in Arms. Allies exchange hit points and Str between themselves.

NEW DRUID SPELLS

1ST-LEVEL DRUID SPELLS

Evan's Minor Guardianship. Summons animal guardian to watch over sleeping caster.
Hand of Vengeance. Grants attack bonus to natural weaponry attacks.
Map Minion. Minor elemental that maps.
Ordain. Sanctifies an item or place.
Shapero's Buckler of Thorns. Creates a shield for use by caster.
Shock Bolt. Electricity deals 1d4 damage/level.

2ND-LEVEL DRUID SPELLS

Commanding Presence. Subject gains 1d4+1 Cha for 1 hr/level.
Divine Wisdom. Subject gains 1d4+1 Wis for 1 hr/level.
Fenrir's Breath. Creates cold mist, 1d6 damage + 1d4/round.
Loki's Spasm. Localized earthquake knock down opponents.
Loss of Hope. Subject loses 1d4+1 Wis for 1 hr/level.
Repulsive Presence. Subject loses 1d4+1 Cha for 1 hr/level.

3RD-LEVEL DRUID SPELLS

Tree Walk. Move through trees as if on ground.

NEW PALADIN SPELLS

1ST-LEVEL PALADIN SPELLS

Ordain. Sanctifies an item or place.

2ND-LEVEL PALADIN SPELLS

Commanding Presence. Subject gains 1d4+1 Cha for 1 hr/level.
Divine Wisdom. Subject gains 1d4+1 Wis for 1 hr/level.
Loss of Hope. Subject loses 1d4+1 Wis for 1 hr/level.
Repulsive Presence. Subject loses 1d4+1 Cha for 1 hr/level.

3RD-LEVEL PALADIN SPELLS

Holy Water Rain. Inflicts 2d4 damage to undead.

4TH-LEVEL PALADIN SPELLS

Brothers in Arms. Allies exchange hit points and Str between themselves.
Cloak of Righteousness. Creates shining rainment, blinding opponents and encouraging allies.
Heimdal's Eyes and Ears. Confers enhanced vision and hearing.

NEW RANGER SPELLS

1ST-LEVEL RANGER SPELLS

Evan's Minor Guardianship. Summons animal guardian to watch over sleeping caster.
Hand of Vengeance. Grants attack bonus to natural weaponry attacks.
Map Minion. Minor elemental that maps.
Shapero's Buckler of Thorns. Creates a shield for use by caster.

2ND-LEVEL RANGER SPELLS

Divine Wisdom. Subject gains 1d4+1 Wis for 1 hr/level.
Loki's Spasm. Localized earthquake knock down opponents.
Loss of Hope. Subject loses 1d4+1 Wis for 1 hr/level.
Repulsive Presence. Subject loses 1d4+1 Cha for 1 hr/level.

3RD-LEVEL RANGER SPELLS

Tree Walk. Move through trees as if on ground.

4TH-LEVEL RANGER SPELLS

Heimdal's Eyes and Ears. Confers enhanced vision and hearing.

NEW SORCERER SPELLS

1ST-LEVEL SORCERER SPELLS

CONJ	**Map Minion.** Minor elemental that maps.
	Rime Weapon. Hoar-frost coats weapon for bonus 1d6 dmg.
EVOC	**Pain Ray.** Subject suffer -2 to all skill checks.
	Shock Bolt. Electricity deals 1d4 damage/level.
TRANS	**Hand of Vengeance.** Grants attack bonus to natural weaponry attacks.

2ND-LEVEL SORCERER SPELLS

ABJUR	**Iron Doesn't Bite.** Immunity to iron weapons.
CONJ	**Fenrir's Breath.** Creates cold mist, 1d6 damage + 1d4/round.
ENCH	**Cloudy Memory.** Subject loses 1d4+1 Int for 1 hr/level.
	Commanding Presence. Subject gains 1d4+1 Cha for 1 hr/level.
	Repulsive Presence. Subject loses 1d4+1 Cha for 1 hr/level.
	Tanin's Blasphemous Taunt. Divine spellcaster suffers -10 to Concentration checks.
EVOC	**Loki's Spasm.** Localized earthquake knock down opponents.
TRANS	**Debilitate.** Subject loses 1d4+1 Str for 1 hr./level.
	Exhaust. Subject loses 1d4+1 Con for 1 hr/level.
	Hypothermia. Target suffers -4 to initiative.
	Perfect Recollection. Subject gains 1d4+1 Int for 1 hr/level.
	Worm's Grace. Walk on walls as if they were level.

3RD-LEVEL SORCERER SPELLS

EVOC	**Voice of Tenek.** Word of unmaking causing 1d6 damage/level to inanimate objects.
TRANS	**Heimdal's Eyes and Ears.** Confers enhanced vision and hearing.
	Illusory Guard Dog. Creates illusion of ferocious dog.
	Tree Walk. Move through trees as if on ground.
	Wall Walk. Subject loses 1d4+1 Dex for 1 hr/level.

4TH-LEVEL SORCERER SPELLS

ABJUR	**Shield of Demeter.** Rebounds ranged weapon against attacker.
	Toughened Bones. Protects from bludgeon attacks.

5TH-LEVEL SORCERER SPELLS

ABJUR	**Counter-magic.** Negates enemy's magic attack or AC bonuses.
TRANS	**Frost Giant's Fist.** One unarmed attack at 29 Str.
	Hollin's Magic Missile Enhancer. Removes maximum cap on magic missile spell.

NEW WIZARD SPELLS

1ST-LEVEL WIZARD SPELLS

CONJ	**Evan's Minor Guardianship.** Summons animal guardian to watch over sleeping caster.
	Map Minion. Minor elemental that maps.
	Rime Weapon. Hoar-frost coats weapon for bonus 1d6 dmg.
EVOC	**Pain Ray.** Subject suffer -2 to all skill checks.
	Shock Bolt. Electricity deals 1d4 damage/level.
TRANS	**Albion's Cantrip Recall.** Recalls a 0-level spell *(wizard only)*.
	Hand of Vengeance. Grants attack bonus to natural weaponry attacks.

2ND-LEVEL WIZARD SPELLS

ABJUR   **Iron Doesn't Bite.** Immunity to iron weapons.
CONJ   **Fenrir's Breath.** Creates cold mist, 1d6 damage + 1d4/round.
ENCH   **Cloudy Memory.** Subject loses 1d4+1 Int for 1 hr/level.
     Commanding Presence. Subject gains 1d4+1 Cha for 1 hr/level.
     Repulsive Presence. Subject loses 1d4+1 Cha for 1 hr/level.
     Tanin's Blasphemous Taunt. Divine spellcaster suffers -10 to Concentration checks.
EVOC   **Loki's Spasm.** Localized earthquake knock down opponents.
TRANS   **Debilitate.** Subject loses 1d4+1 Str for 1 hr./level.
     Exhaust. Subject loses 1d4+1 Con for 1 hr/level.
     Hypothermia. Target suffers -4 to initiative.
     Perfect Recollection. Subject gains 1d4+1 Int for 1 hr/level.
     Worm's Grace. Walk on walls as if they were level.

3RD-LEVEL WIZARD SPELLS

EVOC   **Voice of Tenek.** Word of unmaking causing 1d6 damage/level to inanimate objects.
TRANS   **Heimdal's Eyes and Ears.** Confers enhanced vision and hearing.
     Illusory Guard Dog. Creates illusion of ferocious dog.
     Tree Walk. Move through trees as if on ground.
     Wall Walk. Subject loses 1d4+1 Dex for 1 hr/level.

4TH-LEVEL WIZARD SPELLS

ABJUR   **Shield of Demeter.** Rebounds ranged weapon against attacker.
     Toughened Bones. Protects from bludgeon attacks.
TRANS   **Sustenance.** Can live without food and water for 1 week.

5TH-LEVEL WIZARD SPELLS

ABJUR   **Counter-magic.** Negates enemy's magic attack or AC bonuses.
TRANS   **Frost Giant's Fist.** One unarmed attack at 29 Str.
     Hollin's Magic Missile Enhancer. Removes maximum cap on magic missile spell.

SPELL DESCRIPTIONS

Albion's Cantrip Recall

Recalls a 0-level spell *(wizard only)*. Transmutation
Level: Wiz 1 Components: V, S
Casting Time: 1 action
Range: Personal
Target: You
Duration: Instantaneous

You instantly recall any one 0-level spell that you have cast during the past 24 hours and add it to your prepared spells list. If the recalled cantrip requires material components, you must have them to cast the spell.

Brothers in Arms

Allies exchange hit points and Str between themselves.
Transmutation
Level: Clr 5, Pal 4, Strength 5 Components: V, S, M, DF
Casting Time: 1 full round
Range: Close (25 ft. + 5 ft./2 levels)
Target: One creature per 3 caster levels
Duration: 1 round/level (D)
Saving Throw: Will negates (harmless)
Spell Resistance: Yes (harmless)

Any targets affected by this spell may donate a number of hit points per round equal to the caster's level to other targets of the spell that are in the donator's line of sight. The donator takes those hit points as damage, while the recipient receives the hit points first as healing and then as additional temporary hit points, up to a maximum of the caster's level. One point of Strength may be similarly donated, with the donator taking a temporary loss of Strength and the recipient gaining a +1 Strength enhancement. Strength enhancements are cumulative, up to a maximum bonus of half the caster's level. Hit points are not returned to the donor when the spell expires, but Strength returns to the donor. Temporary hit points are lost when the spell ends.

Material Component: A drop of blood of a hero of the caster's faith that died honorably. The hero must be dead, so using the blood of one who has been resurrected doesn't work.

Cloak of Righteousness

Creates shining rainment, blinding opponents and encouraging allies. Abjuration [Good]
Level: Clr 4, Good 4, Pal 4 Components: V, S, DF
Casting Time: 1 action
Range: Personal
Target: You
Duration: 1 round/level
Saving Throw: Fortitude negates (see text)
Spell Resistance: Yes (see text)

When cast, this spell appears as a shining silver-white cloak and aura surrounding the caster. All of the caster's foes who can see the cloak must make Fortitude saves or be blinded for the duration of the spell. Allies of the caster or those she is defending are automatically affected as if by a Bless spell.

This spell is primarily used by paladins, but clerics who serve good deities are sometimes granted this spell as well.

Cloudy Memory

Subject loses 1d4+1 Int for 1 hr/level. Enchantment (Compulsion) [Mind-affecting]
Level: Brd 2, Sor/Wiz 2 Components: V, S, M
Casting Time: 1 action
Range: 20 ft.
Target: One creature
Duration: 1 hour/level
Saving Throw: Will negates
Spell Resistance: Yes

The subject's memory and ability to focus is weakened. The subject suffers an enhancement penalty to Intelligence of 1d4+1 points, subtracting the usual benefits normally gained by her Intelligence modifier.

The subject may lose spells as the result of having a lower Intelligence score. For each spell less per day that the subject can prepare as a result of a lowered Intelligence modifier, one random spell of the same spell level is lost from the character's prepared spells.

Material Component: A piece of wool from a sheep.

Commanding Presence

Subject gains 1d4+1 Cha for 1 hr/level. Enchantment (Compulsion) [Mind-affecting]
Level: Brd 2, Clr 2, Drd 2, Pal 2, Sor/Wiz 2 Components: V, S, M/DF
Casting Time: 1 action
Range: Touch
Target: Creature touched
Duration: 1 hour/level
Saving Throw: None
Spell Resistance: No

The subject is better able to exert his will and personality. The spell grants an enhancement bonus of 1d4+1 points to Charisma, adding the usual benefits to ability and skill checks, as well as turning attempts, DCs of spells (where applicable), etc.

An increased Charisma score may allow the subject to prepare more spells. When the spell's duration ends, one random spell of the same spell level is lost from preparation, as if it had been cast, for each additional spell prepared by virtue of the recipient having a higher Charisma than normal.

A creature cannot benefit from another casting of this spell for one week after receiving the spell.

Arcane Material Component: A small wooden token carved in the likeness of the sun or a lock of hair from a being with a Charisma score of 18 or higher.

Counter-magic

Negates enemy's magic attack or AC bonuses. Abjuration
Level: Clr 7, Sor/Wiz 5 Components: V, S, M/DF
Casting Time: 1 action
Range: Personal/Touch
Target: You/Creature touched
Duration: 1 round/level
Saving Throw: Will negates (harmless)
Spell Resistance: Yes (harmless)

This spell creates an aura around the recipient which negates certain magical enchantments and special abilities. There are three variations of the spell and the caster must choose one when the spell is cast. The counter-magic only suppresses the opponent's magic. It does not dispel it. Dispel magic can remove a counter-magic aura. Artifacts and divine creatures of demigod or higher status are unaffected.

Defensive: You or the creature touched are surrounded by a blue counter-magic aura which negates magical attack bonuses up to +3 from magic weapons, spells, or supernatural or spell-like abilities while you engage them in melee combat. Thus, an enemy's +3 sword acts as a normal sword against a person protected by a Defensive Counter-magic spell. The spell has no effect on bonuses received from Strength, skills, feats, or natural ability.

Arcane Material Component: A small, palm-sized silver shield (50 gp cost).

Offensive: You or the creature touched are surrounded by a red counter-magic aura which negates an opponent's magical AC bonuses up to +3 from magic armor, items, spells, or supernatural or spell-like abilities while you engage them in melee combat. Thus, an enemy's +3 chainmail only confers protection as normal chainmail. The spell has no effect on bonuses received from Dexterity, skills, feats, or natural abilities.

Arcane Material Component: A small, palm-sized silver gauntlet (50 gp cost).

Reduction Nullification: You or the creature touched are surrounded by an orange counter-magic aura which nullifies any enhancement bonus, up to +3, needed to inflict damage upon a creature with the damage reduction special ability while you engage them in melee combat. For example, you attack a creature with 10/+2 damage reduction while wielding a normal longsword. Typically, the creature would ignore the first 10 points of damage inflicted by you. If the counter-magic is in effect, however, your sword acts as a +2 weapon, thus negating the creature's damage reduction ability.

Arcane Material Component: A small, palm-sized silver weapon (50 gp cost).

Consecrate Weapon

Confers attack bonus on cleric's weapon. Transmutation
Level: Clr 1 Components: V, S, DF
Casting Time: 1 action
Range: Touch
Target: Weapon touched
Duration: 1 minute/level
Saving Throw: None
Spell Resistance: No

The spell bestows an attack bonus to the cleric's non-magical weapon when used against an opponent diametrically opposed to the cleric's alignment. The weapons gains +2 attack bonus for each alignment aspect opposite the cleric casting the spell. The bonuses stack. Example: A lawful good cleric casting the spell on his mace gains a +2 bonus against chaotic creatures, or a +2 bonus versus evil creatures, or a +4 bonus versus chaotic evil creatures. True neutral clerics gain a +2 bonus against all alignments.

Material Component: Cleric's weapon.

Debilitate

Subject loses 1d4+1 Str for 1 hr./level. Transmutation

Level: Brd 2, Clr 2, Sor/Wiz 2 Components: V, S, M/DF
Casting Time: 1 action
Range: 20 ft.
Target: One creature
Duration: 1 hour/level
Saving Throw: Will negates
Spell Resistance: Yes

The subject becomes weaker, suffering an enhancement penalty to Strength of 1d4+1 points. The subject must adjust melee attack rolls, melee damage rolls, and other uses of the Strength modifier accordingly.

Arcane Material Component: A few hairs from a small mammal.

Divine Wisdom

Subject gains 1d4+1 Wis for 1 hr/level. Transmutation

Level: Clr 2, Drd 2, Pal 2, Rgr 2 Components: V, S, DF
Casting Time: 1 action
Range: Touch
Target: Creature touched
Duration: 1 hour/level
Saving Throw: None
Spell Resistance: No

The subject gains a greater sense of inner balance and mental strength as well as a tangible connection to her god. The spell grants an enhancement bonus of 1d4+1 points to Wisdom, adding the usual benefits to ability and skill checks, as well as Will saves.

An increased Wisdom score may allow the subject to prepare more spells. When the spell's duration ends, one random spell of the same spell level is lost from preparation, as if it had been cast, for each additional spell prepared by virtue of the recipient having a higher Wisdom than normal.

A creature cannot benefit from another casting of this spell for one week after receiving the spell.

Evan's Minor Guardianship

Summons animal guardian to watch over sleeping caster. Conjuration (Summoning)

Level: Clr 1, Dream 1, Drd 1, Rgr 1, Wiz 1 Components: V, S, M
Casting Time: 1 round
Range: Personal
Target: You
Duration: 4 hours + 1 hour/level

When the spell is cast, you summon a small animal in the vicinity to watch over you as you sleep. The type of animal summoned will be dependant upon the surrounding environment, although birds, snakes, toads, rabbits, and squirrels are common. It will take up to 10 minutes for the animal to reach your location. You have no control over the animal, and the animal may not reveal itself. Once the animal approaches within 100 ft., you become aware that it is nearby and acting under the spell.

The guardian animal will circle the caster's resting place for the duration of the spell. It will detect any animal or creature, from frogs to giants, that approach within 300 ft. of the caster. If you are asleep when an animal or creature approaches, the guardian will convey a mental image of the spotted intruder into your dreams. If the intruder would normally invoke a fight or flight reaction from you, then you will be awakened by the dreamvision (DM's perogative).

Material Component: A small amount of food that must be eaten by the caster while casting the spell.

Exhaust

Subject loses 1d4+1 Con for 1 hr./level. Transmutation

Level: Clr 2, Sor/Wiz 2 Components: V, S, M/DF
Casting Time: 1 action
Range: 20 ft.
Target: One creature
Duration: 1 hour/level
Saving Throw: Will negates
Spell Resistance: Yes

The subject loses vitality and endurance. The subject suffers an enhancement penalty to Constitution of 1d4+1 points, subtracting the usual benefits normally gained by her Wisdom modifier.

Hit points lost by a temporary decrease in Constitution are not temporary hit points. They return to normal when the spell's duration ends.

Arcane Material Component: A few hairs from a tired animal.

Fenrir's Breath

Creates cold mist, 1d6 damage + 1d4/round. Conjuration (Creation)

Level: Drd 2, Sor/Wiz 2 Components: V, S
Casting Time: 1 action
Range: Medium (100 ft. + 10 ft./level)
Effect: Mist that spreads in a 30-ft. radius, 3 ft. high
Duration: 1 minute/level (D)
Saving Throw: Reflex half
Spell Resistance: Yes

This spell emulates the breath of fenrir, the bestial wolf and child of Loki. The spell creates a knee-high mist of extreme cold around the caster. The ground frosts over. The cold causes no damage to the caster, but it causes 1d6 points of damage to any creature entering the area, and thereafter causes 1d4 points of damage for every round the creature remains in the area.

Moderate winds (11+ mph) blow away the mist in 4 rounds, and strong winds (21+ mph) will do so in 1 round. The spell will not function underwater.

Frost Giant's Fist

One unarmed attack at 29 Str.

Transmutation
Level: Clr 5, Sor/Wiz 5 Components: V, S
Casting Time: 1 action
Range: Personal
Target: You
Duration: 1 rd.
Saving Throw: None
Spell Resistance: Yes (harmless)

You gain a 29 strength for one round, but you may only make a single unarmed attack. The spell grants the usual benefits to melee attack rolls and melee damage rolls only. Attacks with a weapon receive no attack bonuses.

Hand of Vengeance

Grants attack bonus to natural weaponry attacks. Transmutation

Level: Clr 1, Drd 1, Rgr 1, Sor/Wiz 1 Components: V, S, M
Casting Time: 1 action
Range: Touch
Area: One creature
Duration: 1 rd./level
Saving Throw: None
Spell Resistance: Yes (harmless)

Grants an attack bonus to creatures using natural weaponry such as horns, teeth, claws, or hands for unarmed attacks. The attack bonus is dependant on the casters's level: +1 at first level, +2 at fourth level, +3 at seventh level, +4 at eleventh level, and +5 at fourteenth level or higher.

Material Component: Holy water sprinkled over recipient.

Heimdal's Eyes and Ears

Confers enhanced vision and hearing. Transmutation

Level: Brd 4, Clr 3, Pal 4, Rgr 4, Sor/Wiz 3 Components: S
Casting Time: 1 action
Range: Personal
Target: You
Duration: 1 rd./level
Saving Throw: None
Spell Resistance: Yes (harmless)

Heimdal guards the rainbow bridge to Asgard, never sleeping. He can see at night as well as in the day, and can hear the wool growing on the back of sheep.

The recipient of this spell gains enhanced vision and hearing. Normal vision becomes darkvision 360 feet and low-light vision. You also receive a +30 bonus to Spot checks.

Hearing is sharpened to the point that surprising you is almost impossible. You can hear creature's attempting to Move Silently. You may make a Listen check with a +30 bonus against an opposed Move Silently check.

You can also use the enhanced hearing to find invisible creatures, making a Listen check as a free action each round with a result equal to or higher than the invisible creature's Move Silently check indicating that the invisible creature stands revealed. A successful check reveals the invisible creature's exact location.

Hollin's Magic Missile Enhancer

Removes maximum cap on magic missile spell.

Transmutation
Level: Sor/Wiz 5 Components: V, S
Casting Time: 1 minute
Range: Personal
Target: You
Duration: 1 day
Saving Throw: None
Spell Resistance: No

This spell increases the maximum number of magic missiles each Magic Missile spell evokes. The mage casts this spell upon herself, and any Magic Missile spell cast in the following 24 hours will evoke more than 5 missiles if the caster is 11th level or higher. For every two levels of experience past 9th, the mage gains an additional missile (no maximum).

Holy Radiance

Allows multiple Turning checks against same creature.
Abjuration [Good]
Level: Clr 4, Good 4 Components: V, S, DF
Casting Time: 1 full round
Range: Close (25 ft. + 5 ft./2 levels)
Targets: Undead within 60 ft.
Duration: See text (D)
Spell Resistance: No

Holy radiance creates a sphere of holy energy around the caster's holy symbol that repels or destroys undead or other creatures just as if the cleric were Turning. The Turning effect, however, lasts for the duration of the spell. Thus, multiple Turning attempts may be attempted against the same creature. You may cast the spell in two ways.

One, you may cast the spell and suspend a holy symbol in the air 5 ft. off the ground. Once suspended, it cannot be moved. If used in this manner, the duration of the spell is 1 round for every 2 levels of the cleric. As such, the cleric is free to move and attack under the safety of the spell, and the holy symbol may attempt a Turning check once per round.

Two, if the cleric maintains a grasp on her holy symbol and concentrates (unable to cast spells, move, defend, or attack), the spell's duration is 1 round per level and the cleric may attempt a Turning check every round until the spell ends.

Holy Water Rain

Inflicts 2d4 damage to undead.

Conjuration (Creation) [Good]
Level: Clr 3, Pal 3 Components: V, S, M, DF
Casting Time: 1 action
Range: Medium (100 ft. + 10 ft./level)
Area: Cylinder (20-ft. radius, 20 ft. high)
Duration: Instantaneous
Saving Throw: None
Spell Resistance: Yes

This spell causes a brief rain of holy water. Any undead or evil outsiders caught within the area suffer 2d4 points of damage.

Material Component: A vial of holy water.

Hypothermia

Target suffers -4 to initiative. Transmutation
Level: Bard 2, Sor/Wiz 2 Components: V, S
Casting Time: 1 action
Range: Close (25 ft. + 5 ft./2 levels)
Target: One creature
Duration: 1 minute/level
Saving Throw: Fortitude negates
Spell Resistance: Yes

This spell causes a drastic drop of body temperature in a single target creature. The target's actions become slow and sluggish, causing a _4 to initiative.

Illusory Guard Dog

Creates illusion of ferocious dog. Illusion (Figment)
Level: Brd 3, Sor/Wiz 3 Components: V, S, M
Casting Time: 1 action
Range: Long (400 ft. + 40 ft./level)
Effect: Figment guard dog
Duration: 1 day/level (D)
Saving Throw: Will disbelief
Spell Resistance: No

This spell creates an illusion of a dog of a ferocious breed. The illusion acts like a dog, and will move, make sound, smell, and emanate heat. The dog will stay within 10 feet of where the spell is cast, and the caster cannot move the illusion once it is cast. The dog will smell and sense anyone approaching within 200 ft., at which point it will bark until they leave its sensory range. Any touch or successful attack against the dog will dispel the illusion.

Arcane Material Component: A few dog hairs wound in fleece.

Iron Doesn't Bite

Immunity to iron weapons. Abjuration
Level: Sor/Wiz 2 Components: V, S, M
Casting Time: 1 action
Range: Touch
Target: 1 creature
Duration: 1 rd./level
Saving Throw: None or Will negates (harmless)
Spell Resistance: Yes (harmless)

The recipient gains resistance to weapons made of iron, gaining damage reduction 10/+1 each time it takes damage from an iron weapon. The recipient ignores the first 10 points of damage each time it takes damage from an iron weapon. A +1 weapon bypasses the damage reduction. The damage reduction increases with the caster's level to 10/+2 at 5th, 10/+3 at 10th, 10/+4 at 15th, and 10/+5 at 20th.

Material Component: Water from a smithy's shop.

Loki's Spasm

Localized earthquake knock down opponents. Evocation
Level: Clr 2, Drd 2, Earth 1, Rgr 2, Sor/Wiz 2 Components: V, S
Casting Time: 1 action
Range: Close (25 ft. + 5 ft./2 levels)
Area: 5 ft./level radius burst
Duration: 1 round
Saving Throw: See text
Spell Resistance: No

Odin imprisoned Loki at the center of the earth and placed the Midgard Serpent over him, its venom dripping. Loki's wife, Signe, stays at his side catching the poison in a cup. When the cup fills, she empties it. When she does so, a single drop strikes Loki's exposed skin before Signe can once again catch the venom. Loki's pain causes a spasm powerful enough to shake the world.

When cast, this spell creates a very localized and violent upheaval of the earth that knocks any creature medium or smaller creature within the area of effect from his feet, during which time they cannot move or attack. Spellcasters must make Concentration checks (DC 15 + spell level) or lose any spell they were trying to cast. The upheaval will affect terrain, but without any significant damage or long-term effect.

Loss of Hope

Subject loses 1d4+1 Wis for 1 hr/level. Enchantment (Compulsion) [Mind-affecting]
Level: Clr 2, Drd 2, Pal 2, Rgr 2 Components: V, S, DF
Casting Time: 1 action
Range: 20 ft.
Target: One creature
Duration: 1 hour/level
Saving Throw: Will negates
Spell Resistance: Yes

The subject's mental strength becomes weaker, even causing a loss of connection with their deity. The subject suffers an enhancement penalty to Wisdom of 1d4+1 points, subtracting the usual benefits normally gained by her Wisdom modifier.

The subject may lose spells as the result of having a lower Wisdom score. For each spell less per day that the subject can prepare as a result of a lowered Wisdom modifier, one random spell of the same spell level is lost from the character's prepared spells.

Map Minion

Minor elemental that maps. Conjuration (Summoning)
Level: Brd 1, Clr 1, Drd 1, Rgr 1, Sor/Wiz 1 Components: V, S, M
Casting Time: 1 full round
Range: Close (25 ft. + 5 ft./2 levels)
Effect: One summoned minion
Duration: 1 hour/level (D)
Saving Throw: None
Spell Resistance: No

The spell summons a minor air elemental that will draw a map of the area in which the caster is traveling. The minion is invisible. The minion must be supplied tools to inscribe the map, and the map that it draws will be accurate.

Material Component: Drawing tools such as quills, ink, and parchment.

Ordain

Sanctifies an item or place. Transmutation
Level: Clr 1, Drd 1, Pal 1 Components: V, S, M, DF
Casting Time: 1 full round
Range: Close (25 ft. + 5 ft./2 levels)

Area: Object or Spread (one place)
Duration: Permanent
Saving Throw: None
Spell Resistance: No

This spell is used to sanctify an item or place, investing it with ministerial or sacerdotal functions. Any item *ordained* gains a +2 on all saving throws (A person wearing an *ordained* item does not get the saving throw bonus, nor can these saving throws be 'stacked'). The spell is used for other priestly purposes as well, such as making holy water, consecrating a grave site or laying the dead to rest.

Material Component: A holy item of some sort, such as sacred earth or holy water.

Pain Ray

Subject suffer -2 to all skill checks. Evocation
Level: Sor/Wiz 1 Components: V, S
Casting Time: 1 action
Range: Close (25 ft. + 5 ft./2 levels)
Target: One creature
Duration: 1 round/level
Saving Throw: Fortitude negates
Spell Resistance: Yes

A yellow ray emanates from the caster's pointed finger to strike one creature. A targeted creature that fails a Fortitude saving throw suffers intense pains. While affected, the target suffers -2 to all skill checks.

Perfect Recollection

Subject gains 1d4+1 Int for 1 hr/level. Transmutation
Level: Brd 2, Sor/Wiz 2 Components: V, S, M
Casting Time: 1 action
Range: Touch
Target: Creature touched
Duration: 1 hour/level
Saving Throw: None
Spell Resistance: No

The subject is better able to recall distant memories and focus on mentally challenging tasks. The spell grants an enhancement bonus of 1d4+1 points to Intelligence, adding the usual benefits to ability and skill checks.

An increased Intelligence score may allow the subject to prepare more spells. When the spell's duration ends, one random spell of the same spell level is lost from preparation, as if it had been cast, for each additional spell prepared by virtue of the recipient having a higher Intelligence than normal.

A creature cannot benefit from another casting of this spell for one week after receiving the spell.

Material Component: A few feathers from an owl or a small figurine in the shape of an owl.

Repulsive Presence

Subject loses 1d4+1 Cha for 1 hr/level. Enchantment (Compulsion) [Mind-affecting]
Level: Brd 2, Clr 2, Drd 2, Pal 2, Rgr 2, Sor/Wiz 2 Components: V, S, M/DF
Casting Time: 1 action
Range: 20 ft.
Target: One creature
Duration: 1 hour/level
Saving Throw: Will negates
Spell Resistance: Yes

The subject's personality, persuasiveness, attractiveness, and leadership ability becomes weaker. The subject suffers an enhancement penalty to Charisma of 1d4+1 points, subtracting the usual benefits normally gained by her Charisma modifier.

The subject may lose spells as the result of having a lower Charisma score. For each spell less per day that the subject can prepare as a result of a lowered Charisma modifier, one random spell of the same spell level is lost from the character's prepared spells.

Arcane Material Component: A small token carved in the likeness of a goblin or a few hairs from a being with a Charisma score of 5 or lower.

Rime Weapon

Hoar-frost coats weapon for bonus 1d6 damage. Conjuration (Creation) [Cold]
Level: Sor/Wiz 1 Components: V, S, M
Casting Time: 1 action
Range: Close (25 ft. + 5 ft./2 levels)
Target: One weapon
Duration: 1 rd./level
Saving Throw: None
Spell Resistance: No

The spell coats a weapon in a layer of hoar_frost. A successful attack with the covered weapons results in an extra 1d6 points of damage.

Shapero's Buckler of Thorns

Creates a shield for use by caster. Transmutation

Level: Drd 1, Plant 1, Rgr 1 Components: V, S, M

Casting Time: 1 action

Range: Personal

Effect: Creates one shield

Duration: 1 minute/level

Saving Throw: None

Spell Resistance: No

Upon uttering the spell, the caster's arm is woven about with a thick shield made from coiling bramble vines. The resulting shield type is detailed in the chart below. The shield created always weighs as a buckler (5 lbs.). The caster may always choose a shield type of a level lower than her caster level.

Caster's Level	Shield Type
1st	Spiked Buckler
3rd	Spiked Small Wooden Shield
5th	Spiked Large Wooden Shield
7th	Spiked Tower Wooden Shield
9th	Any preceding with spikes coated in paralysis is poison (Fortitude DC 18, paralysis last 2d6 minutes).
11th	Any preceding with additional +1 enchantment bonus to Armor Class and spikes with +1 to attack rolls
13th	Any preceding with spikes coated in venom (Fortitude DC 24; 1d6 Str initial damage; 2d6 Con secondary damage)
15th or higer	Any preceding with additional +3 enchantment bonus to Armor Class and spikes with +3 to attack rolls

Material Component: Length of bramble vine twisted in a loop that is worn as a bracelet prior to casting.

Shield of Demeter

Rebounds ranged weapon against attacker.

Abjuration [Force]

Level: Sor/Wiz 4 Components: V, S

Casting Time: 1 action

Range: Personal

Target: You

Duration: 1 round/level

The spell creates an shimmering green cone around you. Any ranged weapon thrown at you will rebound towards the attacker. The attacker's to hit roll is used to determine if the attacker is struck by his own weapon.

Shock Bolt

Electricity deals 1d4 damage/level. Evocation [Lightning]

Level: Drd 1, Sor/Wiz 1 Components: V, S

Casting Time: 1 action

Range: Close (25 ft. + 5 ft./2 levels)

Target: 1 creature

Duration: Instantaneous

Saving Throw: Reflex half

Spell Resistance: Yes

You channel energy into a bolt of electricity and cast from your hands at a single target. The shock bolt deals 1d4 points per caster level (maximum 10d4). It does not set fire to combustibles or damage objects in its path.

Sustenance

Can live without food and water for 1 week. Transmutation

Level: Wiz 4 Components: V, S, M, F

Casting Time: 1 hour

Range: Touch

Area: Object (focusing item)

Duration: 1 week or until discharged

Saving Throw: None

Spell Resistance: No

The Sustenance spell is a common, well known spell often employed during times of war or covert action. It is especially coveted by adventurers.

The caster focuses and casts the spell upon an item of her choice. Any person that carries that item with them at all times thereafter will have the ability to live without food and water. The magic lasts for one week or until food or drink touches or passes the gem carrier's lips. Even too much salivation, or perhaps rain, will break the spell.

Material Component: A good meal (5 sp).

Tanin's Blasphemous Taunt

Divine spellcaster suffers -10 to Concentration checks. Enchantment

Level: Sor/Wiz 2 Components: V

Casting Time: 1 action

Range: Close (25 ft. + 5 ft./2 levels)

Target: One divine spellcaster

Duration: 1 round/level

Saving Throw: Will negates

Spell Resistance: Yes

You enrage a divine spellcaster by blaspheming their deity. The enraged divine spellcaster suffers a -10 to concentration checks if they fail a Will saving throw.

Toughened Bones

Protects from bludgeon attacks. Abjuration

Level: Sor/Wiz 4 Components: V, S, M

Casting Time: 1 action

Range: Touch

Target: Creature touched

Duration: 10 minutes/level or until discharged

Saving Throw: Will negates (harmless)

Spell Resistance: Yes (harmless)

This spell increases the durability of bones, giving the warded creature resistance to bludgeon attacks. While in effect, all bludgeoning blows which could break bones are deflected. Also, the subject gains damage reduction 10/+5 versus bludgeon attacks, ignoring the first 10 points of damage each time it is struck by a bludgeoning weapon unless the weapon has a +5 enchantment bonus. Once 10 points of damage per caster level have been prevented (maximum of 150 points), the spell is discharged.

Material Component: A bone from an ogre, gnoll, or giant wrapped in platinum wire (cost 50 gp).

Tree Walk

Move through trees as if on ground.
Transmutation
Level: Clr 3, Drd 2, Plant 3, Rgr 3, Sor/Wiz 3 Components: V, S
Casting Time: 1 action
Range: Touch
Target: Caster + 1 touched creature/level
Duration: 10 minutes/level
Saving Throw: Will negates (harmless)
Spell Resistance: Yes (harmless)

Tree Walk allows the caster or recipient to move freely along branches of trees as if moving on normal ground. Thin branches may bend and twigs will break, but otherwise, movement is the same as travel by foot on solid ground. Consider the recipients weight as far as effect on branches to be equivalent to a squirrel. The spell only allows movement along trees and vines, not roof tops or tightropes.

Vigor of the Paladin

Combat allowed to -6 hit points. Enchantment (Compulsion) [Mind-affecting]
Level: Clr 7, Good 6, Law 6 Components: V, DF
Casting Time: 1 action
Range: Touch
Target: One touched creature
Duration: 1 minute/level
Saving Throw: Will negates (harmless)
Spell Resistance: Yes (harmless)

The spell's subject is overcome with a feeling of invincibility and vigor for combat. The subject's will becomes so strong that he can continue to fight until reaching -10 hit points, and will not die unless he reaches -20 hit points. Upon reaching -10 hit points, the subject becomes disabled. At -11 or below, the subject falls unconscious. If -20 hit points is reached, the subject dies.

Once the spell's duration expires, the recipient must rest for one full day unless a healing 6th level or higher healing spell is cast upon them.

Voice of Tenek

Word of unmaking causing 1d6 damage/level to inanimate objects. Evocation [Death]
Level: Sor/Wiz 3 Components: V, S
Casting Time: 1 action
Range: Close (25 ft. + 5 ft./2 levels)
Area: One object in a 20 ft. square area
Duration: Instantaneous
Saving Throw: See text
Spell Resistance: Yes

Uttered in a barely audible whisper, this spell focuses a word of unmaking. It deals 1d6 points of damage per caster level to one inanimate object in the area (maximum 10d6). Unattended objects receive no saving throw. Attended objects receive a Fortitude saving throw as if the character were making the saving throw. Magic items receive Fortitude saving throw with a bonus equal to 2 + one-half its caster level. Attended magic items either make a saving throw as their owner or on their own.

Wall Walk

Walk on walls as if they were level. Transmutation
Level: Brd 3, Sor/Wiz 3 Components: V, S, M
Casting Time: 1 action
Range: One touched creature/level
Target: One creature
Duration: 1 hour/level
Saving Throw: Will negates
Spell Resistance: Yes

The spell allows the caster or recipient to walk on walls as if they were level. The recipient can walk, run, charge, or otherwise move across the surface as if it were normal ground.

Worm's Grace

Subject loses 1d4+1 Dex for 1 hr/level. Transmutation
Level: Brd 2, Sor/Wiz 2 Components: V, S, M
Casting Time: 1 action
Range: 20 ft.
Target: One creature
Duration: 1 hour/level
Saving Throw: Will negates
Spell Resistance: Yes

The subject becomes clumsy and less coordinated. The subject suffers an enhancement penalty to Dexterity of 1d4+1 points, subtracting the usual benefits normally gained by her Dexterity modifier.
Material Component: A live worm.

The DM's Handbook

Herein are listed items specific to the World of Erde, from the powerful to the Mundane. The Book of Lies - Cloth of Hylde - Fonts of Narrheit - Gorgorthorium - The Holy Flame & Others Besides. Too, there are Monsters, eldritch creatures that stalk the landscape of Erde.

At last, the task finished he held up his greatest creation and was smitten with love for it and desired it in his heart for it was made of the stuff of the earth and therefore separate from the horned god's black soul. And he called it the Krummelvole, the Crown of Sorrow, or as the Hill Dwarves would say, the Crown of Tears.

from the "Making of the Crown, Dolgan's Tale"

CHAPTER 5: MAGIC ITEMS

Erde. A world forged under a thousand years of ice. A world of epic adventure and high fantasy. A world filled with promise of battle and glory, and of lost treasure and power arcane.

Epic adventure is incomplete without weapons of high sorcery, items of wonder and power, and potions of marvelous effect. Since the dawn of fantastic storytelling, the battles between hero and villain have, in some way, employed magic items to tell a tale.

Below appear magic items specific to the World of Erde, from the powerful to the mundane. Players exploring the World of Erde will of course covet and seek out magic items. As a DM, you have the duty to ensure that the magic items that enter the campaign do not imbalance game play or the level of power within the party. The following descriptors of each magic item will help you do so. More information regarding the handling of magic items within a campaign, their use under the rules, their creation, and more can be found in Chapter 8 of the *DMG*.

Name (type): The item's name and type (Armor, Artifact, Cursed, Potion, Ring, Rod, Scroll, Staff, Wand, Weapon, Wondrous, or, Special Material).

History: The history of the item as related to The World of Erde.

Description: The physical description of the item.

Powers: The affects on game play bestowed by the item.

Caster Level: The power of the item, similar to a spell's caster's level. The caster level determines the item's saving throw bonus, as well as range or other level-dependent aspects of the powers of the item (if variable). It also determines the level that must be contended with should the item come under the effect of a dispel magic spell or similar situation.

Prerequisites: The requirements that must be met in order to create the item.

Cost to Create: The cost in gp and XP to create the item.

Market Price: The going price in gp to buy the item. Market price for unique items includes inflation for rarity and demand, but the DM may raise the market price by 2d10 x 1000 gp more to account for increased demand.

Damage: The damage caused by the item.

Weight: The weight of the magic item in U.S. pounds. An entry of "—" indicates that an item has no weight worth noting (for purposes of determining how much of a load a character can carry).

Treasure Classes: Treasure Classes indicate the power level, uniqueness, and origins of the magic item. The eight treasure classes are Major Artifact, Minor Artifact, Unique, Arcane, Divine, Heroic, Tragic, Celestial, Infernal, Lawful, Neutral, and Chaotic. Magic items are often categorized by more than one treasure class.

Major Artifact: Unique items of extreme power, some of which are intelligent entities from other times or planes. Most are incapable of explanation or understanding by any, including most deities. Major artifacts are, for the most part, not intended for possession by player characters. An item's description may note otherwise. DMs should use major artifacts to drive epic storylines and for background information.

Minor Artifact: Unique items of extreme power that DMs might allow player characters to possess.

Unique: A one of a kind item that cannot be duplicated by characters or mortals.

Arcane: Items of arcane origin are typically enchanted or created by mortals.

Divine: Items of divine origin become magical via the workings of the deities or other forces of the universe.

Heroic: Items of heroic origin become magical through the noble or idealistic actions of their possessors.

Tragic: Items of tragic origin become magical via a tragic occurrence, typically tied in some way to their possessors.

Celestial: Items of celestial origin become magical via the workings of an entity residing on good aligned planes connected to a prime plane.

Infernal: Items of infernal origin become magical via the workings of an entity residing on evil aligned planes connected to a prime plane.

Lawful, Neutral, or Chaotic: Items of these origins become magical via the workings of an entity residing on a plane that is concerned with neither good or evil.

Treasure Level: DMs can use this indicator if unsure as to whether to include a magic item as treasure in an adventure. A magic item with a higher level than the character who possesses it is potentially unbalancing to game play.

Alignment: The alignment of the item, if any.

Magic Item Descriptions

Arrows of Weakening (Weapon)

History: These otherwise normal appearing arrows contain powerful debilitating magic. The necromancers of the Twilight Elves crafted these arrows to combat the Dwarven army during the Three-towers Campaign.

Description: Slightly longer than typical arrows, the shafts of the arrows are very tensile and are crowned by steel tips.

Powers: These arrows are +2 weapons. Upon a successful hit, an arrow releases a black flash of magic and inflicts a sorcerous strike requiring the wounded victim to make a Will Saving Throw (DC 15). A successful saving indicates normal arrow damage. Failure results in damage and causes the loss of 1 point of Str per round for 1d4+1 rounds. In addition, upon the round following the last round of Str loss, the victim must make a Fortitude Saving Throw (DC 15) or lose consciousness for 1d4 minutes. Lost Str points cannot be healed magically. They must be recuperated through normal rest, with each full day of rest restoring 1 point of Str.

Caster Level: 5th

Prerequisites: Craft Magic Arms and Armor, *Bull's Strength*, *Sleep*

Market Price: 8,350

Damage: –

Weight: 3 lb. (20 arrows)

Treasure Class: Arcane

Treasure Level: 4th

Blade of Rhealth (Weapon)

History: In the Age of Heroes, Malhavok was reputed to be the greatest thief in all the west. His travels brought him into contact with Luther, the Count of Pendegrantz, and eventually, into battle with that paladin. When Malhavok's treason against Pendegrantz was discovered, he was captured and subjected to the law of the land. Luther's enmity of Malhovak was so strong that he had the thief's body ground into dust and cast to the winds. Malhavok's spirit, however, lived on.

The dark deity Rhealth captured Malhavok's raging, avenging spirit and imprisoned it in the sword he carried in life. Malhavok had recovered the enchanted blade from a ruined temple of Rhealth in his early days. The blade is now forever cursed.

Description: A finely worked short sword that glows with a yellowish light when commanded (10 ft. radius).

Powers: The sword had a +3 enhancement bonus. The sword grants a +2 modifier to Balance, Climb, Decipher Script, Disable Device, Escape Artist, Hide, Jump, Move Silently, Open Lock, Pick Pocket, Read Lips, Search, Spot, and Tumble skill checks. When drawn, the wielder gains +4 to AC against all missile and ranged weapon attacks. The blade grants fire resistance 20. Once per week the wielder can summon the spirit of Malhovak and command it to fight for him for up to 15 rounds.

Malhavok, Wraith: CR 5; Med-Size Undead; HD 5d12; hp 32 hp; Init +7 (+3 Dex, +4 Imp. Init.); Spd 30 ft., fly 60 ft. (good); AC 15 (+3 Dex, +2 deflection); +5 melee (incorporeal touch 1d4 and 1d6 permanent Con drain); SA Con drain, create spawn; SQ undead, incorporeal, +2 turn resistance, unnatural aura, daylight powerlessness; Fort +1, Ref +4, Will +6; Str -, Dex 16, Con -, Int 14, Wis 14, Cha 15; AL LE; Skills: Hide +11, Intimidate +10, Intuit Direction +6, Listen +12, Search +10, Sense Motive +8, Spot +12; Feats: Alertness, Blind-Fight, Combat Reflexes, Improved Initiative.

Caster Level: 13th
Market Price: 98,000
Damage: 1d6; 19-20/x2 crit.
Weight: 3 lb.
Treasure Class: Tragic/Unique
Treasure Level: 9th
Alignment: Lawful Evil

Bloodline Weapon

History: A weapon passed from father or mother to a son or daughter. These weapons are typically not enchanted or magical in any way, but they become imbued with power when the original wielder retires or dies a heroic death if the wielder had won many battles of importance with the weapon. The magical weapons of orcs and other humanoid bands often originate in this way.

Description: Any common, non-magical sword or other weapon.

Powers: The sheer force of will of the original wielder infects the weapon over time of battle. When the sword passes on to a succeeding generation, the sword makes a Saving Throw (DC 18,

no modifiers). A successful save turns the weapon into a magical +1 weapon. Only the original bloodline gain the benefits of the powers of the weapon. Each time the weapon is passed to the next or a succeeding generation, it again saves to determine if it gains another plus (stacks). Weapons passed through many generations may become intelligent or develop other special abilities as detailed in the DMG.

Caster Level: Dependant upon powers. *See DMG, chapter 8.*
Market Price: Dependant upon powers. *See DMG, chapter 8.*
Damage: as per Weapon type
Weight: as per Weapon type
Treasure Class: Heroic or Tragic
Treasure Level: 1st

Book of Lies, The (Artifact)

History: The origin of the Book of Lies is unknown, although legend holds that the book came into existence around the time that Thorax slew his sister, Mordius.

Description: This pages of this dark tome are made from a variety of papers and skins, each bearing inks of many colors and stains. The book's cover is composed of some unknown metal with a greenish sheen, covered in gems and gold formed in faces of mockery.

Powers: This book contains every untruth ever uttered upon the planes by any being, be they mortal or god. To access the book, the reader need simply open it and announce the being or creature whose lies they wish to view.

Weight: 15 lb.

Treasure Class: Major Artifact

Treasure Level: Characters should never be allowed unfettered access to this book. Such use will often turn to abuse, and interrupt the flow of the adventure. The book is more properly used as a hook or plot device to drive the storyline.

Alignment: Radiates all alignments.

Charles's Bane (Weapon)

History: Dolgan King forged this sword for Lord Charles's ill fated duel with Kain the Godless. The blade was such a perfect expression of the sword_maker's art that Wenafar the Faerie Queen sent a benevolent faerie to live within the sword to aid its wielder.

But Charles's pride kept him from wearing a protective neckguard (see *Neckguard of Charles the Confessor*), and he was beheaded by Kain's vorpal blade. Charles's body fell upon his sword, and his blood stained the blade and the faerie within. The faerie's anguish and rage at Charles's defeat twisted him into a dark faerie who craves blood and souls. Kain took the sword of his defeated enemy. None know where the blade lies today.

Description: This wide claymore sports a well_balanced thin blade of Iergild Steel. A gold cross-guard and platinum wrapped handle highlight its look. The blade of the sword is now stained a dull red color.

Dwarves have a chance to recognize the blade upon sight (Wisdom check at DC 11). A lawful good character who grips the blade will know its story, seeing it her mind's eye in a moment in time.

Powers: This +3 sword is a *wounding* weapon. Its alignment is chaotic evil. As a weapon of *wounding*, this sword deals damage such that a wound it inflicts bleeds for 1 point of damage per round thereafter in addition to the normal damage the weapon deals. Multiple wounds from the weapon result in cumulative bleeding loss (two wounds for 2 points of damage per round, and so on). The bleeding can only be stopped by a successful Heal check (DC 15) or the application of any cure spell or other healing spell (heal, healing circle, and so on).

If the faerie within the sword is restored, the sword will become a *Flaming* sword.

Role-playing Effect: The dark faerie in the sword constantly whispers to the wielder, urging him to commit evil deeds with the sword.

Restoring the Faerie: The tormented faerie can be restored to his benevolent self by redeeming the frustrated quest of the sword's former wielder. Successfully facing the knight's slayer in combat (surviving without being killed) will lift the blood lust from the faerie, allowing it to return to the realm of the fey. Defeating a major creature of evil such as a dragon or demon may also lift the curse. The DM is encouraged to design a quest for a character who bears the cursed blade if they seek to lift the curse.

Caster Level: 11th
Market Price: 50,000
Damage: 2d6; 19-20/x2 crit.
Weight: 15 lb.
Treasure Class: Arcane/Tragic/Unique
Treasure Level: 7th
Alignment: Chaotic Evil

Cloth of Hylde (Major Wondrous)

History: When Fyorgyn of Eisenheim fell to the flames of a ancient Worm, her companions fled the field with her body and her two war hammers (see *Harg & Hylde*). One hammer, Hylde, was wrapped in a wool cloth. When Fyorgyn returned from Asgard, she used the cloth to rub away blood and ash left by the dragon. In time, she lost the cloth, not knowing that it had been transformed by the powers of dragons and heroes.

Description: The cloth is a simple wool square, 2 ft by 2 ft, grey-blue in color.

Powers: The cloth possesses the power to heal wounds three times per day. When applied to an open wound for 2 rounds, it burns infection and casts *Cure Moderate Wounds*, healing 2d8+8 points of damage. The cloth also had the ability to restore lost limbs; if applied to such an area for 10 days, the limb will regenerate.

Caster Level: 13th
Market Price: 85,000
Weight: –
Treasure Class: Tragic/Unique
Treasure Level: 6th

Discerpo, The Emperor's Sword (Artifact)

History: The Emperor's Sword was forged in the days between discovery of the Paths of Umbra and the summoning of the Dark. Suspecting that the Dark may be as great a threat to him as an ally, Sebastian Oliver I, created this sword as a safeguard.

Description: This long sword, 3 ft. 4 in. in length, is perfectly weighted. A simple cross-guard fashioned from Iergild Gold (the rarest of all substances) frames its blade of adamantine steel. It glistens with an emerald tint.

Powers: The sword acts as a +5 longsword of *dancing*, but it is also intelligent and possesses many other abilities. The sword speaks the common tongue. It can Read Magic, including any ancient script

in the old magical tongue. The sword can communicate telepathically, but rarely does so. The sword is neutral in alignment. Its wielder can *Detect Magic* and see invisible at will. Th sword glows with an orangish light as a torch (20 foot radius).

As a *dancing* sword, the weapon can be loosed (requiring a standard action) to attack on its own. It fights for 4 rounds using the base attack bonus of the one who loosed it and then drops. It never leaves the side of the one who loosed it (never straying more than 5 feet) and fights on even if that creature falls. The wielder who loosed it can grasp it while it is attacking on its own as a free action, but when so retrieved it can't dance again for 4 rounds.

Combating the Dark: When used to fight the dark god or his servants, the sword acts as a bane sword and can also paralyze them upon a successful hit. The paralyzation power is commanded by the wielder of the sword and can be used once per day. The paralyzation automatically succeeds and lasts for 1 round. Once per week the wielder of the sword may cast a special Imprisonment spell upon the dark god alone which will cast him into the Void.

Ego: 23; *Int* 17, *Wis* 15, *Cha* 17.
Caster Level: 30th
Market Price: 350,000
Damage: 1d8; 19-20/x3 crit.
Weight: 4 lb.
Treasure Class: Arcane/Minor Artifact
Treasure Level: 15th
Alignment: Chaotic Good

Durendale, The Avenging Sword (Artifact)

History: The physical form that the deity takes before mortals. Durendale was fashioned by Corthain and cast into Erde; it is the god of law, order, goodness, and the sun, and it seeks to deal justice across the lands (reference Cosmology, p. 56). The powers below are the only powers a mortal may access when wielding the sword.

Description: This holy longsword is made of Iergild Gold wrapped or covered in places with Iergild Silver. The blade has a silver sheen to it, and is a full two inches in width. The angled cross-guards are gold, and resting below them is golden hilt and pommel wrapped in silver wire. The pommel bears the symbol of a burning flame. Despite its simplicity of design, the sword radiates an aura of awe and power.

Who can wield: Only lawful good beings may wield this sword to its full affect. Even so, the sword will not allow itself to be used by all lawful good persons. In the past, the sword has been wielded by kings, mighty paladins, and great knights, but has also been seen in the hands of people of lower standing who were true of heart or showed great promise.

Other good and neutral beings may pick up the sword, but they do not gain the ability to use all of its powers.

If an evil being attempts to wield the sword, it bestows three negative levels on the evil wielder. The negative levels remain as long as the weapon is in hand or possessed by the bearer. The sword will remove itself from the possession of any evil being that holds it for longer than 1 round by teleporting to a safe place (or the nearest lawful good being worthy of wielding it). One negative level becomes permanent one day later if the evil wielder fails a Fortitude save (DC 23). The other two levels lost return in 1d20 rounds. While held, the level loss cannot be overcome in any way (including restoration spells).

Powers: This +5 sword is intelligent and *holy*. Against evil beings, it deals a bonus +2d6 points of damage. The wielder can cause the blade to glow with a whitish-blue light up to twice the intensity of a torch (40 foot radius) at will.

The following powers are gained only if the sword is wielded by a paladin. The sword will grant a spell resistance of 20, and will *Dispel Magic* in a 5 foot radius at the class level of the paladin (usable every other round, and only the area dispel is possible, not the targeted dispel or counter spell versions of dispel magic). The sword speaks four languages (see above), and can *Read Magic*. The sword's wielder can also *Detect Magic*, *Detect Traps*, see invisible, *Detect Illusion*, and *Detect Alignment* at will. The blade can communicate by speech or telepathy. Once per day, the wielder of the sword may *Teleport*.

Ego: 34; *Int* 14, *Wis* 18, *Cha* 25.

Combating Chaos: Against chaotic evil beings, the sword inflicts a bonus +10 points of damage.

Caster Level: 40th

Damage: 1d8; 19-20/x3 crit.

Weight: 4 lb.

Treasure Class: Major Artifact, but an experienced DM might allow a player character to come into its possession.

Alignment: Lawful Good

Eye of Thorax (Artifact)

History: Thorax's duel with Trilikorr, the blue dragon, led him to great loss. He sought to drag the beast to the underworld, and he wrestled with her. She tore from his grasp and ripped his left eye from its socket. She took the eye to the heights of the world, and there she swallowed it. It burned within her and solidified, until she vomited it forth. The resultant jeweled eye has ever been sought for by man, dwarf and beast, for legend holds it is filled with wondrous power.

The legends hold true. Upon utterance of the command spell, "Unto death of Corthain I do summon thee," the eye will come alive with power.

Description: An eye-shaped, multifaceted ruby.

Powers: This eye must be placed in an empty eye socket. Once placed, the eye attaches itself and cannot be removed until the death of the bearer. Upon utterance of the command spell, the eye comes alive, granting its host darkvision and low-light vision. The host can *Detect Alignment* at will. Once per week, the host can command the eye to cast a death ray (*Finger of Death*), however, a failed Fortitude saving throw against DC 20 results in the eye casting the death ray upon the host instead.

Role-playing effect: The possessor becomes irritable and quick to temper.

Caster Level: 15th

Market Price: 135,000

Weight: —

Treasure Class: Divine/Minor Artifact

Treasure Level: 10th

Alignment: Chaotic

Fonts of Narrheit (Major Artifacts)

History: During the Winter Dark, Unklar bound Narrheit, the god of chaos, in a great tower in the wilderness of Erde. Narrheit did not fight his imprisonment for he knew that he was no match for the God of Eternal Darkness. With him was bound Imbrisius, his consort.

For a thousand years Narrheit served as entertainment for the lords of Unklar. The lords of Unklar's realm frequently came to the tower of Narrheit to overcome the challenges of unmitigated chaos. Countless anti_heroes of the Dark fell, but some escaped into the world beyond the Tower of Delight and with each went a gift of Narrheit, Knight of Chaos. Each bore with him or her a Font, made by the hands of Narrheit, a reward of sorts.

Through the Fonts, Narrheit leaked into the world the power of chaos, for within their making he placed bits of himself and so gained certain freedoms in the world of men. Later, after Unklar's fall, he came to Erde and set about gathering these cups in order to be whole again. The 13 grails possess power with a price.

Description and Powers: Each is separately described below. The DM is encouraged to play up the power of the fonts and their effect upon those that possess them. Most importantly, every font creates chaos wherever it is carried. When reference is made to the font's possessor, the font need not be on the person's body at all times, although they will desire to stay close to the font or look upon it at least once per week.

Each font will fill with liquid upon command of its possessor. The type of liquid is noted parenthetically after the font's name, along with any special notes about the liquid.

Reference should also be made to the *Truncheons of Narrheit*, detailed below. Some fonts will be found with their companion *Truncheon*.

Font of Hope and Loss (warm mead). This wooden grail is plain in appearance, and has no handles. Despite the losses that come with possession of the grail, the possessor will be struck with an enduring optimism that "better days are coming soon." A number of losses will strike any person possessing this font for more than one month, a period in which the possessor will feel ecstatic and as if they are invincible.

First, they will lose all wealth and real property. This effect, however, is not immediate. Over a period of a few months, money (including all gems, jewelry, treasure, and art objects) will either become lost, stolen, or taxed. All land owned will be struck by blight, natural disaster, taxation, ruin, war or attack by monsters, or overtaken by enemies.

Second, after three months time, the possessor will become very sick or diseased. They will recover in one month's time, but will lose 2 points of Str and Con permanently.

Third, after six months time, a close friend to the possessor (an NPC if possessed by a character) will meet a gruesome death.

Finally, after one year, the possessor will die a premature, but natural death.

Absent a wish by another person or the equivalent, it is extremely difficult for a possessor to loose themselves from this font's possession. Any person possessing the font may attempt to do so one time only by making a Will save (DC 35).

Font of Lust (fine champagne). A silver grail with maidens fair and comely warriors upon its surface, the *Font of Desire* acts similar to a *Potion of Love*. This causes the possessor (or anyone drinking from the font) to become charmed with the first creature she sees after consuming the dräft (as charm person; the drinker must be a humanoid of Medium-size or smaller and receives a Will save (DC 14)). She actually becomes enamored if the creature is of similar race or kind. The charm effects wear off in 1 day, but the enamoring effect is permanent. Thus, anyone possessing the font may potentially become charmed, and/or enamored, with a new person everyday.

The desires created by this font can become overpowering, and become the possessor's sole purpose in life. However, because the possessor also loses 5 points of CHA (temporarily while possessing it), the affections they seek are rarely given. The beneficial powers of this font are that it acts as a *Ring of Warmth*, and grants a continuous *Mind Blank* spell upon its possessor.

Once the possessor has become enamored with 3 persons, there is a 50% chance each day that he will lose interest in the font and abandon it.

Font of Longing (cool water). This sand colored glass is emblazoned with a thirsty man. It causes an insatiable longing in the possessor for their heart's desire. As each person is unique, the boundaries of the font's effect cannot be readily defined. The DM is advised, however, to play up the affect upon the possessor to the extreme, such that they would change the course of the life. Two side effects are that the possessor becomes constantly thirsty. Each time a new person takes possession of the font, they will find the *Truncheon of Longing* resting at the bottom of the glass. Because of the nature of the font, the possessor will not easily part with this treasure.

Font of Sorrow (whiskey). This pewter cup bears the visage of an old man on one side, and a mother with dead child on the other. It has two triangular handles. The possessor of this cup labors under a constant melancholy, sorrowful over past deeds, love ones lost, or failures. The initial sorrow will set in after possessing it for one week, and in one month's time, the possessor becomes unable to do anything more than sit about talking or thinking about his sorrow. The sorrow will last until death or until broken by powerful spell or other intervention. The font grants no powers or other effects.

Font of Greed (thimble size volume of exquisite wine). This squat cup of brass and iron has strands of fool's gold within it, and a singular oval handle. It creates overwhelming greed in its possessor, causing them to become consumed with material wealth. The possessor's personality should thus be appropriately affected. Once per week, the possessor may cast the following spells: *detect magic, Nystul's undetectable aura, locate object, obscure object,* and *shrink item*. The possessor will not willingly give up this font.

Font of Gluttony (sweet white wine). This font is tall and round, and has no handles. The indentation of hands are on either side of the font, as if someone lifted it from the forge before it cooled. The possessor of this font will become addicted to its wine. In one week, they will gain 5% of their normal body weight. After one month, their weight will have increased 15%, and after one year by 50%. In addition, the possessor will slowly become *Incorporeal*, becoming fully *Incorporeal* (no physical body; immune to all nonmagical attack forms; harmed only by other incorporeal creatures, +1 or better magical weapons, spells, spell-like effects, or supernatural effects) after the passage of one year's time. Upon becoming *Incorporeal*, the possessor will no longer be able to handle the font and it will be ready for another owner.

Font of Jealousy (fine red wine). A tall silver grail with a ghostly woman coiling around it, the font affects both the possessor and those that drink from it. Anyone possessing this grail will instantly have their strongest jealousy heightened to an overpowering level. They will seek to obtain any object or station of which they are jealous, or to eliminate anyone of whom they are jealous. Actions taken to achieve these goals will vary from possessor to possessor, ranging from outright, instantaneous combat to carefully devised plans that take years to succeed. If and when the possessor satisfies their jealously, the sorcery of the font will be broken. The font will then find itself another victim. Those who drink from the font will become jealous of its possessor, and they will seek to obtain possession of the font through either direct or indirect means.

Anyone possessing the font gains *Fast Healing* (5 hp).

Font of Madness (good ale). A broad golden grail decorated by indecipherable runes, any person possessing this font will be struck by the following diseases which cannot be cured while maintaining possession of the font. After one week, the possessor becomes diseased with *Cackle Fever* (minus 1d6 Wis). After one month, the *Shakes* set in (minus 1d8 Dex). After three months, *Mindfire* strikes (minus 1d4 Int). If the possessor is still alive after six month's time, they are struck by a major mental disease such as schizophrenia.

Absent a powerful spell on the level of a *wish*, the madness of the font cannot be cured. However, after possessing the font for one week, the possessor may roll a Will save (DC 18). Success indicates that the possessor is aware of his predicament and may freely pass on the font to another person for one day's time. When the font is given to another person, the former possessor suffers a permanent loss of 2 points of Int and will require one week of bed rest.

Font of Vanity (water). This Font is like a cube, open on one end. Each face is a mirror, and the whole is held together with platinum workings. Any person possessing this font for more than one day permanently gains 2 points of CHA, and becomes consumed with their appearance. They will spend one year fulfilling this addiction to its extreme, at which time the font will lose itself from its possessor and find another victim. Upon losing the font, the former possessor will age 10 years.

Font of the Lost (dry white wine). An old wooden cup with iron bands, this Font leaks its contents slowly. Its possessor will slowly lose purpose, become muddled in thought and action. The possessor, however, will always offer a drink from the font to most everyone they come into contact with.

The possessor of this font will have no desire to rid themselves of it. Indeed, the Truncheon of the Lost will always be found with this font and the possessor will use it to defend the font. A *wish* or similar spell cast upon them will break the font's hold.

After possessing this cup for one day, the possessor becomes *Fatigued* (cannot run or charge; suffer an effective penalty of -2 to Str and Dex; becomes exhausted by doing something else that would normally cause fatigue). The possessor remains so as long as they own the font.

Font of the Abandoned (possessor's choice). A battered cup of copper, this font carries a sadness with it. Its possessor feels as if they are alone in the world, no matter their station, number of allies and friends, family, or quest. They go about their way unaffected except for a deep emptiness of unfulfillment that is always present.

As with any treasure, the possessor will not gladly part with the font, but they may do so freely if they make a successful Will save (DC 14). If they do part with the font, however, they will meet their death in one day's time, be it natural or violent. Powerful divinations or other sorceries will reveal this fate, even to the possessor. Thus, most possessors will walk the world unfulfilled, knowing that the only cure lies in death.

The possessor of this font gains *Low-light Vision* at 90 feet range, +1 to all ability scores, and +1 to all saving throws.

Font of Hate (fine red wine). This font is a square cup of wood with no adornment. It fills its possessor with hate for a race, guild, order, or group (randomly determined or a logical extension of the character's background). The possessor will then live out his life attempting to destroy the persons he hates. The possessor gains the *Scent* ability (ex), but it may only be used to scent the hated persons. After possessing the font for one day, the Truncheon of Hate will appear in the possessor's belongings.

Font of Pride (brandy). This narrow chalice made of an unearthly, greenish steel holds little liquid. If any font possesses intelligence, this chalice would be it. Unsatisfied with allowing any to grasp it, the *Font of Pride* seeks out those who have accomplished great things. Its favorite targets are the humble.

The chalice subtly affects it possessor. It slowly causes pride to well up in the possessor, pride over his great life deeds. In time, typically over the course of months, this pride becomes arrogance. The possessor's self-importance grows daily and becomes so strong that even friend and family will begin to turn against them or avoid their company. In this way, the font erodes reputations and lives. The font has no other powers.

Caster Level: 30th
Weight: 1/2 lb.
Treasure Class: Major Artifacts
Treasure Level: The Fonts of Narrheit are properly used as adventure hooks, plot devices, or as an overall campaign storyline. Any possession of a font by a character should be closely controlled, and again, are more properly used to drive the story and for character development.
Alignment: All radiate pure chaos.

Gloves of True North (Minor Wondrous)

History: The origin of these gloves can be traced to an obscure battle between the Watchers in the Wood and a large force of goblin bandits that had infested the Darkenfold forest. The ranger commander, Auric Treeshield, led his company into the encampment of the goblin brigands who had raided the lands, killed at random, and terrified the populace. The rangers scattered the goblins, only to learn that the bandits regrouped on the southern edge of the forest, fleeing into the Great Soup Marsh.

Auric led his company into that poisoned swamp where all manner of foul beast made its home. They trailed the goblin marauders, their pursuit taking them deeper and deeper into the swamp, where the sun was permanently shrouded by leaden skies and swirling tendrils of fog that obscured safe pathways through quicksand laden waters. It was then that the goblins sprung their trap.

Having lured the human pursuers into the swamp, the goblins took to the offensive. Auric and his company were pressed to give ground to overwhelming numbers. They eventually were forced to flee entirely. Lost in a hostile environment and under constant attack, they fought a retreating battle lasting two full days. Eventu-ally, Auric and one other surviving ranger escaped from the goblins and the swamp.

Much later, Auric commissioned a wizard to imbue his leather gauntlets with an enchantment. One, he hoped, that might forestall similar circumstances happening again. Now, years later, gloves of Auric's type, while not common, are not unheard of either.

Description: Any glove or gauntlet.

Powers: These enchanted gloves, as the name implies, enable the wearer to determine the direction they are traveling in and the orientation toward north three time per day. In addition, the gloves convey a +1 to initiative, lessening the chance of being surprised in an encounter.

Caster Level: 3rd
Prerequisites: Craft Wondrous Item, *know direction, guidance*
Market Price: 1,250
Weight: –
Treasure Class: Arcane
Treasure Level: 2nd

Gorgorthorium (Weapon)

History: This wicked biter was forged by the enemies of St. Luther during the Age of Heroes. The spear was given to Luther's half-demon son, Morgeld, in hopes that it would be used to slay the paladin of light. Morgeld wielded the weapon to bloody effect, but he never used it to draw a drop of blood from his father.

Description: This long spear has a wide blade surrounded by four smaller blades jutting outward and upward. The blades are Iergild Gold, and the shaft of the spear is dragon bone. When forged, the spear was cooled in the blood of a paladin.

Powers: The fear of the dragon was bound into this +5 spear along with many other sorceries. Once per day the wielder can call forth the dragon's fear and inflict it upon his enemies. Creatures within a 30 feet radius of the spear are subject to the effect if they have fewer HD than the wielder. A potentially affected creature that succeeds a Will save (DC 10 + 1/2 wielder's HD + wielder's Charisma modifier) remains immune to the dragon fear for one day. Failure has the following effects: creatures with 4 or fewer HD become panicked for 4d6 rounds, and those of 5 or greater HD become shaken for 4d6 rounds.

The wielder can *Fly* (no time limit) at will, and may *Teleport without Error* three times per day. The spear is also a weapon of *distance*, having twice the range of a normal spear. The wielder can create *Darkness 10 ft. radius* three times per day upon command.

The spear has a special *returning* power. Similar to a *returning* weapon, the spear will returns to a creature that throws it. It returns, however, by using its teleportation power upon the command of the wielder. The wielder can command it to return before his turn, thus its throwing creature's turn. It is therefore ready to use again that turn. Commanding the spear to return uses one of the three *Teleports without Error* that can be used each day.

The spear also contains animation and summoning powers. Three times per week, the bearer of the spear can *Animate Dead*. Once per month, the wielder can summon a medium-size Vrock (see MM).

Caster Level: 18th
Market Price: 275,000
Damage: 1d8; x3 critical
Weight: 5 lb.
Treasure Class: Infernal/Unique
Treasure Level: 13th
Alignment: Evil

Grail of Jaren (Artifact)

History: "Jaren *One Hand is crucified above the high gates of Aufstrag. His blood flows from wounds on his hands and feet and pools upon the ground at the gate's opening. Unbeknownst to him, a supplicant of the old ways, Andulf, comes with a cup. Hidden from the eyes of the Dark he fills the cup with the blood of Jaren and it becomes a Holy Vessel of Peace, of Power, and Holiness. Into it, the hopes of the World are poured.*" – Excerpt from "Book of the Millennial Darkness" as compiled by Bernard of Oix.

Andulf, a monk in the service of Toth, and a servant of Master Jaren, did not witness his master's fall in the Halls of King Robert Luther. When the final battle came, Andulf was caught in the mountains making meditation. He could not, in the final years, make his way through the armies of Unklar to fight at his master's side. So he waited.

There he had a dream of a woman riding a Unicorn, and she bade him travel to distant Aufstrag and await his master's coming. Then, take from his body what he could, and keep it safe from the harm of the world.

And so he did. For seventeen years he waited in the outskirts of the city, living as a beggar. At last he saw his master brought forth and during much tribulation, Jaren was crucified to the wall above the gate. The high monk did not cry in pain, but his mind failed him and he drifted on seas of agony. His blood spilt freely upon the ground and a great horde of evil folk gathered and bathed in the elixir of his pain. Amidst this chaos none saw the small thin beggar approach with a mud covered cup, which was in truth a grail of platinum and gold, and fill it with the blood of master.

The grail took on a holy aspect for Jaren was a Saint in the ethos of the old gods and Andulf fled with it to the east to keep it safe and to worship it as the last manifestation of Jaren upon Erde. The grail never emptied of its liquid and it served Andulf as a vessel of healing. A few drops from the grail and a man's wounds were cured and his disease abated. Eventually Andulf built a shrine to the grail and placed the cup on high. This was done upon an island, lost now to time, though suspected to be near the lands of Aenoch and the straights of Ursal. The isle, called Ibernia, was inhabited by fierce warlike people who payed homage to distant spirits. They treated Andulf as one of these spirits and worshiped him and the grail. The worship of Jaren Falkynjager began.

While worship of the grail and Jaren flourished on Iberia, another cult sprung up at Aufstrag. The Cult of the Hanging God looked ever skyward upon their master, hanging upon the gates of Aufstrag. And legend grew of a holy grail located on the distant shores of a lost lands.

That was a thousand years gone by. Memory and sources fail to report where the isle of Ibernia can now be found.

Description: An exquisitely worked grail of platinum and gold, perhaps encrusted in mud.

Powers: A few drops of blood from the grail acts as a *Heal* spell upon good and neutral creatures. A creature may only receive this blessing once per day. Legend holds that the grail had many other divine powers as well (as determined by the DM to fit his campaign).

Caster Level: 30th

Weight: 1/2 lb.

Treasure Class: Minor Artifact/Divine/Tragic

Alignment: Lawful Good

Harg & Hylde (Weapon)

History: 'Tis said that the gods Harg and Hylde are the children of the god Mimir and the goddess Freya. Beneath the branches of Yggdrasill, when the world was young, those two loved one another, and Freya gave birth to the twins, Harg and Hylde. This was before Mimir lost his head to the vengeance of the Vanir, and before he drank from the cup of wisdom which ever after allowed him to know what men and gods were forbidden to know.

When their father died, Harg and Hylde set about avenging him, and swore to unmake Vanaheim and start the wars anew. Their plots were uncovered by their mother, however, and she made a pact with the Giant Hrunganir to bind them in sorceries that could keep them from their sworn task. Hrunganir invited the warrior sons of Mimir to his deep halls with promises of weapons to destroy Vanaheim. Harg and Hylde came to Hrunganir's chambers, and were drugged by the giant, who in turn bound them in two great hammers.

Freya took the hammers, her children, to Asgard. But Loki stole them from her and brought them to the world of humankind, hoping to unmake them and gain the loyalty of the twins. He was undone when Thor found him upon the heights of Klarnacht Mountain. Great and thunderous the battle raged between the storm god and the trickster, but in the end, Thor smote Loki such a blow that he dropped Harg and Hylde into the world and they were lost in the deeps. Legend holds that the eldritch goblins found them and took them to their dread King.

Descrip-tion: The heads of these massive warhammers are made of some unearthly blue-steel metal, while their handles are Iergild Gold wrapped in a leather-like substance crafted from skin shed Jormungand, the Midgard Serpent. The emblazoned faces of Harg & Hylde decorate the sides of each hammer's head. When the hammers are used against enemies, mortal or divine, they howl and moan, longing to go to Vanaheim and destroy the Vanir who dealt so cruelly with their father.

Powers: These +5 hammers are unbreakable and do not shed light. When employed in combat, they take on a life of their own, seemingly guiding their wielder's blows. When used in tandem (two weapon fighting), the hammers reduces the primary hand penalty and the off-hand penalty by 4, not including their normal +5 bonus to attack rolls.

The hammers deal bonus damage upon striking a successful critical hit. Harg deals a *Flaming Burst* when a critical hit occurs, causing +2d10 points of bonus fire damage. Hylde deals an *Icy Burst* when a critical hit occurs, causing +2d10 points of bonus cold damage. In both cases, the fire and frost do not harm the wielder's hands. The hammers do not otherswise act as flaming or frost weapons to any extent.

The will of the imprisoned twins also transfers to their wielder. They provide a +2 bonus to all Will saves, and a Spell Resistance of 25 against all charm and sleep type spells.

Caster Level: 16th

Market Price: 120,000

Damage: 1d8; x3 crit. (each)

Weight: 8 lb. (each)

Treasure Class: Divine/Unique

Treasure Level: 10th

Havoc (Weapon)

History: This mighty dwarven waraxe is an artifact of the Winter Dark wars. King Dolgan secretly fashioned the cleaver during his bondage as the Smith of Aufstrag. Elvish legend holds that during the deep of Unklar's winter, the last of the great unicorns, the Mare, quested to find Dolgan. In her dying breath she bade the dwarf to forge a weapon to bring freedom back to the world. Dolgan wielded the fell axe to wicked effect throughout the wars of the Winter Dark. Dolgan bound his loathing for Unklar into the axe, imbuing it with great magic to combat the Mogrl of Unklar (*see special purpose below*).

Some say that the King lost his axe in the far north in combat with one of the Elder Mogrl. The elves of the Eldwood, however, maintain that Dolgan unmade the axe and thus returned the unicorns to the world.

Description: This mighty weapon is an Iergild steel double-bladed dwarven wares. The haft is made of a 3 ft. long unicorn horn.

Powers: The axe acts as a +4 *defending* weapon with the following additional powers that are constantly in effect: the wielder cannot be flanked, immunity to disease, immunity to sleep and sleep effects, and empathy (50 ft. range). Also, twice per day the wielder can cast *Dimension Door*.

As a *defender*, the axe allows the wielder to transfer some or all of the sword's enhancement bonus to his AC as a special bonus that stacks with all others. As a free action, the wielder chooses how to allocate the weapon's enhancement bonus at the start of his turn before using the weapon, and the effect to AC lasts until his next turn.

Special purpose: When used against Mogrl, the axe grants a +2 luck bonus to all saving throws, a +2 deflection AC bonus, and a spell resistance of 15.

Caster Level: 16th
Market Price: 128,000
Damage: 1d10; x3 crit.
Weight: 15 lb.
Treasure Class: Arcane/Unique
Treasure Level: 10th

Holy Flame (Artifact)

History: The most sacred item of the Holy Defenders of the Flame, the Holy Flame resides in the Paladin's Grove in Kayomar. Legend holds that this flame is the last spark of the All Father's language of creation, and thus, is far more powerful than any other force in The World of Ede. It is good personified. (See further history in Chapter 2, *Holy Defenders of the Flame*)

Description: The blue-white flame dances upon silvery water within a broad, shallow dish of platinum and gold.

Powers: The water possesses divine healing powers, but they only have effect upon good aligned beings. Any good creature that drinks of the water is cured by the following spells, all to their maximum effect: *Atonement, Heal, Greater Dispelling* (only negates detrimental magic), *Greater Restoration, Neutralize Poison, and Regenerate*. If a cup of water is poured upon the remains of a good being, it acts as a *Resurrection* spell (no other components needed).

Any evil being that drinks from the water is cursed by an unquenchable thirst. The being must drink twice as much water as is normal each day. Breaking the curse is within the DM's discretion, but the cure should be on the magnitude of a greater quest.

The Flame also acts as an instrument of judgment and atonement. Those seeking true atonement will be judged by the Flame based upon their life's work or potential, their discipline to their convictions, or their simply capacity for goodness. The DM maintains complete discretion in such matters. Those that drink from it with ulterior motives should suffer accordingly.

Caster Level: 40th
Treasure Class: Major Artifact
Alignment: Lawful Good

Holy Icon (Minor Wondrous)

History: These holy items are typically given to clerics who perform great service to their church or order.

Description: A small holy symbol on a chain or leather necklace, or a decorated and inlaid cloak brooch or ring.

Powers: Grants +1 to Wisdom.
Caster Level: 7th
Prerequisites: Craft Wondrous Item, *commune*
Market Price: 2,000
Weight: –
Treasure Class: Arcane
Treasure Level: 2nd

Horn of Breaking (Wondrous)

History: This horn of old was fashioned by the goblin smiths during the Goblin-Dwarf wars. Unclear's trusted goblin servant, Erix, bore it for years.

Description: A black bull's horn inlaid with silver.

Powers: When directed toward an item and sounded, the blast from the horn can shatter any item, magical or not. So powerful is the horn that only items with a +3 or better enchantment can save. A failed Fortitude save (DC 20) automatically inflicts enough damage to render the item useless, including artifacts! The horn has no effect if sounded against creatures.

Caster Level: 20th
Market Price: 60,000
Weight: 1 lb.
Treasure Class: Arcane/Minor Artifact
Treasure Level: 20th

Horn of Sounding (Wondrous)

History: This summons the god Utumno, the son of Daladon Lothian and Wenafar, the Faerie Queen. Daladon forged the horn to call to his son on the Sea of Dreams.

Blowing it once summons Utumno' Knightmares, dark faeries who bear dark dreams to mortals. Blowing the horn twice will drive off the Knightmares. Blowing the horn three times will summon Utumno's sea-craft, the "Dream Horn."

Description: A silver-coated ram horn, eighteen inches in length, wrapped in platinum-laced iron bands. A leather strap is attached to either end.

Powers: The dark faeries hound the blower in his sleep and haunt his waking until the recipient's Endurance is overcome, at which point he goes mad. He loses one point of Endurance a day. Endurance is figured by adding Constitution and Wisdom.

Caster Level: 15th
Market Price: 100,000
Weight: 1 lb.
Treasure Class: Divine/Minor Artifact
Treasure Level: 7th

Iergild Metal (Special Material/Artifact)

History: Shards of the All Father's great hammer which he used to shape creation. He shattered it while making the Dwarves and it fell to the earth. There are three varieties: Iergild Gold, Iergild Silver, and Iergild Steel.

Powers: The following bonuses are conferred to weapons and other objects constructed from this metal: Iergild Gold +5, Iergild Silver +4, and Iergild Steel +3. The hardness and hit points of each is:

Iergild Gold has a hardness of 30 and 50 hit points per inch of thickness.

Iergild Silver has a hardness of 20 and 40 hit points per inch of thickness.

Iergild Steel has a hardness of 15 and 30 hit points per inch of thickness.

Market Price: A 1 pound block of the metal is valued in gold pieces as follows: Gold 25,000; Silver 16,000; and Steel 9,000.

Jackal Sword (Weapon)

History: Hundreds of these swords were created during the Winter Dark Wars to outfit halflings troops. With the aid of their Jackal Swords, warriors of that race were able to more readily hide from the Ungern. The halflings effectively used the swords for infiltration and sneak attacks.

Description: A nondescript, battered short sword of common steel.

Powers: Within these +1 swords live jackal-like outsiders. By speaking the command word, "Hunt," in the halfling tongue, the wielder summons forth the "jackal".

Celestial Jackal, outsider: CR 1/3; Small Outsider; HD 1d8+2; hp 8; Init +3; Spd 40 ft.; AC 15; +2 melee (1d4+1 bite); SA smite evil; SQ darkvision 90 ft, scent; Fort +4, Ref +5, Will +1; Str 13, Dex 17, Con 15, Int 6, Wis 12, Cha 7; AL G; *Skills*: Hide +5, Listen +5, Spot +5, Wilderness Lore +5; *Feats*: Track. *Smite Evil (Su)*: Once per day may inflict additional damage against an evil creature upon a successful attack equal to HD total.

Caster Level: 3rd
Prerequisites: Craft Magic Arms and Armor, *summon monster I*
Market Price: 8,000
Damage: 1d6; 19-20/x2 crit.
Weight: 3 lb.
Treasure Class: Arcane
Treasure Level: 2nd

Krummelvole (Artifact)

History: In DY 898, Dolgan, son of Hirn, slave of Mithgefuhl, crafted the Crown of Sorrow, the Krummelvole, for his Dark Master Unklar. The mage Kraxel recorded King Dolgan's remembrance of the crown's making during a visit to Grundliche Hohle during one of the king's more talkative moods . . .

"Upon a high day in my 400th year of life and 357th of captivity, the great and terrible Dark Lord summoned me to his throne and bid me craft him an iron crown, adorned with the greatest jewels of the world. So I left away to the dark regions beneath Mitgefuhl, the pits wherein my foundry lay, named dark Klarglich, the pit of Woe, and I bid all leave until the task was done. So great in the councils of the Dark had I grown that the hosts of Darkness followed my bidding.

"And there in the dark solitude I bent iron and shaped the great crown to hold the jewels of Unklar's desire. I crafted the shape with magics held in the deeps and released by the might of the Dark God. For twelve days I labored, until my brow was weighted and frowned. But at last the task was finished, and I held up my greatest creation. And I loved it and desired it for it was made of the stuff of the earth, and altogether separate from Unklar's black soul. I called it The Krummervoll in the ancient tongue of the dwarves, the Crown of Sorrow."

The power to *Gaze upon the Planes* was imbued into the Crown by Unklar without Dolgan's knowledge.

Description: The Crown is fashioned of iron and its brow bears 16 stones of incomparable value. Fifteen *Ioun Stones* sit in the crown's band. Riding above them all, upon the ridge of the crown, is the *Heart of Darkness*, a star ruby almost 6 inches in height.

Powers: The powers of the crown originate within the *Ioun Stones* and the *Heart of Darkness*.

Unlike the *Ioun Stones* detailed in the DMG, the *Ioun Stones* residing in this crown cannot be destroyed and never burn out. Their powers are:

Color	Power
Dusty rose	+1 deflection bonus to AC
Clear	Sustains creature without food or water
Pale blue	+2 enhancement bonus to Strength
Scarlet and blue	+2 enhancement bonus to Intelligence
Incandescent blue	+2 enhancement bonus to Wisdom
Deep red	+2 enhancement bonus to Dexterity
Pale red	+2 enhancement bonus to Constitution
Scarlet and green	+2 enhancement bonus to Charisma
Dark blue	Alertness (as the feat)
Vibrant purple	Stores six levels of spells
Iridescent	Sustains creature without air
Pale green	+1 competence bonus to attack rolls, saves, and checks
Pearly white	Regenerate 1 point of damage/hour
Pale orange	Absorb 24 levels of spells up to 4th level
Milky white	Absorb 24 levels of spells up to 8th level

The *Heart of Darkness* grants the following powers: *Animate Object* upon command three times per day (command word is Munterkeit), and *Flesh to Stone* upon command three times per day (command word is Fliesch zu Stein).

In addition, the wearer can *Gaze upon the Planes* at will. The wearer of the crown can cast his mind into the planes and see as if actually there. He can locate objects and creatures (unless they are magically hidden and then it acts the same as a crystal ball), and can commune with them if he chooses. A wearer possessing a combined intelligence and wisdom of 40 or greater can launch a psychic attack on the mind of a creature located while "walking." This attack combines and affects as *Causes Fear, Hold Person*, and *Nightmare*.

Using this power, however, is very dangerous. The beauty of the interlocking dimensions of the planes are such that they can be mesmerizing and catch the weak of will, potentially leading to madness. If one cannot control the "walking," then they may become consumed with it and lost forever. Spirit and mind become bound to the planes, and the mortal body is left a gibbering madness. Each time the possessor attempts the "walking," their mind is battered by the psychic gales of the planes. The possessor must immediately make a Will save (DC 35). A failed save results in any number of catastrophic ailments at the DM's discretion (such as insanity), including effective Intelligence and Charisma Decrease to 7 for 4 weeks.

Caster Level: 35th
Weight: 3 lb.
Treasure Class: Major Artifact

Lucky Whetstone (Minor Wondrous)
Description: A typical looking whetstone.
Powers: These whetstones grant the possessor a +1 to all saving throws.
Prerequisites: Craft Wondrous Item, *Guidance*
Market Price: 1000
Weight: –
Treasure Class: Arcane
Treasure Level: 2nd

Mammoth Scrolls (Artifact)
History: The Mammoth Scrolls are that knowledge written upon the steps of the brass rings connecting the World of Erde to the World of Inzae. Each step bears thousands of runes recounting the histories of the world and the Language of Creation.

The dwarf Angrim coveted their knowledge and quested for them. After many long years, Angrim discovered them within the brass rings, and he copied many runes onto large stone tablets. These he transported to Erde, storing them in first home, Gorthoraug. He went mad shortly thereafter, and was known thenceforth as Angrim the Black.

These stone tablets are a compilation of tens of thousands of scrolls which recount the history of the world as reckoned by the dwarves. It is the only reliable information that exists concerning the early ages of Erde. They are bound within a temple constructed into the ruins atop Mount Austrien at Gorthoraug. There they are studied by dwarves and goblins alike.

Description: Massive stone tablets covered in runes of the Language of Creation and dwarvish.
Powers: The knowledge one gains from reading these scrolls is limitless. A character who spends 1 full year studying the scrolls gains 4 points of wisdom. Three further years of study increases the readers intelligence by 4 points.
Caster Level: 40th
Treasure Class: Major Artifact

Mantle of Confession
History: St. Luther came into possession of this great cloak at the conclusion of the Winter Dark Wars when he surrendered Durendale to its next bearer. The greater Lords of Law granted him the Mantle when he became the Lord of Dreams. He uses the Mantle to better see into the hearts of mortals and to understand them, what he calls "Confessing."
Description: A fur-lined cape made of heavy wool.
Powers: The mantle may only be used by a Lawful creature. It allows the wearer to see with keen vision (upon active concentration, allowing for no other action during the round). The wearer gains dark vision with a 120-foot range. The wearer can also see invisible, displaced, and out of phase creatures and objects at 240-foot range (or 120-foot if dark vision is needed). This includes seeing those affected by invisibility potions and rings, dust of disappearance, a robe of blending, or a similar magical item. Camouflaged or hidden things can also be seen. Astral and ethereal objects cannot be seen, nor does the mantle increase the chance to find secret doors.

The wearer of the mantle cannot be surprised, and they gain the following: Spell Resistance 13, Armor Class 18 (cannot be used with any other form of magical defense, other than a Defender sword), and +2 on all saving throws.

The Mantle bears special properties which allow the wearer to see into the hearts of men. When the wearer makes a concentrated effort to hear "Confession," these spell-like abilities operate simultaneously (cast as 20th level cleric): 0 – *Detect Magic, Detect Poison*; 1st – *Cause Fear, Command, Detect Chaos/Evil/Law/Good, Detect Poison, Remove Fear*; 2nd – *Augury, Calm Emotions, Death Knell, Consecrate, Zone of Truth*; 3rd – *Speak with Dead*; 4th – *Discern Lie, Sending, Tongues*; 5th – *Atonement, Commune (with recipient), Greater Command, Mark of Justice, True Seeing*; 6th – *Banishment, Geas/Ques*; 7th – *Dictum, Repulsion*; 8th – *Holy Aura*; 9th – *Implosion (upon recipient), Miracle, Soul Bind*.

    Caster Level: 22nd
    Market Price: 225,000
    Weight: 5 lb.
    Treasure Class: Lawful/Minor Artifact
    Treasure Level: 15th
    Alignment: Lawful

Neckguard of Charles the Confessor (Armor)

    History: Long before the Battle of Olensk, Kain the Godless appeared in the halls of Grundliche Hohle. Kain, bearer of Omdurman (see below), bade the dwarven king to send forth a champion or face Kain himself. Dolgan, not knowing Kain nor his blade, made to take up Havoc and strike down the interloper.

    But the Confessor Knight, Charles, knew that battle with Kain meant certain death. He requested that the king name him champion. The King, feeling the righteousness of Luther emanating from the knight, agreed.

    Hence, Dolgan forged this magical neck_guard so that Charles could fight Kain without fear of being beheaded. Charles refused the gift, claiming that his paladin's "honor" forbade him to wear it. The result was predictable, and Charles's tomb stands now at the foot of Grundliche Mountain. Dolgan forged several more Neckguard in the years following this incident in honor of the knight who sacrificed himself so that the king could live.

    Description: A decorated Neckguard made of Iergild Silver that can be fitted to a suit of plate mail.

    Powers: This neckguard grants +1 to the AC of the wearer. If a foe wielding a vorpal blade scores a critical hit against the wearer of the neckguard, the wearer's head is not automatically severed. If the wearer successfully makes a Fortitude saving throw (DC 25), the vorpal blade will rings off the neckguard with a mighty reverberation. While the wearer retains his head, the neckguard is destroyed. If the saving throw is unsuccessful, the wearer is decapitated and the neckguard is destroyed.

    Caster Level: 9th
    Market Price: 60,000
    Weight: 4 lb.
    Treasure Class: Arcane/Tragic/Unique
    Treasure Level: 6th

Noxmurus, "Night of the Dead" (Weapon):

    History: When Unklar came to the world of Erde, the elven folk fled, hiding themselves in magical realms. Some elves, however, stayed behind. They hated Unklar and fought him at every turn.

But as their losses mounted and the world suffered, they began to hate their own kin even more. And in time these folk turned their vengeance on their own.

    The Elf Prince Meltowg Lothian, brother to Daladon, was one of these elves. He forged the sword Noxmurus and bound within it the spirit of his rage and hate. When he died in the Winter Dark Wars his brother took up the blade.

    Within the blade lurks the corporal manifestation of Meltowg's madness, Bodach the imp. When held by any elf but a high elf (or half-elf who is not the offspring of a high elf) the sword becomes a living thing and will talk to its "master," trying to influence the wielder.

    Description: A great two-handed claymore, the blade is deep green in color. Its grip is of black wire wrapped tightly around an iron base, the pommel a dark green opal, and the great cross-guard is made of steel colored black with coal dust. The sword does not become worn with time, for the spirit of the elves lies within it. It is always sharp, immune to notches and scratches.

    Powers: The +5 blade is unbreakable. When unsheathed, the sword bestows the Move Silently skill (10 ranks), and if in a forest environment, the bearer can become invisible at will to all beings less than 15 hit dice and to all elves.

    The sword has two enemies to which it always manifests, orcs and elves. Against orcs, the wielder always gains initiative. Against elf or fey, the blade has malevolent effect. On a roll of natural 20, the elf or fey's spirit is forever destroyed, thus cursing them to live out their day under a cloud of gloom and depression.

    When borne by any elf but a high elf (or half-elf who is not the offspring of a high elf), the sword bestows the power of *Glamour*, allowing the wielder to make himself seem greater than he is. This acts similar to the Frightful Presence of Dragons (Ex). The *Glamour* unsettles creatures within 120 feet if they have fewer than 12 HD. A potentially affected creature that succeeds at a Will save (DC 20) remains immune to the *Glamour* for one day. On a failure, creatures with 4 or fewer HD become panicked for 4d6 rounds and those with 5 or more HD become shaken for 4d6 rounds.

    Also, elves and half-elves wielding the blade may summon and command Bodach the Imp (see Devil, Core Rulebook III) upon command. Bodach acts as a familiar in all respects.

    Caster Level: 19th
    Market Price: 160,000
    Damage: 2d6; 19-20/x2 crit.
    Weight: 15 lb.
    Treasure Class: Arcane/Tragic/Unique
    Treasure Level: 11th
    Alignment: Chaotic

Omdurman (Weapon)

    History: Kain the Godless wields this eldritch blade with ferocity. It has been with him for over one hundred and forty years, and the two have become symbiotic, acting as one.

    Description: A excellently crafted longsword of simple design that is made from an unknown metal.

    Powers: This blade is +5 *vorpal* sword. It is intelligent and evil. When drawn, the wielder gains dark vision and low-light vision at a range of 240 feet, and a +3 to Charisma. The sword speaks the common tongue, and can communicate telepathically.

Vorpal enchantment: This enchantment allows the weapon to sever the heads of those it strikes. Upon a successful critical hit, the weapon severs the opponent's head (if it has one) from its body. Some creatures, such as many abominations and all oozes, have no heads. Others, such as golems and undead creatures other than vampires, are not affected by the loss of their heads. Most other creatures, however, die when their heads are cut off, but that is left to the DM's judgment.

Ego: 22; *Int* 14, *Wis* 13, *Cha* 16.
Caster Level: 20th
Market Price: 225,000
Damage: 2d4; 19-20/x2 crit.
Weight: 6 lb.
Treasure Class: Infernal/Unique
Treasure Level: 10th
Alignment: Chaotic Evil

Pride of the Goblins (Artifact)

History: A simple trunk of wood and iron holds the greatest magic of the Eldritch Goblins. Their pride is here bound in a jewel of amber, for therein rests the soul and power of Ondluche, that most fell of goblin mages. To break the spell which binds him would bring back the power of evil that only the dwarves of old battled. The Goblin Pride is ever sought after by the goblin folk, for to possess it would mean they could resume their war upon the dwarves.

Description: A fist-sized piece of uncut amber that emanates a slight, sinister glow.

Powers: This powers of this artifact can only be accessed by an Eldritch Goblin. The immediate affect of the jewel is that it enhances the natural hatred of Dwarves innate to all Eldritch Goblins. Even non-evil Eldritch Goblins that call Dwarves friends may be turned by the Pride against their forefather's enemy.

Most of the powers of the Pride are ephemeral in that they enhances the innate powers of the Eldritch Goblin possessing it. As each Eldritch Goblin is unique, so are the powers bestowed upon the possessor of the Pride. The DM should determine the affect of the jewel upon any Eldritch Goblin that possesses it.

Notwithstanding the unique effect the Pride has on its possessor, it will also bestow the following upon Eldritch Goblins: +1 Int, +1 Wis, +3 Cha, SR 10, *Stoneskin* (3 times per day, wielder only, 10 minutes), *Detect Thoughts* (at will), *Detect Dwarves* within 1 mile (at will), Alertness (as Feat), All Armor and Weapon proficiencies, Deflect Arrows (as Feat), Great Cleave vrs Dwarves only (as Feat).

Caster Level: 35th
Weight: 1 lb.
Treasure Class: Major Artifact.
Alignment: Evil

Rilthwood (Special Material)

History: Rilthwood trees grow in the Red March, and they provide ideal wood for the construction of bows, especially composite bows, and arrows. The wood absorbs stain easily, highlighting the natural swirls of the grain, which vary from tree to tree.

The stains applied typically make Rilthwood bows unique to their owner. Kings often equip their troops with bows stained in the color of their coat-of-arms. Nobility and adventurers often commission skilled artisans to stain Rilthwood bows with patterns and symbols.

Arrows made from Rilthwood also absorb stain, and they seldom snap or splinter unless scoring a deep strike. Roland's Raiders, an infamous mercenary troop, were known for their half-red, half-white Rilthwood arrows.

Description: The slender Rilthwood trees have stark white bark and shiny, broad green leaves. In the Fall, the leaves turn a brilliant red. Every Rilthwood tree has a unique swirl to its grain.

Powers: Composite bows made from Rilthwood are *masterwork* items and their range increment is increased by 20 feet. Arrows made of Rilthwood have a hardness of 5, 2 hit points per inch of thickness, and a Break DC of 12.

Market price: 3x Masterwork price
Weight: 3/4 normal

The Ring of Gruach the Goblin Lord

History: Forged in the depths of time during the First Goblin-Dwarf War, this ring is an artifact of eldritch power with a long and bloody history. It most recently served as a symbol of peace between goblin and dwarf.

During the War of the Pit, Dolgan dwarf_lord forged a friendship with a fellow slave, the Eldritch Goblin Agmour. Dolgan fought side by side with Agmaur for ten years beneath the tree, and upon their eventual escape, they pledged blood brotherhood to one another and peace between their peoples for so long as Dolgan sat upon the throne of Grundliche Hohle.

But Praeconius, an Eldritch Goblin whose memory stretched long and long back to wars, sought to break the peace. He bade Dolgan to prove his worth by placing upon his finger the Ring of Gruach. When Dolgan did this and mastered the ring, Praeconius stood dumbfounded and named Dolgan the War Chief of the Goblin Horde. Dolgan's dwarves fought alongside Agmour's goblins for the remainder of the Winter Dark Wars.

After the banishment of Unklar, Dolgan surrendered the ring to his brother Agmaur, who wore it for many years until it was lost during one of Agmour's many journeys across the breadth of Erde. Agmaur is the rightful owner of the ring.

Description: This ring is irregularly shaped and made from a strange, greenish organic-metallic substance. It pulsates with warmth and power.

Powers: The ring bestows the following powers: time stop 1/week, word of recall 1/day, suggestion 3/day, detect lie 3/day, true seeing 1/day, detect magic continuous, detect invisibility continuous. The ring also carries the curse of the Goblin Bane.

Goblin Bane: Any wearer who bears a substantial enmity toward goblins will become instantly inflicted with the insanity of suicidal tendencies (no save, magic resistance at ½). Remove curse is ineffectual. The name and location of any bearing the ring under such an affliction will become known immediately by its rightful owner, who will seek the wearer out. Any other Eldritch Goblin seeing such a character will instantly know the same whether or not the ring is openly displayed, and they will attack unquestioningly in an attempt to gain ownership of the ring. A wish or limited wish (treat as a dispel magic vs. lesser god) might remove the ring, but not the insanity.

Rightful Owner: The rightful owner of the ring remains as such until such time as they name a new rightful owner. If they die before doing so, then the first Eldritch Goblin to possess the ring becomes its rightful owner.

Caster Level: 15th
Weight: –
Treasure Class: Major Artifact

Statue of Well Tiding (Wondrous)

History: These statues appear now and again across the world. They are evidently gifts from the gods.

Description: Small statues made of a variety of substances. They typically resemble a place or creature.

Powers: Any character possessing one of these statues is allowed one dice re-roll in a gaming session. The item never radiates magic.

Market Price: 1000 gp
Weight: 1 to 3 lb.
Treasure Class: Divine
Treasure Level: 3rd

Stones of Guiding (Special Material)

History: The Dwarves of old took indigenous rocks of a region and placed them contrary to the lines of geographical development, hiding them among rock. In this way, they developed a message system and guide trails permanent but utterly hidden to all but their kin. Only Dwarven master-stonemasons are capable of inscribing and laying these stones. Any Dwarf can read and follow them.

Description: Indigenous slabs, tablets, or monoliths of rock that appear to be natural to the terrain.

Powers: None.

Shield of Illumination (Armor)

History: These shields originated in Tagea. Tagean troops often employ them to blind their foes before loosing their Tagean Hounds upon them.

Description: A black border edges the bronze face of these small iron shields. Embedded within the center of the shield's face lies an oval crystal.

Powers: A bearer of one of these shields gains +1 AC. In addition, when activated, the crystal unleashes a blinding flash of light. The *Blinding* ability, which may be released once per day, requires enemies within 20 ft., except the wielder, to make a Reflex Saving Throw (DC 14) or be blinded for 1d4 rounds.

Caster Level: 7th
Prerequisites: Craft Magic Arms and Armor, *blindness/deafness, searing light*
Market Price: 4,000
Weight: 6 lb.
Treasure Class: Arcane
Treasure Level: 3rd

Shield of Shattering (Armor)

History: Dwarven wizards created these shields during the Great Goblin-Dwarf Wars to help the Dwarven infantry break the spear hedges of the goblins.

Description: Any shield.

Powers: A non-magical weapon striking this shield must make a saving throw (DC 12) or it is broken.

Note on Creation: These shields cannot be created by characters or NPCs.

Caster Level: –
Market Price: 4,000
Weight: as Shield type
Treasure Class: Arcane
Treasure Level: 3rd

Shroud of Aiden (Wondrous)

History: For a time, Aiden served as the alter-ego of Aristobulus. His blood was linked to the arch-magi's, being the descendent of his brother. When Aiden died by dragon acid, the daughter of Daladon, Fedalia, laid a cloth across his body to cover his horrible scars. The cloth served as the boy's funeral shroud when the Watchers in the Wood buried him. Being a frugal folk, they kept the shroud, for it was still a good piece of cloth. Unbeknownst to any, a piece of Aiden's soul became entwined with the cloth, giving it a life of its own.

Description: A white cloth of irregular size about six feet in length.

Powers: When worn the cloth grants the recipient visions into the outer planes, even the lands of the dead. It allows the character to *Know Alignment, Detect Thoughts* (100 ft. range), and *Sense Motive* (10 ranks) at will with concentration.

Caster Level: 10th
Market Price: 40,000
Weight: –
Treasure Class: Tragic/Unique
Treasure Level: 5th

Skruel's Climbing Spikes (Wondrous)

History: Fashioned with goblin magic during an assault on the fortress of the fire giant king, Nurrich, Skruel's Climbing Spikes allowed the intruders safe descent down a thousand_foot escarpment to attack the fortress from within.

Description: Iron spikes with an eyehook and the goblin rune for "hold" on the shaft.

Powers: When the command word, "hold," is spoken in the goblin tongue, a spike will embed itself into the hardest stone, wood, or even ice and support up to 1500 pounds of stress. They also magically strengthen any rope passed through the eyehook to support 1500 pounds, even thin twine. The use of the spikes grants a +10 modifier (non-stacking) to all Climb checks. Typically, 1d8 of these spikes will be found. Once embedded, it takes great effort to remove a spike.

Caster Level: –
Prerequisites: Craft Wondrous Item, *Freedom of Movement, Stone Shape*
Market Price: 4,500 per bundle
Weight: 1/2 lb. each
Treasure Class: Arcane
Treasure Level: 2nd

Sword of Crateus   (Cursed Weapon)

History: Crateus was an anti-hero bound in this sword by the wizard Zaos. The sword is altogether evil, and Crateus constantly seeks to break out of his prison.

Description: A massive, two-handed greatsword with glowing red runes along its sides. It's scabbard is plain steel.

Powers: This +3 great sword radiates neutrality if its alignment is detected. In truth, it is chaotic evil.

When unsheathed, the sword must draw blood or it will attempt to slay its wielder. If the wielder fails to draw blood with the blade after it is loosed from its scabbard, the sword becomes a *dancing* sword and attacks the wielder, fighting until the wielder is slain or 20 rounds have elapsed.

Caster Level: 10th
Market Price: 20,000
Damage: 2d6; 19-20/x2 crit.
Weight: 15 lbs.
Treasure Class: Arcane/Unique
Treasure Level: 7th
Alignment: Chaotic Evil

Truncheons of Narrheit (Weapons)

History, Description, Powers: Each of these weapons is somehow connected to one of the 13 Fonts of Narrheit. In some cases, they were created to protect and serve their corresponding font. Others came about because of its Font's affect upon its environment. Each truncheon is separately described below. For those weapons that mirror magic items detailed in the DMG, reference should be made to that book for further description and details such as caster level and market price.

Truncheon of Hope and Loss (Spiked Gauntlet and Punching Dagger). To relieve him of his agony, a loyal friend of the first possessor of the *Font of Hope and Loss* killed him with these weapons. The spiked gauntlet is a +3 *defending* weapon. The +2 punching dagger acts as a *Rapier of Puncturing* (three times per day it allows the wielder to make a touch attack with the weapon that deals 1d6 points of temporary CON damage by draining blood).

Truncheon of Lust (Light Mace). This silver mace's former wielder possessed it and the *Font of Desire*. He was killed by the lover of a recent conquest. It is a +1 *bloodline* weapon (reference above). Once per day its wielder may cast *change self*.

Truncheon of Longing (Ring). An unadorned, copper *Ring of Shooting Stars*.

Truncheon of Sorrow (Net). This net became associated with the Font of Sorrow when one of its possessors hung himself with it. It acts as *ghost touch* weapon, although it entangles instead of dealing damage to incorporeal creatures.

Truncheon of Greed (Morningstar). The first possessor of the *Font of Greed* hired a guardian to watch over it. That guardian was armed with this weapon, a +3 *Morningstar of Flaming*.

Truncheon of Gluttony (Greatclub). The relationship of this weapon to the *Font of Gluttony* is unknown. It is a +2 *Greatclub of Thundering*.

Truncheon of Jealousy (Wand). This wand acts like a *Rod of Negation*. It will appear in the possessions of anyone who maintains ownership of the *Font of Jealously* for one week.

Truncheon of Madness (Battleaxe). This weapon was used by an angry and resentful dwarf that had once possessed the *Font of Madness*, but had rid himself of it. Once recovered from the font's effects, the dwarf traveled the lands following the passage of the font from hand to hand. If the afflicted possessor did not rid themselves of the font within a week's time, the dwarf would slay them. The dwarf was eventually brought to justice. The location of his axe is unknown. The axe is a *Battleaxe of Life Stealing*.

Truncheon of Vanity (Rod). This *Rod of Splendor* has been wielded by at least five of the past possessors of the *Font of Vanity*.

Truncheon of the Lost (Ring). A *Ram Ring* with unlimited charges.

Truncheon of the Abandoned (Broadsword). A *bloodline* weapon (reference above) used by a paladin to slay a friend who had been possessed by the Font of the Abandoned. The wielder of this Broadsword may cast *remove curse* once per week.

Truncheon of the Hate (any). This weapon takes the form of the primary weapon used by the possessor of the *Font of Hate*. It is a +3 weapon granting free use of the following feats: Combat Reflexes, Improved Initiative, Mobility, and Uncanny Dodge (as 5th level barbarian).

Truncheon of Pride (Bastard Sword). This weapon always travels wherever the Font of Pride goes. It acts as a *Sword of Terror*, except that it is +4 and there is no chance that the wielder will permanently lose any points of Cha.

Twig of the Banshee (Wondrous)

History: This twig fell from the Great Tree long ago. It possesses several powers.

Description: A small twig roughly six inches long.

Powers: When held in hand, the twig allows the possessor to automatically Turn a Banshee or Ghost as a cleric. The twig can also conjure the thoughts of the undead; the wielder need but concentrate on a lost soul and he will see the former creature's last thoughts. To use this power, the possessor must have some familiarity with the undead's background or situation. The twig also bestows a +1 to Saving Throws versus any special attacks by undead (such as ghoul paralysis).

Caster Level: 10th
Market Price: 5,250 gp
Weight: –
Treasure Class: Unique
Treasure Level: 6th
Alignment: Neutral

Winter Rose (Special Material)

History: A magical plant found only the environs of a Unicorn's domain. The Winter Rose thrived during the Age of Winter's Dark. It is now extremely rare. Known to grow in the Detmold.

Description: A rose with white petals and blue stems, covered in a multitude of small thorns resembling ice.

Powers: The petals of the rose carry strong magic. A drink of wine brewed from the petals bestows one point of Con in one day. The effects of the Winter Rose may only be gained once in a lifetime.

Market Price: 10,000 gp/rose
Treasure Class: Divine

CHAPTER 6: MONSTERS

A variety of monsters, creatures, and races populate the World of Erde. This chapter contains entries for some of the creatures and animals that live in the lands, but DMs should not feel limited as they populate their campaigns with fiends to do battle with the Players. The present time, After Winter Dark, provides fertile environments for all walks of life, and unlife. Reference should be made to the *MM* for reading the statistics blocks of the monsters detailed here.

CHARON FIEND
Large-size Magical Beast

Hit Dice:	5d10 (27 hp)
Initiative:	+5 (+1 Dex, +4 Improved Initiative)
Speed:	40ft
AC:	16
Attacks:	2 claws +4 melee, bite +4 melee
Damage:	Claws 1d6+1; bite 1d10+1
Face/Reach:	5ft. by 10ft/5ft
Special Attacks:	Poison
Special Qualities:	Scent, Darkvision 60 ft., Low-light vision
Saves:	Fort +5, Ref +3, Will +1
Abilities:	Str 13, Dex 13, Con 13, Int 10, Wis 12, Cha 10
Skills:	Hide +9, Listen +5, Move Silently +10, Spot +12
Feats:	Improved Initiative
Climate/Terrain:	Any land or underground
Organization:	Solitary or pair
Challenge Rating:	2
Treasure:	None (standard in lair)
Alignment:	LE
Advancement:	4-5 HD (Large), 6-8 (Huge)

Also known as Spirit Fiends, these grim beasts served the Mogrl as pets and hunting companions. With Unklar's fall and the end of the Winter Dark Wars, these beasts slipped from Aufstrag and into the world. The terror of their passage left a mark upon the people of Erde, for their depredations knew no bounds. Eventually, they vanished into the dark places of the world and became legends of the Age of Winter Dark. On occasion, one or two are seen, wreaking havoc upon the world at large.

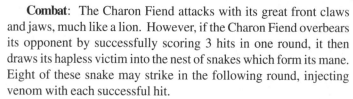

Description: Charon Fiends resemble a cross between a large, otherworldly dog and a great male lion. Upon closer examination, the Charon Fiend's mane is revealed to be a writing mass of snake heads, each about 2 ft. in length. Charon Fiends are close cousins of chimaeras.

Combat: The Charon Fiend attacks with its great front claws and jaws, much like a lion. However, if the Charon Fiend overbears its opponent by successfully scoring 3 hits in one round, it then draws its hapless victim into the nest of snakes which form its mane. Eight of these snake may strike in the following round, injecting venom with each successful hit.

Poison (Ex): Those struck by a snake must succeed at a Fortitude save (injury DC 14) or become poisoned. Though not fatal itself, each failed save results in 1d2 Con initial damage and 1d2 Str secondary damage. The infected area will also swell for 1 day.

CHIMAERA, LESSER
Medium-size Magical Beast

Hit Dice:	2d10+4 (15 hp)
Initiative:	+2 (+2 Dex)
Speed:	50ft
AC:	14 (+2 Dex, +2 natural)
Attacks:	Bite +3 melee, 2 claws +3 melee
Damage:	Bite 1d6+1, claws 1d4+1
Face/Reach:	5ft. by 5ft/5ft
Special Attacks:	Tail strike +3 melee (1d3, Poison)
Special Qualities:	Darkvision 60 ft., Low-light vision, Scent
Saves:	Fort +5, Ref +5, Will +0
Abilities:	Str 13, Dex 15, Con 15, Int 4, Wis 12, Cha 10
Skills:	Hide +3, Listen +5, Spot +5
Feats:	Multiattack
Climate/Terrain:	Any land or ruins
Organization:	Pack, 3-12 (1d10+2)
Challenge Rating:	1
Treasure:	None (standard in lair)
Alignment:	NE
Advancement:	4-5 HD (Large)

These vile creatures are minor cousins of the legendary Chimaeras. Halfling legends hold that the beasts are the result of a mating between a wolves and Charon Fiends.

Description: Lesser Chimaeras have the body of a large wolf with a multi-colored snake tail.

Combat: These beasts cunningly attack as a group. A lesser chimaera bites, attacks with two forepaws, and whips its tail around for another bite attack. Anything bitten by the snake tail must make a successful Fortitude save against poison (injury DC 13) or suffer 1d2 Dex initial damgae and 1d4 Str secondary damage.

Skills: Lesser chimaeras speak a crude form of the common tongue. They receive a +2 racial bonus to listen and spot checks.

DARK FAERIE
Medium-size Fey

Hit Dice:	5d6 (20 hp)
Initiative:	+ 6 (+2 Dex, +4 Improved Initiative)
Speed:	20 ft., fly 40 ft. (perfect)
AC:	15 (+2 Dex, +3 natural)
Attacks:	Short sword +0 melee, short bow +3 ranged
Damage:	1d6
Face/Reach:	5 ft. by 5 ft./5 ft.
Special Attacks:	Spells
Special Qualities:	Darkvision 60 ft., Low-light vision, SR 18
Saves:	Fort +1, Ref +4, Will +4
Abilities:	Str 11, Dex 15, Con 11, Int 16, Wis 14, Cha 11
Skills:	Hide +8, Jump +6, Listen +6, Move Silently +8, Spot +8
Feats:	Improved Initiative, Dodge, Point Blank Shot, Rapid Shot
Climate/Terrain:	Temperate forest, the Dreamscape
Organization:	Individual, Band (6-12), or tribe (20-80)
Challenge Rating:	2
Treasure:	Standard
Alignment:	E
Advancement:	By character class

Dark Faerie are outcasts from the land of Faerie and for this reason, they hate beauty of any sort. They work to undo all that is good in the world and they long for the return of Unklar and the Age of Winter's Dark.

Dark Faerie have an inexplicable hatred, which borders on fear, of birds.

Description: Dark Faerie take many shapes and forms. Their natural form is that of a small winged creature, mottled dark green in color. Frequently, however, they take on the shape of deformed gnomes.

Combat: Dark Faerie rarely stand and fight unless they feel that they have a better than average chance of overcoming the enemy. The prefer hit and run tactics that keep an enemy unbalanced, gradually weakening them until chances of a successful attack improve.

Polymorph Self (Su): Dark Faerie have the ability to *Polymorph Self* twice each day as a 7th level caster.

Spell-like Abilities: Once per day – *flare, obscuring mist, entangle, pass without trace, light and silent image*. Cast as by a 6th level sorcerer (save DC 10 + spell level).

DREAM WARRIOR
Large-Size Outsider

Hit Dice:	9d8+27 (68 hp)
Initiative:	+ 5 (+1 Dex, +4 Improved Initiative)
Speed:	30 ft., fly 30 ft. (perfect)
AC:	27 (+1 Dex, +16 natural)
Attacks:	Dreamscape weapon +14/+9 melee
Damage:	1d8+5
Face/Reach:	5 ft. by 5 ft./10 ft.
Special Attacks:	Spells
Special Qualities:	Dream-mist, Fear, Darkvision 60ft, Incorporeal
Saves:	Fort +9, Ref +4, Will +4
Abilities:	Str 20, Dex 13, Con 16, Int 10, Wis 12, Cha 10
Skills:	Hide +15, Listen +10, Move Silently +12, Sense Motive +15
Feats:	Cleave, Improved Initiative, Power Attack
Climate/Terrain:	The Dreaming Sea
Organization:	None, 2-5
Challenge Rating:	7
Treasure:	Standard
Alignment:	LE
Advancement:	None

When Unklar discovered the Dreaming Sea and became aware of Luther's presence there he cast himself upon that wild expanse and fashioned warriors from his own dreaming. Luther called them "slivers of Unklar's imagining," and they traveled the dreamscape hunting the paladin. Luther and the dream warriors battled on many occasions. While the paladin proved too strong for them, the dream warriors gained some of his powers and came to understand him better.

The warriors have since scattered across the far wide expanse of the Dreaming Sea, haunting only the unwary. Having gained some of Luther's power, they can affect another's dreams. They haunt the prime material world, occasionally enticing people onto the Dreaming Sea and their destroying them.

Description: Dream Warriors appear as swirling columns of white mist, having no corporal bodies to speak of. As they engage in combat they take on corporal forms in their upper torsos. In this form they appear as tall, heavily armored men in heavy plate, shield and helm, tendrils of mist always coiling about them. They do not bleed.

Combat: Dream warriors use any variety of weapons in combat, preferring those of their enemy, St. Luther, to all others: swords, axes and lances. Their weapon of choice is fashioned from the

Dreamscape when the creature alters itself from its mist form. They wield these as +2 weapons.

Spell-like abilities: Dream Warriors can become *Incorporeal* 3 times per day. It takes 4 melee rounds for them to change into mist from their corporal form or vice versa.

They also employ the powerful illusionary spell, *Dream-mist*, to trap their prey. This spell plays upon the victim's own desires, creating minor illusions of them. The illusions react upon the opponent's weaknesses and needs: food and water, or gold for example. The spell is instantaneous. They can cast *Fear* as 10th level Wizard 3 times per day.

ELDRITCH GOBLIN
Small Humanoid

Hit Dice:	1d8 (5 hp)
Initiative:	+1 (Dex)
Speed:	30 ft.
AC:	12+ (+1 size, +1 Dex, + armor modifier)
Attacks:	By weapon +1 melee, +2 ranged
Damage:	By weapon type +0
Face/Reach:	5 ft. by 5 ft./5 ft.
Special Attacks:	+1 to attack rolls against Dwarves
Special Qualities:	Darkvision 60ft, Eldritch Goblin Qualities
Saves:	Fort +3 , Ref +4, Will +0
Abilities (average):	Str 10, Dex 13, Con 11, Int 12, Wis 11, Cha 10
Skills:	Hide +6, Listen +3, Move Silently +5, Search +4, Spot +4
Feats:	Alertness
Climate/Terrain:	Any
Organization:	Typically solitary or tribe (40-400)
Challenge Rating:	1
Treasure:	Standard
Alignment:	Neutral to any Evil
Advancement:	By character class

The Eldritch Goblins were First-born Dwarves corrupted by Thorax in ancient times. He twisted them and made them hate their Dwarven brethren. He taught them a vile sorcery, and in time, their form became deformed. Too, the Eldritch Goblins saw into Thorax's memory, and there they found the secret of immortality and other dark powers. Most are evil and vicious, ever seeking to begin again the great wars between Dwarf and Goblin.

Eldritch goblins live forever, although they can be slain in combat or by spell. Each Eldritch Goblin also possesses a power unique to itself.

All Eldritch Goblins have a character class. Each uses only their character levels because they are 1 HD. They may be any character class.

Description: Eldritch Goblins appear as typical goblins (lesser goblins) in most respects, though their features are more exaggerated and unique. Unlike lesser goblins, Eldritch Goblins often have green skin color.

Combat: The goblins utilize the same tactics as their lesser brethren, but they are even more vile and wicked in doing so. Unlike lesser goblins, Eldritch Goblins can match strategy with any Dwarf, and they are not cowardly.

Skills: Eldritch Goblins gain a +4 racial bonus to Move Silently checks, and a +6 bonus to Ride checks and the Mounted Combat feat if mounted on Worgs.

Eldritch Goblin Qualities: Every Eldritch Goblin possesses a unique ability. The individual abilities greatly range in power, from simple mimicry of a spell, class ability, magic item, or feat, to extremely powerful, extraordinary powers comparable to those exhibited by artifacts or deities.

For quick and low-level encounters, DMs should generate Eldritch Goblin abilities by randomly rolling for or picking lower level spells and feats, or the powers of minor magic items. Mid-level encounters, and encounters intended to generate story hooks and plot require more careful planning by the DM and should be predetermined and worked into the adventure's story. For high-level encounter, espe- cially those involving the elite Eldritch Goblins leaders, the DM should create abilities comparable to the following examples: invulnerability to all weapons; can only be killed by a singular attack type; extremely high spell resistance; or polymorph at will. Indeed, the most evil and powerful Eldritch Goblins can prove to be the most deadly antagonists in the lands who possess a unique power bordering on godlike proportion.

Eldritch Goblin Society: Eldritch Goblins are tribal, but a good portion rise to become leaders of lesser goblins, other goblinoid races, or even humans. Unlike lesser goblins, the Eldritch Goblins are the most civilized of any goblinoid race.

Eldritch Goblin tribes are led by the strongest and smartest among them, although history and great deeds are part of the equation. They sometimes employ Worgs as mounts. There will be an equal number of lesser goblin combatants and noncombatant young in any Eldritch Goblin tribe.

Eldritch Goblins cannot spawn their own kind without a Queen. Instead, a mating of Eldritch Goblins results in a typical goblin ("lesser goblin"). Only a Queen lays eggs from whence Eldritch Goblins hatch. Hundreds of years passed without a Queen, but a new Queen has appeared, and the race is spreading again across Erde. The race worships Oglotay, the first Queen, the reincarnation of Oglotay herself.

Eldritch Goblin Characters: The race's favored class is fighter, but clerics, rangers, rogues, and sorcerers, or mulit-class combinations, are prevalent as well. Eldritch Goblin clerics that worship Oglotay can choose two of her domains. Most Eldritch Goblin spell-casters are sorcerers, but those in tune with magic are wizards.

HOBGOBLIN (Ingoezlin/Inzoelin)

Medium Humanoid

Hit Dice:	2d8+2 (10 hp)
Initiative:	+2 (Dex)
Speed:	30 ft.
AC:	17 (+2 Dex, +4 scale mail, +1 small shield)
Attacks:	By weapon +2 melee, +2 ranged
Damage:	By weapon type +2
Face/Reach:	5 ft. by 5 ft./5 ft.
Special Attacks:	+1 to attack rolls against Dwarves
Special Qualities:	Darkvision 60ft, Eldritch Goblin Qualities
Saves:	Fort +3 , Ref +2, Will +0
Abilities (average):	Str 13, Dex 15, Con 13, Int 11, Wis 11, Cha 11
Skills:	Hide +2, Listen +3, Move Silently +4, Spot +3
Feats:	Power Attack
Climate/Terrain:	Any
Organization:	Single or small bands (5-20), but usually hobgoblins travel with other demihumans or goblinoids. For every 5 encountered, there will be a 3rd-level sergeant. For encounters of 10-20, there will also be a 5th-level leader. For groups numbering between 20 or more there will be 7th-level leader. Leaders are cumulative and in addition to the number encountered. Example, for an encounter of 20 hobgoblins, there will be the following leaders: four 3rd-level, two 5th-level, and one 7th-level.
Challenge Rating:	1
Treasure:	Standard
Alignment:	Lawful Evil
Advancement:	By character class

Note: This description of Hobgoblins replaces that found in the MM.

Hobgoblins are generally thought to be greater cousins to the goblins or lesser cousins to the orcs. This is far from the truth though.

Hobgoblins are rare in the world and their origin and making are shrouded in mystery. No females are known to exist and it is believed they come from the breeding pens of the Orcs or goblins. The Hobgoblins are thought to be mutations or permutations that occasionally rear their ugly heads in orc broods who embody the foulest and most cruel characteristics of that vile race.

When a Hobgoblin is born, it is set aside, raised separately, and revered. They are cast in with the shamans or the warriors, and raised to exemplify those classes. There seems to be an intimate connection between the Hobgoblins and the gods the Orcs pay their dark homage, for they make some of the most powerful warriors and religious leaders of the Orcs. Their prowess on the battlefield brings them great status and many become renowned warlords and leaders of some of the most nefarious orc nations and tribes the world over.

They travel with bands of Orcs, Ungern and others, and usually act as their leaders. They are even found with trolls and the crueller giants. It is not unknown for them to serve in some human armies, though this practice is rare. They are consummate warriors or religious zealots.

Description: Hobgoblins are thick and sturdily muscled in their upper bodies, yet have rather thin and short legs making them seem smaller than they truly are. They typically stand between 6 1/2 to 7 ft. tall. Their skin is light brown to orange, leathery, and very hairy. Upon their torsos rest a peculiar head. Large thrusting jaws lined with jagged teeth sit beneath a broad bulbous nose and thin piercing eyes. Their foreheads are large affairs, sitting over their eyes like a battlement over a wall. The shocks of hair upon their head are usually shaved to small stubbles.

Combat: Hobgoblins are martial creatures and natural leaders. Though their battle plans tend to lack sophistication and nuance, they do have a firm understanding of the basic principles of war and through their constant and steady application, prove themselves time and again on the battlefield.

Hobgoblin Society: There is no true Hobgoblin society as they are raised within and live within the Orc social structure. They are a breed apart though. At birth they are removed from the common milling grounds and placed in special training arenas and with the most powerful leaders. There, they are encouraged to fight amongst one another for positions of leadership. These positions can be obtained through guile, force, or religious intervention. However they are attained, only the strongest and most intelligent survive the ordeal.

Hobgoblins are self-disciplined. They curiously tend to live a spartan existence, eschewing the gross accumulation of treasures and wealth. They prefer living above ground, but are not averse to the dark caverns and black halls of the deep delving Goblins and Orcs. They are well know for their gladiatorial pits where many a slave, prisoner, and volunteer are encouraged and forced to compete for their lives.

Hobgoblin Characters: Most Hobgoblins are either barbarians or clerics. Their warlords tend to be barbarians and focus on exotic weapons that deal tremendous amounts of damage. They would, for instance, favor the heavy crossbow over any other ranged weapon. The clerics worship the gods of war and conquest, and the less well known ancient lords and celestial beings lingering along the edges of existence. The clerics generally lead solitary lives of desperate searches to dark questions. Occasionally, one returns from the wilderness after some epiphany to lead their brothers on crusades

HOUNDS OF DARKNESS
Gargantuan Magical Beast

Hit Dice:	16d10+112 (200 hp)
Initiative:	+1 (Dex)
Speed:	60 ft., running jump 200 ft.
AC:	22 (-4 size, +1 Dex, +25 natural)
Attacks:	Bite +26 melee
Damage:	Bite 4d8+12
Face/Reach:	20 ft. by 40 ft./20 ft.
Special Attacks:	Swallow whole
Special Qualities:	Darkvision 60ft, Low-light vision, Scent
Saves:	Fort +16 , Ref +5, Will +4
Abilities:	Str 34, Dex 13, Con 25, Int 11, Wis 10, Cha 10
Skills:	Intuit Direction +5, Jump +15, Listen +5, Spot +10
Feats:	Alertness, Power Attack, Run

Climate/Terrain:	Any
Organization:	Solitary or pair
Challenge Rating:	17
Treasure:	None
Alignment:	LE
Advancement:	None

Unklar first used the his forge Klarglich to ring forth these fiendish beasts. The evil hounds were forged from the tortured bodies of the fey, and are driven by hate. Their only purpose was to root out the high elves from their places of hiding. With the banishment of Unklar, they roam the world without a master, seeking elves to kill or a new master to follow. Some lair in dark places to abide their days in misery.

Description: These malevolent hounds tower above the earth, standing 32-35 feet at the shoulder and weighing over 32,000 lbs. They resemble bulldogs covered in a otherworldly reddish-brown fur. A magical energy, orange in color, emanates from their eyes. Their breath is a gale of fetid stink. When they walk the world rumbles, when they leap it shakes, and when they do battle it quakes.

Combat: The hounds typically leap upon their prey and attempt to swallow them whole.

Swallow Whole (Ex): Can try to swallow a Medium-size or smaller opponent by making a successful grapple check. The swallowed creature takes 3d8+7 points of crushing damage per round plus 8 points of acid damage from the hound's gizzard. A swallowed creature can cut its way out by using claws or a Small or Tiny slashing weapon to deal 25 points of damage to the gizzard (AC 20). Once the creature exits, muscular action closes the hole; another swallowed opponent must again cut its own way out. The gizzard can hold three Medium-size, six Small, ten Tiny, twenty Diminutive, or forty Fine or smaller opponents.

LORE DRAKE
Huge Dragon

Hit Dice:	12d12+48 (120 hp)
Initiative:	+4 (Improved Initiative)
Speed:	40 ft., swim 60 ft.
AC:	31 (-2 size, +33 natural)
Attacks:	Bite + 13 melee, 2 claws +8 melee, tail slap +8 melee, crush +8 melee
Damage:	Bite 2d8+6; claw 2d6+3; tail slap 2d6+9; crush 2d8+9
Face/Reach:	10 ft. by 20 ft./10 ft.
Special Attacks:	Breath weapon (6d6)
Special Qualities:	SR 23, damage reduction 5/+1, and see below
Saves:	Fort +10, Ref +8, Will +11
Abilities:	Str 23, Dex 10, Con 19, Int 18, Wis 19, Cha 20
Skills:	Bluff +10, Concentration +9, Diplomacy +10, Knowledge (pick 5) all at +20, Listen +14, Spot +9, Search +14, Spellcraft +14
Feats:	Extend Spell, Improved Initiative, Quicken Spell-like Ability, Snatch

Climate/Terrain:	Underground, ruins
Organization:	Solitary
Challenge Rating:	9
Treasure:	Quadruple standard
Alignment:	Always neutral
Advancement:	Young (7-8 HD), Adult (12 HD), Ancient (14-16 HD)

Lore Drakes are a rare breed of dragon, almost to extinction. Most encountered are at least 1000 years old. The drakes are naturally curious and have the ability to retain history and lore without error. They make places of knowledge their lair, sometimes even making their home in a place of civilization, such as a Dwarven kingdom, a wizard's tower, or an active temple.

Dwarven legend holds that Lore Drakes were forged by the Greater Dwarves in the image of Inzae, and that the eldest of these dragons possess some knowledge of the language of creation. An elder Lore Drake laired in Grundliche Hohle during the reign of King Dolgan.

Description: Although huge in size, Lore Drakes are long and sinewy, with small vestigial wings. Their fangs, claws, and tails are still deadly. Not of any uniform color or striation, Lore Drakes are often mistaken for young dragons of color. As they age, however, the scales of a Lore Drake begin to grow a crystalline covering mimicking their most prevalent color. This gives the appearance that they are covered in thousands of tiny, glittering jewels.

Combat: Although the drakes do not typically seek out combat, like any dragon, they are fearsome warriors if they choose to engage.

Bite and Claws: The dragon also can use its bite or claws to snatch opponents (as a feat).

Breath Weapon (Su): The drakes breath a cone of sound 50 ft.

in length that deals 8d6 damage (DC 20). Using a breath weapon is a standard action, and once a dragon breathes, it can't breathe again until 1d4 rounds later. If the breath weapon deals damage, creatures caught in the area can attempt Reflex save to take half damage.

Crush: Lore Drakes can jump and land on opponents as a standard action, using its whole body to crush them. Crush attacks are effective only against opponents three or more sizes smaller than the dragon (though it can attempt normal overrun or grapple attacks against larger opponents). A crush attack affects as many creatures as can fit under the dragon''s body. Creatures in the affected area must succeed at a Reflex save against a DC equal to that of the dragon''s breath weapon or be pinned, automatically taking bludgeoning damage during the next round unless the dragon moves off them. If the dragon chooses to maintain the pin, treat it as a normal grapple attack. Pinned opponents take crush damage each round if they don't escape.

Frightful Presence (Ex): Unsettles foes with its mere presence. The ability takes effect automatically when the dragon attacks or charges. Creatures within a radius of 240 feet are subject to the effect if they have fewer HD than the dragon. A potentially affected creature that succeeds at a Will save (DC 20) remains immune to that dragon's frightful presence for one day. On a failure, creatures with 4 or fewer HD become panicked for 4d6 rounds and those with 5 or more HD become shaken for 4d6 rounds. Ignores the frightful presence of other dragons.

Grappling: Dragons do not favor grapple attacks, though their crush attack and Snatch feat use normal grapple rules. If grappled by a creature the same size or larger, a dragon can return the attack with its bite and all four legs (the rear legs deal claw damage). If snatched or crushed by a larger dragon, a dragon can respond only with grapple attacks to try winning free, or with bite or breath weapon attacks. If grappled by a creature smaller than itself, the dragon can respond with any of its physical attacks other than a tail sweep. The dragon can always use its breath weapon while grappling, as well as its spells and spell-like or supernatural abilities, provided it succeeds at Concentration checks.

Tail Slap: The dragon can slap one opponent each round with its tail.

Blindsight (Ex): Can ascertain creatures by nonvisual means (mostly hearing and scent, but also by noticing vibration and other environmental clues) with a range of 240 ft.

Immunities (Ex): Sleep, paralysis, and cold.

Keen Senses (Ex): Sees four times as well a human in low-light conditions and twice as well in normal light. It also has darkvision 600 feet.

Water Breathing (Ex): Can breathe underwater indefinitely and can freely use its breath weapon, spells, and other abilities while submerged.

Spell-like Abilities: Caster level 11th. 3/day – *suggestion, detect thoughts*; 2/day – *stone shape*; 1/day – *wall of stone*.

Lore Memory (Ex): The drakes retain any history, legend, or rumor told or read without error. They can recount this knowledge with great flair, even detailing each derivation of tale or story they know.

Note: Lore Drakes, although dragons, do not conform to all specifications of a typical dragon as detailed in the MM. The Lore Drake's complete specifications are detailed above.

MIIWEEN
Tiny-size Fey

Hit Dice:	½d6+1(2 hp)
Initiative:	+ 4
Speed:	10 ft., fly 60 ft. (perfect)
AC:	16 (+2 size, +4 dex)
Attacks:	Dagger +0 melee
Damage:	1d4
Face/Reach:	2 1/2 ft. by 2 1/2 ft.
Special Attacks:	Spells, Fascinate
Special Qualities:	none
Saves:	Fort +0, Ref +6, Will +4
Abilities:	Str 4, Dex 18, Con 10, Int 12, Wis 15, Cha 16
Skills:	Animal Empathy +6, Craft +5, Escape Artist +9, Heal +5, Hide +10, Listen +6, Move Silently +7, Sense Motive +4, Spot +2, Wilderness Lore +5.
Feats:	None
Climate/Terrain:	Winter only, any terrain with snow fall
Organization:	Individual, Band (4-10), or tribe (10-40)
Challenge Rating:	1/2
Treasure:	Standard
Alignment:	NG/CG
Advancement:	By character class

Miiween are tiny, female snow-fairies. They are friendly but usually timid. Those to whom they take a liking will reap the benefit of their help, which they offer without expectation of recompense. However, if they have any suspicion of selfishness, cruelty, or other maleficent personality trait of those who they encounter, they quickly abandon them. Often they are found with their pets, the colorful Yaalings.

Miiween only appear during winter and then only after snow has fallen on the ground. None know where the Miiween go when the snows leave, nor has anyone ever found a Miiween habitation.

Description: Miiween appear as small females with pointed ears, skin as pale as the moon, fiery red hair, large eyes, and broad wings of the most brilliant colors. They speak in very high pitched tones that sounds like singing. They are tiny in size.

Combat: Miiween sometimes employ daggers, but usually utilize one of these abilities:

Fascinate(Sp): Myweens can cause a single creature to become fascinated with them. The creature to be fascinated must be able to see and hear and must be within 90 feet. The distraction of a nearby combat or other dangers prevents the ability from working. The target can negate the effect with a Will saving throw (DC 15). If the saving throw fails, the creature sits quietly and listens to the song for up to 4 rounds. While fascinated, the target's Spot and Listen checks suffer a -4 penalty. Any potential threat allows the fascinated creature a second saving throw. Any obvious threat, such as casting a spell, drawing a sword, or aiming, automatically breaks the effect.

Adept Spells (3/1): 0 – *purify food and drink, ghost sound, light*; 1st – *cure light wounds(x2).*

MOGRL
Huge Monstrous Humanoid

Hit Dice:	18d8+90 (216 hp)
Initiative:	+ 8 (+4 Dex, +4 Improved Initiative)
Speed:	40 ft., Fly 120 ft. (poor)
AC:	36 (-2 size, +4 Dex, + 34 natural)
Attacks:	Weapon +24/+19/+14/+9 (or 2 claws +24 melee, bite +22 melee, tail +22 melee)
Damage:	Weapon (Greataxe 1d12, Greatsword 2d6) +8, or claw 2d4+8, bite 1d8+4, tail 3d4+4
Face/Reach:	10 ft. by 5 ft./15 ft.
Special Attacks:	Spell-like abilities, breath weapon
Special Qualities:	Damage Reduction 20/+3, SR 30, and see below
Saves:	Fort +18, Ref +10, Will +13
Abilities:	Str 27, Dex 18, Con 25, Int 24, Wis 24, Cha 17
Skills:	Bluff +12, Climb +10, Concentration +20, Jump +10, Listen +22, Move Silently +10, Search +20, Sense Motive +15, Spellcraft +16, Spot +24
Feats:	Cleave, Great Cleave, Improved Initiative, Multi-attack, Power Attack
Climate/Terrain:	Any
Organization:	Solitary
Challenge Rating:	19
Treasure:	Double coins, goods, and items, plus 1d8 magic items
Alignment:	Lawful Evil
Advancement:	19-20 HD (Huge), 21-30 HD (Huge)

Unklar forced Dolgan to forge twenty-four of these dark servants from the spite contained in Unklar's mind. Fierce and crafty in war, these creatures of fire and ash are the most feared beasts upon Erde other than the Dragons. Some are worshiped as gods.

Native to Erde, they do not travel to any other planes. Coming into life during the height of the Winter Dark, Mogrls have no memory of what came before. They consider any attempt to conquer the plane a direct threat to what is rightfully theirs. They particularly hate the first-born, the Dwarves.

Mogrl live in deep places under the earth away from the sun, where they lord over many diverse creatures through spite and mal-

ice. They have mastered the forge and often craft weapons of power. The Greater Mogrl have mastered the act of creation, and they populate their realms with creatures of their own evil imaginings.

While some Mogrl were slain in the Winter Dark Wars, some remain. Rumor holds that the Greater Mogrl have forged a new lineage of these wicked creatures, and that more than 24 now exist in the deep pits of Erde.

Description: These huge creatures emanate fear and hate. The smell of blight precedes their shadowed form, towering 20 ft. in height (ranging upwards to 32 feet) above the earth. Their mass is supernatural, averaging around a ton, and they use it to its full effect in battle.

Combat: These wicked beasts usually carry a magical weapon, preferring the Greataxe or Greatsword. The primary weapon will always be at least +2 in enchantment, and the attack and damage bonuses above should be adjusted accordingly. Some will additionally carry a +2 cat-o-nine tails (as whip, but 2d4+10 damage).

Though they prefer to fight while on ground with their weapons, their great wings enable them to fight airborne as well. When doing so, their favorite tactic is to hover over their opponent while striking with claws, tail, and a horrific bite.

In all cases, they utilize walls of fire, fireballs, and flame strikes to full advantage.

Breath Weapon (Su): The creature breathes a cone of fire and ash 30 ft. in length that deals 4d10 damage (DC 26), four times per day. Using a breath weapon is a standard action. Creatures caught in the area can attempt a Reflex save to take half damage. Those that fail their Reflex save suffer the secondary effect of constricted air and limited visibility, thus reducing their attack rolls by -2 for 2d4 rounds.

Fear Aura (Su): Can create an aura of fear in a 20 foot radius as a free action. Identical to the fear spell as cast by a 18th level sorceror (DC 16). A successful save indicates that the opponent cannot be affected again by the fear aura for one day.

Immunities (Ex): Immune to fire and poison.

Resistances (Ex): Cold and acid resistance 20.

See in Darkness (Su): Can see perfectly in darkness of any kind, even if created by spell.

Spell-like Abilities: Cast as a 18th level Sorceror (DC 13 + spell level). At will – *charm person, detect chaos/evil/good/law, create greater undead, desecrate, detect magic, dispel magic, hold person, produce flame, pyrotechnics, teleport without error* (self plus 50 pounds of objects only), *see invisibility,* and *wall of fire*; 3/day – *flame strike*; 6/day – *fireball.*

Once per year, the creature can use *wish* as a spell cast by a 20th level sorceror.

Summon (Sp): Twice per day, they can automatically summon 1d2 of their kin.

Telepathy (Su): Can communicate telepathically with any creature within 100 ft. that has a language.

Note: Mogrl are native to Erde. As such, they cannot be turned.

They were terrible to behold and Dolgan knew fear as he had when he wrestled with the black god himself. Their coming was a weighty thing in the world, and Unklar named them Mogrl, and they were demons of horror. And the Mogrl rose one by one and lifted themselves from the halls and strode forth into the world. They were four and twenty in number.

SENTIENT
Huge Plant

Hit Dice:	5-18d8+40 (80-140 hp)
Initiative:	+0
Speed:	30 ft.
AC:	22 (-2 size, +14 natural)
Attacks:	2-12 branches +4 melee
Damage:	1d4 per branch
Face/Reach:	10 ft. by 10 ft./15 ft.
Special Attacks:	Devour (see below), Acid (1d8)
Special Qualities:	SR 25, Branches have 2d8 hp separate from Sentient and are AC 13, Low-light vision, Plant qualities
Saves:	Fort +10, Ref +2, Will +7
Abilities:	Str 18, Dex 14, Con 13, Int 14, Wis 17, Cha 12
Skills:	Knowledge (any four) +10, Listen +6, Spot +6, Wilderness lore +12
Feats:	Alertness, Iron Will, Power attack
Climate/Terrain:	Any forest
Organization:	Solitary
Challenge Rating:	7-12
Treasure:	Standard
Alignment:	Any
Advancement:	5-18 HD (Huge), 19-23 HD (Gargantuan)

Sentients are intelligent trees whose history predates recorded time. They were the first creatures to live in the world and are old beyond reckoning. Few remain and most that do are benevolent creatures who simply enjoy the waning years of their lives. Some are helpful, the Great Oak of the Druids being the most prominent example. Still others have grown old, twisted and evil, and they seek to weave dark plots and carve out domains. Sentients are extremely rare.

Description: Sentients appear as very old trees.

Combat: A Sentient will attempt to *Devour (Ex)* a victim (*Improved Grab (Ex)* and *Swallow Whole (Ex)*), drop it in the maw of its bole, and crush the life from it (maximum 1000 lbs). It takes 4 rounds to move a victim from the ground up to the mouth. The unfortunate character takes 1d4 dmg per round. Upon the fifth round the victim is dropped into the Sentient's maw where he receives 1d8 dmg per round, doubling each round until dead. Escape is impossible short of splitting the tree open. The Sentient can ooze an acidic secretion once per day. The acid will eat through any non-magical weapons. Any contact made with the acid will cause 1d8 hp dmg.

Plant, Elemental Vulnerability (Ex): Ssuffers double damage from elemental attacks like lightning and fire; cold attacks shocks into state of dormancy until thawed.

Plant Qualities: Immune to poison, sleep, paralysis, stunning, and polymorphing. Not subject to critical hits or mind-influencing effects (charms, compulsions, etc...).

SIENNA OLGDONBERG
Large Animal

Hit Dice:	4d8+20 (36 hp)
Initiative:	+2 (+2 Dex)
Speed:	60ft
AC:	15 (-1 size, +2 Dex, +4 natural)
Attacks:	2 hooves +7 melee, bite +5 melee
Damage:	Hoof 1d6+4; bite 1d4+2
Face/Reach:	5ft. by 10ft/5ft
Special Attacks:	-
Special Qualities:	Scent
Saves:	Fort +8, Ref +6, Will +2
Abilities:	Str 18, Dex 14, Con 18, Int 3, Wis 13, Cha 7
Skills:	Listen +7, Spot +7
Feats:	-
Climate/Terrain:	Any land
Organization:	Domesticated
Challenge Rating:	2
Treasure:	None
Alignment:	Always neutral
Advancement:	-

The most magnificent warhorses on the face of Erde are the Sienna Olgdonbergs. Stronger than a heavy warhorse and with the speed of a light warhorse, the Sienna Olgdonbergs have carried the day in more than one battle. They are an exceptionally strong and aggressive breed, and they live longer than most other breeds. Their trainers are held in high renown in Sienna, and raising and selling them is considered an honorable profession. The Count however, controls the herds, allowing only loyal lords to utilize his stock.

Sienna Olgdonbergs have a flare for parading which has been transformed with training into intricate combat maneuvers. Although they mature late, they show obedience, intelligence and a willingness to learn. The philosophy of their trainers is to treat each horse as unique, allowing each to develop movements for which it is best adapted. Olgdonbergs are trained for seven years before they are allowed to enter combat.

Description: These horses emote an aura of beauty and nobility. Short powerful necks sup- port a noble head, and sits atop a strong body with rounded quar- ters, athletic shoulders, and strong legs. The pre- dominant colors are gray; bay, and chestnut, with brown being rare. Their tails and manes are luxuriant. These horses average 15-16 hands in height, and weigh around 2000 lbs.

C o m b a t : Olgdonbergs can fight while carrying a rider, but the rider can- not also attack unless he or she succeeds at a Ride check (DC 9).

Carrying Capacity: A light load for an Olgdonberg is up to 350 pounds; a medium load, 351-700 pounds; a heavy load, 701-1000 pounds. They can drag 5,000 pounds.

TAGEAN HOUND
Medium Magical Beast

Hit Dice:	3d10+6 (21hp)
Initiative:	+2 (+2 Dex)
Speed:	50ft
AC:	15 (+2 Dex, +3 natural)
Attacks:	Bite +5 melee
Damage:	Bite 1d8+2
Face/Reach:	5ft. by 5ft/5ft
Special Attacks:	Trip
Special Qualities:	Low-light vision, scent, telepathy
Saves:	Fort +5, Ref +5, Will +1
Abilities:	Str 14, Dex 15, Con 15, Int 3, Wis 12, Cha 7
Skills:	Hide +3, Listen +6, Move Silently +4, Spot +4, Wilderness Lore +1
Feats:	Weapon Finesse (bite)
Climate/Terrain:	Any forest, plains, hills
Organization:	Domesticated
Challenge Rating:	2
Treasure:	None
Alignment:	Neutral
Advancement:	3 HD (medium, 4-5 HD (large)

The Tageans are known for these fearsome war dogs. The Tagean Hound is a highly sought after battle companion because they can communicate telepathically with their masters and convey images,

sounds, smells, and even taste. They are sold to a select few for no less than 5,000 gp. The strongest have sold for up to 25,000 gp.

Description: These hounds have a compact build and great strength, dexterity, and constitution. They have a large frame and heavy bones. They tend to be black or deep brown in color, with lighter shades on their muzzles, chest and legs. Their hair is coarse and straight, and of short length.

Combat: These hounds are trained for war and can make trip attacks. They receive a +4 racial bonus to Wilderness Lore checks when tracking by scent.

    Trip (Ex): A hit with a bite attack allows an attempt to trip the opponent as a free action without making a touch attack or provoking an attack of opportunity. If the attempt fails, the opponent cannot react to trip the hound.

    Telepathy (Su): The hounds can communicate telepathically with their masters up to 1000 feet. The master can receive images, sounds, smells, and even taste, although they cannot "see" through the hound. Because of this link, the master has the same connection to an item or place that the hound does. For instance, if the hound has seen a room, a master can teleport into that room as is he has seen it too.

Master of the Tagean Hound: The person wishing to become a master of one of these hounds must partake in 2d6 months of training with the hound under the tutelage of a Tagean trainer.

TROLL LORD

Large Giant

Hit Dice:	11d8+36 (80 hp)
Initiative:	+ 2 (+2 Dex)
Speed:	30 ft.
AC:	19 (-1 size, +2 Dex, +8 natural)
Attacks:	2 Fists +11 melee, huge great club or stone axe +11 melee, or rock +9 ranged
Damage:	Fist 1d6+5, huge great club 2d6+5, or rock 2d6
Face/Reach:	5 ft. by 5 ft./10 ft.
Special Attacks:	Bear hug/pummel (3d6)
Special Qualities:	Damage Reduction 12/+1, Darkvision 60 ft.
Saves:	Fort +7, Ref +5, Will +3
Abilities:	Str 20, Dex 14, Con 16, Int 10, Wis 11, Cha 10
Skills:	Hide +5, Listen +6, Spot +5
Feats:	Alertness, iron will, spring attack
Climate/Terrain:	Any
Organization:	Individual, gang (2-4)
Challenge Rating:	7
Treasure:	Standard
Alignment:	E
Advancement:	By character class

Troll Lords are rare, solitary creatures, never traveling in groups larger than four. They inhabit wilderness regions where they are not likely to be disturbed. Occasionally they raid farming communities for their favorite food, billy goats. Troll Lords are evil with a mean disposition. They keep to themselves and avoid contact with others. They are of average intelligence, but can see in the dark as easily as they can in the day and have keen senses of smell.

Description: Troll Lords are massive creatures with a taste for raw meat. They stand 12 feet tall, their huge bellies only matched by their large hands and feet.

Combat: In combat they use small trees for clubs or crude stone axes. They also use their huge fists to pummel an opponent senseless or squeeze them like fruit. If the troll lord scores two successful hits with his fists, he can grab an opponent an opponent in a bear hug or pummel him (DM's choice) for 3d6 points of damage.

UNGERN

Medium-size Humanoid

Hit Dice:	3d8 (14 hp)
Initiative:	+ 6 (+2 Dex, +4 Improved Initiative)
Speed:	30 ft.
AC:	16 (+2 Dex, +4 natural)
Attacks:	+4 melee (weapon of choice), +2 great bow, or 2 claws +4
Damage:	Weapon of choice +2, great bow 2d8, claw 1d2+2
Face/Reach:	5 ft. by 5 ft./5 ft.
Special Attacks:	Gore +2 (1d6+2)
Special Qualities:	Darkvision 60 ft., Scent, SR 20
Saves:	Fort +5, Ref +3, Will +1
Abilities:	Str 15, Dex 15, Con 14, Int 12, Wis 11, Cha 10
Skills:	Hide +3, Listen +3, Spot +3
Feats:	Alertness, Combat Reflexes, Improved Initiative
Climate/Terrain:	Any
Organization:	Individual, Band (6-12), or tribe (20-80)
Challenge Rating:	2
Treasure:	Standard
Alignment:	LE
Advancement:	By character class

In the black days of the Winter Dark when the Horned God, Unklar, ruled the land, the ungern issued forth from the fortress of Aufstrag. They served Unklar as soldiers and captains, and spread his evil throughout the lands. Some say that they were born of a union between the dark fay and wild evil men enslaved in Unklar's service. Whatever their origin, they are always the same: evil with an undying lust for destruction.

Description: Ungern mimic the guise of their maker, Unklar. They stand about 6 feet on average and are generally humanoid in shape. They have dark brown or red skin. Their hands are clawed, their feet cloven hooves. They have wolf like heads with long tooth filled snouts. Long black horns rise from their backs and over their brows.

Combat: In battle, Ungern always dress in armor, helms and shields. They wield axes and other heavy cleaving weapons such as bardiches or halberds. Their archers are famed for using great horned bows, and though they can only fire one arrow a round, the damage they do, 2d8, more than makes up for it.

UNKLAR'S BREATH
Medium-size Magical Beast

Hit Dice:	1d10 (7hp)
Initiative:	+1 (+1 Dex)
Speed:	15ft.
AC:	18
Attacks:	Special
Damage:	Special
Face/Reach:	5ft. by 5ft/5ft
Special Attacks:	Paralysis
Special Qualities:	None
Saves:	Fort +2, Ref +0, Will -1
Abilities:	Str —, Dex 12, Con 13, Int 8, Wis 8, Cha 10
Skills:	None
Feats:	None
Climate/Terrain:	Any
Organization:	Solitary
Challenge Rating:	1/2
Treasure:	None
Alignment:	N
Advancement:	None

These creatures were created by the Arch-Mage Nulak-Kiz-Din to guard treasure. An Unklar's Breath manifests wherever a drop of Nulak's blood has been placed and the proper incantation laid upon it. Nulak was known to supply his precious commodity to his more powerful guild houses and to some of his greater servants, so the number of Unklar's Breaths is limit-less. The creatures are often placed on the locks of chests and spell books.

Description: When the enchanted drop of blood is disturbed by touch or spell, the Breath pours forth as a medium-sized purple mist.

Combat: The Breath attacks by entering the mouth or nostrils of its victim, infecting his/her blood and thereby paralyzing them. Holding one's breath will not keep the creature from entering the body. Though the creature can be hit by normal weapons, the most effective way of combating the creature is by casting a Dispel Magic, Neutralize Poison, or Remove Disease upon it. These spells instantly destroy it. The same spells cast on the drop of blood, if undisturbed, will destroy the Breath as well. Once disturbed, the Breath will attack until destroyed or until it overcomes all of its opponents.

Paralysis (Sp): Those that inhale an Unklar's Breath become paralyzed for 2d4 rounds if they fail their Fortitude save (DC 20). For each round paralyzed, the victim takes 1d4 damage. Elves are vulnerable to this paralysis.

WITCH ORB
Medium-size Aberration

Hit Dice:	2d8+3 (12)
Initiative:	-1 (-1 Dex)
Speed:	fly 20 ft. (poor)
AC:	12 (+3 natural, -1 Dex)
Attacks:	none
Damage:	–
Face/Reach:	5 ft. by 5 ft./5 ft.
Special Attacks:	Spells
Special Qualities:	Fly, SR 5
Saves:	Fort +2, Ref +0, Will +4
Abilities:	Str 3, Dex 8, Con 11, Int 11, Wis 14, Cha 6
Skills:	as Cleric level
Feats:	as Cleric level
Climate/Terrain:	Any
Organization:	Solitary, pair, or cluster (3-6)
Challenge Rating:	1
Treasure:	None
Alignment:	Any
Advancement:	By character class

These bizarre aberrations were once the devoted clerics of Unklar, transformed into a new form. Once a cleric of Unklar had risen in the ranks of the devoted, they were changed into Witch Orbs. In this new form, they became the servants of the most honored and respected Unklarian priests, the Beholders. Those that were faithful eventually were transformed into Beholders themselves.

Description: A Witch Orb is a rubbery green sphere roughly 2-3 ft. in diameter that flys above the ground. Most have 3d4 mouths and 1d8+4 eyes. Unable to speak, they cast spells by releasing wisps of colored smoke from their mouths. The sight is sinisterly disturbing.

Combat: These creatures are clerics. Most all of this race that are encountered will be between levels 1-6.

All-around vision (Ex): The creature's many eyes give them a +2 racial bonus to Spot checks. They cannot be flanked.

Flight (Ex): A natural buoyancy allows them to fly as the spell, as a free action, at a speed of 20 feet. The buoyancy also grants a permanent feather fall effect with personal range.

Spells: Can use divine spells as a cleric of their level.

Skills and Feats: Skills and feats should be assigned as would be appropriate for a cleric of the Witch Orb's level. Obviously, skills or feats requiring arms or legs should not be assigned.

TEMPLATES

ORINSU

Orinsu are lost souls spawned from those who suffered a horrible death due to torture, starvation, or other evil circumstances. The spirit, wracked by earthly pain, is unsure as to whether it should pass on from the realm of the living. It remains in the foggy middle, tied to its place of death as undead.

"Orinsu" is a template that can be added to any corporeal creature or object. Objects with this template are considered constructs. An Orinsu uses the base creature's physical statistics, but not any former special abilities. Orinsu have the special abilities detailed below.

Description: Orinsu are ethereal spirits without form or substance. If spied on the ethereal plane, they appear as pain-wracked versions of their former hosts.

Combat: In combat the Orinsu animate the nearest, most threatening object and attack. They gain all of the combat abilities of the host they animate. Once the host is destroyed, or near destruction, the Orinsu flees it and searches for another host to animate. If none exist, it returns to its earthly remains.

Animate (Su): Orinsu remain near the remains of their former host, but they manifest in a number of ways. They may be appear as simple poltergeists, moving candle sticks and books in the late of night, or they may walk the earth, haunting the living. When desiring to affect the living world, Orinsu manifest themselves by animating objects. The bodiless spirits worm their ways inside a statue, a figure in a painting, or their former bodies (treat as zombie, lesser zombie, or skeleton). The more powerful Orinsu may even animate a fallen character. The animation process takes one round, both to enter and to leave a host. Orinsu Animates may never venture more than 1 mile from the earthly remains that once housed their uncorrupted spirit.

Saves: Same as base creature or object.

Abilities: Same as base creature or object, but no Con or Int, and Wis and Cha are 1.

Skills: Same as base creature.

Feats: Same as base creature.

Climate/Terrain: Any.

Organization: Solitary or group.

Challenge Rating: As base creature, or object at: up to 3 HD is 1/2, 3-6 HD is 1, 6-8 HD is 2, 8-10 HD is 3, and so on.

Treasure: Same as base creature.

Alignment: Always NE.

Advancement: Same as base creature or object.

Defeating an Orinsu: If the Orinsu animates the earthly remains of its former host, it is treated as undead. The undead host can only be permanently destroyed by a cleric through turning. A successful turning check, regardless of turning damage inflicted, consigns the Orinsu to oblivion and destroys it. If the undead host is physically defeated, burnt, or otherwise destroyed, the Orinsu will seek out another host to animate. If no host is available, the Orinsu remains bound to the area as an ethereal spirit.

The only way to destroy the Orinsu itself spirit is to "lay it to rest." To do so, the Orinsu's former living host must be recognized by name. Then consecrated earth must thrown upon them, and some sort of burial consecration spell must be cast. Any number of spells will serve the purpose (Bless, Consecrate, Prayer,

Remove Curse, Sanctuary, or similar spell). Characters that succeed in laying an Orinsu to rest receive x2 xp value.

Sample Orinsu Creature
Orinsu Animated Statue (non-magical gargoyle)
Medium-size Construct

Hit Dice:	2d10 (11)
Initiative:	+0
Speed:	30ft, fly 60 ft.
AC:	14 (+4 natural)
Attacks:	2 Claws +2 melee
Damage:	Claw 1d6+1
Face/Reach:	5 ft. by 5ft/5 ft.
Special Attacks:	–
Special Qualities:	Damage Reduction (Hardness) 8, Immunity (Critical hits), Immunity (1/2 damage) from acid, fire, and lightning)
Saves:	Fort +0, Ref +0, Will -5
Abilities:	Str 11, Dex 11, Con – , Int –, Wis 1, Cha 1
Skills:	none
Feats:	none
Climate/Terrain:	Any
Organization:	Solitary or group
Challenge Rating:	1
Treasure:	None
Alignment:	NE
Advancement:	–

The Tale of Sagramore & the Coming of the Vampire

"Do not judge a man by the role he was made to suffer!"
— St. Luther, Lord of Dreams

Vampires are a rare creature in Erde. They owe their existence to a strange myriad of events occurring a thousand years in the past, during the Age of Heroes.

In those days, before the coming of the Dark, there existed that council of mages called The Council of Patrice (*reference The Age of Heroes, p.26*). They came together under the tutelage of Patrice, the Arch-magi and Master of Prophecy, the most reasoned voice in the world. Twelve sat upon the Council and they counted amidst their numbers Aristobulus the White, the stygian Crisigrin, the mysterious Greymantle, and Sagramore the Great. This last man, Sagramore, was a powerful mage, crafty and able, who heralded from the north lands. He was quiet, speaking only when the need arose. It was a trait many said came from his Northern blood.

Sagramore dabbled in the fates. He spoke with gods, perhaps even the supreme deities, ever seeking what paths man should take to lessen his burden in life. This magic led to his downfall and the creation of the most horrid of apparitions to walk the face of Erde.

In time of years Sagramore uncovered the plot of the Emperor and Nulak-Kiz-Din (*reference The Age of Heroes, p.26-27*). He saw the future and witnessed the end of the world. He tried in vain to bring this calamity to the attention of his fellow magi, but the Emperor and his lackey already were making war on the powers of the world. Several Council members had been slain, and the most active and knowledgeable in the movements of gods, Aristobulus, was lost. So Sagramore attempted to divert the power of Nulak, but the dark mage proved too powerful and bent Sagramore to his will. Sagramore thus became a traitor to the Council, and he led Patrice into the trap that destroyed him. Bound to the prophecy he helped to write, Patrice was broken and hurled into the heavens.

When Unklar stepped upon Erde, summoned via the Paths of Umbra, Sagramore became his slave. He became a toy, tortured and maligned by his masters until at last, 300 years into Unklar's reign, he rose in revolt. At that time, Unklar held unchallenged control over all the world. He was powerful and filled with the rage of youth. Sagramore's efforts thus came to nought, and he was cast down, beaten and broken. Unklar gathered the remnants of the once proud mage and carried him far to the north where he bound him in a cave with great, unbreakable chains steeped in sorcery.

Unklar then cursed him, "Ever shall you thirst for the power you cannot have! Ever shall you gain that which you do not seek!" And he marked him with the gift of immortality, bound to a chain in a cave under a mountain in the frozen north.

Thus Sagramore suffered for eight hundred years. He became mad and raged against the walls of his prison, thirsting for sustenance that he could not have. He learned simple tricks of the mind to call small animals and unsuspecting humans or Orcs who wandered nearby, and he lured them into his den. He made use of wolves and bats to bear his will-o-wisps into the mountains and lure others to his cave. There he slaughtered them, and feasted on them, ever trying to satisfy his hunger and thirst. In time he drew strength by devouring their souls. Sagramore became a monster, a wretch, a horrid thing of grim purpose, a mad man who feasted on the blood and souls of his victims.

When the Winter Dark Wars began, the fates guided Jaren Falkhynjager and Aristobulus to the far north. Questing for a place to hide from Unklar, they found Sagramore and made to rescue him. Jaren, filled with his own rage against a thousand years of torment, wept at Sagramore's plight and would not allow Aristobulus to slay him. Instead, they cured Sagramore of his madness and set him free. They bore him to a far off land and hid him away, promising to aid him when he called. They could do no more, for the addiction of flesh and blood had grown great in Sagramore.

As the wars took the Council of Light away, Sagramore was left to his own, hungry and thirsty, but now utterly cured of his affliction. So he stalked the forests of the north for feasts. He prayed only on those doomed to die, the weak, the elderly, and the sick. Even this he regretted and pitied himself all the more.

But he found that he was powerful in certain ways. He could charm with a look, fade into the mist, and from his old alliance with certain creatures, change into the shapes of bats, wolves, and other creatures of the north. But the worst of his powers came when Naarheit, god of Chaos, revealed to Sagramore that he could alleviate his loneliness by spreading his disease to others.

At first he did so reluctantly, for he was ever a good man, and knew in his heart that what he did was a crime. He felt also that he owed Jaren a debt. But his loneliness overcame his reluctance, and he eventually made others like himself.

But, to his shock, they were not so alike. They were the living consigned to a living death, and they did not possess Sagramore's magic and knowledge. A rage took them, a hatred of their creator and of life, and they stalked the lands, killing in secret, drinking the blood of their victims, and leaving hidden memories of their passing. They longed again for the warmth of life, for the undead are ever cold.

These creatures were named by the folk of Demeter. They were called Ordog (devil), necuratul (unclean), or if female, strigoiaca. But most common name was vampyr, which is vampire in the Vulgate tongue.

In recent times the vampires have been hunted by a breed of professional soldiers who stalks them and kills them in peculiar manners. This has forced the vampires to unite in small family groups, or cabals, which serve to protect their kind and make the more flagrant abuses of lust seem less so. These families discourage rouge vampires, though many are known to exist. They have divorced themselves from their master, knowing of his hatred, but they long to consume him, for it is said, amongst their kind, that his soul is still bound within him and the power of it is unimaginable.

What became of their master, Sagramore, few know, but in truth he stalks the northern wastes, hating himself ever more. He dwells in an old castle that once belonged to the Council of Patrice. From time to time he leaves it and hunts in the southern land, but if ever he comes across one of his cursed "children," he slays them outright. He is still the most powerful of the vampires for he has a soul within him, stained though it is.

Chronology

Events	Dwarf Kalandar df	Elven Year ef	Olden Year oy	Millennial Dark md
The Making of First Home.	1			
Crowning of the Dwarf All Father Argrind; founding of 13 tribes.	76			
The Great Migrations; Mordius settles among the men of the north.	1000-3400			
The war between Argrind King and Thorax.	1400			
Coming of the Goblins.	3400			
Grausumhart Founded under Uthkin the All Father; The murder of Mordius by Thorax and the bringing of evil into the world.	3800			
The Founding of the Dwarf Realms throughout and under the world.	3400-4750			
Grundlich Hohle (Gondolim) Founded under Aegold the All Father	4609			
The free Dwarves of the Sea Kings unite and create the Realm of Alanti, which is upon the Sea.	4956			
Herein are the ages of Peace and Dwarven craft.	4750-5050			
First mention of the Goblins, the Kav-Orun, "cave dwellers."	5123			
The Death of the line of Argrind Darkeye and the beginning of the Kinship disputes inaugurating 200 years of warfare between the various kingdoms.	5207			
The Sundering of Realms and the end of the First Age.	5457			
First Goblin Dwarf War.	5590-92			
The Second Goblin-Dwarf War wherein the Dwarves are driven to their holds, but for the Sea Kings of Alanti.	5616-5640			
The Reign of the Goblin King and the coming of WitchCraft.	5640-6010			
Men begin to track the stars.	5704			
The fleets of Alanti come to the mainland and begin building fortified estuaries and towers in defiance of the Goblin hordes.	5725			
Ondluche becomes servant to the Goblin King Ichlun.	5804			
The Third, or Great Goblin-Dwarf War in which at last the Goblin Kings are thrown down and driven to the far reaches of the world. The Field of the Ravens and the death of King Ichlun. The Second Age of Dwarf is ended.	5812-6010			
The Peace of Tunnels, The Golden Age. Tribes of men spread to the four corners of the world.	6010-6600			
The rise of the Sea Kings of Alanti. All the world is mapped and the stars besides. Great wonders enter the world and the gates immortal are opened and the Dwarves know peace again.	6600-8000			
Ondluche is named Goblin King.	8603			
Fourth Goblin Dwarf War begins.	8613			
The plundering of Alanti.	8645			

Events	Dwarf Kalandar df	Elven Year ef	Olden Year oy	Millennial Dark md
Gorthurag is destroyed, the Seven Swamps created.	8693			
Ondluche's sorcery shatters the Realm Physical opening the Gates of Forever.	8733			
Ondluche is slain by Dognur VII ending the Third Goblin-Dwarf War.	8735			
The coming of the Elves.	8735	1		
The Goblins rise in force to plunder the world and the Stone Wars begin The rise of men.	9804	1069		
The Stone Wars in which the Goblins are at last destroyed but not before the realms of the Dwarves are looted and plundered and the Dwarves broken forever in numbers and strength.	10302	1567		
The plundering of Grausumhart & the end of the Songs of the Dwarves.	10302	1567		
The rise of Aenoch & Thorax. The rule of the God Emperors. The War of the Gods.	10650-11012	1915-2277		
The reckoning of men under the Olden year.	11388	2653	1	
The founding of the Twin Kingdoms of Aenoch and Ethrum.	11480	2745	92	
The crowing of Olivier I, Emperor of Aenoch.	11595	2860	207	
The conquest of Ephrum.	11629	2894	241	
The Festival of Clowns and Marking of the Emperors.	11864	3129	476	
The founding of the White Order.	11791	3202	549	
The Imperial Wars.	11818-11822	3229-3234	576-580	
Beginning of the Wars of Liberation.	11821	3233	579	
The death of the Emperor Marcus Owen I.	11977	3242	589	
The fall of the Aenoch and the rise of the Middle Kingdoms.	11978	3243	590	
First mention of the Halfling folk.	12002	3267	614	
Founding of the Defenders of the Holy Flame.	12026	3291	638	
Nulak-Kiz-Din discovers the Paths of Umbra.	12064	3329	676	
The Council of Patrice.	12081	3346	693	
The Age of Heroes, Aristobolus, Luther, Daladon; Elven migrations.	12081-12124	3346-3389	693-736	
The rise of Rapscallion.	12094	3359	706	
Baron Petrovich becomes keeper of the Cunae mundus Usquam.	12095	3364	711	
Sebastian Olivier I, crowned Emperor.	12102	3371	718	
The Durendale found by Luther.	12116	3385	732	
The Holy Alliance.	12120	3389	736	
Enslavement of Aristobulus, Luther to the Dreaming Sea.	12123	3392	739	
Death of Daladon Half-Elven.	12123	3392	739	
Jaren founds the Order of the Scintillant Dawn.	12128	3397	744	
Through the Paths of Umbra Unklar is brought to Erde.	12136	3401	748	

Events	Dwarf Kalandar df	Elven Year ef	Olden Year oy	Millennial Dark md
War of the Gods.	12138-12149	3402-3413	750-761	
The Elven quarrel and divide, Shindolay & Fontenouq.	12140-12144	3404-3408	752-756	
The Siege of Avignon.	12149-12151	3413-3415	761-763	
The Catalyst War	12149-12188	3413-3452	761-800	
The Age of Winter Dark begins, Unklar crowned God Emperor of Erde.	12188	3452	800	1
Grundliche Hohle overrun; Unklar begins remaking the world.	12313	3577	925	125
The Cold Mist and the Shroud of Darkness.	12563	3827	1175	250
Solarium Empire founded by Kayomar refugees, Aristobulus returns.	12490	3704	1102	302
Elven Quest Knights arrive on Erde.	12586	3800	1198	398
Bending of Oerth.	12699	3913	1209	409
The Flame removed to Du Guesillon.	12713	3927	1223	423
Hounds of Darkness released to sniff out those who resist the dark.	12660	3874	1272	472
Melius hides the portals to Shindolay	12842	4056	1454	654
Aristobolus founds the Mystic enclave.	12882	4096	1494	694
The Uneasy Peace is shattered by Unklar's return.	12888	4102	1500	700
The return of Luther and Daladon; Aristobolus convenes the Council.	13307	4521	1919	1119
The Winter Dark Wars.	13307-324	4521-4538	1919-36	1119-36
The birth of the Young Kingdoms.	13324-385	4538-4599	1936-97	1136-97

Index

THE ECONOMY OF ERDE

The Economy of Erde is well developed. The thousand year reign of the horned god, Unklar, established an orderly world with both land and sea trade routes that were monitored and managed by the efficient imperial bureaucracy. When Unklar's reign ended much of the efficiency was lost, but nevertheless, the Young Kingdoms adopted some of the commercial sophistication that developed in the Age of the Winter Dark.

Most work in Erde is done by free men, however, slavery is common in the east and along the southern coasts of both the Ethrumanian and Aenochian land masses. Erde is in a pre-industrial stage with craftsman producing the goods. Trade is generally shifting from the southern climes to the more northerly ones. The countries in the north such as the Hanse City States, Avignon, and Aachen, are changing the nature of commerce by producing large quantities of manufactured or luxury items.

Each country in Erde is assigned a tier of trade/commercial development indicating the state of its economy and industry, whether it engages in long distance trade, and average taxation. Icons located in each country's information table indicate its economic tier. The tiers range from one to five, with each tiers being cumulative. Thus, the descriptions of tiers one to four would be applicable to a tier four country.

Tier One: foodstuffs, clothing, and essentials; local trade.

For the most part, trade within the countries of Erde consists of local trade of bare essentials such as foodstuffs, clothing, simple furnishings, and tools. Much of the trade occurs as barter, being confined to a local level. Virtually every country is capable of feeding and clothing itself. Taxes are paid in commodities, not money. Most peasants thus pay their taxes in livestock, bales of hay, or sacks of foodstuffs.

In Tier One areas, adventurers will find simple weapons, light armors, leather helms, wood shields, adventuring gear costing 5 gp or less, and mounts costing 30 gp or less.

Tier Two: luxury items and raw industrial material; short to medium distance trade.

Merchants and middlemen become involved in the long distance trade of industrial goods. The industrial goods making up the bulk of the second tier of trade includes timber, metals (iron, copper, tin), oils, coal, salt, and barley and wheat. It also includes slaves in those regions where it is not outlawed. The trade routes for these items are usually short, with several rare exceptions, due to the high cost of transportation and its necessary substructure of armies for protection, buildings for storage, and general infrastructure. Industrial goods are subject to moderate taxation, with traders typically paying in coin or barter.

In Tier Two areas, adventurers will find simple weapons, light to medium armors, wood helms and shields, adventuring gear costing 10 gp or less, and mounts costing 75 gp or less.

Tier Three: processed goods and luxury items; long distance trade.

The next tier is luxury items, and their trade generates the greatest wealth for the coffers of the importing and exporting countries. Luxury items include spices and fine cloths such as silk, wool, cotton, and linen, rare food stuffs (fruits), wines, beers, and finished goods such as weapons, furniture, rope, and fittings for ships. Because these items are relatively easy to transport compared to raw industrial goods, the return on investment is potentially high. Hence, these items are traded across the known world and merchants brave dangerous lands to gather them. The high profit margins induce high taxation. The taxing authorities, however, will typically accept payment by barter as they are always in need of many of the tier three processed goods.

In Tier Three areas, adventurers will find martial, exotic, and renaissance weapons costing 100 gp or less, medium to heavy armors, steel helms and shields, adventuring gear costing 100 gp or less, mounts costing 200 gp or less, and special and superior items costing 150 gp or less.

Tier Four: speciality & rare items; long distance trade.

Tier four encompasses speciality and rare items such as artwork, gold, finely smithed goods, tapestries, rare animals, books and paper, and large items such as ships, wagons, or elaborate stonework. These valuable items fetch quite a sum, usually being made to order. Vast sums of wealth may be exchanged for these items, and of course, begat high taxation. Taxes on these items are almost exclusively paid in coin.

In Tier Four areas, adventurers will find all weapons, armors, gear, mounts, special items, and siege weapons.

Tier Five: magic items & services.

The final tier includes those countries where the traffic of magic items and specialty services occurs. Specialty services include divinations, healing, resurrections, and other magical spells, or the practice of sages. Although the sale of magic items or cialty services might occur on an infrequent basis in tier two to tier four countries, only in tier five countries will be found an active marketplace dedicated such trade. Magic items sales attract high taxation. Specialty services are taxed moderately, but religious specialty services, such as healing, are not taxed at all.

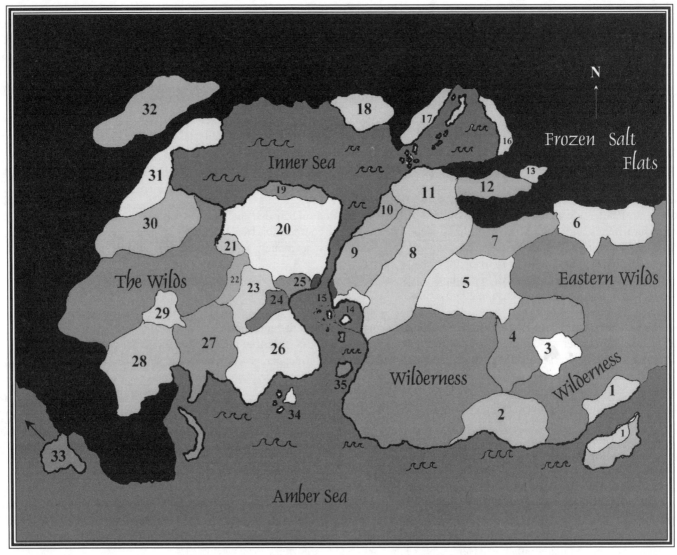

Boundries of the Realms of the Lands of Ursal

1	Outremere	18	Holmgald
2	United Kingdoms	19	Hanse City States
3	Aufstrag	20	Angouleme
4	The Toten Fields	21	Cleves
5	Luneberg Plains	22	Sienna
6	Punj	23	Twilight Elves
7	Rhuneland	24	Fontenouq
8	Augsberg	25	Karilia
9	Aachen	26	The Gelderland
10	Eisenheim	27	Maine
11	Zeitz	28	Kayomar
12	Grundliche Hohle	29	Norgorad Kam
13	Ngorondoro	30	Burnevitse
14	Tagea	31	Gottland
15	Avignon	32	Moravan Plains
16	Trondheim	33	Brindisium
17	Haltland		

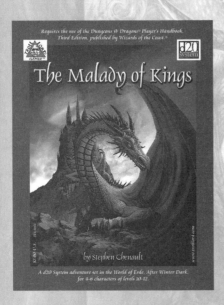
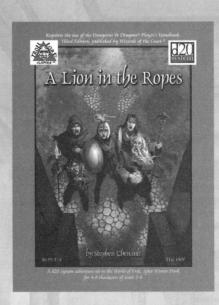
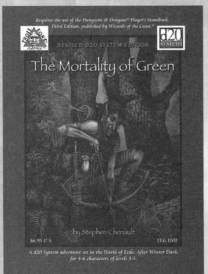

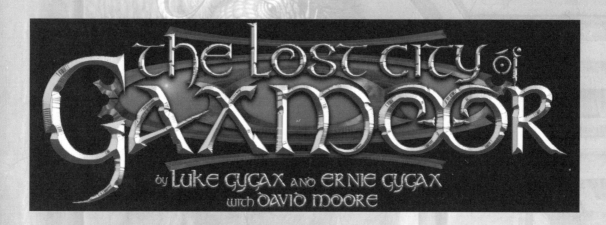